LECTIONARY
of MUSIC

ALSO BY NICOLAS SLONIMSKY

Perfect Pitch: A Life Story
Lexicon of Musical Invective
A Thing or Two about Music
The Road to Music
Thesaurus of Scales and Melodic Patterns
Music of Latin America
Music Since 1900

EDITED BY NICOLAS SLONIMSKY

Baker's Biographical Dictionary of Musicians
International Cyclopedia of Music and Musicians

LECTIONARY
of MUSIC
by NICOLAS SLONIMSKY

McGraw-Hill Publishing Company

New York   St. Louis   San Francisco   Bogotá   Hamburg   Madrid   Mexico
Milan   Montreal   Paris   São Paulo   Tokyo   Toronto

1 2 3 4 5 6 7 8 9 DOC DOC 8 9 2 1 0 9

ISBN 0-07-058222-X

Library of Congress Cataloging-in-Publication Data
Slonimsky, Nicolas
Lectionary of music.

1. Music—Dictionaries.   I. Title.
ML100.S637   1989   780′.3   89-2515
ISBN 0-07-058222-X

Book design by Sheree L. Goodman

Exordium

The title of this book, *Lectionary of Music*, comes from the Latin *lectio*, "the act of reading," a more adequate description for a reference work than *dictionary*, derived from *dictio*, "the act of speaking." Through the centuries, however, the word *lectionary* has acquired the specific meaning of a reading in church of sacred texts from the Scriptures. The present publication is an attempt to restore the word *lectionary* to its original sense.

This *Lectionary of Music*, however, is not proposed to be an all embracing encyclopedia of things musical. Rather, it is intended to be a menu of aperitifs preliminary to a rich gastronomic repast. (*Menu* is French for something minute or selective; *aperitif*, also French, is a drink of liquor for the stimulation of the appetite.) The present book, then, is an introduction to extensive reading on the subject of music, but it contains quite a bit of pertinent terms and titles, for example Fioritura and Coloratura, Belly Dance and *Billy Budd*, *Aniara* and *Arcana*, Sonata and *Traviata*, Musette and Muzak, Castrati and Miserere, Bar and Barbershop Harmony, *Ave Maria* and *The Mother of Us All*, Cacophony and Dodecafonia, Olla Podrida and Paradiddle, Ocarina and Carioca, Charivari and *Chopsticks*, Flute and Lute, *Nixon in China* and *The Turn of the Screw*. And there are extensive (well, semidemiextensive) articles on such dignified musical terms as Symphony, Opera, Oratorio, Cantata, Partita, Counterpoint, Canon, Fugue, Melody, and Harmony, and all that jazz, crowned by a grandiose disquisition on Music itself, which is bound to raise some bushy musicological eyebrows.

Hopefully,

The Compiler
El Pueblo de la nuestra Señora
La Reina de Los Angeles, 1988–89

A

A. The initial note of the alphabetical scale. Its alphabetical primacy was established in the 16th century. In German and English terminology, A corresponds to the note La of France, Italy, Spain, Portugal, Latin America, and Russia. Glareanus, in his *Dodecachordon* (1547), fixed A as the tonic of the Aeolian mode. In 1571 Zarlino elevated the Ionian mode to primacy, relegating A to the sixth place of our C major scale. A is the note used for tuning an orchestra, and it is usually given out by the oboe because the oboe is the least affected by humidity or other weather conditions of all wind and string instruments. The frequency for A above middle C is 440 vibrations per second.

A major. A key often associated with springtime. Mendelssohn's *Spring Song*, in his *Songs without Words*, is cast in the key of A major, although the title is not Mendelssohn's own (it was probably an invention of one of his publishers). Mendelssohn's *Italian* Symphony is in A major, as is Tchaikovsky's *Italian Capriccio*, for Italy was poetically associated in the minds of men of the North with sun and spring, the land "wo die Zitronen blühen." Beethoven's most joyful symphony, No. 7, is in A major; Wagner grandiloquently described it as "the apotheosis of the dance." Many classical works, nominally catalogued as being in A minor, end in A major; among them are the Piano Concerto of Schumann and the Violin Concerto of Glazunov, with their tonally assertive fanfares in the finale.

A minor. The key of resignation. Few symphonies are set in it. And yet the A-minor key is technically advantageous for string instruments, with the upper violin strings providing for the tonic and the dominant of A minor and the upper strings of the viola and cello offering the ready recourse to the tonic and the subdominant. Mozart avoids A minor as a principal key, as does Beethoven. Mahler's Symphony No. 6, a work of mental depression in which Mahler wrestles with Fate, is in A minor, as is Sibelius's Symphony No. 4, which sounds strangely unlike the robust Sibelius of Finnish inspiration and

1

must be regarded as an exception among his works. It is difficult to say why so few violin concertos exist in this eminently violinistic key. Glazunov wrote a Violin Concerto in A minor that is a repertory piece in Russia, and Ernest Bloch and Dvorak each wrote one. Two great piano concertos are in A minor, one by Schumann and one by Grieg. The introspective and essentially pessimistic key suits Tchaikovsky perfectly. His Piano Trio opens with a phrase on the cello in A minor, and it comes nearest to the sound of sobbing in music. (Tchaikovsky dedicated the Piano Trio to the memory of his friend Nicholas Rubinstein, director of the Moscow Conservatory.)

The Abduction from the Seraglio. An opera by Mozart, produced in Vienna on July 16, 1782, under the German title, *Die Entführung aus dem Serail*. A fair damsel is captured by a Turkish pasha. A youth in love with her tries to rescue her, but his attempt is foiled by the wily Turk. In the finale, the Turk yields to a sudden magnanimous impulse and lets her go with her lover. Apart from the treasure of Mozartean *melos*, the score is interesting in its stylization of "Turkish" tunes and rhythms—for example, movements *alla turca* in slightly syncopated 2/4 time.

L'Abeille. A popular violin piece by a Dresden violinist whose name was, unfortunately for him, Franz Schubert. He never tried to capitalize on the excusable confusion with his immensely greater namesake, only 11 years his senior, but confusion persisted. He even wrote an open letter to music editors shortly before his death in 1878, persisting in his claim that he was as good a composer as Franz Schubert the Great ever was.

Academic Festival Overture. A musical acknowledgment by Brahms of the honorary degree of Doctor of Philosophy conferred upon him by the University of Breslau in 1879. The Latin diploma describes Brahms as *artis musicae severioris in Germania nunc princeps*, "now the foremost composer of serious music in Germany." But the overture itself is not serious in the deadly sense of the word. It is based on student songs, some of them of frivolous nature. Its finale is a brilliant orchestration of the lugubrious university song *Gaudeamus igitur*, with its sepulchral reminder that in the end *nos habebit humus*, "the earth will have us." It was first performed in Breslau on January 4, 1881, with Brahms conducting.

Accidentals. A sign placed in front of a note to alter its pitch. Sharps, flats, naturals, double sharps, and double flats are among accidentals commonly used. Triple sharps and triple flats are theoretically conceivable. There are no known instances of the use of a triple flat. The only occurrence of a triple sharp, which is marked by a sharp next to a double sharp, is in the second scene of the fourth act of Rimsky-Korsakov's opera *The Legend of the Invisible City of Kitezh and the Maid Fevronia*. The rationale for its use in this particular instance is that it constitutes a lower auxiliary note in the dominant of the key of C double-sharp minor, which theoretically has 11 sharps in its key signature.

The flat sign takes its origin from the small *b*; it was introduced as early as the 11th century to provide the perfect fourth over the major tetrachord on F, to obviate the danger of the forbidden tritone, which was considered by medieval scholars as the "devil in music." The flatting of B in the F tetrachord was regarded as such an obvious necessity that it was dubbed *signum asininum*, "the mark of the ass," for only hopelessly stupid students had to be told to put in this flat. To this day, B-flat is designated in the German musical alphabet simply as B. In medieval Latin music books, this crucial B-flat was called *b rotundum*, that is, a "round B," or *b mollis*, a "soft B." (Thus the French term *bémol* for "flat.") When it became necessary to devise a symbol for B-natural, a square was substituted for the gentle oval of *b*. This nonflatted note received the name *b quadratum*, that is, a "square b," or *b durum*, a "hard b." Because in Gothic script the square *b* looked like the letter *h*, the square *b* was eventually substitued for the sign of B-natural. As a result, the German musical scale has been extended to eight letters of the alphabet, wherein B stands for B-flat and H for B-natural. Hence, the musical theme for BACH is B-flat, A, C, B. Sharps originally appeared in medieval notation to cancel previously used flats; a sharp was therefore called *signum cancellatum*, "sign of cancellation." (In French such a canceling sign was called *b carré*, "squared b," so the French term *bécarre* stood for a natural sign.) Further modifications of the signs for a sharp and a natural were necessary to differentiate between them. The sharp assumed the shape of a crisscrossed lattice, and the natural was represented by a rhombus, with an upward stem to the left and a downward stem to the right. Some old American music manuals used the term *cancel* for a natural. Double sharps were represented by a cross resembling the letter *x*.

Accidentals usually retain their validity throughout one bar, but the rules are not absolute. To add to uncertainty, flats and sharps in Baroque music are sometimes retroactive. The player is supposed to know, or to guess, where the leading tone leads, or a passing note passes, taking a hint from the future accidentals. In fact, Baroque composers and copyists often omitted self-evident accidentals that the player was supposed to supply, relying on general usage. A typical *casus belli* is the ambiguous double sharp on the third beat of the third bar in the C-sharp-major fugue of the first book of Bach's *Well-Tempered Clavier*. If a genuine modulation into the dominant is presumed to take place on this particular semiquaver, then the note in question must be the leading tone to the new key of G-sharp major, in which case F-double-sharp is in order. If a modulation is not implicit, then F-sharp should be allowed to stand without further alteration. Modern composers are not always strictly logical in their use of accidentals. Charles Ives upbraided a conscientious copyist for trying to correct a seemingly wrong accidental by scribbling in the margin of his manuscript: "Please don't correct the wrong notes. The wrong notes are right." Schoenberg sacrified logic in bar 22 of his piano piece, op. 33a, where an irregular A-natural appears instead of the dodecaphonically correct A-flat. Yet Schoenberg most definitely put down an A-natural, allowing, *horribile dictu*, an illicit recurrence of a note within the tone row for the sake of euphony. After a brief skirmish in the correspondence columns of a British publication, the advocate of the strict dodecaphonic orthodoxy recognized Schoenberg's right to disrupt the continuity of his own tone row and withdrew his proposed correction. In atonal music, and, *a fortiori*, in dodecaphonic works, double sharps or double flats have no *raison d'être* because only the absolute pitch counts, not the notation. Still there are some preferences. Just as in tonal music B-flat and F-sharp are the harbingers of keyed tonality, so in atonal music B-flat is used more often than its enharmonic equivalent A-sharp, and F-sharp is used in preference to G-flat.

Accorde di stupefazione. "Chord of stupefaction," a colloquial term used by Italian opera composers to describe the "stupefying" effect produced by the persistent use of the diminished-seventh chord to illustrate a scene of dramatic tension.

Acoustics. The science of sound that establishes the laws of the vibrations of strings, the transmission of air movement in the organ and wind instruments, and the effect of the superposition of the resulting sound waves on consonant or dissonant intervals and harmonies. It also establishes the causes of different tone colors and related problems, which constitute the physical basis of music. Since ancient times, it has been known that pitch depends on the length and tension of a vibrating string, the length and diameter of the air column in a pipe of the organ, or the size of a bell or a drum. The height of pitch is proportionate to the frequency of vibrations. If the thickness of a string remains the same, the frequency of vibrations increases with its length. If a string is set in motion with a greater force so that the amplitude of its vibrations is increased, then the resulting sound becomes louder without changing the actual pitch. The range of audible sounds for the human ear is between 16 and 25,000 cycles per second, a cycle being a complete vibration of a string oscillating up and down. Dogs hear sounds far above the human range; high-pitched whistles, inaudible to humans, are used by handlers to summon dogs.

Each string or each air column naturally divides itself into component parts that produce overtones, or partials. Theoretically, each complete vibration produces also two vibrations of one-half that of the sounding body, three vibrations of one-third that of the sounding body, and so on. The sound of one-half of the string registers in the human ear as the interval of the octave, one-third of the string as the interval of the twelfth, and so forth, forming the harmonic series of intervals. The simpler the fraction produced by the divided string, the more euphonious is the interval created by such overtones. Thus the perfect octave produced by the division of a string into two equal parts is the most consonant interval; the interval between one-third of the string and one-half of the string produces the interval of the perfect fifth; the interval between the division of the string into three parts and four parts produces the interval of the perfect fourth; the interval between the division of the string into five parts and four parts produces the major third. These intervals together constitute the major triad, which is acoustically the most natural consonant triad. Wind blowing across the strings of an Aeolian harp hung on the branches of a tree produces a harmonic series that forms a major chord. If there were enough wind on the surface of Mars, and if Martians were to develop harmony, the major chords would still be at the foundation of their musical system.

To the diapason of humanly audible sounds must be added a whole series of combinational sounds produced by the difference or the summation of two tones, particularly those sounded in perfect tuning. A violinist playing the double-stop E and G on the two high strings in the perfect acoustical ratio of a minor third will hear, to his annoyance and surprise, an unwelcome C below the G string. Aware of this parasitic phenomenon, string players instinctively avoid using such acoustically pure double stops. Furthermore, combinational tones form between overtones of the individual sounds. The most common of such intrusive sounds are Tartini tones, so named because Giuseppe Tartini was the first to describe them in detail in the 18th century; they are also known as differential tones. It is fortunate that they cannot be heard in performances. Indeed, a veritable pandemonium would result if musicians could, and did, play perfectly in tune. The combinational tones would then cling to the basses of the harmony like barnacles to the bottom of a ship, and an additional maze of nonharmonic sounds would plunge the orchestra into a sonic fog. Thus, it is the very imperfection of manufactured instruments and the limitations of the human performers to play in perfect tuning that saves music from chaos.

For more than 2,000 years theorists have wrestled with the problem of equalizing the perfect octave by having the ratio of vibrations 2:1 commensurate with that of a fifth that has a ratio of vibrations 3:2. In the traditional cycle of fifths, twelve perfect fifths on the keyboard of the piano, as in all instruments built on the tempered scale, is supposed to aggregate to seven octaves. But this is obviously an impossible equation, because two to the seventh power cannot equal 3:2 to the twelfth or any other power. Therefore an adjustment had to be made; the perfection of the perfect fifth was sacrificed in order to fit twelve fifths into the compass of seven octaves. A similar adjustment had to be made in other intervals. The result is that what we call a major chord is not a nontempered harmony but an artificially adjusted harmony, or "tempered pitch." When the piano tuner tunes a fifth, it is actually a slightly flattened fifth. Violinists and players of other string instruments, however, tune their strings in nontempered perfect fifths. If a violinist plays a fifth on the open strings and the piano accompanist plays the same fifth, a disagreeable discrepancy results. It was not until Bach's time that acousticians finally abandoned all hope of reconciling the pure harmonic series with practical instruments, and the famous "well-tempered" clavier became universally accepted. The word *acoustics* comes from the Greek adjective meaning "audible." This science of sound has come to be the connecting link between physics and musical aesthetics.

Adagio for Strings. A transcription of the slow movement of Samuel Barber's String Quartet made by the composer for Arturo Toscanini and the NBC Symphony. It was performed for the first time in New York on November 5, 1938, and it subsequently has become not only the most popular piece by Barber but probably the most frequently played short work by any American composer. Because of its finely sustained mood of modal harmonies, it is often performed at funeral occasions, including the services for Franklin Delano Roosevelt in April 1945. Appropriately, Barber's own funeral in 1981 was also accompanied by this somber invocation.

Adeste Fideles. The Latin words of this hymn are usually attributed to St. Bonaventura, who lived in the 13th century. The musical setting is dated much later and is variously ascribed to the Portuguese composer Marcus Portogallo and even to King John IV of Portugal. The English text *O Come All Ye Faithful* was first published in London in 1760.

Les Adieux. Beethoven's Piano Sonata in E-flat major, op. 81a. The full title is *Les Adieux, l'Absence, et le Retour.* The French titles were given by Beethoven himself, who also added an alternative title, *Sonate caractéristique.* The words "Farewell," "Absence," and "Return" refer to a vacation taken by Archduke Rudolph, a friend of Beethoven. The opening theme imitates the postillion horn (descending major third, perfect fifth, and minor sixth, from the mediant through the supertonic to the tonic). French titles were fashionable in 1809 when Beethoven composed *Les Adieux.* Napoleon's star was high in the political firmament, and German vernacular was considered inelegant. The situation changed radically after the fall of Napoleon, when Beethoven pointedly entitled his Piano Sonata, op. 106, in German vernacular, *Hammerklavier* Sonata, as if it were necessary to mention that a piano operates with hammers.

Adriana Lecouvreur. An opera in four acts by Francesco Cilèa. The libretto deals with a historical figure, an 18th-century Parisian tragedienne engaged in crisscrossed amours. She is poisoned by a bouquet of lethal violets. Cilèa's most famous opera, it was performed in Milan on November 6, 1902.

Adventures in a Perambulator. An amusing orchestral suite by the American "modern" composer John Alden Carpenter, who was also a railroad executive.

The orchestra is supplemented by tinkling, jingling, and jangling percussion instruments such as triangle, xylophone, glockenspiel, and bells. Six movements supposedly represent a child's view of the world while being wheeled around in a baby carriage; the most spectacular of these impressions are a policeman and a dog. The suite was first performed in Chicago on March 19, 1915. Its cuteness soon became too fulsome for sophisticated consumption, and it became a seldom-revived period piece.

Aeolian mode. The ecclesiastical mode corresponding to the modern natural minor scale. Projected onto the diatonic scale on the white keys of the piano keyboard, its range is from A to A. The Hypoaeolian mode is a later construction that is rarely encountered in ecclesiastical chants. It extends from E to E and is identical with the Phrygian mode, except that its tonic remains A, as in the authentic Aeolian mode.

Affects. The doctrine treating the relationship between music and emotions. The word comes from the Latin *affectus*, "state of the soul." St. Augustine wrote, "*Musica movet affectus.*" The Doctrine of Affects, as it was known, goes back to Greek antiquity when the correlation between music and the soul was accepted as a scientific fact. The Greek word for *affectus* is *pathos*, which conveys the meaning of deep emotion. (The adjective *pathétique* still retains the meaning of "full of feeling" and is used in the title of Tchaikovsky's Symphonie No. 6, *Symphonie Pathétique*.) In medieval Latin treatises, the term *musica pathetica* was attached to music that represents emotions. The most "scientific" of these tracts is *Istitutioni harmoniche* by Zarlino, 1558, in which all consonant intervals are divided into two categories: Those consisting of whole tones (major seconds, major thirds, and their inversions) reflect the feeling of joy, whereas intervals containing fractional tones (minor seconds, minor thirds, and their inversions) express sadness. The establishment of major and minor tonality brought about the most durable *affectus*, associating major keys with joy and minor keys with sorrow. This dichotomy persists even in our own day. One cannot imagine Schumann writing *The Happy Farmer* in a minor key, or Chopin composing his *Funeral March* in a major key. The theorists of the Renaissance expanded the Doctrine of Affects to include tempo, rhythm, registers, and dynamics. If some of these scholastic elucubrations have retained their validity, it is because they generally correspond to observable physiological or psychological conditions. Rapid passages cannot very well portray illness or death, and slow progressions in static harmonies cannot represent anger. Even Schoenberg, who rejected programmatic interpretations of musical tones, yielded to the temptation to writing descriptive music in his score *Accompaniment to a Cinema Scene*, in which the subsections titled *Imminent Danger*, *Anxiety*, and *Catastrophe* follow in their dynamic content the precepts of the Doctrine of Affects. The selection of registers by Romantic composers also frequently follows these psychological associations. The preference of Sibelius for the somber sonorities of the low register may be indicative of the severity of the landscape of his native Finland. In a very general manner, it can also be said that the music of the North tends toward a greater exploitation of low registers, slower tempi, and minor modes, whereas the music of the South cultivates high registers and fast tempi.

The Doctrine of Affects greatly influenced the melodic structure of vocal works. The symbolism of states of mind is in evidence in the works of Bach. Thus the verbal injunction "Get up, Get up!" is expressed by the ascending major arpeggio; the phrase "Follow me" is illustrated by a very long ascending scale passage; suffering is depicted by narrow chromatic configurations; the fall into hell is punctuated by a drop of the diminished seventh. The medieval description of the tritone as *diabolus in musica* is an early precursor of the Doctrine of Affects. The diminished-seventh chord, often used to enhance the dramatic tension in opera, received the nickname of *accorde di stupefazione*, a designation related to the Doctrine of Affects. During the Baroque period, some musical philosophers actually drew comparative tables between states of mind and corresponding intervals, chords, tempi, and the like. The famous 18th-century lexicographer Mattheson stated in his treatise *Die neueste Untersuchung der Singspiele*, 1744, that "it is possible to give a perfect representation of the nobility of soul, love and jealousy with simple chords and their progressions." This exaggerated notion of the precise correspondence between emotions and musical progressions was tenaciously upheld in the annotations, mostly by German writers, of programmatic works. One such literal analyst even found in a perfectly innocuous descending interval near the end of Beethoven's *Egmont Overture* the representation of the beheading of the historical Egmont. The elaborate enumerations of leading motives and the analysis of their intervallic content by annotators of Wagner's music dramas and the tone poems of Richard Strauss are remnants of the Doctrine of Affects. In the 20th century the theory of affects has practically disappeared and has been replaced by a structural analysis unconnected with emotional content.

A-flat major. A key of joyous celebration and human devotion. Also an eminently pianistic tonality having four black keys and three white keys, a convenient digital disposition for melodies and harmonies. It lies uneasily for string instruments, however, and is therefore rarely if ever selected as the principal key for a large orchestral work; among individual symphonic movements in A-flat major, the third movement of the Symphony No. 1 of Brahms is notable. A-flat major describes a festival mood in Schumann's *Carnaval*, and it is a romantic invocation in Liszt's *Liebestraum*.

L'Africaine. Meyerbeer's last opera, performed posthumously in Paris on April 28, 1865. The African girl of the title is Selika, whom Vasco da Gama brings back to his native Portugal from his African adventures. Becoming aware of the racial barrier, she sacrifices her life so that Vasco da Gama can marry his former white mistress. The opera takes nearly six hours to perform, but it attained tremendous popularity with sentimental audiences of the last third of the 19th century. It has exotic flavor, Italianate bel canto, thunderous sunderings of love, and loud orchestration, all qualities that made Meyerbeer the idol of his time.

African music. To the white people of Europe and America, during the centuries of colonialism, Africa was "a dark continent." Stanley, who "found" Livingstone in a remote African village and extended his famous, superfluously genteel salutation, entitled his book *In Darkest Africa*. Joseph Conrad, who actually traveled in Central Africa, summarized his experience in his novel *Heart of Darkness* with the words of its central character, "The Horror! The Horror!" With the availability of modern transportation and the development of ethnological research, it became possible to examine the reality of Africa beyond the figures of witch doctors and local chiefs holding court under an umbrella. It also became possible to notate and record indigenous music of Africa. Indeed, the motion picture, *The African Queen* includes a large section in which the natives play drums and chant authentic music. As a rule, the deeper we penetrate into the interior of Africa, the more authentic is the music. During colonial rule, the populations of the African littorals absorbed the cultures, including music, of the various European and Asian powers. On its Mediterranean coast, in Morocco, Algiers, Libya, Egypt, and Ethiopia, Arabian modalities in song and dance held sway. The British influence was paramount on the coast of the Indian Ocean; the Portuguese were the colonial powers in Mozambique and Angola. The Dutch and the English established their artistic influence in South Africa. France and Belgium spread their cultures on the Ivory Coast and the Congo. The islands in the Indian Ocean, Madagascar and St. Mauritius, developed a unique mixture of European and Arabian musical cultures. How powerful the role of singing and beating the drum is in African life is indicated by the fact that plaintiffs are known to submit their claims in court by chanting, and the judges deliver their sentences to the accompaniment of gongs and drums. The truth of the briefs is measured by the expressiveness of the lilting phrase.

In colonial times, European opera composers eagerly exploited reports from the mysterious "dark continent" as material for exotic libretti. Verdi's *Aida* is a prime example of a melodramatic story of the collision of two civilizations. In Meyerbeer's opera *L'Africaine*, the lady of the title is a Madagascar beauty. Composers of such operas did not even attempt to find out what real African music was. Yet the diversity of African chants and rhythms is extraordinary. The tonal progressions allow a great variety of pitch, quasi-diatonic and ultrachromatic scales alternating with wide intervals, but rarely exceeding a fifth. Remarkably, the tritone, once described as *diabolus in musica*, is freely used in African song cadences. The rhythmic figures are mostly asymmetric and syncopated, at least when notated in Western nomenclature. The strong beat may be emphasized by loud claps. The texts are invócations to the gods of the village, laments when disaster strikes, and celebrations for important local events, marriages, or the inauguration of a new chief. There are hundreds of dialects among African tribes, and the language itself serves as a dynamic means of communication. Thus the unique click of the Bushmen and others may serve to mark the ending of a musical phrase. Intonation is of prime significance; a slight rise or drop in pitch may change the meaning of the phrase. The African ensemble contains drums of various sizes, gourds with rattling beads attached as shakers, metal bells, and various manufactured products. One interesting drum, known as the talking drum, is in the form of an hourglass with long strips of leather stretching down the sides from the head so that when the drum is squeezed under the arm it changes pitch; it is played with bent sticks. Another native instrument is the thumb piano, or *mbira*, a small wooden box with flexible nails or prongs of various lengths that are thumbed to produce sounds. For a large diapason, harp lutes are widely used, the largest being the *cora* with 21 strings. The neck of the cora has a number of notches that increase the register.

The time has finally come, toward the end of the 20th century, when Africa has ceased to be merely a receptacle of the white man's music but is itself the source of a new art deeply influencing the debilitated European and American music ways. Western musicians now go to Africa to learn their music. The American composer Steve Reich took a summer course in African percussion techniques at the Institute for African Studies at the University of Ghana, and upon return to the United States wrote a piece for voices and drums entitled *Drumming*.

Afro-beat. Generic name of popular music of Nigeria combining elements of primitive dance rhythms of Africa with jazz and rock. It emerged in Nigeria in the last quarter of the 20th century.

The Age of Anxiety. A work for piano and orchestra by Leonard Bernstein; his Symphony No. 2. The title is from the poem by W.H. Auden. The work is a musical summary of the unquiet mid–20th century. Bernstein makes use of a variety of techniques and styles—jazz, neo-Baroque commotion, and occasional episodes of dodecaphony—all this enlivened by pungent rhythms. The work was first performed by the Boston Symphony Orchestra on April 8, 1949, with Serge Koussevitzky conducting and Bernstein playing the redoubtable piano part.

The Age of Gold. A ballet by Shostakovich; first performed in Leningrad on October 26, 1930. The title refers to a festival at which the soccer teams of the Soviet Union and those of an unnamed capitalist nation participate, and which end in a triumphant procession of all workers of the world united in a common cause. A polka from this ballet ridicules an early disarmament conference at Geneva in 1920.

Agogic. A legitimate performing practice in which melodically important notes are allowed to linger without disruption of the musical phrase. Rubato is an agogical practice. Introduced by the German music theorist Hugo Riemann in 1884, the term derives from the Greek word "to lead." In musical rhetoric, it is opposed to the concept of dynamics, which provides accentuation by varying the degree of intensity.

Aida. An opera in four acts by Verdi. It is one of the most melodramatic operas, written to the most tragic and most implausible of all librettos ever contrived. Radames, commander of the ancient Egyptian army, falls in love with a captive Ethiopian princess, Aida, and inadvertently reveals a crucial military secret to her while her father, the king of Ethiopia, also captured anonymously, listens from behind the bushes. Amneris, the Egyptian king's daughter, who is affianced to Radames, discovers the treachery but is willing to save Radames if he relinquishes Aida. Radames refuses and, joined by Aida, is buried alive in a stone crypt. *Aida* was commissioned by the Khedive of Egypt for the inauguration of the Cairo Opera House. The outbreak of the Franco-Prussian War delayed the delivery of the costumes from Paris, which was under siege, and the production was postponed until Christmas Eve, 1871. It was one of the most spectacular opera premieres, with shiploads of notables and music critics converging on Cairo. But peasantlike Verdi, ever unsocial, declined the invitation to attend. Egyptian scholars regarded *Aida* as a popular European spectacle quite unauthentic in its story and music, and it never entered the regular repertoire of the Cairo Opera House until May 3, 1987, when it was lavishly staged in ancient Luxor, with the participation of some 150,000 Egyptian soldiers and hundreds of singers in the chorus, not to mention the horses. The role of Radames was performed by Placido Domingo. The price of a single ticket was $750, and several supersonic Concorde planes were rented to transport wealthy opera lovers. Note: *Aida* does not require a diaresis in Italian; *Aïda* with the diaresis is the French spelling.

Aida trumpet. A long trumpet specially constructed for use in Verdi's opera *Aida*. The original, manufactured in France, was called *trompette thébaine*, "a trumpet of Thebes." It was capable of sounding four tones: A-flat, B-flat, B-natural, and C.

The Airborne. An aeronautical symphony by Marc Blitzstein that traverses the history of aviation since the historic flight of the Wright brothers. Blitzstein wrote it while serving with the U.S. Air Force during World War II. It had its first performance in New York on March 23, 1946.

Akathistos. A Byzantine hymn to the Virgin that originated in the seventh century, supposedly to give thanks for the lifting of the Persian siege from Constantinople. The Greek name, which means "not seated," is explained by the injunction that the congregation should remain standing throughout the service. Structurally, the *Akathistos* follows the Byzantine poetic form Kontakion, with 24 stanzas, the initial letters of each adding up to the entire Greek alphabet.

Alba. A Provençal morning song, very popular with the troubadours, that corresponds to the serenade, or evening song. *Alba* means "light of dawn." See also *Aubade*.

Albert Herring. An opera in three acts by Benjamin Britten that is based on a Maupassant story centering on a contest in a small village for the most demonstrably virtuous young man. The contest is won by Albert Herring, but his immaculate virginity is immediately undermined by an alcoholic potion, and he goes morally berserk. The opera was produced at the Glyndebourne Festival in England on June 20, 1947, the composer conducting.

Alberti bass. A type of tonal accompaniment in broken triads and even tempo, traditionally for the piano left-hand accompaniment. It was popularized by Domenico Alberti early in the 18th century and used extensively by Haydn, Mozart, and Beethoven, among others.

Alceste. An opera in three acts by Gluck that is based on a play of Euripides'. It was produced in Vienna on December 16, 1767. The mythological story deals with Alcestis, who volunteers to enter Hades in place of her dead husband; she is saved from the nether region by Hercules. Handel wrote an opera on the same subject long before, and Lully even earlier, but Gluck's *Alceste* remains historically the most important. Much more significant than the opera itself is Gluck's preface to the published score in which he states his opposition to the preponderance given to performers, scenery, and costumery, and maintains that the dramatic and poetic content should be a paramount consideration in any artistic stage work.

Alcione. An opera by Marin Marais, produced in Paris on February 18, 1706. It contains a symphonic tempest, the first attempt at realistic effects in the orchestra. The orchestral score also includes, for the first time, a part for the snaredrum. Alcione, or Alcyone, was a daughter of Aeolus, the keeper of the winds; she was transformed into a halcyon bird (kingfisher) for defying the gods. The expression "halcyon days" stems from the belief that the seas are becalmed when the halcyon broods on her eggs.

Aleatory music. Aleatory music is chance music, random composition generated by the throw of dice or some other way of producing numbers by chance.

It is nothing new, having been practiced as early as the 18th century. Mozart amused himself by writing a piece with numbered bars that could be put together by throwing dice. Aleatory music in modern times, however, is a very serious business especially cultivated by the American composer John Cage, who has used for material the numbers derived from the Chinese I Ching. His classic aleatory works are *Music of Changes* for piano and his Piano Concerto. The German composer Karlheinz Stockhausen wrote numerous aleatory pieces for piano and chamber ensembles, as did his many disciples and followers in Europe and Japan. The term *aleatoric* is sometimes used.

Alessandro. An opera in three acts by Handel that deals with the conquests of Alexander the Great. Its Italian libretto by the celebrated Metastasio was subsequently used by several dozen other composers.

Alessandro Stradella. An opera in three acts by Friedrich von Flotow that is based on legends of the loves and murders of the 17th–century Italian composer Alessandro Stradella (1642–1682), whose own operatic output was significant in the development of the Neapolitan school of composition. Stradella was actually murdered by a hired assassin at the behest of a jealous rival in love. In the opera, Stradella soothes the savage breasts of the would-be murderers by singing arias from his operas; they are so deeply moved by the music that they desist from their dastardly deed—hence the subtitle, *The Power of Song*. The opera abounds in sentimental arias and dramatic episodes. It was first performed in Hamburg on December 30, 1844, and enjoyed an unusual success in Europe for a number of years before lapsing into innocuous desuetude.

Alexander Nevsky. A cantata by Prokofiev, first performed in Moscow on May 17, 1932. The score grew out of the music Prokofiev wrote for a motion picture based on the Russian hero who routed the German invaders in 1242. The production was a gentle caution to the Nazis not to tempt fate by another invasion. The rest is history.

Alexander's Feast. An oratorio by Handel; also known as *The Power of Music*. The text is derived from the famous ode by John Dryden. The oratorio was first performed in London on February 19, 1736, and it would have been forgotten were it not for Handel's happy thought of adding the Concerto Grosso in C major to the score. In fact, the oratorio itself has been forgotten except for a reference to it whenever the Concerto Grosso is programmed as *The Celebrated Concerto* from *Alexander's Feast*.

Alexander's Ragtime Band. An early song hit by Irving Berlin, written in 1910. Actually, the piece is not in ragtime but is a march, and there was no bandleader named Alexander. It became tremendously successful. A Broadway musical of this name was produced in 1938.

Aliquot strings. Sympathetic strings sometimes placed above the strings of the upper register of the piano to round out the sound. In mathematics, *aliquot* means an exact and proper divisor; in acoustics it applies to a sound that produces overtones.

Alle Vorschläge stets vor dem betreffenden Taktteil. "All notes and appoggiaturas always to be played before the corresponding beat of the measure." A remark found in one of Mahler's symphonies, showing that he did not follow the Baroque practice of putting appoggiaturas on the strong beat.

Alleluia. A Latin acclamation, much used in liturgical music, corresponding to the Hebrew evocation *hallelujah*, meaning "praise Jehovah." Alleluia in Gregorian chant usually concluded some of the responds. Naturally, an alleluia has to be set to joyful music. When joy is inappropriate, as in Requiem Masses, it is replaced by the tract, a psalmodic interlude in the Roman Catholic liturgy.

Almira. An opera in three acts by Handel, his first, produced in Hamburg on January 8, 1705, when he was 19 years old. It is actually a medley of German and Italian arias and recitatives.

Aloha. A Hawaiian song composed by the Princess Regent of Hawaii in 1878 while she was imprisoned by the Republican government of the island. The melody of the refrain is taken from a popular ballad by George F. Root that was originally published in 1847 under the title *There's Music in the Air*.

Alphorn. A wooden horn used by shepherds in the Alps, able to produce harmonics up to the 12th partial. Brahms noted the tune of such an Alpine horn on a postcard he sent to Clara Schumann on September 12, 1868, to words of his own: *Hoch auf'm Berg, tief im Tal, grüss' ich dich viel tausendmal!* ("High on the mountain, deep in the valley, I greet you many thousand times.") Eight years later, 1876, he made use of it in the famous flute solo in the last movement of his Symphony No. 1. This melody contains an approximation of the 11th partial note, F-sharp.

Alpine Symphony. A tremendous orchestral panorama unfolded by Richard Strauss and first conducted by him with the Berlin Philharmonic on October 28, 1915. It depicts the ascent of an Alpine peak and a fearful thunderstorm near the summit, conglomerating into chords containing all seven notes of the diatonic scale. A thunder machine and a wind machine for realistic effect are aluded in the huge score.

Also sprach Zarathustra (Thus Spake Zarathustra). A tone poem by Richard Strauss. The score was inspired by the philosophical poem by Nietzsche and was first performed with the composer conducting in Frankfurt on November 21, 1896. The opening is set in a proclamatory C major. There follow sections on religion, passions, science, and other matters. The fugal theme of science is an interesting anticipation of 12-tone composition, and the coda, combining the basic key of C major with a B-major triad in the highest treble, ventures into polytonality; it represents Nietzsche's World Riddle. The musical solution of this riddle lies in the fact that a very high B-major triad is actually composed of the highest overtones of the fundamental low C. The main theme of the work became a thematic signature of the futuristic film *2001: A Space Odyssey*.

Alto. Also *contralto*, the lowest female voice. Its range is from about G below middle C to two octaves upward. A group of instruments of the middle range are designated as alto—for instance, alto saxophone, alto recorder, and alto flute. The alto clef sets middle C on the third line of the staff. *Alto* is the French word for "viola."

Amahl and the Night Visitors. A one-act opera by Gian Carlo Menotti to his own text, suggested by the painting *The Adoration of the Magi* by Bosch. The earliest operatic work ever written specially for a television production, it was first shown on Christmas Eve, 1951, by NBC Television, and its success was so extraordinary that it has become an annual Christmas presentation. The story deals with the crippled boy Amahl who is miraculously healed when he gives his crutches to the visiting Three Wise Men as a gift for the Christ child.

Amateurs. A noble word degraded during the past couple of centuries to connote persons who dabble in the arts without requisite skill or understanding; it is often used synonymously with dilettante, which itself has been unjustly degraded from its original meaning of a person delighting in the arts. (The Italian word *diletto* means "delight.") In the 18th century, the word *amateur* had a complimentary meaning. There was a flourishing society in Paris called Concerts des Amateurs. Composers dedicated their works to persons described as amateurs in the dedication. Such works were alternatively called "music for ladies." Bach's son Carl Philipp Emanuel entitled his Clavecin Sonata No. 6, "*À L'Usage des dames*." Several royal personages were amateurs in the best sense of the word, among them Frederick the Great of Prussia. Of all professions, medical doctors are the most enthusiastic amateurs of music. There are doctors' symphony orchestras in several major cities of the United States and in other countries. A story is told about a famous pianist who played a concerto with a doctors' orchestra. Shortly afterward he suffered an attack of appendicitis; several surgeons from the orchestra volunteered to operate on him, but he declined. "I prefer to have my appendix removed by a member of the New York Philharmonic," he declared in all solemnity. Mathematicians and physicists like to play chamber music. The great scientist Albert Einstein was quite proficient on the violin, although a story goes that when he played a Mozart sonata with the famous pianist-pedagogue Artur Schnabel, he could not keep time. "For pity's sake, Albert," Schnabel exclaimed, "can't you count?" Chess players love music. The 18th-century composer Philidor earned a place in chess history by his opening known as Philidor's Defense. Prokofiev reached the rank of a top chess player in Russia. Painters, too, are often musical. The famous French artist Ingres loved to play the violin, even though he could never quite master it. Hence, the expression *violon d'Ingres* is applied to a passionate but inefficient amateur. Conversely, many musicians show a respectable talent for painting. Arnold Schoenberg and George Gershwin had exhibits of their art in public galleries. The Italian Futurists, among them Luigi Russolo, painted canvases in an expressionistic manner that fetched high prices after their deaths. The American composer Carl Ruggles devoted himself entirely to painting and stopped writing music during the last 40 years of his very long life. Dane Rudhyar, the French-American astrologer and composer, painted hundreds of pictures symbolic of his mystical beliefs. Some statesmen were accomplished music amateurs. Francis Hopkinson, a signer of the Declaration of Independence, claimed the distinction of being "the first Native of the United States who has produced a Musical Composition." Thomas Jefferson played the harpsichord, violin, and recorder. Benjamin Franklin perfected the glass harmonica. Presidents Harry Truman and Richard Nixon played the piano, but their repertory was limited. The great Polish patriot Paderewski was a pianist first, a statesman second. A story is told that when he met the French prime minister Georges Clemenceau at the Versailles Peace Conference following World War I, Clemenceau exclaimed: "So you are the famous pianist, and now you are prime minister! What a comedown!"

Ambrosian chant. A system of plainchant traditionally associated with the fourth-century bishop of Milan, St. Ambrose. It preceded by two centuries the codification of Gregorian chant. Some music historians regard the Ambrosian chant as an inchoate predecessor of Gregorian chant; others find in ancient Ambrosian ways a refreshing freedom from the strict Gregorian doctrine. Still others connect the Ambrosian chant with the oriental sources of liturgy and cite in support the use of florid quasi-exotic melismas that adorn the melodies of the Ambrosian Mass (some such fiorituras comprise more than 100 notes). Perhaps the most rational historical theory about the place of the Ambrosian chant in Christian liturgy is that it is a Milanese branch of the hymnal ritual, whose other three main branches are the Gregorian of Rome, the Gallican of France, and the Mozarabian of Moorish Spain. This division is analogous with the emergence of Romance languages from their common source, the Roman Latin. Whether Ambrose actually composed the traditional

"Ambrosian hymns" credited to him is a moot question, but there can be no doubt as to their great importance.

Amelia Goes to the Ball. A one-act opera buffa by Gian Carlo Menotti, his first, to his own libretto in Italian. In it the ambitious Amelia is eager to get to the ball on time but is delayed by a violent encounter between her husband and her lover. She finally is escorted to the ball by a friendly policeman. The opera was first performed in Philadelphia on April 1, 1937.

America. Patriotic song to words written by Samuel Francis Smith in 1832. As a student at the Andover Theological Seminary, he was commissioned to write a chorus for children. He selected a German song with the original words, *Heil, dir im Siegerkranz.* Smith's first line was "My Country 'tis of Thee," which became universally popular. The only reason it was not chosen as the national anthem of the United States was that the tune was identical to that of England's *God Save the King. America* was first performed by a children's choir at the Park Street Church in Boston on July 4, 1832.

America is also the name given to a symphonic rhapsody by Ernest Bloch, a work grandiloquently tracing the history of the United States from the landing of the Pilgrims to the dawn of the 20th century. Bloch won a prize instituted by the magazine *Musical America* for this work, and it had a few well-publicized performances, the first of them by the New York Philharmonic on December 20, 1928. Bloch made use of all kinds of American tunes, ending with a synthetic hymn of his own dedicated to his adoptive land. The work sank into oblivion despite its patriotic proclamations.

America the Beautiful. A set of words written by Katherine Lee Bates, professor of English at Wellesley College. The inflated patriotic verses were inspired in her heaving bosom in 1893 by the view from Pikes Peak in Colorado. Her poem was published in the Boston religious periodical *The Congregationalist* on July 4, 1895, producing a national uplift. Several songwriters vied to set the inspirational words to music, but none could find a sufficiently powerful melody. Despairing of finding a suitable musical setting to express the purple majesty of these shining words, the seekers turned to the time-honored tune *O Mother Dear Jerusalem* by Samuel Augustus Ward, commonly known as *Materna,* and the hymn became an obligatory effusion at patriotic gatherings. Katherine Lee Bates lived long enough (until 1929) to see her work enshrined as an American classic.

American Festival Overture. An orchestral work by William Schuman, first performed in Boston on October 6, 1939. In it he uses the vernacular and provocative calls of small American boys at play.

An American in Paris. A tone poem for orchestra by George Gershwin, in which he introduces realistic noises such as Paris taxi horns and Parisian popular songs of the time. It was first performed in New York on December 13, 1928, Walter Damrosch conducting.

American Quartet. Dvořák's String Quartet in F major, op. 96, which he wrote during his sojourn in the United States. It was originally nicknamed the "Nigger Quartet" because its syncopated themes suggested Negro spirituals. This familiar title was not changed until the 1930s, when blatant forms of racism finally became unacceptable.

Amériques. A symphonic panorama of the Americas, both North and South, composed in the United States by Edgar Varèse between 1918 and 1922. It was first performed by the Philadelphia Orchestra with Leopold Stokowski conducting on April 9, 1926. The score abounds in resonant discords and is built on a gargantuan scale of instrumental sonorities.

El Amor brujo. A ballet by Manuel de Falla. The title means *Love, the Magician.* The ballet was first performed in Madrid on April 15, 1915; a successful symphonic suite was drawn from it. The romantic scenario deals with the posthumous pressure of a dead gypsy lover upon his surviving beloved not to yield to any living human. But a new love conquers the spectral prohibition; hence the title.

Anabasis. An ascending musical figure, usually associated in Baroque composition with concepts of ascent, such as the resurrection or spiritual enlightenment. *Anabasis* means "ascension" in Greek; its opposite is *katabasis.*

Anamorphic transformation. A technique applied by some Renaissance painters by which the true image can be obtained from a distorted representation by projecting it on the surface of a cylinder or a cone. Similarly, in music an anamorphic transformation may be achieved by altering the component intervals of a melody, telescoping the rhythmic values, and performing similar distortions upon the harmony. The concept may be useful in analyzing works by modern composers.

Anchors Aweigh. A marching song of the American Navy, written in 1907. Both the music and the words are by Charles Zimmerman, who was musical director of the Naval Academy at Annapolis, but Alfred H. Miles is sometimes credited with joint authorship.

Andrea Chénier. A grand opera in four acts by Umberto Giordano, produced in Milan on March 28, 1896. The libretto by Illica deals with the tragic fate of the poet André Chénier, condemned to the guillotine by the revolutionary tribunal in 1793. His beloved contrives to incriminate herself and to die with him. The spectacular success of this opera established Giordano as one of the finest Italian opera composers of his time.

Angelito. Spanish for "little angel." In Venezuela, Colombia, and some other South American countries, a funeral chant for a dead child who upon ascent to heaven becomes a guardian angel for the family. As befits this kind of song, it is slow and mournful, suggesting a liturgical cantillation. Among South American Negroes, a curious game accompanies the ritual with the attendants trying to blow out a candle held over the dead child's head.

Aniara. An opera by Karl-Birger Blomdahl, after the novel by Harry Martinson. Described as "a revue of mankind, in space-time," it was first produced in Stockholm on May 31, 1959. After an atomic war, survivors from Earth emigrate to Mars in the spaceship *Aniara.* They become demoralized during the long journey and fail to achieve the new way of life that they seek. The score employs electronic sounds, but its tonal fabric is derived from the *Grossmutterakkord*, which consists of 12 different notes separated from each other by 11 different intervals.

Animal voices. Because birds are the primordial musicmakers of the animal world, it is to be expected that composers have for centuries imitated bird calls in their works. The cuckoo has the most immediately identifiable leitmotif, a falling major third. Beethoven immortalized it, along with the trilling nightingale and the repetitive quail, in his *Pastoral* Symphony. The 18th-century French composer Louis Claude Daquin wrote a harpsichord piece entitled *The Cuckoo*, which became a universal favorite. The contemporary French composer Olivier Messiaen expanded the musical aviary by filling his compositions with accurately notated exotic bird calls. The rooster is glorified in Rimsky-Korsakov's opera *Le Coq d'or*; he sounds his cockadoodle-doo on the muted trumpet. The bleating of sheep is imitated by a cacophonous ensemble of wind instruments in the symphonic poem *Don Quixote* of Richard Strauss. Villa-Lobos reproduces the piercing cry of the jungle bird araponga on high B-flat in one of his *Bachianas Brasileiras*. Saint-Saëns has a whole menagerie in his *Carnival of Animals*. Buzzing insects provide an obvious source of animal onomatopoeia. Rimsky-Korsakov's *Flight of the Bumble Bee* is a famous example. A more esoteric illustration is Béla Bartók's *Diary of a Fly* from his *Mikrokosmos*. In the score of his pantomime *L'Enfant et les sortilèges*, Ravel includes a couple of meowing amorous cats.

Sometimes special instruments are invented to imitate animal sounds; there is the toy cuckoo used in Haydn's *Toy* Symphony. Actual reproductions of animal noises on a phonograph disc or tape are used in some modern scores. Ottorino Respighi was the first to introduce a recording of a nightingale in the orchestration of his symphonic poem, *The Pines of Rome.* Two American composers, George Crumb and Alan Hovhaness, use recordings of the sounds of humpback whales. These giant marine animals have no vocal cords but are capable of producing tones covering the entire human range; furthermore, the whale voice has a tremendous endurance and can carry a tone as long as 18 minutes.

Are animals themselves sensitive to music in any selective way? Experiments conducted on dairy farms in New Zealand in 1947 seemed to show that cows produce more milk when jazz is played. On a New Jersey farm, 2,500 pigs were exposed to a constant flood of jazz in 1950, and they put on weight faster than pigs not otherwise favored. A farmer in Surrey, England, wrote to the British Broadcasting Corporation that his cows gave their highest milk yield when Haydn's string quartets were played for them. The curator of reptiles at the Brookfield Zoo in Chicago noted that the alligator mating calls approximated the pitch of B-flat below middle C. He hired four French horn players and instructed them to play B-flat in unison, but no visible mating ensued. All these and numerous other attempts to connect music with physiological processes in animals have failed, proving, if proof were needed, that animals lack music appreciation. Perhaps the most vocal animal is the Siamang (*Symphalangus syndactylus*), a large gibbon of Sumatra. Its throat sac swells like a red balloon during vocalization, and it has the loudest voice among primates, not excluding coloratura sopranos.

Anna Magdalena Books. A common name for Bach's *Klavierbüchlein* (*Little Clavier Book*), a collection of keyboard music that Bach composed for his young second wife, Anna Magdalena.

Années de pèlerinage (Years of Wandering). A collection comprising three series of piano works by Liszt, each piece bearing a descriptive title. The most famous of them are *Au bord d'une source* (*By the Bank of a Brook*), *Venezia e Napoli* (*Venice and Naples*), and *Les Jeux d'eau à la Villa d'Este* (*Fountains at the Villa d'Este*).

Annie Laurie. An Irish song composed by Lady John Scott in 1835. Annie Laurie may have been a real person whose unhappy romance with a member of a rival Scottish clan was the subject of the poem reputedly written by her lover.

Anteludium. Literally, in Latin, "foreplay." An older term for *praeludium*, "prelude."

Anthem. A hymnal song performed by a chorus. The word is derived from the Latin *antiphone*, and liturgically the form corresponds to the Roman Catholic motet. Anthem singing arose in the Reformation; consequently, it had its most fruitful development in the Lutheran and Anglican churches. More widely, the term came to signify any solemn song performed by a community. National anthems are the patriotic extensions of the prayerful religious anthems.

Antiphon. In common usage, a choral response after the singing of a psalm. It is usually sung in a plain syllabic manner. In large polyphonic compositions an antiphon may become an elaborate setting vying in importance with the main section. Etymologically the term is traceable to the early Christian singing of the same phrase an octave higher by another chorus composed of women and boys. *Antiphonium* literally means "countersound" in Greek.

Antony and Cleopatra. An opera by Samuel Barber, with a libretto that faithfully preserves selected scenes from Shakespeare's play. The work was commissioned by the Metropolitan Opera for the inauguration of its new house at the Lincoln Center for the Performing Arts in New York and was produced there on September 16, 1966. Despite, or perhaps because of, the unabashed romantic flow of operatic cantilena, *Antony and Cleopatra* was generally damned by the critics. Barber revised the score in 1975.

Anvil. A percussion instrument in the form of an actual anvil, consisting of a metal bar struck by a hammer. It was first used in an opera by Auber, *Le Maçon*, 1825, and was popularized in the famous *Anvil Chorus* in Verdi's *Il Trovatore*. In *Das Rheingold* Wagner introduces 18 anvils to illustrate the forging of the ring of the Nibelung. Varèse has a part for the anvil in *Ionisation*, and Carl Orff employs it in his opera *Antigony*.

Anvil Chorus. Common designation of the scene in a gypsy camp in the second act of Verdi's opera *Il Trovatore*, in which the blacksmiths strike anvils in time with the chorus. It is one of the most celebrated single passages in all opera, even though the stage description of the *Anvil Chorus* appears nowhere in Verdi's score. During the celebration of the Peace Jubilee in Boston in 1872, 100 city firemen beat anvils in a monster extravaganza during the performance of this number.

Apache Dance. A spirited tune by Offenbach, originally published as a piano piece entitled *Valse des Rayons*. Early in the 20th century, the tune acquired a sudden popularity under the unjustified title *Apache Dance* to accompany Paris cabaret dancers, with the male partner simulating extreme violence purported to represent the savagery of Apache Indians.

Apocalyptic Symphony. The title attached to Bruckner's Symphony No. 8 in C minor to point out its religious depth and expectations of eternity. Actually, it is not overlong and is quite tolerable to an unprejudiced listener. It received its first performance in Vienna on December 18, 1892. A thoroughly revised version premiered in London on September 2, 1973.

Apollon musagète (Apollo, Leader of the Muses). A ballet with string orchestra by Stravinsky, first performed in Washington, D.C., on April 27, 1928. This work marks Stravinsky's transition to a neo-Classical method of composition: the score is emphatically diatonic in texture and all attempts at purely coloristic effects are abandoned.

Aposiopesis. A Greek term in rhetoric denoting an interruption of a sentence under the influence of a sudden emotion. In sacred oratorios the aposiopesis is often expressed by a general pause at a climactic point, particularly after a reference to death.

Appalachian Spring. A ballet by Aaron Copland, with choreography by Martha Graham, first performed in Washington, D.C., on October 30, 1944. The title is from a poem by Hart Crane, but the music has only a peripheral contact with the text of the poem. There are eight sections, descriptive of a wedding celebration on a farm in the Appalachian hills. As with most of his ballet scores, Copland drew an orchestral suite from it and this was first performed in New York on October 4, 1945.

Appassionata. The title given by Beethoven's publisher to his Piano Sonata in F minor, op. 57. Beethoven entitled it simply *Grande Sonate pour piano*. There is certainly enough passion in the work—somber and subdued in the first movement, stormy and unrestrained in the last, with a lyrical movement in between—to justify the publisher's title.

Applause. From the Latin verb *plaudere*, "to clap hands," an instinctive reaction to an excellent artistic performance. Shouts of "bravo" often join the applause. Outside Italy, "bravo" is shouted equally at men and women performers, although the proper grammatical form for a female artist should be "brava." In Moslem countries, audiences cry out "Allah, Allah" to commend a singer; in Spain it is "olé, olé!" At the opera, applause often greets the entrance of a favorite singer. When there is an orchestral coda after a particularly successful aria, it is often drowned out by intemperate applause. (An example is the soft instrumental conclusion to the famous tenor's aria in *Pagliacci*.) A tug-of-war ensues when the conductor makes a definite effort to proceed with the music and the singer is eager to prolong the applause. Sometimes a singer, expiring at the end of an aria, is forced to rise from the scene of death and bow to the public. Cries of *bis* ("twice"), that is, encore, might bring a repetition of the aria. It was once a common practice among opera singers, especially in the 19th century, to hire people to applaud them. The hired group was known as a *claque*. A peculiar type of what may be called responsorial applause developed in Russia toward the middle of the 20th century, when the artists themselves applauded the audience, usually in a rhythmic measure of one long and two short claps. The origin of this custom can be traced to the practice of political leaders returning the applause of an enthusiastic audience. It is interesting that whistling, which is the expression of the most passionate pleasure at a performance in England and America, is equivalent to hissing in France and particularly in Russia. When, shortly after the victorious conclusion of World War II, American soldiers greeted the

Russian dancers in Berlin with whistling, the performers were in tears, believing that they had been hissed down. The so-called Bronx cheer, produced
by sticking out the tongue between closed lips and exhaling vigorously, is the
most emphatic way of expressing displeasure at the quality of performance.
At commercial musical programs on the radio and television, at which timing
is essential, the amount and the loudness of applause is precisely proportioned
by signs passed in front of the audience; an even safer practice is "canned
applause," the time and volume of which can be controlled by the studio
engineers. However, unrestrained outbursts of adulation are usually welcomed
by highly paid popular singers.

Après une Lecture de Dante. Liszt's grand piece for piano, subtitled *Fantasia
quasi sonata* (as contrasted with Beethoven's *Sonata quasi una fantasia*). It
is also known simply as *Dante Sonata*. Its opening tritones suggest the inferno
of Dante's *La divina commedia*, the tritone being the *diabolus in musica* of
the musical theologians of the Middle Ages. Since the work is called "Upon
Reading Dante," Liszt progressed from infernal tritones and their derivatives,
the diminished-seventh chords, to the celestial harmonies of Paradise, passing
through the tortuous path of dissonant Purgatory.

April in Paris. Vernon Duke's most famous song, to words by Edgar Harburg;
originally heard in the Broadway show *Walk a Little Faster*, which opened
on December 1, 1932. The phrase was supposed to be from a remark made
by Dorothy Parker during a rehearsal in bleak and cold New York December:
"I wish I were in April in Paris." An anecdote is also related that a New
York dandy, inspired by the song, went to Paris in April, found the city damp
and chilly, and reported his disillusion to Duke, who said, "Okay, so Paris
is miserable in April. It is lovely in May, but I needed a word with two
syllables for the rhythm."

Arab music. It must be said at the outset that authentic Arab scales, rhythms, *weak*
and polyphonic combinations are as transcendental to European modes and
time measures, as, let us say, the periphery of a circle is incommensurate to
its radius. What we know about Arab music is contained in a considerable
number of theoretical studies by Arab mathematicians and philosophers. Notation of Arab chants and rhythmic modes is largely given in terms of positions
on native instruments, which have undergone practically no changes in their
construction and tuning throughout the centuries. The tones of Arab music
rarely coincide with the Western system of tetrachords; major and minor
tonalities are nonexistent in the Western application of these terms. There are
12 basic modes (known as a *maqām*) in Arab music, which tend to emphasize
the minor third. The melodies are short and are followed by long inhalations
serving to scan the prosody; indeed, the intonation of muezzins chanting

prayers from their tall minarets is greatly impressive. Harmonization in the Western sense of the word is also nonexistent; the only combination of tones in Arab music results from simultaneous accompaniments on Arab lutes to a singing voice. The melodies themselves register to a Western-trained ear as progressions of quarter tones, semitones, and other divisions of a whole tone. The incidence of the "oriental" interval of a tone and a half occurs in many religious chants in Arab countries. In addition to the lute, or *'ūd*, native Arab musicians typically use a variety of vertical flutes (*nāy*), the violin (*rabāb*), the zither, a vase-shaped drum, and the tambourine. Several Russian and French composers wrote pieces purporting to be of Arabian inspiration, and their melodies invariably emphasize the orientally inflected tonal progressions. Tchaikovsky included an Arabian Dance in the score of his *Nutcracker* ballet, in which the only suggestion of an exotic atmosphere is the avoidance of a perfect cadence and a continuous organ point on the tonic and dominant in a minor mode. The most famous Arabian tale in music is Rimsky-Korsakov's symphonic suite *Scheherazade*, inspired by the *Arabian Nights*, but there is no attempt in the score to imitate Arabian modalities.

Arabesque. A character piece, marked by an ornamental melodic figuration, usually in a pronounced rhythmic manner in 2/4 time. The etymological reference to Arabic designs reflects the Romantic infatuation with exotic art. Arabesques by Schumann, Tchaikovsky, and others are engaging solo pieces for piano.

Arcana. A symphonic poem by Edgar Varèse. The title, meaning "mysteries," is inspired by the hermetic philosophy of Paracelsus. The score uses 40 percussion instruments besides a huge orchestra. It was first performed by Stokowski with the Philadelphia Orchestra on April 8, 1927. The music critics vented a torrent of invectives. A quarter of a century later the work became an acknowledged classic of modern music.

Arciorgano. A type of organ constructed in the 16th century, with manuals containing a great number of keys to the octave, manufactured in the vain attempt to incorporate all the theoretical scales of ancient Greek music, the diatonic, chromatic, and enharmonic, so that modulation could theoretically be performed in all keys without yielding to the artificial division of equal temperament. The most ambitious of the category of arciorgano was the grandly named *clavicymbalum universale*.

Aria. A word common to all European languages; etymologically derived from the Latin *aer*, "air," which in music came to signify a manner or a model of performance or composition. In 17th-century England the spelling "ayre" was used to designate a variety of songs, whether serious or popular. The most common association of the word *aria* is with a solo song in opera. An important development was the formation of the *da capo* aria, popularized by the composers of the Neapolitan school in the second half of the 17th century. It was in a symmetric three-part form, with the third part being the exact repetition, or a slight variation, of the first part (*da capo* means literally "to the head"). It became the most common form of the operatic aria, especially among Italian composers of the 18th and 19th centuries and their many followers in other nations. Specialized categories of such arias came to be used in Italian opera; among them are the following:

Aria cantabile. A "songful" aria, expressing sorrow or yearning.

Aria d'abilità. An aria requiring especial ability to sing properly.

Aria di bravura. A rapid virtuosic song expressing violent passion.

Aria di mezzo carattere. An aria of a medium type, flowing melodically but not too passionately.

Aria d'imitazione. An imitation aria, in which the melody imitates singing birds, hunting horns, marching trumpets, or anything else that can be imitated.

Aria parlante. An aria in the manner of declamation. Sometimes a composer would write a double aria for a virtuoso singer, one of a passionate nature and one in a contemplative mood. Instrumental pieces of a songful character were often called arias in Baroque music.

Ariadne auf Naxos. A one-act opera by Richard Strauss to a libretto by Hugo von Hofmannsthal, first performed in Stuttgart on October 25, 1912. The extremely involved story consists of three superimposed plots: A bourgeois gentilhomme, annexed from Molière's play, engages an opera company and a commedia dell'arte troupe. A philosophical, methodological, and aesthetical imbroglio ensues in which the impractical composer of the opera to be performed preaches pure art; that opera centers on Ariadne abandoned on the island of Naxos praying for death to release her. In the finale, Ariadne ascends to the skies with the opportunely arriving Bacchus. The watchers of the opera within the opera signalize approval.

Ariadne auf Naxos is also a scenic melodrama by the Czech composer Jiří Benda, first produced in Gota on February 27, 1775. It is one of the earliest examples of true melodrama, in which the text is recited with musical accompaniment. Mozart heard it in 1778 and said that opera recitatives should be treated as a melodrama of this type and sung only when the words are in perfect agreement in mood and rhythm with the musical accompaniment.

Ariane et Barbe-Bleue (Ariadne and Bluebeard). An opera in three acts by Paul Dukas after Maeterlinck's drama, to the familiar story of an uxoricidal castelan. His last wife outwits the villain after she discovers the dead bodies of his previous six wives. The opera was first performed in Paris on May 10, 1907.

Arkansas Traveler. An American dancing song of 1847. Its composer is unknown and its attribution to Colonel Sanford D. Faulkner of Arkansas is highly dubious. *Arkansas Traveler* is also an American square dance of unknown origin that acquired popularity in the middle of the 19th century. Its syncopated design, like that of the dancing song that shares its name, presages ragtime rhythms.

Arlecchino. Italian for "harlequin." In medieval commedia dell'arte, the character of a buffoon, usually wearing a mask. In musical comedies Arlecchino is the lover of Colombina. *Arlecchino* is also the name of a "theatrical" capriccio by Ferruccio Busoni, in which the harlequin assumes different guises, some virtuous, some sinful. It was first performed in Zürich on May 11, 1917.

Armide et Renaud. Lyric tragedy by Lully, first performed in Paris on February 15, 1686. The subject is taken from the famous poem by Tasso, *Gerusalemme liberata*, which forms the libretto of many other operas. The Crusader Renaud is bewitched by the charms of Armide, who lures him to her magic garden. But after lengthy dalliance, Renaud feels a need of further heroic deeds and leaves Armide. Despondent, she destroys her garden with its memories of love. This work is regarded as one of the greatest achievements of the French lyric drama.

Arpeggione. A string instrument about the size of a cello, having six strings and a guitar-like shape. Invented in 1823, its vogue was of a short duration, but Schubert wrote a sonata for arpeggione and piano.

Arrangements. Reductions of classical symphonies for piano four-hands that proliferated in the 19th century when mechanical recordings did not exist. They served a laudable purpose: piano albums published under such ingratiating titles as *Brother and Sister* made it possible to acquaint pianistic boys and girls with popular arias of the operatic repertoire and, indeed, with complete movements of classical symphonies. Professional composers were called upon to make such arrangements, and they did not regard it as beneath their dignity to do so. A special form of reduction was the so-called theater arrangement, which was adapted for performance of symphonic works by small ensembles for amateur productions. Theater arrangements usually contained indications for optional substitutions of one instrument by another, with the piano part filling in the harmonic vacuum. When Rachmaninoff played his Piano Concerto No. 2 in Los Angeles, a lady rushed to him after the show, exclaiming, "Beautiful! Who is your arranger?" "Madam," Rachmaninoff replied, "in Russia, we composers were so poor we had to write our own music." A more dignified term for an arrangement is *transcription*. Busoni's famous version for piano solo of Bach's *Chaconne* has become an independent virtuoso piece. Brahms arranged Bach's *Chaconne* for piano left-hand. Musical literature abounds with such examples, but publishers must be careful not to infringe on the copyright of popular pieces. An American publisher who issued a song called *Avalon*, based on Cavaradossi's aria from Puccini's *Tosca*, was obliged to pay a heavy fine for such an infringement. On the other hand, nothing could be done by the perpetrators of the song *I'm Forever Chasing Rainbows*, based on the middle section of Chopin's posthumous *Fantaisie-Impromptu* because Chopin's music was not protected by copyright law. Neither could Mozart be spared the depredation of his C-major Piano Sonata in a song entitled *In an 18th-Century Drawing Room*. The person who added these particular lyrics made more money than Mozart made from all his piano works.

Ars Antiqua. A Latin term meaning "old art," traditionally applied by historians to musical developments of the 12th and early 13th centuries. Ars Antiqua had its inception in France; its great early representatives were the masters of the Notre Dame school, or the Paris school, Leoninus and Perotinus. Leoninus was called *optimus organista*, "the best composer of the organa," and Perotinus was described as *optimus discantor*, "the best composer of discantus," a form that used florid melismas in the upper voices. An intermediate system between organum and discantus was *copula*, coupling two voices in various combinations. In the course of time, the organa generated the *clausulae*, short pieces in two parts serving as surrogates for the organa. When a liturgical text in Latin was added to the upper voice of the clausula, it evolved into the motet, which introduced the seemingly chaotic practice of appending different texts, in the French vernacular as well as in liturgical Latin, to the upper voices. It was a striking departure from the "pragmatic" or "rational" polyphonic forms, but it proved the most fertile development in medieval music. The *cantus firmus*, the "solid song," retained its dominant position in all musical forms during the Ars Antiqua, with the exception of *conductus*, which used free improvisation.

The metrical system of Ars Antiqua is confined almost exclusively to ternary groupings in the *tempus perfectum*. Binary meters were used in the *tempus imperfectum*, "incomplete time," without the connotation of being intrinsically imperfect. The preference for the ternary metrical division had a theological significance for medieval theorists to whom triple time symbolized the perfection of the Trinity. The theoretical doctrine of Ars Antiqua was provided by Franco of Cologne, active in the 13th century, in his treatise *Ars Cantus mensurabilis* (*The Art of Measured Song*). In it he codified the rhythmic modes of Ars Antiqua, indicating the relative note values of mensural notation.

Ars Musica. The "art of music." In medieval universities, music was regarded as one of the *septem artes*, the seven liberal arts. Taught in the Latin language, it was a part of the *quadrivium—arithmetica, geometria, musica*, and *astronomia*. The remaining *trivium* of the *septem artes* included *grammatica, rhetorica*, and *dialectica*. In medieval Latin the word *ars*, "arts," stood below the more elevated concept of *scientia*, "science," and above the more common category of *usus*, "usage." When Guido d'Arezzo taught his singers with the aid of his Guidonian Hand, he was following the precepts of practical *usus*. When he introduced neumes, first without lines (*neumae usuales*) and later with lines (*neumae regulares*, from *regula*, "line"), he elevated the Ars Musica to the point of *scientia canendi*, "science of singing." This innovation marked the beginning of musical notation, which received its medieval culmination in the treatise *Ars nova*, completed in 1320 by Philippe de Vitry. Indeed, an alternative title of this work was *Ars nova notandi*, "the new art of notating music." As the scientific aspect of music began to be developed further in the medieval universities, it became subdivided into special branches, such as *Ars cantus plani*, "art of plain chant," or *Ars componendi*, "art of composing." Bach called his *Musikalisches Opfer*, "*Ars canonica*," or "the art of writing canons."

Ars Nova. A Latin term meaning "new art" or "new method." The name stems from the treatise of Philippe de Vitry, compiled about 1320, and from a work by Johannes de Muris, *Ars novae musicae*, dating from 1321. Actually, the new art had much more modest aspirations than its title suggests; it was merely a new way of notating music (*Ars nova notandi*). It is historically important in its extension of mensural notation to include small note values, down to the semiminima, and the expansion of practical metrical systems. Its greatest innovation was the formal acceptance of binary division of the measure, as contrasted with the conventional designation of ternary division as the only "true art." The composers of Ars Nova, on the other hand, described music in ternary division as Ars Antiqua, "old art," and, by implication, an inferior art. Besides accepting binary division, the *tempus imperfectum*, as of equal validity as the ternary division, the *tempus perfectum*, the composers of Ars Nova introduced other innovations. Of these, the most significant was the acceptance of thirds and sixths as consonances and the resulting toleration of the *fauxbourdon*, the use of sixth chords as concords. These "novelties" aroused opposition by adherents of the Ars Antiqua. Thus Jacques de Liège in his treatise *Speculum musicae (Mirror of Music)* declares ruefully, *"Regnat nova ars, exulat antiqua"* ("New art reigns, old art is exiled"), and then proceeds to excoriate the "unnatural" novelties of the *moderni*. Curiously enough, today the technique of Ars Antiqua appears more progressive with its quartal harmonies than the *fauxbourdon* peculiar to Ars Nova. In rhythmic patterns, too, Ars Antiqua cultivates a more "modern" type of syncopated iambic prosody of a short note followed by a long note, whereas Ars Nova uses the more "natural" trochaic rhythmic figure of a long note followed by a short one. There is a tantalizing parallel with this inversion of the concepts of new and old in the emergence of *Nuove musiche* at the threshold of the 17th century introduced by the Florentine school of the Camerata, which gave rise to the art of opera. The "new" musicians of this group renounced the complex contrapuntal art of the great polyphonic school of the Renaissance in favor of monodic usages, in which contrapuntal voices are subordinated to the melody. The theorists of the Camerata described their music as *stile moderno*, in contradistinction to the *stile antico* of their polyphonic predecessors.

The most important representatives of the Ars Nova were Guillaume de Machaut in France and Francesco Landini in Italy. The great accomplishment of Machaut was the introduction of the rhythms and folkways of popular dances, including ballades, rondeaux, and virelais. Landini is known for the "Landini cadence," which detours from the direct resolution of the leading tone into the tonic by first retreating to the submediant. Johannes Ciconia, a Flemish composer who was active in Italy, was instrumental in reversing the trend of Ars Nova toward further simplification and returning to the exploration of new polyphony. In this sense he was a forerunner of the great contrapuntal school in the Netherlands that reached its flowering in the Renaissance. Thus, Ars Nova, which arose as a movement of simplification, became in a single century the harbinger of new complexity, which reached the saturation point and precipitated another historical simplification, that of the Florentine school of the 17th century.

The Art of the Fugue. In German, *Die Kunst der Fuge*. The last great work of Johann Sebastian Bach, which remained unfinished. It was issued posthumously, edited by Bach's son Wilhelm Friedemann Bach, who inscribed these words after the last fugue, based on Bach's own name, B-A-C-H: "During the composition of this fugue the author died," and who attached the title *Die Kunst der Fuge* to the work. Bach's original was set simply as a collection of contrapunti—canonic and fugal samples all based on the same subject in D minor. It actually is a manual of composition in a contrapuntal style and not necessarily meant for performance. Inevitably the work became the target of experimenters, theorists, and scholars who tried to read Bach's mind and decide for him in what form his contrapunti should be performed.

As Time Goes By. A song by Herman Hupfeld written in 1931 for the musical *Everybody's Welcome*. Its popularity was boosted when it was used in the 1942 movie *Casablanca*.

ASCAP. The acronym for the American Society of Composers, Authors, and Publishers, an organization that was established in 1914 to protect the rights of American composers and lyricists against copyright infringement. The first test came in 1917 when ASCAP tried to collect royalties from a New York restaurant that had an orchestra perform selections from Victor Herbert's operetta *Sweethearts*. After much litigation, ASCAP won the case. In subsequent years, ASCAP extended its operations to include hotels, theaters, radio, and motion pictures. As a result, ASCAP itself became a formidable monopoly. As such, it was challenged by another organization established for the same purpose, Broadcast Music Inc., or BMI, which was formed in 1940. Instead of collecting royalties, BMI licensed radio and later television stations, charging them for the use of works by composers and lyricists represented by BMI. Eventually a competitive coexistence was arrived at between ASCAP and BMI.

Ashmedai. An opera by Joseph Tal, first performed in Hamburg on November 9, 1971. Ashmedai, or more commonly Asmodeus, is a minor demon who takes possession of a peaceable kingdom, ostensibly for a year, but who manages to corrupt the populace into voting for him as president for life. The score is ultramodern, atonal, and obsessively discordant, with a liberal application of eerie electronic effects.

Asleep in the Deep. A lugubrious sea song written by H.W. Petrie in 1897, sung mostly by low basses who can hit deep C.

Asymmetry. A departure from the natural binary or ternary rhythm. Asymmetry can be easily felt by making a step with the same foot while walking, thus adding a beat to the natural walking pace. Asymmetry is common in non-Western music and is artificially imposed in modern primitivistic music (that is, music deliberately imitating exotic sounds). One of the clearest illustrations is provided by Stravinsky's *L'Histoire du soldat*, in which an asymmetrical melodic line is projected upon a steady bass, creating a constant arrhythmia and suggesting a missed heartbeat.

Atonality. A term current among progressive musicians in Vienna at the turn of the century. As its etymology suggests, *atonality* means the absence of tonality, the avoidance of a historic relationship between members of major and minor scales. The technique of atonal writing derives from the chromatic scale, and shuns the use of consecutive steps of semitones. Thus Rimsky-Korsakov's *Flight of the Bumblebee* is not an example of atonality; the foundation of the running chromatic scale is decisively underlined by the tonal accompaniment. Schoenberg is credited (or blamed) for the invention of the method of atonal writing, but he expressly denied this honor (or dishonor). True, he avoided in his music the use of triadic constructions, and he ceased to employ the key signature in his works, letting the melody flow freely, unconstrained by the rigid laws of modulation, cadence, sequence, and other time-honored devices of tonal writing. It was not until 1924 that he reached the logical development of his system of composition, known as the 12-tone technique, in which all members of the given melody are related to each other without reference to a tonal center or epicenter.

Atonicality. The term suggested by Schoenberg in place of "atonality," which he thought was illogical. Atonicality would properly imply, so Schoenberg argued, only the absence of the tonic, typical of the works of the Second Vienna School, whereas atonality would suggest the absence of tones themselves. Schoenberg's logically argued term never took root.

Attila. An opera by Verdi, first performed in Venice on March 17, 1846. The libretto draws its subject from the final struggle of Rome against the invading hordes of Attila and his Huns. Contemporary audiences found a parallel with the subjugation of Italy by Austria in the middle of the 19th century, and patriotic sentiment contributed to the opera's temporary success.

Aubade. French for morning music, corresponding to the Spanish *alborada*, and contrasted with serenade, evening music. The word comes from *aube*, "the dawn." Aubades were popular in the 18th century when they were composed and played in place of pastorales. See also *Alba*.

Aucassin et Nicolette. A French *chanson de geste* of the 13th century, illustrating the tale of a young Provençal prince who falls in love with a slave girl captured by the Saracens. The lovers are united after many vicissitudes when Nicolette is revealed to be of noble blood. Several modern composers have used this subject to evoke the medieval period.

Audience reaction. The response of an audience to a new work or to an artist's debut is of crucial significance to public success. Yet there are numerous cases in which the first performance of a famous work was a fiasco: Rossini's *Barber of Seville*, Puccini's *Tosca*, Debussy's *Pelléas et Mélisande*, Wagner's *Tannhäuser*. On the other hand, rapturous applause has greeted many an artistic failure. The reaction of music critics has been even less indicative of final judgment than that of the audience. Generally speaking, audiences in England, America, and Germany are restrained in their vocal expression of disapproval; in France, audience reaction, particularly to opera, is more pronounced; most exuberant and uninhibited of all are the audiences of Italy. Because Italian opera-goers often know the music as well as, or better than, the singers themselves, they often shout encouragement or condemnation. When a tenor sang flat at a Naples performance, a listener pointed his index finger upward and shouted: *"Su! Su!"* ("higher, higher"). When in a scene of romantic discovery the leader of brigands warned his followers not to attack the lady of the castle whom he recognized as his half-sister by saying, "Desist! On the same milk were we nurtured!", a member of the audience shouted, "You bastard! You must have lapped up all the cream!" (The male singer was inordinately fat, the lady quite slender.) In an inverse situation, when the male singer was slightly built but the prima donna was ample, and the scenario required him to carry her off the stage, someone in the audience encouraged him, shouting, "Make it in two trips!" At a Futurist concert in Paris in 1913, several people actually mounted the stage and attacked the performers physically. The Futurists, however, fought back; a dozen members of the audience had to be hospitalized. Enthusiasm for popular pianists, violinists, and particularly singers often carried the audience away to extremes. At the height of the golden age of opera, admirers were known to unharness the carriage of a prima donna and pull it to her home or hotel. In the 1890s young girls with scissors invaded the stage after a Paderewski concert intent on cutting off a lock of his flowing hair. The adulation for serious artists in Russia was extraordinary both before and after the Revolution. Music lovers used to stand in line all night to get a ticket for a recital by Chaliapin, and were known as Chaliapinists. One crooked entrepreneur in Leningrad collected a considerable number of rubles in the 1920s by selling tickets for a piano recital by Josef Hofmann, a great favorite in old Russia, that was never planned. Russian audiences, insatiable in demands for encores, sometimes refuse to leave the hall until the lights are turned off.

Audition. A test given to an aspiring actor, singer, orchestral musician, and even a symphony conductor, preliminary to the offer of a contract. The fate of a trembling (or occasionally cocky) postulant usually lies in the hands of an all-powerful manager (particularly on the lower entertainment level) in hiring chorus girls, electric guitar players, ballad singers, and the like. Such a person, whose total absence of all artistic sense is compensated for by a more valuable gift of precognition of commercial success, is usually a heterosexual male, unscrupulous in his dealings, devoted only to the service of his overbearing self. He is apt to approach ever so delicately, or bluntly, a female contestant with an offer of an exchange of favors, trading her natural endowments for a job, on the principle best enunciated in the medieval subjunctive injunction, *do ut des* ("I give that you should give"). In more "artistic" auditions, a jury of professional musicians, usually consisting of retired concert players or obsolete opera singers, is engaged to sit in judgment. Some members of such a jury like to exercise their temporary power by interrupting a hapless singer, violinist, cellist, or pianist in the middle of a rendition, with a curt dismissal, "Thank you," first flashing a glance at their colleagues of the jury for anticipated approbation of the verdict. The annals of the opera and concert hall are full of stories about budding celebrities ignominiously cast out only to rise to the heights as critically acclaimed artists and commercially successful stars.

Aufstieg und Fall der Stadt Mahagonny (The Rise and Fall of the City of Mahagonny). An opera by Kurt Weill, to the libretto by Bertolt Brecht, first performed in Leipzig on March 9, 1930. The action develops in a Miami-like city in which justice is meted out according to the ultimate capitalistic creed, with murder and rape punished lightly and crimes against property penalized by execution. The first production was accompanied by shouts from the audience: *"Es stinkt!"* and *"Schweinerei!"*

Augmentation. A simple arithmetical device that looms large in contrapuntal and, particularly, fugal writing as a highly scientific accomplishment. It is nothing more complex than presenting the melodic subject in half the speed by doubling the note values. In Bach's fugues, augmentation is employed with a didactic purpose to illustrate resources of tonal counterpoint. In his C-minor Fugue in the second book of *The Well-Tempered Clavier*, Bach combines the original theme with itself at half the speed. Augmentation lends itself naturally to the expression of Gothic grandiloquence, particularly in the concluding section of a work. Max Reger and Anton Bruckner produced fine effects with augmentation. In organ works, augmentation can be used impressively in the bass register of the pedals. A rather unusual type of augmentation occurs in Debussy's *La Mer*, where the pervading whole tone harmonies secure a needed euphony.

Auld Lang Syne. A famous valedictory song with words by the Scottish poet Robert Burns. *Auld Lang Syne* means "old long since." The melody, of unknown origin, underwent many changes until it assumed its present form. It is set in the pentatonic scale, a circumstance indicative of its antiquity.

Aus Italien. An early symphonic fantasy by Richard Strauss, first performed in Munich on March 2, 1887. The score contains the tune of *Funiculì, Funiculà*, which Strauss believed to be a Neapolitan folksong; it was actually the composition of one Luigi Denza.

Authentic modes. In Gregorian chant, the four most frequently used modes are the Dorian, Phrygian, Lydian, and Mixolydian. To convert them into plagal modes, the prefix "hypo" (indicating its initial position as below the corresponding authentic mode) is used, as, for example, Hypodorian. The range of authentic modes in such a classification is from the tonic to the tonic; that of plagal modes from the dominant (a fourth below the tonic) to the dominant. In the early practice of church singing and music theory, authentic modes were named by Latinized pseudo-Greek ordinal numbers: Protus, Deuterus,

Tritus, and Tetrardus. At a later time, authentic and plagal modes were both incorporated into a system that became traditional. The four authentic and four plagal modes were originally called Tonus, with the pseudo-Greek numerals translated into accurate Latin: Primus tonus, Secundus tonus, and so on, corresponding respectively to Protus authentic, Protus plagal, and so on. In the 16th century four more modes were added: Aeolian, Hypoaeolian, Ionian, and Hypoionian, aggregating in all to 12 modes; hence, the title of the famous treatise of Glareanus, *Dodecachordon*, wherein the particle *chord* means a tone, not a chord, and *dodeca* means 12.

Avalon. A song brazenly concocted by Al Jolson and Vincent Rose in 1920 from Cavaradossi's aria from Puccini's opera *Tosca*. Puccini's publishers sued the musical hijackers and collected damages.

Ave Maria. One of the most celebrated religious tunes, adapted by Gounod to the first prelude of Bach's *Well-Tempered Clavier*. Its original version (1853) was *Meditation* for violin and piano. It is not known who adapted the Latin words from the Archangel Gabriel's Annunciation to Mary to Gounod's tune.

Avec. French for "with." Some of the most imaginative directions beginning with this word are found in the works of Scriabin:

> **Avec défi.** "Defiantly," and **Avec délice**, "with sensual delight," in *Prométhée*.

> **Avec entraînement et ivresse.** "With impetuosity and inebriated abandon," in *Le Poème divin*.

> **Avec une ardeur profonde et voilée.** "With a profound but veiled ardor," in the Piano Sonata No. 10.

> **Avec une chaleur contenue.** "With contained passion," in the Piano Sonata No. 6.

> **Avec une douce ivresse.** "With tender inebriation," in the Piano Sonata No. 10.

> **Avec une douce langueur de plus en plus éteinte.** "With sweet languor gradually fading away," in the Piano Sonata No. 10.

> **Avec une douceur de plus en plus caressante et empoisonnée.** "With a tenderness ever more caressing and venomous," in the Piano Sonata No. 9.

> **Avec une ivresse débordante.** "With overflowing inebriation," in the Piano Sonata No. 3.

Avec une joie débordante. "With an overflowing joy," in the Piano Sonata No. 7.

Avec une joie éteinte. "With an extinguished joy," and **Avec un intense désir**, "with an intense desire," in *Prométhée*.

Avec une passion naissante. "With a nascent passion," in the *Poème Nocturne*.

Azmari. An indigenous name for an Ethiopian minstrel. The word comes from the Amharic verb *mezemer*, "to sing"; a "song" is *mezmur*. According to an attractive conjecture, azmari singing preserves in an unpolluted form the ancient psalmody of King Solomon. The Ethiopian kings are reputed to be descendants of Solomon and the Queen of Sheba, who was supposed to have been an Ethiopian.

B

B. The second note of the alphabetical musical scale and the seventh note of the C-major scale. It is called Si in French, Italian, Spanish, and Russian; and in the English and American tonic sol-fa method it is sung to the syllable ti. In German terminology, however, the letter *B* signifies B-flat, a very important bit of idiosyncratic nomenclature that must be heeded by musicians, teachers, and students in the Anglo-Saxon realm. Thus *B dur* in German is B-flat major; *B moll* is B-flat minor. The availability of the letter *B* in its musical guise of B-flat in German makes it possible to render Bach's name in musical notes (since the letter *H* corresponds to B-natural). The historical and theoretical importance of *B* as B-flat is further emphasized by its position as the fourth note in the F-major tetrachord, necessary in order to avoid the forbidding and forbidden B-natural placed in confrontation with F, which would form the dreaded *diabolus in musica*, as the medieval scholars described the tritone.

B major. A key of velvety warmth, rich in texture and emotionally ingratiating. The scale of B major, numbering all five black keys and two white keys, is eminently pianistic, but the tonality is not suited for orchestral works. Only the subdominant of B major is represented by an open string on the violin. As for brass instruments, they are all flat-oriented, and B major is preeminently a sharp key, having five sharps in the key signature. Its enharmonic equivalent, C-flat major, with its seven flats in the key signature, has a certain affinity with the standard tune of the transposing wind instruments. Stravinsky's ballet *The Firebird* has seven flats for C-flat major in its key signature, a rarity in orchestral scoring.

B minor. The 17th-century French composer Marc-Antoine Charpentier described the key of B minor as *solitaire et mélancolique* ("solitary and melancholy"). The description holds true remarkably well, as composers throughout the centuries seem to have agreed. Tchaikovsky's *Pathétique* Symphony, certainly one of the most melancholy pieces ever written, is in the key of B minor. So are Mendelssohn's overture *Fingal's Cave*, which suggests aloofness and remoteness, and the bassoon solo in the second movement of Rimsky-Korsakov's *Scheherazade*. Perhaps the epitome of dolorous melodies is achieved in the first movement of Schubert's Symphony in B minor (the *Unfinished*).

Baba Yaga. A symphonic poem by Anatoli Liadov, first performed in St. Petersburg on March 18, 1904. Baba Yaga is a notorious Russian witch who navigates the skies on a mortar. Liadov makes use of modernistic whole-tone scales to convey weird eeriness.

Baccanale. French for "bacchanalia," a celebration of Bacchus, the god of wine. Bacchanalias were introduced into music for the first time by the pianist Daniel Steibelt, who composed 12 bacchanalias for piano with the accompaniment of the tambourine; these curious pieces enjoyed great success in Paris during the time of Napoleon. Cherubini featured a bacchanalia in his ballet *Achille à Scyros*, produced in 1804. Several famous opera-ballets in the form of bacchanalias afford effective interludes in several famous operas. A most provocative bacchanalia is in Wagner's *Tannhäuser* in the scene in the grotto of Venus, and also in the overture. There is also a bacchanalia in the ballet *Walpurgis Night* in Gounod's opera *Faust*, as well as in *Samson et Dalila* of Saint-Saëns and in Glazunov's ballet *Raymonda*.

Bachianas Brasileiras. Villa-Lobos had a whimsical idea that there was a link between Brazilian folk rhythms and Bach counterpoint. This quaint notion resulted in his composing nine pieces for various instrumental and vocal combinations. One of the most engaging of these is No. 5, for voice and eight cellos.

Bagatelle. Literally, a "trifle," a short composition, usually for piano solo. Couperin wrote a group of bagatelles for the clavecin. Beethoven's bagatelles for piano, however, belie the connotations of the name; they are far from trifling.

Bagatelle ohne Tonart. A piano piece by Liszt, written in his old age, around 1880, and not published until many years after his death. It is remarkable because of its explicit indication, "without tonality." Indeed, it lacks a time signature, and it cultivates tritones, major sevenths, and other "atonal" intervals.

Bagpipe(s). An ancient wind instrument, equipped with several pipes, with single or double reeds affixed to a windbag. One of the pipes has six to eight holes played with the fingers and is called a "chanter," or melody pipe. The three other pipes produce the "drones," sustained notes that impart the instrument's characteristic sound. Although the bagpipe is the national instrument of Scotland and Ireland, there are varieties of such blowing instruments in many other countries. A bagpipe is called *musette* and *cornemuse* in France, *Dudelsack* in Germany, and *zampogna* in Italy. In Russia the popular instrument of the type is called *volynka* or *duda*; it is also called *duda* in Czechoslovakia. In Bulgaria it is known as *gaida*, and in Poland as *koza*.

Le Baiser de la fée (The Kiss of the Fairy). An allegorical ballet by Stravinsky on themes of Tchaikovsky, first performed in Paris on November 27, 1928, with Stravinsky conducting. The scenario is freely arranged from an Andersen tale. A fairy kisses a baby boy, and this kiss gives him happiness throughout his life. Stravinsky restructured assorted pieces by Tchaikovsky, changing the meter and the harmony but preserving the essence of Tchaikovsky's music. This is a most curious score, signifying Stravinsky's turn toward rococo mannerisms on borrowed material. So great is Stravinsky's mastery, however, that Tchaikovsky's melodies become transmuted into something new and strange rather than deformed into something old and ugly.

The Ballad of Baby Doe. A folk opera by Douglas Moore. Baby Doe is a historical figure, the wife of the rich owner of a silver mine in Colorado who lost his fortune when gold became the official U.S. currency. After his death, she stubbornly remained in her dilapidated house in Leadville, Colorado, and there she froze to death in 1935. The world premiere took place appropriately in another ghost city, Central City, Colorado, on July 7, 1956.

Ballad opera. A stage genre popular in 18th-century England that is stylistically close to vaudeville. The work that precipitated the development of the English ballad opera was *The Beggar's Opera* by John Gay, 1728. Subsequent English ballad operas drew freely on arias and choruses of old composers. The genre exhausted itself toward the end of the 18th century and gave way to the fertile development of the German *Singspiel*. After about 150 years, it was revived in Germany by Kurt Weill and others who used the mixed English-German designation *Songspiel* (the English word *song* acquired a slang meaning in Germany for musical entertainment of any kind).

Ballade. A French term of widely ranging connotations. It applies to vocal compositions of the masters of Ars Nova and the songs of the troubadours. Although the word is derived from the Latin verb *ballare*, "to dance," the choreographic aspect of this genre disappeared at the time of the Renaissance. Among the most significant ballades in a polyphonic vocal form are those by Guillaume de Machaut; later development of the French genre were bergerettes (from *bergère*, "a shepherdess") and pastoral songs of the 18th century. A totally different type of vocal composition designated by the same word, *Ballade*, are German Gothic poems of the strophic structure popularized by

Goethe and Schiller. Schubert and Schumann were particularly fond of these poems and set a multitude of strophic songs in which all stanzas were sung to the same music. The most prolific composer of German ballades was Karl Loewe, who published 17 volumes of such songs, most of them in strophic form. A more elaborate type of ballade was *durchkomponiert* ("through-composed"), in which each stanza was set to a different accompaniment. Instrumental ballades were designed as wordless narratives. Chopin's ballades for piano are the greatest examples of this genre. Piano ballades were also written by Liszt, Brahms, and Grieg. The Russian composer Nicolai Medtner introduced a combined form of a sonata-ballade for piano. Nicolai Miaskovsky wrote a ballade-symphony, and Alexander Glazunov composed a ballade concerto for cello and orchestra.

Ballet mécanique. A celebrated piece by George Antheil that shocked Paris at its first performance there on June 19, 1926. It shocked the American public even more when it was staged the following year in New York, where Antheil used airplane propellers, buzz saws, and loud drums. Several revivals of *Ballet mécanique* were attempted some decades later, but it sounded like a period piece, and the only shock that the audience experienced was from the knowledge that this music ever shocked anyone at all.

Un ballo in maschera (The Masked Ball). An opera in three acts by Verdi. The libretto by Scribe was based on the assassination of King Gustavus of Sweden in 1792. Regicide was no longer regarded as a fitting subject for a stage spectacle when Verdi's opera was produced in Rome on February 11, 1859, so the locale was changed to the distant land of America, and the victim of the plot was the "Governor of Boston," a nonexistent title. He consults a fortune teller for a reading of his future, and she tells him that he will be murdered. Operatic fortune tellers are never wrong, and the unfortunate governor is stabbed to death at a masked ball by his male secretary with whose wife the governor had been consorting. In 20th-century productions, when royal personages were no longer untouchable, attempts were made to restore the original libretto, but somehow they were not successful. Opera audiences prefer romantic nonsense to historic truth.

Band. An instrumental ensemble consisting of brass, woodwind, and percussion instruments, to the exclusion of string instruments. The term is used specifically for such groups as military bands, jazz bands, dance bands, and brass bands. In jazz, a distinction exists between big bands and small bands. Big bands are scored for several trumpets, trombones, clarinets, and saxophones, and the rhythm section (piano, guitar, percussion, and double bass), while small bands employ one player for each instrument. In Italian the term *banda* is applied to only the brass and percussion section of the entire orchestra. In the hierarchy of musical ensembles, the term *band* occupies an inferior position vis-à-vis an orchestra. A band leader who has symphonic ambitions prefers to be called *conductor*. However, English kings had their royal designation. Lully's group of *24 violons du roy* was called *La grande bande*.

Military band. Since time immemorial, military activities have been accompanied by brass instruments, drums, and cymbals. "If the trumpet gives an uncertain sound, who shall prepare himself to the battle?" the Apostle Paul asked rhetorically. He must have understood the importance of music when he said that unless one had love, he would become "as sounding brass or a tinkling cymbal." Military bands in the modern sense of the word arose in Europe in the Middle Ages. Frederick the Great enlarged military bands to include "melody" instruments such as oboes and clarinets. Napoleon extended the instrumentation of military bands to include "Turkish" music resonant with drums and bells. About the middle of the 19th century, Adolph Sax enriched the sonority of French military bands by adding instruments of his own invention, which came to be known as saxophones. As a rule, each branch of the military service had its own military band. In the United States the bands of the Marines, the Army, the Navy, and the Air Force maintain a high professional standard of performance. In England there are several excellent military bands, notably that of the Scots Guard Royal Artillery. In France the Garde Républicaine presents regular concerts.

Symphonic band. A term applied to English and American bands capable of playing symphonic music; an equivalent term is *concert band*. A large symphonic band maintained by an American college or high school includes many more wind instruments than does a regular symphony orchestra. A large symphonic band may have as many as 24 clarinets, a lot of brass, a number of saxophones, and an impressive contingent of percussion; double basses may also be included. A considerable literature for the symphonic band exists, beginning with the pieces Haydn wrote for the Prussian regimental bands, which were the predecessors of the modern concert band. Among modern composers, Vaughan Williams, Hindemith, Stravinsky, Prokofiev, and Darius Milhaud contributed to the symphonic band repertory, and Arnold Schoenberg made a significant departure from his method of composition in 12 tones by writing a perfectly tonal piece for an American school band.

Bandonion. An accordion or concertina built by a German instrument manufacturer who was actually named Herr Band. A similar instrument, usually spelled *bandoneon*, is in vogue in South America.

Banjo. An American folk instrument with five strings plucked by the fingers and made popular in Negro spirituals, hillbilly music, Dixieland, and early jazz.

Bar. The dividing line (barline) between two measures; also a measure of music itself.

Barbe-Bleue. An opéra-bouffe by Offenbach, produced in Paris on February 5, 1866. The monstrous Bluebeard wins his sixth wife in a lottery. Unaware that his previous wives were merely drugged and not poisoned by an alchemist in his employ, he casts a lustful glance on a potential Wife No. 7, when his former wives make their sudden reappearance. As a result, Bluebeard has to be satisfied with Wife No. 6, who is no longer afraid of him now that he has been exposed as a wretched bungler in uxoricide. There is a love duet.

The Barber of Bagdad. An opera in two acts by Peter Cornelius, first performed in Weimar on December 15, 1858. The story is based on the *1001 Nights*, wherein an Arab swain in love with the Caliph's daughter is thrown into a dungeon. He is rescued by a court barber, who persuades the Caliph (who has hundreds of virgin daughters anyway) to bless the loving pair.

The Barber of Seville. An opera in two acts by Rossini after the famous comedy of Beaumarchais. Rossini was only 23 years old when he wrote it. It was first produced in Rome on February 20, 1816. The original name was *Almaviva, ossia L'Inutile precauzione* (*Almaviva, or A Futile Precaution*). Count Almaviva is in love with Rosina, ward of Doctor Bartolo, who plans to make Rosina his own bride. The versatile barber Figaro arranges various disguises for Almaviva to pursue his quest. After much chicanery, the lovers are united by Bartolo's own notary. Rossini's opera was not the first to be based on the Beaumarchais play; it was preceded by one by Giovanni Paisiello (1782), which enjoyed considerable sucess.

Barbershop harmony. A type of close harmony arrangement once popular in America, stylized from amateur performances by singing barbers. In modern performances, this type of arrangement is usually presented as a parody, with the singing barbers costumed and gesticulating in mock eloquence.

Barcarole. A boating song. The name is derived from the Italian words *barca*, "bark," and *rollo*, a "rower." This genre is inseparably associated with the songs of the Venetian gondoliers who entertained and delighted tourists in the 19th century. Gilbert and Sullivan turned the gondoliers into sentimental lovers in their operetta *The Gondoliers*. The barcarole is usually set in 6/8 or 12/8 time, suggesting a lulling motion of the rowers along the Venetian canals. The most famous operatic barcarole is in Offenbach's *Tales of Hoffmann*. Chopin wrote a poetic barcarole for piano, in which the accompaniment maintains a constant movement from the tonic to the dominant, and the melody engages in artful fiorituras. Mendelssohn has three gondola pieces in his *Songs Without Words* for piano. Barcarole may also be spelled barcarolle.

Bard. A name given to officials of Ireland and Wales who were poets and musicians. The tradition of the bards goes back to the British Druids. Their folk instrument was the crwth, the Irish lyre. The Welsh bards established an annual festival, Eisteddfod, which was revived in the 19th century.

Bärentanz. Literally, "bear dance." A German peasant dance accompanied by drums and piccolo, or a sophisticated composition trying to imitate primitive rhythms.

Barform. The medieval German name for a poem consisting of several stanzas, each one subdivided into two sections, all of which together constitute the *Aufgesang* ("on song"), followed by an *Abgesang* ("off song"). The term would have been long relegated to limbo had it not been for Wagner, who inserted a surprisingly logical definition of the barform in *Die Meistersinger von Nürnberg.*

Baritone. The medium-range male voice, lower than the tenor and higher than the bass. The term is a literal translation from the Greek, meaning "deep" (*bari*) "sound" (*tone*). The compass of the baritone voice is from C an octave below middle C to about F or G above middle C. An ideal baritone voice possesses the character of lyric masculinity, with the tessitura corresponding to that of an average married male. Baritones are rarely given leading roles in opera, which are usually assigned to tenors, yet Mozart entrusted the role of Don Giovanni to a baritone. Character baritones range from villainy to piety, from nefarious Scarpia in *Tosca* to saintly Amfortas in *Parsifal*. The imperious Wotan in Wagner's *Ring* is a bass baritone. The most famous dramatic baritone part is that of the toreador in *Carmen*. Baritones are often given comic parts. For example, an amusing baritone part is assigned to Mr. Lavender-Gas, a mincing homosexual professor of literature in Menotti's satirical opera, *Help! Help! The Globolinks!*

Baroque music. An arbitrary term used to describe the musical style that dominated the years from 1600 to 1750. The origin of the word is mysterious, and feuding music historians can pick their choice. It may derive from the Portuguese adjective *barroco*, "irregular shape." The term was first used in a derogatory sense; in his *Dictionnaire de Musique*, Jean-Jacques Rousseau wrote: "Une Musique Baroque est celle dont l'harmonie est confuse, chargée de modulations et de dissonances, le chant dur peu naturel, l'intonation difficile." The expression *goût baroque* for nearly a century meant having a taste for fanciful design in architecture and painting. A change of attitude came about in 1900 when German writers on aesthetics decided to rehabilitate the *style baroque* as a technically advanced art. About then, music historians assigned the term *Baroque* to the period of the greatest flowering of contrapuntal, instrumental, and vocal art. The same period comprised the evolution of opera, from the rudimentary form of the Florentine Camerata to the fine ripening of Italian bel canto. It was during the Baroque era that a symbolic link was drawn between tonalities and musical intervals with the words in the text. Major keys became the expressions of joy, fortitude, and determination, whereas minor keys expressed melancholy, dejection, and depression. Melodic intervals conveyed the meaning of the text even when words themselves could not be clearly understood. In Bach's cantatas, words descriptive of the act of arising in the morning were set to music by ascending passages in a major key; a descent into the nether regions was illustrated by a mournful falling figuration. Acute agony was invariably rendered by chromatic ornamentation.

The popular notion that Baroque music is analogous to architecture, that the metrical units in a melody corresponded to the severe proportions of a Doric column, that the melodic ornaments of a Baroque phrase should be measured as precisely as the fanciful incrustations of a Gothic cathedral, is belied by the contemporary descriptions of the state of mind and bodily actions of performers of the music that we now call Baroque. To judge by these reports, instrumentalists of the Baroque era behaved more like corybantic orgiasts than professional players. In *Principles of Musick*, a manual published in London in 1636, at the very inception of the Baroque era, the author Charles Butler commented: "The composer is transported as it were with some musical fury, so that he himself scarce knoweth what he doth nor can presently give a reason for his doing." In *Musick's Monument*, published in London in 1676, Thomas Mace described the mental state of the listener to Baroque music in these words: "Sensibly, fervently, and zealously captivated, we are drawn into raptures and contemplations by those unexpressible rhetorical, uncontrollable persuasions and instructions of musick's divine language, to quietness, joy, and peace; absolute tranquility." Bach's son Carl Philipp Emanuel declared: "An artist cannot move his listeners unless he himself is moved. He must experience the same feelings that he intends to arouse in them: in displaying his own emotion, he evokes the same emotion in his hearers." The anonymous English translator of a French treatise published in 1702 described his impression of the playing of Arcangelo Corelli: "I never met with any man that suffered his passions to hurry him away so much whilst he was playing on the violin as the famous Arcangelo Corelli. His eyes will sometimes turn as red as fire; his countenance will be distorted; his eyeballs roll as in an agony; and he gives in so much to what he is doing that he doth not look like the same man." This was the same Corelli to whom a German musician said after he heard him play: "Your first name may be archangel, but you play like an archdevil." The great lexicographer Samuel Johnson, who was notoriously unmusical, commented on the performance of a contemporary violinist: "They say this piece is very difficult to play. I wish to God it had been impossible." A century later, Emperor Franz Josef of Austria, wishing to compliment a musician who gave a command performance at the court, observed: "I have heard many musicians play, but I never before saw anyone perspire so profusely." In light of these reports, it seems ironic that the 20th-century standard of performance of Baroque music should be commanded by the rigorous observations of the written notation, that no deviation from the mathematical precision of meters and rhythms should be tolerated, and that no personal or collective emotions should intrude into the marmoreal immutability of the music of Baroque masters. The names of Monteverdi, Bach, and Handel, and their lesser contemporaries, Vivaldi and Telemann, Buxtehude and Scarlatti, dominated the firmament of the Baroque era. Several generations of earnest musicians devoted themselves to the true worship of these musical deities with a singleness of purpose worthy of Torquemada. Bach became the Jehovah of music; to alter a single note in Bach's music was a blasphemy. Inevitably, conflicting factions arose among the specialists; no two music editors agree on the proper execution of trills, mordents, and other ornaments in Bach's works. Wanda Landowska, a blithe and independent spirit, proposed that a performer of Bach should conduct himself like a civilized guest, to feel free to engage in conversation and partake of the food but not to put his feet on the table. Yet diversity ruled the performance of Baroque music in its own time.

The inception of the Baroque era coincides with the birth of opera, an art that arose as a reaction to the overly intricate polyphony of the Renaissance. The melodic content of operatic arias was essentially monodic; the voice and the text were determining factors of harmony, whereas harmony itself was determined by the bass line. Similar developments took place in instrumental music. The great accomplishment of Baroque music was the decisive retreat from the ambiguous modality of the Renaissance period to definitive tonality, culminating in the creation of Bach's *Well-Tempered Clavier*.

Barrelhouse. A type of early ragtime, in vogue in the most squalid recesses of New Orleans and later Chicago. Barrelhouse rhythms are set by barrelhouse pianos, with the main beat in quickstep time and with the pedal used for percussive effects rather than for the enhancement of harmony.

The Bartered Bride. An opera in three acts by Smetana, first produced in Prague on May 30, 1866. The Czech title is *Prodaná nevěsta*, literally, *The Bride Which Is Sold*. The action takes place in Bohemia early in the 19th century. The parents of a young girl intend to give her in marriage to a rich man's son, but she loves another. The wily marriage broker attempts to bribe the girl's lover to surrender her, but he indignantly refuses to trade love for money.

A happy ending ensues when the lover proves that he is himself wealthy, being a prodigal son of the village headmaster.

Bass. The deepest male voice; its range extends from D below the bass clef staff to F two octaves above. There have been exceptional bass singers, particularly Russian, who could shatter the air by going even below this range. In his drama *The Sea Gull*, Chekhov tells the story of an Italian bass singer who sang at the Imperial Opera in St. Petersburg, rousing the audience to admiring frenzy when he reached low C, whereupon a choir bass singer in the audience shouted "Bravo!" an octave below that C. Some ethnomusicologists speculate that the vast expanse of the Russian landscape somehow contributes to the formation of powerful chest cavities, whereas the cerulean waters of the bay of Naples favor the development of the lyric tenor voice. Bass parts are usually assigned to the roles of sinners or devils. Mephistopheles in Gounod's *Faust* is a bass; so are the villainous Czar in Mussorgsky's *Boris Godunov* and the treacherous Hunding in Wagner's *Die Walküre*. Then there is the comic bass part (*basso buffo*) of the music master Don Basilio in Rossini's *Barber of Seville*. *Basso profondo*, a deep bass, is often misspelled *basso profundo*.

Bass drum. The largest and the lowest-pitched drum, used particularly in military bands and employed in orchestral works for special effects. It gives out no definite pitch. Beethoven introduced the bass drum in the finale of his Symphony No. 9. The dramatic and often ominous sound of the bass drum was used for dramatic purposes by Richard Strauss. Mahler liked to punctuate his symphonies with single strokes of the bass drum. In Leoncavallo's opera *Pagliacci*, the bass drum is part of the equipment of the clown who was tormented by jealousy. In Litolff's overture *Robespierre*, the bass drum illustrates Robespierre's beheading.

Bass line. Although the bass is generally regarded as a subsidiary component of a musical composition in determining the harmonic progression, in actual composition, since the time of Bach and Handel, the bass line has served as the determinant of the melody. One of the most common guiding lines in bass parts is the descending figure from the tonic to the dominant. Sometimes the bass follows an entire diatonic scale, from the tonic to the lower tonic, in even notes. Thus the second theme in Franck's Symphonic Variations in E-flat minor is formed as a derivative from the descending bass line. A remarkable example of the bass diatonically descending for several octaves is the accompaniment of Rachmaninoff's song *A Little Island*, with the bass notes in even rhythm while the melody forms counterpoint of several species, including syncopation. The groups of sixteenth notes, descending from the tonic to the dominant in the middle section of Chopin's Polonaise in A-flat major, must be regarded as expansions of the tonic-dominant pedal points. Many descending basses are set in chromatic motion, invariably in even notes. In such cases, it is the bass line that governs the melody, resulting in a modulatory chromatic sequence. An excellent example is the opening of Grieg's Ballade in G minor for piano.

Basso continuo. A specific Italian term that means literally "continued bass" but is more accurately described by the English term "figured bass." This method was widely used in the educational system in Baroque music and retained in musical training throughout the 19th century. The numerical figures in basso continuo indicate the intervals above the bass, thus spelling out stenographically the harmony within a given tonality. It is important to point out that the number of notes, or the position of the voices, is not specifically marked. Historically, the basso continuo developed as an aid to improvisation and as an indicator of the main harmony in the cembalo part, which supplied the accompaniment. Thus 6/4/2 over the bass D in the key of A major or minor would indicate the notes D, E, G-sharp, and B, whether in closed or open harmony, and with any number of duplications of these notes. In old English practice, also adopted in America, the basso continuo is called "thoroughbass." The adjective "thorough" is an archaic form of "through."

Basso ostinato. An Italian term that means literally "bass obstinate." True to the sense of the term, it consists of a repeated motive as the foundation for variations in the upper voice. A fine basso ostinato can be greatly diversified both in rhythm and melody, differing in this from the English ground bass, which is static. The passacaglia and chaconne are examples of musical forms that use a basso ostinato.

Bastien und Bastienne. A Singspiel by the adolescent Mozart, with a simple tale of young love for a plot. It was produced in Vienna in 1768 when Mozart was only 12 years old, at the home of Dr. Franz Mesmer, the protagonist of the famous method of therapy known as mesmerism.

Baton. A conductor's stick. From the French *bâton*, but the French word for the conductor's baton is *baguette*. In America, the word *baton* is also used, in a less exalted way, for the twirling stick of a drum majorette.

Battaglia. The Italian word for "battle." In musical usage, battaglia applies to compositions featuring trumpet flourishes, fanfares, drum rolls, and similar explosions of sound. The genre evolved in the 14th century; battle pieces were invariably in march time in the *stile concitato*, with a typical rhythmic figure consisting of a half note followed by two quarter notes. A characteristic piece of battle music of the Renaissance period is *La Guerre*, a four-part chanson by Jannequin, descriptive of the battle of Marignano. Instrumental battaglias were written by Byrd, Sweelinck, Frescobaldi, and Couperin. Possibly the most durable battaglia is the representation of the combat between David and Goliath in the Piano Sonata No. 1 by Kuhnau. During the Baroque period, battaglias were favorite dramatic scenes in operas and oratorios. *The Battle of Prague* for piano by the Czech composer Franz Kotzwara still furnishes its element of bland amusement. Beethoven's notorious battle symphony, entitled *Wellington's Victory*, originally written for a mechanical instrument, is often cited as a paradigm of exceptionally bad music written by an exceptionally great composer. Tchaikovsky wrote a celebrated symphonic battle piece, *1812 Overture*, commemorating the Russian victory over Napoleon. Some musical nitpickers point out the anachronism involved in quoting in the *1812 Overture* the Russian national anthem, *God Save the Tsar*, which was not written until 1833. One of the best operatic battaglias is the orchestral interlude in Rimsky-Korsakov's opera *The Legend of the Invisible City of Kitezh*, describing the battle between Russians and Mongols.

The Battle Cry of Freedom. A Civil War ballad composed by George Frederick Root in 1863. It became a rallying song in the Union camp. President Lincoln wrote to Root saying that his song had done more for the cause of the Union than 100 generals and 1,000 orators.

The Battle Hymn of the Republic. The words of this song were written by Julia Ward Howe in 1862, to the already famous tune of *Glory, Glory, Halleluluh!* The composer of the music is unknown. Another set of words to the same tune is *John Brown's Body Lies A-Mouldering in the Grave*.

The Bear. Symphony No. 82 in C major by Haydn, written in 1786. Why bear? There is no rational explanation, but there is an imitation bagpipe section, and circus bears were often made to dance to the accompaniment of Scottish bagpipes. The symphony was written for a Paris performance and is therefore often listed in Haydn's catalogues under its French name, *L'ours*.

Beautiful Ohio. A song by Robert King, published under the female pseudonym Mary Earl in 1918. First issued as a waltz, it was later supplied with verses. The vocal version sold more than 5 million copies. No less a person than Fritz Kreisler was sufficiently impressed by the tune to arrange it as a violin solo, which he also recorded.

Beer Barrel Polka. A song that achieved tremendous popularity in America when it was interpolated into the musical *Yokel Boy* in 1939. The music is by the Czech composer Jaromir Vejvoda.

The Beggar's Opera. A satirical ballad opera to the text by John Gay, with music collated in the manner of pasticcio by the German composer resident of England, John Pepusch. The spectacle was usually introduced by an actor dressed as a beggar announcing the wedding of two popular ballad singers. The musical score mixed street tunes with French airs, and the text contained undisguised persiflage of British political figures along with highwaymen and other common criminals. The first production was in London on January 29, 1728, staged in a theater frequented by the poor rather than by members of the aristocracy who patronized performances of Italian opera. The satirical impact of the opera moved the Lord Chamberlain to forbid the production of its sequel, *Polly*. The music historian Sir John Hawkins wrote in all solemnity, "Rapine and violence have been gradually increasing ever since the first representation of *The Beggar's Opera*," and Dr. Johnson opined that there was in the work "such a labefaction of all principles as might be injurious to morality." The idea of mixing rogues and politicians in a play accompanied by light music is as attractive in the 20th century as it was in the 18th. Kurt Weill, in collaboration with the radical German dramatist Bertolt Brecht, adapted *The Beggar's Opera* to a satire on world conditions in 1928, under the title *Die Dreigroschenoper*. The American composer Marc Blitzstein adapted the opera into colloquial American and called it *The Threepenny Opera*.

Beguine. A Latin American dance in a lively syncopated rhythm. Cole Porter made a brilliant play on words in his *Begin the Beguine*, a song imitative of Latin rhythms. He composed it after hearing the beguine during a cruise in the West Indies in 1935.

Bel canto. Literally, "beautiful song," a term representing the once-glorious tradition of vocal perfection for beauty's sake. The secret of bel canto was exclusively the property of Italian singing teachers who spread the technique all over the world—to Russia, to England, and to America. It was, above all, applied to lyric singing, particularly in opera. The art of bel canto is still being taught in conservatories and music schools as a necessary precondition for an operatic career.

Bell Song. The aria for coloratura soprano in Delibes's opera *Lakmé*, in which the heroine, a daughter of a Brahman priest, unhappily in love with a British officer in old colonial India, sings to the resonant accompaniment of temple bells. The necessary purity of intonation in performing the song was underlined by the American author of detective stories Raymond Chandler, when he alluded to the piece in a spoof on a typical British murder mystery, in which the soprano is stabbed with a solid platinum poniard when she sings flat on the top note of the *Bell Song*.

Bells. A generic name for church bells, carillons, and tubular chimes. For church bells, the collective name is a *ring*, and the sound they make together is a *peal*; "the peal of a ring of five bells" is a correct phrase. The largest church bell was the Czar Bell, which was cast in Moscow in 1733, but fell and cracked. It weighed nearly 500,000 pounds and was about 20 feet in diameter. Church bells are rarely used in musical scores except for special spectacles. Tubular bells, or tubular chimes, are suspended from a horizontal bar and struck with a hammer. Sleighbells, such as are attached to the harness of a horse-drawn sleigh, are included in the scores of Mozart, Mahler, and Varèse. Cowbells, heavier bells with a clapper, are also found in a few scores. Domestic handbells are used for special effects in some operas; a handbell orchestra consisting of a number of handbells of varying pitches is popular in churches in America. The glockenspiel is a set of bells in the form of metal bars.

Belly dance. A provocative oriental solo dance, usually performed by a young female strenuously exerting the abdominal muscles around her bellybutton. The music to which belly dancers exercise their attractions is usually a whining monotone, intended to conjure up the humid air of an oriental bazaar.

Belshazzar's Feast. An oratorio by William Walton to the text from the Bible, opening with the choral lament, "By the Waters of Babylon We Sat Down and Wept." The oratorio is in a neo-Handelian manner. It was first performed at the Leeds Festival on October 8, 1931.

   Belshazzar's Feast is also a suite by Sibelius, written for a play by Procopé. The composer conducted its first performance in Helsinki on November 7, 1906.

Berceuse. A cradle song; the name is derived from the French word *berceau*, "cradle." It is usually set in 6/8 time, suggesting the rocking of a cradle, with an ostinato accompaniment on the tonic and the dominant. Chopin's famous Berceuse for piano has an ingeniously variegated melody against a steady accompaniment on a pedal point. Stravinsky wrote in 1915 a group of four berceuses to words about cats. The cats in these songs are distinctly Russian, and their meowing distinctly Stravinskian.

Bergamasca. Originally, merely a geographic indication of certain types of songs and dances popular in the North Italian town of Bergamo that were characterized by a symmetrically structured duple time. In the 19th century the bergamasca changed its character to a tarantella-like fast dance in 6/8 time. Debussy's *Suite Bergamasque*, of which *Clair de Lune* is the most famous part, has no relation to the old Italian dance but is, rather, a poetic reminiscence of the alliterative verse of Verlaine: *que vont charmant masques et bergamasque* "parading and bewitching masks and bergamasques." The spelling *bergomask* occurs in Shakespeare's play *A Midsummer Night's Dream* ("Will it please you to hear a bergomask dance?").

Bergerette. A pastoral song (*berger* is French for "shepherd," *bergère* for "shepherdess") popular in the 18th century. In earlier centuries, bergerette was a type of lyric French poetry accompanied by pastoral music.

Die Bernauerin. An opera by Carl Orff, to his own libretto written in the Bavarian dialect, first produced in Stuttgart on June 15, 1947. The story tells of the medieval married woman Agnes Bernauer, commonly known as Bernauerin, who is terrorized and finally drowned by her tyrannical father-in-law. The music is ostentatiously static with an emphasis upon relentless monochromatic repetitions.

Le Bestiaire (The Menagerie). A song cycle with the accompaniment of a small ensemble by Poulenc, composed in 1919. Six animals, from a dromedary to a crayfish, are depicted.

B-flat major. If any key can claim to be the key of the universe, it is B-flat major. Most machines of modern industry—such as electric motors, fans, and washing machines—buzz, whir, and hum on the 60-cycle B-flat, corresponding to the lowest note of the bassoon, with its natural overtones forming the triadic complex of B-flat major. The transposing instruments of the orchestra, particularly the trumpets and the clarinets, are most often in B-flat. This tuning enables them to be played in the key of B-flat major with the same digital facility that C major gives pianists. B-flat major is the key of fanfares and of festival and military marches, in which natural trumpets in B-flat play such an overwhelming role. The march of the soldiers in Gounod's *Faust*, the return of Radames from the conquest of Ethiopia in *Aida*, the march of the children and the signal call summoning Don José back to the barracks in *Carmen* are all in B-flat major. The dramatic trumpet call in Beethoven's *Fidelio*, announcing the arrival of the governor, is in B-flat major. In the purely symphonic repertory is Schubert's romantic Symphony No. 5 in B-flat major. In a more introspective mood is Bruckner's Symphony No. 5 in B-flat major. Beethoven selected this key for his rather lackluster Symphony No. 4, but for Schumann the key must have signified the joy of life for he wrote his Symphony No. 1, which he called *Spring* Symphony, in this key. Prokofiev described the blinding pagan sunrise at the end of his *Scythian Suite* in blazing B-flat major. Standard arrangements of national anthems, including *The Star-Spangled Banner* and the *Marseillaise*, are in B-flat major. The song *Over There*, imitating the bugle calls of the doughboys of World War I, is in B-flat major, as is the bugle call that announces the opening of horse races. And then there is that gloriously uninhibited upward sweep of the clarinet (a B-flat clarinet, of course) that opens Gershwin's *Rhapsody in Blue*. Can there be a special psychological reason in Mahler's exclusion of B-flat major as the principal tonality in any of his symphonies? Was he inhibited by its aggressive character? Was he subconsciously concealing his darksome inner self from the intrusion of the brilliant illumination of B-flat major? It might be a tantalizing subject for a psychomusical study.

B-flat minor. The key of B-flat minor is pianistically desirable as a first cousin of D-flat major, both scales having five flats in the key signature. Tchaikovsky's famous Piano Concerto No. 1 is nominally in the key of B-flat minor, but after a few perfunctory measures in the principal key, it explodes into action with the famous optimistic D-flat major theme. Chopin favored B-flat minor; he wrote a scherzo and a piano sonata in this key. The slow movement of the sonata is the solemn but depressing *Funeral March*. It is difficult to find any symphonic works, however, that are unambiguously set in B-flat minor. A good example is the *Alpine* Symphony by Richard Strauss, in which the ascent and the descent to and from the summit are illustrated by the correspondingly ascending and descending scales of B-flat minor. Miaskovsky assigned the key of B-flat minor to his Symphony No. 11, but then he wrote symphonies in virtually every key.

Bibelregel. "Bible regal," the German name for a small portable organ that could be folded like a book in use in Germany in the 17th century.

Bicinium. A term, meaning literally "double song," that became current in Germany in the 16th century to designate a composition for two voices or two instruments. The first significant collection of such two-part compositions was *Bicinia Gallica, Latina, Germanica*, 1545. The popularity of bicinium rose, mainly owing to the reaction against the prevalent polyphonic structures of the Flemish school of the Renaissance. A revival of the bicinium took place in the early 20th century, when Bartók and Hindemith composed pieces in this genre using dissonant harmony.

Biedermeier. A genre of domestic furniture that became standard in petit bourgeois homes in Germany in the middle of the 19th century. The term subsequently expanded in its meaning to include sentimental literature, painting and music; as such, it acquired derogatory implications. The name was the pseudonym of the writer of ostensibly naive and implicitly satirical stories that were published in the German humorist magazine *Fliegende Blätter*. The stories were written in the first person of a fictional character, Gottlieb Biedermeier.

Bigotphone. A mirliton, or a kazoo, invented by a Frenchman named Bigot. It consists of a tube with a vibrating membrane at each end. When one sings into a perforation in the membrane, the voice becomes grotesquely high-pitched. For this reason, it is also known as the Eunuch flute.

Bill Bailey, Won't You Please Come Home? An old-fashioned ragtime song by Hughie Cannon, written in 1902. Bailey was a real person, a vaudevillian, but the text concerned a fictitious story of his being locked out of his house for a night by his temperamental wife.

Billion-Dollar Baby. A musical comedy by Morton Gould, first produced in New York on December 21, 1945. A simple girl from a middle-class home becomes involved with gangsters, unsuccessfully competes in a Miss America contest, eventually connects with a tycoon just as the stock market crashes in 1929, and the poor billion-dollar baby loses her last million. Several ballet numbers in the score are notable, among them "Miss America Pageant" and "Gangster Funeral and Wake."

Billy Budd. An opera by Benjamin Britten, scored for men's voices and orchestra, after Melville's unfinished novel of a mutiny on the British warship *Nore* in 1797, during which the young sailor Billy Budd kills his brutal superior officer and is hanged for it. The work opened in London on December 1, 1951. The Italian composer Giorgio Federico Ghedini wrote an opera on the same subject that was produced in Venice on September 7, 1949.

Binary. A term applied in music to twofold rhythms or forms. Binary rhythms contain two subdivisions in a beat. In Gregorian chant, binary division in metrical time was called *tempus imperfectum*, "incomplete rhythm," the complete division being ternary. Binary forms are represented in songs and dances of the Baroque period that lacked the contrasting middle section. The harmonic plan in binary composition is symmetrical. The first section proceeds from the tonic to the dominant, and the second section begins on the dominant and ends on the tonic. The allemande is typical of the binary form. Although most compositions are set in ternary forms, the nucleus is always binary, with the third section being the repetition, either literal as in da capo songs, or oblique as in the sonata form where the recapitulation differs in tonality and sometimes in structure from the exposition. It is always possible to convert a composition in binary form to one in ternary form by repeating, with or without variations, the first section and adding a cadence leading back to the tonic. It is difficult, if not impossible, however, to shorten a ternary composition to the binary without performing major surgery. Stravinsky is quoted, perhaps apocryphally, that Mozart's music would gain if the contrasting middle sections were removed from all his works to reduce them to the binary structure.

Biomusic. Biological events are electrochemical in nature. Because energy in any form can be transmuted into sound waves, musically inclined biologists have experimented in converting the electrical energy in the brain, heart, lungs, eyeballs, and blood into signals that can be perceived through the auditory nerve. The brain activity, as recorded in an electroencephalogram, can be electronically metamorphosed into sounds. The brain as a musical composer is a fascinating notion for musicians who hope that their art can be scientifically reduced without losing its human quality. Brain signals, and consequently brain music, are transmitted through electrodes attached to the skull, and at best reflect cranial rather than cerebral states. Indeed, the Parisian music hall artist Jacques Perrot, known as "Tête de bois," composed and performed in 1962 a concerto for the cranium, producing the scale by tapping different parts of his skull bones with a mallet, using his mouth cavity as a resonator. The Aztecs had percussion ensembles consisting of the skulls of their defeated enemies. Catgut is used for violin strings, horsehair for the violin bow, and animal hides for the membrane of a drum. All these forms may be described as biomusical.

In a modern sense, biomusical experimentation is concerned with measuring the stimuli of sounds upon the auditory organs and the electrical signals produced by the organs of the body, whether human or animal. The ultimate aim of these studies is to connect emotional states with the sound waves produced by electronic transformation of the original biological impulses. The acceleration of the pulse under the influence of a powerful emotion has an obvious counterpart in music as accelerando and crescendo, and the reduction in pulse rate can be likened to a ritenuto and diminuendo.

A Bird in a Gilded Cage. A sentimental ballad written by Harry von Tilzer in 1900. It bemoans the fate of a girl who married a millionaire. It is reported that von Tilzer first played it for the ladies in a bordello and that they wept. The sheet music sold 2 million copies.

Bitonality. The employment of two keys simultaneously is often termed *polytonality*, but bitonality is a more accurate description. Before the advent of modern music in the 20th century, playing in two different keys at the same time could be regarded only as a joke. Mozart wrote a piece entitled *Ein musikalischer Spass* (*A Musical Joke*) that can be cited as an example of bitonal writing, but the subtitle of the piece, *Dorfmusikanten* (*Village Musicians*), betrays his sly purpose to ridicule the inability of rustic players to perform music correctly. Bitonality is no longer a joke in the 20th century but a well-established practice calculated to add spice and sparkle to singular tonality. The most euphonious type of bitonality is achieved by combining two major chords with tonics separated by a tritone; Stravinsky's "Petrouchka" chord combines C major with F-sharp major. This type of bitonality is akin to the technique of the Neapolitan sixth chords, because the lowered supertonic triad is related to the dominant triad in the cadence by the tritone —for instance, D-flat major to G major in the key of C major. There is also some mysterious relationship between bitonality and the progression of intervals when each interval diminishes by a semitone. Starting on C-sharp in the low register and beginning with a major sixth and ending with a minor third, we obtain the following series: C-sharp, A-sharp, F-sharp, C-sharp, G, C, E,

G, which is a bitonal chord consisting of the second inversion of the F-sharp major triad in open harmony and the second inversion of the C major triad in close harmony. The increasing intervallic progression beginning with a minor third and ending with a major sixth will form a bitonal chord of two minor triads distanced by a tritone—for example, C, E-flat, G, C, F-sharp, C-sharp, A, F-sharp. In this case, the lower chord will be in close harmony and the upper chord in open harmony. The wonders of arithmetical music will never cease. But then the archaic word for music was Numbers, originating in the theories of Pythagoras, and used as late as the 17th century in poetry.

The Black Crook. A musical extravaganza put together from miscellaneous popular numbers, first produced in New York on September 12, 1866. The Black Crook of the tale is endowed by the devil with preternatural powers, but in exchange he must annually deliver a Christian soul. His first payment is a noble prisoner whom he liberates and then sends in search of a hidden treasure. On the way the prisoner saves a dove who turns out to be a fairy princess. She redeems his soul from the devil. The show featured a daring display of uncovered female skin, which led the official and self-appointed guardians of public morality to demand its suppression. The producers assuaged the clamor by substituting a chorus of infants for the nubile maidens. The trashy score featured a *March of the Amazons*.

Blackbirds of 1928. One of the most successful Negro revues, with music by Jimmy McHugh. Produced in New York on May 9, 1928, the revue is a series of topical skits. The score includes the famous madrigal, *I Can't Give You Anything but Love, Baby*.

Blaise le savetier. A comic opera by François Philidor, first performed in Paris on March 9, 1759. The cobbler Blaise is threatened with eviction by his landlord. To evade payment, he accuses the landlord of illicit advances to his wife. After the landlord is caught in a compromising situation, he is blackmailed into letting Blaise use the apartment rent free.

Blaník. An opera by Zdenko Fibich, first performed in Prague on November 25, 1881. The libretto is based on the national Czech legend of Czech patriots, followers of the religious reformer Jan Hus, who take refuge on Mt. Blaník and who emerge and liberate the country from Austrian rule.

Blindness. It is well known that musically gifted blind children develop more rapidly than normal children as performers on a musical instrument. Blind organists in particular often achieve great distinction in their profession. The blind pianist Alec Templeton made a lucrative career as an entertainer. The jazz pianists Ray Charles and George Shearing are blind. The British composer Frederick Delius lost his sight because of a syphilitic infection but continued to compose by dictating music, note by note, to a musical amanuensis. The Spanish musician Joaquín Rodrigo became blind early in his childhood but was able to compose for guitar. A curious case of a blind musical genius was a former Negro slave known as Blind Tom, whose pianistic talent was discovered when he was a small child. He was "leased" to one Perry Oliver who arranged concerts for him, including an appearance at the White House.

The Blue Danube. The most celebrated of all waltzes, written by the "Waltz King," Johann Strauss, Jr., in 1867. When Brahms was asked for an autograph by a music lover, he wrote down the initial two bars of *The Blue Danube* waltz and signed, "Unfortunately, not by Brahms." The original German title is *An der schönen blauen Donau.*

Bluebeard's Castle. An opera by Béla Bartók, produced in Budapest on May 24, 1918. The justly infamous Bluebeard (possibly a historic character) lets his last bride open seven secret doors of his castle that conceal torture chambers and the dead bodies of his previous wives. Although Bluebeard protests his love for his last bride, she joins the dead wives behind the last door. The music is appropriately dissonant, stressing the cumulative melodramatic events.

Bluegrass music. A type of rustic music that originated in the mountain country of Kentucky, a state famous for its rich bluegrass fields on which thoroughbred horses are raised. It is marked by an unsophisticated, easygoing, and unaggressive Americanism that appeals to country folks rather than the urban listener. Native performers of bluegrass music, albeit untutored, have developed an instinctive skill of contrapuntal improvisation resulting occasionally in stunning polyphony. The instrumentation includes the fiddle, banjo, double bass, and guitar, supplemented by such homely devices as jugs to be blown into, washboards to be scraped, and bones to be rattled.

Blues. An authentic form of American popular music that emerged early in the 20th century. The colloquialism "blues" for sadness is long-standing in the American language, but the musical form of blues was a genre influenced by the Negro spirituals and popularized by the black composer and trumpet player W.C. Handy, who published his *Memphis Blues* in 1912. The scale structure of the blues is characterized by a "blue note," which is the lowered seventh degree; its existence may be accounted for as being an approximate seventh partial tone of the natural trumpet. Some blues also have a lowered mediant, coexistent with the natural mediant in the accompaniment. Like its direct predecessor, ragtime, the fundamental tonality of the blues is in major. Untutored popular musicians refer to the seventh chord containing the blue note as the tonic seventh, whereas this chord would be analyzed by an academically trained person as the dominant-seventh chord of the subdominant of the principal key. The traditional refrain of the blues contains 12 measures, harmonized by the tonic, the subdominant, and the dominant. The first piece of symphonic jazz rooted in the blues was Gershwin's *Rhapsody in Blue*, composed in 1924. Even before that Darius Milhaud had made use of the genre in his ballet *La Création du monde*. Ravel also wrote music of the blues type, as did Samuel Barber in his piano suite *Excursions*.

BMI (Broadcast Music Incorporated). A music licensing organization founded in New York in 1940 as an alternative collecting agency to ASCAP. It operates by granting licenses to entertainment businesses, including radio and television stations, hotels, restaurants, ballrooms, airlines, even circuses—wherever music is performed. BMI purchases the rights from publishers, who in turn pay royalties to composers and lyricists. In other words, BMI serves as an intermediary between the composer of music, or writer of words used with music, and the public users of such productions. Since BMI started out as a rival organization to ASCAP, it naturally tried to attract composers with prestigious names but who did not command a decent income from royalties for performances. In its early years, BMI offered large sums of money to such composers, up to $10,000 a year.

Bockstriller. In German, "goat's trill." A curious vocal effect produced when a singer repeats a note very fast and catches a breath after each note. It was introduced by Monteverdi for dramatic purposes; Wagner also used it in *Die Meistersinger*. In Italian this effect is called *caprino*, "little goat."

Le Bœuf sur le toit (The Bull on the Roof). A rollicking musical entertainment by Darius Milhaud, with the music derived mainly from Brazilian dances. (Milhaud served as an attaché to the French Embassy in Rio de Janeiro during World War I.) It was first performed in Paris on February 21, 1920, as a stage show; the original score was for two pianos. So popular did the piece become that a Paris bartender named his establishment "Le Bœuf sur le Toit."

Bogdan Khmelnitsky. An opera by Konstantin Dankevich, first performed in Kiev on January 29, 1951. In deference to criticism in the Soviet press for the erroneous representation of the relationship between the Ukraine and Russia in the 17th century, the composer radically revised the score. The new version was performed for the first time in Kiev on January 21, 1953. Bogdan Khmelnitsky, a historical figure, was the hetman of the Ukraine who successfully defeated the then-powerful Polish kingdom and in 1654 effected the reunion of the Ukraine with Russia.

La Bohème. An opera by Puccini, produced in Turin on February 1, 1896. It depicts the life of two impoverished but amorous Paris artists (known as Bohemians in the 19th century). They befriend a neighboring girl who falls in love with one of them, but she is consumptive and dies at the end of the opera. The realism of the subject and the relative modernity of the score made *La Bohème* a landmark in opera. Leoncavallo produced an opera on the same subject with the same French title a year after Puccini, in Venice, on May 6, 1897; although meritorious, his *La Bohème* was eclipsed by Puccini's masterpiece.

The Bohemian Girl. An opera by the Irish composer Michael William Balfe, on a subject ultimately derived from *La Gitanella* by Cervantes. The much-revised libretto deals with a girl abducted by gypsies from her socially important father but finally restored to him and allowed to marry her Polish lover. The opera was first produced in London on November 27, 1843, and has clung firmly to the British stage ever since. It includes the famous nostalgic aria *I Dreamt That I Dwelt in Marble Halls*.

Boléro. The most celebrated musical composition by Maurice Ravel, written for the dancer Ida Rubinstein. It had its first performance in Paris on November 22, 1928. The melody (inspired by the Spanish popular dance) and the harmony never change. The extraordinary variety is provided by diversified instrumentation and colorful dynamics. With the exception of a brief deviation to E major before the coda, the entire piece is maintained in C major, a veritable tour de force of modernity made simple.

Bomarzo. An opera by Alberto Ginastera, based on the legend of an Italian nobleman who constructed giant statues of volcanic stone in his garden near Rome in the 16th century. The score includes electronic sounds, quartertones, tone clusters, and improvisational episodes. The opera was first performed in Washington, D.C., on May 19, 1967. Previously, Ginastera wrote a cantata on the same subject that was performed for the first time in Washington, D.C., on November 1, 1964.

Boogie-woogie. A rhythmic development of jazz that made its appearance in Chicago and quickly spread to New York and elsewhere. Its characteristic feature is the accompaniment of rapid eighth notes in broken octaves, a rhythm that is suggested by a boogie-woogie song, *Beat Me, Daddy, Eight to the Bar*. Its harmonic scheme is close to the blues, consisting of a 12-bar section with alternating harmonies of the tonic, subdominant, and dominant. The Dutch painter Mondrian, who lived in New York, drew an abstract painting in straight lines that are interrupted by blank spaces crossing at right angles another set of broken straight lines, and called it *Broadway Boogie-Woogie*.

Boris Godunov. A music drama in four acts by Modest Mussorgsky that is based on the historical tragedy of Pushkin; it was composed in 1869 and produced in St. Petersburg on February 8, 1874. The action takes place during the interregnum of 1598–1605. Boris is tormented by the murder of the young Czarevitch Dmitri, lawful heir to the Russian throne, which was perpetrated by assassins acting ostensibly to remove a possible rival of Boris's. A young monk, Gregory, conceives the idea of pretending that he is the true Dmitri and that he was miraculously saved from his assassins. The Polish government backs Gregory's claim and leads the army to Moscow with Gregory as the pretender to the throne. Boris demands proof from his henchmen that it was the child Dmitri who was actually slain. The opera ends with Boris's death and the expectation of the pretender's entry into Moscow. After its original production in 1874, *Boris Godunov* was radically revised by Rimsky-Korsakov, and it is in this version that the opera is usually performed. An original score was republished in 1928.

Boston (Valse Boston). A slow waltz with jazz-like inflections. It emerged as a popular dance in Europe after World War I, but it is practically unknown in America and least of all in Boston.

Bouche fermée. French for "mouth closed." An effective device used in choral singing and in opera as a manner of vocalization without words. A famous example occurs in Verdi's *Rigoletto*, in the last act, where it is used with great dramatic effect.

Boulevard Solitude. An opera by Hans Werner Henze, first produced in Hannover on February 17, 1952. The libretto is the modern interpretation of the story of Manon Lescaut, in which she is deflowered, debauched, and humiliated, but eventually is returned to her now-penitent seducer and dies in his arms. The musical score is extremely dissonant and abounds in nervous syncopated rhythms.

Bowing. The action of playing on string instruments depending on the manner of applying the bow to the strings. Because a bow is of a finite length, a melody must be played alternately with upbows and downbows. Upbows move against gravity, therefore more effort must be applied to the movement than to a downbow, which follows the direction of gravity. When a composer wishes to produce a succession of strong sounds, downbows are indicated by a specific sign that looks like a square bracket turned 90 degrees to the right. A succession of upbows, used to produce lighter sounds, is indicated by a capital letter V above the note. When several notes are used in the same stroke of a bow, the first and last notes are connected by a curved line. It is not generally realized that because of the need to change direction of the bow, rhythmic figures such as a quarter note followed by an eighth note, when not played by the same type of bowing, cannot be performed evenly with the same amount of pressure and consequently with the same amount of tone. In actual performance, therefore, a string player automatically changes such rhythmic figures to two eighth notes separated by an eighth-note rest, making legato quite impractical. Apart from legato, which in theory should not have any interruption of the sound, the most common stroke is staccato, an Italian word for "detached." For special effects, the player is instructed to bow *sul ponticello*, "close to the bridge," *sul tasto*, "on the fingerboard," or *col legno*, "with the wooden part of the bow."

Brandenburg Concertos. A set of six concerti grossi for various instrumental combinations that Bach wrote and dedicated to the Margrave of Brandenburg in 1721. Two of them are in F major, another pair is in G major, and the remaining are in D major and in B-flat major. Strictly, only three of them belong to the category of the concerto grosso, characterized by contrasts between the *concertino*, a small group of solo instruments, and *ripieno*, "replenishing instruments," (i.e., a full ensemble). Bach's flowery dedication to Brandenburg is an extraordinary example of the verbal genuflection of a great composer before a member of petty royalty who vouchsafed him an emolument.

Break. A short and lively improvised instrumental solo in jazz that momentarily breaks the continuity of the tune without upsetting the symmetric period of the whole. Breaks can be improvised by several solo instruments in prearranged harmonic changes, and they often result in extremely ingenious and even complex contrapuntal settings.

Break the News to Mother. A sentimental ballad (words and music by Charles K. Harris) in which a wounded drummer boy of the Confederate Army whispers these words to a Negro slave. Composed in 1897, it became popular during the Spanish-American War.

Die Bremer Stadtmusikanten. An opera by Richard Mohaupt, produced in Bremen on June 25, 1949. The libretto is derived from a folk tale by the Brothers Grimm. Six musically gifted domestic animals, a cat and a dog, a rooster and a hen, a donkey and a bear, rescue the animal-loving daughter of the burgomaster of Bremen from her abductors. In gratitude, the burgomaster appoints them *Stadtmusikanten*, "town musicians." The score makes use of multinational dances, the waltz, and the polka.

Breve. A note value which, when it was introduced into medieval mensural notation, had the etymological meaning of a short note. In subsequent centuries, however, a whole generation of shorter notes made their appearance, and as a result the breve became incongruously the longest note in modern notation. This unnatural terminology is retained in contemporary British usage. The breve equals two whole notes and can be used only in the time signature of 8/4. It is written as an oblong, not blackened in.

Brindisi. A salutatory drinking song; an operatic toast. The word apparently comes from the German *bring' dir's* ("I bring it to you") and is not connected with the port town of Brindisi in Apulia. The earliest known operatic brindisi occurs in Donizetti's *Lucrezia Borgia.* The most celebrated example is in Verdi's *La Traviata: "Libiamo!"* ("Let us drink!").

Brothers Ulyanov. An opera by Yuli Meitus, first performed in Ufa on November 25, 1967. The libretto traces the early years of the Ulyanov family and the revolutionary development of Vladimir Ulyanov, the future Lenin, whose brother Alexander is implicated in a terrorist conspiracy against the czar. Alexander is offered clemency if he names his accomplices, but he proudly refuses and is hanged. Lenin enters revolutionary apprenticeship as a university student in Kazan. In the last act of the opera, he predicts the collapse of the Russian monarchy and the rule of the proletariat. The score represents the first attempt by a Soviet composer to portray Lenin in opera in a singing part.

Bruder Lustig. An opera by Siegfried Wagner, son of Richard Wagner, to his own libretto from a medieval German legend. The score is written in an emphatic Wagnerian idiom, with 88 leitmotifs facilitating comprehension of the story. It was first performed in Hamburg on October 13, 1905.

Bühnenweihfestspiel. The description given by Wagner to his opera *Parsifal*; literally, "stage-sacred-festive-play."

Bunt Zakow (The Rebellion of Students). An opera to a Polish text by Tadeusz Szcligowski, first performed in Wroclaw on July 14, 1951. The libretto depicts the rebellion of students and clerks in 1549 in Cracow against the oppressive rule of the Polish King Sigismund II. The score makes use of authentic student songs of the time and also rhythms of various Polish and European dances. The dramatic style of the opera reveals the influence of Mussorgsky.

La buona figliuola (The Good Little Daughter). An opera by Niccolo Piccinni to a libretto after Richardson's novel, *Pamela, or Virtue Rewarded.* It was first produced in Rome on February 6, 1760, and proved to be Piccinni's greatest success. He wrote a sequel to it, *La buona figliuola maritata (The Married Good Daughter).* Hoping to capitalize on Piccinni's success, another Italian composer, Gaetano Latilla, continued the series by writing *La buona figliuola supposta la vedova (Presumed Widow),* but it foundered.

Burgundian school. The ill-defined name of the school of composition that formed a natural transition from the Ars Nova, in which the motet was the crowning achievement, to the great Flemish school, which achieved its luxuriant polyphonic flowering during the late Renaissance. The justification for the term *Burgundian* is that most of the musicians who created this intermediary style of composition served at the various courts in the large geographical dominion that comprised, under the benevolent rule of the Dukes of Burgundy, Philip the Good and Charles the Bold, much of the Netherlands and Belgium, as well as Burgundy proper in central France. Against this stood the embarrassing fact that not one of the masters of the Burgundian school was born in Burgundy. To mitigate this ambiguity, some music historians designated the entire 15th century, in which the Burgundian school flourished, as the Burgundian epoch. To emphasize its role in the inception of the Flemish school, other historians suggested replacing the term *Burgundian school* by *First Flemish school*. Still others, particularly Belgian musicologists, felt that the contribution of the French speaking Walloons of Belgium should be noted, and they suggested the name *École franco-flamande*. To point out the important role played in the development of the Burgundian school by Italian musicians, it was also proposed to describe the Burgundian school as "Italo-Burgundian." Finally, a compromise was achieved by retaining the name Burgundian school, or Burgundian music, to denote the art of the courtly chanson, which was indeed cultivated primarily at the various courts of the sprawling Duchy of Burgundy, and by restoring the general description of the Netherlands or Flemish school for other musical forms that were developed under the aegis of Burgundy, such as the Mass with a definite cantus firmus, and the peripheral secular forms of the narrative ballade and the popular virelai. Perhaps the most practical means of resolving this problem of nomenclature would be to call the period in question the Quattrocento school, that is, the 1400s, the school of the 15th century.

The greatest masters of this period were Guillaume Dufay, whose life covered the first three-quarters of the Quattrocento, and Gilles Binchois, whose lifetime embraced the first 60 years. Dufay was known as *Cantor illustrissimi ducis burgundie*, "court musician of the illustrious Duke of Burgundy," although his term of tenure at the duchy was relatively short. The Burgundian school had many features in common with the developing style of English polyphonic music; it was during this cosmopolitan Quattrocento that thirds and sixths were definitely accepted as consonant intervals, parallel to the acceptance of the *fauxbourdon*. The tonic and dominant triads became the mainstays of the harmonic texture, particularly in cadences. Also the major key, described a century before by the pejorative term *modus lascivus*, now became frequently used, particularly in secular music. Generally speaking, the Burgundian school contributed much to the relaxation of the rigid theological rule that hampered the natural development of musical composition. This was invariably accompanied by the simplification of the prevalent contrapuntal idiom to clear the way for the advent of the new art of the great polyphonic school of the Netherlands in the Renaissance.

Burlesque. A popular type of theatrical entertainment that flourished in the 18th century parallel to the ballad opera; it usually included comic recitatives and songs with original texts set to preexisting popular tunes. In the 19th century, the genre of burlesque was lifted from its vulgar connotations and became a dignified instrumental or vocal form. Richard Strauss wrote a *burleska* for piano and orchestra, as did Bartók and other modern composers. Stravinsky's ballet *Petrouchka* is subtitled *Scènes burlesques*.

Byzantine chant. The church system of modes as established in the Byzantine Empire of Constantine the Great in A.D. 330 and continued until the fall of Constantinople to the Turks in 1453. Byzantine hymnody is similar to Gregorian chant in its monophonic melos, diatonic structures, and asymmetrical sequences unsubordinated to a generic meter. The development of Byzantine chant can be summarized by considering the successive emergence of various types of hymns: Kontakion in the 6th century, Troparia in the 7th century, and Kanous in the 8th century. The essentially syllabic chant began to be adorned with flowery melodic elaborations, but even these embellishments were sung to syllabic verbal formations, having no meaning in themselves. Byzantine music masters outlined a system of modes, or *echoi*, that paralleled the system of modes in the Western church. The language of Byzantine chant from its inception to its decline remained Greek, but there is no formal, tonal, or structural link between the Byzantine *echoi* and the ancient Greek modes. It is, rather, an autochtonous Christian type of hymnody. Its dependence on Oriental rites, particularly Jewish, has been a matter of speculation among scholars.

C

C. The first note of the C major or C minor scale, and therefore also the tonic of the first scale in the cycle of scales. There are no sharps or flats in the key signature. In French, C is Ut, the syllable assigned to it in the *Hymn* of Guido d'Arezzo. In other Romance languages, and in Russian, it is Do.

C. A time signature indicating 4/4. It is not, as is sometimes ignorantly suggested, the phonetic sign for the Spanish *cuatro*, Italian *quattuor*, French *quatre*, or the English Common Time, but is a relic of the medieval half circle, meaning "imperfect time," perfect time being triple time. A time signature marked by a crossed C designates the tempo *alla breve* (literally, "in brief time"), corresponding to 2/4 time.

C major. In common musical association, the key of exultant joy, triumphant jubilation, and communal celebration. Multitudes of piano studies by Czerny and others are set in C major. Beethoven selected this key for his Symphony No. 1 and his Piano Concerto No. 1, as well as the finale of his Symphony No. 5. The most Olympian of all Mozart's symphonies, the *Jupiter* Symphony, is also in C major. When Schumann completed his own C-major Symphony, he must have been aware of the splendors of Mozart's symphony in that key, for he remarked to a friend, "Yes, I think it will be a regular Jupiter." Wagner set the Prelude to his only comic opera, *Die Meistersinger von Nürnberg*, in C major. The key may be solemn and proclamatory, as in the opening of *Also sprach Zarathustra* of Richard Strauss. Scriabin ended his *Le Poème l'extase* with 53 measures of C major. Prokofiev was fond of C major. His most popular piano concerto, No. 3, goes on for pages of music on white keys before modulating. In Prokofiev's fairy tale *Peter and the Wolf*, Peter's opening theme is set in undiluted C major; the coda of the march from his opera *Love of Three Oranges* ends on a C-major triad. It is natural that pianists should love C major; it is the first scale they practice when they begin their lessons, being innocently free from bothering with black keys. Composers of atonal music are apt to exclude C major from their musical vocabulary altogether. Schoenberg used occasional triadic formations, but it would be difficult to find a single use of an unadulterated C major chord during his atonal and dodecaphonic period. Yet Schoenberg's faithful disciple Alban Berg did not hesitate to use C major in his atonal masterpiece *Wozzeck*, in the recitative *Da wieder ist Geld, Marie* ("Here is money again, Marie"), to underscore, the vulgar essence of money. Curiously enough, Mozart's C-major string quartet acquired the sobriquet *Dissonance* Quartet, owing to some perfectly innocent and plainly resolvable melodious ornaments in its introduction.

C minor. The key of concentration in solemnity, of philosophical introspection, quite different from its major homonym, C major. But the two are intimately related, by virtue of the *tierce de Picardie*, in which the minor third at the root of a minor triad is replaced by a major third. Thus, no matter how sepulchral, how lugubrious, how morbid an opening C minor can be, there is always a promise of C major in the finale. The most famous symphony in C minor is unquestionably Beethoven's No. 5, with its "fateful" opening of four notes falling from the dominant to the mediant in C minor. But we can confidently expect the glorious explosion of a C-major finale. Perhaps less predictable is the last movement in C major of the Symphony No. 1 of Brahms, the C-minor symphony, but the apotheosis is nonetheless redeeming. For Mozart, the key of C minor had tragic connotations, or so we are inclined to think from the angular convolutions of the opening theme of the first movement of his Piano Concerto in that key, which travels into the alien region of chromatic modulations. Beethoven's *Pathétique* Sonata is in C minor, and the tragic connotations of its slow opening are unmistakable. Schubert's Symphony No. 4 was inscribed "Tragic" in the manuscript and is set in C minor. Bruckner must have been possessed by this key; his first and second Symphonies are in C minor and so is his eighth, which, paraphrasing what Schumann said about Schubert's "Symphony of Heavenly Length," may be called the Symphony of Infernal Length. Mahler was also partial to C minor. His Symphony No. 2, which rivals in length the interminably revolving symphonies of Bruckner, is in that key. And it is little consolation to the listener that the choral finale of that symphony proclaims the dubious promise, "You must die to live." Scriabin selected the key of C minor for his two consecutive symphonies, the second and the third, which he named *Le Poème divin*; both end in redeeming C major. The most frequently performed Saint-Saëns symphony, No. 3, with organ, is in C minor; but this symphony teleologically directs itself toward a C-major finale, with the organist literally pulling out all the stops. C minor, with its centrally positioned black keys, is eminently pianistic. Beethoven's great Piano Concerto No. 3 is set in that key. And can one speak of C minor without mentioning the most popular piano concerto of modern times, the second by Rachmaninoff, with its overwhelming C major ending? The tone poem *Tod und Verklärung* of Richard Strauss is in the key of C minor, representing the corruption of death but concluding in triumphant C major depicting transfiguration.

Ça ira. A French revolutionary song that became popular after the fall of the Bastille during the Revolution in 1789. The tune was taken from *Le carillon national*. The opening words mean "It will be all right."

Caccia. An Italian medieval musical form that originated in Florence in the 14th century. Initially, the caccia ("chase") used words concerned with hunting, and therefore it was often arranged in the form of a canon in which one voice chased another. The popularity of the caccia grew when renowned composers wrote vocal works in this form. It was often combined with a madrigal; such compound forms became known as canonic madrigals. Motets containing canonic imitation were called caccia motets.

Cacophony. In Greek, "bad sound," but as applied by music critics whose untutored ears are incapable of perceiving concord of a different sort, cacophony is new music. Thus, an English writer reviewing Chopin's recital in London in 1842 described his music as "excruciating cacophony." Nikita Khrushchev, expressing his opinion of 12-tone music, said, "To you it may be dodecaphony, but to me it's plain cacophony." Dodecaphony and cacophony rhyme in Russian.

Cadence. A generic term denoting the conclusion of a musical phrase; it derives from the Latin verb *cadere*, "to fall." The purpose of a cadence is to establish the terminal key of a musical composition. Its minimal length contains the dominant triad followed by the tonic triad; such a dominant-tonic cadence is called an *authentic cadence*. A cadence consisting of a subdominant triad leading to a tonic triad is called a *plagal* (oblique) *cadence*. Sometimes, to circumscribe the tonality more fully, three chords are used: the subdominant, the dominant, and the concluding tonic. This is a full authentic cadence, which includes all seven notes of the scale, thus outlining the key unambiguously. To enhance the tonality in a cadence, the second inversion of the tonic triad (or tonic 6/4) is inserted between the subdominant and the dominant triad. Various surrogates of these fundamental chords are commonly adopted. Thus the subdominant harmony can be substituted by the use of the second inversion of the supertonic triad, which has the same bass as the root of the subdominant triad. In the so-called Neapolitan cadence, the supertonic and the submediant are flatted; this chord then moves through the dominant to the tonic. The dominant triad can be extended by adding the seventh, forming the dominant-seventh triad.

During the Ars Nova, the Italian musician Landini introduced a cadence which bears his name; in it the leading tone in the melody is diverted to the submediant, a degree below, before resolving into the tonic. This melodic divagation creates a momentary impression of a plagal cadence. An important cadence is the so-called *deceptive cadence* in which the dominant-seventh chord leads into the submediant triad instead of the tonic triad, thus "deceiving" the expectant ear. In a major key, such a deceptive submediant is a minor triad; in a minor key, the submediant triad is major. Cadences can be endlessly ornamented and the final resolution into the tonic chord tantalizingly delayed, creating a harmonic suspense. A common device is the insertion of a florid cadenza over the tonic 6/4 chord in anticipation of the inevitable dominant harmony on the way to the resting point of the tonic. The concluding tonic chord is then repeated a great number of times, in varying rhythmic figures and harmonic positions, so that the melody may be traversing through the third or the fifth note of the tonic triad before arriving at the fundamental note of the key in the melody. It would be most instructive to compile a statistical table of the number of such tonic chords in the cadential sections of Classical symphonies. In the resonant C-major coda of Beethoven's Symphony No. 5, the tonic chord is repeated, after alternating with the dominant triad, 15 times, and in Beethoven's Symphony No. 8, 24 times.

In modern compositions, cadences are apt to be abrupt. The march from Prokofiev's opera *Love for Three Oranges* ends in a single C-major chord preceded by the briefest appearance of the dominant. Although in Classical and Romantic music the final chord cannot possibly consist of more than three notes of the tonic harmony, 20th-century composers have introduced a pandiatonic type of cadence in which the tonic triad is supplemented by the submediant, supertonic, or tonic seventh in a major key. Thus the C-major triad blossoms out into a chord of C-E-G-A, C-E-G-B, or C-G-E-A-D, or other combinations of those ingredients, comprising every degree of the scale except the subdominant (because the subdominant cannot be derived from the fundamental tone by an expansion of the overtone series). Jazz musicians popularized the "added sixth," "added seventh," or "added ninth" chords, all technically classified in academic harmony as dissonances, but all sounding to the modern ear more satisfyingly concordant than the sterile triadic tonic harmony.

Cadenza. In Italian, cadenza means "cadence." In English, Russian, and other languages, it signifies an improvised interpolation in an instrumental or vocal work that is mainly intended to demonstrate the technical brilliance of the performer. Solo cadenzas in Classical concertos were rarely written by the composer but were contributed by performers. Among writers of cadenzas, the most notable were Hummel, Moscheles, and Reinecke for piano concertos and Joachim for violin concertos. Still, their products were not always compatible with the style of the original work, and the emphasis on technical display sometimes proved jarring. Beethoven wrote his own cadenzas in his piano concertos, and so did Schumann and Brahms. Chopin and Liszt avoided long cadenzas in their concertos, preferring to interpolate brief fiorituras, or amplified embellishments. Most 20th-century composers have abandoned the cadenza as unnecessary. During the so-called golden age of opera, coloratura sopranos were expected to roll out a formidable line of trills and arpeggios.

Café chantant. A "singing café" that flourished during the Second Empire in Paris between 1852 and 1870. The repertoire usually consisted of sentimental ballads. Such cafés eventually evolved into large places of entertainment of which the most celebrated is the Folies-Bergère, where increasingly explicit sexuality reigned. When the "singing café" transferred to England, it assumed the name "music hall" and was scorned by Victorian society as a most shocking institution of sensuality.

The Caissons Go Rolling Along. A song composed by Edmund Gruber in 1907 for the Fifth U.S. Artillery in the Philippine Islands. John Philip Sousa arranged it for band. Eventually the song became a semiofficial march for the Artillery.

Cakewalk. An American dance in quick 2/4 time that became popular among blackface comedians about 1870; its vogue soon spread all over the world. Its rhythm is essentially that of ragtime. Debussy included a cakewalk in his piano suite *Children's Corner*, entitled *Golliwogg's Cakewalk*.

Calliope. A large circus organ with very loud whistles activated by steam. Raucous and vulgar, the calliope became a musical symbol of the swashbuckling and aggressive society of the late 19th century. It went into a limbo of nostalgia with the advent of the modern sophisticated age. Calliope was the Greek Muse of heroic poetry.

Callithumpian. A not-very-ingenious theatrical slang word for cacophonous. It comes from the Greek word *kallos*, "beautiful," and the English word "thump."

Calumet Dance. An American Indian peace-pipe dance, or a walk about the fire. *Calumet* is the French word for a long, ornamented, ceremonial pipe for smoking tobacco.

La cambiale di matrimonio. A "merry farce" by Rossini, first performed in Venice on November 3, 1810, when Rossini was only 19 years old. The daughter of a British banker is traded without her consent to a Canadian merchant, but she loves a young employee of her father. When the Canadian, improbably named Slook, arrives in Europe to claim her hand, she explains to him that she is already "mortgaged." Moved, he writes off his own capital to her and her lover as a matrimonial "bill of exchange" (*la cambiale*). The work is full of jollity. It was republished in 1970, and revived on the stage to considerable acclaim.

Camerata. A historically important society organized in Florence late in the 16th century by a group of aristocratic poets, philosophers, and music lovers. Its aim was to reinstate the pure singing practice without accompaniment as it was believed to have been used in ancient Greek drama. Renouncing the florid art of polyphonic writing, the Camerata cultivated lyric melody and homophony, leading to the genesis of opera.

Campanella. Italian for "little bell." It is the name of one of the most brilliant piano compositions of Liszt, *La Campanella*, arranged by him from a caprice by Paganini. Liszt expanded the tune into a veritable carnival of tintinnabulations in high treble.

Canary. An American slang word, with derogatory undertones, for a female vocalist in a dance band; another ornithological appellation of the species is thrush, also somewhat demeaning.

Cancan. A lively and somewhat salacious dance that emerged in Paris about 1830, set in rapid 2/4 time, similar to a gallop. At the height of its popularity under the Second Empire, the cancan, as danced by girls on the vaudeville stage, shocked the sensibilities of French audiences because the dancers lifted their skirts above the knees in time with the music. Early editions of the *Oxford Companion to Music* characterized the cancan as "a boisterous and latterly indecorous dance, of the quadrille order and including high kicking," and demurred at further elucidation by stating that "its exact nature is unknown to anyone connected with this *Companion*."

Cancel. A term used in music courses in American schools in the second half of the 19th century; it meant a natural sign.

Canción. Spanish for "song," applied specifically to the poetic type of 15th-century Spanish popular ballad, but semantically given a more dignified standing than the rustic *villancico*. The verse is usually strophic, and the musical setting strictly symmetrical. Its derivative, *cancionero*, is a collection of such songs.

Candide. A musical comedy by Leonard Bernstein, first performed in New York on December 1, 1956. It is derived from Voltaire's famous story of a Westphalian youth learning the sordid side of life. There are several lively tunes. Bernstein later revised the orchestration and text into an "opera-house version" that was produced in New York on October 13, 1982.

Canon. A contrapuntal composition of two or more voices in which a subject introduced by one of the voices is imitated by another voice. The most common type, canon in unison, is imitation on the same pitch or an octave higher. A more difficult imitation is the canon at the fifth, which gave rise to the fugue. (In a classical fugue, the imitating voice is in the key of the dominant, and it may enter either a fifth higher or a fourth lower than the main subject.) The most popular canons are in two voices, but the earliest canon ever written, *Sumer is icumen in*, is set for four voices. Examples are known of canons in 8, 16, 32, and even more voices, but the subjects of such canons are inevitably reduced to a series of broken tonic triads, with a few auxiliary notes, and so contribute little to the contrapuntal essence of the form. There are also canons in which the subject is imitated by augmentation (by doubling the note values of the original theme) or by diminution (halving the note values). In canon by inversion, the imitating voice inverts the melodic intervals of the subject; such canons are also called mirror canons. The most ingenious, the most artificial, and the most difficult to compose is the canon *cancrizans*, a crab-walking canon, in which the melody is imitated by playing it backward. (Actually, crabs do not walk backward; they walk sideways, but the old contrapuntists were not acquainted with the walking modes of such creatures.) If the crab-walking voice is inverted, the result is imitation by retrograde inversion, or inverted retrograde. Most canons are furnished with an ending by way of an authentic cadence. Canons that return to the beginning, called perpetual canons, or rounds, are very popular group songs. Baroque composers found pleasure in asking the performer or the person to whom the canon was dedicated to decide at what particular beat the imitating voice should enter, with a suitable Latin quotation, such as "Seek, and ye shall find." Bach's *Musikalisches Opfer* (*Musical Offering*), which he wrote for Frederick the Great, is full of such verbal riddles. For example, *Ascendenteque modulatione ascendat gloria regis* ("With an ascending modulation, Let the King's glory ascend also") meant that the canon must modulate by ascending degrees. This type of canon is fittingly called a *riddle canon*. The masters of the Baroque developed fantastic ingenuity in writing canons in all conceivable forms, and in carefully attending to the proper resolution of dissonances without breaking the established rules of harmony and counterpoint. The art of canon suffered an inevitable decline in the 20th century when dissonances became emancipated and canons could be written at any interval and in any form of inversion, retrograde, or the inversion of the retrograde, without fear of violating harmonic conventions.

Canope. One of Debussy's piano Preludes in Book II, a dirge evoking the Canopic vase, used in ancient Egypt as a container for the entrails of an embalmed body.

Cantabile. In a songful manner, singingly. This Italian term received its currency in the 18th century when it became a criterion of beauty in music. As applied to vocal compositions, cantabile appears redundant, but it became of aesthetic importance as an expression mark in instrumental writing. A cantabile was often part of the name of the movement itself, as in Mozart's *Andante cantabile con espressione* in his A-minor Piano Sonata, and in Beethoven's *Adagio cantabile* in his Violin Sonata No. 2. Romantic composers made use of the term with increasing frequency, as Tchaikovsky did in the *Andante cantabile* of his String Quartet. In the piano music of Chopin, Schumann, and other Romantic composers, cantabile is synonymous with legato.

Cantata. A musical form of fundamental historical importance, written for solo voices, chorus, and instruments, that developed parallel to the emergence of opera and oratorio at the threshold of the 17th century. The Italian word *cantata* means "a work to be sung," as opposed to *sonata*, "a work to be sounded or played." In contrast to the oratorio, which had a religious origin, the cantata appeared first as a secular composition, a series of vocal stanzas in the strophic form. Only later, mainly through the works of Bach, did it become the medium of religious composition. The early cantata embodied varied characteristics, making use of both polyphonic and monodic construction. A cantata is usually of a shorter duration than an oratorio; its form is flexible, so that it can admit both lyrical and dramatic elements and appear as a series of extended arias or else as an operatic scene with recitatives. Bach contributed decisively to the standardization of the form; at his hands the common type of monodic cantata grew to dimensions of fervent religious devotion and dramatic grandeur within a polyphonic framework of incomparable mastery. Bach was not averse to writing cantatas of a topical nature, such as his entertaining *Coffee Cantata*. Beginning early in the 19th century, the composition of cantatas was obligatory in order to obtain the Prix de Rome at the Paris Conservatory. Since practically all French composers worth their bouillabaisse competed for the Prix de Rome, the number of prize-winning and prize-losing French cantatas reached tens of thousands in a mere 100 years. Mozart wrote a Masonic cantata; one aria from it became the Austrian national hymn after World War I.

In the 20th century, the borderline between an oratorio and a cantata has become difficult to trace. Prokofiev's patriotic suite *Alexander Nevsky* has the features of both an oratorio in the solemnity of its invocation and a cantata in the brevity of its individual numbers. Benjamin Britten wrote two particularly memorable cantatas: *Cantata Accademica*, first performed in Basel on July 1, 1960, which was written for the quincentennial of the University of Basel, to the Latin text of Carmen Basiliense; and *Cantata Misericordium*, to commemorate the centennial of the International Red Cross. The latter's text is also in Latin and glorifies the humanitarian deed of the Good Samaritan. It was first performed in Geneva, the birthplace of the Red Cross, on September 1, 1963. Béla Bartók's *Cantata Profana* is a choral work with orchestra, with text and musical themes borrowed from Rumanian folksongs. (Bartók was a Hungarian born in Transylvania, which later became part of Rumania.) It was first performed in London on May 25, 1934. The word *Profana* in the title means "secular," that is, not sacred. Alberto Ginastera wrote quite an effective cantata, *Cantata para America Mágica,* for soprano and percussion; the melodies and rhythms in the score are drawn from chants of South American Indian tribes. It was first performed in Washington, D.C., on April 30, 1961.

Canti carnascialeschi. Polyphonic songs performed at Florentine festivals that flourished during the reign of the murderous but artistically minded house of the Medicis in the 15th century. *Canti carnascialeschi* are historically important because they include work songs, such as those of tailors, scribes, perfume makers, and so on. Their form approximates that of the frottole.

Canticle. From the Latin *canticum,* "a song." Used in early Christian liturgy, the texts are in the nature of psalms, taken from the Bible but not from the *Book of Psalms* itself. Canticles are called major when they are taken from the New Testament, and minor when they are derived from the Old Testament. Texts from the *Song of Solomon* are often used in motets.

Canticum sacrum ad honorem Sancti Marci nominis. A sacred cantata in honor of St. Mark composed by Stravinsky for the Venice Festival. The text is in Latin, and the prosody is Gregorian. Stravinsky conducted its first performance in the Basilica of St. Mark in Venice on September 13, 1956. This is the first work of Stravinsky in which he uses Schoenberg's 12-tone system of composition.

Cantiga. A medieval Spanish song to texts in the vernacular. Secular cantigas were subdivided into several categories according to their content, such as *cantiga de amor, cantiga de amigo,* and the like. Religious cantigas most often praised the Virgin Mary. The theory that they were of Arabic origin and brought to Spain by the Moors is unfounded; most probably they are varieties of villancicos.

Cantillation. Religious chanting in the Jewish synagogue service, usually a recitative with a text from the Hebrew Bible. The manner of the cantillation is peculiarly rhapsodic and is often set in the style of a lamentation. Its rhythm follows the natural accents of the text. The word itself comes from the Latin verb *cantillare,* "to sing softly."

Cantor. In the Roman Catholic church, the cantor is the soloist in the liturgical chants, and the chorus is called *schola.* In Lutheran liturgy, the cantor is the music director as Bach was in Leipzig. In the Jewish synagogue, the cantor is the soloist who chants the cantillation. Cantor derives from the Latin verb *cantare*, "to sing."

Cantus firmus. Literally, a "firm chant." Historically, the term for the main musical subject in a polyphonic work, a plainsong melody in Gregorian chant. It originated in the organa of the Notre Dame school of Paris in the 12th century and continued to appear in the motets and Masses of the Renaissance. In the Quattrocento Masses, the melody of the cantus firmus was often taken from secular popular songs, such as *L'homme armé*. A cantus firmus is usually given to the tenor part and consists of long notes of even values. In the 18th century the cantus firmus was often placed in the bass, as in the organ chorales, where it was played by the pedal.

> **Cantus fractus.** Literally, a "fractured chant" consisting of notes of different metrical value as if broken away from even notes. In Elizabethan times, the expression "broken music" (found in Shakespeare) meant cantus fractus.

> **Cantus gemellus.** Literally, "twin chant," a type of two-part writing in thirds or sixths. In England this technique became known as *gymel*.

> **Cantus Gregorianus.** Latin for "Gregorian chant."

> **Cantus mensuratus.** A chant consisting of precisely measured notes, usually of equal duration.

> **Cantus planus.** Plainchant; Gregorian chant, with notes of equal duration.

> **Cantus transpositus.** A term used in the theory of mensural notation to indicate the alteration of a given meter.

Canzona. An Italian term, a cognate of the French *chanson*. The plural of canzona is canzone, but canzone is also used as a singular noun, in which case the plural is canzoni. In Dante's time, canzona was a lyrical Italian poem of several stanzas. Originally a vocal composition, *canzona* began to be used over the course of time as a title of works for lute or keyboard instruments. During the Renaissance, the canzona acquired traits of a folksong melody in monodic settings; such a canzona became known as a *canzona alla napoletana*, a designation applied to a lyric ballad. The instrumental canzona became differentiated into the form of *canzona francese*, or *canzona alla francese*, "a canzona in a French manner." An instrumental canzona for several instruments was also called *canzona da sonar*, "a canzona to be played," as distinguished from one to be sung. As canzonas became more complex in contrapuntal settings, they came to be identified with the ricercar, eventually giving rise to a hybrid form of variation canzona, with a single theme followed by a free fantasy in variation form. Later still, the term *canzona* began to be used interchangeably with *sonata*, in the sense of a piece to be played on an instrument, without any connotation, however, of the classical sonata form.

Capolavoro. A masterpiece. In Italian *capo* means "chief," and *lavoro* means "labor."

Capotasto. A metal bar placed on the fingerboard of a guitar or lute to shorten the length of all strings and raise their pitch. This enables an uncertain player to transpose to other keys without changing the fingering. American guitarists often use the slang abbreviation *capo*, pronounced "kaypo."

Cappella. Italian and Latin for "chapel." Through the centuries, the word has been used in two senses: as the place of worship, and as persons participating in the church service. *A cappella* is music composed and performed in the way it was done in a chapel. Because such performances were, beginning with the 16th century, mostly polyphonic choral works, the term has come to mean an unaccompanied chorus.

Capriccio. Italian for "caprice," from the Latin *caper*, "goat." Thus, a capriccio is a sort of musical caper. Capriccio originated in the Renaissance as a lively instrumental composition in a free improvisatory style. In the 19th century the term reasserted its capricious character. Beethoven, Weber, Mendelssohn, Brahms, Reger, Dvořák, Tchaikovsky, Rimsky-Korsakov, Saint-Saëns, and Richard Strauss wrote instrumental capriccios. Paganini composed 24 capriccios for solo violin that were arranged by other composers for various instruments. Bach entitled one of his few unabashedly sentimental pieces *Capriccio on the Departure of a Beloved Brother*. Beethoven notated his rondeau subtitled *Rage Over a Lost Penny*, "quasi un capriccio." The free form of capriccio makes it especially suitable for works of national color. Tchaikovsky wrote a *Capriccio Italien*, Rimsky-Korsakov a *Capriccio Espagnol*, and Saint-Saëns a *Capriccio Arabe*. Richard Strauss composed an opera called *Capriccio*; the title seems to denote an uninhibited whimsical production, a musical play within a musical play, with various theatrical and operatic characters discussing the problem of whether words or music are more important. With the accentuation of a neo-Classical trend in the 20th century, the term *capriccio* regained its original meaning as a contrapuntal instrumental piece in the manner of a ricercar. Stravinsky's *Capriccio for Piano and Orchestra* is an example. The proper Italian plural of capriccio is *capricci*.

Capriccio brillante. A work by Mendelssohn for piano and orchestra, first performed in Leipzig on November 9, 1835. The soloist was Clara Wieck, future bride of Schumann. The adjective *brillante* describes the nature of the work, but the noun *capriccio* does not necessarily imply any capriciousness in the music. On the contrary, the piece is highly organized in a symmetric, formal fashion.

Capriccio espagnol. A symphonic suite on Spanish themes by Rimsky-Korsakov, first performed in St. Petersburg on November 12, 1887. Rimsky-Korsakov borrowed the themes and harmonies from a collection of authentic Spanish songs and dressed them up in a multicolored panoply of instrumental timbres. The result was a triumph of sonorous orchestration.

Capriccio italien. A symphonic fantasy by Tchaikovsky, first performed in Moscow on December 18, 1880. The work is based on authentic Italian songs that Tchaikovsky heard during his sojourn in Italy. Included are a bolero, a Neapolitan ballad, and a tarantella.

Capricorn Concerto. A piece that Samuel Barber wrote in the form of a concerto grosso, with the flute, oboe, and trumpet being the concertante instruments. It is in three sections, alternately meditative and playful. He named it after a house he owned near New York City with a fellow composer, Gian Carlo Menotti. The work was first performed in New York on October 8, 1944.

The Captain's Daughter. An unsuccessful opera by César Cui, first performed in St. Petersburg on February 27, 1911. The libretto is drawn from a short story by Pushkin and centers on the romance of two Russians helped by the rebellious cossack chieftain Pugachov.

I Capuleti ed i Montecchi. An opera by Bellini, produced in Venice on March 11, 1830, to a libretto derived from Shakespeare's tragedy *Romeo and Juliet*. Bel canto arias and conventional Italian recitatives being adaptable to different words and lyrico-dramatic situations, Bellini made use of portions of his earlier unsuccessful operas, *Adelson et Salvini* and *Zaira*. The part of Romeo was written for a female alto, a surrogate for the quondam male castrato of the Baroque opera. The spectacle of a richly bosomed female making like Romeo jarred literal-minded opera-goers of the 19th century, and eventually the role had to be given to a tenor. The result was a misalliance of registers, unisons becoming octaves, and, worse still, consecutive thirds being stretched to tenths. Attempts to return to the nonrealistic but melodically superior original were made during the last quarter of the 20th century with dubious results.

Cardillac. An opera by Paul Hindemith, after a fantastic story by the fabulist E.T.A. Hoffmann, in which a wily craftsman murders his customers after they buy his jewels. It was first performed in Dresden on November 9, 1926.

Caresse dansée. A short piano piece written by Scriabin in 1908. Scriabin was at that time infatuated with the idea of writing music for all five senses; he preferred to call the sense of touch a "caress."

Carillon. A set of church bells suspended from a beam in the belfry, operated either manually by persons pulling on ropes to swing them, or mechanically from a keyboard connected to the clappers of the bells. Modern carillons may have as many as 50 bells and are capable of playing rapid scales, complex harmonies, and facile trills. Large organs have a special stop that plays a carillon timbre.

Carioca. A Brazilian dance in a fast 2/4 time that is derived from the rhythm of the samba but originated in the vicinity of Rio de Janeiro. *Carioca* is a colloquial term for an inhabitant of Rio de Janeiro.

Carmagnole. A French revolutionary song that became popular in Paris after the storming of the Tuileries palace in 1792. The name came from the town of Carmagnola in Piedmont, Italy; the song was probably carried to Paris by Italian street musicians.

Carmen. An opera by Georges Bizet, produced in Paris on March 3, 1875. The oft-repeated story that *Carmen* was a fiasco and that Bizet expired of chagrin over it is contradicted by chronology. Bizet died on the night of its 31st performance, three months after its premiere, surely a very satisfactory run. With Gounod's *Faust* and Verdi's *Aida*, *Carmen* became one of the most successful operas in the repertory, continually produced all over the world. Nietzsche counterposed the spirit of *Carmen*, with its Mediterranean gaiety, passion, and drama, to the somber creations of the Nordic Wagner, once his idol. The action of *Carmen* takes place in Seville around 1820. Don José, a soldier, falls in love at first sight with a gypsy cigarette girl, Carmen, and deserts the army. This is all in vain, for Carmen abandons him for a bullfighter. Distraught, Don José stabs her to death. The most famous arias in *Carmen* are the bullfighter's victory song, *Toreador* (the correct Spanish word is *torero*), and Carmen's song *Habanera* (too often misspelled Habañera, with a tilde, despite its obvious derivation from *Havana*). The Habanera was borrowed by Bizet from a Cuban song by Sebastian Yradier. Just how a Cuban song got into an opera taking place in Seville is a mystery.

Carmen Jones. A musical play with a text by Oscar Hammerstein II and a score preserved almost intact from Bizet's *Carmen*, first performed in New York on December 2, 1943. In his modern version, Hammerstein shifted the scene from Seville to a southern American town during World War II. Carmen is a worker in a parachute factory, Don José a black corporal, and the toreador a prize fighter. Don José kills Carmen outside a Chicago arena during her lover's fight for the heavyweight championship.

Carmina Burana. A scenic cantata by Carl Orff, first performed in Frankfurt on June 8, 1937. The texts, in rhymed verse in a variety of dialects, Latin,

French, and Provençal, date to the 12th and 13th centuries. They were discovered in the Benedictine Cloister in Bavaria, and the collection became known as *Burana Sancti Benedicti*. Despite linguistic difficulty and occasional profanity in the texts selected by Orff, *Carmina Burana* became extremely popular.

Carnegie Hall. The most famous concert hall in the United States, opened in New York in 1891 through endowment from the wealthy Scottish-born magnate Andrew Carnegie (1835–1919), who built an immense fortune from successful investments in steel and oil. Before becoming a multimillionaire, Carnegie published an essay, *Gospel of Wealth*, in which he outlined his philanthropic program of supporting education and art by establishing financial foundations. Tchaikovsky was the guest conductor at the opening of Carnegie Hall, which was then called Music Hall. Carnegie Hall is beloved by concert performers for its remarkable acoustics. In the subculture of movies and rock, the name Carnegie Hall has assumed a magical aura as a passport to greatness in music.

Carnival. The etymology is interesting: *carne* is "meat," and *vale* is from the Latin verb *levare*, "to abandon," so that carnival means, in effect, "goodbye meat." Carnival is the occasion for eating meat for the last time before Lent. Many composers wrote pieces glorifying the carnival season: Berlioz produced a popular concert overture, *Le Carnaval romain*; Liszt's Hungarian Rhapsody No. 9 is subtitled *Carnaval de Pest*; Saint-Saëns wrote an ingenious suite, *The Carnival of the Animals*; and Schumann wrote a piano suite, *Carnaval*, subtitled *Scènes mignonnes sur quatre notes*. Considering the extraordinary popularity of Schumann's *Carnaval*, it is mind-boggling that all its romantic display is manufactured artificially on the thematic foundation of four notes that spell Asch, a town where Schumann had a girlfriend. These thematic notes are, in the German musical alphabet, A, S (or Es, German for E-flat), C, and H (German for B-natural). The same town can also be spelled in three letter notes, AS (or As, German for A-flat), C, and H. Schumann weaves a colorful tapestry from these letter-notes, creating 21 sections that include musical portraits of Chopin, Paganini, and Schumann's beloved wife, Clara. There is also a "silent" section entitled *Sphinxes*, which notates the "riddle" of the piece, that is, the four notes of the subtitle.

The Carnival of the Animals (Le Carnaval des animaux). A marvelously witty and musically enchanting "grand zoological fantasy" by Saint-Saëns, for orchestra, piano, xylophone, and metal plates struck with a mallet. There are 14 pieces, making delicious fun of the animals, among which the composer includes pianists playing asinine scales. The cello solo for the 13th piece, entitled *The Swan*, has become a celebrated concert piece, also serving as an accompaniment for a ballet scene, *The Dying Swan*. Although he completed the score in 1886, Saint-Saëns did not allow it to be published during his lifetime; it was first performed in Paris on February 26, 1922, two months after his death.

Carnival of Venice. Originally a set of 20 variations for violin and piano by Paganini, based on a popular Venetian tune. Ambroise Thomas wrote an opera entitled *Le Carnaval de Venise*, produced in Paris in December 9, 1857.

Carol. A Christmas song; the name may be derived from the French medieval *carole*, a round dance often accompanied by singing. The most common form, established in the 19th century, is in four-part harmony, symmetrical in structure, and most often in a major key. More ancient forms preserve the style of polyphonic modality.

Carré. A work for four orchestras and four choruses by Karlheinz Stockhausen. The audience is seated in a *carré* ("square") of chairs, hence the title. The work was first performed in Hamburg on October 28, 1960.

Carry Nation. An opera by Douglas Moore, first performed in Lawrence, Kansas, on April 28, 1966. The heroine of the opera, a historical figure, was a fanatical woman who devoted her life to the fight against "demon rum," carrying a small axe with which she bashed in the glass doors of saloons in her native Kansas. The libretto adds an apochryphal episode about her marrying an unregenerate alcoholic.

Casey Jones. A popular American railroad ballad, paying tribute to the heroic locomotive engineer of the Cannonball Limited who on April 29, 1900, remained at his post during a fatal crash after warning the passengers to get out and was scalded to death by the steam. He was known as Casey Jones because he came from Cayce, Tennessee. It is disputed who wrote the ballad, but it was made popular by a pair of vaudevillians, Lawrence Seibert and Eddie Newton.

Cassation. An 18th-century instrumental form that combines the traits of an outdoor serenade, a suite, a divertimento, and a symphony. The etymology of the term is obscure. Some suggest that it comes from *cassa*, Italian for "drum," a conjecture supported by the character of two of Mozart's cassations, which open with a military march. Or it may be derived from the legal term *cassation*, "appeal." Whichever it may be, a cassation is a welcome addition to musical nomenclature to denote a wide spectrum of instrumental works ranging in character from a serenade to a short symphony.

Castrati. Male singers castrated at puberty in order to inhibit the maturation of their sexual glands so as to preserve their high voices. This barbarous practice originated in the 17th century along with the development of opera, which created the demand for "angelic" voices in certain mythological roles such as Orpheus. In the 18th century, the castrati became so famous that they could command large fees to sing in opera houses. Handel wrote special parts for the famous castrato Francesco Senesino. Perhaps the most celebrated castrato singer was Carlo Farinelli. He was engaged by the court of Philip II, King of Spain, who suffered from melancholy. Farinelli sang the same four songs for Philip every night for 25 years. Operatic castration was forbidden with the advent of the 19th century, although occasional cases of castration persisted. The story is often told of a pharmacy in Naples around 1820 that bore the sign, *"Qui si castrati ragazzi"* ("Boys are castrated here"). A famous case of incomplete castration was that of the Italian singer Tenducci, who was a triorchis. So manly did he become that he managed to elope with a mayor's daughter in England, eventually coming to America. She wrote a memoir in which she described her family life (they had children, too). The last castrato singer was Alessandro Moreschi, who died in 1922 and who was known as Angelo di Roma because of his celestially pure voice. Recordings of Moreschi's singing made in 1903 are extant.

Catcalls. Loud and raucous cries to express disapproval at a performance. The term is unfair to cats who never meow derogatorily.

Catch. A popular type of English social song, usually in three parts and often in the form of a canon or round. Catches were the favorite songs in the aristocratic clubs of London in the 18th century, along with glees. Such clubs often commissioned celebrated composers to write catches for them. Purcell contributed many catches, as did Handel after him. Among the earliest catches was *Three Blind Mice*. One catch begins with the famous line, "Catch That Catch Can." The texts often contained humorous allusions to topical events, puns, and even mild obscenities, usually of a scatalogical character. The word *catch* is probably derived from the Italian *caccia*, "chase," because one voice "chases" another as in a canon.

Cats. *Katzenmusik* was the ultimate term of opprobrium used by ailurophobic critics; cat lovers were alienated by such comparisons. In his singing ballet *L'Enfant et les sortilèges*, Ravel introduces an amorous baritone tomcat and a nubile mezzo soprano kitten singing a fine atonal duet.

Cats is an Americanism for musicians in popular bands, and by extension is applied to any humans, mostly of the masculine gender. The term carries a bantering but friendly and even affectionate connotation.

Cat's Fugue. A popular nickname for a harpsichord piece by Domenico Scarlatti with a theme based on curiously unrelated rising intervals. According to a common story that has never been verified, this theme was inspired by a domestic cat's walking on Scarlatti's keyboard. The British professor Edward Dent tried to coax his cat to walk up Scarlatti's scale but failed.

Cavalleria rusticana. An opera by Pietro Mascagni. The title means rustic chivalry, not rural cavalry. *Cavalleria rusticana* launched the vogue of operatic verismo after its first production in Rome on May 17, 1890. The drama takes place in Sicily and is based on an actual event. A young villager is emotionally torn between his attachment to a local girl and his passion for a married woman. The unfortunate lover is confronted by the husband; a duel ensues, and he is killed. Because *Cavalleria rusticana* is unusually short, it is often paired in the same evening with Leoncavallo's *Pagliacci*; in America, the two are affectionately referred to as *Cav* and *Pag*.

Ce qu'on entend sur la montagne (What One Hears on the Mountain). A symphonic poem by Liszt, first performed in Weimar on January 7, 1857. The title is taken from a poem by Victor Hugo. The two principal voices heard on the mountain represent the joyous song of nature and the depressed lament of man.

Cecilianism. A reform movement in Roman Catholic church music, intended to restore Catholic choral polyphony in all its purity, as opposed to the romantic treatment of religious themes. Named for St. Cecilia, the patron saint of music, the Cecilian movement had its inception in Germany in the 19th century, where numerous choral organizations were founded. Later in the century Cecilianism spread into the United States, cultivated mostly by German emigré societies and their publications.

Celesta. A keyboard instrument built on the principle of a glockenspiel, with the keys activating hammers that strike the steel bars in its mechanism. It is limited to four octaves and has a soft ingratiating sound, which was the reason for naming it celesta when it was invented in 1886. Tchaikovsky discovered the celesta during his visit in Paris and was so enchanted with its sound that he warned his publisher not to tell any composers about its existence, specifically naming Rimsky-Korsakov and Glazunov as those who might use it before him. Tchaikovsky included a part for celesta in the movement describing the sugar-plum fairy in his ballet, *The Nutcracker*.

Les Cents Vierges. An opéra-bouffe by Charles Lecocq, produced in Brussels on March 16, 1872. A bevy of young maidens becomes excited over an advertisement for 100 virgins wanted in marriage by 100 colonists on a tropical island. The plot is complicated by numerous cross-amours, but the bridal ship finally arrives, and the colonists are enabled to legally gratify their marital impulses.

A Ceremony of Carols. A work by Benjamin Britten for high voices and harp. There are nine carols and a recession, that is, a repetition of the opening procession. The melodies all come from medieval chants. The work was first performed in Norwich, near London, on December 5, 1942.

Chanson. French for "song," used in music history as a generic term for songs of any description, but specifically to describe the songs cultivated by the polyphonic school of the 15th and 16th centuries in France and the Netherlands. Such chansons were usually strophic in structure, with the same melody repeated for different stanzas. *Chansonette* is a French song of a light nature, often containing scabrous verses. The genre flourished in France in the 19th century in cafés chantants.

Chanson de geste. A medieval "poem of deeds" of which *Chanson de Roland* is the most famous example. Such poems are fantastically long, sometimes numbering more than 20,000 lines in an unchanging meter. They were usually sung to monotonous melodic phrases intoned by professional minstrels. Improvisation was apparently an integral feature of the *chanson de geste*. Some melodic lines are preserved through quotations in *Jeu de Robin et Marion* by Adam de la Halle.

Chansons de Bilitis. A set of songs by Debussy to the sensuous poems by the French poet Pierre Louÿs, in imitation of Greek lyric poetry. Debussy wrote these songs in 1897 using neo-Grecian modalities. Another work of the same title by Debussy is a melodrama for a reciting voice and a small ensemble, composed in 1901.

Chanterelle. The French term for the highest string on a string instrument, as the E string on the violin. Chanterelle is derived from the French verb *chanter*, "to sing."

Character piece. A musical genre cultivated in the 19th century. The pieces were usually for the piano and were given titles suggesting a mood, landscape, or pictorial subject. Among typical titles are *Bagatelles*, *Impromptus*, *Moments musicaux*, *Lieder ohne Worte*, and *Albumblätter*. Schumann composed a number of character pieces under the titles *Fantasiestücke*, *Nachtstücke*, *Kinderszenen*, *Waldszenen*, and *Carnaval*. The genre was anticipated by Couperin and Rameau, who used such descriptive titles as *Les langueurs tendres* and *La triomphante*. Character pieces are usually short, symmetrically constructed, and not too difficult to perform. Modern composers abandoned the German model of character pieces but were not averse to using imaginative titles, as illustrated by Prokofiev's *Visions fugitives*. Scriabin appended titles of a mystical nature to some of his short piano pieces, *Flammes sombres*, *Désir*, and even *Poème satanique*. The German designation is *Charakterstück*.

Charivari. A cacophonous serenade performed by a group of young people to mock and embarrass a pompous official or honeymooning couple, a type of entertainment that arose in France in medieval times. The term is derived from the Latin *carribaria*, which in turn came from the Greek etymological roots *kara*, "head," and *barys*, "heave" (as in "barometer" or "baritone"). In other words, *charivari* is a musical, unmusical, or at any rate acoustical headache.

Chaser. In musical parlance, an orchestral peroration at the end of a theatrical performance to chase out the lingering members of the audience.

La Chasse. A title frequently used for pieces depicting the hunt. Among them are Haydn's String Quartet No. 1, subtitled *La Chasse*, and Mozart's *Jagd Quartett*. Both are in the key of B-flat major, which is the tonality of the natural horn used in the hunt and military exercises. Both pieces have melodic and harmonic figures evoking hunting horns.

Chef d'attaque. Literally, "chief of the start," that is, a term occasionally used by French orchestral players for the concertmaster; a more common term is *premier violon*, "first violin."

Chef d'orchestre. In French, "chief of the orchestra," that is, conductor. It is occasionally abbreviated to *chef*.

Chester. An early American Revolutionary song by William Billings, written in 1778. Although the tune is of a hymnal nature, it was adapted to the ringing revolutionary words, "Let Tyrants Shake Their Iron Rod."

Chevrotement. A rather uncomplimentary reference to a singer trilling like a goat (goat in French is *chèvre*). Chevrotement is occasionally used for special comic effects in opera.

Chiavette. Literally, "little clefs"; commonly used in the 16th and 17th centuries to change the range of the standard clef to avoid the use of extra lines above or below the staff. The baritone clef, with the F on the third line instead of the more common position of the F clef on the fourth line, is an example. However, the C clefs placed on different lines of the staff, which are standard, are not classified as chiavette.

Chicken flip. An American ballroom dance that became popular in the 20th century, along with other "animal dances" such as the turkey trot and the grizzly bear. It was accompanied by ragtime music.

A Child of Our Time. An oratorio by Michael Tippett, to his own text inspired by a tragic episode when a young Jew killed a Nazi diplomat in Paris shortly before World War II. To underline the theme of racial persecution, Tippett included in the score several quotations from Negro spirituals. It was first performed in London on March 19, 1944.

Children's Corner. A suite of piano pieces written by Debussy in 1908 for his little daughter. The English title is explained by the fact that she had an English governess. There are six movements: the first is called *Doctor Gradus ad Parnassum*, emulating Clementi's famous piano studies, and the last one, *Golliwogg's Cakewalk*, is a rollicking pseudo-American ragtime.

Die chinesische Flöte. A chamber symphony by Ernst Toch for soprano and 14 instruments, to words from ancient Chinese poetry, first performed in Frankfurt on June 24, 1923.

Chironomy. An ancient system of leading a choir with the aid of a sign language in which movements of the fingers indicate the tempo, intervals, and rhythm. It is conceivable, if not plausible, that the musical notation used by Jews, Egyptians, and some Slavic nations was the pictorial representation of chironomy. The term is Greek meaning the "law of the hand" (*cheiro*, "hand"; *nomos*, "law").

Chopsticks. This celebrated children's piano exercise is played by two hands, each using a single finger, or else with both hands turned sideways imitating the chopping of wood, which explains the origin of the name. The piece was first published in England in 1877 under the title *The Celebrated Chop Waltz*, without an inkling of the composer's name. The piece was known in Germany as *Koteletten Walzer*, from the French *cotelette*, "cutlet." Several Russian composers published a set of variations on *Chopsticks*, and Liszt added a variation of his own.

Choral Symphony. The popular name for Beethoven's mighty Symphony No. 9 in D minor, op. 125, with a final chorus on Schiller's *Ode to Joy*. Beethoven worked on this symphony for nearly ten years and completed it barely in time for the scheduled first performance in Vienna on May 7, 1824. It is easy to call the work a sublime masterpiece 165 years after its creation, but originally it appeared as a curious challenge to an established tradition: a choral ending seemed unfit for an instrumental work. And what an ending! Beethoven forced the singers into the upper region of their ranges with a massive accompaniment of the orchestra. In fact, the entire symphony seems to partake of the spirit of a solemn oratorio. It opens with a series of open fifths as if Beethoven hesitated to commit himself to a definite tonality. There is another departure from tradition: Beethoven places the scherzo as the second instead of the third movement, as in his previous symphonies. There follows the slow movement, leading to the choral finale, which opens with a horrendously dissonant chord containing all seven notes of the D-harmonic-minor scale. Academic music analysts should not interpret this chord as Beethoven's anticipation of total dissonance, however, for it is nothing more than a suspended-in-midair diminished-seventh chord on the seventh degree of the scale resolving to everyone's satisfaction into the tonic.

Chorale. A generic term for religious choral compositions employed in the German Lutheran church. The word comes from the Latin adjective *choralis*, "belonging to the chorus." The development of the chorale as a fundamental musical form of the Protestant service in Germany is intimately connected with the activities of Martin Luther himself, who caused the Latin hymns of the Roman Catholic church to be translated into the vernacular and made it possible for the congregation to take part in the singing. Most of these texts were direct translations from Latin, so that *Te deum laudamus* became *Herr Gott, Dich loben wir*, and the *Credo* became *Wir glauben all' an einen Gott*. But the Lutheran church also boldly borrowed the melodies from secular songs of the people. One of the most popular was *Durch Adams Fall ist ganz verderbt* (*Through Adam's Fall We Sinned All*). Collections of Lutheran chorales were published in Germany as early as 1524, when the Protestant movement was still fighting the stigma of heresy. Soon these chorales became the sources for polyphonic compositions, thus effecting a link between chorale and instrumental music. The chorale reached its peak in the works of Bach, who harmonized hundreds of known chorale melodies and composed many more. Thus the purely practical movement of the Protestant chorale, begun in the early 16th century with the purpose of forming a repertory of songs in the German tongue in order to bring sacred music closer to the people, grew into a great art, embracing all genres of sacred and secular music.

Chorale cantata. A term applied to cantatas in which harmonized chorales are used in some or all divisions of the cantata, along with free recitatives and homophonic arias. Most of Bach's cantatas are of this type.

Chorale prelude. A composition for organ without a chorus that opens a service in Protestant churches. In Roman Catholic usage, the chorale preludes correspond to organ hymns.

Chorale variations. A common term for variations on a chorale tune. Such variations proliferated, particularly in the 17th and 18th centuries, in the form of keyboard compositions. The theme was usually selected from organ chorales.

Chord. A generic term covering all tonal combinations containing three or more different notes. The major triad is colloquially described as a common chord; this does not mean that other chords are uncommon. Before the advent of modern music in the 20th century, triadic chords—that is, chords derived

from triads by inversion and distribution in various registers—constituted a
statistical majority in all Classical and Romantic music. The final chords in
a cadence in every composition written before 1900 are necessarily tonic triads
or a unison, discounting duplications in octaves. Any chord with more than
three different notes was regarded as a dissonance, requiring resolution into
a consonance according to traditional academic rules. Discrimination against
unrestricted use of dissonant chords has been abolished in the 20th century.

Chôros. A generic term used in Brazil to describe street bands playing native
melodies. Villa-Lobos wrote 14 works for various instrumental groups under
the title *Chôros*, which to him meant a composition in the authentic Brazilian
spirit. The most engaging of the *Chôros* is No. 5 for piano, subtitled *Alma
Brasileira* ("Brazilian Soul"), which he wrote in 1926.

Chorus. An ensemble of voices, consisting of sopranos, altos, tenors, and
basses, abbreviated SATB. A female or boys' chorus consists of sopranos and
altos; a male chorus consists of tenors, baritones, and basses. The word *chorus*
is also used for a refrain in popular songs, show tunes, and similar light music.

Chout. A ballet by Prokofiev, produced by the Ballet Russe in Paris on May
17, 1921. The title is the phonetic French transliteration of the Russian word
shoot, "buffoon." The complete and very long Russian title is *A Tale of a
Buffoon who Outwitted Seven Other Buffoons*. To attempt to report the plot
derived from a Russian fairy tale in any rational manner would be futile, but
the music is exciting, with rhythms pushing and pulling in different directions
and lyric passages full of poetic self-ridicule.

Christmas Symphony (Weihnachtssymphonie). Haydn's Symphony No. 26 in
D minor, composed in 1768. There is nothing in the music that would suggest
the Christmas spirit; in fact, it is sometimes called *Lamentations*.

Chromaticism. From the Greek *chroma*, "color." In music theory, a consistent
and frequent use of chromatic progressions, that is, a systematic insertion of
intermediary notes between two diatonic degrees. In the key of C major, every
sharp and every flat would constitute a chromatic note a semitone apart from
the preceding diatonic degree or the following one. A distinction ought to be
made between a chromatic and a diatonic semitone. The interval from E to F
is a diatonic semitone, but the interval between F and F-sharp is a chromatic
one because the same letter note F is used twice, first as a diatonic degree of
the scale, and then as a "colored" or chromatic note, F-sharp. In the progression F–F-sharp–G, the F-sharp constitutes a chromatic passing note.
    In analyzing a musical composition from the viewpoint of chromaticism,
it is necessary to consider the prevalence of diatonic melody and harmony
relative to the frequency of chromatic passages. A convoluted melody weaving
its way around principal triadic tones impresses the ear as highly chromatic,

even when two consecutive semitones do not occur. On the other hand, a clearly tonal melody with a plethora of chromatic passage notes will register as diatonic if such a melody is harmonized in triads or seventh chords belonging to the principal key. Even such an obvious chromatic run as that in Rimsky-Korsakov's *Flight of the Bumblebee* cannot be classified under the rubric of chromaticism because the underlying harmonies are triadic. There can be no question as to the chromatic "color" of the prelude to Wagner's *Tristan und Isolde*, for the harmonies proceed by semitones. In Bach's *Chromatic Fantasy*, the bass line moves upward in chromatic semitones, but because triadic harmonies occur on the strong beats of each measure, the feeling of tonality persists.

The music of the post-Wagnerian era was swept by a tidal wave of chromaticism; many composers abandoned key signatures altogether because the triadic resting point occurred too infrequently to justify their use. Chromatic melody and chromatic harmony achieved their ultimate development in the method of composition that used 12 different notes of the chromatic scale related to one another, as formulated by Schoenberg. As a *coup de grâce* to diatonicism, and particularly triadic diatonicism, Schoenberg avoided triads and their inversions, particularly the major triads. Still, chromaticism was not Schoenberg's aim. Having rejected tonality as a governing principle, he organized both harmony and melody according to the new dodecaphonic principle uniting both melody and harmony within the framework of the 12 chromatic tones.

Chronochromie (Color of Time). An orchestral work by Olivier Messiaen, first performed in Donaueschingen on October 16, 1960. Instrumental sonorities represent the color, and the rhythms represent time.

Cimbalom. A Hungarian zither commonly used in gypsy bands in southeastern Europe. In the form of a trapezoid, it is placed on a table or other flat surface and is played with two mallets. Kodály uses the cimbalom in his orchestral work *Háry János*, and Stravinsky employs it in his symphonic fairy tale *Le Renard*. Liszt imitates the sound of the cimbalom in his Hungarian Rhapsody No. 11 for piano, specifically indicating the passage as *quasi-Zimbalo* (Italian word for cimbalom).

Les Cinq Doigts (Five Fingers). A group of eight piano pieces by Stravinsky. Ostensibly written for little children, the pieces are dissonant and rhythmically difficult. Once the five fingers are set on five keys of the piano, their position does not change. Stravinsky wrote these pieces in 1921; they illustrate his desire to create a new simplicity in music without sacrificing novel content.

Circle of fifths. A circular chart showing the 12 major and 12 minor keys arranged by ascending fifths and represented graphically by the face of a clock beginning at 12 o'clock with C major and A minor, each having no sharps or flats. The direction of sharp keys is clockwise; the direction of flat keys is counterclockwise. When the 6 o'clock position is reached, going in the sharp direction, the key of F-sharp major enharmonically meets G-flat major; similarly, its relative key, D-sharp minor, is changed to E-flat minor. It is theoretically possible to continue the accumulation of sharps in key signatures, moving clockwise, reaching the key of B-sharp major at the 12 o'clock position; such a scale would have 12 sharps in the key signature. Similarly, it is possible to continue accumulating flats in key signatures moving counterclockwise, making a full circle at the position of 12 o'clock in the key of D-double-flat major, which would have 12 flats in the key signature, counting each double flat as two flats. Key signatures of more than seven sharps or flats are totally impractical and are rarely found in actual usage. Among the exceptions are the scale passages in B-sharp major, enharmonically equal to C major, in the four-hand piano arrangement of Stravinsky's *Le Sacre du printemps*; Ravel has a D-double-flat-major scale in the piano part of his Piano Trio. And in one amazing instance, in the score of his opera *The Legend of the Invisible City of Kitezh*, Rimsky-Korsakov modulates clockwise until he is forced to use an accidental triple-sharp.

Circus Polka. An orchestral sketch by Stravinsky originally written for piano, commissioned by the Ringling Brothers' Circus to accompany the entrance of the elephants. It was arranged for band by David Raksin in 1942. Stravinsky conducted its first performance for symphony orchestra in Cambridge, Massachusetts, on January 13, 1944.

Clair de lune. The third piano piece from the *Suite Bergamasque* by Debussy, and one of the most famous modern pieces written for the instrument. Debussy sold its rights to a Paris publisher for the equivalent of about $15. *Clair de lune* means, of course, the "Light of the Moon." Debussy took the title from a poem by Paul Verlaine.

Claque. French for "clapping." Mercenary applause hired by operatic stars, bosomy prima donnas, self-inflated tenors, and occasionally even seemingly normal pianists and some desperate violinists. The practice of engaging a claque began in the early 19th century in Italy; it rapidly spread into France, even into otherwise snooty Victorian England, and by international infection caught on in America. Claques failed to prosper in Germany, perhaps because Germany took its music seriously. Occasionally, an ambitious opera star would engage an anticlaque to drown out a rival's claque. A list for services circulating in Paris in the middle of the 19th century quoted the following prices:

Applause sufficient for a single curtain call .... 150 francs
Overwhelming applause .... 225 francs
Hissing a rival singer .... 250 francs

Ovation after the last act, serenading before the window of the artist's home, price by special arrangement.

The claquers were officially banned at the Metropolitan Opera House in New York in 1935 but apparently still prospered as late as 1960, at the cost of up to $100 for a group of vociferous young males on Saturday afternoons.

Clarinet. One of the most important woodwind instruments in the orchestra. The clarinet is a single-reed instrument (that is, it has only one vibrating reed in the mouthpiece), as contrasted with the oboe and the bassoon, which are double-reed woodwinds. The clarinet is a vertical pipe with a beak at one end and a bell-shaped aperture at the other. The word *clarinet* derives from *clarinetto*, the Italian diminutive of *clarino*, connected with the Latin adjective *claro*, or "clear." The low register of the clarinet is called *chalumeau*, which was the name of a 17th century clarinet prototype. The modern clarinet is a rather late addition to the woodwind family; as an orchestral instrument it did not come into use until the middle of the 18th century. The Bohemian composer Johann Stamitz was the first to include a clarinet part in an orchestral score; in 1755 he wrote a symphony with a clarinet and double basses. The clarinet is the most expressive and the most versatile instrument of the woodwinds; it is capable of attaining a zephyr-like waft in the low and middle registers, and an overwhelming fortissimo in the upper register.

The written range of the clarinet is from E below the treble clef to the high E or beyond above the treble clef. It is a transposing instrument, which means that the written note is automatically raised or lowered. The most commonly used clarinet is the one in D-flat, so that the written note C sounds B flat; in the clarinet in A, the written C sounds A. The clarinet in B-flat automatically provides two flats in the key signature, and the clarinet in A provides three sharps in the key signature. Thus, the player uses the B-flat clarinet for scores that have flats, and the A clarinet for those that have sharps. If an orchestral work is written in the key signature of, say, five flats, the clarinet in B-flat economizes on three flats, for two flats are already built into the instrument. When a clarinet player has to play a work written in, say, a key of four sharps, the clarinet in A will automatically deduct three sharps (the key signature of A major) and leave the clarinet player with only one sharp in the key signature. That is why in orchestral scores key signatures in the clarinet parts differ from those in the strings. Some modern composers prefer to write orchestral clarinet parts in the conductor's score without transposition, while writing the individual clarinet parts in B-flat and A.

The clarinet family includes two small clarinets, tuned in D and E-flat, that transpose, respectively, a major second and a minor third up. A most striking example of the clarinet in D appears in the score of *Till Eulenspiegel* by Richard Strauss, where it portrays the unfortunate schlemiel strangling while he is being hanged. The clarinet in F transposing down a fifth is called the *basset horn*. The bass clarinet transposes an octave below the common clarinet. There is also a double-bass clarinet that transposes two octaves lower than either of the common clarinets in B-flat and A. Playing on the double-bass clarinet requires exceptionally strong lungs, and there is usually a special pedal provided that blows in additional air.

A large repertory of clarinet music exists. Among the most popular clarinet concertos are those by Mozart, Weber, Spohr, Nielsen, and Debussy. Gershwin's *Rhapsody in Blue* is practically a double concerto for clarinet and piano; the opening clarinet solo reaches a high B-flat, approached by a glissando, an effect that only modern virtuosos are capable of achieving. The clarinet is a basic instrument in jazz bands. Stravinsky wrote his *Ebony Concerto* for the clarinetist Woody Herman; the title uses a slang term for clarinet, "ebony stick."

Classical Symphony. A work by Sergei Prokofiev that he conducted in Petrograd (formerly St. Petersburg, later Leningrad) for the first time on April 21, 1918, six days before his 27th birthday. The title *Classical Symphony*, given by Prokofiev himself, is fully justified. The work is set in four movements, following the Haydn model, and it is ostentatiously tonal, keeping within the key of D major. It was to become Prokofiev's most popular symphonic work.

Classicism. Etymologically, the words *classic*, *classical*, and *classicism* denote membership in a high class. In literature, art, and music, classicism came to mean purity of design, perfection of form, and the ability to gratify high aesthetic demands. These qualities were connected in the minds of historians with the remote ages, particularly of Greece and Rome. Negative aspects of ancient society were overlooked, so as not to detract from the artistic glory that was Greece and the grandeur that was Rome. The flowering of the arts during the Renaissance was marked by the renascence of interest in the Greek and Roman cultures. The emergence of the art of opera at the threshold of the 17th century was the intellectual outgrowth of the search for the artistic essence of Greek tragedy. Because the dramatic performances in ancient Greece were accompanied by music, the theorists of opera urged a return to monodic simplicity in melody and rhythm and the abandonment of intricate polyphony.

Historians place the era of Classicism in the 18th century and early decades of the 19th century. It was preceded by the ornate Baroque style and ended with the expansion of the Romantic period. Stylistically, Classical music is distinguished by the symmetry of form, set in either binary or ternary structures, strict observance of the proper sequence of tonalities in modulation, incisive but relatively simple rhythms, articulate polyphony, and harmonic euphony. Instrumental technique in the Classical era was conservative; virtuosity was encouraged as long as it served the dignified formality of the general design. The Romantic period that followed shifted the emphasis from clarity of form to a humanistic concern for emotional expression. Because the formulas of Classical harmony, melody, and rhythm were standardized to a considerable degree, composers of the period were able to turn out hundreds of symphonies, concertos, sonatas, and dozens of operas, cantatas, and other works, all tailored to a fairly uniform model, no matter how different were their stylistic contents.

The external attire of men of the 18th century was an aspect of their artistic uniformity. Portraits of 18th-century composers show them invariably adorned with wigs; the Classical era itself has become known derisively as the *Zopf* ("wig") era. Wigs, perukes, and pigtails disappeared early in the 19th century. The paintings of Beethoven show his tousled hair, which he did not try to cover with a wig. Like all historical concepts, Classicism does not yield to temporal delimitation. The roots of Beethoven's music were firmly lodged in the spirit of Classicism, and his last period bears the traits of Romanticism. A similar dichotomy applies to the music of Schubert. To account for this historic indeterminacy, the term *Vienna Classics* was introduced to describe the productions of composers active in Vienna between 1800 and 1830. Inevitably, composers of the 20th century, weary of the endless self-projections of the Romantic composers, turned to the clear, unambiguous, and, in some respects, impersonal ways of the 18th century. A modern version of Classicism arose under the guise of neo-Classicism.

Clausula. A Latin term describing certain formalized endings in medieval vocal polyphony. Clausulae are usually sung to a single vowel or syllable derived from a melisma of a sacred chant such as alleluia. The singing of a clausula signaled the termination of a chant or a polyphonic work, and thus served a definite function in performance. During the Renaissance, the distinction between the clausula and the cadence tended to disappear. Yet there is a distinction, namely that the cadence signifies a homophonic, rather than a polyphonic, ending in a harmonic setting.

Clavichord. A keyboard instrument popular during the Renaissance and Baroque periods, particularly in Germany where it was the favored domestic instrument. Its name comes from the Latin *clavis*, "key," and the Greek word *chorda*, or "string." It differs in construction from its musical siblings, the harpsichord and the virginal, in that the strings are not plucked but struck with brass tangents. The clavichord has a delicate, intimate sound much softer than that of the harpsichord, and it possesses the unique capacity of producing a peculiar vibrato that can be governed by varying the pressure on the keys even after they have been depressed. Its range is between three and five octaves.

During the Baroque era, composers designated keyboard music as for *Clavier*; it may have been valid for both harpsichord and clavichord. The problem of precise attribution remains ambiguous. The harpsichord has retained its significance in historical contexts, but the clavichord has all but disappeared from actual practice.

Clavier. A generic term for all keyboard instruments. The word comes from the Latin *clavis*, "key." This spelling was used in the 18th century; in Germany it was later changed to *Klavier*, which applied exclusively to the piano.

Clef. French for "key." A sign placed at the beginning of a composition to determine the pitch of the notes. Two clefs are used in piano music: the G clef, indicating the position of the note G above middle C on the second line, and the F clef, indicating the position of the note F below middle C on the fourth line. The G clef is also called the treble, or violin, clef because it is used primarily for the violin; the F clef is called the bass clef because it covers the bass register. The present shape of these clefs evolved from Gothic capital letters.

There is also a group of clefs that indicate the position of middle C on the staff. The present shape of the C clef evolved from the letter C. The most common C clefs are the viola clef that sets middle C on the third line, and the tenor clef that sets middle C on the fourth line. The viola clef is used in viola parts and occasionally in trombone parts; the tenor clef is occasionally used in the cello and bassoon parts. Several C clefs are obsolete, among them the soprano clef, with middle C on the first line, and the baritone clef, with middle C on the fifth line of the staff. Obviously, the lower the clef is posted the more room it affords to high notes; conversely, when a clef is placed high on the staff the available range lies in the low register. A combined form of the tenor clef and the treble clef is sometimes used in the tenor parts of operatic scores to replace the inaccurate G clef, which covers the register an octave above the common tenor range and is reserved for soprano parts. Bach made use of various C clefs even in his keyboard compositions. His Invention No. 15 in F major is notated in the soprano clef for the right hand and in the tenor clef for the left. This notation is apt to startle a piano-minded clef reader who happens to come upon Bach's Inventions in the facsimile edition.

La Clemenza di Tito. Mozart's last opera, produced in Prague on September 6, 1791. The libretto by Metastasio deals with the generous clemency granted by the Roman Emperor Titus to those who plotted against him. The same libretto was set to music by a dozen or more composers, before and after Mozart. The opera has been filmed by Franco Zefferelli.

The Clock. Symphony No. 101 by Haydn, in the key of D major. It is listed as the 9th of Haydn's 12 symphonies written for London, where it was first performed on March 3, 1794. The symphony is called *The Clock* (*Die Uhr* in German) because of a pendulum-like accompanying figure in the slow movement.

Coda. Italian for "tail." An appendage to the end of a musical composition that usually consists of a repetition of the concluding section of the main subject. The imminent arrival of a coda is usually signaled by a deep pedal point on the dominant in the bass; other ways to announce a coming coda are a rapid acceleration followed by a prolonged retardation, a forceful crescendo, or an equally eloquent diminuendo. In fugal writing, the coda often annexes additional voices, forming a harmonic section, with the pedal point on the tonic. Bach's Fugue No. 2 in C minor in the first book of *The Well-Tempered Clavier* is an example.

Coffee Cantata. A rare example among Bach's works of a light, vocal composition in a style approaching opera buffa, written about 1734 when coffee was still regarded, along with tobacco, as an exotic product. The cantata deals with an attempt of the father of a willful young woman to persuade her to refrain from drinking coffee. As a reward, he promises to find her a personable husband and actually produces a suitable candidate. She likes his looks, but she likes drinking coffee even more. Bach's score is set in an elevated style. Indeed, if the text were to be rewritten, the music could be appropriate for a solemn, although occasionally vivacious, oratorio.

Col pugno. Italian for "with the fist." A percussive effect on the piano keyboard. Prokofiev marked *col pugno* in a certain episode in his Piano Sonata No. 6, and it is probably the sole example of fist pounding in concert literature for piano. This effect is similar to the tone clusters that are played with forearms or fists introduced by Henry Cowell.

Collective composition. Parceling the composition of an opera or another large work among several composers. Handel, Bononcini, and Amadei wrote in 1721 one act each for the opera *Muzio Scaevola* dealing with a heroic Roman soldier who, when captured, refused to forswear his allegiance to Rome and to prove his fortitude put his right hand into a fire, burning it to the bone; he received the nickname *Scaevola*, left-handed. The brothers Paul and Lucien Hillemacher collaborated on a number of operas and even adopted a joint signature, P.L. Hillemacher. Collective composition is frequently the *modus operandi* of writers of popular musical comedies. Sometimes several names are given as composer of a successful song. During the early years of ragtime in the Soviet Union, the idea of musical collectivism fascinated student composers at the Moscow Conservatory, and they formed the Productive Collective of Student Composers of the Moscow Conservatory (PROCOLL). Its announced aim was to represent the collectivism of the masses. Chinese musicians have also contributed to musical collectivism. *The Yellow River Concerto* for piano and orchestra, produced by the Peking Opera Troupe in Shanghai, was purportedly written by a committee, but only four musicians, presumably members of the committee, acknowledged the applause after its production.

Collegium musicum. The Latin name for a group organized to make music for pleasure. The first collegium musicum was formed in 1616 in Prague; a similar group was organized by Bach in Leipzig. A contemporary description of the collegium musicum in Frankfurt in 1718 stated that its purpose was "to quicken the spirit after a day of work by providing innocent pastime." At such gatherings, amateur musicians were given an opportunity to play instrumental music and discuss musical matters. The practice was revived in colleges and universities in Europe and America in the 20th century.

Color hearing. The psychological and aesthetic association between sound and color. The first scientific (or pseudoscientific) treatment of this supposed association was given by the English rationalist philosopher John Locke in *An Essay Concerning Human Understanding*, published in 1690. An English ophthalmologist, Theodore Woolhouse, drew up an arbitrary comparative table of sounds and colors, asserting, for instance, that the sound of a trumpet is red. But mostly the parallelism of hearing and seeing arose from speculation about the unity of the senses. Mathematical symbolism also played a part. The magic number 7 determined both the number of degrees in the diatonic scale and the number of colors of the spectrum as outlined by Isaac Newton. Scriabin, who was a profound believer in the unity of all senses, inserted a part for a color organ in the score of his last orchestral work, *Prométhée*. It was to inundate a concert hall with changing colors correlating to keys struck on the organ manual.

It is notable that the dual sense of sound and color is claimed mainly by musicians who possess perfect pitch. Indeed, it cannot be otherwise, for how can one perceive a definite color for a note or tonality without being able to identify the note as immediately and unhesitatingly as one does a color? Random testing of color hearing among persons having perfect pitch, however, shows no demonstrable coincidences in color designation. There is a signal exception, however. Most pianists perceive the key of C major as white, and the key of F-sharp major as black. Obviously, this association is owing to the fact that the C major scale is played on the white keys and the F-sharp major scale is played on the black keys, with white keys used for only two notes. It would be interesting if such an association were valid for harpsichords on which the white keys are manufactured in color, and the black keys are actually painted white. If a true correspondence existed between tones and sounds, then the ascending chromatic scale should register as the spectrum from red to violet, from low to high frequency of vibrations, which is not the case. It follows, therefore, that color hearing is a purely subjective impression, similar to color perception by sensitive persons (particularly children) who are apt to describe natural sound phenomena in terms of color (thunder is gray, crying is red). In Tolstoy's *War and Peace*, the sensitive young Natasha describes Pierre and other friends in terms of color. Such psychological coloring is akin to color hearing; the voice of a child may be associated with yellow; the wrinkled face of an old man with brown; the meow of a cat with silver blue. A convincing argument against the objective existence of correlation of sounds and colors can be proffered in the history of pitch, which has been consistently on the rise for more than a century. Should Mozart come back to life and hear the performance of his *Jupiter* Symphony, which is in C major, he would hear it as being in D-flat. Would he then cease to hear that work in white as proper for C major?

Coloratura. A colorful, ornamental passage in opera, consisting of diversified, rapid runs and trills, often used in cadenzas and occurring in the highest register. A coloratura soprano is a singer capable of performing virtuoso passages in high treble. Famous examples of such passages are in the arias of the Queen of the Night in Mozart's *The Magic Flute*, and in Verdi's *Rigoletto*. In modern times Rimsky-Korsakov wrote a highly chromatic coloratura part for the Queen of Shemaha in his opera *Le Coq d'or*.

Colour Symphony. An orchestral work by Arthur Bliss, first performed in Gloucester, England, on September 7, 1922. The colors of the title are heraldic, not acoustic. There are four movements: *Purple*, *Red*, *Blue*, and *Green*.

Columbia, the Gem of the Ocean. It is remarkable that a song as popular as this one, composed in the mid-19th century and so full of patriotic pride, should be an orphan, contested by two English-speaking nations and having several claimants for paternity. It is known in England under the title *Britannia, the Pride of the Ocean*, but several editions of the song were published under the title, *Red, White and Blue*, the colors of both the American and British flags. An English actor, Thomas à Becket, claimed its authorship, but he could produce no corroborating evidence.

Il combattimento di Tancredi e Clorinda. A dramatic cantata by Claudio Monteverdi, first performed in Venice in 1624. Tancredi is a Christian knight in the first Crusade in the 11th century. Clorinda, whom he loves, is a non-Christian Persian maid who combats the Crusaders. Tancredi mortally wounds her during an encounter near Jerusalem and recognizes her only when he lifts the visor of her armor. He then laments his and her fates. The work is historically important because in it Monteverdi introduces a type of composition that he called *stile concitato* ("agitated style"), set in the meter of two rapid beats.

Tancredi is also an opera by Rossini, produced in Venice on February 6, 1813.

Combinational tones. Parasitic tones that are generated when two notes are played simultaneously very loudly, known as *differential tones* if the emergent sound's frequency is the difference of the frequencies of the two original sounds, and as *summation tones* if the resulting sound's frequency is the sum of the two original sounds. Differential tones are heard with particular distinction when a consonant interval is sounded in a near-perfect tuning. Such differential tones are known also under the name *Tartini tones*; Giuseppe Tartini is reputed to have been the first to describe them. Theoretically at least, differential tones form a supplementary relationship with summation tones, so a new parasitic tone may emerge from this interference. The overtones that are the natural extension of a single sound also enter into this multilateral combination. If all these parasitic tones were to materialize audibly, even the simplest piece of music would degenerate into a monstrous jangle of mutually discordant sounds. Fortunately, the principal tones are so clear and loud in comparison with their combinational sounds that musical pollution is not a real threat.

Comédie-ballet. A type of scenic performance cultivated by Lully and Molière for the court of Louis XIV. It included, besides the dialogue and ballet, arias and choral pieces.

Comma. A minute interval in Pythagorean tuning, resulting from the difference between seven octaves and twelve perfect fifths, which is equal to about one-eighth of a whole tone. In tempered tuning, the fifths are adjusted to become commensurate with octaves, avoiding the difficulty of handling the comma.

Comme. A French conjunction meaning "as" or "like," used in some expression marks, particularly by Debussy and Scriabin:

Comme des éclairs. "Like lightning flashes," in Scriabin's Piano Sonata No. 7.

Comme un cri. "Like a cry," found in one of Scriabin's last piano preludes.

Comme un écho de la phrase entendue précédemment. "Echoing the phrase previously heard," Debussy's suggestion to the performer in his piano piece *La Cathédrale engloutie*.

Comme un murmure confus. "Like an indistinct murmur," in Scriabin's piano piece *Poème-Nocturne*.

Comme un tendre et triste regret. "Like a tender and sad regret," in Debussy's music.

Comme une buée irisée. "Like a rainbow-colored mist," in Debussy's music.

Comme une lointaine sonnerie de cors. "Like a distant sound of horns," in Debussy's piano music.

Comme une ombre mouvante. "Like a moving shadow," indicating the mood in Scriabin's *Poème-Nocturne*.

Commedia dell'arte. Literally, an "artistic play." An Italian genre of theatrical performance that emerged at the time of the Renaissance and incorporated versatile elements of pantomime, acrobatics, masks, music, and dance. Most of the action was improvisational, but the main characters were clearly delineated. They usually included a cuckolded husband, a handsome gallant, an accommodating servant, a wily lawyer, and an incompetent doctor. Later on, the stock characters had definite names: a grumbling old Pantalone, his beautiful daughter Columbina, her lover Arlecchino (Harlequin), and Pulcinella (Punchinello), a grotesque clown with a long nose. Some composers have used these characters in their own operas, pantomimes, and plays. Leoncavallo built his opera *Pagliacci* as a play within a play, in which a circus clown discovers that his wife, performing the part of Columbina, has a lover. Stravinsky emulated commedia dell'arte in his ballets *Petrouchka* and *Pulcinella*, and partly also in his *L'Histoire du Soldat*.

Compensation. The principal elements of a musical composition are melody, harmony, rhythm, dynamics, form, and instrumental arrangement. As music evolved toward a greater complexity, only one of these at a time tended toward a maximum of technical involvement. When modern melody abandoned tonality and gradually assumed an atonal aspect, the elements of rhythm, harmony, and orchestra remained relatively stable. In dodecaphonic composition, harmony is a function of the tone row, incorporating the horizontal melodic elements in a vertical dimension, but rhythm, meter, and form are independent in their development. It is indeed remarkable that composers of the dodecaphonic school are very conservative in the matter of form, sometimes prescribing classical repeats in dance movements. Alban Berg maintained the form of a classical instrumental suite even in his operas. When rhythm is paramount and metrical exchanges are frequent, as in Stravinsky's *Le Sacre du printemps*, the melody and harmony become remarkably static, even in highly dissonant settings. The Law of Compensation is at work in canonic movements, when the orderly procession of voices in mutual imitation creates at times surprisingly dissonant combinations. It is sufficient to play the development section of some of Bach's fugues in a very slow tempo to realize how many vertical discords are created in the canonic process. Here the formal dissonances are justified by the strong linear counterpoint. The unifying strength of the pedal point on the dominant in the deep bass register allows modulation into remote keys without discomfort. In the wedding procession in Rimsky-Korsakov's opera, *Le Coq d'or*, with the steady dominant pedal point on G in the bass, there are modulations into the remote keys of A-flat major and D-flat major. An exception to the Law of Compensation is exemplified by totally serial works, in which rhythm, dynamics, melody, harmony, instrumentation, and form are organized to prevent any compensation for unrelieved diversification. Paradoxically, this exclusion of compensation leads to a unification *sui generis*, with the totality of musical elements regarded as a single entity.

Composer. The etymological root of this word implies nothing more exalted than the ability to "put things together," *componere*. The term *composer* in the musical sense is at least 1,000 years old. Guido d'Arezzo included it in his Latin treatise *Micrologus*, establishing the necessary properties for a melody to be well "put together" (*componenda*). The medieval Latin term for composer was *compositor*, a word now reserved in English for typesetters. The designation *compositor* is preserved in Spanish in its original Latin sense, that is, composer. Tinctoris, the author of the first dictionary of music, describes the composer as a writer of a new melody. Later theorists drew the distinction between *compositio*, a conscious act of composing, and *sortisatio*, a random improvisation. The rules for composition vary enormously through the centuries. Dissonances of yore are acceptable to modern ears, but changes, however momentous, have not altered the basic definition of a composer as a person who puts notes together in a logical and coherent manner.

Compound meters. Time signatures with the numerator in prime numbers greater than 3 are often termed compound meters because they represent the sum of commonly used meters. 5/4, 7/4, 11/4, and 13/4 are compound meters. Ideally, there should be only a single accent on the first beat, but in practical use compound meters are divided into two simple meters. Thus 5/4 is perceived as 3/4 plus 2/4 or 2/4 plus 3/4; 7/4 as 4/4 plus 3/4 or 3/4 plus 4/4, and so on. It has been asserted, on inadequate evidence, that a bar of five beats is a natural metrical unit in Russian folksongs. But it is true that Russian composers introduced whole sections in 5/4 meter into their works, the most famous example being the waltz in 5/4 time in the second movement of Tchaikovsky's

Pathétique Symphony. The compound meter of 7/4 is also found in many Russian compositions. The meter 11/4 is used in Rimsky-Korsakov's opera *Sadko*; Russian chorus singers used to sing the Russian equivalent of the sentence in 11 syllables: "Rimsky-Korsakov is altogether mad," to cope with the unusual count. Some dictionaries of music list all time signatures with a numerator that is not a prime number (such as 6/8, 9/8, and 6/4) as compound meters, but this classification would include 4/4 time, often called "common time," as a compound meter, which conflicts with the historical conception of this traditional time signature. Early in the 20th century, compound meters were used by numerous composers as novelties. This tendency was particularly enhanced by the great diversification of time signatures in Stravinsky's works, especially in *Le Sacre du printemps*. An important category of compound meters is represented by the symmetric division of traditional time signatures (for instance, the sum of 2/8, 3/8, 2/8, and 2/8, aggregating to 9/8, which was used by Rimsky-Korsakov), or time signatures in 10/8, being simply the coalescence of two bars of 5/8. Compound meters are sometimes masked by the use of dotted notes and rests within a traditional time signature. An interesting example of this metrical distribution is George Gershwin's song *I Got Rhythm*, which is notated in 4/4 time, with four dotted eighth notes flanked by two eighth-note rests. When written out, the measure could be differentiated into one bar of 2/16, four bars of 3/16, and one bar of 2/16. The value of the denominator (which is always a power of 2) has no bearing on the nature of the compound meter, because doubling or halving the duration of the note value in the denominator makes no difference to the ear. Thus 3/4 with a metronome mark of a quarter note equalling 60 would sound the same as 3/8 with an eighth note equaling 120.

Computer music. For many centuries, music theorists and composers have cherished the notion that beautiful melodies and luscious harmonies could be produced by mathematical means. Such musical alchemy fascinated the masters of polyphonic music of the Renaissance, who eagerly experimented with inversion, retrograde movement, interval extension, rhythmical expansion, and the like—all basically mathematical concepts. It was only natural that when digital computers were perfected in the middle of the 20th century, musicians began to explore electronic resources for the creation of scientific "music of the spheres" that would provide composers with new resources. Alas, digital computers and other electronic devices cannot produce any output more valuable than the input fed into them by the human programmers. Programming a computer by a series of numbers is no different from the process of writing notes on paper. Let us take the mathematical formula G, 0, 0, −4, in which zero denotes the repetition of sound, the minus sign denotes a downward direction, and the number 4 is counted in semitones. When this formula is fed into a digital computer, it will produce the famous theme of Beethoven's Fifth Symphony. The computer can even be programmed to play the actual notes G, G, G, E-flat, and it can be instructed to orchestrate it electronically for clarinet and strings, which is the way Beethoven orchestrated it. In one of the earliest computerized compositions with a relatively primitive computer called Illiac, two programmers produced an *Illiac Suite*, which ended with a lengthy coda in C major. Obviously, the Illiac did not select C major in preference to some other chord. The "input" was very scientific-looking, expressed in a pseudo-algebraic equation: $C (4 + 3 + 5) \times 2^8$. It designates a chord formed by the consecutive intervals of 4, 3, and 5 semitones from C, which results in a C major triad, with the fundamental tone doubled, repeated 256 times. The duration in seconds may be added, indicating the length of the chord.

Even though a digital computer is helpless without a programmer (who himself may be helpless as a composer), it still can be a fascinating resource for the composition of instantaneous canons or similar contrapuntal forms. The computer is given a subject and is instructed to cause the subject to enter in another voice after a given time lapse at an octave or another interval. The result can be tested by immediate playback. Computers can also solve specific problems, such as the possibility of forming a dodecaphonic series consisting of two major and minor triads consecutively arrayed with either a minor or a major third separating these triads from one another. The answer to the problem is in the affirmative, but whereas a human must rack his brain for days to find a solution, a computer can give an answer within microseconds: F-sharp, A-sharp, C-sharp, E, G-sharp, B, D, F, A, C, E-flat, G. This is the only possible solution, but of course the series can be transposed to any other note of the chromatic scale.

In musical analysis, a computer can be most useful. Suppose a music scholar undertakes to compare the main subjects of a number of sonatas and symphonies of the Baroque period to prove a certain point and to trace coincidences and unconscious borrowings. By devising a relatively simple code, indicating the duration of each note in the melody with the plus and minus signs respectively for ascending and descending intervals and using the semitone as a unit, the motives can be tabulated and the degree of similarity among them determined statistically. A criterion of similarity can be measured by the number of steps necessary to convert one melody into another, with each semitone of alteration counted as a melodic unit and each difference in an assigned note value counted as a rhythmic unit. Such an anamorphic alteration is one of the basic principles in the science of topology. Scientific checks of this sort would be particularly valuable to composers of popular songs who are periodically sued in court for pilfering someone else's tunes. A recent example was the case of the popular song *Hello, Dolly!* by Jerry Herman, the melody of which turned out to be practically identical with the tune of *Sunflower*, published several years earlier by Mack David, who lost no time suing for plagiarism. The suit was settled out of court to the tune (which is the *mot juste*) of half a million dollars. If all popular songs were to be stored away in code in a digital computer's memory bank, composers with retentive memories of other tunes would be saved a lot of work. On the other hand, such a computerized memory bank could turn out to be a Frankenstein monster. The number of tunes and rhythms, many of them revolving around the major triad, with rhythms kept to the simplest proportions of relative note values, is limited, and the time may not be far away from the Doomsday of popular music that was predicted by John Stuart Mill more than a century ago: "I was seriously tormented by the thought of the exhaustibility of musical combinations. The octave consists only of five tones and two semitones, which can be put together in only a limited number of ways of which but a small proportion are beautiful; most of these, it seemed to me, must have been already discovered."

Le Comte Ory (Count Ory). An opera by Rossini, first produced in Paris on August 20, 1828, and the first of Rossini's two operas to French texts. The story deals with a licentious count's attempt to seduce a woman whose husband is out on a current Crusade.

Con. Italian for "with," used in many phrases, such as:

Con amore. With love, affectionately, tenderly.

Con anima. With soulful feeling.

Con brio. With spirit, brilliantly.

Con due pedali. Holding both the loud and soft pedals of the piano simultaneously, producing the effect of muted resonance.

Con duolo. Dolorously; with suffering.

Con eleganza. Elegantly.

Con espressione. With expression.

Con tutta forza. With all possible force.

Con una certa espressione parlante. With a certain speech-like expression. This is the curious phrase found in Beethoven's *Bagatelle*, op. 33, no. 6.

Con una ebbrezza fantastica. With a fantastic sense of drunkenness. An expression mark found in Scriabin's Piano Sonata No. 5.

Concert. A universally accepted word for a musical performance in the presence of an audience. Public concerts were first organized in Italy in the early 17th century; solo performances and chamber ensemble concerts were popular in London in the 18th century. In France a series of concerts was established in 1725 under the name Concert Spirituel; in the 19th century concerts became part of cultural life in every part of the world. The word *recital* for a solo concert came into vogue in the middle of the 19th century; it was invented by the London manager of Liszt. Regular symphony concerts were organized in Paris in 1828; later they spread to England, Russia, and all over the continent of Europe. America became the El Dorado of concert artists in the second half of the 19th century.

Concertmaster. The name commonly used in America for the first violin player in an orchestra; the word is a direct transplant from the German term, *Konzertmeister*. In England, however, the first violinist in the orchestra is called leader; in France, it is *premier violon*, or *chef d'attaque*; in Italy, *violino primo*; in Spain, *concertino*.

Concerto. A composition for a solo instrument with orchestra. A concerto for orchestra without a soloist is called *concerto grosso*, a "grand concerto." The etymology of the word *concerto* is subject to debate. The most logical origin is from the Latin verb *concertare*, "to compete," "to contend." The word is also a cognate of *concerto*, in the sense of agreement, as in "concert of nations." Another conjecture is that concerto comes from the Latin verb *conserere*, "to come together." In fact, the spelling *conserto* is found in some Italian manuscripts of the 17th century. The word *concerti* is a proper plural in Italian, but in English it should be concertos. We do not use the Italian plural *opere* for operas, or *orchestre* for orchestras; there is no reason to follow the Italian plural for concertos.

The form of the Classical concerto is similar to that of a sonata. Most concertos are in three movements that are commonly marked Allegro, Andante, and Allegro. A minuet is often inserted after the second movement; in later works it may have been replaced by a scherzo. The chief characteristic of a concerto is antiphony, with the soloist and the orchestra alternating in presenting the main themes. Classical concertos usually feature a cadenza for the solo instrument inserted in a cadence between the tonic 6/4 chord and the dominant. A good cadenza should be confined to the tonic harmony with the bass on the dominant, so as not to interfere with the sense of an interrupted cadence, and any intervening modulations ought to be handled with caution.

The length of an orchestral introduction to a concerto varies widely. A story is told about a near disaster that befell the famous violinist Mischa Elman during one of his concert tours. Mistakenly believing that the Beethoven concerto was scheduled on the program, he relaxed, letting his violin rest loosely on his left arm in the expectation of a long orchestral *tutti* ("all"), and was rudely jolted out of his siesta when the orchestra struck the opening chord of Mendelssohn's Violin Concerto, which has only a brief introduction. Conditioned by countless performances of this work, he launched into his part by automatic reflex. Piano concertos seldom begin with a solo passage, although a striking exception is Beethoven's Piano Concerto No. 4 in G major. Rachmaninoff's Piano Concerto No. 2 opens with a short prelude in the solo part, letting the orchestra present the main theme.

Numerically piano concertos are in the majority. Composers who are pianists themselves naturally give preference to their own instrument in writing concertos. Among piano concertos that have been permanently enshrined in the repertory are those of Mozart, Beethoven, Chopin, Schumann, Mendelssohn, Liszt, Saint-Saëns, Brahms, Tchaikovsky, Grieg, and Rachmaninoff. The piano concertos by Anton Rubinstein, which enjoyed great popularity in the 19th century owing to Rubinstein's own virtuoso performances, went into limbo in the 20th century, except in Russia. Piano concertos by Dvořák, MacDowell, and such minor figures as Thalberg, Moscheles, or Litolff occasionally appear on concert programs. Modern piano concertos tend to be less discursive and more compact than their Romantic predecessors. Following the example of Liszt, they are often compressed into a single movement subdivided into several sections that allow changes of tempo and character. Piano concertos by Ravel, Prokofiev, and Béla Bartók have become firmly established in the modern piano repertoire. Schoenberg's Piano Concerto is slowly gaining ground despite the unfamiliarity of its idiom and its tremendous technical difficulties. A special kind of piano concerto is those for left hand alone, which were commissioned by the Austrian pianist Paul Wittgenstein, who lost his right arm on the Russian front in World War I. Ravel, Richard Strauss, Prokofiev, Korngold, and several other composers obliged him with one-hand works.

String instruments have provided the vehicles for a magnificent repertoire of concertos. The number of violin concertos written during the three centuries of the violin as a virtuoso instrument is almost as large as that of piano concertos. Among the most celebrated violin concertos are those by Mozart, Beethoven, Mendelssohn, Brahms, Tchaikovsky, and Sibelius; Paganini's concertos are brilliant virtuoso pieces. Glazunov's Violin Concerto enjoys an unabated popularity in Russia; concertos by the violin virtuosos Wieniawski, Vieuxtemps, and Bruch are also popular. Among modern violin concertos those of Prokofiev, Bartók, and Khachaturian are often heard. Alban Berg's Violin Concerto has earned a permanent place in the repertory of modern violinists. Schoenberg's Violin Concerto has yet to achieve a comparable public acceptance. Stravinsky's Violin Concerto enjoys respectability but offers little attraction to performers. Among cello concertos of the Classical period, those by Haydn and Boccherini are well established; the best known 19th-century cello concertos are those by Saint-Saëns and Dvořák. Tchaikovshy's *Variations on a Rococo Theme* for cello and orchestra can be classified as a concerto; equally qualified is Ernest Bloch's *Schelomo* for cello and orchestra. The main character in *Don Quixote* of Richard Strauss is portrayed by the cello solo, but the work is in the form of a programmatic tone poem rather than a true solo concerto. The viola is the orphan of the string family; there are few composers who are charitable enough to write concertos for this instrument. Berlioz assigned a concertizing part to the viola in his symphonic poem *Harold in Italy*, and the work may be classified as a viola concerto. In modern times, Hindemith and William Walton have written viola concertos. Béla Bartók worked on a viola concerto but did not finish it by the time he died; his faithful disciple Tibor Serly completed the score. Koussevitzky wrote a concerto for double bass, an instrument on which he was a virtuoso.

In the woodwind department, there are concertos for practically every instrument. Quantz, who was the court flutist for Frederick the Great, wrote a plethora of flute concertos for himself and for his sovereign to play. Eugene Goossens wrote an oboe concerto for his brother, an oboe player. Richard Strauss wrote an oboe concerto in his later years. Clarinet concertos are not lacking in quantity; there are some by Mozart, Weber, Carl Nielsen, and one by the 20th-century composer Thea Musgrave, written in an ultramodern idiom. Stravinsky composed an *Ebony Concerto* for clarinet and jazz ensemble. There are several bassoon concertos available for ambitious performers. Glazunov composed a saxophone concerto. Haydn's Trumpet Concerto is a brilliant virtuoso piece. Richard Strauss wrote two concertos for horn and orchestra (his father was a renowned horn player). There are a few scattered trombone concertos. Vaughan Williams wrote a concerto for tuba. Concertos for harp and orchestra are not numerous, but Ravel's *Introduction et Allegro* for harp and instruments is one in effect. The modern harpist Carlos Salzedo wrote a harp concerto accompanied by wind instruments. Guitar concertos have been written by Manuel Ponce, Castelnuovo-Tedesco, and José Rodrigo. Glière wrote a concerto for voice and orchestra. Henry Cowell composed a concerto for the koto, a Japanese string instrument. There is even a concerto for kazoo with orchestra, concocted by the American composer Mark Bucci.

Double concertos are those in which two instruments are soloists on an equal standing. The Double Concerto for Violin, Cello, and Orchestra by Brahms is an example. Bartók orchestrated his Sonata for Two Pianos and Percussion into a Concerto for Two Pianos and Orchestra. The category of triple concerto is represented by Bach's mighty Concerto for Three Harpsichords and Orchestra, and by Beethoven's Concerto for Violin, Cello, and Piano with Orchestra. Spohr wrote a quadruple concerto for string quartet and orchestra. Such multiple concertos effectively cross the line of demarcation separating solo concertos from the class of the concerto grosso.

Concerto grosso. The "grand ensemble" of the Baroque period. It differs from a solo concerto because in it an instrumental group, called *concertino*, "little concerto," functions as a multiple soloist, antiphonally supported by the concerto proper, designated by the Italian terms *tutti*, "all; every instrument," and *ripieni*, "the replenishing ones." The instruments in the concertino usually comprise two violins and a cello, with the harpsichord furnishing the harmony indicated by figured bass. The *tutti* consist of a fairly large ensemble of strings supplemented by trumpets, flutes, oboes, and horns. The earliest works in this genre were Corelli's *Concerti Grossi con duoi violini e violoncello di concertino obbligati e duoi altri violini, e viola, e basso di concerto grosso ad arbitrio*, which were probably composed in 1680 but not published until much later. Torelli wrote a group of concerti grossi about 1690. The concerto grosso was standardized by Vivaldi; it consisted of three cyclic movements: Allegro, Adagio, Allegro. Bach's *Brandenburg Concertos* are basically of the concerto grosso type, but Bach often diversified the concertino parts in the manner of a solo concerto. Handel's concerti grossi observed the formal elements of the type more strictly than Bach. In the second half of the 18th century, with the growing tendency toward Classical symphonic forms, the concerto grosso evolved into the symphonie concertante and eventually into a full-fledged symphony without individual solo groups. In the 19th century, the concerto grosso became almost totally obsolete, and it was left to the 20th century to revive it in the original Baroque form. A typical example is Max Reger's *Konzert Im alten Stil* (*Concerto in the Old Style*), in which the Classical structure is tinted with Romantic colors.

Concord Sonata. The second sonata for piano by Charles Ives, subtitled *Concord, Mass.: 1840–60*. Its four movements are named after the Concord transcendentalist writers, *Emerson, Hawthorne, The Alcotts*, and *Thoreau*. Ives published the *Concord* Sonata at his own expense in 1920. The difficulties of the music were insurmountable to ordinary piano virtuosi, and it took the stamina and perseverance of John Kilpatrick to give its first complete performance in New York on January 20, 1939. Eventually, the work became a standard of pianistic technology, performed by a number of pianists in America and in Europe.

Conducting. When a number of singers or instrumentalists perform together, it is convenient to have a leader whose function is to give the signal to begin the music and to indicate the tempo. In Baroque practice, it was usually up to the *maestro al cembalo*, the "master at the keyboard," to give these directions. When performing groups evolved into multimusical bodies, the

first violinist usually initiated the proceedings with a motion of his bow. An
alternative was for the composer-conductor to beat time on the desk with a
small stick or a roll of paper, occasionally emphasizing the beat by stamping
his foot on the floor. Legend has it that Lully, who was the leader of the *petits
violons du roi* for Louis XIV, struck his foot with the sharp point of his
conducting baton, causing a fatal gangrene.

The present tradition of conducting with a wooden baton originated early
in the 19th century. Mendelssohn mentions in one of his letters that he conducted an orchestra in London "with a white stick." Although the baton is
the sceptre of conductorial authority and the emblem of the art of conducting,
some conductors dispense with it and lead with their hands. The Russian
conductor Wassily Safonoff was the first to become batonless; he said that in
abandoning the baton, he acquired ten batons with his fingers. Leopold Stokowski did away with the baton during his entire career in America and made
eloquent use of his long, aristocratic fingers. In the early days of professional
conducting, it was a general custom for conductors to face the audience rather
than the orchestra, and indeed it would have been regarded as uncivil to turn
one's back to the public. But because such a fashion of polite conducting
made it virtually impossible for the conductor to control his players, the
orchestral leaders gradually decided to "face the music." Yet as late as 1925
Walter Damrosch would turn toward the public for the grand finale in Beethoven's Symphony No. 5. Beards on conductors were common in the 19th
century, and some also sported flowing hair. Such adornments disappeared in
the first half of the 20th century, but the hirsute fashions were revived later
on. Natural hair, whether groomed or flowing, seemed to be a condition *sine
qua non* for conductors; sartorial elegance was also *de rigueur*. With the
advent of the age of functional efficiency, capable conductors were often bald.

As with many branches of music, it was in Germany that the art of conducting was formalized. A whole generation of impeccably tailored conductors
set the tradition of "dictators of the baton," commanding their players in the
manner of a feudal lord ordering about his vassals. Hans von Bülow in particular was as famous for his Prussian brutality as for his superior musicianship.
A typical anecdote deals with his dislike of two members of his orchestra
named Schulz and Schmidt. One day the manager announced to him that
Schmidt had died. "Und Schulz?" Bülow asked coldly. Another time he
remarked to his soprano soloist that she was not pretty enough to sing so badly
out of tune. When major symphony orchestras organized themselves into
unions, the orchestra members began to assert their human dignity. Toscanini
was probably the last conductor who could afford to hurl insulting epithets at
orchestra members with impunity. At the last rehearsal for his last concert in
New York, he shouted at his men: "Imbecili! Tutto è scritto. La più bella
musica del mondo!" ("Imbeciles! All is written. The most beautiful music

of the world!'') In deference to Toscanini's great age and supreme musician-ship, the orchestra fell silent at his imprecations, and Toscanini slowly walked off the podium.

The art of conducting is the most elusive of musical pursuits. Ideally, it requires a total mastery of the musical score and an ability to coordinate the players and singers so that they create a euphonious ensemble. The tempo must be established with a wave of the hand that is clear without being obtrusive. The subtlest nuances must be communicated to the players with a gentle motion of the fingers or a suitable facial expression. A common gesture (often immortalized on professional photographs) is to put the index finger of the right hand on the lips to indicate pianissimo. An imperious thrust of the right hand toward the brass section indicates fortissimo. Conductors of the Romantic type, such as Arthur Nikisch and Serge Koussevitzky, used to address the orchestra with a great expenditure of bodily motion, often changing their angle of direction. Toscanini usually bent his left arm and kept it almost immobile, pressed against his left side. Idiosyncrasies are many. Some conductors move their lips as if trying to speak; others hum with the melody, often out of tune. Histrionic and elegant conductors were the most successful in earlier times, but some remarkably ungainly orchestra leaders have attained great renown. Old-fashioned conductors were often moved to explain the imaginary meaning of the music. When the famous Willem Mengelberg exhorted the solo cellist, pointing out that the music expressed the yearning of the soul for happiness and redemption, the cellist looked at him quizzically and said, ''You mean mezzoforte?''

Although a pianist or a violinist must practice for years to build even a passable technique, a conductor may begin a career without any preparation, for his instrument is an orchestra on which he cannot practice at home. The basic technique of conducting can be learned in a few lessons. As traditionally established, conductors must give the downbeat on the first beat of the measure and an upbeat on the second beat when the measure is 2/4. In 3/4 his stick must describe a triangle with its lowest apex always downward. In 4/4, after the mandatory downbeat, the hand moves northwest, then across to northeast, then at an angle to north, and down south for the next downbeat. Compound measures combine these fundamental motions. There was a time when apprentice conductors had trouble with the 5/4 movement in Tchaikovsky's *Pathétique* Symphony. A tale is told about a French conductor who counted the time allowed as *un, deux, trois, quatre, cin-que*, thus converting the 5/4 measure into one of 6/4. He could not understand why the orchestra stopped and waited for his next downbeat. Some would-be conductors do not realize that in order to give the downbeat, one must first lift the conducting hand in an anticipatory upbeat, which also sets the tempo. However, some very great conductors allow themselves the luxury of starting a pianissimo movement by gradually lowering the hand without a discernible upbeat. If the orchestra cooperates with a nervous or hesitant conductor, then even the rankest amateur can get through an overture or a movement from a symphony without suffering a major disaster. Danny Kaye, the talented American comedian who could not read music, managed to lead a whole symphonic movement with an impressive show of command. Mayor Fiorello LaGuardia of New York liked to conduct *The Star-Spangled Banner* during World War II, but he could not master the trick of beating triple time and conducted the national anthem in 2/4, with the result that his downbeat was coming successively on the third beat of the first bar and on the second beat of the second bar. Hans Richter, the celebrated Wagnerian conductor, was once asked how he succeeded in maintaining the tempo with such metronomic precision. "Simple," he said. "My upbeat always equals my downbeat." Some conductors prefer imperceptible movements, and sometimes stop beating time altogether to demonstrate their full control of the orchestra. Such ventures, however, only strengthen the cynical notion that conductors are useless at best and nuisances at worst. An interesting experiment was made in Russia after the Revolution to dispense with a conductor as an undemocratic vestige of musical imperialism. Indeed, a conductorless orchestra of Moscow lasted for ten seasons until it was abandoned as a perverse distortion of socialism, and the conductors returned to the Soviet podium to exercise their authoritarian power over the downtrodden musical masses. Even the most vocal skeptics about the role of conductors agree, however, that a musical coordinator is necessary to lead the highly complex orchestral scores of modern works.

Whatever the technique used by a professional conductor, his prime duty is to translate the written notes in an orchestral score into an effective panorama of sound, faithfully rendering the composer's creative designs. The art of conducting is unique in that it requires the musical, psychological, and intellectual ability to coordinate the instruments and voices in such a way as to create a perfect euphony of the ensemble incorporating a great variety of dynamic nuances and timbres, and to maintain a balance of contrapuntal components within the general harmonic framework and the animating flow of propulsive rhythm. Paradoxically, composers are rarely the best interpreters of their own works. Perhaps only Wagner, Berlioz, and Mahler, who were excellent conductors in their own right, gave full justice to their own masterpieces. Tchaikovsky conducted his passionate music in a singularly pedestrian manner. Rimsky-Korsakov never knew how to bring out the brilliant sounds of his operatic suites in actual performance. Debussy lacked the sensitivity required to project the impressionistic colors of his scores when he was called upon to act as composer-conductor. Ravel was so uncertain on the podium that he was content with just managing to finish beating time when the orchestra played the last bar of his score. No wonder, then, that composers have had to have their interpreters, much as presidents must have their speech-writers. It is in this sense that one talks about "Toscanini's Beethoven," "Bruno Walter's Mozart," or "Furtwängler's Brahms." Considering the tremendous difficulties in controlling a large body of musicians by the wave of a hand, it would seem hazardous to conduct without a score. Toscanini was the first to lead operas and symphonic works from memory; he was compelled to do so, it is said, because of his poor eyesight. But Toscanini's repertory was limited to Classical and Romantic works which he had absorbed by musical osmosis. When he attempted to conduct Stravinsky's *Petrouchka*, he had several memory lapses. The pioneer in conducting from memory was Dimitri Mitropoulos, who led rehearsals as well as concerts without a score. Now such feats of memory have become a matter of routine; reviewers do not, as a rule, mention such accomplishments.

In the 19th century, the majority of conductors were Germans, not only in Germany and central Europe, but also in Scandinavia, Russia, England, and the United States. When Major Henry Lee Higginson decided to finance the Boston Symphony Orchestra in 1881, he stipulated that conductors must be German by origin. It was a profound shock when, at the outset of World War I, the great German conductor of the Boston Symphony Orchestra, Karl Muck, was arrested and interned as an enemy alien. Similar fates befell most German-born conductors of American orchestras during the war. A few who had become American citizens, among them Walter Damrosch, were spared the disgrace of internment and continued in their profession, although they were warned not to play German music. French, British, and Russian conductors filled the vacated posts. Another wave of political discrimination arose in 1933 when some great German conductors such as Furtwängler were unable to obtain American engagements because of their alleged collaboration with the Nazi government. German conductors of Jewish origin, however, being victims of the Hitler regime, were welcome in the United States. An extraordinary development ensued in later decades of the century when two of the most important conducting positions in the United States were entrusted to Asians: Zubin Mehta of Bombay was appointed music director of the New York Philharmonic, and Seiji Ozawa of Japan became head of the Boston Symphony Orchestra. Gradually, even women conductors began to be recognized as worthy candidates for conducting posts.

Confinalis. The secondary final tone, usually the dominant, in ecclesiastical modes. The confinalis of the Dorian mode is particularly important because it corresponds to A, which in the 16th century became the primary tone of the scale.

Connotations. An orchestral work Aaron Copland wrote for the opening of Philharmonic Hall at the Lincoln Center for the Performing Arts in New York on September 23, 1962. This was the first work in which Copland used an explicit technique of 12-tone composition.

Consecutive fifths. The progression of two voices moving in the same direction at the distance of a perfect fifth, strictly forbidden in conventional harmony. The importance attached to this prohibition among academic teachers was paramount. Rimsky-Korsakov was extremely careful in this respect and double-checked his students' exercises by handing them over to his trusted pupil and assistant Glazunov, who enjoyed the reputation of an expert in ferreting out such fifths. Yet there is parallel movement of two consecutive fifths in the coda of Liszt's *Liebestraum.* To amend it, some editors removed one of the voices, even though the result was that the customary four-voice harmony was left incomplete.

The progression of consecutive fourths was also not allowed in two-part counterpoint, unless it was protected by overlapping consecutive sixths, in which case the result was a progression of two sixth chords in three-part harmony. Likewise, the use of consecutive octaves, particularly between the two outer voices, was strictly *verboten*, with the exception, of course, if two voices were mere duplications of each other. In the 20th century, the prohibition of these consecutive intervals was quietly dropped.

Consolations. A cycle of six piano pieces by Liszt that was inspired by the romantic musings of the French literary critic Sainte-Beuve and composed in 1850. The characteristic epigraph of the cycle is *"Notre bonheur n'est qu'un malheur plus ou moins consolé"* ("Our happiness is nothing but sorrow which is more or less consoled"). The symbolism of the tonalities is interesting; four numbers are in E major and two in D-flat major, which to Liszt symbolized, respectively, the concepts of love and meditation.

Consonance. A combination of sounds that is harmonious and pleasing to the ear, as opposed to dissonance, which is presumably unpleasant to the ear. The Latin etymology of *consonance* corresponds precisely to the Greek *symphonia* (con = sym, "together"; sonance = *phonos*, "sounding"). A more poetic synonym of consonance is concord, the "agreement of hearts," as opposed to discord, "disagreement of hearts." Early in musical history only the intervals of the octave, the fifth, and the fourth, were considered consonant. Thirds and sixths were cast out as dissonances and were not accepted into the realm of consonances until well into the 13th century. The separation of consonances from dissonances is not entirely frivolous. The concept of harmonious consonance is based on the laws of acoustics. According to historical practice, consonances are those combinations of tones whose mutual ratios of vibrations do not exceed the fractions formed by numbers 2 to 6 in the numerator and the denominator. The smaller these numbers are, the more perfect is the consonance formed by such fractions. Thus the octave is the most perfect consonance, representing the ratio of vibrations 2/1. The fifth corresponds to the ratio of 3/2; the fourth to 4/3; the major third to 5/4; and the minor third to 6/5. The ratio of vibrations 5/3 corresponds to a major sixth, also a consonance. The acoustical point of these ratios is that consonant intervals are among the first six tones of the overtone series. It is significant that the first five partial tones of the series form a major triad, which may therefore be quite properly described as "a true chord of nature."

There are paradoxes aplenty inherent in the overtone series; indeed, all intervals in the series theoretically form a consonance with the fundamental note. Consider, for example, the demonstrable fact that if we play the C-major scale in the lowest register of the piano simultaneously with the B-major scale in high treble, the two scales will form consonances. The reason? The B in the middle octave of the piano forms the 15th partial tone of the lowest available C; the B an octave higher is the 30th partial; the B one more octave higher is the 60th partial. Ragtime and jazz pianists who introduced unresolved dissonances into harmony did so spontaneously in blissful ignorance of the overtone series, but—and this is remarkable—they invariably placed dissonant notes higher in the treble where they became acoustically consonant with the bass note. The "added sixth" over the major triad forms the 27th overtone from the fundamental bass note. The tonic-seventh chord is a favorite among jazz pianists for the final cadence; when the seventh is placed in the high treble at a distance of nearly four octaves, it is the 15th overtone of the fundamental bass note. Other cadential chords employed by popular musicians contain the 9th overtone, which is the supertonic of the major scale counting from the fundamental tone. But no jazz player would ever put a perfect fourth on top of the harmonic pile. Why not? Because no matter how high we go in the overtone series, we will never reach a perfect fourth from the bass. Other unavailable intervals from the bass in the overtone series are a minor second and a minor third. However, the dissonant interval of the augmented fourth is, *mirabile dictu*, a part of the overtone series; it is the 45th partial tone. If we play the C-major scale in the low bass register and the F-sharp-major scale in the highest treble, the effect will be a progression of theoretical parallel consonances.

The Consul. An opera by Gian Carlo Menotti, to his own libretto, first produced in Philadelphia on March 1, 1950. This is the most dramatically powerful work by Menotti. It is focused on the desperate effort of a man and his wife to escape from an unidentified fascist country. They are doomed when the consul (who never appears on stage) of an unnamed great transoceanic nation refuses to grant them a visa.

Contredanse. An old type of French salon dance similar to the quadrille. It is conjectured that the word *contredanse* does not mean a counter-dance but is a corrupted form of *country dance*. Indeed, there are in existence collections of *contredanses anglaises*, published in France in the 17th century. Beethoven wrote several contredanses and used one of them in the finale of the *Eroica* Symphony.

Cool. A term introduced by New York jazz players about 1940. Paradoxically, it is synonymous with the designation "hot" as applied to jazz of the 1930s, as if the faucets running hot and cold water have been interchanged by accident. Through another paradox, cool jazz cultivates an evenly flowing mood of relaxation, in serene legatissimo, replacing the frenetic syncopated beat of early jazz by an emphasis on the strong parts of the measure. Cool jazz rejects the big bands of the swing era, being more adaptable to smaller ensembles that offer greater freedom for solo improvisations. It seeks a rapprochement with Classical music. Among sophisticated practitioners of cool jazz, there is a tendency to flaunt the names of Bach and Vivaldi (and among the hyper-sophisticates, even that of Schoenberg) as models.

Coppélia. A ballet by Delibes, first produced in Paris on May 25, 1870. Its subtitle is *La fille aux yeux d'émail* (*The Girl with Enamel Eyes*). The story is derived from a fantastic tale by E.T.A. Hoffmann, dealing with a toymaker Coppélius whose creations are magically lifelike. Of these, the most entrancing is the doll Coppélia. A village youth is so struck with her beauty that he abandons his human girlfriend Swanhilda, who in a fit of jealousy intrudes into the house of Coppélius and accuses Coppélia of alienation of affection before she realizes that Coppélia is a doll. Swanhilda marries her suitor, and Coppélia and her fellow dolls arrange a celebration. The first Swanhilda was a 16-year-old ballerina named Giuseppina Bozacchi. Tragically, she fell victim to malaria after a few performances and even more tragically, the Prussians laid siege to Paris a few weeks after that. *Coppélia* survived both disasters and became one of the most celebrated ballets of all time. Among separate numbers, there are an energetic mazurka, an entrancing waltz, an intoxicating csárdás, and an impetuous gallop. When Tchaikovsky heard the performance of *Coppélia* in Paris, he wrote to a friend that he felt ashamed of his own ballets when he compared them with the glorious music of Delibes.

Copyright. The legal right to an individual production. It applies to musical compositions and is recognized by the laws of most nations. The oldest performing rights society is the French *Société des auteurs, compositeurs, et éditeurs de musique*, formed in 1851. Although Great Britain passed its first copyright act in 1709, musical works came under its protection much later. In the United States, the American Society of Composers, Authors, and Publishers (ASCAP) was founded in 1914. A rival organization, Broadcast Music Incorporated (BMI), was organized in 1938, originally concentrating on broadcasting fees. Russia did not join the international copyright convention until

1914. The Soviet government abolished all international copyright law after the Revolution but joined the International Copyright Convention in 1972. As a result of these delays, many celebrated Russian works were published and performed without any payment to the composers; Rachmaninoff never collected a penny for his Prelude in C-sharp minor and his first three piano concertos; Prokofiev's *Classical* Symphony was pirated freely. No protection existed for Shostakovich and other Soviet composers, but a gentleman's agreement was made with publishers to collect fees for performances of major works by Soviet composers. To regain copyright for his most popular works, published but not properly copyrighted before the Revolution, Stravinsky revised his ballet *The Firebird* and other scores, but most conductors use the original uncopyrighted editions, not to avoid copyright payments but out of preference for a simpler version of the work. The Mexican composer Manuel Ponce failed to copyright his popular song *Estrellita*, thus losing substantial income. Numerous lawsuits were fought over popular American songs pirated because of inadequate copyright protection. A rather celebrated case is that of the song *Happy Birthday To You*, freely used until a clerk in a Chicago music company discovered that the tune was written by two sisters, Patty and Mildred Hill, to a different set of words ("Good morning, dear teacher"). The Western Union Company, which used the tune for its singing birthday telegrams, had to pay a substantial sum of money for the newly discovered copyright. And a movie depicting a father whose family forgot his birthday and who sings "Happy Birthday to Me" all alone had to change the words and the tune to "For He's a Jolly Good Fellow," an uncopyrighted song, to escape the penalty for infringement of a valid copyright.

Le Coq d'or (The Golden Cockerel). An opera in three acts by Rimsky-Korsakov, produced posthumously in Moscow on October 7, 1909. The libretto is drawn from a fairy tale by Pushkin. The czarist censor prescribed some modifications in the text to soften the resemblance between the bumbling ruler of the fairy tale and the bungling Czar Nicolas II, who had just lost a war with Japan. Rimsky-Korsakov refused to submit, and the opera was not performed during his lifetime. His heirs, however, decided that it was more important to have the opera produced and accepted the censor's rather mild alterations.

Cornett. Unlike the cornet, an instrument of noble lineage and multiple mutations. It is shaped like a straight pipe and is made of ivory or strong wood. Some cornetts are bent to provide a more convenient placement of fingerholes. During the Renaissance, there were cornetts of different registers, one for soprano, called *cornettino* (little cornett) and one of the tenor pitch, called *cornone* (big cornett). The bass size, which was added to the cornett family in the 16th century, was bent in the shape of an *S* to enable the player to reach the appropriate holes. It was called "the serpent" because of its shape, but it had a melodious tone that was anything but reptilian. Disregarding the curse put on the serpent in Genesis, the instrument made regular appearances in church music. In France, it bore an explicit designation, *serpent d'Eglise*. The serpent underwent another change of shape in the 18th century when a section of it was bent back so as to form two adjacent tubes. In this shape it became known as the Russian bassoon. Other varieties of the serpent were the English bass horn and ophicleide. Eventually, all these quaint instruments lapsed into disuse.

Corno di bassetto. Basset horn, or alto clarinet. This Italian term would have long become obsolete had it not been for George Bernard Shaw, who whimsically used it as a *nom de plume* for his music criticism in London papers a century ago, undoubtedly with the intent of comparing the rarity and unconventional quality of the instrument with his style of writing.

Cornu. A tremendously impressive metal horn of ancient Rome, more than three meters in length, curved in the shape of a *G*, and for this reason known also as *tuba curva*. Two authentic specimens were found in the excavations of Pompeii. The cornu was used in Rome at ceremonial occasions and was revived during the classically minded French Revolution. When Voltaire was solemnly reburied in the Panthéon (he died before the Revolution), Grétry wrote a special fanfare to be played on a modernized recreation of the cornu.

Coro dei Morti (Chorus of the Dead). A dramatic madrigal by Goffredo Petrassi, scored for male chorus, brass, double basses, three pianos, and percussion, and first performed at the Venice Festival on September 28, 1941. The text by Leopardi propounds the idea that the dead are as horrified of life as the living are of death.

Coronach. A Scottish funeral procession. Sometimes the term is applied to the cries of the women mourners. Schubert composed a coronach for women's chorus, using the verses from Walter Scott's poem, *The Lady of the Lake*.

Le Corsaire. An overture by Berlioz, first performed in Paris on January 19, 1845, with Berlioz himself conducting. The work was inspired by the famous Byron poem depicting the picaresque adventures of a gentleman pirate. Disconcertingly, Berlioz first entitled the work *La Tour de Nice*, then changed it to *Le Corsaire rouge*, finally abbreviating the title to *Le Corsaire*.

Così fan tutte. An opera buffa by Mozart, first produced in Vienna on January 26, 1790. The title is untranslatable into languages that do not distinguish between male and female nominative plural. The literal translation would be *Thus Do All*, but *tutte* being a feminine plural, the translation would have to be paraphrased as *Thus Do All Women*. The plot is even more nonsensical than those of most comic operas. Two soldiers taking leave of their sweethearts test the girls' fidelity by appearing in disguise as a couple of Albanians, and each proceeds to make love to the other's girl. They nearly reach the point of double marriage but finally confess the trickery and thus secure a happy ending.

Cosmic A. Berlioz tells in his memoirs that Jullien, the French conductor, used to stop his ears with his fingers and listen intently to the blood flowing through his carotid arteries. He believed that he was hearing the cosmic A sounded by Earth rotating around its axis.

Council of Trent. A gathering of dignitaries of the Roman Catholic church held in Trent from 1545 to 1563, part of which was devoted to condemning the use of secular melodies and rhythms in sacred works. A decree was issued under the title *Abusus in sacrificio missae* ("Abuse in the Sacred Mass"). Some members of the council advocated a total elimination of polyphony from the Mass and a return to plainchant, but the final verdict was to recommend that the Mass be primarily free from popular motifs. Palestrina composed his celebrated *Missa Papae Marcelli* in a purified type of polyphony as a demonstration of a possible reform without destroying the underlying structure. Exuberant music historians describe Palestrina's accomplishment as the "salvation of church music" from obscurantist forces.

Counterculture. In modern sociology, counterculture embraces all manifestations of the rebellious young generation counterposing their own concept of social behavior, art, and even science in opposition to the establishment. In music, counterculture uses the techniques of the avant-garde calculated to irritate, exasperate, and stupefy the bourgeoisie and academic listeners. The most violent expressions of counterculture, reaching their climax in the 1960s, included the destruction of musical instruments, exemplified by burning an upright piano, drowning it, or dropping it from a helicopter at the altitude of 300 feet (as was actually done near Detroit under the auspices of the radio program "Detroit Listener's Digest").

Counterpoint. From the Latin, *punctum contra punctum* ("point against point," or "note against note"). Eventually, two or three or more "points" were used against one point, and that principal point became *cantus*, "song," and by extension, *cantus firmus*, "a firm singing line." This terminology came from the hymns of the Christian church. It was also in the tenets of the church that the domination of so-called perfect intervals—the octave, fourth, and fifth—was firmly established. Early contrapuntal usages, such as those of the Notre Dame masters Leoninus and Perotinus, who flourished in Paris in the early centuries of the second millennium of our era, introduced dissonant ornaments on the basic cantus. However, the interval of the third, fundamental in common chords, was still regarded as a dissonance to be used only as a concession to advanced tastes in the *fauxbourdon* (false bass). The early stage of counterpoint was the tool of Ars Antiqua, as it was described by the later "enlightened" theorists of the Ars Nova. But Ars Nova itself was still a body of composition abounding in contradictions.

True counterpoint belongs to the great age of the Baroque. The foundations of this mighty art can be summarized as follows: (1) several voices, above or below the basic theme, engage in an ensemble of mutually consistent figurations; (2) consonant intervals—the octave, fifth, major and minor thirds and sixths—form a tonal fabric, aiming at the foreseeable cadence and the final triadic chord; (3) rhythmic imitation among several interconnected voices creates a sense of unity in variety; (4) dissonant intervals that participate in a pattern of intermingling voices must be resolved into consonances, even though such resolutions can be delayed by the introduction of numerous passing notes or ornamentation; (5) the bass plays a commanding role establishing the fundamental tonality of the whole composition.

Bach's great collections *The Well-Tempered Clavier* and the *Art of the Fugue* were designed as didactic works, specifically described as an aid to study. They summarized the practice of counterpoint as well as its development in mutual imitation of its component parts. By Bach's time, a number of scholastic works had been published by various theorists establishing the rules of counterpoint of five kinds: note against note; two notes against note; three or more notes against note; syncopated counterpoint; and, finally, florid counterpoint. These species of counterpoint were fundamental to courses in music schools until the most recent times. Several attempts were made to unite counterpoint with harmony by means of figured bass. In the 19th century, a number of learned professors of music, mainly in the German conservatories, spread their influence throughout educational institutions of Europe, including Russia and America, inaugurating what may be called the Art of Pedantry, with the harmonic rules, by way of figured bass, being paramount. The British music theorist Ebenezer Prout introduced the principle of assumed fundamental bass to prove that all counterpoint, and indeed all harmony, should be derived from the tonic and dominant. Thus, a chord of the supertonic seventh was indicated in such a treatise as an incomplete dominant-eleventh chord.

Countertenor. A very high male voice. Ideally, a countertenor sings in the contralto or soprano range, while retaining a masculine tone quality. Highly praised in the Middle Ages, countertenors were replaced in the Baroque era by the castrati. When the practice of emasculation came to an end in the 19th century, composers resumed the use of countertenors.

Country-and-western music. Indigenous musical Americana that has been so highly commercialized that its Celtic roots in the music of the Scottish and

Irish pioneers have been all but forgotten. The geographic center of country-and-western music is Nashville, Tennessee, where country ballads are seemingly spontaneously generated by both congenial smiling males, mostly blond, mostly very young, mostly in possession of a full complement of 32 shining teeth without a single cavity, and radiant females, all with luxuriant hair and looking through beautiful eyes at the world with marvelously simulated naiveté. The songs themselves are uniformly set in easy-going square time, with the simple melody occasionally saved from stultifying monotony by the freedom from academic restrictions and richness of artless syncopation, enlivened by audacious melodic triadic harmonies. Country-and-western texts are both sad and worldly; the singers even lament the departure of their beloved into the mist, but they are ever hopeful. They never use mind-altering drugs, and they always bless the joy of living.

Coup de glotte. Literally, "a stroke of the throat," a curious vocal device in which a singer simulates suffocation from despair. Caruso's *coup de glotte* in the aria *Ridi, pagliaccio*, moved audiences to tears.

Courtship. Charles Darwin wrote in *The Expression of the Emotions in Man and Animals*: "Music has a wonderful power of recalling in a vague and indefinite manner those strong emotions which were felt during long-past ages, when, as is probable, our early progenitors courted each other by the aid of vocal tones." Literature and art abound in stories of courtship and love engendered and encouraged by musicmaking. Winged cupids anachronistically played the lute to speed Venus and Adonis on the road to erotic consummation. Apollo played the lyre to win the hearts of nymphs. Orpheus, son of Apollo, enchanted nymphs by his lyre and even reclaimed Eurydice from the nether regions by singing. The forest god Pan used his vocal powers to attract the reluctant nymph Syrinx, and she sought refuge in a pond where she was metamorphosed into a field of reeds. Frustrated, Pan collected the reeds and made a pipe out of them—hence, panpipes.

Composers of historical times wrote symphonies to attract their distant objects of adoration. Berlioz wrote his *Symphonie fantastique* as an offering of love to the Shakespearian actress Miss Smithson. But he could not speak English and she could not speak French, so they had to wait. He finally married her, but their life together was miserable. According to a sentimental legend, Schubert began writing his *Unfinished* Symphony as a dedication piece for young Princess Esterházy, hoping to win her heart. When she responded negatively to his verbal advances (he was portly and wore glasses), he declared dramatically: "Since my love is destined to remain unfinished, let my symphony be unfinished also." (The story lacks all documented evidence.) Schumann paid tribute to his love for Clara by inserting a brief elegy to her under the Italian form of her name "Chiara" in his piano work *Carnaval*. Tolstoy, who in his old age came to regard art, literature, and music as conduits of immorality, drew a horrendous picture in his novel *The Kreutzer Sonata* of the aphrodisiac power of the last movement of Beethoven's *Kreutzer* Sonata by throwing together the female pianist and the male violinist. A famous 19th-century French painting, representing a similar outburst of passion between a mustachioed violinist and a fragile girl pianist, has been used commercially to advertise perfume. A painting by the British artist William Holman Hunt, entitled "The Awakening Conscience," shows a well-petticoated Victorian damsel rising distractedly from the lap of her designing piano teacher. Indeed, a great number of male piano teachers married their pupils. Theodore Leschetizky married at least four of his. Other music teachers took their nubile pupils as temporary outlets for their artistic passions.

The Creation (Die Schöpfung). An oratorio by Haydn, who conducted its first public performance in Vienna on March 19, 1799 (Salieri played the clavier). Interestingly, the original text was in English, compiled mainly from Genesis and Milton's epic poem, *Paradise Lost*; it was then translated into German. The oratorio is grandiose in conception; the section entitled *Representation of Chaos* is particularly remarkable in its orchestral coloring.

La Création du monde. A ballet by Darius Milhaud, first performed in Paris on October 25, 1923. The music was inspired by Milhaud's 1922 visit to Harlem in New York; the jazz bands he heard there impressed him greatly. *La Création du monde* is the Negro version of the Biblical story of the creation. The score is historically important as the first example of "symphonic jazz," appearing a full year before Gershwin's *Rhapsody in Blue*.

Creativity. The musical profession is sharply divided into two categories: creative work, that is, individual composition, and performing interpretation. Because the interpreter is only a servant of the composer, it is natural that performing artists should be placed lower in the philosophical estimate of music than creative musicians. As far as worldly success is concerned, famous interpreters by and large gain greater fame and much greater fortune, but it is the composers whose names are in gold letters on the illuminated pages of music history, not the interpreters. Fortunately for the cause of music, many composers were also great artists who could perform their own works as pianists, violinists, or conductors. In rare instances, the composer's talent as an interpreter matches his genius as a composer. Chopin, Liszt, and Paganini were such complete men of music. In the 20th century, perhaps the only composer who was also a great performer was Rachmaninoff. Most composers can play only their own compositions and avoid the careers of performing artists. Such were Scriabin, Debussy, and Bartók. Stravinsky played the piano in some of his works, but he was not a professional pianist. Many musicians known chiefly as interpreters also compose music on the side, but it is generally of a fairly low quality. Symphonies written by professional conductors are often derisively described as *Kapellmeistermusik*, "conductor's music." Some pianists have written technical studies and minor pieces of excellent value and of great popular appeal. The case of Anton Rubinstein is curious. He was undoubtedly one of the greatest pianists who ever lived, but in his lifetime he was also an extremely successful composer of operas, symphonies, and concertos. The judgment of posterity greatly devalued his importance as a composer; his name is rarely even mentioned in histories of composition. He remains a disembodied phantom of great pianism, for he died before the advent of the phonograph. His solo piano pieces, however, are still played and admired.

The question whether the art of composition is superior to the interpretive art has been at least partly answered by recent investigations into the physiology of the brain. In normal right-handed individuals, the left hemisphere of the brain is the seat of higher intellectual qualities, governing speech, analytical reasoning, and other attributes of the active intellect, whereas the right hemisphere controls emotions, gestures, and the passive appreciation of the arts. It is, therefore, in the right hemisphere that the performing ability has its nerve centers. If the right hemisphere is damaged, the artist can no longer express himself in music and is unable even to remember the simplest melodies. But if his musical intellect, which is located in the left side of the brain, is untouched, he will be able to compose music even if he cannot remember the notes he writes down. The process of musical invention remains mysterious. Although it has been established that the musical impulses are generated in the right hemisphere of the brain, which governs emotion and the fine arts and other nonverbal capacities, it is the intellectual left side that must arrange and organize the raw creative material. This process probably underlies the nature of inspiration. If this analysis is correct, as recent physiological studies of the brain suggest, then inspiration, or the creative impulse, is generated vaguely and almost unconsciously in the right side of the brain and is then "brained over" to the rational left side. It is then the right side that figuratively exclaims "Eureka!", and the left side that develops this stroke of genius, rationally and intellectually. Even the development of an idea needs periodical impulses of creativity at important points, however. Every person working in an abstract field experiences a series of such spurts of inspiration, following the primary "eureka" type of impulse. It is not inconceivable that these impulses can eventually be measured in terms of electrical units and that the chemical changes effected by them can be analyzed. It will then be possible to draw an electroencephalograph of inspiration. Such a drawing of inspiration may not be inspiring as a design, and it seems probable that there is no quantitative or qualitative difference between the inspirational impulse of a Beethoven and an amateur. It is interesting that in German the word for inspiration is *Einfall*, "falling in." The remaining mystery involves the peculiar nature of the electrochemical condition that creates favorable circumstances for a "eureka" in the right hemisphere of the brain to occur.

Crépuscule matinal (de midi). The nonsensical title of a piano piece by Erik Satie, written in 1914 with the purpose of ridiculing the impressionistic precision of landscape tone painting. This "morning twilight at noon" is the second piece in a group under the general title, *Obstacles vénimeux* ("Poisonous Obstacles").

Crescendo. Literally, "growing"; a gradual increase in loudness. The abbreviation is *cresc.*, followed by lines or dots to indicate the duration. The word itself can also be broken up by several dots or hyphens: *cres . . . cen . . . do*. The effect of gradual swelling up of the sound was primarily cultivated by the Mannheim school in the 18th century. A musician who heard the Mannheim players perform wrote that the power of their crescendo made the audience rise from their seats in response to the music. A brief outburst of crescendo may be indicated by two lines diverging at an acute angle from a point.

Cri de la belle-mère. A rather colorful popular French name for the friction drum, which produces a kind of querulous squeaking sound when the stick perforating the membrane is rubbed by a wet finger. But why should it be described as the cry of a mother-in-law?

La Croisade des enfants (The Children's Crusade). A cantata by Gabriel Pierné for solo voices, children's choir, and orchestra, descriptive of the historic voyage of 1212 when thousands of children embarked on a crusade. Most of them perished at sea and never reached the Holy Land. The work was first performed in Paris on January 18, 1905.

Cross-relation. A progression, sometimes called *false relation*, in which a chromatic passing tone occurs not in the same voice but in another, a modus operandi strictly *verboten* in proper scholastic exercises. In the very opening of his Symphony No. 3 in F major, however, Brahms violates the pedantic prohibition by having the melody descend via F major—F, C, A, G, F— while the bass defiantly rises from the low F to A-flat, a minor third above it.

Crumhorn. An obsolete double-reed wind instrument of the oboe family, gently curved upward at the bell. Its sound was angelically pure and sweet; angels in Renaissance paintings were often shown playing crumhorns. Crumhorn is a common English spelling; an alternative form is cromorne. In German, it is *Krummhorn*; in French, *tourebout* ("turn-end"); in Italian, *cornomuto toto* ("a twisted horn").

Crwth. Pronounced "crowd"; the national instrument of Wales. In its modern form it has a fingerboard and usually six strings. It is rectangular in shape and is topped by a wooden board. The body is carved from a single piece of wood.

Csárdás. A fast Hungarian dance in 2/4 time. The term comes from the Hungarian word *csárdá*, "village inn." The dance consists of two parts, a slow introduction, called *lassu*, which is danced by men only, and the csárdás proper, also called *friss* or *friszka*, a lively dance for both men and women in accentuated 2/4 or 4/4 time. The csárdás became popular in Hungary as a salon dance toward the middle of the 19th century. Liszt stylized the csárdás rhythms in his whimsically named piano pieces *Csárdás macabre* and *Csárdás obstiné*. Csárdás numbers are often included in ballets; one of the best known is the csárdás in *Coppélia* by Delibes.

C-sharp minor. This key, to judge from its use by composers, particularly in piano pieces, has a meditative, somewhat somber nature. Typical in this regard is the first movement of Beethoven's *Moonlight* Sonata, which suggested to an imaginative critic the surface of a moonlit lake in Switzerland. The famous Prelude in C-sharp minor by Rachmaninoff is an example of the use of this key for solemn evocation of old Russia, with bells ringing over the resonant harmonies. Schumann's *Études symphoniques*, also in C-sharp minor, fit into the description of meditative recollection. There is an evocative Tchaikovsky Nocturne in C-sharp minor. This tonality is rarely encountered as the principal key of a symphonic work. The most outstanding example is Mahler's Symphony No. 5, which begins with the funereal measures of doom, but modulations are frequent in the score. Prokofiev set his last symphony, No. 7, in C-sharp minor; he called the work a *Youth Symphony*, glorifying the spirit of the young Soviet generation. The finale is in the major tonic of the key, enharmonically notated as D flat major. What is most intriguing in this work is that its opus number is 131, which is the opus number also of one of Beethoven's last string quartets, also in C-sharp minor. Prokofiev, ever alert to numerical parallels and contrived coincidences, could not have been unaware of this double identity of key and opus number, but apparently he decided to enjoy the joke in private. Not one of the usually alert Soviet analysts of Prokofiev's works has noted this similarity.

Cuauhnahuac. A tone poem for orchestra by Silvestre Revueltas in which Mexican percussion instruments play a dominant role. *Cuauhnahuac* is the Indian name for Cuernavaca, a Mexican tourist resort. Revueltas described this piece as "music without tourism" and said that it represents "anticapitalist agitation." It was first performed in Mexico City on June 2, 1933.

La Cucaracha. A famous Mexican song that became popular about the time of the Mexican revolution of 1910. La Cucaracha, meaning "the cockroach," was the nickname of the girl in the song. The words vary, those of the modern version complaining that La Cucaracha will not go out because she has no marijuana to smoke.

Il Curioso Indiscreto. An opera by Pasquale Anfossi, produced in Vienna on June 30, 1783. The libretto is typical of a multitude of operas. A suspicious suitor, desiring to test his fiancée's loyalty, asks a friend to pay court to her. The two promptly fall in love, defeating the suitor's intention. The opera survives in music history because Mozart's sister-in-law sang in it, and Mozart wrote two special arias for her to be inserted into the performance.

Curlew River. A parable for church performance by Benjamin Britten, first performed at the Aldeburgh Festival in England on June 12, 1964. The subject derives from a Japanese miracle play in which a mother searches for her son who was taken away from her on the Curlew River. She finds that he is dead, and his grave becomes an object of pilgrimage. The text is in Latin.

D

D. The fourth note of the alphabetical scale. In French, Spanish, Italian, and Russian nomenclature, this note retains the name Re, derived from the first syllable of the second line of the millenarian hymn, *Ut queant laxis. Resonare libris* . . . .

D major. The key of classical vigor and clarity of expression, particularly suitable for string instruments. The D major tonic and dominant can be played on open strings in the violin, viola, and cello, so triadic and scale passages can be executed with natural facility in rapid tempo. Many violin concertos are written in D major, those by Beethoven, Brahms, and Tchaikovsky are the most famous examples. Mozart set his *Prague* Symphony and the endearing *Haffner* Symphony in D major, both works exuding the joy of musicmaking. One of the most frequently played Haydn symphonies, written for his London concerts and catalogued as No. 104, is in D major. An American music critic once wrote that the fire exit signs in the then newly built Symphony Hall in Boston should be marked "Exit in Case of Brahms." He later qualified his anti-Brahms sentiment when he wrote that the Symphony No. 2 of Brahms in D Major is "the most genial of the four, and the most easily accepted by an audience." When Prokofiev determined to show to the world that he could emulate Haydn *à la moderne*, he wrote his *Classical* Symphony in the key of D major.

D minor. The key of repressed passion. The greatest of all works written in D minor, Beethoven's Symphony No. 9, opens with an allusion rather than an overt declaration, exposing vacant fifths, with the full triadic conjunction disclosed only when the listening ear can no longer endure the ambiguity. The last symphony of Schumann is also in D minor, but he let it lie fallow for many years before completing it. Bruckner selected the key for his most lugubrious inspiration, his Symphony No. 3. Yet Mahler's Symphony No. 3 (and Mahler is commonly regarded as a kindred spirit to Bruckner), also set

121

in D minor, expresses joy in the presence of nature. César Franck's Symphony in D Minor is philosophically restrained; the use of an English horn, never regarded as a symphonic instrument, reveals an emotional strain. In his popular Piano Trio No. 1 in D minor, Mendelssohn represses his passion almost to the point of rupture. Why is the D-minor triad commonly used by pianists to tune up string instruments in playing chamber music? Why not D major? The explanation may be in the neutral character of the sound of D minor, which is more suitable to the nontempered natural pitch of the violin and the cello.

Dalibor. An opera by Smetana, first performed in Prague on May 16, 1868. Dalibor is in prison for rebellion against the king of Bohemia. A sister of the Burgrave of Prague, in love with Dalibor, is determined to rescue him. She manages to pass him a handsaw and a violin; when he begins to play as a signal of his readiness to flee, she joins him. There are three variants of the finale, all of them tragic: (1) both Dalibor and the girl are killed trying to escape; (2) the girl is slain and Dalibor commits suicide over her body; (3) she is killed and Dalibor is led to execution.

La damnation de Faust. A dramatic legend by Berlioz, first performed in Paris on December 6, 1846. Berlioz added to Goethe's classical poem a sequence placed in Hungary that includes the celebrated *Rákóczy March*. There is also an effective choral pandemonium in which minor devils converse in an agglutinative tongue resembling Turkish, the Turks being notoriously non-Christian. Gretchen goes to Heaven, airborne by angels, but Faust, as indicated in the title, is damned.

Danse du ventre. A fanciful French name for a meretricious oriental belly dance performed by a seductively denuded and often occidental Caucasian female to provide titillation to tourists by a series of suggestive circumumbilical gyrations.

Danse sacrée et Danse profane. A piece for harp and strings by Debussy, first performed in Paris on November 6, 1904. The *Sacred Dance* is pentatonic and rhythmically static; the *Profane Dance* is set in mundane syncopation.

Danse sauvage. A piano piece written by Leo Ornstein in 1913, when he was 21 years old. Its savagery is expressed by a series of rhythmic, dissonant chords. The piece shocked listeners when Ornstein played it in New York and London on the eve of World War I, causing one bewildered English critic to describe Ornstein as "a new star in the musical sky that effectually pales the fires of Schoenberg and Stravinsky."

Daphnis et Chloë. A ballet by Ravel, recounting in sensuous instrumental colors the mutual love of Daphnis and Chloë, who tend sheep. It was first performed by Diaghilev's Ballet Russe in Paris on June 8, 1912.

Dardanella. A celebrated foxtrot with a repetitive bass figure of eighth notes *check* that later became known as boogie-woogie. Composed in 1919 by Johnny S. Black, it was originally called *Turkish Tom Tom* because the Dardanelles separate Europe from Asian Turkey.

Dargason. An English country dance that originated in the 16th century; its tune was also sung to the words, "I was a maid of my country." Holst used it in his *St. Paul's Suite.*

Dark Eyes. One of the most popular Russian songs, along with the *Volga Boatman.* Upon investigation it appears that the romantic waltz-time tune in a minor key is derived from a violin piece, *Hommage*, by a German musician named Florian Hofmann. It was set to the sentimental words, "Dark eyes, passionate eyes," and was published in 1897 in a Russian collection of gypsy songs.

Davidsbündler-Tänze. A piano suite of 18 pieces, written by Schumann in 1837. Davidsbund, the imaginary "David's band," is dedicated to overcoming the Philistines in the musical world. The cryptic initials E. and F. that appear as signatures after each piece stand for Eusebius and Florestan and represent the dual personalities of Schumann's nature—Eusebius as an earnest student of music and Florestan as a romantic youth.

Deaconing. A common usage in English and American colonial parish churches for the preliminary reading by a deacon, or a lay singer, of a line from a hymn before the entire congregation sings it. The practice was also called "lining out."

Deafness. No greater misfortune can befall a musician than the loss of hearing. Beethoven gave an eloquent expression of this horror in his famous *Heiligenstadt Testament.* He was willing to consult every Viennese quack who promised a cure. In his conversation books is this pathetic notation: "There is in Vienna a Dr. Mayer who is employed by a sulphur vapor company which uses vibrations to cure sufferers from hearing impediments when no organic fault is found in the tissues. His electrovibratory machine works by counteracting rheumatic ear infections, hardness of hearing and deafness." Some critics of Beethoven's last works blame their strangeness on Beethoven's deafness. "Beethoven's imagination seems to have fed upon the ruins of his sensitive organs," wrote William Gardiner of London in 1837. Another victim of ear ailments was the Czech composer Smetana. Pressure on the auditory nerve made him hear a constant drone on a high E; he memorialized this affliction in his string quartet, entitled *From My Life*, in which he has the violin play a persistent high E. Schumann suffered from a similar disturbance, technically known as tinnitus; during his last years he heard a constant A-flat.

Gabriel Fauré became almost totally deaf toward the end of his life, but he succeeded in hiding his condition sufficiently to continue as director of the Paris Conservatory.

Death and Transfiguration (Tod und Verklärung). A tone poem by Richard Strauss, first performed in Eisenach on June 21, 1890. The music depicts the struggle of a sick man with approaching Death. It is set in the lugubrious key of C minor, the tonality of quiet horror and dissolution. The death motive is transfigured at the end into C major as the liberated soul departs from the body.

Death in Venice. An opera by Benjamin Britten after the novella of the same name by Thomas Mann, first performed in Aldeburgh on June 16, 1973. An aging German writer, Gustav Aschenbach (his name means "brook of ashes"), goes to Venice in search of emotional experience. There he watches an adolescent Polish boy on a vacation with his family, admiring his Platonic purity and Apollonian beauty. An epidemic of cholera breaks out in Venice; Aschenbach listlessly stays on after the boy's departure and becomes a victim of the dreaded disease. Mann himself visited Venice in 1911 and was impressed by a vacationing Polish boy who became the prototype of his novella. A motion picture has been made of *Death in Venice*, in which the character of Gustav Aschenbach was changed to that of a composer, strongly suggesting Gustav Mahler, and which uses Mahler's music on the soundtrack. Friends of Mahler's family vigorously protested this unwarranted approximation. It was also discovered that this Polish boy was still living in Sweden as late as 1970 and remembered having seen Thomas Mann in Venice 60 years before. Britten's opera is austere and yet dramatic, even monodic in its structure. The part of Aschenbach is set almost entirely in accompanied recitative.

Death of the Bishop of Brindisi. A dramatic cantata by Gian Carlo Menotti, based on the actual children's crusade organized by the Bishop of Brindisi in A.D. 1212, in which the children perished when their ship sank on the way to the Holy Land. The cantata was first performed in Cincinnati on May 18, 1963. Gabriel Pierné's opera on the same subject was performed nearly 60 years earlier.

Decibel. The minimal increment of sound energy perceptible to the human ear; 1/10 of a bel, the arbitrary unit of sound named for Alexander Graham Bell, the American acoustician. The range of tolerable loudness of sound varies from 25 decibels to about 100 decibels, corresponding to the sound of a full orchestra. Rock 'n' roll bands, in their pursuit of deafening noise, reach 120 decibels. The pain threshold is 200 decibels, which can cause physical damage to the eardrum.

Dedications. Composers since time immemorial have dedicated their works to the high and the mighty. The honor could be bought for a few florins or ducats. Every music lover knows Mozart's *Haffner* Serenade; through this piece of sublime music an insignificant Salzburg functionary achieved immortality. Bach's *Goldberg* Variations obliquely glorified Bach's pupil Johann Gottlieb Goldberg, who requested Bach to write these extremely difficult and lengthy keyboard compositions to help Goldberg relieve the insomnia of one of his patrons. Bach was rewarded for his work with a golden goblet and 100 louis d'or. Goldberg himself received a life stipend, but he died at the age of 29. Beethoven's *Kreutzer* Sonata, written for the virtuoso violinist Rodolphe Kreutzer, was never actually played by him in public, but his name was not only made glorious through the tremendous eloquence of Beethoven's music but also became a symbol of Tolstoy's antisexual obsession, as expounded in his novel *The Kreutzer Sonata*. Beethoven dedicated several of his works to titled benefactors and foreign dignitaries, among them the string quartets of op. 59 for the Russian ambassador in Vienna, Count Rasoumowsky, *Wellington's Victory* inscribed to King George IV of England, and his last trio, the *Archduke*, for Archduke Rudolf. His most famous dedication was a failed one, the fulsome tribute to Napoleon in the *Eroica* Symphony, which he later retracted. Dedications were usually written in extremely flowery and obsequious language, with the exalted status of the royal or aristocratic person to whom the work was dedicated symbolized by large capital letters, and a contrasting self-effacing signature emphasizing the comparative humbleness and insignificance of the composer. Bach's dedication to the Margrave Brandenburg is striking in this respect:

Since I had a couple of years ago the fortune of having been heard by Your Royal Highness at your express command and since I noticed then that Your Highness took some pleasure at my small talents which Heaven endowed me in music, and since upon taking my departure from Your Royal Highness, I was given the honor of receiving from Your Highness a command to write some pieces of my own compositions, I therefore according to these gracious orders, took the liberty of rendering my very humble tasks to Your Royal Highness by way of the present concertos which I arranged for several instruments beseeching Your Highness not to make judgment of their imperfection because of the rigor of the fine and delicate taste in music which the whole world knows that Your Highness possesses in the highest degree, but rather to take into benign consideration the profound respect and the most humble obeisance which I have attempted to express by this offering. For the rest, Monseigneur, I beseech most humbly Your Royal Highness to have the goodness to continue your good graces towards me and to be persuaded that I have nothing as much to my heart than the capacity to be employed in occasions more worthy of Your Highness and in the service of Your Highness, I am, Monseigneur, with total devotion, a very humble and very obedient servant of Your Royal Highness, Jean Sebastian Bach, Coethen, 24 March 1721.

Schumann dedicated many of his works to his wife Clara. Beethoven liked to inscribe his piano sonatas to his favorite female pupils. At the age of 51, the English composer John Ireland dedicated his piano concerto to his 20-year-old pupil but removed the dedication when she married someone else. Tchaikovsky dedicated his last symphony, the *Pathétique*, to his adored nephew Bob, who did not even bother to acknowledge receipt of the score. Finally, a unique negative dedication should be mentioned. Kaikhosru Sorabji dedicated his monumental *Opus Clavicembalisticum* "to the everlasting glory of those few men blessed and sanctified in the curses and execrations of those many whose praise is eternal damnation."

Deep in the Heart of Texas. A song by Don Swander, a Californian who never went to Texas. Nevertheless, the song became a hit in numerous Texas-colored movies, beginning with *Heart of the Rio Grande* (1942), in which it was sung by Gene Autry.

Deep Purple. A piano piece by Peter De Rose (1939), regurgitated from disjointed fragments of Rachmaninoff's Piano Concerto No. 2, later provided with lyrics as a treacle-dripping, maudlin ballad. Babe Ruth of baseball fame had it performed for him on every birthday until he died. When a new wave of blubbering sentimentality swept over America in 1963, the song became a hit once again.

Deidamia. An opera by Handel, first produced in London on January 10, 1741, to an Italian libretto. It was Handel's last opera, and its complete failure made him turn toward oratorio, a felicitous development for him and for music in general. *Deidamia* was revived in London in English more than 200 years after its original production, with a new appreciation for its musical qualities. The libretto is from Homer. Deidamia was a companion of Achilles and bore him a son.

Les Demoiselles de la nuit. A ballet by Jean Françaix, first performed in Paris on May 20, 1948. A youth marries his favorite cat, who is instantly transformed into a female beauty, but she retains her feline habit of prowling around at night. She dies; he dies. They become transfigured in some sort of ailurophiliac heaven and live happily ever after.

The Demon. An opera by Anton Rubinstein, first produced in St. Petersburg on January 25, 1875. The libretto is extracted from a romantic poem by

Lermontov. Tamara, beauteous daughter of a Caucasian prince, is engaged to a brave nobleman who unfortunately perishes in an ambush in the mountains. A dark vision appears to Tamara in the night; it is a disfranchised demon, who declares his love for her. Horrified, she seeks refuge in a convent, but the demon pursues her even in that holy retreat. He begs her for a kiss, which would redeem his formerly angelic soul. She yields, but his demoniacally virile kiss is lethal and Tamara dies. The score is saturated with singable tunes. There is a spirited Lesghinka dance by the *corps de ballet*. The demon's aria, introducing himself as a "free spirit of the air," continues to be a favorite with old-fashioned Russian singers. The opera is never heard outside Russia.

Density 21.5. A work for solo flute written by Edgar Varèse for the virtuoso Georges Barrère to mark his acquisition of a platinum flute. Barrère performed it for the first time in Carnegie Hall on February 16, 1936. The title designates the specific gravity of platinum, which is 21.5 times as dense as water. In the work, tritones proliferate and the melodic line is angular but strangely affecting.

Derangements. In the pernicious practice of some commercially successful arrangers and antiquated organ soloists in decaying provincial churches, the mutilations practiced upon the dead bodies of works by great composers by means of stuffing the melodic intervals of their tunes with chromatic passing notes, or filling the open harmonies with supernumerary thirds and sixths. Pseudopianists, such as Liberace, made a career of virtuoso derangements.

only Slonimsky

Déserts. A work written by Edgar Varèse for instruments and prerecorded electronic tape. One of the first attempts to combine live players with a recorded electronic score, it was first performed in Paris on December 2, 1954.

Désir. A very short piano piece by Scriabin, composed in 1908, in which he equalized dissonances with consonances. The desire seems unfulfilled on the last chord, which is rooted in deep C but tapers off in an unresolved dissonance.

Ein deutsches Requiem. The *German* Requiem by Brahms. This title merely indicates that the text is in German, from Luther's translation of the Latin Bible. An erroneous theory proliferated that Brahms wrote the work to glorify the German soldiers who fell in the Franco-Prussian war. In fact, Brahms wrote the Requiem in 1867 in memory of his mother, and it was first performed in the Bremen Cathedral on April 10, 1868, a year before the war broke out.

Deutschland, Deutschland über alles. A nationalistic German poem written by a well-meaning German university professor at the time of the political disturbances of 1848, to the tune of Haydn's Austrian national anthem, *Gott erhalte Franz den Kaiser.* The words were generally misapprehended to mean "Germany above all," and as sung by the Nazis acquired an ominous meaning,

"Today Germany, tomorrow the world." Actually, *über alles* means "first of all." After the downfall of the Nazi regime, the song could not be used in this ambiguous form and the words *über alles* were taken out, but the noble tune was kept as the national anthem of West Germany.

The Devil and Kate. An opera by Antonin Dvořák, first produced in the Czech language in Prague on November 23, 1899. Kate, a middle-aged and garrulous woman, vows to dance with the devil himself if she cannot find a partner at a country fair. The devil obligingly materializes and carries her off to hell, but Kate talks so much that the devil gets a headache and sends her back to earth.

The Devils of Loudon. An opera by Krzysztof Penderecki, first produced in German, in Hamburg on June 20, 1969. The libretto is based on an Aldous Huxley novel about an actual event in Loudon, France, in 1634. A handsome lay cleric was accused by hysterical nuns of being a sexual incubus who was bothering them in their dreams; he was eventually burned at the stake. The opera applies the most extreme devices of the avant-garde in its vocal and instrumental parts to portray adequately the *furor uterinus* of the erotic nuns.

Le Devin du village (The Village Diviner). An *intermède*, or comic opera, by Jean-Jacques Rousseau (who was not only a philosopher but a composer and theorist of music), first produced in Fontainebleau on October 18, 1752. The story was written by Rousseau himself. A village girl suspects her sweetheart of infidelity; she consults a wise friend who advises her to pretend she is in love with another. The stratagem works, and the couple is reunited. The unpretentious score is important historically because it breaks away from the French tradition of mythological grand opera and presents theatrical music as part of common human experience.

D-flat major. A key descriptive of wide-open spaces, capable of a great variety of expressions. The scale of D-flat major is marvelously pianistic, covering all five black keys and making room for two white keys at strategic positions. What wealth of resonance in Liszt's Etude in D-flat major, in which the left hand goes over the right hand to maintain the requisite fullness of euphony! And on the other side of the spectrum, there is Debussy's *Clair de lune*, delicate and subtle in its evocation of a moonlit landscape. The celebrated principal theme of the first movement of Tchaikovsky's Piano Concerto, nominally described as being in B-flat minor, states its theme in unambiguously triadic D-flat major. A remarkable episode occurs in the 18th variation of Rachmaninoff's *Rhapsody on a Theme of Paganini*, in which he ingeniously inverts the principal A-minor theme to become D-flat major. Amateur composers who pollute the shelves of American music stores with creations under such titles as *Deep Purple Hills*, *Red Sunset*, and the like, tend to favor the key of D-flat major. This key is difficult to handle in orchestral writing, particularly in string instruments. Only one composer, Miaskovsky, has ever written a symphony, his 25th, in D-flat major.

Di Tre Re. The subtitle of Arthur Honegger's Symphony No. 5, first performed by the Boston Symphony Orchestra on March 9, 1951. The last note of each of the work's three movements is a D, hence the Italian title, meaning *Of Three D's*.

Diabolus in musica. A nickname for the tritone that is laden with theological connotations and found in many medieval treatises on music. The tritone was a forbidden interval because it did not fit into the basic hexachord of ancient musical theory. In Bach's time, school boys were rapped on the knuckles with a ruler for any accidental uses of the tritone in musical exercises. It was to be expected that an interval bearing such a diabolical designation would be used by composers to characterize sinister forces. Examples are many: the violin tune in *Danse macabre* by Saint-Saëns; the leitmotif of the dragon Fafner in Act II of Wagner's *Siegfried*, consisting of a running Locrian pentachord followed by a staccato interplay between F and B; the motives of the three magical winning cards in Tchaikovsky's opera *The Queen of Spades*; the devil's motto in Howard Hanson's opera *Merrymount.* The Polish composer Witold Lutosławski used an overlapping series of tritones in an elegy on the death of Béla Bartók. The *diabolus in musica* is the formative interval of the diminished-seventh chord, a favorite device of Romantic operas for suggesting mortal danger. Ironically, this interval became the cornerstone of the modern techniques of polytonality and atonality; it is also the basic element of the whole-tone scale used for coloristic effects in impressionistic works.

Diapason. As applied to Greek music, this term meant the interval that "ran through all the tones," that is, the octave. In subsequent centuries, it acquired the meaning of the range of the voice and is used in this sense in French and Russian theory books. The French word for the tuning fork is *diapason*. The diapason is also the principal pipe of the organ, usually 8 feet long; the double diapason is a pipe 16 feet long.

Dido and Aeneas. An opera by Purcell after Virgil's *Aeneid*, first performed in a school for young gentlewomen in London in 1689. It deals with the love of Dido, Queen of Carthage, for the Trojan hero Aeneas, and her self-immolation when he abandons her. About 60 composers of many nations have written operas on the same subject.

Dies Irae. The most famous Christian doomsday hymn, the Day of Wrath, painting the apocalyptic picture of the dissolution of the world into ashes and imploring the Lord not to cast the repentant sinner into outer darkness. Both the words and the melody are attributed to the 13th-century musician Thomas of Celano. It is monodic and not easily classified as to its modality. In the 16th century, *Dies Irae* became an obligatory part of the Requiem Mass. In numerous polyphonic versions, *Dies Irae* is a symbolic invocation of millennial resignation and appears in many allusions, including the last movement of Berlioz's *Symphonie fantastique* and Saint-Saëns's *Danse macabre*. It is also incorporated into the Requiems of Mozart, Cherubini, Berlioz, Verdi, and many others.

Diminution. A common device in Baroque polyphony whereby the theme is played twice as fast as its initial appearance, so that quarter notes become eighth notes, eighth notes sixteenth notes, and so on. The effect is that of a stretto, a melodic precipitation in a hurried statement that heightens the rhythmic tension, usually raising also the dynamic level, and anticipating a decisive ending. In its formal and emotional respects, diminution performs the function opposite to that of augmentation.

Directional hearing. An ability common to all animals, including humans, to judge the direction and the relative intensity of sound. It evolved from the biological need to anticipate danger. This faculty plays an important role in stereophonic sound reproduction and also in the newly developed spatial music in which the placement of individual performers or performing groups is prescribed by the composer.

Dirge. A funeral song, usually for chorus *a cappella*; sometimes also an instrumental composition of a funerary nature. The word is a corruption of the opening of the Matin of the Office of the Dead, *"Dirige Domine Deus Meus in conspectu tuo viam meam."* In *Romeo and Juliet* there is a line: "Our solemn hymns to sullen dirges change." Stravinsky wrote a dirge, *In Memoriam Dylan Thomas*.

Dirty tones. A jazz effect producing an unnatural alteration of the instrumental timbre by muting, damping, or "wa-wa" techniques. When a jazz leader of the swing era (1925–1940) urged his players to "throw some dirt in," they used such special effects.

The Disappointment, or the Force of Credulity. A ballad opera by Andrew Barton, composed in 1767 for the opening of a Philadelphia theater but cancelled by the censors because the text contained satirical references to important colonial officials. The libretto deals with a group of practical jokers who persuade greedy Philadelphians to dig for buried treasure on the banks of the Delaware River. The tunes are melodies that were popular in colonial times, including an early version of *Yankee Doodle*. A reconstructed score, with a specially composed overture and three instrumental interludes by Samuel Adler, orchestrated for a typical Baroque ensemble, was produced at the Library of Congress in Washington, D.C., on October 29, 1976, as part of the U.S. bicentennial celebration.

Discant. A term of diverse connotations, whose meaning has changed throughout history. In the Middle Ages it was applied to a contrapuntal voice of the cantus firmus, as the abbreviation of the Latin word *discantus*, which is itself a translation of the Greek term *diaphonia*. Discant is related to organum, but it is limited to a counterpoint of the first species, note against note, whereas organum developed eventually as a free counterpoint of the fifth species. Originally, the term *discantus* designated the upper voice; its etymological meaning was "countervoice." In the late Middle Ages, the term was semantically expanded and appeared in the Gallicized form of *dechant* or *deschaunt*. It was also used interchangeably with the term *motet* and even, unjustifiably so, with *fauxbourdon*. Finally, already in modern times, *discant* was commonly used to denote the highest part in a choral composition.

Discourse. A musical sketch by Arthur Bliss that emulates an argumentative discussion among a group of intellectuals. The work was first performed in Louisville, Kentucky, on October 23, 1957.

Dissonance. A generic term for a combination of sounds that is not harmonious. Etymologically, dissonance means "not sounding together" (*dis* = "not together"; *sonans* = "sounding"). A more poetic term for dissonance is discord, literally a disagreement of hearts (*corda* = Latin plural of "heart"). The antonym of *dissonance* is *consonance*, "sounding together," of which the synonym is concord. In Greek terminology, dissonance is *diaphonia*, whereas consonance is *symphonia*.

The concept of dissonance has varied greatly through the millennia of musical history. From the standpoint of acoustics, the line separating dissonance from consonance is as indefinite as the demarcation between two neighboring colors of the spectrum. The greater the numerator and denominator of a fraction representing the ratio of vibrations between two sounds, the more acute the resulting dissonance. A minor second, represented by the ratio 16/15, constitutes a sharper dissonance than a major second, whose ratio of vibrations is 9/8. The presence of a single dissonant interval in an otherwise consonant chord converts it into dissonance. In traditional harmony, a dissonant chord must be resolved into a consonance. The story is told that Bach, who was a compulsive sleeper, was awakened in the morning by his second wife playing a dominant-seventh chord on the harpsichord in the music room. Alarmed by the unresolved dissonance, Bach jumped out of bed still wearing his nightcap, rushed to the harpsichord, and resolved the dominant-seventh chord into the tonic triad. In

his song *The Classicist*, Mussorgsky ridicules the abhorrence of dissonance by delaying the resolution of a transient dissonance. No composer
before 1900 dared to leave a dissonance unresolved. Liszt was perhaps
the first to break this absolute prohibition when he used a dissonant combination of notes of the so-called gypsy scale in a final cadence.

The concept of inherent dissonance is not arbitrary. There are solid
scientific reasons for the traditional division of intervals into consonances
and dissonances, depending on the degree of interference of sound waves
in a given harmony. The octave sounds harmonious because two waves
of the upper note correspond to a single wave of the lower note when
the crests of the waves coincide and reinforce each other. However, in
a dissonant interval, the sound waves overlap, creating oscillations of
dynamic strength. When a minor second is sounded, the higher note produces 16 waves per time unit as against 15 waves of the lower tone. This
means that only one wave out of 15 or 16 coincides with the other waves,
creating an interference that registers as a dissonance in our ears. That
the ear can get accustomed to dissonance and treat it as a consonance
is proved by the common practice of tonic-seventh chords in cadences
in jazz music. Actually, the major seventh, when placed in the treble in
the tonic-seventh chord, forms a consonance with the bass on the tonic,
with which it has the ratio of vibrations 15/1. No jazz pianist would think
of placing that major seventh in the bass register where it would create
an acute dissonance with the bass, generating a number of "beats" of
interference. Another technical dissonance commonly used in contemporary practice is the so-called added sixth. This is a note lying a dissonant major second above the top note of a major triad. But placed, as
it usually is, in the treble, it forms a 27th overtone in relation to the
bass note, thus producing the sensation of a consonance because 27 sound
waves emanating from this "added sixth" coincide with a single wave
of the bass sound.

Early in the 20th century composers finally recognized the art of dissonance as a legitimate idiom that no longer required the crutch of consonance. Inevitably, by the dialectics of the antithesis, dissonances became
paramount. The hegemony of consonance gave way to the dictatorship of
dissonance. It was now the turn of consonant combinations to resolve into
a dissonance. Schoenberg, working contrapuntally in the thematic development of his music, went so far as to exclude all triads from his vocabulary,
allowing only occasionally the acceptable concords of the minor sixth and
minor third; he totally banned perfect octaves. Thus Schoenberg reacted
with horror when a conductor found an unexpected C-sharp in both the first
and second trumpet parts in the score of Schoenberg's symphonic piece
Begleitungsmusik zu einer Lichtspielszene. "Das ist falsch!" Schoenberg

exclaimed. After a thorough workout of the relevant tone row, it was found that the improperly doubled C-sharp in the higher trumpet should be C-natural, making the result a proper dissonance. Another example of the relativity of consonance: In the score of his grandiose symphonic poem *Arcana*, Edgar Varèse introduced a chord consisting of a perfect octave and a perfect fifth. He explained this peculiar consonant intrusion into his integrally dissonant work by his desire to create an effect of contrasting dissonance!

There is a horrifying tale of a young woman whose father, a deranged biologist, fed her a diet of poisonous herbs to prove his theory of physiological adaptation. When a student fell in love with her and brought her fine tropical fruit, a box of chocolates, and a plate of French pastries, she feasted on them and died, poisoned by their tasty delights. But is there a new light dawning on the world of dissonance? Yes, the danger lies in a renascence of undiluted triadic harmonies. Several modern composers are celebrating this new bulimia, so far without lethal consequences.

Dissonanzen Quartett. The strange nickname for Mozart's String Quartet in C major, K. 465 (1785), which was foolishly criticized by some contemporaries for Mozart's alleged indulgence in dissonant counterpoint. It requires a very fine ear to discern any real dissonances in this piece.

Il Distratto (The Absent Minded One). Haydn's Symphony No. 60 in C major. There is nothing particularly distracting in this symphony, which proceeds unimpeded through its six movements. The musical material was originally intended to accompany a comedy of the same title produced in Vienna in 1776.

Diva. "Divine woman." A term introduced by Italian impresarios to describe a female opera singer for whom even the description *prima donna assoluta*, "absolute prima donna," seemed inadequate. The term was popular in the 19th century but disappeared from publicity campaigns early in the skeptical 20th century.

Divertimento. "Diversion" or "entertainment"; its plural is *divertimenti*. The term began to be used in Italy in the 17th century as the title of collections of music for entertainment; such a miscellany contained instrumental or vocal pieces of various genres. Toward the end of the 18th century, however, the divertimento acquired considerable dignity and was used for instrumental compositions similar to classical suites. In the 20th century the genre of instrumental divertimento was revived by Stravinsky, Bartók, and others.

Divertissement. A brilliant orchestral work by Jacques Ibert, replete with familiar quotations such as Mendelssohn's *Wedding March* and the *Blue Danube Waltz*, first performed in Paris on November 30, 1930.

Divided stop. An ingenious mechanical arrangement in the organs made in Spain in the 17th century that allows the use of different registrations, and therefore different timbres, in the treble and the bass. In England, divided stops are often called half-stops; in France they are termed *régistres coupés*.

Divina commedia. A symphony by Liszt, inspired by Dante's great epic, first performed in Dresden on September 7, 1867. The symphony has two movements, *Inferno* and *Purgatorio*. Dramatically, the best music is, of course, in the *Inferno*; *Purgatorio* is necessarily bland. Liszt was apparently moved too strenuously by demonic impulses to complete the planned third section, *Paradise*.

Dixie. A song associated with the Southern cause in the American Civil War. It was actually written by a Northerner, Daniel Decatur Emmett of Ohio, and was published a year before the Civil War.

Dixieland. A ragtime Southern-style jazz in binary meter with syncopated stresses. A Dixieland group usually consists of a piano, clarinet, cornet, trombone, and drums. The cadence formula is usually C, G, G, A-flat, G, B, C; the lowered submediant is a lasting idiosyncrasy that has endured for decades and has been incorporated into rock music.

Le Docteur miracle. An early opera by Bizet, produced in Paris on April 9, 1857, when Bizet was only 18. The plot employs an old device: The lover of the town mayor's young daughter introduces himself as a doctor who promises to cure the mayor's gout provided he be allowed to marry the daughter. The mayor signs the necessary contract and then is told the painful truth—the alleged cure is a hoax. The music is not worthy of Bizet, whose fresh and appealing Symphony in C major was written about the same time. Charles Lecocq wrote an operetta on the same subject, competing for a prize that he won jointly with Bizet. Lecocq's operetta was produced one day before Bizet's premiere.

Dodecachordon. A famous Latin treatise of Glareanus published in 1547. Its historical achievement consists in extending the system of eight authentic modes—the Dorian, Phrygian, Lydian, and Mixolydian, with their plagal dependencies—to twelve by adding the Ionian and Aeolian modes, with their plagal derivations. In addition, it contains important analyses of works by contemporary masters of polyphony. The title means "twelve modes" (not twelve chords; the Greek word *chord* refers to a string of a musical instrument, as in monochord, or to a tone, and by extension, to a mode).

Dodecafonia. Italian for "dodecaphony." The term was used for the first time in print in an article by Domenico Alaleona published in *Rivista Musicale* in 1911, in the sense of the chordal use of all 12 tones of the chromatic scale rather than in the later Schoenbergian sense of the method of composition with 12 tones.

Doktor Faust. An opera by Ferruccio Busoni, left incomplete but performed posthumously with an ending by Busoni's pupil Jarnach, in Dresden on May 21, 1925. Faust appears as a magician and artist. With its complex harmonies and Bach-like counterpoint, the opera represents the culmination of the grandiloquent Romantic ideal in musical composition.

Doktor und Apotheker. An opera by Karl Ditters von Dittersdorf, first performed in Vienna on July 11, 1786. A pharmacist's daughter loves the son of a local doctor, but her father wants her to marry a captain of the Austrian army. The libretto resorts to the time-honored ploy of having a marriage contract drawn by a false notary, while the lover puts on a captain's uniform to fool the old man. A happy ending is vouchsafed to all except the pharmacist and the real captain. The opera underwent numerous revivals and was even favorably compared with Mozart's masterpieces.

Don Carlos. An opera by Verdi, first produced in Paris on March 11, 1867. Don Carlos is the heir to the Spanish throne and is in love with Elisabeth de Valois, but his father King Philip II decides to marry her himself. Young Don Carlos continues his clandestine trysts with his stepmother, both appropriately disguised. They are eventually found out, and the sinister Grand Inquisitor directs the king to put his son to death. The final confrontation takes place at the tomb of Philip's father Emperor Charles V, but at the crucial moment a monk dressed as the late emperor emerges from behind the tomb, scaring everyone. Don Carlos takes advantage of the confusion and flees. The libretto, modeled after Schiller's drama, is the most hopelessly confused of all Verdi's operas.

Don Giovanni (Don Juan). Mozart's greatest opera, described as *dramma giocoso*, "merry" or "jocose drama," although the subject is anything but merry. The libretto, in Italian, is by the famous Lorenzo da Ponte. The alternative title was *Il Dissoluto Punito* (*The Dissolute One Punished*). The opera was first produced in Prague on October 29, 1787. A Vienna production was announced under the title *La Statua parlante* (in German, *Die sprechende Statue*), that is, "the speaking statue." Obviously, the producers intended to sensationalize the attraction; the speaking statue was that of the Commendatore, whom Don Juan slew in a duel. There are many masquerades, charades, disguises, and mistaken identities. Don Juan's sidekick Leporello, in the famous "catalogue aria," gives the exact number of Don Juan's conquests in various countries, culminating with the record of *"mille e tre"* (1,003) seductions in Spain. In an act of supreme effrontery, Don Juan challenges the statue of the slain Commendatore to have supper with him. With trombones sounding ominously in the orchestra, the statue accepts Don Juan's defiant invitation, and in a deep bass voice speaks his determination to carry Don Juan to Hell.

Don Juan. A tone poem by Richard Strauss, first performed in Weimar on November 11, 1889. This is his first important work, written at the age of 23, and is still one of his most frequently performed compositions. The score was inspired by a poem of Lenau in which Don Juan atones for his sins by death.

Don Quixote. The pathetic, heroic "knight of the sorrowful countenance" of the great novel of Cervantes, who appears as the principal character of several operas: *Don Quichotte* by Massenet, produced in Monte Carlo on February 19, 1910; *Don Chisciotte* by Caldara, Philidor, Piccinni, Salieri, Donizetti, and others. Don Quixote is also the hero of the puppet play *El Retablo de Maese Pedro* by Manuel de Falla, and of a Broadway musical, *The Man of La Mancha*. There is a ballet *Don Quixote* by the Russianized 19th-century Austrian composer Minkus, and *Don Quixote* is also the title of a tone poem for cello and orchestra by Richard Strauss, subtitled "Fantastic variations on a theme of knightly character." The latter's first performance was in Cologne on March 8, 1898. Ten variations depict various adventures of the hero. The bleating of the sheep, when Don Quixote charges into the herd, is represented by a cacophonous commotion in muted brass. The cello dies at the end in a downward glissando toward the tonic D.

Don Rodrigo. An opera by Alberto Ginastera, first produced in Buenos Aires on July 24, 1964. Don Rodrigo is the Visigoth king in Toledo, Spain, in the eighth century. The governor of Ceuta, whose daughter is raped by Don Rodrigo in the opening scene, avenges her honor by invading Spain and defeating Rodrigo's army. The victim forgives Rodrigo, and he dies in her arms. The score is written in a dodecaphonic system with the application of stereophonic techniques, and the form is built on the classical divisions of an instrumental suite. The idiom is uncompromisingly dissonant, but tonality is not avoided.

Donnermaschine. German for "thunder machine," a rather primitive device used to imitate thunder by rotating a barrel with pebbles inside. It was first used by Richard Strauss in his *Alpine* Symphony, composed in 1915. There are not many instances of its subsequent use, except for special effects in old movies.

Dorian mode. The basic mode of Gregorian chant; originally named *primus tonus* in the system of church modes. The ecclesiastical Dorian mode is not identical with the ancient Greek mode of the same name. If projected onto the diatonic scale represented by the white keys of the piano, the Dorian octave would extend from D to D. It is the only mode that is self-invertible without a change in the order of intervals when played downward. The plagal derivation of the Dorian mode is Hypodorian, which ranges from A below the tonic D to A an octave above.

Dorian Toccata and Fugue. A great organ work by Bach, mistakenly classified as being in the Dorian mode. In reality it is simply in the key of D minor. In Bach's time B-flat (*B* in German nomenclature) was taken for granted and was not necessarily inserted into the key signature. All modern editions of the work supply the key signature.

Dot. In music, more than a mere punctuation mark. When placed after a note, it increases the note's value by one half; a dotted quarter note equals a quarter note plus an eighth note. In the 17th and 18th centuries, dotted notes had an indeterminate prolonged value. To avoid uncertainty, the double dot was introduced late in the 18th century, the value of the second dot being half the value of the first. Thus a quarter note with a double dot equaled seven sixteenth notes. A triple dot is occasionally encountered; a quarter note with a triple dot equals fifteen thirty-second notes (one quarter note, one eighth note, one sixteenth note, and one thirty-second note).

Double Concerto for Harpsichord, Piano, and Two Chamber Orchestras. A work by Elliott Carter, first performed in New York on September 6, 1961. The score, ostensibly in a Baroque form, is a formidable attempt to organize musical ingredients in which each instrument and each group of instruments play distinct individual roles in dissonant counterpoint. Stravinsky described it as the first true masterpiece by an American composer.

Double stops The technical name for playing two notes simultaneously on string instruments of the violin family. The easiest double stops are in sixths, but thirds and octaves are also entirely playable even in consecutive progressions. To depress three strings simultaneously in triple stops is difficult for it requires considerable pressure, the strings not being on the same plane. Quadruple stops on all four strings are practically impossible without playing an arpeggio.

Doxology. A hymn of praise to God. The word is from the Greek: *doxa*, "glory"; *logos*, "discourse." In church services, there are three doxologies: the greater doxology represented by the Gloria in the Roman Catholic liturgy; the lesser doxology, Gloria Patri, used at the end of the psalmody; and the variant of the lesser doxology, metrical doxology, used in the Anglican liturgy. Of this type, the most common is the metrical hymn by the 17th-century divine Thomas Kent: "Praise God, from whom all blessings flow/ Praise Him all creatures here below/ Praise him above ye heavenly Hosts/ Praise Father, Son, and Holy Ghost.''

Drag. A very slow dance in which the feet are dragged rather than moved on the floor. Scott Joplin wrote a "real slow drag" for his opera *Treemonisha*.

The Dreadnaught Potemkin. An opera by Oles Tchishko, first performed in Leningrad on June 21, 1937. The libretto is based on a historical incident: the rebellion of the crew of the Russian Dreadnaught *Potemkin* against the Czarist navy commanders in the harbor of Odessa in 1905. The opera is in a realistic vein, even to the point of setting to music such lines as "Our borscht is full of worms!"

The Dream of Gerontius. An oratorio by Edward Elgar based on the religious poem of Cardinal Newman. Gerontius is any dying man (the name is derived from the Greek root *geront*, "old man") who is conducted through Purgatory by the angel of Death. Elgar was a Catholic, and to him such a subject was congenial. The work was performed for the first time in Birmingham, England, on October 3, 1900. George Bernard Shaw declared it a masterpiece. Its choral writing is expert.

Dream of St. Jerome. How this piece was attributed to Beethoven and sold as such by an unscrupulous publisher is a story of musical gullibility that is as irritating as it is sad. Somebody adapted the poem of that name by Thomas Moore to the first subject of the slow movement of Beethoven's Symphony No. 2. Thackeray contributed to the misattribution by mentioning in a novel a young lady playing Beethoven's *Dream of St. Jerome*. An enterprising publisher cashed in on the confusion by adding to the piece a genuine Beethoven song and a Welsh folk tune. The collage enjoyed considerable popularity about 100 years ago.

Drehleier. A player on the hurdy-gurdy. The sound is immortalized in Schubert's song *Der Leiermann* and in Hindemith's viola concerto *Der Schwanendreher*.

Die drei Pintos. An unfinished opera by Carl Maria von Weber, completed and orchestrated (using materials from Weber's other vocal works) by Mahler and conducted by him for the first time in Leipzig on January 20, 1888. The story deals with romantic adventures in Spain in which three pintos (i.e., mottled horses) play a part. The opera failed. As Hans von Bülow said, *"Wo Weberei, wo Malerei, einelei"* ("Whether weaving, or painting, it's all the same")— a pun on the names Weber, "weaver," and Mahler (*Maler*), "painter."

Die Dreigroschenoper (The Threepenny Opera). An opera by Kurt Weill, first produced in Berlin on August 31, 1928. It is a modernized version of *The*

Beggar's Opera, with a new text by Bertolt Brecht, denouncing the social hypocrisy of modern life. The score includes blues and ragtime. The concluding chorus enjoins the audience to "pursue injustice, but not too much." In an English version, the mocking ballad "Mack the Knife" has become a perennial favorite in America.

Drumroll Symphony. The traditional nickname for Haydn's Symphony No. 103 in E-flat major. It is the 11th of Haydn's 12 London symphonies composed for the Salomon series in London in 1795. The symphony opens with a roll on the kettledrum.

I Due Foscari. An opera by Verdi based on Byron's play *The Two Foscari*, first produced in Rome on November 3, 1844. The story recounts a mortal feud between two Venetian families. The two Foscari of the title, father and son, are innocent of suspected murders but die from mental anguish and chagrin.

I Due Litiganti. An opera by Giuseppe Sarti, produced in Milan on September 14, 1782. The complete title is *Fra Due Litiganti il Terzo Gode (Between Two Litigants, the Third Profits)*. The opera was extremely popular in its time; Mozart quotes a tune from it in *Don Giovanni*.

Dugazon. Louise Dugazon (1755–1821) was a French soprano who excelled particularly in the roles of soubrettes. So great was her fame that her last name became synonymous with the kind of parts she sang. In published French operetta scores is often found the listing *première Dugazon, seconde Dugazon* for first soprano, second soprano, and so on. This is the only case in the history of opera in which the name of a singer has become a generic noun. One cannot very well imagine the listing *primo Caruso, secondo Caruso*, and the like.

Dulcimer. A predecessor of the harpsichord and the piano. It is in trapezoid form resembling the psaltery, or zither, but with the strings activated by mallets. In Hungary it is known as the *cimbalom*. A 17th-century musician named Pantaleon Hebenstreit manufactured an instrument like a dulcimer that became known under his first name, Pantalekon. It is quite different from the historical dulcimer, a folk instrument popular in the Appalachian Mountains in the United States, and consists of an elongated soundbox with a fretted fingerboard and, usually, three strings. In contradistinction to the dulcimer and the zither, the strings in the folk instrument are plucked. The folk dulcimer is frequently used to accompany singers or dancers at American country festivals.

Dumb piano. A piano keyboard with no strings, used for practicing by aspiring pianists whose crowded lodgings do not permit the joyful noise of pounding

great

on the keys. George Bernard Shaw, as "Corno di Bassetto" (his *nom de plume* of 1888), reports an inquiry from a correspondent as to whether there is such a thing as a "dumb horn." He claimed that no such contrivance was needed because a French horn is so difficult to play that it remains naturally dumb in the hands of inexpert hornists.

Dumbarton Oaks. Stravinsky's Concerto in E-flat major, scored for 14 instruments and commissioned by a rich American music lover who lived on an estate called Dumbarton Oaks, in Georgetown, a neighborhood of Washington, D.C. It was first performed in Washington, D.C., on May 8, 1938. The work is written in a distinct neo-Baroque style characteristic of Stravinsky's music of the period.

During the Storm. An opera by Tikhon Khrennikov, first produced in Moscow on May 31, 1939, under the title *Brothers*. The action takes place during the decisive phase of agricultural collectivization in Soviet Russia. When an acquisitive kulak (an overprosperous muzhik) treacherously knifes a Bolshevik, young Natasha kills him with a single shot from her trusty rifle. The score introduces, for the first time on the Soviet stage, the character of Lenin in the cast (but he does not sing).

E

E. The fifth note of the alphabetical scale and the third note, or mediant, of the C-major scale. In Italian, Spanish, French, and Russian, E is Mi.

E major. With four sharps in its key signature, E major was difficult to handle in the Classical period, which employed natural brass instruments normally tuned in flat keys. The grandest symphony in E major is Bruckner's No. 7, both in length and in its ambitious concept. In composing this symphony, Bruckner's imagination was possessed by Wagner, and he said that the second movement, the Adagio, in the relative key of C-sharp minor, presaged Wagner's death. Wagner himself favored the key of E major; he wrote the overture to *Tannhäuser* in that key. To Romantic composers, E major was the key of spiritual transfiguration. The Symphony No. 1 of Scriabin is in that key, and it ends with a choral paean to art. The key of E major is *de rigueur* in the final sections of orchestral works nominally in E minor. The last movement of Mendelssohn's Violin Concerto ends that work in E major.

E minor. The tonality of contemplative calm, if we are to judge by the works written in this key. It is not frequently used by the great composers of the Classical period: Mozart neglected it, as did Haydn and Beethoven. But the Romantics loved it. Mendelssohn's Violin Concerto is in E minor. Perhaps the best known symphony in E minor is Brahms's Symphony No. 4, with its spacious narrative development. Tchaikovsky couched his Symphony No. 5 in the key of E minor, and the finale, as tradition demanded, is set in the major tonic of the key. Mahler's most serene symphony, No. 7, is in E minor. Even though there are lapses into darkness, the finale in unambiguous C major reasserts the optimistic aspect of the music, so unusual in Mahler's works. The river Moldau in Smetana's symphonic cycle *Má vlast* flows poetically in E minor. Dvořák's *New World* Symphony is in E minor, and the nostalgic quality of this work written during his sojourn in the United States fits the

141

key. Perhaps the most congenial use of E minor is in Rimsky-Korsakov's symphonic suite *Scheherazade*. Although the motto of the work for solo violin is in A minor, the listener's ear registers it as the subdominant of the principal key of E minor.

Ear training. A generic description of educational methods employed to improve the appreciation of intervals and rhythms. Students who have the precious gift of perfect pitch (which cannot be trained artificially) have a tremendous advantage over others not so favored by nature—in recognition of intervals, chord formation, melodic structure, counterpoint, and so on—but a child with perfect pitch is not necessarily superior musically to another without it. Ear training, therefore, must be highly selective. Memory is another valuable asset in ear training; here again, individual gifts may differ greatly. An otherwise unmusical child may have a natural ability to remember popular tunes he hears in the street, whereas a virtuoso violinist or pianist may be devoid of such instinctive memorization. The ability to carry a tune is also highly individual; some children can pick up melodies and sing or whistle them with extraordinary accuracy, while some experienced musicians cannot. Maurice Ravel would have probably failed a test of memory or even pitch recognition; Toscanini sang embarrassingly off pitch when he wanted to instruct the orchestra in shaping a musical phrase. Stravinsky had an unusually poor memory even in reconstructing his own works; his ear training by any educational standard was surprisingly deficient. On the other hand, jazz musicians innocent of strict academic training often display amazing capacity for picking up and reproducing complex melodies and rhythms.

Ebony Concerto. A jazz piece Stravinsky wrote for the clarinet player Woody Herman. "Ebony stick" is a jazz term for clarinet. The piece was first performed by Herman and his band in New York on March 25, 1946.

Echo. The natural reflection of sound in mountain landscapes inspired many composers to use canonic imitation. In Greek mythology, the nymph Echo languishes in unrequited love for Narcissus; only her voice remains as an echo. Gluck wrote an opera, *Écho et Narcisse*, in which he made ingenious use of canonic imitation. The device of canonic echoes is employed in many madrigals; in some cases the echo repeats the last syllables of the preceding word when it makes sense (e.g., *esempio*, "example," answered by *empio*, "empty"). In the last movement of his Partita in B minor, Bach makes use of a similar echo effect. In Mozart's *Notturno en Echo*, there is an antiphonal interplay of groups of four instruments in a quadruple echo.

Echoi. The Greek term for melodic formulas of Byzantine music, paralleling closely the system of modes in Gregorian chant. Collectively they are known as *oktoechos*, "eight modes." Their emergence has been traced to Syrian chant, which is much more ancient than Gregorian chant. It is historically probable that both Byzantine and Gregorian chants were ultimately derived from a Syrian source.

Éclogue. A French term for a type of literary composition of a pastoral nature that was cultivated by Virgil and other Roman poets and revived by the dramatists of the Renaissance. Musical éclogues were precursors of opera. Éclogues became practically extinct in the 19th century, but were revived by Stravinsky and his followers. Modern éclogues are slow, introspective movements often set in modal structure. In Italian, éclogue is *egloga*.

Ecuatorial. A symphonic poem for bass voice, brass instruments, piano, organ, percussion, and thereminovox by Edgar Varèse, to Spanish texts from the sacred book of Mexican priests. It is one of the earliest works to employ an electronic instrument, first performed in New York on April 15, 1934.

Edgar. An opera by Puccini, first produced in Milan on April 21, 1889. Edgar loves two women, a wild one appropriately called Tigrana and a faithful one appropriately named Fidelia. As Edgar vacillates, Tigrana descends on Fidelia and stabs her to death. The opera lacks distinction, and its rare revivals are done out of curiosity to see what kind of music Puccini wrote before *La Bohème*.

E-flat major. The natural brass instruments are keyed either in B-flat or E-flat major, which are the keys of festive serenades, military marches, and solemn chorales. Works in E-flat major are suitable for heroic, patriotic, and religious themes. Beethoven's *Eroica* Symphony cannot be imagined in any other key; neither can Beethoven's *Emperor* Concerto (although the title was not Beethoven's own). One of the greatest Mozart symphonies, No. 39, is set in E-flat major. Although this key is not particularly violinistic, for the upper two strings are not part of the scale, Mozart and several other Classical composers wrote violin concertos in E-flat major. It is not by accident that Schumann's Symphony No. 3 in E-flat major is surnamed *Rhenish*, for it reflects life on the Rhine river, with its constant traffic and postillions in E-flat major signaling the departure of stagecoaches. Beethoven's piano sonata nicknamed *Les Adieux* begins with an imitation of the postillion's signal in "horn fifths" in that key. Bruckner's *Romantic* Symphony, his Fourth, is also in this key, as is Mahler's grandiose Eighth, known as *Symphony of a Thousand*. The key is peculiarly suited to the piano keyboard; its full octave scale runs symmetrically through alternating pairs of white keys and black keys. Piano works in E-flat major number in the thousands. Liszt set his Piano Concerto No. 1 in E-flat major, but he avoided introducing the key in a triadic exposition; rather, he teased the listener with syncopated descent from the tonic into the dominant. This figure generated the abusive words supposedly addressed to the orchestra:

"Sie sind alle ganz verrückt" ("You are all quite off your wits"). In his egocentric tone poem *Ein Heldenleben*, Strauss writes a violin solo in the vainglorious key of E-flat major to represent his own self. When Hans von Bülow was asked what his favorite key was, he replied "E-flat major, for it is the key of the *Eroica* Symphony, and it has three Bs [B in colloquial musical German signifies a flat] for Bach, Beethoven, and Brahms." This was the origin of the famous grouping, the "Three Bs in music."

E-flat minor. The key of seclusion and aristocratic retreat from the common elements of harmony. With six flats in the key signature, it lends itself to brilliant technical devices for a piano virtuoso, but it is utterly unsuitable for orchestral writing. A rare instance of an orchestral work set in E-flat minor is Miaskovsky's Symphony No. 6.

Egmont Overture. A movement from Beethoven's music for Goethe's drama *Egmont*, which was first performed in Vienna on June 15, 1810. Egmont was a Dutch patriot who organized resistance to the Spanish invaders of the Netherlands. Factitious analysis may be offered, explaining the ponderous chords of the opening as the oppressive Spanish Duke of Alva, and the main movement as exemplifying the patriotic fervor of the nation. Egmont's lamentable death may be seen in a melancholy coda of the violin solo, and the triumphant ending is easily interpreted as the eventual victory of the people. Musically speaking, the overture is constructed according to tradition, and it may bear any other name just as easily, for there are neither quotations from Dutch folksongs nor any other identifying marks.

1812 Overture. A work commemorating the defeat of Napoleon's armies in Russia in 1812. Tchaikovsky wrote it for the consecration of the Church of Christ the Savior in Moscow, and the first performance was given in the outdoors on August 20, 1882. The score included such special effects as church bells and even cannon shots. The Overture opens with a Russian religious hymn. Then the *Marseillaise* intrudes—at first remotely, then menacingly. The Russians respond with a folksong and a prayer, whereupon the *Marseillaise* wilts in a minor key. Finally, a czarist anthem, "God Save the Czar," sounds forth in triumph. The use of this hymn is anachronistic, because it was composed 20 years after Napoleon's invasion of Russia. Tchaikovsky thought poorly of the work. "My Overture is loud and noisy," he wrote, "and I composed it without any feeling of affection for the music; it is therefore devoid of artistic value." Posterity disagreed. After the Revolution, the *1812 Overture* was not performed because of the political associations of the hymn, at the sound of which the post-Revolutionary Russians saw red. But as the patriotic wave rose on the eve of the Nazi attack on Russia, the Overture returned to the Russian concert halls, with the significant change that the

Czarist anthem was replaced by the tune from the final chorus of Glinka's opera, *A Life for the Czar* (the title of which was itself changed to *Ivan Susanin*, the opera's central character). Fortunately, the harmonies fitted.

Eine kleine Nachtmusik (A Little Night Music). A suite for string instruments that Mozart wrote in 1787. The work is in four movements, in symphonic form. Mozart's genius is particularly expressive in this little symphony. A modern work entitled *A Little Night Music* was produced by the American popular composer Stephen Sondheim on Broadway on February 2, 1973. Among its numbers was *Send in the Clowns*, which won a Grammy award in 1976. The music has nothing to do with Mozart.

El Capitan. A comic opera by John Philip Sousa, first produced in Boston on April 13, 1896, and the most successful of his ten comic operas. The story is heroic. The Viceroy of Peru foils a conspiracy against him by joining it in disguise as El Capitan, a legendary bandit. When he reveals his real identity, the plot against him collapses. Besides the marching chorus *El Capitan*, there is a song, *A Typical Tune of Zanzibar*.

Élégie. One of the most popular cello solos, by Jules Massenet, originally published under the title *Mélodie* for piano solo. Massenet used it in incidental music he wrote for the play *Les Érinnyes* in 1873, to illustrate Elektra's Invocation. It was renamed *Élégie* in 1875.

Die Elegie für junge Liebende (Elegy for Young Lovers). A chamber opera by Hans Werner Henze, first produced in Schwetzingen, Germany, on May 20, 1961. It has a German libretto translated from the original English play by W. H. Auden and Chester Kallman. The story deals with a poet living in the Swiss Alps who deliberately sends his stepson and his own mistress to the mountains during a raging snowstorm. They die as expected, and their fate gives him the necessary inspiration to write his poem, "Elegy for Young Lovers." The brutality of the protagonist is expressed by atonal angularities and acrid harmonics in the score.

Elektra. An opera by Richard Strauss, to a libretto after Sophocles by Hugo von Hoffmannsthal, first produced in Dresden on January 25, 1909. In this work, Strauss reaches greatness; the classical Greek drama of lust and murder, of brother and sister killing their mother to avenge the mother's murder of their father, is set to a musical score of awesome power, filled with excruciating discords and demanding the utmost exertion of vocal resources.

L'Elisir d'amore (The Elixir of Love). An opera by Donizetti, first produced in Milan on May 12, 1832. The inpecunious nephew of a wealthy man produces an aphrodisiac to charm the girl of his dreams. She rejects him but he tries again, serving her another love potion. Opportunely, his uncle dies and he inherits a fortune. The elixir suddenly proves potent as the girl realizes that he is now rich. The opera is one of the most successful in Donizetti's large catalogue of works.

Elytres. A work for 11 or more instruments by Lukas Foss. *Elytre* is French for the exterior wings of certain insects that protect their fragile interior. The scoring exploits the most anxious modalities in the most uncomfortable instrumental registers to portray the repulsive creatures with utmost realism. The first performance took place in Los Angeles on December 8, 1964.

Embryons desséchés. A piano piece in three movements by Erik Satie, purported to represent the musical impressions of desiccated embryos. In the second movement he inserts a quotation from Chopin's funeral march with a footnote identifying it as a mazurka by Schubert. In 1913, when he wrote the piece, this sort of thing was regarded as wit.

Empfindsamer Stil. An aesthetic movement developed in the middle of the 18th century in Germany. *Empfindung* means "feeling." Its adjectival form, *empfindsam*, was launched by the German writer Lessing as the German counterpart of the English word "sentimental," popularized by Laurence Sterne's unfinished novel *A Sentimental Journey*. This "sensitive" or "sentimental" style superseded the Aristotelian striving for compositional unity that characterized the Baroque musical style. It stood in opposition to the contemporary French *style galant* and the Rococo, which emphasized elegance of form and substance rather than feeling.

Endless melody (unendliche Melodie). A term introduced by Wagner to describe an uninterrupted melodic flow unhampered by sectional cadences. With the decline of the Wagnerian cult in the 20th century, the *unendliche Melodie* lost much of its attraction; modern operas now gravitate toward a Verdian concept of operatic numbers.

L'Enfant et les sortilèges (The Child and the Things of Magic). A lyric fantasy by Ravel, to a libretto by Colette, first produced in Monte Carlo on March 21, 1915. In a dream, broken dishes, mutilated toys, and torn books come to haunt the destructive boy who owns them. There is a duet of meowing cats complaining of ill treatment. When the boy awakens from this nightmare of destruction, he is totally reformed. The score bristles with ingenious sonorities and subtle rhythms.

English horn. The alto instrument of the oboe family which transposes a fifth below the written note. It is not clear why this instrument acquired its name; it certainly did not originate in England. The French name for it is *cor anglais*, which may well be a corruption of *cor anglé*, the angled horn, but the mouthpiece of the English horn is curved rather than placed at an angle. Like the oboe, the English horn is a double-reed instrument. Its sound suggests a variety of moods, from a pastoral scene to an ominous premonition of unknown danger. Its range is from E below middle C to about C an octave above middle C. The English horn does not coalesce very well with other instruments in an ensemble and is used mostly for solo parts. It is the English horn that intones the Alpine song after the storm in Rossini's Overture to *William Tell* and that sounds the shepherd's pipe in the third act of Wagner's *Tristan und Isolde*. César Franck shocked the French academicians by including the English horn in the score of his only symphony, for the instrument was regarded as unsymphonic. Sibelius assigns to the English horn the role of the mortuary messenger in his tone poem *The Swan of Tuonela* (Tuonela is the kingdom of death in Finnish mythology).

Enharmonic equivalents. Notes that sound the same in the tempered scale but are notated differently. C-sharp and D-flat are enharmonically equal, as are E-sharp and F. Pianists do not have to bother about enharmonic equivalents on the well-tempered keyboard. String instrument players, however, have to grope for their sharps and flats to stay within the tempered scale. Many violinists and cellists believe that the descending augmented second, say from E to D-flat, is actually larger than the minor third from E to C-sharp, even though the two intervals are enharmonically equivalent. In chromatic modulation, proper enharmonic notation is essential. A dominant-seventh chord is enharmonically equal to a chord containing a doubly augmented fourth and an augmented sixth, which is the signal for the mandatory resolution into the tonic 6/4 chord of the new tonality. Such an enharmonic change occurs, with brilliant effect, in the coda of Chopin's Scherzo in B-flat minor, where a chord that the ear perceives as the dominant-seventh chord in the key of D is suddenly transformed into its enharmonic equivalent, the augmented-sixth chord, leading to the cadential tonic 6/4 chord in the key of D flat major. Robert Browning, who had a keen musical sense, described a modulation from D-sharp minor into D major by enharmonic change as follows:

> *The augmented-sixth resolved—from out of the straighter range*
> *of D-sharp minor—leap of disimprisoned thrall*
> *Into thy life and light, D major natural.*

Chromatic harmony thrives on enharmonic chords; of these the most chameleonic is the diminished-seventh chord, which can be written in 24 ways. Depending on the arrangement of sharps and double-sharps, flats and double-flats, it can lead into any of the 24 major and minor tonalities. This ambiguity and unpredictability made the diminished-seventh chord the darling of the Romantic composers. The equivalence of the augmented fourth (the forbidden *diabolus in musica* of the Middle Ages) and the diminished fifth, a perfectly respectable interval, is of fundamental importance in the theory of scales. The leap upward from the subdominant to the leading tone was taboo in strict counterpoint, but the downward skip from the subdominant to the leading tone, with its inevitable resolution to the tonic, is a cliché of Classical music.

The doctrine of enharmonic equivalence lost its practical significance in musical notation with the advent of organized atonality as promulgated by Schoenberg in his method of composition using 12 tones related only to one another. Sharps and flats became interchangeable; double flats and double sharps were discarded, and such remote sharps in the cycle of scales as B-sharp or E-sharp and similarly remote flats such as F-flat and C-flat also vanished from modern spelling.

> *B is a B is a B is a B,*
> *And never C-flat will it be.*
> *C is a C is a C is a C,*
> *And never B-sharp will it be.*
> *B-double-flat is nonsensical*
> *When we know it's just plain old A.*
> *And why be unduly forensical,*
> *Insisting that G-double-sharp is not A?*

Enharmonic scale. The ancient Greek scale which included two consecutive divisions smaller than a semitone, approximating quarter-tones. The Greek word itself means "in the melody."

Enigma Variations. A remarkably clever set of theme and 14 orchestral variations by the British composer Edward Elgar. Each variation bears initials or nickname of one of Elgar's friends, the first being those of Lady Elgar. Some titles contain sly literary allusions; for instance, the ninth variation is entitled *Nimrod*, the "mighty hunter before the Lord" in Genesis, and the variation is supposed to represent Elgar's friend Jaeger, whose name means "hunter" in German. But why is the theme itself described as an enigma? Elgar invariably parried inquiries by spoofing the inquirers and compounding the confusion with even darker allusions, declaring that the enigma theme may be a hidden counterpoint of a famous classical melody. The work was first performed, under its complete title, *Variations on an Original Theme, "Enigma,"* in London on June 19, 1899.

Ensalada. The Spanish word for salad, particularly a tossed salad. As a musical form, *ensalada* originated in Spain in the 16th century as a potpourri of various popular melodies, sometimes commingled with sacred themes.

Epigonism. The original meaning of the word *epigones* is "those who were born later." In Greek mythology and history, it was applied to descendants of the seven heroic warriors who conquered the city of Thebes. In modern usage, epigonism has acquired derogatory connotations; an epigone is seen as a mediocrity in the following of greatness. An example of musical epigonism is illustrated in the career of Siegfried Wagner, the "little son of a great father." He wrote operas tantalizingly Wagnerian in their libretti and in their music but totally lacking the greatness that Wagner infused into his music dramas. When Hans von Bülow called Richard Strauss "Richard the Second," it was not, however, with the purpose of derogation but with the intention of elevating him to the great legacy of Richard the First, Wagner. Even though Richard Strauss himself adopted many Wagnerian dramatic devices, he created works so powerful and so individual that it would be wrong to apply the term *epigone* to him. A typical Wagnerian epigone was August Bungert, who wrote two operatic cycles built on the model of the *Ring*, to libretti drawn from Homer's epics; his efforts are pathetic examples of intertile futility. The adoption of a certain method of composition first established by a great master is not necessarily the mark of an epigone. Many contemporary composers have adopted Schoenberg's method of composing with 12 tones, among them such superb musicians as Anton von Webern and Alban Berg, and they certainly cannot be described as epigones. Nor does a return to the technique of composers of a much earlier era constitute epigonism. Stravinsky adopted the techniques of the Baroque, but it would be a mistake to regard his neo-Classical works as the products of an epigone. However, the imitators of Stravinsky's emulation of the Baroque are typical epigones, or rather epigones of the second remove. To justify the introduction of a historical or aesthetic category such as epigonism, it is necessary to establish a direct line of succession from a great master to his less significant followers. Furthermore, a great master must also be a great innovator in order to generate a line of epigones. Debussy was such a great master, and his epigones are legion. Mere imitators are not epigones in the historical sense of significant succession. Thousands of composers in the second half of the 18th century imitated Handel without creating a distinct movement of epigonism. Thousands of composers imitated Mendelssohn in the second half of the 19th century, but they could not be called Mendelssohn's epigones in the aesthetic sense. Boccherini was derisively described as "the wife of Haydn" because of the close kinship of his musical idiom to that of Haydn, but again it would be misleading to call him an epigone of Haydn.

To conclude: Epigonism, a historical phenomenon in the arts, is characterized by the emergence of artists, writers, or musicians who consciously or unconsciously adopt a mode of formal composition that constitutes a logical continuation of the artistic accomplishments of a master who inspired them. Such a group, furthermore, must create a certain aesthetic atmosphere in which they can breathe freely and contribute signally to the formation of a school possessing distinct stylistic features. It would not be difficult to compile a suggestive list of composers during the past century who were true epigones of a great master. Such a classification would be more enlightening and conducive to the proper understanding of stylistic evolution than the commonly used practice of relegating such *di minores* of the arts to the rubric of "other contemporary composers." Max Reger was an epigone of the Romantic movement. Arensky and Kalinnikov were epigones of Tchaikovsky's Russian Romanticism. But it would be misleading to describe Rachmaninoff and Glazunov as epigones, because they elevated themselves above pure imitation of their predecessors and created their own distinguishd style of composition.

Equal temperament. A precise division of the octave into 12 equal semitones that is the foundation of all Western music since the time of Bach. It enables the performer to play a tune without melodic distortion in any key, but it inevitably departs from the acoustical purity of all basic intervals except the octave itself. Numerous and sometimes desperate methods were undertaken by practical musicians through the centuries to reconcile these incommensurate intervals. Accordingly, the tuning of keyboard instruments must be made deliberately off pitch for the intervals of the perfect fifth, the perfect fourth, thirds, and seconds. The deviations are small, and the musical ear easily accommodates itself to the margin of error, but the impurity of intervals within equal temperament is easily perceived by playing a fifth on the piano and listening to peculiar acoustical "beats" that occur 47 times a minute. Because violins and other string instruments are tuned in pure fifths, string players naturally avoid playing double stops on open strings when they play chamber music with piano accompaniment; otherwise the difference between their untempered intervals and the equal temperament of the piano can be plainly heard. Some modern theorists propose a return to pure untempered pitch and are apt to refer to equal temperament as "tampered." An untempered scale known as the Pythagorean scale is based on the cycle of acoustically pure fifths; however, because 12 fifths are not equal to 7 octaves, there is an unavoidable residue at the end of the cycle.

Ernani. An opera by Verdi, after Victor Hugo's drama *Hernani*, first produced in Venice on March 9, 1844. The libretto is the quintessence of pseudohistorical nonsense. Ernani is a banished scion of the royal house of Aragon; his beloved is inexorably placed on the apex of a tangled love triangle, being loved by Ernani, an elderly grandee, and the future Emperor Charles V. In the end Ernani stabs himself and dies in her arms. The original production of Hugo's play in Paris in 1830 gave impetus to the Romantic movement in art. Hugo himself expressed his dislike of Verdi's opera.

Eroica Symphony. Beethoven's Symphony No. 3 completed at the age of 33. When it was published two years later, in 1806, the title page bore a cryptic designation in Italian: *Sinfonia eroica composta per festeggiar il sovvenire d'un grand' uomo*. But who was the *grand' uomo* whose memory was celebrated by Beethoven in this "heroic symphony"? The answer is Napoleon!

Indeed, the original title was *Sinfonia grande: Buonaparte*. On the manuscript title page, which is in Vienna, the name of Buonaparte is still visible, but the rest is carefully crossed out in spiraling chains of the quill pen. Books on Beethoven relate how, when he was told that Napoleon had proclaimed himself Emperor in May 1804, Beethoven flew into a rage, tore up the dedication page, and exclaimed: "Then he is a tyrant like all conquerers!" The story is first told in the autobiography of Beethoven's student Ferdinand Ries, which he apparently dictated a third of a century after the event, shortly before his own death. Beethoven's official biographer Anton Schindler popularized the scene in which Beethoven denounced Napoleon. How old was Schindler at the time of the *Eroica*? Born in 1795, he was 9 years old; obviously his testimony would not stand the test of even hearsay evidence. Worse still for biographical fantasy: In a letter to his publishers dated August 1804, after Napoleon had already had himself crowned by the Pope, Beethoven still referred to the Symphony as "really named Buonaparte." If the *Eroica* was to celebrate Napoleon's victories, why is its first movement written in 3/4 time rather than in a march tempo? And in whose memory was written the funeral march that constitutes the second movement? The ensuing Scherzo, also in 3/4 time, reveals no possible connection to the career of Napoleon. As for the finale, Beethoven used thematic materials that he had previously used in the finale of his unimportant ballet score, *The Creatures of Prometheus*, and in his variations for piano that were written before the composition of the *Eroica* but that afterward acquired the title *Eroica Variations*. Any other theory? Yes, here's one: Beethoven was a friend of the French ambassador in Vienna, and it is possible that a suggestion was made to him to write a symphony about Napoleon, then first consul of the French Republic. When Napoleon became emperor, he was too high to reach even for Beethoven, who may have been annoyed by the apparent inattention and decided to change the dedication from Napoleon to a Vienna music patron, Prince Lobkowitz. At its first public performance in Vienna on April 7, 1805, conducted by Beethoven himself, it was described as "a new grand Symphony in D-sharp." No mention was made in the initial announcement that it was Beethoven's Symphony No. 3 and that its opus number was 55. The listing of the key as D-sharp is incongruous to a modern musician; the key of D-sharp would require nine sharps (including a couple of double sharps) in its key signature. Such enharmonic usage was not uncommon in Beethoven's time. The key is, of course, E-flat major.

Erwartung (Expectation). A monodrama by Schoenberg, first produced in Prague on June 6, 1924, nearly 15 years after its completion. The score has only one singing part, that of a woman who finds the dead body of her lover in a forest and muses over the circumstances that led to his death after he had abandoned her for another woman. The idiom is permeated with atonal anguish; the monologue is an inflected speech song (*Sprechstimme*).

***Estampes*.** French for "engravings," "prints" or "etchings." A piano suite by Debussy containing three picturesque movements: *Pagodes*, *Soirée dans Grenade*, and *Jardins sous la Pluie*. The suite was first performed in Paris on January 9, 1904.

Estampie. A medieval instrumental composition developed by the troubadours in the 13th and 14th centuries. It is divided into several sections called *puncta*. Different endings are provided for the repetitions of the puncta, similar to the indications of *prima volta* and *seconda volta* in the repeat sections in Classical music. It is most likely that the original estampies were dances. *Estampie* is the most common French spelling; the Spanish and Italian forms of the term are respectively *estampidas* and *stampitas*.

Ethos. A doctrine in musical philosophy postulating that each mode corresponds to a particular state of mind. Its classical exposition was given by Plato, who taught that the Dorian mode was noble, elevated, and masculine; the Phrygian mode passionate; the Lydian mode feminine, plaintive, seductive, and so on. Medieval theorists adapted this system to ecclesiastical modes, not realizing that the ancient Greek modes were scaled in descending order so that the progression of intervals was reversed. Thus, the masculine virtue of the Greek Dorian mode of Plato, representing the descending E, D, C, B, A, G, F, E, was attributed to the ecclesiastical ascending scale on D. The doctrine of ethos was applied with great changes in Classical music. Many composers of the Classical and Romantic periods, impressed by the whiteness of the C-major scale on the piano keyboard, often selected that key to represent immaculate virtue, magnanimity, and strength. The key of F major was associated with pastoral scenes, whereas minor keys were generally reserved to the themes of melancholy, unrequited love, and world malaise. Tchaikovsky, who was obsessed by the inexorability of Fate, used a disproportionate percentage of minor keys in his music.

***Étrangeté*.** One of the two "poems" for piano written by Scriabin in 1912. The "strangeness" of the music consists of its vague tonality and a willful disjointedness of musical phrases.

Étude. An exercise or study; in French, it is *étude*, in Italian, *studio*. Originally, the term was applied exclusively to technical exercises. In the 19th century, its connotations were enlarged. Études proper, designed for improving technique, were called exercises and were usually in the form of simple melodic and rhythmic sequences, scales, trills, arpeggios, and other technical passages. Études evolved into full-fledged compositions, often brilliant displays of instrumental technique in the bravura style. Clementi's *Gradus ad Parnassum* (*Steps to Mount Parnassus*) (the dwelling of the Muses) and Czerny's numerous collections of piano exercises established a higher type of étude in which the purely technical devices were subordinated to the musical conception. Czerny's most famous collection is *Die Schule der Fingerfertigkeit*, also called *The School of Velocity*. Études fit for public performance were called concert études. Chopin elevated the genre to romantic grandeur in his two series of études for piano. Schumann's *Études symphoniques* for piano are neither études nor symphonic compositions but variations on a theme. Liszt produced a superior kind of piano étude in his 12 *Études d'exécution transcendante*. Scriabin followed Chopin's model in his own group of piano studies, as did Debussy. In all these advanced forms, the technical aspect of the étude became merely the means toward the creation of piano works in a bravura manner. Violin virtuosos, above all Paganini, wrote brilliant études for the violin; cellists and other instrumentalists composed études for their own instruments.

Études d'exécution transcendante. A series of 12 piano compositions by Liszt, called "transcendental" because of the virtuoso technique required for their execution. Originally, Liszt let the studies speak for themselves as pure music, but in his later revisions he added programmatic titles to some. The most popular among them are *Feux follets* (*Will o' the Wisps*), which translates into sounds and rhythms of the lambent fires of the *ignis fatuus*; *Mazeppa*, which depicts the fate of the Ukrainian cossack leader who opposed Peter the Great; *Wilde Jagd* (*Wild Hunt*); and *Eroica*, which is set in E-flat major, the key of Beethoven's *Eroica* Symphony. The entire series is dedicated to Liszt's piano teacher Czerny, "in token of gratitude, respect, and friendship."

Études symphoniques. A series of piano studies composed by Schumann in 1834, originally titled *Études of an Orchestral Character* to emphasize the advanced polyphony employed. The story of their inception is unusual. For one thing, the theme is not by Schumann but by the adoptive father of Schumann's first fiancée, Ernestine von Fricken. The final title was *Études en forme de Variations (XII Études symphoniques) pour le Pianoforte*. The variations are extremely free, and the last one is based on an aria from the opera *Der Templer und die Jüdin* by Marschner. Why the unexpected intrusion of a borrowed song? Because Marschner's opera was based on Walter Scott's novel *Ivanhoe*, and the aria used by Schumann began with the words, *Du stolzes England, freue dich!* ("Thou proud England, rejoice!"). Schumann dedicated his *Études symphoniques* to his friend, the English composer William Sterndale Bennett, and he wished in this manner to gratify Bennett's patriotic feelings. Five more variations not used in the original edition were published posthumously and are often added by modern pianists to the original twelve.

Eugene Onegin. An opera in three acts by Tchaikovsky, after Pushkin's poem, first produced in Moscow on March 29, 1879. Two young friends, Onegin and Lensky, are visiting the summer estate of a family with two daughters, Tatiana and Olga. Tatiana is fascinated by the posturing Byronic Onegin and confesses her love to him in a passionate letter. The next day he explains to her in a condescending declaration that he is not created for the simple domestic happiness of marriage. At the family ball he pointedly dances with Olga to taunt Lensky, her fiancé. Lensky accuses him of callous immorality and challenges him to a duel. Onegin kills Lensky and, torn by remorse, departs on a long journey abroad. Returning to Russia several years later, he again meets Tatiana, now the wife of a retired general. Perversely he is seized with passion for her and begs her to leave her husband for him. She rejects his belated entreaty and he leaves her forever. The music is suffused by lyric melody. *Eugene Onegin* is a perennial favorite in Russia but, like Tchaikovsky's other opera, *Queen of Spades*, it is seldom heard elsewhere.

Euphonious harmony. Tonal combinations that contain only concords and mild discords and do not contain major sevenths or minor seconds, which are acoustically the sharpest dissonances. Thus all chords consisting of whole tones or their multiples are by this definition euphonious. All seventh chords built on the supertonic, mediant, dominant, submediant, or the leading tone in a major scale are also euphonious, but the tonic and the subdominant seventh chords, which have a major seventh from the base, are not euphonious. All diminished-seventh chords are euphonious. An example of euphonious harmony in a chromatic setting is the introduction to Wagner's *Tristan und Isolde*—containing chords having multiples of whole tones and dominant seventh chords.

Europera. A unique theatrical genre created by John Cage that comprises all conceivable elements of the stage production for which he designed, directed, and programmed the actions of the dramatis personae. He gathered musical materials from a number of 19th-century European operas (hence the title) that are in public domain—arias, choral ensembles, instrumental interludes, all assembled and mutally superimposed according to computerized chance operations initially derived from the I Ching. As a result, unrelated musical numbers form unexpected ensembles. Each listener is free to direct attention to the more familiar melodies from various operas. *Europera* is in two parts, with an intermission between *Europera I* and *Europera II*. The first performance was scheduled to take place at the Frankfurt Opera House on November 15, 1987, but an unscheduled fire consumed much of the materials assembled, and the premiere had to be postponed until December 12, 1987.

Euryanthe. An opera by Weber, first performed in Vienna on October 25, 1823, under Weber's direction. It was announced as "grand heroic romantic opera,"

but some critics said that *Euryanthe* should be called *Ennuyanthe* ("the annoying one"). The libretto is taken from an old French legend in which the
enemies of the virtuous Euryanthe charge her with infidelity. Although the
opera failed, its vivacious overture became a favorite concert piece. Weber
himself declared that *Euryanthe* should have for its proper presentation "an
allied coalition of all sister arts." This seems to presage Wagner's idea of the
Gesamtkunstwerk.

Executed queens. Beheaded queens have a morbid attraction for poets, dramatists, and opera composers. Henry VIII, the champion decapitator of consorts,
had to work hard to find legal reasons to have his second wife, Anne Boleyn,
axed in the Tower of London on May 19, 1536. Her chief insubordination
was her failure to give birth to a male child. So Henry charged her with
adultery, a capital crime. Anne Boleyn was the mother of Elizabeth I, who
herself had her rival queen, Mary Stuart of Scotland, executed. The story of
Anne Boleyn was put in operatic form by the Italian composer Gaetano Donizetti, under the Italian title *Anna Bolena*. It was first performed in Milan on
December 26, 1830. The uxoricidal king had his obsequious parliament pass
a bill of attainder declaring it treason for an unchaste woman to marry the
king, and this allowed him to do away with his fifth wife, Catherine Howard,
who was proved to be impure. She was beheaded expeditiously on February
13, 1542, but nobody wrote an opera about her. Perhaps the most sanguinary
execution was administered to the mistress of Pedro I of Portugal, Ines de
Castro. When her lover ascended the throne, he had her body exhumed and
crowned as an empress, with her suspected murderers forced to kiss her skeletal
hands in solemn procession. At least two composers wrote operas about Ines
de Castro, Giuseppe Persiani (produced in Naples on January 27, 1835) and
Thomas Pasatieri (produced in Baltimore on March 30, 1976). Mary Stuart
was also popular with playwrights and composers. Even a Soviet composer,
Sergei Slonimsky, was inspired by the tragic fate of the Scottish queen and
wrote an opera on the subject. It had considerable success in Russia and in
August 1986 was produced in Edinburgh, Mary's former capital.

Exoticism. A movement in Western art in which coloristic devices are borrowed
from native practices as perceived by a visitor. In the transfer of exotic samples
from a faraway country, the actual scales and rhythms are distorted, so that
Western exoticism becomes a refracted image hardly recognizable to those
who ostensibly inspired it. The main resource of exoticism in the 18th century
was Turkish music, characterized by a simple binary meter. (*Alla turca* is
often found in tempo indications in Classical music.) India, China, and Japan
provided inspiration for French opera and ballet. Russian composers were fond
of exotic subjects; Rimsky-Korsakov's *Scheherazade* is based on *The Arabian
Nights*. The Mongolian invasion of Russia during the Middle Ages gave a
historic background for stylized Tatar ballet episodes in Russian operas. When

authentic gamelan performers from Indonesia appeared at the Paris International Exposition in 1889, Debussy and Ravel became inspired to make tasteful impressionistic renditions of these exotic rhythms and melodies in their works. Because ethnic scales are not readily adjustable in terms of traditional diatonic and chromatic intervals, Western musicians created their own exotic tonal progressions. The aria of the Queen Shemaha in Rimsky-Korsakov's opera *Le Coq d'or* forms an ingenious web of such "exotic" arabesques. Less literal and more abstract is the orientalism of Stravinsky's ballet-opera *Le Rossignol*. The orientalism of Chinese and Japanese subjects is expressed in the pentatonic scale; examples are in *Madama Butterfly*, *The Mikado*, and various chinoiseries of other composers.

". . . explosante/fixe . . .". A work for vibraphone, harp, violin, viola, cello, flute, clarinet, and trumpet by Pierre Boulez. The "explosive" element is provided by the entry of each instrument on cue from another instrument; the "fixed" element refers to the individual continuity of each. It was first performed in New York on January 5, 1973.

Expressionism. Whereas impressionism is an artistic technique of visual perception in colors or auditory perception in sounds, an external phenomenon recorded internally, expressionism is an internal state of mind transmuted into a palpable object of art or audible phenomenon of organized sound. Thus expressionism is reciprocal to impressionism, both in the source of inspiration and in the reception of artistic results. The source of impressionism is visible or audible, and its result is artistically comprehensible; the source and revelation of expressionism is hidden in the psyche. In music, impressionism projects luminous polyharmonic euphony; expressionism explores severe counterpoint within the dissonant, atonal, and ultimately dodecaphonic system. In terms of national preference, impressionism is Gallic, whereas expressionism is Germanic, arising in central Europe early in the 20th century. The essence of expressionism was *Angst*, an internal disquiet often with suicidal overtones. In painting, the most revealing exposition of Angst was the work of the Norwegian artist Edvard Munch, who painted macabre images of men and women wracked by suffering, physical deformity, and unrequited love. Among composers the most profound expressionist was Schoenberg, who was also a painter of considerable talent; his self-portrait could serve as a conspectus of expressionist Angst.

Expression marks. Verbal instructions indicating the recommended type of performance. The earliest expression marks appeared in keyboard compositions in the 16th century and were limited to the signs for *forte* and *piano*, usually abbreviated to the initials *f* and *p*. A curious expression mark was *E* for echo, in 17th-century works; it was equivalent to *piano*. The Florentine composers who pioneered the art of opera used elaborate verbal descriptions such as *esclamazione spiritoso*, "like a jocular exclamation," and *quasi favellando*, "almost like speaking." In the 20th century verbal expressions achieved extravagant forms, particularly in Scriabin's music—for instance, *presque en délire*, "almost in a delirium"—and in the picturesque descriptions of Debussy, such as *ce rhythme doit avoir la valeur sonore d'un fond de paysage triste et glacé*, "this rhythm must have the sonorous validity of a sad and icy landscape." The signs of *crescendo* and *diminuendo* did not achieve currency until the late 18th century. The various gradations of *forte* and *piano* were increasingly cultivated by Romantic composers; the ending of Tchaikovsky's *Pathétique* Symphony is marked *pppppp*.

Eye music. Composers are often tempted to use a visual representation in their scores to express the mood of a song or instrumental composition. Renaissance composers of madrigals used blackened notes to express death, dark of the night, or grief whenever such sentiments were found in the text, disregarding the fact that such blackening affected the time values in mensural notation. Bach used melodic figures that suggested the cross in his *Passion of St. Matthew*. The appearance of the score in the storm scene in Beethoven's *Pastoral* Symphony actually suggests vertical rainfall in the wind instruments, swirling streams in the basses, and bolts of lightning in the rapid violin passages. There is no denying that the visual aspect of a piece of music somehow relates to the auditory impression of it. Brahms used to say that music that looks good will sound good. Some modern composers have advanced the paradoxical argument that music should not be heard at all but be regarded as a pictorial art. Experienced readers of scores claim that they obtain greater satisfaction and pleasure from reading music and idealizing the sound in an impossible euphony than from hearing it. "Heard melodies are sweet, but those unheard are sweeter," Keats said. Critics sometimes use the term "eye music" (usually in its German form, *Augenmusik*) as an opprobrium.

In the second half of the 20th century, *Augenmusik* became a trusty tool of avant-garde composers. Geometric lines and curves mark the scores of John Cage. Sylvano Bussotti composed pieces that look like illustrated catalogues. An extraordinary innovation was introduced by the Greek composer Jani Cristou who included "psychoid factors" in his music, drawing miniature faces portraying rapidly succeeding emotional states from serene happiness to utter dejection. The mystical Russian composer Obouhov replaced sharps by religious crosses and marked rehearsal numbers with his own blood. However, such extreme excursions into the visual field by composers soon began to subside, and *Augenmusik* showed signs of self-depletion.

F

F. The sixth note in the alphabetical scale, and the fourth note of the C major or minor scale. In French, Italian, Spanish, and Russian nomenclature, F is Fa.

F major. Predominantly a key of pastoral music, descriptive of gentle landscapes and lyric, often sentimental moods. Beethoven's *Pastoral* Symphony and the famous *Melody in F* by Anton Rubinstein are paradigms of the natural affinities of this key. The most optimistic of Brahms's symphonies, No. 3, is in F major, as is the merriest Two-Part Invention of Bach. No doubt, examples can be found in which F major suggests an autumnal rather than a vernal mood—a Chopin nocturne, for instance—but they are rare.

F minor. A key of lyric reverie infused with melancholy. Composers writing for string instruments or for orchestra instinctively shun F minor because it is so unwieldy, having only secondary degrees, the supertonic and the leading tone, that can be played on open strings. But F minor is eminently pianistic, and much Romantic music is written in this key. Chopin wrote a piano concerto in F minor; Schubert's most famous *Moment Musical* is in F minor. It is also the principal key of Tchaikovsky's Symphony No. 4, Vaughn Williams's Symphony No. 4, and two Miaskovsky symphonies, Nos. 10 and 24.

Façade. An "entertainment" by William Walton written for a speaking voice and instruments to a text by the English woman of letters Edith Sitwell. The music is a tossed salad of sentimental and provocative vulgar tunes. *Façade* was first performed in London on June 12, 1923, when Walton was only 21 years old.

Fake book. A collection of standard jazz tunes used as "lead sheets" for instrumentalists in a jazz combo, indicating melodies and chord symbols but no other detail, thereby allowing the players to "fake" or improvise their way around a basic framework. Chord symbols use capital *M* for major and small

158

m for minor triads. Numerical figures stand for intervals. A superscript *o* indicates diminished and a plus sign (+) denotes augmented; an *x* is for flat. The fundamental note is given before the indication of the chord symbol. Thus, *CM* is C-major triad; *CM*6 is C-major triad with an added sixth (i.e., the note A); *Cx*7 is C-major triad with a "blue note" flatting the seventh.

Fall River Legend. A ballet by Morton Gould, first performed in New York, April 22, 1947. The subject is derived from the famous murder trial in Fall River, Massachusetts, in which a maiden lady was accused of murdering her stepmother and then her father with an axe (she was acquitted).

Falsetto. The practice of voice production by using head tones rather than chest tones, particularly among tenors, thus producing sounds well above the natural range. Falsetto singing was widely practiced in the choirs at the Vatican and Italian cathedrals when the use of female or castrated male singers was inappropriate. Falsetto singers were also known under the name of *alti naturali*, "natural alto" singers, to distinguish them from *voci artificiali*, the "artificial voices" of the castrati. Another term for falsetto singers was *tenorini*, "little tenors." The word falsetto itself is a diminutive of the Italian *falso*, because the singer, even when not castrated, applies a "false" way of voice production. Falsetto voices are often used in Baroque operas for comic effects. The part of the astrologer in Rimsky-Korsakov's *Le Coq d'or* is cast in falsetto to indicate that he was a eunuch. The falsetto is also used in yodeling.

Falstaff. An opera by Verdi, to a libretto by Boito from the story of Shakespeare's famous fat man, bumbling lover, and cowardly braggart. *Falstaff* was Verdi's last opera and his only comic opera (it was described by Verdi as "lyric comedy"). The statement found in some reference works, even respectable ones, that Verdi wrote *Falstaff* when he was 80 is false. He worked on it from 1890 to 1892 and completed the score when he was barely 79. It was produced at La Scala in Milan on February 9, 1893, several months short of Verdi's 80th birthday. In the opera, Verdi inaugurated a new style, approaching that of music drama; it ends on a magisterial choral fugue with the Shakespearean words, "All the world's a stage."

Falstaff is also the title of a symphonic study by Edward Elgar, first performed at the Leeds Festival on October 2, 1913, with Elgar himself conducting. Elgar was fascinated by the portly figure of the Shakespearean antihero; in this work he outlined in musical images Falstaff's life from his companionship with the future King Henry V to his fall from royal grace and his pitiful death. The music is romantic, with elements of grandeur.

The Family of Taras. An opera by Dmitri Kabelevsky, first performed in Leningrad on November 7, 1950. The action takes place in a Ukrainian city occupied by the Nazis in 1942. A group of young partisans, among them a daughter of Taras, is given an assignment to blow up the Nazi headquarters. They succeed, but she is seized by the Germans amd hanged. Her sacrifice is not in vain; Soviet soldiers soon recapture the town. Old Taras vows to live to see that peace again reigns in the world. The opera is remarkable because it was written so soon after the events it portrays.

La Fanciulla del West. An opera by Puccini, based on Belasco's drama *The Girl of the Golden West.* It was composed for America and produced at the Metropolitan Opera House in New York on December 10, 1910, with Toscanini conducting and Caruso singing the part of the Western badman Dick Johnson. Dick and the sheriff are both in love with Minnie, who owns a saloon. When Dick seeks shelter in her quarters, she challenges the sheriff to a poker game, the stake of which is Dick's freedom. Minnie wins by secreting an extra ace in her petticoat, and together she and Dick ride away. The score contains a number of unintentionally hilarious pseudo-Americanisms, and the poker game itself is quite preposterous.

Fanfare for the Common Man. One of several fanfares commissioned by Eugene Goossens for the Cincinnati Symphony Orchestra, which he conducted during World War II. Written by Aaron Copland for brass and percussion, it was first performed on March 12, 1943, and soon became a perennial favorite. Copland included it in its entirety in the finale of his Symphony No. 3.

Fantasia. A term that implies a free flight of fancy. It has a respectable pedigree, having been applied first to contrapuntal compositions for keyboard instruments, lutes, and viols. Technically, it is marked by a free thematic development and an abundance of florid cadenzas. Jean-Jacques Rousseau, in his *Dictionnaire de musique*, asserts fancifully that a fantasy can never be written down because as soon as it is arranged in notes it ceases to be a fantasy. In the 19th century, instrumental fantasies largely abandoned their contrapuntal character and became works in sonata form. When Beethoven described his *Moonlight* Sonata as "Sonata quasi una fantasia," he apparently intended to impart to the music a romantic image, but it is set in strict sonata form. Chopin's *Fantaisie-impromptu* is organized in a symmetric ternary form.

The word *fancy* is derived from the Italian *fantasia*, and was used in England in the 16th and 17th centuries to represent a freely connected group of tunes in a contrapuntal setting, written for the keyboard or a consort of viols. The form of "fancy" vanished in the 18th century and was replaced by the more international Italian term *fantasia*.

Fantasia on a Theme by Thomas Tallis. One of the most popular works of Vaughan Williams, scored for string orchestra. Tallis was a significant English composer of hymns during the reign of Elizabeth I. Vaughan Williams set his solemn melodies in spacious modern modalities. The *Fantasia* was first performed in Gloucester, England, on September 6, 1910.

Fantasia on Greensleeves. The tune of *Greensleeves* is one of the most ingratiating English folk ballads. Shakespeare mentions it in *The Merry Wives of Windsor*, where Fastaff says, "Let the Sky Thunder to the tune of Green Sleeves." Ralph Vaughan Williams made use of it in his opera *Sir John in Love*. He arranged it as the *Fantasia* for harp and strings and conducted its first performance in London on September 27, 1934.

Farce. A comic intermezzo in medieval plays with music, making use of songs popular at the time, often of lewd, lascivious, or libidinous nature. The word *farce* itself come from Latin *farcire*, "to stuff." In modern times, farce still retains the old meaning of a frivolous comedy of manners.

Farewell engagements. Convenient, though rarely truthful, announcements issued by prima donnas of both sexes at the end of their careers to attract the attention of a vanishing public. Long past her prime, Adelina Patti gave an extended series of "farewell" concerts in the United States.

Farewell Symphony. Symphony No. 45 by Haydn, written in 1772, in the unusual key of F-sharp minor. The work itself is most unusual as well. In it, Haydn instructs one player after another to leave the stage until only the first violinist remains. After the first violinist's last solo, he blows out his candle and makes his departure. Haydn left no clue to the meaning of this pantomime, but in time an elaborate myth was conjured up: Haydn and his little symphony group, who were employed by the Hungarian Prince Esterházy, desired to leave their place of employment and take a little holiday in merry Vienna. The prince took the not-so-subtle hint from this performance and let the musicians go on a well-merited vacation. A much more plausible story is told in a book of memoirs by an obscure friend of Haydn, who relates that the prince was about to dismiss his resident musicians, which saddened them all, for they enjoyed healthy living and relatively generous emoluments. Haydn arranged this little exhibition to tug at the prince's heartstrings. He fully succeeded, and his group remained in the service of the prince for many more contented years. The German title of the *Farewell* Symphony is *Abschiedssymphonie*.

Fasola. A method of teaching singing that was popular in England and in colonial America. The term specified that only three syllables of the Guidonian Hand, Fa, Sol, and La, were to be used to form the major hexachord. By adding the syllable Mi for the seventh degree of the scale, a complete major scale was obtained. To further facilitate the immediate recognition of the degrees of the scale, an American musician William Little notated Fa, Sol, and La in different shapes. This "shape note" notation, also known as "buckwheat notation," was for many years taught in music classes in America, particularly in the Southern states.

Fatum. A symphonic work by Tchaikovsky, first performed in Moscow on February 27, 1869. The title is significant because it shows Tchaikovsky's abiding obsession with the inexorability of fate.

Faust. An opera by Gounod, first performed in Paris on March 19, 1859, and one of the most successful operas of all time. In its melodiousness, harmoniousness, and mellowness, *Faust* has no equal. During the first century of its spectacular career, *Faust* was performed more than 2,000 times in Paris alone. Its libretto emphasizes the mundane aspects of Goethe's great poem. Faust sells his soul to the canny devil Mephistopheles in exchange for the elixir of youth. No sooner is the deal arranged than Faust is shown the image of the virginal, blonde, succulent Marguerite. He is conducted to the girl's abode, sings an aria extolling the chastity of her retreat, tempts her anonymously with jewels (which gives her a chance to sing an aria with coloratura trills and frills), and with worldly advice from the ubiquitous devil, seduces her. Marguerite's brother fights Faust in a duel but is slain. Marguerite bears Faust's child, but goes insane and nine months later kills the child. She is sentenced to die, but a host of cherubim and seraphim carries her to heaven. Faust, however, goes to hell. The Germans were so offended by Gounod's vulgar treatment of Goethe's great classic that the opera was produced in Germany under different titles, *Margarete* or *Gretchen*.

Faust Symphony. First performed in Weimar on September 5, 1857, this work by Liszt is the only true symphony inspired by Goethe's great epic poem *Faust*. It is subdivided into three movements, which are portraits of the main characters: *Faust*, *Gretchen*, and *Mephistopheles*. The ending is choral. The purely musical distinction of the work is its remarkable opening in four mutually exclusive arpeggiated augmented triads, covering 12 notes of the scale.

Fauxbourdon. A technique of composition that evolved in the 15th century. *Fauxbourdon* is an honorable word in music history and theory that is unfortunately self-contradictory in its meaning. There is nothing *faux* ("false") in its harmonic setting, and there is no *bourdon* (in French, "constant drone"). In medieval English, fauxbourdon was spelled *faburden*, "false drone." In actual harmonic usage, fauxbourdon introduced thirds and sixths as consonant intervals and consequently legitimized the use of what was eventually defined as first-inversion triads proceeding in parallel motion and necessarily allowing the use of parallel octaves and fourths, progressions that were at a later time invalidated in music schools of the Renaissance era. The papal authority was still powerful in music when fauxbourdon was emerging, and the "anti-Pope"

Pope John XXII, who held his post not in Rome but in Avignon, France, decreed a return to pure plainchant. Inevitably, the forbidden parallel thirds and sixths emerged in the inner voice parts and, although still called false drones, became sanctified by common usage. Thus, the "bourdon," false in name, became true in actual practice. The terminological confusion remained only in books on music written by authors trying to reconcile the irreconcilables and to contradict the incontradictables.

La Favorite. An opera by Donizetti, first performed in Paris on December 2, 1840; in Italian it is *La Favorita.* The heroine is the favorite mistress of the king of Castile. Unaware of her lofty status, a novitiate monk watches her form in the window. Inflamed with carnal desire, he declares his love to her. The king, eager to rid himself of the embarrassing liaison with his mistress, lets her marry the monk, who soon discovers that he was made a fool by her and returns to the monastery. But she realizes that she really loves the monk and makes her way to his monastic retreat disguised as a young novice. The finale is tragic, as she is overcome by moral scruples and falls dead into his arms.

Fedora. An opera by Umberto Giordano, first produced in Milan on November 17, 1898. Fedora is betrothed to a Russian count, but he is assassinated by a nihilist. Fedora traces the killer to his exile in Paris and flirts with him as a means of making him confess his crime. Inadvertently she falls in love with him and follows him to Switzerland to protect him from the ubiquitous czarist police. But instead of gratitude, the nihilist accuses her of dark betrayal. She takes poison and dies in his arms. The opera is seasoned with pseudo-Russian folk tunes in Italian dressing.

Le Festin de l'araignée. A ballet-pantomime by Albert Roussel, first performed in Paris on April 3, 1913. The scenario depicts the feast of a spider with a menu comprising, among other insects, a butterfly and a mayfly. In the end, the bloated spider is itself devoured by a praying mantis. The music is impressionistic, with dancing tunes for the entomological scenes.

Festivals. A generic name for all kinds of festivities accompanied by singing, playing upon instruments, and dancing. The earliest music festivals were the gatherings of the troubadours in 13th-century France and the Minnesingers in Germany, the latter portrayed in Wagner's operas *Tannhäuser* and *Die Meistersinger.* The oldest regularly produced festival was the Eisteddfod, held in Wales and since revived. England was the first nation to organize music festivals devoted to performances of classical music. The first of these was the Three Choirs Festival founded in 1724, which took place in the three cathedral cities of Gloucester, Hereford, and Worcester. The earliest festival to present the music of a single composer was the Handel Festival, organized in London in the Crystal Palace in 1857. The most grandiose opera festivals devoted to a living composer were the Bayreuth Festivals, begun by Wagner in 1876 with the aid of funds supplied by his fanatical admirer, the young King Ludwig of Bavaria. The opening event presented the complete performance of *Der Ring des Nibelungen*. Music festivals in America in the 19th century tended to emphasize chronological memorialization of great events, as exemplified by the two festivals celebrating the end of the Civil War, held in Boston in 1869 and in 1872, under the name Peace Jubilee. It boasted of an orchestra of 1,000 men and a chorus of 10,000. An important series of music festivals of a high professional order was initiated in Worcester, Massachusetts, in 1858.

In the 20th century, several festivals were organized with the express purpose of promoting modern music. Of these the most ambitious in scope were the festivals of the International Society for Contemporary Music, founded in 1923, and held in the summer or early autumn in various countries of Europe. The Coolidge Chamber Music Festivals were established by Elizabeth Sprague Coolidge, first under the name Berkshire Festival of Chamber Music in Pittsfield, Massachusetts, in 1918, and after 1924, at the Library of Congress in Washington, D.C. In 1930 Howard Hanson inaugurated a series of annual festivals of American music in Rochester, New York. In 1940 Koussevitzky and the Boston Symphony Orchestra established a series of summer concerts in Tanglewood, Massachusetts, in programs of classical and modern music. In 1956 Poland opened an annual series of festivals of modern music under the name Warsaw Autumn. The festivals in Donaueschingen, begun in 1921, produced numerous new works, principally by German composers. The International Festival in Edinburgh, Scotland, founded in 1947, presented programs of opera, symphony, and chamber music. The Maggio Musicale Fiorentino (Florentine Musical May) was established in 1933 in Florence, at first on a biennial and then on an annual basis, with varied programs of opera, ballet, and symphony concerts. The biennial Venice Festival has flourished since 1950. In 1958 Gian Carlo Menotti organized the Festival of Two Worlds in the town of Spoleto, Italy, the two worlds being Europe and America. In 1977 he opened the American counterpart of the festival in Charleston, South Carolina. The Israel Festival has been held in principal cities of that country since 1961; its programs have emphasized Israeli folk music and works by national composers. In 1957 the Armenian industrialist Gulbenkian founded annual festivals in Lisbon and other cities of Portugal, known as Festival Gulbenkian de Musica. The Prague Spring Festivals were inaugurated in 1946. Biennial international festivals of contemporary music are presented in Zagreb, Yugoslavia. The annual Holland Festival, established in 1948, presents music in all genres in Amsterdam and other cities of the Netherlands. In 1948 Benjamin Britten organized annual summer festivals in Aldeburgh, England.

Operas, new and old, are presented during the summer months in Glynde-bourne, England. Regular festival presentations are held in virtually every European city, the most important ones being those in Berlin, Munich, Vienna, Salzburg, Stockholm, and Bergen, Norway. Festivals of the music of Sibelius are given in Helsinki in December to commemorate the month of his birth. In the Soviet Union, ample musical activities are maintained in Moscow, Leningrad, Kiev, Tbilisi, and other musical centers. Festivals of ethnic music, ranging from folksongs to operas and symphonies, are given periodically in Moscow. Japan and Australia contribute to the development of festival music. Jazz festivals in Newport, Rhode Island, held during the summer months, provide special interest, as do those in Monterey, California. Concerts and presentations in multimedia are sporadically given by composers of the International Avant-Garde, in New York, San Francisco, London, Cologne, and Tokyo. Similar events are held annually in a different U.S. city as part of New Music America.

Festschrift. A festive publication in honor of a music scholar or an esteemed pedagogue, issued on the occasion of the 60th, 70th, or 80th birthday of the person thus honored. The custom began in Germany, and the German term is retained for non-German publications as well, particularly in the United States. Festschriften (plural) are usually printed on deluxe paper and adorned by a touched-up photograph of the person showing him or her as bespectacled and corrugated by age and scholarly concentration, suggesting that learned pursuits are physiologically deadening. The contents of such volumes are usually grab bags, if not indeed garbage containers, of discarded PhD theses on jejune subjects, aborted parerga, fetid paralipomena, and fulsome fecundities, laden with footnotes that frequently retract statements made in the text, and couched in a stupefyingly pedestrian style that is often grammatically and syntactically indigestible. Such materials are usually intellectual elucubrations contributed by students of the person so honored. Unintentionally, such editions put in doubt the ability of the master to enlighten or instruct. The Festschriften usually honor men; few deserving women are ever made the subjects of Festschriften if for no other reason than their reluctance to admit to a definite age. Exceptions in this wasteland of depressing dullness are Festschriften for composers, such as the ones for Schoenberg, which contain valuable articles by his faithful disciples.

Feuersnot. An opera by Richard Straus that was described by him as a *Sing-gedicht*, a "singing poem." The title of the opera literally means "fire-famine." The libretto is based on a Flemish legend, *The Extinguished Fires of Audenarde*. A recluse tries to kiss a girl who ridicules him publicly, unaware that he possesses magical power. In revenge he creates a fire-famine that extinguishes all lights in the entire village. The girl quickly repents, and he withdraws his ban on fires. The opera was first produced in Dresden on November 21, 1901, with Strauss himself conducting.

Fiasco. An utter failure of a theatrical or other performance. Music history abounds in stories of fiascos of great masterpieces that eventually became parts of the standard repertory. The fiasco of Wagner's *Tannhäuser* in Paris in 1861 is notorious; he withdrew the opera after three disastrous performances. The first production of Puccini's *Madama Butterfly* in 1904 was a resounding fiasco; Puccini and his librettist notified the publishers that in view of the negative reaction on the part of the audience, they were withdrawing it from further performance. Melodramatic biographies of Bizet describe his anguish at the fiasco of *Carmen*, which supposedly drove him to an early grave. Aside from the fact that nobody, not even a composer, ever died of chagrin, *Carmen* was anything but a fiasco. It had a continuous run of three months after its initial production, and Bizet died on the night of its 23rd performance. The Italian word *fiasco* means a flask or a bottle; just how it acquired the meaning of an ignominious failure is not clear.

Fibonacci-Mobile. A work by Ernst Krenek scored for string quartet and two pianos. Its contrapuntal ingredients are arranged according to the Fibonacci series, in which each number is the sum of its two antecedent numbers. Krenek called his work a mobile because of the various changing combinations that are involved in the technique of its compostion. It was first performed at the Congregation of the Arts of Dartmouth College in New Hampshire on July 7, 1965.

Fidelio. Beethoven's only opera, first produced in Vienna on November 20, 1805. Derived from a French play, it bears the alternative title *Die eheliche Liebe* (*The Conjugal Love*). Florestan is in a dungeon for his opposition to a tyrannical Spanish governor. His faithful wife Leonore enters the jail service in a boy's attire, taking the name Fidelio, symbolic of her fidelity. Political and marital virtue triumphs when a new governor, announced by a resonant fanfare backstage, orders the release of Florestan and the arrest of his tormentor. Beethoven wrote four overtures for the opera, one of them entitled *Fidelio* and three others entitled *Leonore*.

The Fiery Angel. An opera by Prokofiev, performed posthumously in Venice on September 14, 1955. A mystical 16th-century girl becomes possessed by the vision of a former lover whom she identifies as her guardian angel. Exorcism is initiated by the Grand Inquisitor, and when it fails, the unfortunate maiden is accused of carnal intercourse with the devil and is burned at the stake. The underlying satirical intent is suggested in the score by acrid harmonies and angular melodies.

Fifth Symphony. Whenever music lovers speak of the Fifth Symphony, it is tacitly understood to be Beethoven's Symphony No. 5, in which "fate knocks at Beethoven's door.'' But did Beethoven really say anything like that in relation to the portentous four notes of the opening theme? The story originated with Beethoven's biographer, Anton Schindler, but he was only 12 years old when the symphony was written. Carl Czerny, who was very close to Beethoven, asserted that the motif was inspired by the call of the oriole or the goldfinch, the two birds that Beethoven often heard during his walks in the Vienna woods. If it *was* fate, would Beethoven not have orchestrated these notes with a flourish of trumpets or trombones? Yet he did not, preferring to open the symphony with two rather soft clarinet sounds accompanied by strings. Furthermore, when we delve into Beethoven's many hesitant sketches for the opening movement of this symphony, we find the fate motif curiously obfuscated. On the other hand, there is the unmistakable evidence that Beethoven was obsessed with the rhythm of three short notes and one long note during the period when he composed the Fifth. The figure occurs and recurs in the Piano Concerto No. 4, in the *Appassionata* Sonata, and in the String Quartet, op. 74. Remarkably enough, these works are closely related to C minor, the tonality of Symphony No. 5, and in each case the three short notes are eighth notes. Whatever the origin, the fate of the fate motif is awe-inspiring. During World War II, the Allied Propaganda Service broadcast the fate motif to the Nazi-occupied continent of Europe to signal *V* for *Victory* in Morse code, which happens to be three dots and a dash. The second movement of the Symphony is a gentle theme with variations. There follows a Scherzo in triple time. The fate motif makes its appearance once more, scanned persistently in the drums, and, after a dynamic transition, explodes in thundering C major in the finale. The first performance of the Symphony No. 5 took place in Vienna on December 22, 1808. The score is dedicated to Prince von Lobkowitz (the patron of music to whom the *Eroica* Symphony was also assigned), and to Count Rasoumowsky, the Russian ambassador to Vienna.

Other well-known "Fifths" include Tchaikovsky's Symphony No. 5, which, like his Symphony No. 4, is dominated by the sense of fate. Tchaikovsky definitely referred to this "fateful" connection in his notebooks. It is remarkable that the opening theme is syncopated similarly to that of the Symphony No. 4 and that its range is limited to the first tetrachord of the minor scale, as was that of its predecessor. Tchaikovsky's Symphony No. 5 was first performed in St. Petersburg on November 17, 1888, and both it and his Symphony No. 4 have become standard orchestral works. Mendelssohn's Symphony No. 5 in D minor was first performed in Berlin on November 15, 1832. It is nicknamed *Reformation* Symphony because the last movement is based on the Lutheran chorale *Ein' feste Burg*. Mahler's Symphony No. 5 in C-sharp minor, often referred to as the *Giant* because of its length, was first performed in Cologne on October 18, 1904. It is in five sections, forming three larger movements. The first is funereal, passing suddenly to a stormy explosion of sound. The next section is an extended Scherzo, which is followed by an Adagietto. It concludes with a Rondo. The structure of the work is unique, for it has sections in every one of the 24 major and minor scales, each division specifically marked by key signatures.

La Figure humaine. A cantata for double chorus *a cappella* by Francis Poulenc, to a symbolic text voicing the irresistible desire for liberty. (Poulenc wrote it during the Nazi occupation of Paris.) It was first performed in London on March 25, 1945.

La Fille du régiment (The Daughter of the Regiment). An opera by Donizetti, first produced in Paris on February 11, 1840. The romantic story tells of a girl who is brought up by a regiment of soldiers and becomes an army mascot. A crisis occurs when her aunt reclaims her and takes her to her castle. The soldiers lead an assault on her aunt's stronghold, and the girl is reinstated as the "daughter of the regiment."

La Fille du tambour-major. A comic opera by Offenbach, first performed in Paris on December 13, 1879. It was the last work by Offenbach produced in his lifetime. The plot resembles Donizetti's *La Fille du régiment*. The action is set in Lombardy in 1806. Napoleon has just crossed the Alps and been welcomed by the Italian populace as liberator from the oppressive Austrian rule. An errant young convent girl flirts with a French lieutenant; it develops that she herself is the daughter of a French drum major. After a number of melodramatic imbroglios, the young couple is reunited in Milan as Napoleon enters the city. There are merry waltzes and victorious marches in the score.

Film music. During the early days of motion pictures, a theater owner would engage a pianist or an organist to provide appropriate music for the moving images on the screen. The type of accompaniment generally followed the "doctrine of affects." Romantic scenes called for sentimental salon music; themes of sadness were enhanced by passages in a mournful minor key. Danger and tragedy were depicted by chromatic runs harmonized by the diminished-seventh chord, the *accorde di stupefazione*. Realistic sound effects were provided behind the scene by a homemade rain machine, consisting of a wooden cylinder covered with a piece of rough cloth and rotated by a crank mechanism, or a thunder machine making rolling noise by rubbing corrugated metal plates over a washboard. Most silent movie pianists were content with playing standard Classical or Romantic pieces within their meager repertory, but there were also truly inspired artists who improvised self-consistent compositions, faithfully following the action on the screen. To aid silent movie pianists and organists, special collections of sheet music were published with a table of contents indicating subject matter—gladness, sadness, madness, married felicity, faithless duplicity, infatuation, assassination, horse races, balloon ascension—all this garnished by ethnic folk music of many lands.

Apart from such trivialities, respectable composers showed interest in writing movie scores to be played by a movie pianist or to be recorded on the phonograph. One of the earliest cinema scores was composed in 1908 by Saint-Saëns for the French movie *L'Assassinat du Duc de Guise*; it is scored for strings, piano, and harmonium. Another early film score, *Napoléon* by Arthur Honegger, was issued as an instrumental suite in 1922. The first application of a cinematographic scene in the theater was in the ballet *Relâche* by Erik Satie, produced in 1924. Other composers who contributed to the art of early film music were Antheil, Copland, Prokofiev, and Shostakovich. Richard Strauss arranged his opera *Der Rosenkavalier* for a film. With the advent of sound in motion pictures, specially composed background music was provided on the soundtrack. At first it consisted of recorded compositions of a popular genre. Producers and directors quite frequently engaged a "ghost" composer to write music according to specifications. Because most movie directors who appeared in the list of credits as composers of musical scores could not read music, they usually engaged a musical amanuensis; their own part in such "composition" consisted in whistling snatches of tunes or beating the desired rhythm. Thus Charlie Chaplin availed himself of the services of Hanns Eisler and David Raksin for several of his films.

The most successful movie composers in Hollywood were not always the most talented or the most imaginative. Of these, the names of Max Steiner and Alfred Newman are outstanding; they enhanced the sonorities of the soundtrack to the dimensions of a full orchestra that they conducted themselves. When their imagination flagged, they helped themselves by quotations, literal or garbled, from Wagner, Tchaikovsky, and Rachmaninoff. When Stravinsky came to America, an admirer tried to arrange for him to write a movie score. He submitted the offer to a movie mogul. "Stravinsky?" the mogul granted. "Yes, I've heard of him. How much will he charge?" "Well, twenty thousand dollars," suggested the go-between. "Twenty thousand dollars?!" exclaimed the magnate. "For five thousand more I can get Max Steiner!" Stravinsky never wrote a movie score. Before he emigrated to America, Schoenberg composed a work entitled *Accompaniment to a Cinema Scene*; it was subdivided into three sections—*Threatening Danger*, *Anxiety*, and *Catastrophe*. Schoenberg, sincerely or not, tried to emulate the movie formula, but the score was dodecaphonic. Because dissonance was not exactly a movie magnate's cup of tea, the score was never used. An important contribution to film music was made by Erich Wolfgang Korngold, an erstwhile Viennese *Wunderkind* who spent many years in Hollywood. His scores retain their purely musical significance even when detached from their visual counterpart. Bernard Herrmann successfully combined his theatrical sense with progressive techniques. Ernst Toch excelled in scores for movie mysteries. David Raksin wrote numerous remarkable scores for the movies; concert suites of the scores of the films *Laura* and *The Bad and the Beautiful* are frequently performed by major symphony orchestras. Among other film composers, Alex North, Virgil Thomson, and Miklós Rózsa are notable. In films of futuristic content, electronic music has been supplied by several avant-garde composers. Henry Mancini has specialized in movie music of imaginative brilliance. John Williams has become highly successful in providing music for films of blatant heroic content, including such science-fiction hits as *Star Wars* and *Close Encounters of the Third Kind*.

Finale. In instrumental music, the last movement of a composition. In opera, the finale is a summary of all major musical themes and the resolution of tangled threads of the plot. A grand finale is a choral conclusion with the participation of most principal characters. Wagner and his followers, however, regarded the finale as a musical supererogation.

Fingal's Cave. A concert overture by Mendelssohn; a perfect example of a Romantic overture, a paragon of the genre. Unlike most Romantic compositions, *Fingal's Cave* owes its inspiration to an actual visit by Mendelssohn to the Hebrides in Scotland during his concert tour in 1829. Impressed by the somber dampness and mysterious surroundings of Fingal's Cave, Mendelssohn wrote an expertly fashioned piece in the darksome key of B minor. It was first performed in London on May 14, 1832. Queen Victoria loved it.

Fingerboard. The elongated section on string instruments over which the strings are stretched. On the guitar, frets, spaced along the fingerboard, guide the player's fingers. Violins and other string instruments are not equipped with frets, which is a pity, for such string fretting would spare the nerve fretting of those forced to listen to a family prodigy torturing the violin out of tune.

Fingering. The art of fingering on musical instruments assumed an educational importance in the 18th century; editions of Classical music, particularly for piano, rarely indicated what fingers to use and when. The task of fingering was left to editors of the classics published in annotated editions in the 19th century. The rule of thumb for standard piano fingering was not to use the thumb on the black keys except in cases of dire necessity, as in F-sharp major arpeggios, or in Chopin's so-called *Black Key* Etude. The chromatic scale is fingered by pianists using the thumb and the index finger in alternation, and the middle finger when convenient. The problem of fingering on string instruments is not so complex, because the shifts of positions give the player an ample opportunity for technical accommodation.

Finlandia. A symphonic poem by Jean Sibelius, written as an expression of his love for Finland at the time when his country was a part of the Russian empire. After Finland gained its independence the work assumed the importance of a patriotic declaration. It was first performed in Helsingfors (Helsinki) on July 2, 1900, under its original title, *Suomi*, the Finnish word for Finland.

Fioritura. Literally, a florid adornment, from the Italian word *fiore*, a flower; the plural of *fioritura* is *fioriture*. It was a common practice for Italian singers to embellish their arias with arpeggios, gruppetti, and trills, often obscuring the main melodic line by such ornamentation. A story is told about Adelina Patti who, as a young girl, sang for Rossini one of his own arias. Rossini was voluble in praise of her singing. "But, pray, who is the composer of this aria?" he inquired. In modern times, no prima donna would presume to go beyond the printed text of an aria except in cadenzas. Toscanini was known to explode in flowery Italian invective when a singer added as much as an unauthorized grace note to his or her solo.

Fire Symphony (Feuersymphonie). Symphony No 59 by Haydn, written in 1769, in the key of A major. Who gave this name to the work, when and why is a mystery, but perhaps the music has some connection with the play *The Conflagration* that was presented at Esterház where Haydn was employed.

The Firebird (L'Oiseau de feu). Stravinsky's first ballet, produced by Diaghilev's Ballet Russe in Paris on June 25, 1910. Like his predecessors, Stravinsky drew upon Russian folklore for this score. The Firebird gives the heroic Ivan Tsarevich a flaming feather as a reward for his freeing it after capture. The feather is a magic wand that helps Ivan when he himself is captured by the evil magician Kashchey. The infernal dance of the finale is bewitching in its angular rhythms. In 1937 Warner Bros. made a film entitled *The Firebird*, featuring a profligate roué who plays a phonograph recording of the piece that so impresses a virginal maiden who lives on the floor below that she falls into his arms and is promptly deflowered. Stravinsky sued the film company for defamation of character, but the French judge could not understand why Stravinsky became so exercised about it. "Mais c'est le plus grand compliment du monde pour un compositeur quand sa musique peut séduire!" ("But it is the greatest compliment in the world for a composer when his music can seduce!") Stravinsky was awarded the token sum of one French franc for the "moral damage" he suffered.

Fireworks. An orchestral work that young Stravinsky wrote for the wedding of the daughter of his revered master Rimsky-Korsakov. It was first performed in St. Petersburg on June 17, 1908. The score is very much in the tradition of the Russian national school, but its brilliant sparks of rhythmic fireworks presage the Stravinsky of the future.

Fireworks Music. More fully, *Royal Fireworks Music*, or still more precisely, *The Musick for the Royal Fireworks*. An orchestral suite Handel wrote to celebrate the Peace of Aix-la-Chapelle, which ended the protracted and tedious war of the Austrian Succession (also known as King George's War). It was first performed at Green Park, London, on April 27, 1749. The "peace" itself is portrayed by a modest siciliana, which is followed by a fast march entitled, quite properly, *La Réjouissance*, and scored for a large orchestra.

Fish horn. A colloquial American term for the oboe, common since the middle of the 19th century, to judge by a remarkable order issued by Vice Admiral Porter of the U.S. Naval Academy in Annapolis, dated October 25, 1867: "Midshipman Thompson (1st class), who plays so abominably on a fish horn, will oblige me by going outside the limits when he wants to practice or he will find himself coming out of the little end of the horn."

Five Pieces for Orchestra. A remarkable group of pieces by Anton von Webern, written in 1911. They are extremely short. One of them counts barely six bars and lasts 19 seconds and is scored for clarinet, trumpet, trombone, mandolin, celesta, harp, drum, violin, and viola, each of these entering alone and thus creating a chain of sounds that may be described as a melody of timbres (*Farbenmelodie*). Yielding to the temptation of forming symbolic or psychological associations, Webern at first attached descriptive titles to each of the pieces but on sober reflection rescinded them. Originally these designations were *Urbild, Verwandlung, Rückkehr, Erinnerung, Die Seele* (*Initial Idea, Metamorphosis, Return, Recollection, The Soul*). Webern conducted the first performance in Zurich on June 22, 1926.

Flamenco. A popular Andalusian art of singing and dancing, accompanied mainly by guitar and castanets, which gradually developed into an important folk art form. The meters and rhythms follow the Spanish models in triple measures. The lyrics, influenced by gypsy motifs, reflect the sentiments of love, fortune, sorrow, and death. Two genres of flamenco singing are known: *cante jondo*, "deep song," and *cante chico*, "small song." The singing is usually introduced by the stimulating exclamations, "Ay! Ay!" When the singing is accompanied by footstamping, the dance is called *zapateado*, "shoe dance."

Flammes sombres. One of Scriabin's last piano pieces, composed in 1914. It represents his ultimate idiom, almost totally divorced from traditional tonality. There is no key signature.

Flatterzunge. The German term for flutter-tonguing, a method of playing a wind instrument by sticking the tongue in the mouthpiece, or by rolling the tongue as if trying to pronounce the liquid consonants "l" and "r." *Flatterzunge* is vulgarly known among wind players as the "French kiss"; it is also indecorously called *frullato* in Italian, *Zungenschlag* in German, and *coup de langue* in French. The technique has been known since the early 18th century, but it has been eschewed in actual playing as being indecent. Not until the modern music of two centuries later did it come to be accepted as a legitimate effect.

Die Fledermaus (The Bat). An operetta by Johann Strauss, first performed in Vienna on April 5, 1874. The bat of the title is the costume used by one of the characters at a masked ball. An Austrian baron, who is sentenced to prison for a petty offense, eludes the police and goes to a masked ball. His wife, suspicious of his conduct, goes to the same ball disguised as a Hungarian countess. Not recognizing her physical attributes, the baron flirts with her. A series of mistaken identities reaches a climax when the baron exchanges clothes with his own lawyer and enters the jail in order to extract a confession from another suspect and clear himself. A happy ending is vouchsafed when all jail sentences are suspended and guests from the masked ball join the principals to drink a toast in praise of champagne, the king of wines. No matter how impenetrable the plot is, particularly to non-Austrians, *Die Fledermaus* enjoys success everywhere.

Der fliegende Holländer (The Flying Dutchman). An opera by Wagner, first produced in Dresden on January 2, 1843. The libretto is by Wagner himself, after an old legend. Originally, a similar libretto by Wagner was used for the opera *Le Vaisseau fantôme* by an insignificant composer named Dietsch. When that opera utterly failed, Wagner returned to the legend and created his own opera that became a minor masterpiece. *Der fliegende Holländer* is a ship on which a mariner is doomed to sail until he finds a woman capable of total devotion. Stormy seas drive the ship off course to a Norwegian fjord. The voyager hears a Norwegian girl sing a ballad about the doomed ship; he realizes that she would redeem him. In her eagerness, she leaps toward the ship from a cliff and perishes. Her sacrifice is his redemption, and together they are lifted to the skies.

Flores. Latin for "flowers"; used in the Middle Ages for embellishments in vocal and instrumental music. The insertion of supernumerary notes above and below the melody notes was named *florificatio.* Usually such embellishments were added to the discantus, the "upper voice," but sometimes even the ostensibly unalterable cantus firmus was adorned by florid ornamentation with *pulchrae ascensiones et descensiones.* Such "pretty ups and downs" were also called *licentiae* ("licentiousnesses") and *elegantiae* ("elegancies"). The Italian words *fiori* ("flowers") and *fioretti* ("little flowers") were used in the same sense as the Latin *flores.* All these attractive descriptions have been eventually replaced by generic designations of ornaments.

Flügel. The German word for the grand piano, literally a "wing," referring to the wing-like shape of the instrument.

Flügelhorn. A brass instrument closely related to the cornet; the name is also applied to a tuba. The word is probably a corrupted form of *Bügelhorn,* "bugle horn." The flugelhorn first came into use in Austria about 1825.

Flute. The most ancient wind instrument, spontaneously evolved by populations in all parts of the world, from Mesopotamia to the Andes, from China to Central Africa. Primitive flutes were all vertical pipes, of the type that later came to be called recorders. They were made of baked clay or reeds with perforated holes that would change the pitch when one or several of them were covered by a finger. The ocarina is essentially a flute, but it looks like a surrealist sculpture of a goose (hence the name, *oca* being "goose" in Italian).

Musical mythology is strewn with stories about the appearance of the flute. When the cloven-footed god of the woods Pan pursued the nymph Syrinx, she was turned into a reed to escape him. Heartbroken, Pan made a panpipe of reeds to commemorate his beloved. In pre-Columbian South America, Indians made flutes out of bones, samples of which still exist. There is a legend of a Peruvian Indian whose beloved died young. Disconsolate, he went to her place of burial, exhumed one of her legs, and fashioned a flute out of her tibia. He played wistful pentatonic melodies on it, and this intimate contact with a part of the body of his beloved gave him surcease from his sorrow. The Pied Piper of Hamelin lured away the town children by playing on his flute. In Mozart's opera *The Magic Flute*, the hero is saved from disaster by playing a tune on his faithful flute. In poetry, flutes are forever sweet, soft, and pure. Milton speaks in *Paradise Lost* of "flutes and soft recorders moving in perfect phalanx." Swinburne poetizes about "the pure music of the flutes of Greece." In a grim Brothers Grimm tale, a young prince is slain by his brothers in a rivalry for the throne. A shepherd finds one of his whitened bones, makes holes in it, and plays on it. The bone flute tells the story of the unbrotherly deed. Mahler set this tale to music in his choral work *Das klagende Lied*.

The flute seems to embody the legendary harmony of the spheres, for it is laden with rich overtones; an attentive ear can discern even the nontempered seventh partial tone when a flute is played in its low register. The flute is the heavenly bird of the symphony and opera. Birds of the forest speak to Siegfried in Wagner's *Ring* through the voice of the flutes. Stravinsky's Firebird is a flute, and so is the helpful bird in Prokofiev's *Peter and the Wolf*. It is the flute that sings the part of the nightingale in Beethoven's *Pastoral* Symphony and in Stravinsky's *Le Rossignol*. The flute is the most agile of wind instruments, capable of skipping from one note to another with great ease. It mates in perfect harmony with the human voice. When Lucia goes mad in Donizetti's opera, she sings her poignant fioritura accompanied by a solo flute. The modern flute is the transverse, or horizontal, flute in which the sound is produced by blowing across a side hole. Because it was first introduced in Germany, the transverse flute became known as the German flute, whereas the recorder, greatly popular in England, was called the English flute. The transverse flute came of age when Quantz, the court musician to Frederick the Great (who, incidentally, was the best flutist among royalty), published in 1752 his famous treatise on the art of playing the *flute traversière*, as it was known in French. In symphonic works, flute parts are frequently used in pairs, like their fellow wind instruments the oboes, clarinets, bassoons, horns, and trumpets. The use of a single flute in a symphonic score, as in Beethoven's Symphony No. 4, is an exception. Concertos for flute were written by Quantz, Handel, and Mozart. Brahms assigned a pastoral solo in the finale of his Symphony No. 1 to the flute. French composers have been particularly fond of the instrument. Debussy wrote a piece for flute solo entitled *Syrinx* in honor of the nymph so persistently pursued by Pan. His *Prélude à l'après-midi d'un faune* opens with a solo flute. Like all wind instruments, flutes are members of a family. The range of the modern flute, also called concert flute, extends from middle C through three octaves, but it can be overblown to produce the high C-sharp, D, and even E-flat. In modern flutes, a special key is provided to produce the low B. Theobald Boehm, the great German flute manufacturer, enhanced the technique of flute playing by producing a new system of fingering and by rearranging positions of the keys. Most flutes are made of alloys of silver, although some rich amateurs have owned flutes made of gold. The present-day flutist James Galway performs on a gold flute. The modern French flutist Georges Barrère had a flute made of platinum, and Edgar Varèse wrote a piece for him entitled *Density 21.5*, which is the density of platinum.

The familiar modern transverse flute is called *grande flute* in French and *grosse Flöte* in German to distinguish it from *petite flute* or *kleine Flöte*, which is the piccolo flute, or simply piccolo in English usage. In Italian the flute is *flauto*, and the piccolo is *flauto piccolo* or *ottavino* (literally, a "little octave thing"). The range of the piccolo is an octave higher than that of the regular flute, but it lacks the C and C-sharp in its low register. Its range is three octaves, its high C being the same pitch as the highest note on the piano; no other instrument can rise to such stratospheric heights. Beethoven introduced the piccolo in the finale of his Symphony No. 5. The alto flute is a fourth below the regular concert flute; it is also known as flute in G. Ravel's ballet *Daphnis et Chloë* has an important part for the alto flute, which invokes the spirit of Pan. The bass flute is an elephantine, low-voice member of the family, having a range an octave below that of the standard flute. It is a long instrument and requires considerable lung power to blow and superlative lip technique to articulate. The Parisian-American composer Betsy Jolas wrote a piece for piccolo and bass flute. There is also a monster of a flute, the double-bass flute, which theoretically ought to produce a sound two octaves below that of the concert flute. When an American manufacturer of the double-bass flute demonstrated it at a congress of flutists, however, he blew and blew into it without making even a wheeze. The *flûte d'amour* may also be mentioned; in Italian it is *flauto d'amore* and in German, *Lieblichflöte*; there is no English name for it, which is just as well; it would be ludicrous to call it a "love flute." It is pitched a minor third below the concert flute.

Avant-garde composers, annoyed by the "sweet" sounds of the flute, have tried their best (or their worst) to improve on it by instructing the players to blow through the flute without producing a recognizable pitch, or to clap the keys without blowing. Double-tonguing and triple-tonguing, known as the *flatterzunge* or "fluttertongue" technique, are favorites in modern flute parts. Unnatural harmonics have also been coaxed out of it. In the last quarter of the 20th century, the flute has been incorporated into rock and jazz groups, making up for its rather ethereal sound by amplifying it electronically.

Folia. A dance that originated in Portugal about 1500 in popular festivals and theatrical performances, usually accompanied by rhythmic hand clapping and clacking of castanets. The strange name, which means "folly," points at an apparently orgiastic type of the dance, particularly in its Spanish form. One Spanish writer of the early 17th century describes the action of the dancers as if "they have abandoned all reason." In later theoretical references, the folia was usually coupled with sarabandes and chaconnes. Actually, the folia has very little madness in it; it is a rather stately rhythmic dance in triple time with a long second beat, and it is usually in a minor mode.

Foot. The common unit measuring the length of a vibrating air column in an organ pipe. In organ playing the standard is an 8-foot C, corresponding to the pitch of the C two lines below the bass staff, which agitates an air column about 8 feet long. By extension, any organ stop producing the normal pitch of the key depressed on the manual or the pedal is called an 8-foot tone. A 16-foot tone is one octave below this 8-foot tone because the air column activated is twice as long (a 4-foot stop corresponds to a sound an octave above the note representing an 8-foot stop). Sometimes this nomenclature is used for other instruments, so that if the cello is said to produce the normal 8-foot tone, then the double bass can be likened to the organ producing a 16-foot tone, one octave lower than the cello for any given note.

For He's a Jolly Good Fellow. The English version of a satirical French tune, *Malbrouk s'en va-t-en guerre*. The surmise that the Malbrouk in the song was the famous Duke of Marlborough and that the song expressed the French contempt for the great British warrior is not supported by evidence.

Forlana. An Italian dance in sextuple meter that originated in the province of Friuli, popular in Venice in the 18th century. Bach has a forlana in his orchestral suite in C major, and Ravel included one in his *Tombeau de Couperin*.

Form. In music, as in literature, drama, and the pictorial arts, form is equivalent to organization. As in a living organism that is comprised of separate parts performing disparate functions, all of which are coordinated for the normal operation of the entire body, so in music does form assemble all component elements of a given composition to produce the best possible impression of unity. Because only one sense, that of hearing, is the object of a musical form, separate sections must contribute to auditory unification. This may be achieved by means of melodic symmetry, organic alternation of melodic sections, successions of tones within the same harmony, and combinations of tones within a contrapuntal framework—all these animated by a rhythmic flow following a certain natural pulse of strong and weak accents. In high developments of the formal elements, a deliberate departure from the basic form of rhythmic or melodic symmetry, harmonic unity, or contrapuntal concordance results in a new form that may impress a rigid musical mind as being formless. The accusation of formlessness was directed at the Wagnerian "endless melody," the Lisztian symphonic poem, and impressionistic monothematic compositions. In the course of time, such "formless" music becomes itself established as a classical form. Paradoxically, even composers who profess formlessness as their aesthetic aims become inventors of more complex forms based on principles of organization far removed from simple symmetry or thematic development. Thus Edgar Varèse propounded the principle of "organized sound" as the only requirement of formal composition.

Formants. The formative components of a given pitch—that is, a series of natural overtones as it affects the individual instrumental timbre. Stockhausen proposed to specify the term to designate the rhythmic phrases as functions of the overtone spectrum of a given pitch, so that the second partial tone would represent the rhythmic duration of one-half the metric unit, the third partial (that is, a fifth over an octave) would represent one-third of the rhythmic unit, and so on.

La forza del destino. An opera by Verdi, first produced by an Italian opera company in St. Petersburg, Russia, on November 10, 1862. The force of destiny of the title seems to decree that an eager lover accidentally kill the father of his beloved and flee in horror to a monastery. His intended bride follows him there dressed in a man's attire. Her brother, seeking vengeance, also tracks down the killer and, not recognizing his sister under her monastic garb, mortally stabs her before dying himself from a wound inflicted by the now completely disoriented lover. The music is amazingly durable in its uncompromisingly melodramatic lilt, despite the nonsensical libretto.

The Fountains of Rome. A tone poem by Respighi, first performed in Rome on March 11, 1917. Four famous Roman fountains are portrayed in this picturesque scene, forming a fine companion piece for Respighi's *The Pines of Rome*.

Four Norwegian Moods. A symphonic suite by Stravinsky, conceived along nonethnological lines and without any quotations from Norwegian folk tunes. He conducted its first performance in Cambridge, Massachusetts, on January 13, 1944.

Four Saints in Three Acts. "An opera to be sung" by Virgil Thomson, first produced by the Society of Friends and Enemies of Modern Music in Hartford, Connecticut, on February 8, 1934. The libretto is by Gertrude Stein and is in accordance with her irrational tenets. Thus, in the play there are really four acts and a dozen saints, some in duplicate. Her famous nonsensical line, "Pigeons on the grass, alas," is sung. The music is disarmingly triadic and ostentatiously repetitious, but the opera is mesmerizing.

Fourth Symphony in F Minor. One of Tchaikovsky's most famous symphonies, in four movements, first performed in Moscow on February 22, 1878. Its opening syncopated subject was to Tchaikovsky the call of Fate, although he did not use this word as a subtitle.

Fourth Symphony in G Major. The most romantic of Mahler's symphonies. Mahler himself conducted the first performance in Munich on November 25, 1901. The symphony is in four parts, the last movement having a soprano solo. The two principal themes of the first movement are uninhibitedly sentimental to the point of lachrymosity. This quality attracted the producers of the film *Death in Venice*, after a novella by Thomas Mann, and they used the themes as leading motifs in the film score.

Francesca da Rimini. A symphonic fantasy by Tchaikovsky, first performed in Moscow on March 9, 1877. It was inspired by the tragic episode in Dante's *Inferno*, in which Francesca and her lover Paolo die at the hands of her jealous husband. Tchaikovsky was very much impressed by the dramatic illustrations of Dante's poem by the popular French painter Gustave Doré. As an epigraph, Tchaikovsky selected the lines, "*nessun maggior dolore/ Che ricordarsi del tempo felice/ Nella miseria*," which he kept repeating in his letters and conversations as a motto of his own life, in which there was "no greater sorrow than to recall happy times in the midst of misery." The lyric melody of Francesca is one of the most characteristic effusions of Tchaikovsky's melancholy muse. His depiction of the tempestuous winds in Dante's *Inferno*, using running chromatics, is quite dramatic.

Die Frau ohne Schatten (The Woman Without a Shadow). An opera by Richard Strauss, first produced in Vienna on October 10, 1919. A royal princess, married to an oriental potentate, is barren because she cannot cast a shadow, a symbol of fertility. When she is given a chance to buy the shadow of a poor woman, she desists, not wishing to deprive the woman of childbearing. For this noble act she is granted the joy of a shadow by the benevolent spirits so that she can become a mother after all.

Der Freischütz. An opera by Weber, produced in Berlin on June 18, 1821. An ambitious sharpshooter, in love with a country girl, agrees to trade his soul to the devil for seven magic bullets that will guarantee a victory in a shooting contest. The last bullet must go where the demonic purchaser directs. The Freischütz hits his six preliminary marks, but the last is aimed at his bride. She is saved by supernatural intervention; the marksman confesses his deal with the devil and is absolved. *Der Freischütz* is regarded as the first truly Romantic opera. Its vivacious overture is often performed as a concert piece.

French horn. The reason for the name of this instrument of honorable ancestry is unclear. The explanation that it is called French horn to prevent confusion with the English horn is unconvincing, for in other languages this distinction is not made. In German it is called simply *Horn*, in French it is *cor*, in Italian *corno*, and in Spanish it is *tromba*, without the pseudonational adjective. It is sometimes called *Waldhorn* ("forest horn") in German; the Russians transcribe it as *valtorna*. In its modern construction it is also called *valved horn* to distinguish it from the early valveless horns that could produce only a series of overtones from the fundamental sound. Even with valves that enable it to play all chromatic tones (the French actually call it *cor chromatique*), however, the glory of the French horn remains in the production of the natural overtones. Its range is wider than that of any other brass instrument, covering nearly four octaves, with possible extensions beyond the upper limit. Its tone production is most unusual. Its mouthpiece is very small, and its bell is very large. To produce high tones, the player must adjust the lips in a precise acrobatic manner. The danger of hitting a wrong note on the horn in the upper registers haunts even the greatest horn virtuosos. One of the most difficult horn solos occurs in *Till Eulenspiegel* of Richard Strauss, in which the player reaches high into the empyrean regions. The story goes that the hornist told Strauss before the first rehearsal that the passage was unplayable; Strauss retorted that he had gotten the idea for this part while listening to the horn player himself practice during the tuning periods. Some say that the horn is the simulacrum of the gastrointestinal system, for it is coiled like a large intestine, with the mouthpiece representing the colon. Horn players have to empty their instrument periodically to remove the accumulated saliva that is apt to cause tonal constipation. A violinist who was engaged to play the Horn Trio of Brahms demanded a pair of galoshes before he went on stage. Before the advent of the chromatic horn, horn parts were written in Classical scores in the key of the composition. When a modulation occurred, the player had to insert or remove a piece of tubing, called a crook, to obtain the right pitch. In modern practice, however, horns are employed almost invariably in the key of F, and are notated so that the players transpose a fifth down in the treble clef or a fourth up in the bass clef.

Der Friedenstag (The Day of Peace). An opera by Richard Strauss, produced in Munich on July 24, 1938. It deals with the conclusion of the Thirty Years' War, which devastated Europe, and it ends with a choral invocation to peace. Its repeated performances on the eve of Hitler's plunge into total war held especial meaning to Germans deprived of their freedom of speech.

From the Apocalypse. A symphonic poem by Anatoli Liadov, based on Russian hymn tunes and ending with seven apocalyptic thunderclaps in the brass and drums. It was first performed in St. Petersburg on December 8, 1912.

From the House of the Dead. A posthumous opera by Leoš Janáček to his own libretto after Dostoyevsky's partly autobiographical novel of the same name describing his Siberian exile. It was produced in Brno on April 12, 1930.

From the New World. The most famous symphony of Dvořák, so named because he composed the score during his 1893 sojourn in New York. It was first performed by the New York Philharmonic on December 15, 1893. The symphony is in E minor, in four movememts, the most popular of which is the second movement, marked Largo, that suggests a Negro spiritual. Much speculation was aroused by this approximation, but Dvořák denied having used any specific Negro air and insisted that the melody was simply the expression of the homesickness of an uprooted Czech finding himself in a new land. One of Dvořák's American pupils, William Arms Fisher, adapted a set of words to the tune, "Going Home, Going Home." It is interesting that the Largo is set in the key of D-flat major, miles away from the tonic E of the work. The symphony was until recently listed as No. 5. Then four earlier unpublished symphonies of Dvořák were discovered, and the number of *From the New World* had to be changed to No. 9, creating considerable confusion among cataloguers.

From the Steeples and the Mountains. A remarkable work by Charles Ives, scored for church bells and brass. Ives wrote in the score: "After the brass stops, the chimes sound on until they die away. . . . . From the steeples—the bells!—Then the rocks on the mountains begin to shout!" As with most works by Ives, it was not performed until decades after its composition in 1905. Its first public performance was in New York on July 30, 1965.

Froschquartett (Frog Quartet). The nickname of Haydn's String Quartet, op. 50, No. 6, in D major, of 1787. It would take an expert ranunculogist to discern froglike croaking in the music. The quartet is also known under the title *The House on Fire*.

Frottola. A type of accompanied song popular in Northern Italy in the 16th century. The term is probably derived from the Italian word *frotta*, a "flock," because the frottola was composed of unusual or unconnected melodic ingredients. A collection of frottole was published by the famous Venetian music printer Petrucci; they are arranged in simple harmonies with symmetrical rhythms, usually accompanied by the lute or viols. Stylistically, the frottola is related to the Spanish villancico and the Italian strombotto.

F-sharp major. A tonality that has six sharps in its key signature and rarely appears as the principal key of a large work for orchestra, chorus, or piano. Curiously enough, however, it is favored by children of a tender age on account of its digitally convenient pentatonic disposition on the black keys of the piano. The so-called *Black Key* Etude of Chopin is in the key of F-sharp major. Scriabin was very fond of this tonality until he abandoned key signatures altogether. The enharmonic tonality of G-flat major has six flats and enjoys the favor of Romantic composers almost as much as its sharp alter ego.

F-sharp minor. A key characterized by a poetic delicacy of sentiment. There are but few symphonies in this key, but Haydn's *Farewell* Symphony, in which musicians leave the stage one after another until the first violinist is left alone as a mute symbol of the unhappiness of parting, is set in F-sharp minor. Miaskovsky, who wrote symphonies in practically every major and minor key, used F-sharp minor for his 21st symphony, entitled, perhaps significantly, *Symphonie Fantaisie*. It is interesting that two Russian piano concertos, the First by Rachmaninoff and the only piano concerto by Scriabin, are in the key of F-sharp minor; the romantic essence of these two concertos is unmistakable.

Fudging. A rustic form of fuguing, a type of free hymm singing once cultivated in the Ozarks, Missouri, and representing a rudimentary canonic form in unison, with traditional homophonic cadences.

Der Fuehrer's Face. A song by Oliver Wallace, published in 1942. It was a rather futile attempt to make a joke of Hitler in song. When Hitler was finished, so was the song.

Fugue. With the fugue, the art of polyphony reached its supreme achievement. The word *fugue* comes from the Latin *fuga*, "flight"; the metaphor is justified, because in the fugue one voice seems to flee from another. Morphologically, the fugue is a successor to the canon; it is also related to the caccia, a musical form of canonic construction whose title is the Italian for "chase." The fugue is far from being a mere development of the canon, however. The element of imitation is common to both, but whereas the canon is mechanical in its structure, the fugue introduces an entirely new principle of imitation through modulation from the tonic to the dominant. The classical fugue opens with the statement of the principal subject in a single unaccompanied voice. In the old Latin treatises on fugue, this subject is called *dux*, "leader." Its imitation, or answer, in the key of the dominant, is *comes*, "companion." When the *comes* enters in another voice, the part of the *dux* continues as a suitable counterpoint to the *comes*; this continuation of the *dux* is called the counter-subject. Fugues of only two voices are rare because they inevitably degenerate into a canon with the imitation in the dominant. In a fugue for three voices, the third voice enters again in the tonic, imitating the *dux* note by note but in another octave. In the meantime, new contrapuntal material is entered in the original part of the *dux*. If there are four voices, the fourth voice comes in again in the dominant, imitating the *comes* note by note. Fugues of five or more voices alternate in the keys of the tonic and the dominant, following the form of the *dux* and the *comes*.

What distinguishes the fugue from the canon and other types of literal imitation is the peculiar phenomenon of tonal answer. In a tonal answer, the dominant of the *dux* is echoed by the tonic of the original key. This kind of imitation creates a dislocation of the intervallic structure of the *dux*. Just how this peculiarity came into being is explained by the obsession of theorists with the primacy of the principal key and with the echoing relationship between the tonic and the dominant. Let us take a concrete example. The simple triadic phrase C, E, G, would normally be transposed into the dominant as G, B, D, an answer that is termed *real*. The tonal answer requires, however, that the dominant G in the *dux* should be answered not by D but by the tonic C. The tonal answer of C, E, G, therefore, must be G, B, C. Obviously, the "tune" of the *dux*, which is a simple ascending major triad, is radically altered in the tonal answer. Still more perplexing is the specification that after the ritual of answering the dominant in the *dux* by the tonic in the *comes* is completed, the transposition of the original subject, the *dux*, into the dominant key is resumed as if nothing had happened. An example of a fugue subject to which the tonal answer does not work is the first fugue in C major of the first book of Bach's *Well-Tempered Clavier*, for in it the dominant of the key in the *dux* is cluttered up by surrounding diatonic degrees. An example of a natural tonal answer is the second fugue in C minor from the same book, in which the dominant in the *dux* is as free as a mountain bird. It must be emphasized that the fugue is not so rigid a form as its formidable reputation makes out. The entries do not have to follow one another in mechanical succession. Bach, the bellwether of the art of the fugue, never followed the rules that are laid down in pedagogical treatises. His fugues were almost romantic in their flights of fancy, which is revealed in numerous little episodes that are ingeniously inserted between entries. Legend has it that students in the class of the fugue at the Paris Conservatoire in the 1890s were so expert and ingenious that the professors were forced to adopt the inhuman practice of *triage* in order to eliminate as many of them as possible. Accordingly, the professors rigged up fugue subjects so tangled in chromatics that only students possessing a sort of musical legerdemain could extricate themselves from the maze of possible and impossible combinations.

The formal structure of the fugue consists of three sections: exposition, development, and recapitulation. The exposition presents the *dux* and *comes* in the tonic and the dominant. In the development, the subject wanders far from the basic keys. It is then broken up into fragments gleaned from the intervallic ingredients of both *dux* and the tonal answer, appearing in a variety of keys, but not too far from the principal key along the cycle of scales. These thematic bits are tossed about in free interplay until the saturation point is reached when the dominant of the principal key is sounded to herald the entrance of the *dux*. The recapitulation is then celebrated in all solemnity, followed by an extended coda. In the coda, the *dux* and the *comes* are compressed and foreshortened. A stretto may make its appearance, in which the entries are telescoped in close canonic succession. The pedal point is embedded deep in the bass on the dominant, preliminary to the eschatological conclusion on the tonic.

Morphological alterations may take place; the *dux* and *comes* are stood on their heads by melodic inversion, in which the original ascending passages descend, and the formerly descending passages ascend. When such things happen, the harmony is subjected to considerable stress. Bach's Fugue No. 20 in A minor from the first book of *The Well-Tempered Clavier* is a magisterial example of a variety of systematic inversions. Unimaginable dissonances are formed in the process, and yet the teleological drive never falters. To suggest the magnificent symmetry of the main proportions of the fugue and the versatility of its ornaments, Ferruccio Busoni was moved in his monumental edition of Bach's *Well-Tempered Clavier* to give a graphic rendering of the structural elements of the Gothic cathedrals on the title page, which to his mind constituted the architectural counterpart of Bach's grand design. The fugue is indeed a cathedral of polyphony, in which the principal lines are enhanced by the gargoyles of florid ornamentation.

Fuguing tune. An American psalm vocalization that became popular in New England at the end of the 18th century. It is derived from the old English kind of psalmody, in which a hymn has a rudimentary canonic section before the concluding cadence. In America, the fuguing tunes of William Billings became well known; some enthusiastic musicologists describe them as the earliest American musical forms.

Full Moon and Empty Arms. An antimusical outrage, with words and music by Buddy Kaye and Ted Mossman, perpetrated on the lovely second subject in the defenseless and uncopyrighted body of Rachmaninoff's Piano Concerto No. 2. Crooners galore made capital out of it, as did the original graverobbers.

Fünf Orchesterstücke. Five orchestral pieces by Arnold Schoenberg in which he introduces new techniques, such as dissonant counterpoint, atonal melodies, and sequences of tone colors. It was first performed not in Germany, but in London on September 3, 1912. The five divisions of the work bear the following titles: *Vorgefühle* (*Premonitions*), set in melodic tritones; *Vergangenes* (*The Past Time*); *Der wechselnde Akkord* (*The Changing Chord*), a kaleidoscopic interplay of instrumental colors in soft dynamics; *Peripetie*, in rapid motion reflecting the peripeteia of life; and *Das obligate Recitative*, a narrative rondo. The suite was first performed not in Germany but in London on September 3, 1912. The reviews were savage. Here is a sample: "The music of Schoenberg's *Five Orchestral Pieces* resembled the wailings of a tortured soul, and suggested nothing so much as the disordered fancies of delirium or the fearsome, imaginary terrors of a highly nervous infant."

Funiculì-Funiculà. One of the most popular Neapolitan songs, written by Luigi Denza in 1880 to celebrate the opening of the funicular railway leading to the crater of Mt. Vesuvius. Mistakenly believed to be a folksong, it was used as such by Rimsky-Korsakov and Richard Strauss in their orchestral works.

G

G. The seventh degree in the alphabetical scale and the dominant of the C-major scale. In France, Italy, Spain, and Russia, G is called Sol, as it appears in the original syllabic hymn of Guido d'Arezzo. Solmization is the practice of singing scales beginning with Sol, which was the lowest note of the Guidonian Hand.

G major. A favorite key of Classical and Romantic composers and their public. It suggests to the romantic imagination a cloudless landscape and warm sunshine. Not as identifiably pastoral as F major, G major is wonderfully suitable for engaging solos on the oboe or the flute, occasionally echoed by a muted horn. The number of symphonic works in G major is immense: the *Oxford* Symphony and the *Surprise* Symphony of Haydn; Mozart's entrancing *Eine kleine Nachtmusik*; Beethoven's Piano Concerto No. 4; Dvořák's Symphony No. 8; Mahler's Symphony No. 4; and the celebrated Paderewski's *Minuet in G.*

G minor. A key of earnest meditation. Its tonic and dominant are represented by two open strings on every instrument of the string family. As a relative key of B-flat major, it provides for natural modulations, especially for woodwind and brass instruments. One of the greatest symphonies in G minor is Mozart's Symphony No. 40, in which the key is seldom abandoned in the lively first movement, in the minuet, and in the finale. Among Haydn's symphonies the one that bears the name *La poule* (*The Hen*) is in G minor. There are untold numbers of solo pieces for violin and other instruments in the key of G minor, among them the Violin Concerto by Max Bruch. The key also lies well for the piano. Among notable examples are the Piano Concerto by Dvořák and the popular Piano Concerto No. 2 by Saint-Saëns.

G string. The lowest and thickest string on the violin, and the second lowest string on the viola and cello. The vulgar expression "G string," referring to the pubic garment worn by a bellydancer or a stripteaser, was launched by American nightclub customers.

Gaillarde. A vivacious court dance popular in France, Spain, and England during the late 16th century and the early 17th century. The name comes from the French *gai*, "merry." At court occasions, the gaillarde usually followed the stately pavane. The two dances are in fact related melodically, but the gaillarde transforms the symmetric binary meter of the pavane into a lively ternary beat. In England the gaillarde was known under the French name *cinq pas* ("five steps"), so called because it had four strong beats ending with an extra rhythmic step. Elizabeth I practiced the gaillarde for her morning exercises, or so it was reported.

Gallant style. A curious and somewhat disparaging designation for the "elegant style" of composition that followed the strict and purely musical Baroque idiom of Bach and Handel. There is, of course, no "gallantry" in this style; the term denotes music in the salon manner, homophonic rather than polyphonic, serving to entertain rather than to enlighten, evoking sentiment rather than meditation. In this sense it is synonymous with Rococo. Paradoxically, the gallant style was given dignity and even nobility by Bach's sons Wilhelm Friedemann and Carl Philipp Emanuel, who initiated a pre-Romantic fashion of musical "affects" to drive music away from austere formalism toward human expressiveness and the "natural" philosophy of Rousseau and the French Encyclopedists. Instrumental pieces composed in the gallant style were sometimes called "galanteries." Dance movements are the favored forms and brevity the recommended feature.

The Gambler. An opera by Prokofiev, after a story by Dostoyevsky, first performed not in Russia but in Brussels on April 29, 1929. The story deals with a Russian general vacationing at a German resort with his very rich grandmother whose fortune he hopes to inherit. She proceeds to gamble recklessly, however, and he despairs. Fortunately, his aide-de-camp manages to break the bank on his own, but this leads to further imbroglios. The imitation of the roulette wheel in centripetal chromatics is highly effective.

Gaspard de la nuit. A group of three pieces for piano by Ravel, entitled *Ondine*, *Le Gibet*, and *Scarbo*. These pieces are fine paradigms of impressionistic writing, portraying a mermaid, a gallows, and a playful sprite. The entire group was performed for the first time in Paris on January 9, 1909.

Gavotte. One of the most important dance forms of the Baroque period. It is written in alla breve time with two main beats to a measure, with a peculiar upbeat of half a bar. Its formal structure is ternary, the middle section being a musette, usually in the dominant key, which often has a pedal point on the tonic and the dominant in the bass, in imitation of the drone of a bagpipe (*musette* is the French word for "bagpipe"). The derivation of the word *gavotte* is uncertain; it may be an old local name for the natives of the hill country in Provençe.

Gayané. A ballet by Aram Khatchaturian, first performed in the city of Perm by the Kirov Theater troupe of Leningrad (which was evacuated to Perm during the war) on December 9, 1942. Gayané is an Armenian farm worker whose husband is a traitor. His attempt to subvert her is foiled; he is apprehended and suffers the supreme penalty, patriotically approved by Gayané. The score contains the celebrated *Saber Dance*. There are also a nostalgic lullaby and other numbers of immediate popular appeal.

La Gazza ladra (The Thieving Magpie). An opera by Rossini, produced at La Scala, Milan, on May 31, 1817. The French play from which the libretto was extracted was described as a comedy. Some comedy! It tells of a servant girl sentenced to death on suspicion of stealing a spoon! She is saved from the gallows (yes, early in the 19th century they hanged people for petty larceny) when the spoon is found in the nest of an errant magpie. Hence the title.

Gebrauchsmusik. A term that came into use in Germany after World War I, in the sense of utility music, or music for everyday use. *Gebrauchsmusik* must be easy to perform by amateurs, with its texture freed from the strictures of academic usage. Unresolved dissonances are liberally admitted, and the rhythmic patterns emulate the music turned out by untutored composers of popular ballads. To compensate for the abolition of old educational music, composers of *Gebrauchsmusik* promulgated a new academic doctrine of providing easy samples of pleasing melodies for beginners. The earliest example of such neoacademic *Gebrauchsmusik* is Hindemith's piece for school children, *Wir bauen eine Stadt*. Carl Orff succeeded in enlarging the academic routine by composing pieces that were modern in harmony, rhythm, and orchestration but that required some professional skill to perform. Easy humor is an important part of practical *Gebrauchsmusik*. Ernst Toch combined wit with ostensible erudition in his *Geographical Fugue* for speaking chorus, which recites names of exotic places in rhythmic counterpoint. *Mikrokosmos* by Béla Bartók presents *Gebrauchsmusik* of considerable complexity without losing its musical innocence.

Geisslieder. Chants of the flagellants (*Geissler*, from *Geissl*, a "scourge") praying for the cessation of the plague and other calamities during the Middle Ages. These chants became the melodic and rhythmic sources of German folksongs of the Renaissance.

Das Geister Trio (The Ghost Trio). The common German nickname for Beethoven's Piano Trio in D major, op. 70, No. 1. It is attached to the work for no reason other than an imagined mystery suggested in the opening of the second movement.

General Lavine—eccentric. One of Debussy's *Préludes* for piano in Book II. The title is taken from the name of an American vaudeville actor, Edward La Vine, whom Debussy watched perform in a Paris cabaret. The piece is set in ragtime rhythms.

General William Booth's Entrance into Heaven. A rollicking song composed by Charles Ives in 1914 as homage to the founder of the Salvation Army. The words are by Vachel Lindsay.

Genius. An unfortunate term when applied to producers of literature, art, or music. It is derived from the name of a tutelary deity, and in Roman usage it was applied to a person or his habitation. One does not have to embrace Edison's cynical definition, "Genius is 10% inspiration and 90% perspiration," to warn critics and analysts to use the word with caution. Schumann contributed to the use of the word *genius* when he put it in the mouth of the fictional musician Eusebius, who exclaimed, "Hats off, a genius!" as he began to play Chopin's op. 2, Variations on a theme from Mozart's *Don Giovanni*. Another time, as the young Brahms showed to Schumann one of his early works, Schumann noted in his diary: "Johannes Brahms was on a visit. A genius!" When the Vienna music critic Julius Korngold took his 10-year-old son to Mahler and let him play, Mahler became greatly agitated, repeatedly exclaiming, "A genius! A genius!" Young Korngold eventually became known as the writer of idiomatic film music in Hollywood, and his operas, which had created quite a sensation when they were first produced, were forgotten.

Popular mythology prescribes that geniuses behave erratically, eccentrically, and unpredictably. Beethoven fits this description to some extent. Bach, however, upsets the popular picture of a genius. To his contemporaries he appeared as an honest and earnest worker, modestly performing his functions as church composer, organist, and rector of a boys' school. Among virtuosos who looked like geniuses was Paganini, whose press agents spared no effort to represent him as being inspired both by God and Satan in his violin playing. Rachmaninoff, who was a great pianist as well as a highly popular composer, presented a visage, as described by a critic, of a provincial banker. Yet a novel has been published under the title *Rachmaninoff's Eyes*, attributing some magical quality to his eyes. Ravel seemed to lack all external attributes of a great musician; he had a very poor sense of pitch, his memory was not retentive, he was a mediocre piano player, and he was practically helpless as a conductor. Stravinsky was similarly lacking in these external gifts. If one wishes to conjure up the romantic vision of a genius among modern composers,

Scriabin would fit the part. His appearance of a distraught visionary, his delicate physique, his inability to cope with the hard realities of life, his messianic complex, his belief that he was called upon to unite the arts in one mystical consummation, all combined to create the impression of a genius incarnate. But Schoenberg, who came close to reforming music and changing its direction, presented the very opposite to a conventional idea of genius. He was bald and lacked social graces, he was not a good performer on any instrument, and he was only a passable conductor of his own works.

The word *genius* has often been applied to symphonic conductors. Toscanini was not extravagant in appearance, but he possessed magic as a conductor. Hans von Bülow was the first to establish the outward appearance of a genius of the baton—tall, erect, and imperious. The list of flamboyant conductors, in more or less chronological order, ought to include Artur Nikisch, Serge Koussevitzky, Leopold Stokowski, and Leonard Bernstein. As against these, there are a number of masters of the baton whose outward appearance is unprepossessing. The romantic picture of a genius at work may be accepted only as a literary or artistic device. Its definition is vague, and it inevitably overlaps such concepts as virtuosity, stimulating spirit, ingratiating social qualities, and the inability to communicate with people at large. If one wanted to name a real universal genius, the choice would be Einstein. He also was an amateur violinist, but he was weak on rhythm. "Can't you count, Albert?" exclaimed Artur Schnabel, with whom Einstein liked to play Mozart sonatas.

Genoveva. An opera by Robert Schumann, his only complete work for the stage, produced in Leipzig on June 25, 1850. Schumann attempted to counteract the prevailing Italian domination of the European opera stage, emphasizing heavy melodrama in the libretto and using the conventional alternation of arias and recitatives. Genoveva is the young bride of a warrior who entrusts her to his companion while he is away, but the friend betrays his trust by making advances to Genoveva. She rejects him, and, frustrated, he tells the bridegroom upon his return that she was unfaithful. The latter orders her to be executed for breaking faith, but she proves to him medically that she is a *virgo intacta*. The betrayer flees, and the couple's happiness is ensured.

Geographical Fugue. A popular work by Ernst Toch for spoken chorus consisting of a rhythmic recital of geographic names, mostly exotic. It was first performed at a modern music festival in Berlin on June 17, 1930, giving an impetus to similar pieces of spoken music by other composers.

Geomusic. A term herein proposed to define a relationship existing between soil and soul, between land and life. One of the most remarkable geomusical facts is that an area of some 75,000 square miles (about a third of the size of Texas) and comprising such cultural centers as Bonn, Hamburg, Berlin,

Prague, Leipzig, Salzburg, and Vienna, embraces the birthplaces of so many of the world's greatest musicians: Bach and Handel, Haydn and Mozart, Beethoven and Schubert, Brahms, Schumann and Mendelssohn, Wagner and Bruckner, Richard Strauss and Johann Strauss, Smetana and Dvořák, Mahler and Schoenberg. The most accomplished violinists of the 20th century came from Poland, the Ukraine, and Lithuania, among them Heifetz, Elman, Isaac Stern, and father and son Oistrakh, all of them being Jewish. What is the secret here? What is this peculiar affinity between young Jews of Eastern Europe and the violin? The economic factor is a dubious explanation.

The small peninsula of Italy generated the finest flowering of opera, a stage form that was born as an art in Florence and produced through its course of three centuries such masters as Monteverdi, Rossini, Verdi, and Puccini, and such great singers as Caruso, Adelina Patti, and Pavarotti. It also produced the greatest opera conductor, the uncontrollably temperamental Arturo Toscanini. Italians, in fact, have been in charge of most opera houses; the Metropolitan Opera of New York has been in Italian hands ever since its foundation. The most popular opera composer living in America and writing his own libretti in English is Gian Carlo Menotti (who for some reason has never applied for American citizenship).

If Italy produces great tenors, Russia is the land of great basses, the grandest among them being Chaliapin. The Russians did not enter the world scene as composers until the second half of the 19th century. The names of Glinka, Rimsky-Korsakov, Mussorgsky, and Tchaikovsky testify to the natural gift of Russia in all musical fields. And despite the political upheavals of the Revolution, the Russian achievement continued to be great. Stravinsky, Prokofiev, and Shostakovich remain dominant figures in new Russia; Russian pianists, violinists, and cellists continue to win prizes at international festivals.

France contributed to music in a less heroic, less grandiose way. The French of the modern age, Debussy and Ravel among them, provided the music of sensual beauty, leaving the field of symphony and grand opera to the Germans and the Russians. It is the task of geomusic to account for these selective pursuits within particular nations. Besides the music of these nations are the totally different musical arts of North and South America, Asia, Africa, and Australia. Who could imagine until recently that the two greatest American orchestras would be led by Orientals, namely Seiji Ozawa and Zubin Mehta, that the finest cellist after Casals would be a Chinese named Yo-Yo Ma? And it must not be omitted in a study of geomusic that the most vital type of folk music of the 20th century was a product of the United States—jazz.

Gesamtkunstwerk. It was Wagner who promulgated the idea that all arts are interrelated and that their ultimate synthesis should be the idea of each constituent art, that painting and figurative arts should serve the cause of architecture and stage representations, that poetry should relate to philosophical concepts, and that music should be both the servant and the mistress of its sister arts. In his music dramas, Wagner attempted to approximate the ideal of *Gesamtkunstwerk*, a "complete art work," by assigning equal importance to the text, orchestral music, singing, acting, and scenic design.

Der Gesang der Jünglinge (The Song of the Youths). A cantata for boy soprano and children's choir electronically manipulated by Karlheinz Stockhausen, first performed in Cologne on May 30, 1956. The text is composed of disjointed fragments from the Book of Daniel dealing with the three youths Shadrach, Meshach, and Abednego, who were put into a fiery furnace by the Babylonians when they refused to worship a golden image, but "came forth of the midst of the fire with not a blister." The work is transmitted by five groups of loudspeakers surrounding the audience.

Gewandhaus. The Leipzig building in which the famous Gewandhaus concerts were inaugurated in 1781. *Gewandhaus* is the German word for a drapery shop; the Leipzig Gewandhaus was actually a textile workshop before it was converted into a concert hall.

La Giara (The Jar). A ballet by Alfredo Casella. A huge terra-cotta jar is broken by accident and a local peasant is told to repair it. He does so inside the jar itself, and then cannot get out. In the end his friends roll the jar down a hill and it breaks into pieces, releasing him. The music consists of a succession of dances mostly derived from Sicilian folksongs. It was first performed in Paris on November 19, 1924.

Gimmicks. Musical tricks are usually regarded as beneath the dignity of a composer or a performer, but the greatest composers were known to indulge in experimenting with devices that have nothing to do with music as an art. Some popular compositions are based on a fortuitous arrangement of letters of the alphabet translated into musical notes. Mario Castelnuovo-Tedesco programmed names of his friends according to the recurrent series of the English alphabet and wrote variations and fugues for them as birthday greetings. The modern American composer Tom Johnson managed to write a whole opera based on only four notes. The American composer Ernst Bacon developed a rather curious symmetric technique in his piano works in which both hands play simultaneously or successively a series of symmetrically positioned chords or arpeggios, so that E-flat, G, C in the right hand are accompanied or echoed (counting down) by G-sharp, E, B in the left, forming a perfect mirror image of one black key and two white keys.

The aesthetic and technical value of musical gimmicks lies in the adage that art must be difficult in order to be elevating. Numerous examples of deliberately set limitations in various branches of arts and sciences that lead to interesting discoveries can be cited. A peculiarly absurd example is a novel written by an eccentric American who tied down the *e* key on the typewriter and wrote the entire manuscript without using that most common letter in the English alphabet. Visual elements in musical composition are of demonstrable value if for nothing else than the greater understanding of the nature of notation. An 18th-century anonymous score exists that, when lying flat on a table, can be played in perfect harmony by two violinists facing each other. Naturally, the piece is in G major, because the G major triad in close and open harmony in the treble clef does not change when the page is turned upside down. Another ambitious piano piece of more recent origin is entitled *Vice-Versa*. When it is read from page 1 to page 8, or upside down from page 8 to page 1, it comes out precisely the same. Such musical tricks can be compared to paintings on the flat surface contrived by artists of the Renaissance period, which look like so much accidental color spreads but become landscapes or nudes or hunting scenes when reflected in a mirrored cylinder placed in the center of the original. Some apparent gimmicks using the musical alphabet cannot be classified as such. It would be absurd to call the noble theme B-A-C-H a gimmick. Similarly, the *"scènes mignonnes composées sur quatre notes"* ("little scenes composed on four notes") underlying Schumann's *Carnaval* are imaginative *jeux d'esprit* connected with autobiographical episodes in his life, and should not be degraded as gimmicks.

La Gioconda. An opera by Amilcare Ponchielli, first produced in Milan on April 8, 1876. The title literally means "a merry girl" (*gioconda*, "jocund"). The action takes place in 17th-century Venice. The jocund street singer is in trouble when her blind mother is denounced as a witch by the Inquisition. The local Inquisitor is willing to release her if the girl submits to his licentious advances. She rebukes him, and he carries out his threat to have her mother put to death. Thereupon La Gioconda stabs herself and dies. There are also some murky doings around the Venetian palaces involving, among other things, a cuckolded husband who tries unsuccessfully to poison his wife. The score includes the famous *Dance of the Hours*, as rollicking a piece of rhythmic entertainment as was ever produced by an Italian composer.

I gioielli della Madonna (The Jewels of the Madonna). An opera by Ermanno Wolf-Ferrari, first produced in Berlin on December 23, 1911. Two rivals for the affection of a fair damsel vow to prove their love by a deed of sacrilege. The winner steals the jewels from the statue of the Holy Virgin and offers them to his beloved. She rejects the blasphemous gift and in distress drowns herself. The horrified miscreant lays the jewels at the Madonna's feet and stabs himself to death. The score is couched in a grandiloquently dramatic Italian manner.

Un giorno di regno (A Day of Reign). An opera by Verdi, first performed in Milan on September 5, 1840. This is Verdi's first comic opera, and yet it was written at the most tragic period of his life when he lost his wife and two children in an epidemic. The opera tells the story of a courageous Polish officer who travels under the identity of King Stanislaw so that in case of regicide the real king will be spared. He is rewarded by marriage to a young Polish lady.

Giovanna d'Arco. An opera by Verdi, first performed in Milan on February 15, 1845. In it Joan of Arc falls in love with the Dauphin, goes to battle against the English, is wounded, and dies in the arms of her royal lover, now crowned as King Charles VII. This perversion of the historical story of the sainted virgin infuriated the French at the first Paris performance of the opera and was banned from the French stage. Still, the score has some nice tunes.

Giraffenklavier. A vertical piano, manufactured in Vienna during the first third of the 19th century. Its left side was elevated to accommodate the longer bass strings, thus forming a shape suggesting that of a giraffe; hence the name, "giraffe keyboard."

The Girl I Left Behind Me. An old song, probably of Irish origin, popular in the American colonies before the Revolution. At the time of the Civil War a new set of words was adapted to the tune, and it became known as *The American Volunteer*. It is used as the graduating class song at the West Point military academy.

Giselle. One of the most famous French ballets, composed by Adolphe Adam and produced in Paris on June 28, 1841. Its full title is *Giselle ou Les Wilis*; the *Wilis* are the disembodied spirits of young girls who die before their announced weddings.

Giuditta. An opera by Franz Lehár, produced in Vienna on January 20, 1934. The subject is drawn from the apocryphal Book of Judith about the Hebrew maiden who skillfully decapitates the sleeping Assyrian army leader and carries his bearded head back to her city. Finding themselves headless, the Assyrians lift the siege of the Hebrew city. This is the only serious opera Lehár ever wrote, but musically it is much inferior to his sparkling operettas.

Glagolitic Mass. A sacred work by Leoš Janáček, also known as the *Slavonic Mass* or *Festival Mass*, first performed in Brno on December 5, 1927. The text is in old Slavonic, common also to the Russian Orthodox church. The use of the Slavonic vernacular by Janáček was as much of an innovation as the use of the German language by Brahms in his Requiem.

Glass harmonica. In its most primitive form, a set of drinking glasses partially filled with water to provide a complete diatonic scale. A famous concert of

"26 glasses tuned with spring water" was presented in 1746 in London by Gluck. It is said that Benjamin Franklin attended and subsequently constructed a glass harmonica with mechanical attachments. The sound is produced by rubbing the rim of the glass with a wet finger. Because of its clarity and purity of tone, it was called "angelic organ." Musical glasses achieved a great popularity in the 18th century under the Italian name *armonica*. Their use fell into desuetude after the romantic attraction was spoiled by mechanization. Richard Strauss used the mechanized form in his opera *Frau ohne Schatten*.

Glee. A popular type of English choral music *a cappella* for male voices, usually in a series of short movements harmonized homophonically. It reached its flowering in the 18th century. Glee clubs proliferated in England and the United States. Although the word *glee* suggests merriment, its philological ancestor *gleo* meant "music" in Old English.

Gli Scherzi. One of several nicknames for the Haydn String Quartets Nos. 37, 38, 39, 40, 41, and 42. They are so called because their minuets are each marked Scherzo or Scherzando. The same group of quartets is known as *Jungfernquartette* (*Maiden Quartets*), for the title page of the first edition bore a picture of a luscious Teutonic female. They are also known as the *Russian Quartets* because they were dedicated to a Russian grandduke.

Glissando. An etymologically incongruous word, formed from the French *glisser*, "to slide," and the Italian suffix, "*ando*." On the piano, a glissando is an effective ornamental device achieved by sliding the back of the fingernail quickly over the white keys, observing special care not to bruise the finger. Glissando on the black keys is possible but rarely used. Piano virtuosos with fingers of steel manage to make glissandos in octaves, and even in octaves with an interposed third, using the thumb, the index finger, and the little finger. The glissando effect is natural for the harp when played on a single string. Trombone glissandos are applicable for a limited range in the bass. The clarinet glissando, requiring a special manipulation of the keys, opens Gershwin's *Rhapsody in Blue*.

Glockenspiel. Literally, "bell play." A set of steel bars struck by a hammer and producing a bell-like sound. The glockenspiel is included in the score of Mozart's opera *The Magic Flute*, but it is listed there simply as *instrumento d'acciacio* ("steel instrument"). In actual performance it is interchangeable with the celesta.

Gloria. The second main division of the High Mass of the Catholic service. The separate canticles are *Gloria in excelsis Deo* ("Glory to God in the Highest"), *Laudamus te* ("We praise you"), *Gratias agimus tibi* ("We give you thanks"), *Domine Deus* ("Lord God"), *Qui tollis peccata mundi* ("Who bears the sins of the world"), *Qui sedes ad dexteram patris* ("Who sits at the right hand of the Father"), *Quoniam tu solus sanctus* ("For you alone are holy"), and *Cum Sancto Spiritu* ("With the Holy Spirit").

Gloriana. An opera by Benjamin Britten, written for the coronation of Elizabeth II and produced at a special gala performance for the Queen in Covent Garden, London, on June 8, 1953. The gloriana of the title was Elizabeth I; the libretto concerns her romance with the Earl of Essex.

Die glückliche Hand (The Lucky Hand). "Drama with music" by Arnold Schoenberg, to his own text, first produced in Vienna on October 14, 1924. A helpless man, beset by horrible visions, meditates on his search for happiness. A chorus points out the futility of his efforts. The vocal part is half speech, half song. The melody is atonal and the harmony dissonant.

God Bless America. This song by Irving Berlin, a Russian-Jewish American immigrant, has a fascinating history. He wrote it in 1918, intending to use it in a show he staged at Camp Yaphank when he was in the U.S. Army. For some reason the song was withdrawn from the production and lay dormant until 1938, when the American soprano Kate Smith put it on a patriotic radio program on Armistice Day. In an atmosphere charged with the expectations of an imminent war, the song produced a profound impression. During the war it became an unofficial national anthem, and on February 18, 1955, President Eisenhower presented Irving Berlin with a Gold Medal in appreciation of his service to the country in writing *God Bless America*. Petitions are periodically circulated to have *God Bless America* replace *The Star-Spangled Banner* as the national anthem. Indeed, the tune is much more singable, and the words are wider in their patriotic application, devoid of such anachronistic references as "bombs bursting in air." Berlin donated his royalties from *God Bless America* to the Boy Scouts and Girl Scouts of America.

God Save the Czar. A Russian czarist anthem composed in 1833 by Alexis Lvov, the director of the Imperial court chapel, with words set especially by the Russian poet Vassily Zhukovsky. It was almost immediately adopted as a national anthem. Controversy as to Lvov's authorship was aroused by the discovery that the tune was identical with the middle section of a march by a German band leader, Ferdinand Haas, conductor of the Imperial Russian Preobrazhensky Regiment in St. Petersburg. But Lvov's manuscript, set for chorus and orchestra, is extant and bears an earlier date than that of Haas. The consensus of Russian musicologists is, therefore, in favor of its authenticity. Singing the tune was abolished after the Russian Revolution, and its quotation in Tchaikovsky's *1812 Overture* was replaced synharmonically by the concluding chorus from Glinka's opera *A Life for the Czar*, which itself was renamed *Ivan Susanin*, after the name of its hero.

God Save the King. The British national anthem, the tune of which is also used in the United States as *My Country,'Tis of Thee.* It was first published in its present form in 1744, but there were adumbrations and approximations in earlier centuries. Countless attempts have been made to ascertain its origin and identify its author, but all in vain. Later, for Queen Victoria and for Elizabeth II, it was titled *God Save the Queen.*

Goldberg Variations. This famous set of 30 variations for the harpsichord was written by Bach at the request of his pupil Johann Gottlieb Goldberg, purportedly as a soporific for Count Kayserling, Goldberg's insomniac employer. Yet the work demands considerable attention, and it is doubtful whether it could really put anyone to sleep.

Goliards. Wandering minstrels, usually students or monks, who traveled through Germany during the Middle Ages. The celebrated collection *Carmina Burana* consists mainly of goliard songs.

Goodnight Irene. An American folksong that Huddie Ledbetter (Leadbelly) picked up while serving a criminal sentence in the Louisiana State Prison and arranged by him with the help of John Lomax in 1936. The recording sold more than a million copies.

Götterdämmerung (The Twilight of the Gods). The final spectacle of Wagner's great tetralogy *Der Ring des Nibelungen* (*The Ring of the Nibelung*), first performed at Wagner's Festival Theater in Bayreuth on August 17, 1876. The gods, demigods, heroes, a Valkyrie, and the monstrous offspring of the sinister gnome Nibelung all perish in the final conflagration. The Rhine River overflows the funeral pyre erected for the final rites for Siegfried, the god-like hero of the tetralogy, and the Rhine maidens seize the accursed Ring from the murderous son of the dwarf who made it. Malevolent magic wrought by the Nibelungs makes Siegfried forget his beloved Valkyrie, transforms him into the image of another Nibelung, then restores his memory and his physical shape to him before he is slain. A labyrinthine network of leitmotifs guides, and misguides, the listener trying to trace the principal characters. Even such a confirmed Wagnerite as George Bernard Shaw candidly admitted his inability to penetrate the tangled web of the story.

Goya. An opera by Gian Carlo Menotti, to his own libretto depicting the life of the tortured Spanish artist. It includes Goya's unverified romance with the Duchess of Alba (whom he painted both clad and unclad in two separate portraits). A dramatic scene describes Goya suddenly going deaf and, to illustrate this, Menotti makes all music stop while the singers continue to silently open and close their mouths, producing a unique effect. *Goya* was staged at the Kennedy Center Theater in Washington, D.C., on November

15, 1986. Much to Menotti's distress, it was cruelly damned by every music critic as a compendium of mawkish melodies and corny clichés.

Goyescas. An opera by Enrique Granados, first performed in New York on January 28, 1916. The title refers to the famous Spanish painter Goya. The libretto, however, has a peripheral relationship to the subjects of his paintings. The score was put together from the material of Granados's piano suite of the same name, regarded as one of the finest stylizations of Spanish popular music. Granados attended the performance of his opera in New York and perished tragically on his return trip when the British ship on which he sailed was torpedoed by a German submarine.

Gradual. The main book of the Catholic liturgy containing all the principal sections of the Mass; in this sense it is a complement of the Antiphonal, which contains the texts of the liturgy. The word *graduale* is derived from *gradus*, "step," because the chants are sung from the steps of the altar.

Gradus ad Parnassum (Steps to Parnassus). A famous Latin treatise on counterpoint by Johann Joseph Fux, published in Vienna in 1725. Parnassus was the mountain of the Muses in Greek mythology. Fux's work was the textbook for composers and theorists for at least a century. The same title was given by Clementi to his collection of piano studies issued in 1817.

Grand Canyon Suite. An orchestral panorama by the American composer and arranger Ferde Grofé. It musically depicts five scenes of the American desert landscape, from sunrise to sunset. It was first performed in Chicago on November 22, 1931, and eventually became a popular concert number.

Grand Ole Opry. A durable feast of American country music that was initiated on November 28, 1925, in Nashville, Tennessee, and broadcast over radio station WSM. The original name of the program, which was broadcast on Saturday nights, was *Barn Dance*. It received its nickname *Grand Ole Opry* on December 10, 1927, *ole* for *old* and *opry* for *opera* supposedly representing common Southern talk. The programs were made up of ballads sung by country folk uncontaminated by the pretentious claims of grand opera. Also participating were fiddlers, banjo players, guitar pickers, string bass strummers, and handlers of the jew's harp, harmonica, accordion, and other folk instruments. The country orchestra numbered as many as 50 players. Often included were such things as "talking blues," comedy routines, and grandiose jamborees. Amazingly enough, the Grand Ole Opry has managed to keep a faint trace of its rustic purity despite the prevailing commercialism, although much of it is a deliberate spoof of the original designed to dupe gullible outsiders. Not even the advent of television was able to disrupt totally its natural folkways. During jamborees, in the early days, members of the audience would gather onstage, indulging in free comments, while performers continued their acts bent over the microphones.

Graphic notation. In avant-garde music that requires the production of sounds outside the tempered scale and that calls for improvisation as an integral part of the composition itself, it has become necessary to employ special notational symbols. Among those most often used are isosceles triangles indicating the highest or lowest possible sound on a given instrument, with the vortex pointing upward or downward respectively; thick vertical or horizontal lines representing tone clusters, conglomerates of chromatic or diatonic intervals within a certain compass; and four vertical lines with a curve crossing them indicating arpeggios below the bridge of a string instrument. In some scores even the emotions and states of mind are portrayed by smiling faces or expressions of despondency.

Gregorian chant. A system of liturgical chant in the Roman Catholic church. Its codification is generally attributed to Pope Gregory I, about A.D. 600. Devoid of harmonic connotations, it may appear monotonous to the modern ear, but it compensates for the absence of harmony with extraordinary melorhythmic richness. The uncertainties of the notation of Gregorian chant led to the proliferation of different renderings of the same manuscripts. Disconcerted by the ambiguity of the chant and its notation, a group of learned Benedictine monks of the village of Solesmes in France undertook the task of reconciling the different versions of liturgical texts. They prepared an edition of early Gregorian chants that was published as the *Editio Vaticana* with the papal imprimatur.

The text of the Gregorian chant is always in Latin. The syllabic settings are entirely free, so that a syllable may be sung to a single note or to several tied notes. In such climactic passages as the singing of alleluia, a single syllable may be sung to a group of as many as 20 notes. What makes Gregorian chant both intractable and fascinating is that singers must treat a given chant melodically and rhythmically in a variety of ways according to its position in the liturgy. In this respect, Gregorian chant has a striking resemblance to the practice of Indian ragas, which are to be sung differently according to the time of day. It would be a grave mistake, however, to seek melodic and rhythmic similarities between specific samples of Gregorian chant and Eastern melodies, for there is no historical parallel between Roman liturgy and Indian ragas. The improvisatory style of Gregorian melismas is rooted in liturgical prose, as distinct from extemporized instrumental figurations of the Baroque school and the aleatory practices of the 20th century. On the other hand, similarities between ancient Jewish cantillation in the synagogue and Gregorian chant may indeed have a historical foundation in view of the common heritage of the Judeo-Christian tradition. Equally tenable is the theory of the Greek origin of Gregorian chant; the strongest argument of this theory lies in the modal classification of Gregorian chant and ancient Greek music. Indeed, the names of the modes in Gregorian chant are borrowed from Greece, but medieval theorists responsible for this false nomenclature misinterpreted the intervallic structure and direction of the ancient modes (in Greek music intervals were counted downward, whereas in medieval church modes they are scaled upward). Observation of the religious services in the old cathedrals and monasteries in Catholic Europe seems to confirm the conviction that Gregorian chant follows its own intrinsically coherent rules, derived from the reading of religious texts, asymmetrical in musical phraseology, syllabically accentuated according to the primary spirit and relative textual importance, and gravitating toward changing tonal centers in fluid modality.

Great composers throughout history have made use of Gregorian melodies. In such inspired works, the generally asymmetrical melodies of Gregorian chant are arranged in symmetrical measures with harmonic textures. In this aggrandizement and elaboration, Gregorian chant serves as raw material, as does folk music when used for similar purposes. As long as the distinction between the historical art of Gregorian chant and the later art of harmonic and mensural organization is fully understood, the true evaluation and proper interpretation of it is possible.

Griffelkin. A television opera by Lukas Foss, with a libretto from a German fairy tale, first performed by NBC–TV on November 6, 1955. Griffelkin is a young devil who becomes disloyal to Hell after a visit on Earth. An episode in a conservatory includes an entertaining cacophonous ensemble of pupils practicing their scales.

Grossvatertanz (Grandfather Dance). An old-fashioned German salon dance, composed by one Karl Hering about 1800. Schumann used it in the finale of his piano suite *Carnaval*, erroneously identifying it as being a 17th-century folk tune.

Gruppen (Groups). A work designed for "music in space" by Karlheinz Stockhausen, first performed in Cologne on March 24, 1959. It is scored for three chamber orchestras, with three conductors beating three varying tempi.

G-sharp minor. This key, relative to B major and armored with five sharps in its key signature, is not often the principal key of a major work. It has a feeling of bucolic intimacy and is marvelously suitable for short piano pieces. Not even the polysymphonist Miaskovsky, however, ventured to write a symphony in G-sharp minor. Liszt's *Campanella* for piano is in G-sharp minor.

La Guerre des bouffons. Or, more precisely, *querelle des bouffons*. This famous theatrical controversy erupted in Paris in 1752 after a visit of an Italian opera company (*buffi*) whose performance of *La Serva padrona* by Pergolesi aroused the admiration of the pro-Italian faction of the Paris intellectuals. This was opposed by the lovers of French opera, fostered by Louis XV. A whole series of polemical pamphlets followed, including Rousseau's historical paper, *Lettre sur la musique française*.

Guidonian Hand. Named after Guido d'Arezzo, the creator of syllabic solmization, usually called in Latin *Manus Guidonis*, it served mainly to teach a system of closely related hexachords. The lowest G (the gamut) was represented by the upperside of the thumb of the left hand, the notes progressing scalewise across the palm to the tip of the little finger, and continuing along the fingertips to the index finger, then descending and after another turn ending on the top of the middle finger on the E two octaves and a sixth above the initial gamut. In the Middle Ages, the choir director indicated the points on the different joints of each finger to dictate the required notes to the singers.

Güiro. A scratcher or a scraper used in Latin American bands. It is made out of a long gourd with notches on its upper side that are scraped with a stick. Although the güiro is usually classified as a percussion instrument, its sound is actually caused by friction. It is often used in modern scores, most surprisingly at the end of Stravinsky's *Le Sacre du printemps*. It is called *reco-reco* in Brazil.

Guitar. A universally popular string instrument played by plucking or strumming. The guitar is the proverbial instrument of chivalrous courtship. Pictures of swains serenading their lady loves under their balconies and accompanying themselves on the guitar are common. The word *guitar* can be traced to the Greek *kithara*, but there is no similarity in the structure or sound of the two instruments. The guitar in its present form originated in Spain in the 16th century and spread all over the world. The standard instrument has six strings and frets along the fingerboard to indicate the position of the notes of the scale. The strings are tuned in fourths, with the exception of the interval between the fourth and fifth strings, which is a major third: E, A, D, G, B, E, the lowest string being E in the middle register of the bass clef. The notation is an octave higher than the actual sound. By the very nature of the instrument, the guitar is incapable of sustained harmony, but it is brilliantly adapted for arpeggiated chords.

Toward the mid-20th century, the guitar was electrically amplified to compensate for its tonal weakness and became a primary instrument of modern rock musicians. In its new role it underwent a change in anatomy. Its folklike outlines were abandoned in favor of a gaudy androgynous thing, thinner in the middle than the classical guitar but sprouting a pair of tinseled shoulders. Fortunately, the electric guitar failed to displace its noble ancestor. Simultaneously with its degradation by rock musicians, great guitar players such as

Andrés Segovia and Chet Atkins maintained its classical and folk traditions. Numerous modern composers, among them Castelnuovo-Tedesco and Manuel Ponce, have written concertos for guitar and orchestra.

Gurre-Lieder. A cantata for narrator, solo voices, chorus, and orchestra composed by Schoenberg at the turn of the century when he was 25 years old, orchestrated in 1911, and not performed until February 23, 1913, in Vienna. The text is the German translation of a set of poems by the Danish poet Jacobsen. The events unfold in a Danish castle in Gurre, and the songs tell of the love of the Danish king for a commoner. The story is morbid, lugubrious, and impenetrable. The music is glorious, and it absorbs the obscure texts much as Wagner's music dramas overwhelm the obscurities of the plots. In *Gurre-Lieder*, Schoenberg is still very much Wagnerian.

Gypsy music. The nomadic gypsies penetrated many countries in Europe, forming their own communities and "tabors," or camps. They elected their "kings" in colorful rituals, but otherwise adapted themselves to the customs of their adoptive land. The English word for gypsies is a corruption of "Egyptians," but gypsies in all probability came originally from India, where they were treated as untouchable pariahs. In literature, in painting, in theatrical plays and operas, gypsies became stereotyped as clever and devious, practicing their arts upon superstitious men and women. They were known as fortune-tellers and thieves, as seducers and international smugglers. They attracted attention by their colorful wearing apparel and jewelry,

The mysteries that make the plot of Verdi's opera *Il Trovatore* unintelligible are contrived by the gypsies; the famous *Anvil Chorus* in the second act is sung by gypsy blacksmiths. In Bizet's opera, *Carmen* is a gypsy who causes Don José to desert the army and join her in a smuggling ring. In Balfe's opera *The Bohemian Girl*, the heroine is kidnapped by gypsies as a child. Because many gypsies came from Bohemia, the nickname Bohemians was attached to rootless artists and wandering adventurers. Paderewski's opera *Manru* glorifies the leader of a gypsy tribe in the Carpathian mountains. Puccini's opera *La Bohème*, a collective noun meaning Bohemian life, might well be translated "The Gypsies." In numberless literary romances, an aristocratic gentleman of wealth is revealed to be a gypsy, noble of heart if not of pedigree. In the famous operetta by Johann Strauss, *Der Zigeunerbaron*, a young Hungarian is chosen by the gypsies to be their leader and is elevated to the rank of a gypsy baron, hence the title. Above all, the romanticized gypsies were passionate and often sinister lovers, such as Aleko, the gypsy hero of Pushkin's poem *The Gypsies*, which served as the subject for Rachmaninoff's opera *Aleko*. The title of the operetta *Zigeunerliebe* (*Gypsy Love*) by Lehár is typical of the gypsy image.

With all their picturesque folkways, the gypsies failed to develop an autonomous art form. The "gypsy scale," containing two augmented seconds, is a misnomer; it might be more properly called a Hungarian scale. But gypsy music had the capacity for insinuating itself into the musical modalities of other peoples. In the 19th century, gypsy music took root in the Balkans, predominantly in Rumania. In fact, the gypsies call themselves *roman* in allusion to their Rumanian origin. From the Balkans, a horde of gypsy Rumanian musicians invaded Hungary, Austria, and Russia. It is said that when the first diplomatic representative of Rumania, liberated from the Turkish yoke, appeared at the Russian Czarist court, an amazed official wondered aloud: "Rumanian? I thought it was a profession!" The most significant incursion of gypsy music was in Hungary; the national Hungarian form of *verbunkos* was directly influenced by Rumanian gypsy musicians. Liszt was an avid listener to gypsy bands; his *Hungarian Rhapsodies* were mainly derived from these impressions rather than from authentic Magyar folk tunes.

Another curious phenomenon of gypsy adaptation took place in Russia, where groups of gypsy singers, guitarists, violinists, and tambourine players, most of them from the annexed Rumanian border state of Bessarabia, established themselves as popular entertainers in restaurants, cafés, circuses, and various places of amusement. "Gypsy romances" or songs became exceedingly popular in Russia, but their words and music were composed by amateur Russian musicians. "Let us go to the gypsies" became a byword of dissolute revellers in Russian society. The greatest successes in the field of Russian "gypsy singing" were won not by Bessarabian gypsies but by singers, particularly women, of pure Russian stock. One of them, Anastasia Vialtseva, scored triumphs as a concert artist in the repertory of gypsy songs in pre-Revolutionary Russia. So deeply were these "gypsy romances" ingrained in the old regime that after the Revolution, Soviet authorities launched a concentrated campaign against gypsy songs. Musicologists were mobilized to supply dialectical argument to prove that the melodies and harmonies of such songs were not only tasteless but ideologically inadmissible in the new society. Eventually the Soviets yielded to the irrepressible lure of gypsy music. The purveyor of the most decadent songs in the postgypsy style, Alexander Vertinsky (who intoned such lines as "your fingers smell of incense" and recounted an imaginary meeting with an exotic Chinese girl in San Francisco, a place he had never visited), was received with honors in Russia after spending 25 years in exile as an anti-Soviet émigré.

Some music historians deny that gypsy music exists at all as a discernible branch of folk music, asserting that what passes for indigenous gypsy modality is really Hungarian music. However that might be, composers for more than a century have used such expressions as *alla gitana* or *alla zingarese* ("in a gypsy manner") as a definite indication of the intended style of performance. Instrumental works with gypsy titles abound. Among the most famous ones are *Zigeunerweisen* (*Gypsy Airs*) for violin and piano by Sarasate and *Tzigane* for violin and orchestra by Ravel.

H

Habanera. The dance of Havana. There is no tilde on the letter *n* in this word. Regrettably, too many composers, including Ravel, put it on, making the pronunciation "Habanyera," a monstrosity by any count. Perhaps the most famous habanera is the one that Carmen sings in Bizet's opera, but it was not Bizet's own tune. He picked it up from a collection of songs by the Spanish composer Sebastian Yradier, published in 1840, in which it appeared under the title *El Areglito*, with the French subtitle *Chanson havanaise*. Bizet inserted it into the score shortly before the production of *Carmen* in 1875, yielding to the importunities of the opera management clamoring for a singable song.

The origin of the habanera as a folk dance is obscure. The most popular theory, based mainly on the meter and rhythm, is that the habanera was an offspring of the English country dance. According to this theory, "country dance" became *contredanse* in France and *contradanza* in Spain, the latter being abbreviated to *danza* in 1800. In 1825, the habanera appeared in Cuba as *danza habanera*, and later simply as *habanera*. The meter of the habanera is 2/4 and its rhythmic formula is a dotted eighth note followed by a sixteenth note and two eighth notes. Among composers who wrote dances in the rhythm of the habanera are Debussy, Ravel, and Manuel de Falla.

Haffner Serenade. A light and charming piece in D major, written by Mozart at the age of 20 for the wedding of the daughter of Burgomeister Haffner of Salzburg. (Mozart himself had a secret liking for the bride.) Also, Haffner had endeared himself to Mozart by his many kindnesses. Thus was immortality gained by the modest Haffner family. The Serenade has eight movements and lasts longer than some of Mozart's full-fledged symphonies.

Haffner Symphony. Haffner strikes twice. This symphony in D major, the same key as that of the *Haffner* Serenade, was jotted down by Mozart in a couple of weeks in 1782, six years after the composition of the Serenade.

Hagith. A short opera by Karol Szymanowski, produced in Warsaw on May 13, 1922. The subject deals with an old king who seeks to regain his youth through the love of a young girl named Hagith. The score is somewhat Wagnerian.

Hail, Columbia. A patriotic song with words by Joseph Hopkinson, a signer of the Declaration of Independence, to the melody of the *President's March*, attributed to one Philip Phile. It was first sung as a finale to a play *The Italian Monk*, produced in Philadelphia in 1798. It gradually acquired popularity as a patriotic American anthem.

Hail to the Chief. An American marching song of unknown authorship that traditionally accompanies the entrance of the president of the United States on state occasions.

Hair. A rock musical with a score by Galt MacDermot. Described as "the American tribal love-rock musical," it was first performed off Broadway in New York on October 29, 1967, then radically rewritten and presented on Broadway on April 29, 1968. The show represents an anarchistic, dadaistic, and surrealistic subversion of all accepted ideas in the musical theater. It is not only antisocial but antisocialist. Its immorality is total. Reflecting the permissive age of pornographic eruption, the songs impudently flaunt a cornucopia of quadriliteral obscenities for the first time in any musical on stage. Among the more defiant and offensive songs are *Sodomy* and *Colored Spade*. There are several genuine hits, however, such as *Let the Sunshine In* and *Aquarius*. So contagious was the stage show that one New York critic actually undressed during the final nude scene to demonstrate his being "with it."

Halka. The national Polish opera by Stanislaw Moniuszko, produced in its final form in Warsaw on New Year's Day, 1858. Its popularity never abated in Poland, but it is rarely if ever performed elsewhere. The story concerns Halka's eternal love for her seducer; she kills herself when he marries another.

Hallelujah. From the Hebrew *hallel*, "praise," and *Jah*, "Jehovah." There are thousands of hallelujah arias and choruses, but the most famous of them all is the triumphant incantation, the *Hallelujah Chorus*, at the end of the second part of Handel's *Messiah*. When Handel brought out *Messiah* at its first London performance, the entire audience, including King George II himself, rose to its feet, establishing a tradition of standing up during the chorus that is observed in Great Britain to this day.

Hamlet. An opera by Ambroise Thomas, first produced in Paris on March 9, 1868. The libretto faithfully follows Shakespeare's tragedy, and the music overflows with melodious and harmonious arias and ensembles. For some reason the opera failed to achieve the success of *Mignon*, an earlier opera by Thomas.

Hamlet is also the title of a symphonic poem by Liszt, first performed in

Sondershausen on July 2, 1876. It is an expanded version of Liszt's *Overture to Shakespeare's Hamlet*. Tchaikovsky composed an overture-fantasy entitled *Hamlet*, first performed in St. Petersburg on November 24, 1888, in which he followed the principal dramatic points in Shakespeare's tragedy. Over the main theme of Hamlet, he even wrote in English, "To be or not to be."

Hammerklavier Sonata. The title Beethoven gave to his Piano Sonata, op. 106. In the spirit of rising nationalism in Europe, Beethoven pointedly used a German title rather than the Italian word, *pianoforte*. Beethoven's piano sonatas opp. 101, 109, and 110 are also marked *Hammerklavier* by Beethoven, but op. 106 is exclusively referred to as the *Hammerklavier Sonata*. The description *Hammerklavier* means nothing more than a keyboard operated by hammers—in contradistinction to the harpsichord, in which strings are plucked.

Hammond organ. A keyboard instrument invented by Laurens Hammond. It produces definite tones of the tempered scale by means of electrical generators. A special mechanism can alter the relative strength of overtones of each key, thereby making it possible to produce any desired instrumental timbre. The Hammond organ is usually constructed in the shape of a spinet, but it has two manuals and a set of pedals.

Hans Heiling. An opera by Heinrich Marschner, first produced in Berlin on May 24, 1833. An immortal spirit falls in love with a mortal woman. When she discovers his supernatural essence, she leaves him for a human lover, and he vanishes.

Hänsel und Gretel. An opera by Engelbert Humperdinck, first performed in Weimar on December 23, 1893, that became forthwith a universal favorite. The subject is from a Grimm Brothers fairy tale. A witch lures the siblings Hänsel and Gretel to her gingerbread house built out of baked children. Ingeniously, the two intended victims push the witch into the burning oven; she explodes and the gingerbread children all return to life. The score is Wagnerian to the core.

Happy Days Are Here Again. A song written by Milton Ager for the movie musical *Chasing Rainbows* (1930). It accompanies a scene in which the brave doughboys receive news of the Armistice in November 1918. It became the campaign song of Franklin D. Roosevelt in 1932 and of all subsequent Democratic candidates for the presidency.

Harlequin. The central character in the Harlequinade as presented in commedia dell'arte. He is in the service of a villainous Pantaloon and adores Columbine, who is the object of Pantaloon's lust. In vulgar Latin, Harlequinus was a benign demon; hence, the Italian form Arlecchino. The name may also be connected with Erlkönig, the king of the Sprites.

Harmonica. A popular "lip" instrument, also known as mouth organ. It consists of a soundbox with a row of openings that can be played both by drawing out and blowing into a series of metal reeds in scale formation, moving the instrument to the right or left for the appropriate note, each of which is in the treble range. The harmonica used to be considered a children's toy but was elevated to a serious status as serious composers began to write serious works for it.

Harmonics. Tones of the harmonic, or overtone, series that are naturally produced by a vibrating string or an air column in a pipe. What we hear as a single tone is actually a complex of tones produced by the vibration of the string or air column as a whole and also as a half, a third, a quarter, and the continuing subdivisions of the sounding body. If we silently depress a key on the piano keyboard, say a low E, and hold it, and then strike sharply the E an octave higher and let it go, the upper octave will continue to reverberate in the open string of the lower E. A weaker but still audible reverberation can be produced by striking a fifth above the octave sound (that is, B) and possibly even the E, two octaves above the open string. Under ideal circumstances on a very well-tuned piano, even the fifth natural component of the original string, in this case G-sharp, can be detected, thus forming a full major triad. An acute ear will hear the octave and the twelfth (upper E and B on basic E) that are produced by striking the fundamental tone very forcibly and letting it vibrate sonorously.

The harmonics are the formative tones determining the timbre of an instrument, depending on their relative strength in the tone complex. The principal harmonics can be produced on a string instrument by lightly touching the string at a chosen point of division, thus preventing the string from vibrating as a whole. A light touch on the node about one-third of the length of the open violin string E will produce the upper B that is an octave and a fifth above. With some practice, one can produce the harmonic series up to its sixth harmonic on the strings of the grand piano. Indeed, most bugle calls, trumpet flourishes, and fanfares are derived from the natural harmonics; an ingenious experimenter can play a variety of common tunes (even the theme of the last movement of Beethoven's Violin Concerto) by sliding a finger over a piano string. The harmonics of string instruments possess a flute-like quality, which explains the French word for harmonics, *flageollet* (from the old French word *flageol*, "flute").

Harmonies poétiques et religieuses. A piano cycle by Liszt containing ten pieces of which No. 7, *Funerailles*, is most frequently performed. It is dated October 1849 and is usually assumed to refer to the death of Chopin, Liszt's close friend who died then. An alternative theory is that Liszt was mourning the defeat of the Hungarian Revolution of 1848 and the establishment of

Austrian rule over Hungary. No. 1 of the cycle, published in 1834, is auda-
ciously written in constantly changing meters (8/4, 9/4, 10/4, etc.), bears no
key signature, and includes such innovations as the emphasis on the tritone
and an ending marked *"très long silence."* Fifty years later Liszt returned to
the exploration of atonality implied in this piece and actually composed a
Bagatelle ohne Tonart (Bagatelle without Tonality).

The Harmonious Blacksmith. A historically unjustified label for the set of variations from Handel's Harpsichord Suite in E major. It is said that Handel
heard this air sung by a blacksmith near London who was forging iron. To
lend credence to this story, the alleged anvil of the fictitious harmonious
blacksmith was even exhibited in London. A real blacksmith who practiced
his art in the vicinity of London was buried with his tombstone inscribed with
the subject of Handel's Air and Variations. The earliest edition of the music
under the title of *The Harmonious Blacksmith* was published in England about
1819, 60 years after Handel's death.

Harmonium. An organ-like instrument on which the sound is produced by an
airstream generated by a pair of pedals passing through a set of flexible metal
strips. The harmonium became a popular instrument in the 19th century with
a special appeal to amateur performers because one could produce a sustained
tone and rudimentary dynamics by pressing the pedals. It became a perfect
instrument for the home in the Biedermeier culture. The most popular trade-
mark name of the harmonium is the Physharmonica.

Harmony. The word *harmonia* in Greek signified an artful coordination between
high and low sounds and a rhythmic arrangement of the notes of the melody.
In Plato's writings, *harmonia* is a balanced sequence of slow and fast musical
phrases. For at least 1,000 years the word *harmony* has meant the simultaneous
sounding of several voices. When harmony first emerged as a technique of
composition, it was entirely consonant, limited to the use of perfect
concords—the octave and the fifth. Because a fifth subtracted from an octave
forms a perfect fourth, consonant intervals incorporated perfect octaves, fifths,
and fourths. With the emergence of organum, contrary motion was added to
theretofore exclusively perfect intervals in parallel progressions. At the same
time, an almost accidental admixture of heterophony introduced dissonant
intervals such as seconds to the available means of harmonic combinations.
The decisive step toward traditional harmony occurred around 1250, when
thirds and sixths were adopted as acceptable consonant intervals. With the
accession of *fauxbourdon*, triads appeared in the form of the first inversion.
Dissonant passing tones became more and more frequent. Curiously, the cadences of fifths and octaves in the guise of tonic triads continued to be the
rule until about 1500, when triads fully secured the essential mediant. Figured

bass opened the way for the use of triads and seventh chords on all degrees of the scale. In the 17th century, harmonic composition began to separate from contrapuntal techniques and acquired an autonomous style that was governed principally by the laws of chord progressions, with occasional contrapuntal ingredients subordinated to the domination of melody, and with the bass as the formative element of harmony in the classical sense of the word. At the conclusion of the Baroque era, about 1750, harmony finally assumed the familiar four-part setting. A relic of three-part harmony is indicated in the name of the middle section of the minuet, the trio.

Four-part harmony, as it crystallized in Classical and Romantic music, is fundamentally triadic, with the tonic, subdominant, and dominant triads being the main determinants of tonality. These three triads comprise all seven notes of the diatonic scale. In major keys, these triads are major; in minor, the tonic and subdominant are minor, but the dominant is major through the raised seventh degree, which is the middle tone of the dominant triad. When set in four parts, the bass note is doubled in another voice. In the first inversion of the triad, either the sixth or the third above the bass is doubled, less frequently the bass note itself. In the second inversion, the bass is doubled in most cases. Four-part harmony makes it possible to achieve complete sets of seventh chords on all degrees of the scale, as well as the diminished-seventh chord that occurs functionally upon the leading tone in a harmonic minor key. In strict harmony, triads having a diminished or augmented fifth are not allowed. As a consequence, neither a triad built on the seventh degree of the major or harmonic minor mode nor the supertonic triad in minor keys can be used. Parallel (also known as consecutive) fifths or octaves—that is, a perfect fifth or octave moving in the same direction as another perfect fifth or octave, particularly between outer voices—are forbidden. Parallel movement of different intervals toward fifths or octaves, known as hidden fifths or octaves, is also taboo, so that a fifth or an octave can be reached only by contrary motion. Yet a number of examples from Bach's chorales or other sacrosanct sources can be adduced to discredit this stern code of prohibited progressions.

In school exercises, the four component parts are named after the voices in a vocal quartet: soprano, alto, tenor, bass. The most important consideration in four-part harmony is voice-leading. Contrary motion is recommended between the soprano and bass; stepwise motion is preferred in other voices. Thirds and sixths are favored because they can be used in parallel motion. When one voice leaps several scale degrees, the rest of the voices ought to move stepwise to provide a counterbalance and to establish a proper equilibrium. If the soprano has a melodic leap upward, then the bass ought to move stepwise, preferably in the opposite direction. If the bass moves in the same direction, it must avoid landing on a perfect fifth or octave, which would result in hidden fifths or octaves. By and large, an ideal exercise in four-part harmony would present an alternation of thirds and sixths between the outer voices. The octave is *de rigueur* in most final cadences. The middle voices are less mobile and have less opportunity to move by leaps; often they are stationary, maintaining the common tone between successive chords. Each chord can be arranged in six different ways without changing the bass. The distance between soprano and alto or between alto and tenor must not exceed an octave, but the distance between bass and tenor may be as extensive as a twelfth. When the three upper voices are bunched together within an octave, the arrangement is called *close harmony*. When these upper voices are dispersed for a total range of more than an octave, the setting is called *open harmony*.

The notation of four-part harmony in school exercises retains the numerical indexes of figured bass in Arabic numbers. The degree of the scale is represented by a Roman numeral. This combination provides two necessary and sufficient coordinates to indicate the nature of the chord, although they do not specify the spatial arrangement of the component notes. A triad in root position is marked by the superscript 5/3 (which stands for the intervals of a fifth and a third above the given bass note) after the Roman numeral corresponding to the scale degree; the index of a triad in first inversion is 6/3, the second inversion, 6/4. The superscripts for seventh chords and their three inversions are 7/5/3, 6/5/3, 6/4/3, and 6/4/2. When a triad's superscripts are not notated at all, it assumes a triad in root position. Similarly, the superscript for the seventh chord may be abbreviated to the single digit 7, and the last inversion of a seventh chord may be notated simply 2, the other intervals being assumed. Thus, VI signifies the submediant triad, V with the superscript 6/4/2 or simply V^2 denotes the last inversion of the dominant-seventh chord, I with the superscript 6/4 is the second inversion of the tonic triad, and so on. It is taken for granted in traditional harmony that in minor keys the seventh degree is always raised a semitone. Accordingly, VII with the superscript 7/5/3 or simply 7 indicates the leading-tone seventh chord; in the key of A minor it would be G-sharp, B, D, F. In altered chords, such as the chords of the augmented sixths, sharps or flats would have to be noted after the corresponding figure in the superscript. In elementary harmony exercises, however, such alterations that are properly part of figured bass are not indicated. Modulations are notated by equal signs, for instance, I = V, meaning that the tonic of the preceding key becomes the dominant of the key into which it modulates.

Harmony and counterpoint are reciprocal techniques of composition. Contrapuntal elements are present in harmony and harmonic elements in counterpoint. Harmony acquires a contrapuntal quality when individual voices carry horizontal segments of a thematic nature. Counterpoint becomes harmonic in structure when the vertical dimension tends to predominate. Counterpoint thrives on mutual imitation of the constituent voices, whereas harmony, being a vertical compound, cannot handle imitation. A harmonic or contrapuntal quality of writing is often revealed in musical notation rather than in actual sound. A remarkable example of a purely harmonic structure masquerading as counterpoint occurs in the opening bars of the finale of Tchaikovsky's *Pathétique* Symphony. One hears a "pathetic" descending figure in four-part harmony, but upon examination it appears that the first violins repeatedly cross the part of the second violin, and the violas cross the cellos, so that the melodic line is traced by a zigzag. Also in this example, the bass line crosses the two inner voices. This unusual scoring for the string section of the orchestra is explained by Tchaikovsky's reluctance to have a passage in four-part harmony descending in parallel motion, even though no forbidden consecutive octaves or fifths result from these parallelisms. It is interesting that when the same passage occurs in the recapitulation, Tchaikovsky scores it without the crossing of voices, but this time there is a powerful pedal point in the bass that changes the harmonic denomination and relegates the potentially objectionable parallel motion to the upper voices.

The introduction of chromatic harmony in the works of Liszt, Wagner, and César Franck left the tradition of the four-part setting fundamentally unaltered. Contrary motion is still the preferred *modus operandi*. Consecutive thirds and sixths still determine the flow of the music. The polarity of the upper and lower voices is maintained. Consecutive triadic formations occur exclusively in first inversions, which possess the saving grace of parallel thirds and sixths. Diminished-seventh chords in chromatic motion are often used for dramatic effect, but although they make the basic tonality ambiguous, they are compounds of minor thirds, eminently suitable for parallel motion. The dominant-ninth chord, which was a relative innovation in the age of Wagner and Liszt, is treated as a suspension of the dominant-seventh chord and presents no particular problem. Dissonances are still faithfully resolved, and complete tonal cadences happily conclude each important musical section.

A veritable harmonic revolution occurred with an extraordinary suddenness toward the end of the 19th century. In the works of Debussy and his followers, the traditional rules of harmony were revised. Naked fifths and octaves moved in parallel lines as they had a thousand years before the advent of organum. Consecutive triads in close harmony became common, disregarding the fact that such progressions necessarily involve consecutive fifths. Parallel formations of major triads became rampant, as did consecutive 6/4 chords in major keys. Ravel's String Quartet ends in such a cataract of major 6/4 chords. Up to about 1900, every dissonant combination had to be resolved into a consonance. The 20th century brought about an emancipation of dissonances. Scriabin built a "mystic chord" of six notes that would have been regarded in the 19th century as an unresolved suspension of a Wagnerian dominant-ninth chord, but Scriabin used it as a foundation for his mystical harmony, a metatriad. Seconds and sevenths acquired full rights and were no longer treated as ancillary structures. The whole-tone scale established a neutral mode. Poly-tonality licensed the use of two or more tonal triads simultaneously.

Curiously effective is the harmonization in major triads in fundamental positions when close harmony is applied intertonally. This type of harmony can be traced to Renaissance composers for whom considerations of euphony were paramount and tonality was free of restrictive rules for modulation. Briefly, intertonal harmonization is conducted in contrary motion between the melody and the bass. If the melody ascends, diatonically or chromatically, then the bass line descends so that the melodic position (that is, the distance between the melody and the bass) follows the row . . . 835835 . . . , in which 8 represents the octave, 3 represents the major third (since all chords are major triads), and 5 the perfect fifth above the bass note. Starting on any interval in this row, we obtain a progression of unrelated major triads that nevertheless produce a sensation of harmonic cohesion. Thus, the ascending chromatic melody C, C-sharp, D, E-flat will be harmonized respectively by C major (if we choose to start with the octave position), A major (C-sharp being the major third above A), G major, and E-flat major, the bass descending to the roots of these chords. If a melody descends, the succession of chords is reversed, resulting in the order . . . 853853 . . . . If we reverse the direction of the chromatic melody in the preceding example, resulting in E-flat, D, C-sharp, C, and start with an octave position, the harmonization will traverse the same major triads in reverse order: E-flat major, G major, A major, C major. This harmonization is efficient only in close diatonic or chromatic melodies, but these melodies may reverse their direction or repeat a note. (In case a melodic note is repeated several times, the row can be either . . . 358358 . . . or its reverse.) A simple example is C, D, E-flat, D, C, C, C, which would be harmonized C major, B-flat major, A-flat major, B-flat major, C major, F major, A-flat major. The remarkable circumstance about this harmonization in intertonal major triads is its almost infallible regularity. Examples can be found by the hundreds. In the second act of Puccini's *Tosca*, the descending bass in whole tones carries an ascending row of major triads in close harmony, following the regular series 8358358. The dream of Dimitri in the second act of Mussorgsky's *Boris Godunov* contains the harmonization of the ascending melody B, C-sharp, E, F-sharp, G, harmonized by the row 58583. (The omission of 3 between the second and third notes of the melody is explained by the omission of the intervening diatonic degree of D.) Debussy's works contain many examples of melodic phrases of the type C, D, E-flat, D, C, harmonized by C major, B-flat major, A-flat major, B-flat major, C major. Extremely effective fanfares can be written with repeated notes in the melody by constantly changing the triadic harmony, again following the order . . . 835383535353838 and so on, as long as the same melodic position is not used twice in succession.

A most remarkable affinity exists between free modulation and a gradually descending tetrachord in the bass, moving diatonically or chromatically from the tonic to the dominant. An example is found in Beethoven's Piano Sonata No. 21, op. 53, the *Waldstein*, where the descending bass C, B, B-flat, A, A-flat, G, in steady motion, gives rise to a modulation from C major through G major, B-flat major, F major, F minor, and C minor. A chromatically altered descending bass line determines the modulating plan of sections in the finale of Beethoven's *Moonlight* Sonata. Finally, it must be noted that an organ point on the dominant in the bass can sustain a progression of harmonies far removed from the principal key. Examples are numerous. Particularly noteworthy in this respect is the introduction to the wedding scene in Rimsky-Korsakov's opera *Le Coq d'or*, which maintains a steady bass on G, the dominant of C major, while the upper harmonies move freely to A major, E-flat major, and A-flat major.

Diatonic harmony has been enriched by pandiatonicism, which removes prohibitions of unresolved dissonances within a given key and cultivates superimposition of different triadic harmonies. Functionally, pandiatonicism can be traced to the hypertrophic development of the pedal point on the tonic and dominant upon which the subdominant and dominant triads are superimposed. Particularly effective are the superimpositions of the dominant triadic formations in close harmony in the middle register upon the tonic or subdominant triads in open harmony in the bass register. In fact, the functional role of the tonic, subdominant, and dominant triads fundamental to classical harmony is fully preserved in pandiatonic techniques. Pandiatonicism was most fruitfully applied in neo-Baroque music, in which the component notes can be used in quartal harmony. In fact, quartal harmony itself has all but succeeded the tertian harmony of classical music. Chains of fourths such as E, A, D, G, placed upon the pedal tones F-C, is a typical example.

Finally, atonality and its organized development, 12-tone composition or dodecaphony, superseded tonality altogether, replacing it with a new concept of integrated melody and harmony in which harmony becomes a function of the fundamental dodecaphonic tone row. Subdivisions of the tempered scale in quarter-tone music and even smaller microtones have prospered modestly as a monophonic art, and experiments have been made in microtonal harmonies as well. Electronic music has freed harmony of all technical impediments, allowing the use of precisely calculated, nontempered intervals as well as microtones. As cultivated by the avant-garde, electronic harmony has become a structure of fluctuating vertical complexes. The ultimate development of this type of total harmony is reached in "white noise," in which the entire diapason of sounds is employed quaquaversally.

Harmony of the Spheres. An imaginary concordance of sounds produced by the relative positions of the moon, the sun, and the planets. In early philosophy and theology, the seven spheres of the geocentric universe were likened to the diatonic degrees of the scale. This system of tonal cosmos was described by some medieval theorists as *musica mundana*, while larger constellations were elevated to the category of *musica celestis*. Subsequent developments of these theological, numerological, and acoustical speculations led to the concept of a concord of angels (*concentus angelorum*) singing the *musica angelica*. Kepler, who accepted the heliocentric cosmos, still clung to the philosophical reality of the Harmony of the Spheres and endeavored to demonstrate its mathematical applicability to the planetary orbits. Hindemith wrote an opera *Harmony of the Spheres*, based on Kepler's life. In *Gulliver's Travels*, Jonathan Swift writes: "The officers, having prepared all their musical instruments, played on them for three hours without intermission, so that I was quite stunned by the noise. . . . The people of Laputa had their ears adapted to hear the music of the spheres which always played at certain intervals."

Harold in Italy. This work by Berlioz, inspired by Byron, is remarkable because the viola, the most modest instrument among strings, is rarely assigned the solo part, as it is in this work representing Byron's melancholy traveler, Childe Harold. Here Harold travels in Italy, the land of sun, joy, and dance. It was first performed in Paris on November 23, 1834.

Harp. The most ancient and most glorified musical instrument. The word is derived from the medieval Latin *harpa*; in Italian it is *arpa* (hence "arpeggio"). In the Middle Ages, the instrument that David played for Saul was described as a harp, but it must have been the biblical kinnor, a lyre related to the Greek kithara. Harps in the modern sense of the word appeared in Ireland and Wales in the 10th century and were practiced upon by itinerant minstrels. During the Renaissance, the harp was domesticated and became the purveyor of melodious and harmonious music in France, Spain, and Italy. Soon its popularity spread all over the civilized world. The harp was portrayed in Renaissance paintings as the instrument of angels and beautiful young maidens.

The range of the modern harp approaches that of the grand piano; its triangular shape, with a curved neck, is geometrically similar. In fact, if a grand piano were dismantled and stood up perpendicularly on the floor, it would make a fairly good simulacrum of a harp. (Such a disassembly occurs in one of the Marx Brothers' screen comedies, with the silent Harpo, a competent harpist in real life, performing a solo on the disemboweled piano.) The prototype of the harp has only seven strings to the octave; to convert it into an instrument capable of modulation, an ingenious tuning mechanism was constructed around 1810 in the form of pedals that can be depressed one or two notches. Each notch shortens the corresponding string so that it sounds a semitone higher; a "double action" of the pedals, depressing two notches, shortens the string to make it sound another semitone higher. Thus it becomes possible for each of the seven strings of the octave to be raised a semitone or a whole tone. The starting scale for the modern harp is tuned in C-flat major. Because each individual string can be raised a semitone or a whole tone, all major and minor scales become available. But it is still awkward to play a rapid chromatic scale on the harp, for it necessitates a prestipedal (quick-footed) action. By using enharmonic duplication—for example, raising the original D-flat two semitones to D-sharp by depressing the pedal two notches and performing similar operations on the F-flat pedal (depressing it two notches), on the A-flat pedal (depressing one notch), and on the C-flat pedal (depressing one notch)—the harpist can play a most ingratiating glissando along the prepedalled strings in the harmony of diminished-seventh chords. Glissando, in fact, is one of the great exclusive privileges of the harp, an effect that can be produced almost effortlessly.

The harp is plucked with the fingers, never with a plectrum, but modern harp composers have added a whole arsenal of special effects, such as angelic-sounding harmonics, or demoniacal plucking of strings with a nail, or even tapping on the body of the harp. The "key signature" of the harp strikes a nonharpist as the most curious mixture of sharps and flats on the staff, but these "accidentals" are simply indications as to the tuning, not signposts of tonality. A chromatic harp was introduced as an experiment in 1897, doing away with the pedals altogether, but like so many simplified devices, it has found no favor with harpists. Although Mozart and Beethoven occasionally wrote for the harp, it never became a Classical orchestral instrument, but it reached a luxuriant flowering in the programmatic symphonic poems and in operas of the 19th century. The harp was invariably sounded whenever the soul of a female sinner was redeemed in the last act of a Romantic opera. Such celestial implications of harp playing all but disappeared in the less lachrymal and antisentimental 20th century. The harp was metamorphosed into a functional instrument that shuns such time-honored devices as sweeping arpeggios in diminished-seventh chords. It is interesting that Stravinsky had three harps in the original scoring of his early ballet *The Firebird*, but eliminated them in a later revision of the score, an eloquent testimony to the obsolescence of the harp as a decorative instrument in modern music.

Harp Quartet. A highly misleading and unnecessary nickname for Beethoven's String Quartet in E-flat major, op. 74 (1809). It is, of course, not a quartet of harps but a quartet with some tinkling passages in pizzicato arpeggios that may suggest to some literal-minded musicians the sound of a harp.

Harpsichord. The English name for the cembalo. It is a keyboard instrument with one or two manuals and activated by plectrums plucking a set of strings. In former times the harpsichord used to be a popular domestic instrument;

hundreds of pictures represent fair ladies playing on a harpsichord. It was eventually superseded in the home by the piano. It is interesting to note that the "black" keys of the piano (sharps and flats) are often white on some makes of the harpsichord, and the white keys of the piano are colored black or brown on the harpsichord. Instruments closely related to the harpsichord are spinets and virginals; their ranges vary from three to five octaves, and they were manufactured in a variety of styles and shapes. Italian harpsichords with a single manual and Flemish harpsichords with two manuals bore a closer resemblance to the modern grand piano. Old harpsichords were often adorned with curved legs and figures of cupids and mermaids. The lids might have carried inspirational legends in Latin such as *"Musica dulce laborum levamen"* ("Music is a sweet solace from labors") or *"Laborum dulce lenimen"* ("Sweet relief from labors,") a motto adopted also by G. Schirmer, Inc., New York music publishers, for the colophon of their publications.

The harpsichord played an all-important role in Baroque instrumental ensembles, serving as the basis of the basso continuo. Bach and Handel presided over the harpsichord in leading their own works; Haydn was asked to lead his ensemble from the harpsichord during his London visits. The art of playing the harpsichord lapsed in the 19th century with the abandonment of the functional use of figured bass, but a vigorous revival of the instrument took place in the second quarter of the 20th century when dedicated craftsmen, foremost among them Arnold Dolmetsch in England, began manufacturing excellent replicas. Wanda Landowska, master harpsichordist herself, greatly contributed to this revival by teaching harpsichord playing and commissioning contemporary composers (among them Manuel de Falla and Francis Poulenc) to write special works for the instrument.

Háry János. An opera by Zoltán Kodály, first produced in Budapest on October 16, 1926. János Háry (in Hungarian the first and last names are in reverse order) is a fantastic liar who boasts of defeating Napoleon all by himself. The opera opens with a deafening orchestral sneeze to signify utter disbelief.

Hatikva. The national anthem of Israel; originally a Zionist song. The melody is nearly identical to the main theme of Smetana's symphonic poem *The Moldau*.

good point

Hearing. The ancients thought that the exterior ear was the organ of hearing that gathered in the sounds, focusing and amplifying them like the seashell it resembles. Expressions such as "pricking up one's ear" reflect this belief. Centuries passed before scientists looked inquisitively into the middle ear behind the eardrum and discovered there a remarkable recording instrument. A sound wave produces a displacement in the eardrum of less than the diameter of a single hydrogen molecule, but so sensitive is the eardrum that even this submicroscopic distention suffices to produce a distinct sensation of a definite tone. The transmission mechanism of the middle ear consists of three interconnected ossicles that were described by early anatomists as hammer, anvil, and stirrup because of their resemblance to those familiar objects. Their miniaturization is astounding; the stirrup is smaller than a grain of rice. The receptive organ for sound waves so transmitted is a snail-like spiral, the cochlea, in the inner ear. It was the 19th-century Italian physiologist Alfonso Corti who discovered the transmitting point of sound waves in the follicles attached to the bony ridges inside the spiral of the cochlea, the Corti organ. These tiny appendages are the strings of a microscopic harp that vibrate by resonance with the incoming air waves. The Nobel Prize–winning scientist Georg von Békésy of Budapest found by ingenious experimentation that the Corti organ converts the sound impulse into electricity which stimulates the auditory nerve. It was at this point that science established the connection between the physical electrochemical phenomena and the physiological sensation of hearing, generated in the cortex of the brain.

The cortex can discern and discriminate nearly half a million sounds, different as to pitch, tone color, degree of loudness, and the myriad combinations of individual sounds forming additional complexes. It can instantly recognize, analyze, and identify them accurately as the voice of a friend, the meow of a cat, the trill of a bird, or the sound of a trumpet—a feat of classification that even the most modern computers cannot match. The frequencies of vibrations that can be perceived as sounds range from 16 to about 20,000 cycles per second. At levels below this range the tone disintegrates into its component beats. In his short story *The Modern Accelerator*, H.G. Wells tells of an inventor who distilled a potion that accelerated his vital functions a thousandfold, so that he experiences the consecutive sensation lasting a quarter of an hour for every second of real time. He goes to a concert and watches a cellist play but hears only heavy beats because the cello tone splits into its components. The summation of such rhythmic beats forms a low tone of about 16 cycles per second. Such a low tone can be heard even without a "modern accelerator." It can be noticed when riding in an old-fashioned streetcar or another electric vehicle on rails. At first one hears discrete beats; as the speed increases, they integrate into a distinct tone.

Ein Heldenleben (A Hero's Life). A tone poem by Richard Strauss, first performed in Frankfurt on March 3, 1899. Upon examination, it seems clear that the hero is Richard Strauss himself, for he quotes themes from his earlier tone poems. His critics are depicted by disjointed jabbering of high woodwinds, while the hero reserves for himself an imperturbable violin solo in the noble key of E-flat major.

Help, Help, the Globolinks! A satirical opera by Gian Carlo Menotti, to his amusing libretto. Its first performance took place in Hamburg on December 19, 1968. The Globolinks are electronic invaders from outer space bent on converting unwary humans into their own kind. But they are vulnerable to the beautiful sounds of traditional music and are finally routed by school children led by the exquisite Mme. Euterpova (Euterpe was the Muse of music in Greek mythology). The hermaphroditic literature teacher Mr. Lavender-Gas escapes, but the school dean, the unmusical Dr. Stone, becomes a Globolink. The score includes passages of mock-electronic music.

The Hen. Nickname of Haydn's Symphony No. 83, in the key of G minor (1785). The gallinaceous title is explained by an imagined imitation of a hen's cluck in the second subject of the first movement, but it is much less overt than the outspoken hen in one of Rameau's harpsichord pieces. The French title, *La Poule*, is commonly used, since this is the second of Haydn's Paris symphonies.

Heredity. That musical talent is hereditary is a matter of statistical analysis. Bach's genealogical tree presents astonishing proof of the persistence of musical endowments. The gift for music usually manifests itself in early infancy. Musicianship can be perfected by solicitous instruction and encouragement, but it cannot be formed without the genetic complex that underlies it. A scientific study of musical heredity is complicated by the impossibility of experimentation, such as breeding musician with musician and observing the results within a generation. Gregor Mendel experimented with peas before he could formulate his laws of heredity; a music historian can only compile statistics and establish a degree of probability in musical genetics.

It takes several generations of competent but undistinguished musicians to arrive, perhaps by random selection, at a summit of genius. Leopold Mozart was a fine and intelligent musician who gave his genius son the benefits of his musical knowledge. Wolfgang Amadeus Mozart himself had sons who were musical, but their talents were mediocre. Beethoven's greatness was an unpredictable mutation. Wagner had no ancestors who were musicians, either in the line of his legal parents or of his stepfather, who, according to some Wagnerites, was in fact Wagner's seminal father. Siegfried Wagner, "the little son of a great father," wrote a number of operas that were lamentable imitations. An interesting example of Mendelian natural selection is the family of Tcherepnin. Nicolas Tcherepnin was a nationalist Russian composer of the Rimsky-Korsakov school. His son Alexander developed his own modern technique of composition. Alexander's two sons Ivan and Serge plunged headlong into experimental and electronic music composition. Similar progressive trends are sometimes found among performing musicians. Rudolph Serkin is a famed performer of Classical and Romantic piano music; his son Peter turned decisively toward ultramodern works. In the musical theater the inheritance of talent is even more striking. Sons and daughters of famous performers, particularly singers, often start their careers as children in the theater acts of their parents, learning their skills through imitation. George Bernard Shaw was a firm believer in the inheritance not only of musical talent but even of a technical facility in performance. He asserted in the preface to his play *Back to Methuselah* that "a pianist may be born with specific pianistic aptitude which he can bring out as soon as he can physically control his hands."

The Hero. The seventeenth opera by Gian Carlo Menotti, produced in Philadelphia on June 1, 1976. The text is, as in virtually all his operas, his own. The "hero" brings fame to his town as the record-breaking sleeper (actually he wakes up occasionally), whose wife charges tourists two dollars to view him. (The opera is the first stage work to use the expletive "shit" in the text.)

Hérodiade. An opera by Jules Massenet, first produced in Brussels on December 9, 1881. The title, which means "daughter of Herodias," refers to Salomé for whom her uncle Herod, King of Galilee, nurtures an incestuous passion. She rejects him and declares love for the imprisoned John the Baptist. Here the story diverges from the famous *Salomé* by Oscar Wilde that served as the libretto for the opera of that name by Richard Strauss. In Massenet's opera, Salomé wants to die with her adored holy man, but he is executed alone and Salomé stabs herself to death.

Hesitation tango. A tango with a sharper syncopation than the standard form. Samuel Barber included a hesitation tango in his set for piano four-hands, *Souvenirs*.

Hesitation waltz. A type of mildly syncopated waltz, similar to the so-called Boston waltz. Its popularity in Europe can be measured by the traffic signs posted in the 1920s in Paris cautioning the pedestrians, "Ne dansez pas la Valse d'hésitation devant les autos."

L'Heure espagnole. An opera by Maurice Ravel, first produced in Paris on May 19, 1911. The action takes place in Toledo, Spain, in the 18th century. The "Spanish hour" of the title is the period of time during which several successive lovers of the wife of a local clockmaker hide themselves in the cabinets of the large clocks in his shop. When he discovers them, they all claim to be bona fide customers, and the greedy clockmaker accepts the explanations, whereupon they all make merry to the sounds of a habanera. The score is one of the finest examples of Ravel's subtle instrumentation and precise rhythms, for the mastery of which he earned the critical sobriquet, "the Swiss watchmaker."

Hin und Zurück. "A sketch with music" by Hindemith, first performed in Baden-Baden on July 15, 1927. The title means "there and back" in German.

The cuckolded husband kills his cheating wife; then the action reverses itself, cinema-wise; the adulteress returns to life, her husband pockets the gun, and the situation is restored to the *status quo ante*. However, the music is not a precise cancrizans.

L'Histoire du soldat (History of a Soldier). A ballet with narrative by Stravinsky, first performed in Lausanne, Switzerland on September 28, 1918. The score is for seven instruments only, and is a *tour de force* of economy. The story concerns a Russian soldier who sells his soul to the devil. Among the dance numbers are a tango, a waltz, and a ragtime.

Die Hochzeit der Sobeide. An opera by Alexander Tcherepnin, first performed in Vienna on March 17, 1933. The beautiful Sobeide, married to an unloved husband, falls in love with a muscular youth and, horrified by her own depravity, commits suicide. The music of the opera is based on Tcherepnin's nine-note scale, which lends an exotic color.

Hocket. A curious syncopated rhythmic device in medieval polyphonic music in which the cantus firmus is rapidly alternated between two voices that sing a single note or short groups of notes. Often the syllables used are onomatopoeic. The word *hocket* apparently comes from medieval Latin, "hiccup."

Holztrompete. Literally, a wooden trumpet, but actually a clarinet. This is also the name of the wind instrument that has an important solo in Wagner's *Tristan und Isolde*. However, this solo is usually played by the English horn.

Home on the Range. A legendary cowboy song with a dubious etiology. The words were first published in 1873, and the musical setting was attributed to William Goodwin, under whose name the song was published in 1904 with the title *An Arizona Home*. David Guion made a standard arrangement of the song and claims were made for him as the sole author William Goodwin instituted a lawsuit for $1 million in 1934 demanding official recognition of his authorship, but he lost for lack of evidence. Several others managed to put in their claims. In the meantime, *Home on the Range* was proclaimed the official song of the state of Kansas. It joins the honorable company of famous phantom songs, among them *God Save the King*, *Hail to the Chief*, and *Yankee Doodle*, whose authorship is claimed by many but proved by none.

Home, Sweet Home. The standard form of this famous song first sung in the opera *Clari, or The Maid of Milan* by Henry Bishop, produced in London on May 8, 1823. But—surprise!—the tune first bobbed up in a collection of songs published in London two years before the production of *Clari* under the title *Melodies of Various Nations*, where it was described as a Sicilian air, even though there was hardly any Sicilian lilt to it. The words "Home, Sweet Home" were contributed by the American writer John Howard Payne. Bishop jealously maintained his claim as the sole composer of the tune. He even sued Donizetti when he espied a simulacrum of the piece in Donizetti's opera *Anna Bolena*. Whatever its origin, the magic of *Home, Sweet Home* has worked well through the years. When a singer performed it at a concert in an American jail in 1885, the inmates were so moved that seven of them escaped that very night and went directly to their respective homes, where they were apprehended the next day. On the other hand, when an Oklahoma attorney tested its efficacy at a trial in 1935 and sang *Home, Sweet Home* to a jury, pleading for mercy for his client, a bank robber, the jury found him guilty, and the sentence was life imprisonment.

Homerische Welt. An operatic cycle in four parts by August Bungert. The first part, *Kirke*, was produced in Dresden on January 29, 1898; the second part, *Nausikaa*, on March 20, 1901; the third part, *Odysseus Heimkehr*, depicting the homecoming of Odysseus, on December 12, 1896, prior to the performances of the first two parts; and the fourth section, *Odysseus Tod*, describing the death of the hero, on October 30, 1903. The Homeric tetralogy, desperately imitating Wagner's *Ring*, sank without a trace into the Hades of stillborn musical fetuses.

Hommage. French for "homage," a dedicatory inscription to a revered personage in the arts, particularly in music. Usually such compositions are written in the manner of the master who is honored. Aaron Copland wrote a piano piece entitled *Hommage à Ives*, approximating the harmonies of Charles Ives. Debussy always had an ironic sense of devotion to England and thus paid homage to the famous Dickens character in his piano piece *Hommage à S. Pickwick, Esq.*, from his second book of *Préludes*, written about 1913. In it are disguised quotations from *God Save the King*.

Homophony. Literally, "equal sounding." A term applied to the style of composition developed in the 17th century in Florence and generally adopted in early operas, as contrasted with the previously dominating polyphonic style. In homophonic pieces, the component vocal or instrumental parts are subordinated to the melody and form clear chordal harmonies. Parallel formations in thirds and sixths, or in first-inversion triads, are essentially homophonic because there is no contrast between the voices either contrapuntally or rhythmically. The term *homophony* is valid only in historical perspective; it would be misleading to describe a Classical, Romantic, or modern work as being homophonic simply because in it harmony is subordinated to melody and strict polyphony is absent.

Honoraria. A story is told about a self-inflated opera tenor who asked a friend a rhetorical question: "How much do you think they paid me for my last opera appearance?" "One-half," was the sympathetic reply. Opera stars were a greedy lot, collecting as much as the traffic would bear. The manager of

Adelina Patti, perhaps the most divine of all divas, asserted that her pet parrot was trained to croak, "Cash! Cash!" the moment he entered her room.

Hopak. A Ukrainian popular dance in rapid, slightly syncopated 2/4 time, corresponding to the meter of anapest (two eighth notes followed by one quarter note). The word *hopak* comes from the Ukrainian imperative *"Hop!"*, "jump." It is only coincidental that its meaning is the same as that of the English word "hop." Mussorgsky, Tchaikovsky, and other Russian composers wrote hopaks for their operas.

Hora. A Rumanian popular dance, in 6/8 or 2/4 time, in a leisurely tempo. It is usually accompanied on the violin, a native type of flute, and a bagpipe. The hora was imported into Israel, where it became extremely popular. Jascha Heifetz transcribed for violin a hora by the Rumanian composer Grigoras Dinicu and published it under the title *Hora Staccato*.

Horn fifths. A two-part harmonic progression playable on natural horns or trumpets. The intervals formed are a minor sixth, a perfect fifth, and a major third. The term *horn fifth* is obviously inaccurate, but it has been traditionally accepted. Examples can be found in innumerable works written during the past three centuries, in a variety of rhythmic patterns. The trumpet calls in Rossini's overture to *William Tell* are examples of rapid horn fifths. Beethoven's *Les Adieux* Sonata opens with a slow, descending passage of horn fifths, illustrating the postilion horn announcing the departure of a stage coach.

The Horn Signal Symphony. Symphony No. 31 by Haydn, in the key of D major (1765). The reason for the nickname becomes evident as one hears a succession of horn signals. The German title is *Mit dem Hörnersignal*.

Hornpipe. An English sailors' dance that originated in the 16th century, in 2/4 time with characteristic syncopated rhythms. Its choreography reflects the energetic gestures and steps of British sailors at play. Hornpipes, either of folk origin or specially composed dances, have been used frequently in English light operas, as for example in *H.M.S. Pinafore* by Gilbert and Sullivan.

A Hot Time in the Old Town Tonight. A song by a bandleader named Theodore Metz, published in 1896. There is a story that when Metz traveled with a minstrel troupe, his train stopped in Old Town, Louisiana. He noticed several Negro boys trying to put out a fire, and someone remarked, "There'll be a hot time in Old Town tonight"; he fashioned a song out of it. Metz's detractors claimed that he lifted the song from a saloon entertainer in St. Louis. Whatever the case may be, the song, an example of early ragtime, took off spontaneously. When it was published, the cover described it as "an up-to-date, hot-stuff, coon song."

The Housatonic at Stockbridge. A song by Charles Ives, to the words of Robert Underwood Johnson. The same musical material is used in the last movement of Ives's *Three Places in New England*. The haunting tune is taken from an anthem *Missionary Chant* by Charles Zeuner. One can also perceive a similarity with the theme of Beethoven's Symphony No. 5, so beloved by Ives.

Les Huguenots. A grand opera by Giacomo Meyerbeer, first produced in Paris on February 29, 1836. One of the most spectacular of 19th-century operas, it embraces history, religious strife, and family tragedy. The climactic scene occurs during the St. Bartholomew's Day massacre of French Protestants, the Huguenots, in 1572. A Catholic nobleman leads an assault on the house in which the Huguenots make their last stand, realizing too late that his own daughter is among them. She perishes with her Huguenot lover, and her father is left to bemoan his fate.

Humor. Musical humor can be expressed in a variety of ways, from the grossest form of sonorous assault to the subtlest allusion toward some humorous subject by way of quotation. Humor by incongruous quotation is illustrated by the insertion of the thematic leitmotiv from *Tristan und Isolde* into Debussy's *Golliwogg's Cakewalk* in his piano suite, *Children's Corner*, marked "*avec une grande émotion*," and harmonized impertinently by chromatic passages. The story goes that Debussy intended to play a joke on the pianist Harold Bauer, a great admirer of Wagner, who gave the first performance of *Children's Corner*. Debussy made a bet with Bauer that he would force him to make fun of Wagner, and he won his bet when Bauer innocently performed the work without ever noticing the quotation. A purely musical example of humor is represented by Mozart's *Musical Joke*, subtitled *Village Musicians*, in which Mozart ridicules the ineptitude of the rustic players by making the fiddles play a figure in a scale of whole tones and by ending in several different keys. Imitation of animal sounds, such as the bleating of sheep in Richard Strauss's *Don Quixote*, may produce a comical effect. Virtually the entire production of Erik Satie depends for its humor on incongruous titles such as *Crépuscule matinal* and *Heures séculaires et instantanées*.

Humoresque. A fanciful instrumental composition of the 19th century, brief and light in mood. Schumann, Tchaikovsky, and others wrote such pieces. Dvořák's *Humoresque* for piano, op. 101, No. 7, written in 1894 and set on black keys, was made popular through an amusing jingle attached to the tune: "Passengers will please refrain from flushing toilet while the train is standing in the station (I love you)."

Hungarian Rhapsodies. Liszt undertook the composition of these piano works as a "patriotic anthology of the People of Hungary" in 1851. He wrote 15 of them in three years and five more during the last few years of his life.

Some of these Rhapsodies have specific surnames: No. 3 is the *Héroïde funèbre*, No. 9 is *Carnaval de Pest*, and No. 15 is *Rákóczy March*. The most famous of all is No. 2, which opens with a typical Hungarian refrain and erupts in a wild dancing rhythm in the finale. Liszt gleaned the melodic and rhythmic materials for his Hungarian Rhapsodies mainly from gypsy bands; other tunes were borrowed. This dubious practice brought about an embarrassing contretemps when an obscure German musician named Heinrich Ehrlich discovered that the thematic material of Liszt's famous Hungarian Rhapsody No. 2 was lifted in its entirety from his own work, the manuscript of which was in Liszt's hands. Liszt readily acknowledged the borrowing but pointed out that all Hungarian tunes, whether Ehrlich's or anybody else's, derive from the same popular sources.

Hunnenschlacht. Liszt's symphonic poem, first performed in Weimar on December 29, 1857, was inspired by a fresco of the painter Kaulbach that represented the battle between the Huns and the Christians. The latter are helped by supernal spirits hovering over the battlefield. The music alternates between scenes of slaughter and angelic hymnody by using parallel diminished-seventh chords and modal harmonies.

Hurdy-gurdy. A popular medieval instrument that resembled a lute in appearance. It was not played with a bow; the strings were set in vibration by turning a wheel with a handle. It had a double melody string played in unison and bass strings that produced a drone, usually an open fifth. Its usual plebeian employment as a street organ caused discrimination against its use in serious music, but in the 18th century it was renamed *lyra*, and the new appellation imparted some dignity to it. Another name for it is *vielle à roue*, a wheel viol. Schubert's famous song *Der Leiermann* is a nostalgic image of a hurdy-gurdy player, the characteristic open fifths in the bass of the accompaniment imitating the drone.

Hymn. The generic name for songs in praise of God. In early established church services, hymns were confined to chants of adoration, differing in their purpose and their form from the psalms and canticles. Hymnody, that is, the doctrine of hymns and the theory of their composition, was generated in the Christian community of Syria about the fourth century. The earliest authenticated Christian hymn, written in Greek notation, was discovered in the town of Oxyrhynchos in Egypt; it is dated approximately A.D. 200. Latin hymns, which are fundamental to the Roman Catholic church, emerged toward the end of the fourth century in the Christian community of Milan, of which St. Ambrose was the bishop. Hymn tunes of the first millennium of our era were almost exclusively monophonic; contrapuntal settings were limited to the intervals of the octave, perfect fifth, and perfect fourth. Polyphonic hymnody was the fruit of the great school of Notre Dame in Paris in the 11th century, and achieved its flowering with the advent of the so-called Burgundian and Flemish polyphonic systems of composition. The Roman Catholic church retained the Latin form of hymns, but in Germany, even before Luther, a trend developed of writing hymns in the German language and of combining German verses with the Latin ones. A mixture of German and French vernacular with Latin hymns attained a high degree of poetic expression in the *Carmina Burana*, a collection named after the monastery of Benedict Beuren in Bavaria that contains texts and melodies notated in rudimentary neumes, as they were sung by the goliards, young clerics, and itinerant students who wandered over Germany, much in the manner of the troubadours and trouvères of France. The French term for a hymn is *cantique*.

The Lutheran hymnody absorbed some of the vernacular modalities from popular sources, and the product became the foundation of hymn singing and hymn composing in all Protestant nations. The Anglican church adopted many Lutheran hymns in the 16th century, among them the most famous hymn believed to have been written by Luther himself, *A Mighty Fortress Is Our God*. In England and later in America, the Lutheran hymns assumed a metrical form that almost approaches the secular type of song. English and American hymns are invariably set in a chordal style; occasional canons do not disrupt the prevailing homophonic arrangements. A curious departure from this style is the type of hymn called "fuguing tunes," in which the middle section of a homophonic composition contains fugal imitation.

The word *hymn* is the precise transference of the Greek word *hymnos*. In Greek poetry, a hymn was a chant in honor of a god or hero. In Latin, such pre-Christian hymns are usually translated by the word *carmen*, which means "song." The Christians, however, accepted the Latinized form *hymnus*, in the sense of a poem or a song in praise of the Lord. St. Augustine gave a remarkably clear definition of the hymn as a poetic expression that must include three aspects: singing, praise, and God.

Hymnen. An electronic work by Karlheinz Stockhausen that combines the tunes of the national anthems of many lands as a vision of a metaphysical union of all nations. It was first performed in Cologne on November 30, 1967.

Hyperprism. An extraordinary work for wind instruments and percussion by Edgar Varèse. It was first performed in New York on March 4, 1923, and was greeted by the critics with expressions of dismay. *Hyperprism* is a projection of the fourth-dimensional prism upon space in three dimensions.

I Didn't Raise My Boy to Be a Soldier. A song by Al Piantadosi, published in 1915 when the United States was neutral during World War I. The cover showed a gray-haired mother shielding her frightened young son from bombs bursting in air over European boys and their mothers. As the national sentiment began to favor joining the Allies in the war, the same publishing house moderated its total neutrality by putting out a song entitled *I Don't Want My Boy to be a Soldier, but I Will Send My Girl to Be a Nurse*. Still later, the same publishers issued a final version of the song, with the same gray-haired mother on the cover surrendering her by now heroic-looking son to Uncle Sam, with the title *America, Here Is My Boy!*

I Got Rhythm. An ingeniously intricate and yet disarmingly simple song by George Gershwin. Its rhythmical pattern is formed by an eighth-note rest followed by four dotted eighths and another eighth-note rest, all encompassed within a regular 4/4 measure. An earnest modernist addicted to polymetrics would have notated Gershwin's pattern as a bar of 2/16 followed by four bars of 3/16, concluding with another bar of 2/16. Gershwin composed the piece for his musical comedy *Girl Crazy* in 1930 and arranged it in a brilliant piano solo. There is also a version for piano and orchestra.

I Wonder Who's Kissing Her Now. This song was introduced by Joseph Howard in the musical *The Prince of the Night* in 1909, and sold more than 3 million copies of sheet music. Howard's reputation as a composer was built on the success of this song, and it was quite a shock when 40 years later one Harold Orlob brought a lawsuit against Howard, claiming that the tune was written by him when he was employed by Howard as an arranger. Interestingly enough, Orlob did not demand money; all he wanted was a piece of the fame. Howard, old and ailing, conceded Orlob's claim, and the song was republished under both names.

Idomeneo, Rè de Creta (Idomeneo, King of Crete). An opera by Mozart, first produced in Munich on January 29, 1781. Returning from the Trojan war,

Idomeneo's ship runs into a storm. To exorcise the sea god Poseidon, Idomeneo promises to sacrifice the first person who meets his ship at home; it happens to be his own son. When Idomeneo tries to evade his pledge, the gods send a monster to ravage Crete. At this point comes the proverbial *deus ex machina* who magnanimously arranges a compromise: forcing Idomeneo's abdication in favor of his son.

If I Were King (Si j'étais roi). An opera by Adolphe Adam, first produced in Paris on September 4, 1852. The action unfolds in the Indian port of Goa in the 16th century before its capture by Portugal. A fisherman saves a young girl from drowning, not realizing that she is the Princess of Goa. When he recognizes her on the beach, he tells the king's nephew about the rescue. The nephew orders him never to mention it again under penalty of death. Aggrieved, the fisherman traces the words on the sand, *"Si j'étais roi,"* and falls asleep. The king, touched by this sight, orders the sleeping man transferred to the royal palace and lets him rule Goa for a day. The fisherman discovers that the king's nephew has been treacherously conducting negotiations with the Portuguese and preparing to surrender the city. The king expels the traitor, and the Portuguese are repelled. The fisherman marries the princess. The opera is melodious; its overture is often played at popular concerts.

Ilya Muromets. The subtitle of the Symphony No. 3, the most significant work of the Russian composer Reinhold Glière. It was first performed in Moscow on March 23, 1912. In four movements, it depicts the deeds of valor performed by the legendary Russian knight, Ilya Muromets. The music is eminently romantic with some modernistic touches, such as the employment of whole-tone scales to suggest Ilya's unbounded heroism.

I'm Always Chasing Rainbows. A musical travesty perpetrated in 1918 on the melody of the middle part of Chopin's *Fantaisie-Impromptu* by an unscrupulous Broadway manipulator, set to words of emetic saccharinity.

Images. An orchestral suite by Debussy, written between 1905 and 1910. The first section is entitled *Gigues*. In the second section, *Iberia*, Debussy depicts his love of Spain; in its last movement he instructs the violinists to hold their instruments in their arms and strum them like guitars. *Iberia* was first performed in Paris on February 20, 1910. The third section, *Rondes de Printemps*, is especially popular; the "dances of spring" in this score are marked by constantly changing rhythms and colorful orchestral timbres; the composer conducted its first performance in Paris on March 2, 1910. Debussy also wrote two piano suites entitled *Images I* (1905) and *Images II* (1907).

Imaginary Landscape. The generic name for several works by John Cage. Each one makes use of noises and random combinations of sounds produced by various means, including the chance manipulation of a radio receiver. Cage produced the first of these *Landscapes* in 1942.

Imbroglio. The word literally means "a mixture." In music, it is the use of rhythmically contrasting and noncoincident sections within a common meter. A simultaneous use of 3/4 and 6/8 in Spanish music is an imbroglio. A similar combination of meters is found in Mozart's opera *Don Giovanni* at the end of the first act. There is another example in the street scene in Wagner's *Die Meistersinger*. Much more complex examples of imbroglio are exemplified by the second movement of *Three Places in New England* by Charles Ives and in the String Quartet No. 3 of Elliott Carter.

Imitation. The generic term for a repetition, either exact or approximate, in an instrumental or vocal part of the main theme or a motif. It is the most natural and powerful device at the foundation of the canon and fugue and is found in practically all musical forms. Progressing from literal repetition of a musical phrase, imitation evolved into a complex polyphonic art in which themes were inverted, taken at half speed (augmentation) or double speed (diminution), and further embellished by a variety of ornamental devices. The minimum requirement of all types of imitation is the preservation of the rhythmic pattern of the original theme, or else it becomes unrecognizable.

Imperial Maryinsky Theater. The great opera house founded in St. Petersburg in 1783, which received the name Maryinsky after an Imperial dowager named Marie. Catherine the Great engaged famous Italian and French musicians and choreographers as its directors. The czars and assorted grand dukes used to pick up ballerinas from the ballet troupe of the Imperial Theater to be their clandestine concubines. The last one, Ksheshinska, who was a favorite of Czar Nicholas II, died in Paris in 1970 at the age of 99. Her name entered history because Lenin made her villa in St. Petersburg his headquarters after the Revolution. At the same time, the name of the Imperial Theater was changed to the State Academy Theater of Opera and Ballet. In 1935 it was renamed Kirov Theater of Leningrad, to commemorate the Soviet leader Kirov, who was assassinated in 1934. With the transfer of the Russian capital to Moscow after the Revolution, the first place among Russian opera and ballet theaters passed to the Bolshoi Theater in Moscow.

The Impresario (Der Schauspieldirektor). A "comedy with music" by Mozart, commissioned by Emperor Joseph II and first performed at the Imperial Palace at Schönbrunn, Vienna, on February 7, 1786, along with another commissioned opera, *Prima la Musica e poi le parole* ("First the music, and then the words") by Antonio Salieri. Mozart's opera concerns an impresario who has to deal with two rival prima donnas contending for the same role, one of whom is a mistress of the banker who finances his season. The libretto has been variously revised, and several versions are in circulation.

Impressionism. A term that originated in art criticism in Paris in the 1870s, specifically referring to the title of a painting by the French artist Claude Monet, *Sunrise*, subtitled *An Impression*. The work was supposed to reflect an impression on the inner eye, lacking precision or a strong separation of colors. An art critic reviewed this painting in the Paris journal *Charivari* in an article entitled "Impressionism," with an obvious humorous intent. However, the French modernists, including Monet himself, accepted the term *impressionism* as honorable. Inevitably, musical compositions by Debussy, Ravel, and their French companions were also described as impressionistic because of their composers' preference for fluid and colorful harmonies suggesting uncertain, misty images. Indeed, to some modern poets and musicians, colors, and tones were mutually interchangeable. To this equivalence Baudelaire added odors: "Les parfums, les couleurs et les sons se repondent" ("The odors, the colors and the sounds relate to one another"). The aesthetician Huysmans joined gustatory impressions to the rainbow of sensations and spoke of an "organ of liqueurs." He compared the sound of the clarinet to the taste of curaçao sec; the oboe was like kümmel; the flute served anisette; the trombone provided gin and whiskey; and the tuba offered the strong drink of vodka. Just as impressionist painters made use of coalescent colors, so impressionist composers enhanced harmonious sounds by dissonances. Impressionism rejected all utilitarian art. Henri de Regnier spoke of "le plaisir délicieux et toujours nouveau d'une occupation inutile" ("the delicious and always novel pleasure of a useless occupation"). Ravel used this line as an epigraph in the score of his evocative suite *Valse nobles et sentimentales*. The acrid sensation of a musical dissonance attracted many poets. Keats wrote of discords that make the sweetest airs. Verlaine described the sounds of "accords harmonieusement dissonants" ("harmoniously dissonant chords"). Impressionist music was an intimate art that abhorred loud sonorities. Even such a caustic critic of Debussy as his former classmate Camille Bellaigue conceded that Debussy's music made "peu de bruit" ("little noise"), but he added with malicious humor that it was a "vilain petit bruit" ("a vile little noise").

Debussy disliked the term *impressionism*. To him his music was a concord of occidental and oriental art. For the cover of his score of *La Mer* he selected a Japanese drawing of the powerful crest of a typhoon wave. Another source of inspiration for Debussy and his companions was classical Greek music, or rather what French musicians of the time imagined such music to be. Accordingly, the Grecian consecutive fifths and fourths, forbidden by conservatory rules, were accepted by the impressionists as valid harmonic progressions. In all impressionist music, a nuance was preferred to explicit statements. The cadences are brief and concise. Chromatic passages are frequent but never extend to the full scale, and adumbration rather than declaration is favored in both harmonic and melodic formulas.

Impromptu. From the Latin locution *in promptu esse*, "to be at hand," "to be ready." The term, which suggests improvisation, was applied to interludes in theatrical plays in the 17th century, as in Molière's *L'Impromptu de Versailles*. As a form of character pieces, the impromptu became popular in the 19th century. Schubert wrote a number of impromptus for piano. These pieces are indeed "in promptu," for they are built in a symmetric form in which each main section is subdivided into three subsections, and each subsection is subdivided into three subaltern segments, which in turn are split into brief musical phrases in three-part form. The title *Impromptu* was not original with Schubert; it was appended to the music by his publisher. Chopin's impromptus for piano are particularly remarkable in their perfect symmetrical design.

Improvisation. From the Latin *improvisus*, "unforeseen," and *ex improviso*, "without preparation." In music, improvisation denotes the art of a completely spontaneous performance without a preliminary plan. Formerly, improvisation was regarded as integral to the craft of composition. Organists in particular were emboldened to improvise freely on a given hymn tune. Among the greatest improvisers on the organ were Frescobaldi and Buxtehude. Bach was a master of organ improvisation in the fugal style. As a child, Mozart included improvisations at his performances at the European courts. Beethoven's improvisations for his musical friends left an overwhelming impression. At his recitals, Liszt asked musicians in the audience to give him subjects for free improvisations and amazed them by the spontaneity of his invention. Organ improvisations have continued to be the stock in trade of organists in the 20th century, but public improvisations by pianists gradually fell into disfavor. Some doubt persists whether the supposedly spontaneous improvisations were not in fact prepared in advance. One type of talented improviser on the piano, unfortunately extinct, was represented by pianists in the silent movies early in the century. Some of them had a real flair for enhancing the visual image on the screen while producing music of considerable validity. Jazz players have brought the art of improvisation to a new height of brilliance, especially in collective improvisations occurring in jam sessions.

In the Steppes of Central Asia. A symphonic tableau by Alexander Borodin, first performed in St. Petersburg on April 8, 1880. It is a poetic evocation of the oriental atmosphere of Khiva and Bukhara, the Khanates of central Asia absorbed in the middle of the 19th century by the expansionist Russian empire. Moslem chants are imitated in the score, and there are also spacious pentatonic passages that reflect Mongolian modalities.

Incidental music. A set of pieces composed to illustrate selected scenes in a dramatic performance. It is distinguished from an orchestral suite because incidental music is subordinated to the dramatic action; it differs from opera because usually there are no vocal parts. The overture from Beethoven's incidental music to Goethe's *Egmont* is frequently performed as a separate concert piece, as are several numbers from Mendelssohn's score to *A Midsummer Night's Dream*, the *Wedding March* being the most famous. Other examples of incidental music that became popular in concert are *L'Arlésienne* by Bizet and *Peer Gynt* by Grieg.

Incipit. Latin for "it begins." It refers to the first word or group of words of a Gregorian chant and thereby identifies a particular hymn or a cantus firmus. In this sense, Requiem, Magnificat, Kyrie, Gloria, and other parts of the Mass are such incipits. In cataloguing old manuscripts, the incipit identifies the beginning of the first page; the ending of the manuscript is then indicated by the word *explicit*, meaning "it folds out," that is, it ends.

The Incredible Flutist. A ballet suite by Walter Piston, one of the few scores he wrote that was programmatic. The flutist leads a village circus in a series of dances. He is incredible because everyone in the crowd follows his cues. The score ends with an infectious march. It was first performed by the Boston Pops Orchestra on May 30, 1938.

Indian music. As in most ancient cultures, the music of India was closely related to religious rites, with melodies and rhythms subordinated to the verbal content of sacred verses. So strict was the formulation of words and modalities of classical Indian music that even a minor deviation from the chant was thought capable of upsetting the entire balance of the universe. The chants and texts were derived from the Indian Vedas ("wisdom" in archaic Sanskrit). The succession of melodic tones in such chants was arranged in a system of ragas, corresponding to Western scales but greatly diversified to express the states of body and soul, so that a performance of a raga by means of masterful improvisation established the mood of both the singer and the listener, varying from unrestrained joy to deep melancholy. Because of this interdependence, an Indian musician conveys the meaning of the music in a way virtually inaccessible to an uninitiated Western listener. Thus it became a hermetic art of music, based on melodic inflections, quite distant from the art of the West, which maintains a harmonic foundation. Indian ragas originated in the north of the Indian peninsula, which was autochtonous and self-sustaining. With the penetration of Arabic and Persian musical elements from the south and the equatorial islands, the nature of Indian music changed, eventually leading to a coalition of different ingredients. The ragas multiplied enormously and combined with an intricate system of complex rhythmic groupings called *talas*. Indian musicians playing in an ensemble merely counted numbers of metrical units to keep time. The resulting impression is that of asymmetrical structure. The instruments of India are adapted to this tradition of rich yet subtle melodic and rhythmic progressions. Among them the most important is the sitar, a string instrument related to the Western lute. It has 3 to 7 gut strings and several sympathetic wire strings that enhance the sound and provide a tonal basis against the minute manipulations and bendings of melodic pitches. A variety of the sitar is the tambura, with four strings that are played in the backgound as a kind of drone. The South Indian counterpart to the sitar is the vina. A full Indian ensemble similar to the Western chamber music group also includes flutes, horns, and other wind instruments made of bamboo reeds. There are also multifarious drums, of which the most common are the tablas, a pair of small, pitched drums, as well as a great number of bells, gongs, cymbals, and other metal percussion instruments.

Indian Suite. An orchestral work by Edward MacDowell, in five movements, with thematic materials derived from Iroquois, Chippewa, Dakota, and Kiowa melodies. It was first performed in New York on January 23, 1895.

Indianische Fantasie. A work by Ferruccio Busoni for piano and orchestra, which he first performed, as piano soloist, in Berlin on March 12, 1914. Original pentatonic American Indian themes are used as material for the work.

Indonesian music. The state of Indonesia comprises several thousand islands, great and small, straddling the equator. Musically, the most important of them are Java and Bali; each developed its own indigenous type of ensemble, the gamelan, which consists of sui generis xylophones and a variety of bells, gongs, and drums. The basic scales of the gamelan are the five-tone *slendro* system and the seven-tone *pelog* system, with supernumerary tones used as embellishments. No two gamelans are tuned exactly the same, however, which leads to the unique character of each particular ensemble. The intervals of the gamelan cannot be reduced precisely to the Western modes, which makes an impression on the Western ear of both the stimulating exotic quality of the sound and the disturbing feeling that the melodies are off pitch. When the gamelan was introduced at the Paris Exposition of 1889, Debussy and other French composers of the modern school were fascinated by it; Debussy tried to imitate its foreign sound in several of his works. The greatest attraction of the gamelan to Western composers is the seeming promiscuity of its modes, so that there is a prevailing sense of enhanced concord even when dissonant combinations are employed. Furthermore, rhythmic patterns can be used without regard to a prescribed meter. The duration of the basic time unit never changes in a given dance or song with the accompaniment of the gamelan and repeated uniform beats are common, but the complexity is provided by interlocking polyrhythmic patterns. The music heard on the large islands of Borneo and Sumatra is closer to being "primitive," devoid of the gamelan delicacy.

***Ines de Castro*.** An opera by Giuseppe Persiani, first performed in Naples on January 27, 1835, with Persiani's wife Fanny Tacchinardi in the title role. This is probably the bloodiest opera ever produced, for it ends with the assassination of Ines and the slaughter of her children. The assassins act on behalf of the King of Castile, who wants to quash the ambition of Pedro I of Portugal, the consort of Ines, to occupy the throne of Castile. So far the events are based on historical evidence. Ines de Castro was indeed assassinated in 1355. In the opera, as in history, Pedro I finally becomes the King of Castile; in the opera, but probably not in history, Pedro orders the body of Ines to be crowned and forces the courtiers to kiss her dead hands. The work is written in the musical manner of Bellini and Donizetti. The famous Maria Malibran sang the part of Ines in the Paris production of the opera in 1839. Czerny wrote a set of piano variations on the theme of an aria from this opera.

Insanity and suicide. It is a common belief that musicians are more nervous by nature than other professionals, that a greater percentage of performers and composers end their lives in mental institutions, and that only mathematicians and chess players exceed musicians in this melancholy fate. Statistics fail to support this estimate. Among famous composers only Schumann and MacDowell became totally insane and had to be committed. Exaggerated sensitivity to criticism, delusions of grandeur, melancholy, and other aberrations may be typical among artists who are constantly on view before the public, but such neurotic traits do not constitute insanity. Even suicidal impulses are no more frequent among musicians than the law of averages would indicate. Perhaps the most spectacular suicide was that of the pianist Alexander Kelberine, who arranged his last concert program to consist only of works dealing with death, concluding with *Totentanz* by Liszt. Upon returning home, he took a lethal overdose of sleeping pills. Rezsö Seress, the composer of *Gloomy Sunday*, a song that was banned in some European countries because it precipitated a wave of Sunday suicides among young people, himself jumped out of a window and died. In his mental distress Schumann jumped into the Rhine but was rescued by a fisherman. There were unfounded reports that Tchaikovsky committed suicide by poison. Not true. He died of cholera, and there is plenty of medical evidence to prove it.

***Intégrales*.** A work for small orchestra and percussion by Edgar Varèse, constructed according to his ideas of organized sound integrated into one self-consistent formal structure. The piece was performed for the first time in New York under the auspices of the International Composers Guild with Leopold Stokowski conducting on March 1, 1925. The critics exercised their literary wits and power of animal metaphors to describe the music as suggesting an intoxicated woodpecker, an injured dog's cry of pain, or a cat's yell of midnight rage.

Intermezzo. This Italian word literally means an "insertion." Intermezzi date back to the liturgical drama in the 13th century, into which they were interpolated between ritual parts of the religious service. Secular intermezzi provided diversions at aristocratic weddings, coronations, and other formal functions. Invariably they were of a lighter nature than other parts of the occasion, and were not necessarily connected with the action in the drama or religious play into which they were inserted. The genre eventually developed into independent musical presentations, leading ultimately to the formation of opera buffa, that is, comic opera. Because the intermezzi did not have to be connected with the principal spectacle, their authors strove mainly to please the public by whatever means, and the results often succeeded in attracting more attention than did the stage play itself. Thus, Pergolesi inserted an intermezzo *La Serva padrona* into a performance of his serious opera *Il Prigioniero superbo*, with the result that the intermezzo became extremely popular; its performances in Paris precipitated the famous *guerre des bouffons*. Rousseau, who was an ardent partisan of the Italian type of opera, composed an intermezzo (*intermède* in French), *Le Devin du village*, which became quite successful. Richard Strauss wrote an amusing opera of his own in this genre and pointedly entitled it *Intermezzo*. In operas, intermezzi are instrumental interludes, usually of short duration, between scenes. An intermezzo in Mascagni's *Cavalleria rusticana* is often performed as an independent concert piece. A quite different type of intermezzo is a character piece of instrumental music in which the title is understood in the sense of a piece written at leisure between times. It is difficult to justify in this sense the title *Intermezzi* that Brahms assigned to his highly elaborate Romantic piano pieces.

Internationale. The proletarian marching hymn written by a wood carver, one Pierre Degeyter, shortly after the fall of the Paris Commune of 1871. It served as the official anthem of the Soviet Union until 1944

Interval. In music theory, the distance between two notes measured in diatonic degrees. The distance between a note and itself is obviously zero, but it is called prime, or unison, with the symbol 1. The distance between a given note and the next note in the scale is obviously a single unit, but it is called a second, marked with the numerical symbol 2. Thus, the names of the intervals indicate not the distance between two notes, but the numerical order of their positions as we proceed up the scale. The Russian composer and theorist Sergei Taneyev, who was mathematically minded, tried to remedy this heteronomy in his book on mobile counterpoint by constructing a rudimentary mechanical gauge for invertible intervals, in which their numerical cardinal symbols are subtracted from 7, the number of diatonic units in an octave. But his seemingly rational taxonomy failed, and we are forced to accept the established terminology.

The tabulation of intervals, named after the ordinal numbers, is otherwise quite simple: unison, second, third, fourth, fifth, sixth, seventh, and octave. In Italian, the intervals are prima, seconda, terza, quarta, quinta, sesta, settima, and ottava. In French, the order is unisson, seconde, tierce, quarte, quinte, sixte, septième, and octave. In German, the names follow the Italian order: Prime, Sekunde, Terz, Quarte, Quinte, Sexte, Septime, and Oktave. The Russian nomenclature follows the German closely, but the final vowels follow the Italian usage. The Spanish names of intervals are, as in Italian, numerical adjectives in the feminine gender. Much more solemn and learned are the names of intervals in Latin, derived from Greek: unisonus, tonus, ditonus, diatessaron, diapente, tonus cum diapente, ditonus cum diapente, and diapason (octave). Beyond the octave, the intervals are still named by the numerical adjectives in English and in French; they follow Latin forms in German, Italian, Spanish, and Russian.

Intervals are specified as being major, minor, augmented, and diminished. It is most unfortunate that the nomenclature of intervals in English borrows the Latin comparative adjectives major and minor for the size of intervals and that the same terms are also used to indicate major and minor keys. This confuses students who are apt to say that the interval E to C is a major sixth, rather than the correct minor sixth, simply because E and C convey to the ear the feeling of a C-major triad, particularly with C in the melody position. Much more convenient is the German terminology in which the adjectives *grosse* and *kleine* are used for our major and minor, so that *kleine Sexte* is unmistakably a small sixth (E to C as in our previous example), and the ambiguity is avoided. The Russians follow the German usage. The unison, fourth, fifth, and octave are perfect intervals, without a subdivision into major and minor (that is, large and small). Furthermore, all intervals can be augmented or diminished, and some can even be doubly augmented or doubly diminished. A fourth can be diminished, augmented, and doubly augmented; a fifth can be augmented, diminished, and doubly diminished. All these possibilities are governed by the intrinsic development of the tonalities of which the intervals are diatonic parts.

Several intervallic pairs are enharmonic equivalents, containing identical numbers of semitones. And here we enter a knotted web of anomalies. A minor third is a consonance, but its enharmonic equivalent, an augmented second, which sounds exactly the same, is a dissonance, requiring resolution. This seeming anomaly is accounted for by the fact that it is the musical spelling that determines the belonging of an interval or a chord to a particular tonality, and what is consonant in one tonality may be dissonant in another. An analogy from linguistics may help: the word *four* is a number, but the word *for* is a preposition. *Mother* is the sweetest word in English, dripping in sentimentality, which may well be likened to a perfect consonance, but the same word, *mother*, is also defined in Webster's *New Collegiate Dictionary* as "a slimy membrane composed of yeast and bacterial cells that develops on the surface of alcoholic liquids undergoing acetous fermentation and called also a 'mother of vinegar.' "

Introduction. An instrumental prelude before an aria in an opera, or an orchestral *tutti* before the entry of the soloist. Such an introduction may be very brief (e.g., the plagal cadential chords in the opening bars of Rachmaninoff's Piano Concerto No. 2), or else it may fill a lengthy section almost qualified to be called an overture (as in the *tutti* introduction to Beethoven's Violin Concerto). It may be in a parallel minor or major key, as in Beethoven's Symphony No. 4, which opens in B-flat minor in a long preamble before the transition to the principal key in B flat major. Scriabin's Symphony No. 3 has a long introduction in D flat major, the Neapolitan lowered supertonic of the principal key, C minor.

Introduction and Allegro. A piece for harp, string quartet, flute, and clarinet by Ravel, first performed in Paris on February 22, 1907. The music exemplifies a modern, impressionistic treatment of the harp.

Invention. From the Latin verb *invenire*, "to find." In music, a work that has elements of intellectual and artistic discovery. In Renaissance music, the word *invention* still kept its Latin connotation of newness. To the minds of 17th-century musicians, inventions were the product of intuitive observation, both modern in relation to their era and curious with respect to intellectual perception. The theory of the musical invention followed the rules of Latin rhetoric going back to Cicero and Quintilian and was retained in the system of schooling in the Baroque era in a sequence of mental and artistic stages in the following order: Inventio, Dispositio, Elaboratorio, Decoratio, and Executio. The art of invention in music reached its highest expressive mark in Bach's two-part and three-part keyboard Inventions. In the introductory paragraph to his Inventions, Bach states his aims in concordance with the old rhetorical sequence: "A faithful Guide, whereby the lovers of the Clavichord are presented with a plain method of learning not only how to play clearly in two parts, but also to progress toward playing three obbligato parts well and accurately; at the same time striving not only to obtain fine inventions, but also to develop them appropriately, and above all to secure a cantabile style of playing so as to create a strong foretaste of the art of composition itself."

Inversion. Etymologically, this word connotes a turning inside out or upside down. In musical terminology, inversion has two aspects: (1) melodic inversion, in which the ascending intervals of the original melody are inverted to become descending intervals, and vice versa, and (2) harmonic inversion, in which the bass voice is placed on top of the chord.

A melodic inversion is said to be tonal if it follows the tonality of the melody. The second subject of the G-major fugue from Book I of Bach's *Well-Tempered Clavier* is such an inversion of the first subject. In tonal inversions, the intervals are not precise as to the content in semitone units. For instance, the C-major scale when inverted becomes the Phrygian mode, with the initial interval being a semitone rather than a whole tone. A major tetrachord when inverted becomes a minor tetrachord. A broken major triad becomes a broken minor triad when inverted, and vice versa. An interesting example of this reciprocal relationship of major and minor tonalities in inversion is provided by the 18th variation of Rachmaninoff's *Rhapsody on a Theme by Paganini*, in which the original ascending minor tune becomes, in a slower tempo, an emotional romantic theme, descending to the dominant an octave lower.

Inversions of intervals are obtained by placing the low notes an octave above, or (which is the same) the upper note an octave below. When a major interval is inverted, it becomes minor; an augmented interval becomes diminished. To obtain the intervallic inversion arithmetically, the original interval must be subtracted from nine. Thus, a second that is inverted becomes a seventh, a fourth becomes a fifth, and so on. A perfect interval inverts into another perfect interval (e.g., a perfect fifth inverted becomes a perfect fourth). A consonance inverted becomes another consonance (e.g., thirds become sixths); a dissonance inverted becomes another dissonance (e.g., a second becomes a seventh).

Invitation to the Dance. A rondo for piano by Carl Maria von Weber, composed in 1819. A unique composition in its treatment as a concert piece, it became famous in its orchestral arrangement that Berlioz made in 1841.

Ionian mode. A mode corresponding to the structure of the major scale. It was added to the traditional four authentic modes by Glareanus in 1547 and placed at the head of the system of church modes as *primus tonus* by Zarlino in 1558. Ironically, the Ionian mode, which is the starting point of the traditional cycle of scales and the first rudiment of musical education, was described in medieval treatises as *modus lascivus*, a "lascivious" or "lewd" mode.

Ionisation. A unique work by Edgar Varèse, written entirely for percussion instruments and a pair of sirens. Composed in 1931, it was first performed in New York on March 6, 1933. The word *ionisation* is a scientific term that signifies the separation of atoms into charged particles. The rhythmic pattern of the score is extremely complex, and the balance of instrumental timbres, such as wood and metal, is maintained with an extraordinary degree of virtuosity. It is said that a recording of *Ionisation* was regularly played by scientists working on the atom bomb in 1942.

Iphigénie en Aulide. An opera by Christoph Willibald von Gluck, after a play by Racine based on Euripides, first produced in Paris on April 19, 1774. The Greek fleet is in doldrums in the port of Aulis and cannot proceed to Troy because Agamemnon, King of Crete, has killed a sacred animal in the temple of Artemis. A priest warns him that the goddess will not be appeased unless Agamemnon sacrifices his daughter, Iphigénia. He is willing to yield, but her bridegroom, Achilles, voices objections, and Iphigénia is saved. The overture from the opera is famous as a concert piece.

Iris. An opera by Pietro Mascagni, first performed in Rome on November 22, 1898. The action takes place in modern Japan. Iris, pure and innocent, is abducted by a villainous suitor who places her in a bordello. Her blind father curses her, believing her guilty. She throws herself into a sewer but is lifted by a host of angels to Heaven. The music is in the style of verismo; pentatonic progressions are used to suggest Japanese modalities.

Islamey. A popular dance of the Caucasian tribe of the Kabardinians, marked by a drone on the dominant and suggesting the Mixolydian mode. In 1869, Balakirev wrote a piano fantasy entitled *Islamey*, which was regarded for a long time as the most difficult piece ever written for piano. The word *Islamey* is derived from Islam.

The Isle of the Dead. A symphonic poem by Rachmaninoff, inspired by the famous mortuary painting by Böcklin. Rachmaninoff conducted its first performance in Moscow on May 1, 1909. The work is remarkable because of its prevalent meter of 5/8, unusual for Rachmaninoff.

Isorhythm. A Greek term to indicate melodies, particularly the cantus firmus of medieval motets, that are built on the same rhythmic sequence (*iso* means "same").

Israel in Egypt. An oratorio in English by Handel after verses from Exodus and the Psalms, written when he was a resident of London. Its first performance took place there on April 4, 1739.

Israel Symphony. A work by Ernest Bloch, who, although born in Switzerland and living most of his life in the United States, remained faithful to his Jewish heritage. The symphony is in two movements, portraying the contemplative religious mood of the Jewish people and the contrasting dramatic outcry of the nation deprived of a home. It was first performed in New York on May 3, 1917, 30 years before the formation of the state of Israel.

Istar Variations. Orchestral variations by Vincent d'Indy, inspired by the Babylonian myth of the goddess Istar who passes through seven gates gradually shedding her vestments until she is nude. Ingeniously, the work begins with variations and ends with the theme, naked at last. It contains impressionistic elements of tone painting. It was first performed in Brussels on January 10, 1897.

Italian Concerto. A work written by Bach for a harpsichord with two manuals. It is so named because it employs the antiphony of the two manuals, one playing soft and the other loud, in the Italian manner of an instrumental concerto.

Italian Symphony. The usual title of Mendelssohn's Symphony No. 4 in A major, first performed in London on May 13, 1833. The Italian element is apparent in the finale, which is a rapid saltarello, but Mendelssohn himself never authorized the title.

Ite missa est. The valedictory sentence of the Mass: "Go, it [the congregation] is dismissed." This dismissal is etymologically significant, for the Latin term for the Mass is *Missa.*

Izeÿl. An opera by Eugène d'Albert from pseudo-Hindu lore. Izeÿl is an Indian princess whose lips are poisonous. She kills her suitors by kissing them until she dies herself when one of the suitors turns out to be immune to her osculation. *Izeÿl* was first performed in Hamburg on November 6, 1909.

J

The Jakobin. An opera by Dvořák, first performed in Prague on February 12, 1889. The action takes place in a small Bohemian town in 1793. Bogus, a young Bohemian, is denounced by his detractors as a radical Jacobin, an appellation that bore a particular stigma at the time of the French Revolution, when the Jacobins were regarded as violent radicals. Bogus is forced to leave Bohemia for several years, but virtue triumphs in the end when the villainous calumniators are exposed, the purported Jacobin returns home with his French bride, and he inherits a rich patrimony. The name of the dastardly persecutor in the opera is Adolf; the line in the libretto, "Wherever brutality reigns, Adolf is there," was loudly applauded at performances during the Nazi occupation of Czechoslovakia. The Nazi authorities ordered the name to be changed to Rudolf, but that did not help because Rudolf was the name of one of Hitler's henchmen, Rudolf Hess. After several incidents, the opera was banned by the Nazis and not revived until the liberation of Czechoslovakia.

Jaltarang. A set of porcelain cups partially filled with water and tuned according to the intervallic scheme of a specific Indian raga. The scale is played with wooden sticks.

Janizary music. The military music of the Janizary guards of the Turkish sultans. In the wake of the Turkish invasion of Eastern Europe in the 16th century, this type of music—raucous, loud, and enlivened by a strong rhythmic pulse—exercised the imagination of European writers, painters, and musicians. They were impressed by the Turkish drums, triangles, and cymbals. The cymbals were the Turkish crescent, known popularly as Jingling Johnny, which was hung with bells and jingles and crowned with an ornament in the shape of a pavilion. This music penetrated into military bands of Poland, Russia, and Austria in the first half of the 18th century. Big drums, triangles, and cymbals *alla turca* provided exotic color in the "oriental" operas of Gluck and Mozart. Haydn stylized the Janizary rhythms in his *Military* Symphony, which includes triangles, cymbals, and a bass drum in the second movement. The finale of Mozart's Piano Sonata in A major, K. 331, is marked "alla turca." Some piano manufacturers made special attachments to the instruments with bells and cymbals for performances of such "Turkish" music and even supplied clappers to strike at the resonance board of the piano in imitation of the bass drum.

Japanese music. The music of Japan, and of the Orient generally, is derived from ancient pentatonic modes, most commonly of the intervallic type C, D, E, G, A, or C, E-flat, F, G, B-flat, both free of semitones. There is also an authentic Japanese scale of great antiquity that contains semitones of the type C, D-flat, F, G, A-flat. Japanese folk music is invariably homophonic without explicit or implicit harmonic connotations. The cultured music of Japan (particularly Gagaku, the orchestral music of the imperial court) originated in the eighth century and includes concepts of consonance and dissonance. Consonances distribute the intervals of the pentatonic scale in open harmony; dissonances are produced when the harmony includes semitones in close formation. When Gagaku accompanies a dance it is called Bugaku. The indigenous Japanese theater form is Kabuki, a stylized drama including music and dancing with heavily costumed male actors playing the roles of both males and females. String instruments, wind instruments, and percussion appear in Japanese music in original forms, some of them metamorphosed from ancient Chinese and Korean instruments imported into Japan in medieval times. The most popular Japanese string instruments are the koto, a rectangular variety of zither, and the shamisen, a long-necked, three-stringed lute; also commonly used are bamboo flutes (the shakuhachi), small cymbals, bells, and drums.

Like most oriental music, Japanese music is melodic and rhythmic, with harmonic extension formed by intervallic couplings in seconds, fourths, and fifths. Consecutive progressions, particularly in thirds or in sixths, are practically nonexistent; rhythmic patterns have great variety and in ancient music do not follow any binding meter. The most important Japanese composers active in the 20th century include Toshiro Mayuzumi, Yashushi Akutagawa, Ikuma Dan, Yoshirō Irino, Yoritsuné Matsudaira and his son Yori-aki Matsudaira, Shukichi Mitsukuri, Akira Miyoshi, Osamu Shimizu, Yuji Takehashi, and Toru Takemitsu. Kosaku Yamada, educated in Europe, was the first Japanese composer to adopt European methods of composition in opera, symphony, chamber music, and songs. Paul Chihara, an American composer of Japanese descent, employs Japanese modes in an advanced sophisticated manner. Operas by modern Japanese composers usually follow European models. Melodramatic operas on Japanese subjects such as Puccini's *Madama Butterfly* are unacceptable in Japan as perversions of national culture. The operetta *The*

Mikado by Gilbert and Sullivan was forbidden to be performed in Japan until 1945, when it was done by the American Army of Occupation.

Jazz. Jazz is the folk music of America. Its rhythmic and melodic origins go back to the plantation songs of the South, which were rooted in the ancestral African memory of the slaves. The elements of sharp syncopation combined with religious refrains were already evident in this music. The ballads of Stephen Foster, which he called "Ethiopian Songs," contain characteristic syncopation and the melodic "blue" notes—that is, the lowered leading tone in the major scale. Early in the 20th century a modified type of plantation song played by brass bands became known as Dixieland dance music, popular in New Orleans. Another development of syncopated music was ragtime. All these various elements contributed to the formation of what became known as jazz music. The word *jazz* itself first appeared in print in a San Francisco newspaper column in 1913, used as an expression of enthusiasm regarding a baseball game. The transition to a term describing a kind of music occurred when professional dance bands appeared in restaurants, hotels, and music halls in Chicago and New York. At the end of World War I in 1918, American jazz bands traveled to Europe and immediately engaged the attention of the Paris modernists, especially Satie and Milhaud, who welcomed the infusion of new transatlantic rhythms and instrumental sonorities to Europe. In March 1917 the first recording of jazz music was issued by the Victor Company under the title *Dixieland Jass One-Step.* (*Jass* was the original spelling.)

Improvisation is the essence of jazz. Among the great initiators of jazz were Louis Armstrong, Cab Calloway, W.C. Handy, Count Basie, Ella Fitzgerald, Duke Ellington, John Coltrane—all of whom were black musicians whose feeling for the racial roots of their art was paramount. White composers soon developed a modern type of jazz music designed for concert performance. Among them were Benny Goodman, Woody Herman, Guy Lombardo, and Paul Whiteman. The most important contribution to concert jazz was made by George Gershwin, whose *Rhapsody in Blue* became a modern classic. As one critic, not very respectfully inclined toward improvised jazz music, remarked, Gershwin made an honest woman out of jazz. Types of jazz proliferated under such terms as *hot* jazz (improvised and dissonant), *cool* jazz (determined and polyrhythmic), *progressive* jazz (using advanced harmony), and *Third Stream* (combining fundamentals of jazz with classical forms). Ragtime and jazz themes were eagerly employed by modern European composers. An early example of classical modern jazz was *La Création du monde* by Milhaud, descriptive of the Creation in terms of Negro jazz. Ernst Křenek's opera *Jonny spielt auf* glorifies a black jazz player who symbolically conquers the world. Gershwin's *Porgy and Bess*, the first opera based entirely on a story from Negro life, contains a number of jazz-like tunes.

The meter of jazz is invariably square time, with syncopation within each individual bar. Rhythmic arrangements within the bars include boogie-woogie, marked by a bass ostinato, and bebop, characterized by a constant shifting of accents within short note values. All these types put in association in a grand exhibition of rhythms, accents, and blue notes form a style that became known as *swing music*. Swing musicians were referred to as "hep cats." The dancers were the jitterbugs—not the musicians. A jazz group typically contained a solo section, consisting of clarinet, saxophone, trumpet, and trombone, and a supporting rhythm section, comprising piano or guitar (which may also double as soloist), string bass (mostly played by plucking rather than bowing the strings), and drums.

Jazz Concerto. An unauthorized but fairly common description of Aaron Copland's Piano Concerto, which does include elements of jazz. It shocked the Boston audience and critics when Copland performed it for the first time with the Boston Symphony Orchestra, Koussevitzky conducting, on January 28, 1927.

Jeanne d'Arc au bûcher. A dramatic oratorio by Arthur Honegger, first performed in Basel on May 10, 1938, in concert form. Honegger described the work as a mimodrama, or mimed drama. Joan has a speaking part; various allegorical figures appear, symbolizing sins and virtues. The music is a deliberate return to the early type of monodic musical drama.

Jena Symphony. This is one of those misnomers and misattributions that disturb the musical scene once in a while. A manuscript was discovered in the town of Jena in 1910 by the German scholar Fritz Stein, with the name of Beethoven scribbled on some of the orchestral parts. A great deal of excitement was generated, and the *Jena* Symphony was performed as an early work of Beethoven. The sensation was spurious, as anyone examining the work from either a stylistic or aesthetic standpoint should have known. Eventually the original manuscript was discovered, fully signed with the name of Friedrich Witt, the real composer of the misnamed work.

Jenufa. An opera by Leoš Janáček, first produced in Brno on January 21, 1904. This is the German title under which the opera is performed abroad; its original Czech name is *Její pastorkyňa*, which means "Her Foster Daughter." The subject is grisly, as peasant life in Central Europe often was in the 19th century. Jenufa is heavy with child by a Moravian farmhand. When the child is born, the moralistic female sexton of the local church drowns it to save Jenufa from disgrace. The truth is found out, the hideous sexton culprit is taken to prison, and Jenufa marries a stepbrother of her original seducer. The work is one of the most remarkable examples of modern Bohemian music drama. The score underwent several revisions, and not until the performance of the final version in Prague on May 26, 1916, was Janáček recognized as an important national composer.

Jeremiah Symphony. The Symphony No. 1 by Leonard Bernstein for soprano and orchestra with a text from the Bible. It is in three sections: *Prophecy*, *Profanation*, and *Lamentation*. Bernstein conducted its first performance in Pittsburgh on January 28, 1944.

Jericho trumpets. In Chapter 6 of the Book of Joshua, it is related how the Lord instructed Joshua to destroy the city of Jericho acoustically by having seven priests blow seven trumpets made out of ram's horn while the people "shouted with a great shout." The noise was such that the walls of Jericho "fell down flat," letting Joshua's people in, whereupon they proceeded to slay "both man and woman, young and old, and ox, and sheep, and ass" (except a local harlot who hid Joshua's spies in her house). Modern acousticians doubt whether a wall could be brought down by sounding trumpets and shouting; even rock musicians using electric amplifiers never do more than frighten the peaceful bystanders.

great!

Jessonda. This opera by Ludwig Spohr, now a fossil, was once a great favorite, particularly in England. It was first performed in Kassel, Germany, where Spohr was court music director, on July 28, 1823. Jessonda is the wife of the rajah of Malabar; he dies, and she must immolate herself like the good Brahmin she is. But lo! Portuguese fanfares are sounded and no less a person than Tristan da Cunha, the explorer for whom a desolate group of islands midway between South America and South Africa was named (one island of the group is called Inaccessible), enters the scene. He recognizes in Jessonda his ideal woman; she sees in him her ideal man. The chorus of Brahmins urges her to take her rightful place on her husband's funerary mound, but now she wants to live. When the Portuguese marines land in force, the unspeakable Brahmins desist in their foul superstition, and the happy ending is assured. The score sounds like any piece of German music of the time; there is no attempt to introduce exotic tunes.

Le Jeu de cartes (The Card Game). A "ballet in three deals" by Stravinsky, first performed in New York on April 27, 1937, the composer conducting. Stravinsky, a devotee of poker, portrays in this score a poker game, with the joker constantly intruding to confuse the players. The sequence of dances follows the Classical tradition.

Jeunehomme Concerto. The common name for the Piano Concerto No. 9 in E-flat major, K. 271, that Mozart wrote at the age of 21 for a French pianist, Mlle. Jeunehomme, who played it in Salzburg. There is no connection with the meaning of the French family name, "young man."

Jeux d'eau. A remarkable piece by Ravel in which he anticipated Debussy by introducing a new type of piano sonority, spreading across the entire keyboard and emphasizing chords formed by cumulative thirds. At a climax in *Jeux d'eau* Ravel had to replace the required low G-sharp below the range of the keyboard with the lowest available note, A, which coalesced with the intended harmony. The piece was first performed in Paris on April 5, 1902.

Jeux vénitiens. A work for chamber orchestra by the eminent Polish composer Witold Lutosławski, first performed in Venice on April 24, 1961. It is arranged in five panels that are performed either simultaneously or canonically, as the orchestra chooses.

Jew's harp. A vibrating strip of metal, one end being placed between the teeth (the nickname *Jew's harp* may actually be a corruption of *jaw's harp*), and the other end plucked with the fingers. Various pitches are attained by changing the shape of the mouth. The instrument has been included in folk ensembles throughout the world, from China to Borneo, from Northern Europe to Appalachia.

Jig. A lively English dance in rapid square time akin to the hornpipe. The word probably comes from the French verb *giguer*, to move rapidly to and fro. The jig was very popular in the 17th century among lower classes; one writer described it as "only fit for Fantastical, and Easie-Light-Headed People." However, jigs penetrated the Royal British court and became favorites with the English aristocracy. The *Fitzwilliam Virginal Book* includes a jig with the provocative title *Nobodyes Gigge*. The jig died out at the end of the Elizabethan era and was replaced by the more courtly and dignified French gigue.

Jim Crow. A Negro song and dance popularized in 1830 by a white vaudeville performer named Rice. It marked the beginning of the American minstrel show with blackface performers. The final lines, "Ev'ry time I wheel about I jump Jim Crow," gave birth to the expression "Jim Crow" for racial segregation.

Job. A masque by Ralph Vaughan Williams, with a scenario inspired by William Blake's *Illustrations of the Book of Job*. It was first performed as a concert piece in Norwich on October 23, 1930.

Johnny Johnson. A musical fable by Kurt Weill, first produced in New York on November 19, 1936. The story concerns the fate of an idealistic soldier, Johnny Johnson, who fights Germany in World War I, which he truly believes is the War to end all wars. He tries to immunize the military by channeling a laughing gas into them, but in the process of securing world peace he loses his favorite girlfriend and is driven insane. Being an ideological play, it failed at the box office.

Le Jongleur de Notre Dame. An opera by Jules Massenet, first produced in Monte Carlo on February 18, 1902. The action takes place in France in the 14th century, focusing on a street juggler who collapses in front of the statue of the Holy Virgin. Before he dies, the Virgin blesses him with her marble hand, and he becomes, in legend and tradition, "the juggler of Our Lady." This is one of the few operas ever written that has no human female roles.

Jonny spielt auf (Johnny Strikes Up). An opera by Ernst Křenek, to his own text, first produced in Leipzig on February 10, 1927, when he was only 26 years old. It became sensationally successful as the first opera making use of the jazz idiom. Jonny (without an *h* and pronounced "Yonny") is a Negro musician who becomes a famous jazz band leader, captivating audiences around the globe. Fox-trot and Charleston rhythms animate the score, but there are also lyric episodes. The work was translated into 18 languages, and even a brand of Austrian cigarettes was named after it. At its production by the Metropolitan Opera in New York on January 19, 1929, the role of Jonny was performed by a blackface singer to avoid offending the segregationist sensitivities of some of its patrons, particularly in scenes when Jonny consorts with white chambermaids.

Jour d'été à la montagne. A rhapsody for piano and orchestra by Vincent d'Indy, in three sections: *Dawn*, *Day*, and *Night*. One of his most effective works, it was first performed in Paris on February 18, 1906.

Judith. An opera by Alexander Serov, first performed in St. Petersburg on May 28, 1863. The libretto is drawn from the Apocrypha. Judith, a patriotic Jewess, decides to risk her virtue in penetrating the tent of the Assyrian chieftain Holofernes, whose army besieges her city. She plies him with wine, and as he sinks into a drunken torpor, she cuts off his head, packs it into a sack, and comes back home. She holds aloft the bearded head of the enemy king at an assembly, and the Jewish people explode in jubilation. The score contains elements of a monumental oratorio style in the manner of Handel. It once enjoyed great popularity in Russia.

Arthur Honegger's opera *Judith* on the biblical subject was first performed in Monte Carlo on Februry 13, 1926. Although it was originally intended as a drama in 13 scenes, it was eventually made into a full opera.

La Juive. An opera by Jacques-François-Fromental-Elie Halévy, first produced in Paris on February 23, 1835. The Jewess of the title turns out to be the natural daughter of the perfidious French cardinal, the leader of a concentrated campaign against the Jews in the town of Constance in 1414. She is condemned to be thrown into a cauldron of boiling water, and the cardinal learns the truth too late to stop the execution. Halévy, although himself Jewish, does not introduce Hebrew melodies; rather, the score follows the dramatic formula of the period. Once very popular, *La Juive* still enjoys occasional performances in France and Russia.

Jupiter Symphony. Mozart wrote many symphonies in the key of C major, but the greatest of them all is this, his last one, No. 41, K. 551, composed in 1788. The first use of this title was in the program of the Edinburgh Festival in October 1819. The person who assigned the Olympian attribute to the work is unknown, but it became forever connected with the music, one of the few musical works that seem to fit its perennial nickname. The finale is a paragon of fugal construction, with the main subject based on the simple progression of four notes, C, D, F, and E.

K

K. The identifying initial for the Köchel catalogue of Mozart's works, in chronological order, assembled by the Austrian botanist Köchel who applied his taxonomical talents to Mozart's music.

Kaddish. Leonard Bernstein's Symphony No. 3 for female speaker, mixed chorus, soprano solo, a choir of boys, and orchestra. The Kaddish is a Hebrew lamentation for the dead; Bernstein dedicated his score to the memory of President John F. Kennedy. The text is partly in Hebrew and partly in Aramaic, the language Jesus Christ spoke. The first performance of the work took place in Tel Aviv with Bernstein conducting on December 9, 1963.

Kalevala. The great national epic of Finland created in the 14th century. Its verses contain numerous references to therapeutic properties of music; in several passages the wounds of heroes are healed by chanting the history of the wound's infliction. Sibelius and other Finnish composers have drawn widely on the *Kalevala* for the subjects of their symphonic and other works.

Kammersymphonie The original German title for Arnold Schoenberg's Chamber Symphony, written in 1906 and first performed in Vienna on March 31, 1913. In Schoenberg's stylistic evolution, this is a transitional work in which harmonies are built on fourths rather than on thirds, and the use of the whole-tone scale signals a departure from tonality. One bemused German critic suggested that the title should be changed to "Chamber of Horrors" Symphony.

Kapellmeistermusik. "Conductor's music," a derisive term applied to orchestral compositions by professional conductors that are pedantically respectable but devoid of vitality. Hans von Bülow and Furtwängler wrote such works, and attempts have been made to revive them. Toscanini never composed and thus kept his image pure as a performing musician. Mahler was known during his lifetime primarily as a conductor; his symphonies were dismissed by music critics as *Kapellmeistermusik*. Posterity ruled otherwise.

Kashchei, the Immortal. An opera by Rimsky-Korsakov, first performed in Moscow on December 25, 1902. Like her father, Kashchei's daughter is sinister. She uses a magic potion to induce Prince Ivan to forget his beloved bride. This done, she sharpens a sword with which she plans to kill Ivan, but at the crucial moment a tempest clears the air and awakens the prince. He returns to his beloved, and Kashchei's evil domain is blown away. The opera is rarely performed, even in Russia, but it is an important work that influenced a whole generation of Russian composers. Stravinsky's symphonic poem *The Firebird* (which concludes with a dance of Kashchei's pagan hordes) makes ample use of harmonic and rhythmic innovations introduced by Rimsky-Korsakov in his opera.

Key. One of those Janus-like music terms in the English language that create confusion in the minds of innocents. A key is the ivory (or wooden) bar on keyboard instruments that is pressed down to cause a tone. Key is also the tonality of a given composition. The French, Germans, Italians, Spanish, and Russians have different names for keys as tonalities and keys as levers. In French the piano key is *touche*, the touched one, but the key in the sense of tonality is *tonalité*. In German the ivory piano key is *Taste*, but tonality is *Tonalität*, or the more sophisticated term, *Tonart*. In Italian the depressible key is *tasto*, but tonality is *tonalità*. In Spanish the fingerable key is *tecla*, and tonality is *tonalidad*. Keys also designate the clappers, or levers, on woodwind instruments. Names other than English for these levers are *clef* in French, *Klappe* in German, *chiave* in Italian, and *llave* in Spanish.

Key signature. The indicator of the prevalent tonality placed on the staff in the beginning of a composition. Discounting the enharmonically equal keys, there are 12 keys in major and 12 in minor, identified by the number of sharps or flats in the key signature. Key signatures of seven sharps are not infrequent; a famous example is the third fugue in C-sharp major in the first book of Bach's *Well-Tempered Clavier*. An example of seven flats in a key signature is the opening of Stravinsky's *The Firebird*. Changes of key signature in the course of a composition are common, but they are not made frivolously for each passing modulation. Even the extensive exposition of the second subject in a sonata movement, which is usually in the dominant key, seldom carries a change of the key signature. In works not bound by a strict key relationship, in which tonalities range far and wide, composers often prefer to signalize a modulation by changing the key signature. The score of Mahler's Symphony No. 6 includes episodes in all 24 major and minor keys, each marked by an appropriate key signature.

Relative major and minor keys have the same key signature; the customary raised seventh in a minor key is marked by an accidental, as, for instance, a single sharp in the key of A minor or a double sharp in the key of G-sharp minor. In key signatures loaded with flats, the raised seventh in a minor key is the cancellation of the corresponding flat, becoming a natural. Attempts have been made by modern composers, among them Béla Bartók, to place accidentals in the key signature. A piece in G minor would then carry the mandatory two flats but also the extracurricular F-sharp. In 20th-century music, however, the vexing problem of frequent changes of key signatures in a rapidly modulating musical piece has become as irrelevant as a Victorian antimacassar on the back of a modern armchair. Key signatures began to disappear from scores at the end of the first quarter of the 20th century, when they became needless armatures in an atonal ocean.

Keyboard. The board of depressible keys or levers on pianos, organs, and other instruments of similar construction. A large organ may have as many as five keyboard manuals. A special feature on the organ is the pedal keyboard, arranged in rows of large white and black keys that are operated by the feet. Through the centuries the arrangement of the 12 chromatic notes within the octave was formed with seven white keys on the lower level of the keyboard and five shorter black keys on the slightly elevated level. The row of white keys forms a diatonic scale; the row of black keys forms the pentatonic scale. The opposition of the white and the black keys is standard on piano keyboards, but the harpsichord, clavichord, and spinet may have a different coloring. There are antique harpsichords on which the diatonic keys are black and the pentatonic keys white; there are also specimens with red keys in one of the rows, much as in some artistic chess sets that have red and white chessmen instead of the standard black and white. The dimensions of the keys on all keyboard instruments are adjusted to the normal relaxed position of the five fingers of a human player resting on the five consecutive white keys.

In *Gulliver's Travels*, Jonathan Swift describes a Brobdingnagian spinet in vivid detail: "The spinet was near sixty foot long, each key being almost a foot wide, so that, with my arms extended, I could not reach to above five keys, and to press them down required a good smart stroke with my fist. . . . Yet I could not strike above sixteen keys, nor consequently play the bass and treble together, as other artists do; which was a great disadvantage to my performance." Actually, one did not have to go to Brobdingnag to find a gigantic keyboard. The keys of the early organs were so wide that the monks who manipulated them (for it was primarily monkish business to play the organ for the glory of God) had to play their hymns with clenched fists, and even elbows, to depress the keys sufficiently to activate the pipes.

Numerous attempts have been made to make the keyboard more handy, to adapt it for playing scales without a constant change of fingering. It is most intriguing to speculate how a twelve-fingered pianist (there have been such) might play scales using six fingers on each hand. Pending the growth of extra fingers, one might consider using the Jankó keyboard, invented by the eccentric Hungarian pianist Paul von Jankó, who manufactured a keyboard with six different rows of keys, one slightly above the other, with a system of levers making it possible to play the chromatic scale with the greatest of ease by letting the fingers walk from one row to another. The Jankó keys are narrower than those of an ordinary piano keyboard, so that a pianist can easily stretch the interval of a fourteenth, from C to B-flat in the next octave, a great convenience for players who want to execute properly some unbridgeable intervals such as are found in Schumann's *Symphonic Études*. Alas! Poor Jankó died, and the Jankó keyboard died with him; all that remains of it is an incongruous illustrated tombstone on his grave. Then there was the Clutsam keyboard in the form of an arc, with the radius that of an arm's length. A pianist playing it must presumably be placed in the center of the circle, using outstretched arms at all times. The Clutsam keyboard, too, went the way of all impractical ivory toys.

Khovanshchina. A music drama by Modest Mussorgsky, posthumously produced in St. Petersburg on February 21, 1886. The title means "Khovansky-ism," a contemptuous reference by young Peter the Great to the rebellious activity of the followers of Prince Khovansky, the leader of the "Old Believers." Surrounded by Peter's loyal troops, they immolate themselves in fiery death. The score, left unfinished and unorchestrated by Mussorgsky, was revised by Rimsky-Korsakov, who smoothed down Mussorgsky's harmonic asperities and straightened up some awkward melodic progressions.

Kikimora. A fantastic symphonic scherzo by Anatoli Liadov, first performed in St. Petersburg on December 12, 1909. Kikimora is a Russian infant girl who does not live long enough to be baptized. She becomes a mischievous spirit suspended between heaven and hell. The music is alternately tender and boisterous. Kikimora's demoniacal side is depicted by the frequent use of the tritone, the *diabolus in musica* of the Middle Ages.

The King's Henchman. An opera by Deems Taylor, first performed at the Metropolitan Opera in New York on February 17, 1927, one of the few American operas given by that institution. It had 14 performances and then sank into oblivion. The libretto was not American. Its hero was the messenger of the King of England who was sent to fetch the royal bride from overseas. Instead, he appropriates her himself and commits suicide when his treachery is revealed. The score is distinctly Wagnerian, as is the subject.

Kismet. An extravaganza thrown together by a couple of Broadway hacks using materials from the works of the defenseless and uncopyrighted Borodin. The mephitic plot parades the ambitious wife of the Baghdad chief of police; she drowns her husband in a fountain in order to marry the young caliph. The slow section from Borodin's *Polovtzian Dances* is perverted into a loathsome mess of fulsome treacle, "Stranger in Paradise," and the Mongol Polovtzi are transformed into spurious Arabs. Another bit, "This Is My Beloved," is purloined from Borodin's String Quartet. The stench that this iniquitous travesty raised in the nostrils of decent music lovers moved them to an outcry of protest, which must have made the perpetrators smile while counting the ill-gotten shekels at the box office. The word *kismet* (*quismah* in Arabic) means "fate."

Klangfarbenmelodie. A German term meaning a melody of tone colors. This description was first used by Schoenberg in his book on harmony in 1911; he proposed to regard the change of instrumental color as a melodic change. Thus a tone color melody can be created by playing the same note successively on different instruments. Schoenberg never carried out the idea; his disciples Alban Berg and Anton von Webern developed it more fully. It received its complete fruition in serial and electronic music by their avant-garde followers.

The Knot Garden. A remarkable opera by Sir Michael Tippett, first produced at Covent Garden in London on December 2, 1970. The libretto by Tippett depicts a knotty psychological involvement in which a white musician confesses homosexual passion for a black poet, a feminist combats her hidden lesbianism, and a nubile maiden tries to escape the clutches of a married voluptuary, all this set in a perfumed garden of intense eroticism.

Knoxville: Summer of 1915. This piece by Samuel Barber, for soprano and orchestra, is inspired by a passage in *A Death in the Family* by James Agee in which he reminisces about his childhood in Tennessee. It was first performed in Boston on April 9, 1948.

Kol Nidrei. A very old Jewish religious song, sung on the eve of Yom Kippur, the Day of Atonement, set in an expressive minor mode and marked by a profound religious sentiment. The Hebrew term means "all the vowels."

   Kol Nidrei for cello and orchestra by Max Bruch is his most popular work; he wrote it in 1880 for the Jewish community of Liverpool, although he himself was not Jewish.

König Hirsch. An opera by Hans Werner Henze, first produced in Berlin on September 23, 1956, and subsequently revised and staged again under the original name of Gozzi's fable, *Il Re cervo*, on which the opera is based. As the title suggests, the King is transformed into a stag. Eventually he sheds his horns, regains his human shape, and returns to his native town. The musical idiom is dissonant, but the score follows the classical Italian tradition in its arias and ensemble numbers.

Königskinder (The Royal Children). An opera by Engelbert Humperdinck, first produced in New York on December 28, 1910. The libretto reverses the course of events of Humperdinck's famous children's opera, *Hänsel und Gretel*. Here the malevolent witch feeds poisonous candy to the young prince and the girl whom he loves, and they both die. The opera is an expanded version of Humperdinck's incidental music for a play *Königskinder*, produced in 1897, notable for its use of *Sprechstimme* (''speech-voice'') long before Schoenberg, who employed it in several of his works and was reputed as its prime user.

Kontakte. A piece for piano, percussion, and electronic sounds by Karlheinz Stockhausen, first performed in Cologne on June 11, 1960. The contacts of the title signify the coexistence of electronic and traditional acoustic instruments. It is one of the most significant, if not the earliest, experiments in organized electronic music.

Koto. A national Japanese instrument of the zither type, with a rectangular body made of strong wooden planks laid out on the floor. It has seven to thirteen silk strings that are plucked with fingers or a plectrum; some modern kotos may have as many as seventeen strings. The koto is commonly used to accompany Gagaku, the music of the medieval Japanese court. Several Japanese composers have written music for the instrument, making use of modern techniques including dodecaphony. Henry Cowell, among other American composers, wrote two concertos for koto and orchestra.

Kreutzer Sonata. The common name for Beethoven's most famous Violin Sonata, op. 47. Although it bears the name of the French violinist Kreutzer, a close contemporary of Beethoven, he never performed it. The first performance was given on May 24, 1803, in Vienna, with Beethoven himself playing the piano part and George Bridgetower the violin. Tolstoy took it as the title of his famous moralistic novel, *The Kreutzer Sonata*, in which a middle-class Russian woman rehearses the sonata with a dashing violinist and eventually succumbs to his advances. Technically the novel is flawed because the difficulties of Beethoven's work would deter any music amateur from tackling it, and continuous attempts to perform it would have so frustrated the players that they would have probably ended up hating each other.

Krútňava (The Whirlpool). An opera by Eugene Suchoň, first performed in Bratislava on December 10, 1949. The whirlpool of the title is the moral dilemma in which a young village girl finds herself when her lover is killed by an unknown assailant. Suspicion is directed against another villager who succeeds in persuading the bereaved woman to marry him, but when a child is born to her it becomes clear that the child's father was her slain lover. The killer is tortured by his memories and goes back to the scene of the crime to retrieve a gun he buried there. He is apprehended and brought to justice.

L

La. The sixth note of Guido d'Arezzo's hexachord, representing the first syllable of the last line of the hymn to St. John, *"Labii reatum."* La is still used to designate the sixth diatonic degree of the scale in Romance languages and in Russian; it is also used in the system of movable Do.

Lady Macbeth of the District of Mtzensk. An opera by Dmitri Shostakovich, first performed in Leningrad on January 22, 1934. The story depicts adultery and murder in Russia in the middle of the 19th century. The title is hardly justified, because the protagonist conspires with her lover to murder her husband, not her husband's potential rival as in Shakespeare's tragedy. The culprits are convicted and sent to Siberia. When he takes another mistress there, she kills her rival and then commits suicide. The music attains a maximum of realism, including a suggestive sliding trombone passage illustrating the act of adultery itself. Unexpectedly, *Pravda*, the official organ of the Soviet Communist Party, attacked the opera as a product of bourgeois decadence and damned it for its alleged modernity. Shostakovich apologized abjectly for his musical sins and stopped writing operas for a number of years. The opera was eventually revived in a sanitized version under the title *Katerina Izmailova*, the name of the heroine.

Lakmé. An opera by Léo Delibes, first performed in Paris on April 14, 1883. Lakmé, the daughter of a priest of Brahma, is loved by a British officer. He inadvertently profanes the Hindu temple by entering it with his shoes on and is denounced by the priest. In the end Lakmé, realizing the futility of her love, plucks a poisonous flower and dies. The score is permeated with attractive pseudooriental melodies and rhythms. Lakmé's *Bell Song* is a perennial favorite with coloratura sopranos.

Lament. A generic term for dirges chanted upon the death of an important person or a beloved friend. Specimens of such laments date back to the death of Charlemagne in 814. In France the laments bore the names of *deplorations*,

253

tombeaux, and *plaintes*. Thus Ockeghem wrote a lament on the death of Binchois, and was in turn musically lamented by Josquin, who was upon his own death eulogized by Gombert. Couperin le Grand wrote an apotheosis for Lully, but he himself had to wait nearly two centuries to be musically commemorated with comparable grandeur in Ravel's *Le Tombeau de Couperin*.

Lamento. A lamentation; a regular type of aria in Italian opera in which a female expresses her unquenchable sorrow and complains about her misery. *Lamento d'Arianna*, the only surviving segment from Monteverdi's opera *Arianna* written in 1608, is an example of such an aria. In it, Ariadne laments her painful abandonment by the treacherous Theseus.

Landini cadence. A melismatic figure popularized by the 14th century composer and theorist Francesco Landini, in which the leading tone digresses a degree down to the submediant before coming to rest on the tonic in the melody.

Lark Quartet. String Quartet, op. 64, No. 5, in D major by Haydn (1790). The opening tune in the high violin range can be construed as imitative of a lark song. The German title is *Lerchenquartett*; it is also known as the *Hornpipe* Quartet.

Lauda. An Italian term for a hymn of praise; its plural is *laude*. Occasionally the plural form is used as singular, in which case the plural is *laudi*. These hymns were particularly popular with itinerant monastic orders, both the penitents and the flagellants. Because of the peripatetic character of these orders, laude became overgrown with unrelated dance forms, such as the frottola and ballata, without, however, losing their basic religious characteristics. The laude influenced the development of the oratorio in the early 17th century.

Laura. A song by David Raksin, inspired by a letter from a woman in which she bade him an affectionate good-bye (her name was not Laura). Raksin wrote the melody in 1944 for a movie of the same name in which a lovelorn detective makes his professional rounds. The words by Johnny Mercer were added later. In its final incarnation *Laura* sold millions of disks. Cole Porter, when asked what song he would have liked to have written among a multitude of songs on the air, said, "*Laura!*" Irving Berlin, in an interview some decades before he struck 100, said he disliked most of the songs written by others, the sole exception being *Laura*. The melody is unusual in that it traverses chromatic steps suggesting a consanguinity with Wagner's Tristan motif.

Leading tone. This term, the exact translation of the German *Leitton*, denotes the seventh degree of the diatonic scale which, to the modern ear, urges the resolution into the tonic, a semitone upward. In minor keys, the seventh degree in the natural scale is raised to provide the necessary leading tone. In French, the leading tone is called *note sensible* ("sensitive note"); it is *nota sensibile* in Italian.

Ledger lines. Extra horizontal lines placed above or below the regular staff to accommodate high or low notes that exceed the range of the staff. In early music, composers used a great number of clefs for this purpose, thus avoiding the clutter of too many ledger lines. In modern notation, only two clefs, the treble and the bass, are used in piano music. When the notes rise to stratospheric altitudes, then the sign 8----¬, meaning to be played an octave higher, is placed above them to reduce the number of ledger lines. When the notes sink too deeply into the region below the bass staff, the sign 8----⌐ or the words *octave bassa* are used. For very high notes, the symbol 15----¬, meaning two octaves higher, is occasionally employed.

Left-hand music. The Austrian pianist Paul Wittgenstein lost his right arm fighting on the Eastern Front during World War I, was taken prisoner by the Russians, spent a year in Omsk, Siberia, and was repatriated to Austria in 1915 as representing no danger to Imperial Russia. Being of a philosophical bend of mind, he developed a startling virtuosity with his left hand. Wittgenstein took advantage of his family wealth and commissioned a number of important composers—among them Ravel, Richard Strauss, Prokofiev, Erich Korngold, Benjamin Britten, and Franz Schmidt—to write for him concertos for piano left hand and orchestra.

When the Hungarian nobleman and amateur musician Count Zichy lost his right arm in a hunting accident in the summer of 1863, he decided to compose piano pieces for the left hand that he performed at social occasions in Budapest. He also made arrangements for three hands and even played with his left hand the bass line of an arrangement of a patriotic Hungarian march, with Liszt supplying the other two hands.

Scriabin was so eager to become a piano virtuoso in a grand style that, while a conservatory student in Moscow, he strained his right hand trying to compete with his classmate Josef Lhévinne. Lhévinne was physically robust; Scriabin was rather frail and could never rival him on the concert platform. Scriabin bandaged his ailing right hand and as a consolation prize wrote a charming group of piano pieces for left hand alone. Even pianists with both hands in perfect order like to play these pieces.

The Legend of the Invisible City of Kitezh and the Maiden Fevronia. A mystical opera by Rimsky-Korsakov, first produced in St. Petersburg on February 20, 1907. Because of its sustained devotional character and its hymn-like theme, it was often described as "the Russian *Parsifal*." The action takes place in the year 6751 after Creation, at the time of the Tatar invasion of Russia. Fevronia, the bride of the Prince of Kitezh, prays that the city of Kitezh be made invisible to save it from the invaders. Her prayer is answered. As the city vanishes, only the pealing of the church bells reveals its existence. A symphonic interlude, depicting the battle between the Russians and the Tatars, is based on a scale of alternating whole tones and semitones, which in Russia is known as the Rimsky-Korsakov scale.

Die Legende von der heiligen Elisabeth. An oratorio composed by Liszt, in 1857; he conducted its first performance in Budapest on August 15, 1865. St. Elisabeth was the Hungarian wife of a German crusader who perished during the wars. She was expelled by her German mother-in-law, took refuge in a nearby cave, and became a saint.

Legno. Italian for "wood," used in string instrument playing in the expression *col legno*, "with wood," which instructs the player to strike the strings with the wooden part of the bow.

Lehrstück. A teaching piece, cultivated in Germany after World War I, to train musical amateurs to play easy pieces in a modern idiom. A typical example is a play by Bertolt Brecht with music by Kurt Weill entitled *Der Ja-Sager*, produced in 1930, and prefaced by the following declaration of intent: "The pedagogical practice of this music is to let the student bypass specialized study by concentrating intensively on a definite idea presented graphically through the medium of music, an idea that penetrates the student's mind much more strongly than formal learning." Brecht's title means "The Yes-Sayer."

Leili and Medzhnun. An opera by Uzeir Hadzhibekov, first performed in Baku on January 25, 1908. Leili loves a youth who is nicknamed Medzhnun ("madman") because of his unrestrained passion for her. When she is forced to marry a wealthy merchant, Medzhnun seizes every occasion to tell her of his misery, until her heart breaks and she expires in her husband's arms. Medzhnun visits her tomb, now that she belongs to him alone, and he too dies. The work represents the earliest organization in a serious operatic form of *mugam*, the cumulative modality of folk songs of Azerbaijan.

Leitmotiv. The accurate German spelling of "leading motif," from the verb *leiten*, "to lead." The spelling *Leitmotif* can be justified on phonetic grounds, to prevent the pronunciation "motive." (*V* in German is pronounced *f*.) The concept of the leitmotiv is commonly associated with Wagner's music dramas, but the term was first used in an annotated catalogue of works by Carl Maria von Weber, published in 1871, in which it was described as a "strong delineation of each individual character in an opera." The leitmotiv was aesthetically defined and analyzed by the Wagnerian theorist Wolzogen in 1876. Wagner himself never used the term but described the identifying motifs in his operas as "melodic moments," "thematic motifs," "fundamental themes," "idea motifs," or "remembrance motifs." The main purpose in Wagner's application of leading motifs in his operas was to identify each character and each important idea. By employing them in contrapuntal combinations, and by varying the rhythm and sometimes the intervallic structure of these motifs, Wagner intended to establish "a new form of dramatic music, wich possesses the unity of a symphonic movement." This unity can be achieved, Wagner averred, "in a network of basic themes permeating the entire work, analogously to the themes in a symphony. They are contrasted with each other, supplement each other, assume new shapes, separate and coalesce . . . according to dramatic action." Thomas Mann describes the leitmotiv as a "magic formula valid in both the past and the future developments." But Wagner's use of leading motifs is not limited to the characters on the stage. He carefully tabulates the motifs of material objects, such as the ring and the sword in *Der Ring des Nibelungen*, and the abstract concepts of covenant, conflict, transformation, love, and so on. Wagner was not the first to introduce identifying themes in opera. Papageno's appearances in Mozart's *Magic Flute* are announced by a scale on his magic bell. There are definite leading motifs in Weber's *Der Freischütz*. Verdi used leading motifs in several of his operas. Tchaikovsky can hardly be called a Wagnerian, but the presence of identifying motifs in his operas is discerned without difficulty. Before Wagner, Berlioz used the *idée fixe*, a device related to the leitmotiv, in his *Symphonie fantastique*. The true innovation in Wagner's operas is the concious, philosophical affirmation of unity through plurality, the *Gesamtkunstwerk*, an artistic synthesis, which was Wagner's grand ideal. One of the ost fascinating aspects of Wagnerian leading motifs is the unexpected musical similarity of the dramatically contrasting characters or ideas. Thus, by a "topological" alteration, the theme of love-death in *Tristan und Isolde* can be converted into the leading motif of the holy grail in *Parsifal*.

Wagner's influence in the use of leading motifs was enormous. Hardly a single opera written since Wagner has escaped this unifying concept. Faithful Wagnerians compiled catalogues of leading motifs in his music dramas, including melodic fragments that were merely transitional passages. Wagner societies were formed in many countries, even in France which had just been defeated by Wagner's compatriots in the Franco-Prussian war. Among composers who absorbed the Wagnerian gospel was Richard Strauss, who introduced the leading motifs into his symphonic works as well as his operas. Engelbert Humperdinck, Janáček, and to some extent even Debussy, all were influenced by Wagner. Alban Berg consciously outlined the significance of leading motifs in his opera *Wozzeck*, a doctrine that enables the composer "by means of leading motifs, to achieve the connections and relationships and thereby attain again a unity." Schoenberg's 12-tone themes as applied in his operas, particularly in the score of *Moses und Aron*, are logical developments of the leading motifs. A more obvious and vulgar exploitation of identifying motifs is represented by commercial jingles in advertising; a cleverly selected tune is designed to form a lasting association with the advertised product and promote its sales.

Lenin Symphony. The Symphony No. 3 by Dmitri Kabalevsky, subtitled *Requiem for Lenin*. Although numbered as his third, it was written before his Symphony No. 2. It concludes with a solemn invocation of "one who is more alive than ever." The first performance took place in Moscow on the tenth anniversary of Lenin's death on January 21, 1934.

Leningrad Symphony. The commonly accepted name of the Symphony No. 7 of Shostakovich, which he dedicated to the heroes of the defense of Leningrad during its seige in 1941. It was first performed in the town of Kuibyshev (formerly Samara) on March 1, 1942. The finale prophesies the victorious end of the "great patriotic war," as World War II was known in Russia.

Leonora. An opera by William Fry, first produced in Philadelphia on June 4, 1845. Fry announced its production with grandiose fanfare, claiming to be the first composer of a real American opera. He selected an English novel for his libretto, however, and set it to music that is almost a parody of Italian opera. After a brief flurry of publicity, *Leonora* sank into the footnotes of musical history. An attempt to revive it a century later met with condescending dismissal.

Leonore Overtures. Beethoven wrote four overtures for his opera *Fidelio*. The first three are called *Leonore Overture*, after the heroine of the opera, Leonore. The fourth *Leonore* overture is the *Fidelio Overture* proper, for it was used for the first performance of the opera in 1814. *Leonore* No. 3 is the one most often performed as a concert piece.

Let's Make an Opera. "An entertainment for young people" with optional audience participation by Benjamin Britten, first produced at the Aldeburgh Festival in England on June 14, 1949. The organizers of the opera discuss on stage the music, the production, and the story. Then the opera, ostensibly planned in front of the audience, is actually produced; it is entitled *The Little Sweep*. The story recounts the inhumane practice of sweeping the chimneys in Victorian England by lowering children from the roof into the fireplace to clean the soot with their little bodies.

Libretto. Italian for "little book," a diminutive of *libro*. In musical usage, the term applies specifically to the text of an opera. Such librettos (or libretti, to use the correct Italian plural) were distributed to the audience to acquaint them with the subject of the opera. In the 19th century it was common to supply a translation into the language of the country in which the opera was performed. Some of these translations are unintentionally funny, such as the English translation of the exhortation of an operatic bandit to his gang upon recognizing his stepsister in the lady of the manor on which he is leading an assault: "Desist! On the same milk we were nurtured!" Italian libretti usually carried an *argomento* (a "summary") listing the acts and scenes, the cast of characters, and sometimes a *protesta* (a protestation by the author of the libretto that his use of names of pagan deities should not be understood as a lack of Christian faith). A paragon of the art was Metastasio, whose libretti were set to music by some 50 composers, accounting for more than a thousand Italian operas. Some libretti have independent literary value, such as Hofmannsthal's thoughtful texts for Richard Strauss. Then there are Gilbert and Sullivan, in whose comic operas the merit is distributed equally for literature and music. In a class by itself is the composer/librettist, of whom Wagner was the supreme example. In modern times Menotti has distinguished himself as a dramatist as well as a composer.

The plots of most early operas are based on standard formulas. Mistaken identities abound. Rigoletto hires assassins to kill the seducer of his daughter; in the darkness of the night they mortally wound the daughter instead and deliver her body to her father in a sack. A most unlikely story, but plausibility is not a virtue among most librettists. A very common theme is seduction followed by desertion; it is the basis of *Faust*, *La Bohème*, and *La Traviata*. Suicides are common, with female self-destruction exceeding that of the male by a large margin. Examples are the seduced granddaughter in *The Queen of Spades*, the murderess in *Lady Macbeth of the District of Mtzensk*, and *Lakmé*. Lodoletta in Mascagni's opera of that name does not commit suicide but dies in the snow outside her lover's Paris house. Infanticide is the central element in *Jenufa*. Impersonation is a common device in opera plots. The faithful Leonore dresses as a boy, assumes the symbolic name Fidelio, and penetrates the prison in which her beloved is unjustly held. The motif of rescue is so ubiquitous that *rescue opera* has entered the dictionaries of musical terms. Religious fanaticism, particularly in the Inquisition, is a convenient dramatic feature in many operas. Thus, in *La Juive* the fanatical cardinal has a girl boiled in a cauldron moments before he finds out that she is his natural daughter. Superstition plays a helpful role in libretti of all kinds. Operatic murders, particularly by stabbing, are too numerous to tabulate. Insanity should not be overlooked; mad scenes in opera are most effective. Fortunately, most of the victims, practically all of them female, recover their sanity as soon as the dramatic situation is favorable for such a development.

It is easy to ridicule opera; the difficulty is to suggest a rational and sensible substitute for operatic libretti. Of course, it is ludicrous for Verdi to have the king of Ethiopia overhear Radames as he relates military secrets to the king's daughter Aida. The hidden king even offers comments in recitative from behind a potted palm. Here Coleridge's injunction regarding the poetic approach as being a "willing suspension of disbelief" is particularly helpful. An operagoer must leave his skepticism with his hat in the cloakroom. When he attended a rehearsal of the opera *Feramors* by Anton Rubinstein, Tolstoy, great writer as he was, felt insulted by the nonsense on the stage. His humorless account of that occasion in his extraordinary tract *What Is Art* (in which he also demolishes music, ballet, painting, and Shakespeare) is worth quoting:

> The procession began with a recitative of a person dressed up in Turkish costume who with a mouth open at an unnatural angle sings: 'I accompany the bri-i-i-i-de.' After singing this he waves his arm, naked of course, under his mantle. The procession opens, but here the French horn accompanying the recitative does something wrong, and the conductor, suddenly startled as if a disaster had struck, taps on the music stand with his stick, and the whole thing starts all over again. The libretto of the opera is one of the greatest absurdities imaginable. An Indian king wants to marry; a bride is presented to him, and he changes his attire to that of a minstrel. The bride falls in love with the supposed minstrel, and becomes desperate at this development. Fortunately, she soons finds out that the minstrel is the king, and everyone is well content. That such Indians never existed, that the personages in the opera do not resemble any Indians or indeed any people, except those in other operas, can be in no doubt whatsoever; that nobody talks in recitative, that no group of four people place themselves at measured distances from one another to perform a quartet, constantly waving their arms to express their emotions; that nobody, except on the stage, walks in pairs carrying halberds made of foil and wearing slippers instead of shoes; that no one ever becomes angry or tender as in the theater, no one laughs or cries like that, and that no one can possibly be moved by such a spectacle, is obvious. And all this repellent nonsense is being put together not in the spirit of social entertainment and fun, but with malice and bestial brutality.

A historical footnote: The rehearsal in question was conducted by the famous Russian musician Wasily Safonov, and the participants were students of the Moscow Conservatory of which he was director. It was Tolstoy himself who asked Safonov's permission to be present at the rehearsal; his account of it did not endear him to Safonov, who never treated the orchestra or the singers with the "bestial brutality" of which Tolstoy accused him.

Sometimes stories of operas are changed for political or social reasons. Glinka's *A Life for the Czar* could not very well be staged in Russia after the Revolution. The Soviet authorities changed the title to *Ivan Susanin*, and the self-sacrificial peasant hero, instead of saving the Czar, is made to save a patriotic Russian commander. Attempts were made in Soviet Russia to rewrite other libretti to make them revolutionary. Thus *Tosca* became *The Commune*, and *The Huguenots* was changed to *The Decembrists* (the revolutionary Russian group of December 1825 who rebelled against Czar Nicholas I). Some operas cannot be performed in certain countries. *The Mikado* is forbidden in Japan because the Japanese emperor is portrayed in an undignified manner. Gounod's *Faust* was renamed *Gretchen* in Germany because the sentimental treatment of Goethe's great poem in the libretto was an affront to German literature. The libretto of Verdi's *Un Ballo in maschera* was based on a historical event, the assassination of the king of Sweden. The opera was forbidden for performance in Italy for fear of inspiring a regicide in Europe at the time. Accordingly, the libretto was changed, and the mythical "Governor of Boston" was substituted for the Swedish king. Sometimes religious restrictions make it impossible to have an opera performed under any circumstances. For instance, *Samson and Delilah* by Saint-Saëns could not be performed for nearly a century on the British stage because of a regulation that prohibited the representation of biblical personages in the theater. The restriction, however, did not apply to oratorios or cantatas. In czarist Russia there was a rule against the portrayal of a member of the reigning dynasty on the stage. So, when Catherine the Great was to make her entrance in Tchaikovsky's *The Queen of Spades*, the *Imperial March* announcing her presence was played, but the empress herself did not appear. No restrictions were applied to the Russian czars before the Romanov dynasty. In Mussorgsky's opera *Boris Godunov*, Czar Boris is a child murderer. Ivan the Terrible is treated by Rimsky-Korsakov in his opera *The Maid of Pskov* as the brute that he was. Ironically, Stalin decreed rehabilitation of the historic Ivan, perhaps because he felt an affinity with his remote precursor. Prokofiev had trouble in his scenic oratorio *Ivan the Terrible*, trying to conform with the new official attitude. Some minor changes had to be made in Pushkin's verses used as the libretto by Rimsky-Korsakov in his opera *Le Coq d'or* to avoid embarrassing similarities between the bumbling czar of the opera and the last czar, Nicholas II, who was not very bright. A unique hazard requires the adjustment of the texts of some operas when they are performed in a different country. The name of Pinkerton in *Madama Butterfly* had to be changed in German productions to Linkerton because in colloquial German *pinkeln* means to urinate. When *Boris Godunov* was performed in Lisbon in 1921, the dying czar's injunction to his son containing the imperative *karai* had to be changed to another Russian word because *karai* means the male sexual organ in Portuguese. The declaration of the young man in *Iolanthe* of Gilbert and Sullivan that he is "a fairy only down to the waist" makes sophisticated audiences of the 20th century giggle.

Lidice Memorial. A symphonic elegy by Bohuslav Martinů, commemorating the Nazi obliteration of the little Czech community of Lidice in June 1942. Its first performance was in New York on October 28, 1943.

Die Liebe der Danaë (The Love of Danaë). An opera by Richard Strauss, first produced posthumously in Salzburg on August 14, 1952. The premiere was originally scheduled for performanance in 1944, but on the day before the announced opening, the Nazi government closed all theaters because of the rapidly deteriorating war situation. Danaë is in a quandary; she must choose between Jupiter and Midas as a lover. She chooses Midas and does not yield even when Jupiter assumes the shape of Midas to deceive her. Jupiter is compelled to accept defeat.

Liebesfuss. Literally, "a love foot," the bulbous opening at the end of the English horn, which has the effect of damping the sound. The same type of extension was characteristic of the manufacture of a clarinetto d'amore, fagotto d'amore, oboe d'amore, and other "amorous" instruments, now largely obsolete. In French this bulbous extension is called *pavillon d'amour*.

Liebestraum. A group of popular piano pieces by Liszt; the title usually remains untranslated because *Dream of Love* or *Love's Dream* in English would sound pedestrian. Liszt wrote three *Liebesträume* in 1850, originally for voice and piano; No. 3 in A-flat major for piano is particularly favored. Each bore a subtitle *Notturno*, and each was provided with an epigraph from German poetry. The first exalted spiritual love, the second was a meditation on saintly death, and the third sang of earthly love.

Lied. This common German word means nothing more than "song," but in the course of time it has acquired a specific meaning of "art song," that is, a "composed" song as distinguished from a "spontaneous" song of folk origin. To obviate this terminological contretemps, the German word *Lied*, and its plural form *Lieder*, have been generally accepted in English to designate such an art song. Sometimes a further specification, "German Lied," is given. The standard form of the German Lied is for a single voice with piano accompaniment. The structure is usually strophic, requiring only a single musical setting for each stanza of the poem. German poems most suitable for this form are rhymed verses containing the same number of syllables in each line; this symmetry of design in the poem corresponds to the symmetry of the musical setting.

Music historians ascribe the creation of the German Lied to Franz Schubert, who, on October 19, 1814, when he was only 16 years old, wrote his inspired Lied, *Gretchen am Spinnrade* (*Gretchen at the Spinning Wheel*). Schubert did have predecessors, notably Zelter and Reichardt. Both wrote songs to German texts in a manner distinguished by a fluid singing line, poignant lyricism of expression, and a symmetry of rhythmical design. Among other 19th-century composers of Lieder were Mendelssohn, Schumann, Liszt, Brahms, Wagner, Loewe, and Hugo Wolf. Wolf expanded the piano accompaniment into an integral part of the Lied as an art form; he furthermore introduced a chromatic harmony that earned him the sobriquet "the Wagner of the Lied." Mahler, Richard Strauss, and Max Reger, although not primarily composers of Lieder, have contributed to the art. Toward the end of the 19th century, the German Lied went into decline, at least in its structural aspect. Most songs of the period were *durchkomponiert* (literally, "through-composed"), with each stanza written anew. Schoenberg created a novel type of Lied in his 15 settings of poems by Stefan George, *Das Buch der hängenden Gärten*, by introducing a songful narrative, *Sprechstimme* ("speechsong"), in which the text is recited in rising and lowering inflections. Whereas the Romantic German Lied cultivated poems of love, sorrow, and death, the modern German Lied annexed topical elements, often of a political import, as in the songs of Hanns Eisler and Kurt Weill.

Other types of German songs are *volkstümliche Lieder*, folk-style songs, also known as *Lieder im Volkston* ("songs in a folk tone"). Anthologies of German popular songs are replete with Lieder whose composers are easily identifiable. What can be more *volkstümlich* than *Lorelei*, to words by Heine? Yet, it is not a folk song; it was written by an otherwise unremarkable composer named Silcher. Mendelssohn's *Lieder ohne Worte* for piano are aptly named, for they are indeed songs without words in a characteristic Lied manner.

Das Lied von der Erde (Song of the Earth). An unnumbered symphony by Mahler, in six parts, for tenor, contralto, and orchestra. The text is a group of Chinese poems in German translation. The work was first performed posthumously in Munich on November 20, 1911. Despite the Chinese derivation of the text, the music has nothing of the Orient, rather, it is a series of romantic impressions.

Liedertafel. A male choral society organized in Berlin in 1809. Numerous branches of the society sprang up in many other cities of Germany and among German musical groups in America. The original Liedertafel (literally, "song table") was organized in imitation of the legendary King Arthur's Round Table, and the singers, like the knights of yore, were expected to be loyal to their group in serving the cause of music.

Lieutenant Kijé. A symphonic suite from a score by Sergei Prokofiev for the Soviet film of the same name. The suite was first performed in Paris on February 10, 1937, with Prokofiev himself conducting. The name Kijé is a Russian misprint resulting from an accidental joining of a suffix with an expletive. The compound was inadvertently mistaken for a name, and stupid military bureaucrats of Nicholas I promoted the suffix plus expletive to a higher rank. Because the Czar had already appended his signature to the promotion, Lieutenant Kijé became an official person. The music is appropriately grinning, full of vibrant rhythms and mock-sentimental romances. Much of Prokofiev's score was used in the 1959 United Artists film *The Horse's Mouth*, based on a screenplay adapted by Alec Guinness, its star, from the book by Joyce Cary. The film is full of British eccentricity; its theme is essentially the artist's right to self-indulgence in a Philistine world.

A Life for the Czar. An opera by Mikhail Glinka, first produced in St. Petersburg on December 9, 1836. The Czar of the opera is young Michael Romanov, elected in 1612 to rule Russia after a long period of social unrest. The Poles, intermittently warring with Russia, send a group of soldiers to kill Michael. Losing their way, they ask the peasant Ivan Susanin to guide them to the Czar's house, but instead he leads them into an impenetrable forest. The invaders kill him, but the Czar is saved. The opera is regarded as the first theatrical work in a national Russian style, even though its facture is largely Italian. It includes genuine Russian folk songs and a remarkable chorus in 5/4 time. Obviously, the opera could not be performed after the Revolution under its original title; accordingly, the libretto was renamed after the heroic peasant, *Ivan Susanin*. The words in the final chorus, which glorify the Czar, were altered to extol the greatness of Russia itself.

Ligature. A fusion of two or more melodic notes into one symbol as a notational development of the neumes. The component parts of a ligature indicated not only the relative pitch but also the rhythmic values, following an elaborate but sometimes self-contradictory set of rules. Depending on the number of notes in a ligature, they were classified as binary, ternary, quaternary, and so on. The terminology of various ligatures was standardized with the establishment of square-note notation. The most common binary and ternary ligatures correspond to accents and other diacritical signs of the alphabet: *pes* ("foot") corresponds to the acute accent and indicates a rise of a degree; *clivis* ("incline") corresponds to the grave accent and indicates a descent of one degree; *torculus* ("twisted") corresponds to the circumflex accent and denotes a rise and a fall of one degree.

Lincoln Portrait. This piece for narrator and orchestra is one of Aaron Copland's most celebrated works. The text is selected from Lincoln's own speeches, and there are modified quotations from ballads of the time. It was first performed in Cincinnati on May 14, 1942, with the poet Carl Sandburg narrating and André Kostelanetz conducting.

Linus. A mythological Greek hero who tried to teach music to Hercules and was slain by his pupil with his own lyre when he tried to correct an error

Hercules made during a lesson. A Song of Linus was sung each year at harvest time in Homer's day to commemorate Linus's tragic death.

Lion's roar. A special percussion, or, rather, frictional instrument, consisting of a bucket covered with a membrane through which a rosined cord is passed. When the cord is pulled vigorously, a sound resembling the roar of a lion is produced. It is used in the score of Varèse's *Ionisation*.

Lira. Not a lyre but an obsolete violin that did not even look like a lyre. It was of two types: *lira da braccio*, held in the arms, and *lira da gamba*, held between the knees. A *lira organizzata* is a type of hurdy-gurdy in which the sound is produced by a rotating wheel; the name means an "organed" string instrument, equipped with a little organ-like mechanism. *Lira mendicorum* was the "lyre of the mendicants"; it was a plucked string instrument cultivated by street beggars in the Middle Ages.

Litany. A protracted imploration beseeching God, the Blessed Virgin, and assorted saints for clemency or another favor with a promise to repent in exchange for divine intercession. A litany is chanted in an oscillating monotone with the congregation responding wearily. The most auspicious time for a litany is the period of Rogation Days (from Latin *rogare*, "to beg"). The unrelenting repetitiousness of a litany is essential for cumulative impact on the more compassionate saints. Litanies of the Anglican church are less impressive, and the words often have a colloquial inflection, such as "Spare us, good Lord." As a common metaphor, a *litany* is a tedious and repetitive importunity addressed to an influential person in lieu of an inaccessible deity.

Little Russian Symphony. The nickname of Tchaikovsky's Symphony No. 2 in C minor, first performed in Moscow on February 7, 1873. The title, as it commonly appears in English, is misleading; it is not a small, or short, symphony but a symphony of Little Russia, which was an imperialistic name in czarist Russia for the Ukraine. Ukrainian songs are used thematically in the work.

Liturgical drama. A term applied to medieval plays in Latin containing action, dialogue, and occasional singing episodes. Although liturgical drama makes use of biblical subjects, it never became part of the Catholic liturgy. One of the most popular kinds of liturgical drama is the miracle play, in which stories of saints, of whom St. Nicholas was a favorite, are recited. During the Renaissance, liturgical drama developed into mystery plays (a misconstrued title actually meaning ministerial plays, from the Latin word *ministerium*, "a service"). Gradually such plays assumed a secular theatrical role while adhering to biblical subjects. Incidental music such as dances, trumpet flourishes, processions, and the like—even folk songs—was used. In Italy these dramas with music became known as *sacre rappresentazioni* and as *autos* ("acts") in Spain and Portugal. These festivals were true predecessors of scenic oratorios and, by ramification, Wagnerian music dramas.

Liturgy. The most comprehensive term for the official service of the established Christian church. In the Byzantine ritual, the liturgy is synonymous with the Mass. The word itself is Greek, derived from an old Attic word *leos*, "the people," and *ergos*, "work."

Locrian mode. The church mode corresponding to the scale from B to B on the white keys of the piano keyboard. Because its dominant F stands to its tonic B in the relation of a forbidden diminished fifth, the Locrian mode was not used in Gregorian chant.

Lohengrin. An opera by Wagner, to his own libretto, first performed in Weimar on August 28, 1850. Liszt conducted it because Wagner was exiled in Switzerland as a fugitive from Saxony, being sought by authorities for his rather nominal involvement in the 1848 Revolution. In *Lohengrin*, as always, Wagner shows his fascination with Nordic legends. Elsa of Brabant has a mystic dream of a noble knight who will defend her from a monstrous accusation of fratricide. Her dream knight arrives in a boat drawn by a swan. She marries him to the strains of the famous bridal chorus (which in the following years sanctified millions of ordinary marriages in Europe and America). Although he adjures her never to ask his name and origin, she breaks the injunction. He then reveals that he is Lohengrin, the Knight of the Holy Grail, son of Parsifal; his swan is Elsa's brother, believed to be dead. The swan's human shape is restored, but Lohengrin must leave now that his identity is known. Swanless, he summons a dove to draw the boat away. The opera is Wagner's first great masterpiece, and it is impossible to understand why *The Musical World* of London wrote so disparagingly of it in 1855: "*Lohengrin* is an incoherent mass of rubbish. Being a Communist, Herr Wagner affirms that national melody is unhealthy. . . . The true basis of harmony is cast away for a reckless, wild, extravagant and demagogic cacophony, the symbol of profligate libertinage."

I Lombardi alla prima Crociata (The Lombards at the First Crusade). Verdi's fourth opera, first performed at La Scala in Milan on February 11, 1843. In it two crusading brothers from Lombardy are rivals in love. The more ambitious one plans to kill the other but slays their father by mistake. To expiate his sin, he goes to Jerusalem and becomes a hermit. His niece is captured by the infidels but falls in love with her captor's son. Her lover is wounded but is baptized by the hermit just in time to save his expiring heathen soul. As the battle rages, the brothers are reunited; the patricide hermit is forgiven by his brother and dies in peace. In France, Germany, Poland, and Russia the opera played under the title *Jerusalem*, and returned to La Scala as *Gerusalemme*.

London Symphonies. A group of Haydn's 12 symphonies, also known as the *Salomon* Symphonies, beginning with No. 93 and ending with his last symphony, No. 104. Haydn wrote these for the London violinist Salomon, who arranged for Haydn's London tours in 1791–1792 and again in 1794–1795. (It took Haydn 17 days to reach London from Vienna by stagecoach and sailboat.)

A London Symphony. Ralph Vaughan Williams's Symphony No. 2, his most popular, first performed in London on March 27, 1914. It is in four movements; there are realistic musical allusions to the noises of London streets, and the chimes of Big Ben are heard through it all. Vaughan Williams exhorted listeners to treat this symphony as a piece of absolute music, taking in the street cries and other London scenes as incidental.

Londonderry Air. A famous Irish melody, apparently an authentic folksong, first published in 1855. Genuine Irish tunes are pentatonic, so it is probable that the leading tone that opens the melody in the common version of the tune is an adjustment and that the submediant was probably the original tone.

Longevity. A cursory reading of actuarial tables seems to indicate that musicians as a class live on the average about 12 years longer than nonmusicians under similar social and geographical conditions. When an aging symphony conductor showed a desperate reluctance to quit, an unfeeling music critic remarked: "Conductors rarely die and never resign." The greatest conductor of modern times, Arturo Toscanini, continued to lead an orchestra well into his 80s and resigned only after he suffered an embarrassing lapse of memory at a concert. Leopold Stokowski conducted concerts and made recordings after he turned 91. Pierre Monteux had already arranged a program he expected to conduct with the Boston Symphony Orchestra on his 90th birthday, but unfortunately he died a few months before the date. Organists are apt to live longer than symphony conductors. The celebrated French organist Charles-Marie Widor lived to be 93. There are several cases on record of church organists who died at the console. Among them was the blind French organist Louis Vierne, who expired while playing one of his new compositions at Notre Dame de Paris; he was only 66. The record of longevity for pianists is not as impressive as that of organists. The American pianist Henry Holden Huss, who was also a composer of sorts, made a point of playing a program of his works on his 90th birthday. Artur Rubinstein continued to give concerts even after he became blind; he died at the age of 95. Violinists and cellists usually stop playing in public after 70, but the greatest cellist of the 20th century, Pablo Casals, continued to perform publicly until shortly before his death at 97. Among singers, Manuel García lived to be 101, but he had long since abandoned his professional singing career, becoming active mainly as a teacher. Marie Olénine d'Alheim terminated her career as a concert singer in her middle age to enter radical politics; she joined the French Communist party and later went to Moscow, where she died at 100. One has to cite less universally known names to find nonagenarians and centenarians among composers. Havergal Brian reached the age of 96. Henri Busser died at the age of 101, but he was little known outside of France. Carl Ruggles lived to be 95, and he was fortunate in acquiring a solid reputation before he died. Eubie Blake, the American black ragtime virtuoso, appeared on television in his late 90s; he died a few days after reaching his 100th birthday. The most spectacular case of a longevity among popular composers was that of Irving Berlin who reached the age of 100 in 1988. Statistically, mediocre musicians live much longer than men of genius. Among truly great composers, only Verdi lived well into his 80s. Wagner did not even reach the biblically sanctified age of three score and ten. Beethoven, Debussy, Ravel, and Tchaikovsky died before their 60th birthdays. And Chopin, Schubert, Schumann, Mendelssohn, not to mention Mozart, died at the height of their genius. Perhaps angels are eager to carry away the best musicians for heavenly concerts. It is enticing to speculate what would happen to music history if the lives of great composers could be magically extended. Had Mozart lived to the age of 80, he could have been an older friend of Chopin. Had Beethoven lived as many years as Sibelius (91), he might have given advice to young Tchaikovsky. O, dreams of temporal relativity!

Longhair. A derogatory characterization of a person interested in classical music; synonymous with *highbrow*. It derives from the conventional portraiture of musicians sporting luxuriant heads of long hair. Liszt in his last photograph appears as such a longhair.

Loud pedal. The far-right pedal of the piano that releases all dampers normally resting on the strings, allowing the strings that have been struck to continue their vibrations. This makes it necessary to quickly change the pedaling when the harmony changes, to avoid unwelcome cacophony. The handling (or more accurately, the footing) of the loud pedal must therefore be considered with great care on general musical grounds rather than narrowly pianistic grounds. One of the natural safety impulses among pianists unsure of their technique is to step on the right pedal to create a universal resonance in which the annoying wrong notes may be conveniently drowned out. When a composer writes for piano orchestrally and requires sustained tones in changing harmonies, a compromise must be sought using the skill of subtle half-pedaling. An outstanding example is a variation in Schumann's *Études symphoniques* in which the theme occurs in the bass while the harmony changes above, making it extremely difficult to achieve both the legato in the left hand and the changing harmonies in the right hand.

Louise. A realistic opera by Gustave Charpentier, produced in Paris on February 2, 1900, with immediate success; it had nearly 1,000 performances during the first half of the century. It was called "Roman musical" by the composer, who wrote his own libretto dealing with the poverty-stricken life of dressmakers in Paris (Charpentier's mistress was a dressmaker named Louise). The score included the precisely notated cries of vegetable vendors in the streets of Paris.

Louisiana Story. An orchestral suite by Virgil Thomson, drawn by him from the background music he wrote for a documentary film, for which he won the Pulitzer Prize in 1948. The suite was first performed in Philadelphia on November 26, 1948. Thompson wrote a second suite based on the same documentary, entitled *Acadian Songs and Dances.*

Loure. A dance often included in Baroque instrumental suites, and also encountered in French ballets and overtures of the Rococo period. It is usually in 6/4 time, marked with syncopation. The word comes from *lura,* "bagpipe," which also generated the term *louré* as a kind of bowing technique on string instruments in which several notes are played in one bow stroke but in a detached manner.

Love of Three Oranges. An opera by Sergei Prokofiev, first produced in Chicago on December 30, 1921, the composer conducting. A court witch decrees that the young prince who laughed when she suffered an embarrassing fall be doomed to wander in search of three oranges. He finds them, and eventually the oranges split open. Each contains a young girl, and each of the girls asks for a drink of water. The prince has enough water for only one, so he chooses the most beautiful of them and lets the other two perish. The libretto is by Gotti. In the music Prokofiev thumbs his nose at the nonsense of operatic stories. The march from the opera is famous.

Luce. Italian for "light." A part for the luce, a "color organ," is marked by Scriabin in the score of his last symphonic work, *Prométhée.* The color organ, according to Scriabin's unfulfilled hopes, would bathe the concert hall in shimmering hues that would change along with the harmonies.

Lucia di Lammermoor. An opera by Gaetano Donizetti, first produced in Naples on September 26, 1835. The libretto is based on Walter Scott's novel, *The Bride of Lammermoor.* Edgar loves Lucia, but her ambitious brother wants her to marry a British lord. When Edgar goes to the wars, Lucia is told that he was unfaithful to her. When Edgar returns, he finds her engaged to be married to the lord. He pronounces a curse on the whole family, after taking part in a famous sextet, the other five singers being Lucia, her brother, Lucia's husband, his chaplain, and Lucia's lady-in-waiting. On her wedding night, Lucia murders her husband and goes insane. In her celebrated mad scene, she imagines being married to Edgar; she then swoons and dies. Vowing to join her in eternity, Edgar stabs himself to death. The score is one of the most mellifluous products of the Italian art of bel canto.

Lucio Sulla. An opera by Mozart, first performed in Milan on December 26, 1772. Sulla was the Roman general who reached the highest power after he was elected consul in 81 B.C. and then proclaimed himself dictator of Rome. In Mozart's opera he renounces his power and returns it to the people. Mozart was only 16 years old when he wrote this opera.

Lucrezia Borgia. An opera by Gaetano Donizetti, first produced in Milan on December 26, 1833. Lucrezia, the most infamous of the Borgia family in 16th-century Italy, shelters her illegitimate son in the Borgia castle and helps him to elude arrest by her husband's henchmen. While handing cups of poisoned wine to some of them, she unwittingly passes poison to her son. Ostensibly, the libretto was drawn from a tragedy by Victor Hugo, but he was outraged when the opera was produced and demanded a total revision in which Lucrezia became a Turk and the title was changed to *La Rinnegata* (*The Renegade*).

Ludus Tonalis. A piano suite by Paul Hindemith, which he subtitled *Studies on Counterpoint, Tonal Organization, and Piano Playing*. The introductory *Praeludium* is converted into the final *Postludium* by turning the page upside down and reading the music backward, with some liberal dispensation for accidentals. The body of the work consists of 12 fugues with intervening interludes. It was first performed in Chicago on February 15, 1944.

Luftpause. A break between melody notes, particularly at the end of a phrase. The German word means "a rest to catch a breath of air." It is used and abused by pseudoromantic performers, particularly violinists, who either cannot sustain a passage in legato or feel that a melody without a soulful luftpause would lack expressive power.

Lulu. An unfinished opera by Alban Berg, produced posthumously in Zürich on June 2, 1937. The libretto is drawn from two dramas of Wedekind. Lulu, a prodigiously promiscuous lady, spares neither young nor old, neither man nor woman. She meets her doom when she is disemboweled by Jack the Ripper in London. The score is a tour de force. Written in the Schoenbergian technique of 12-tone composition, it preserves the structure of a classical suite. The work was completed by Friedrich Cerha in 1974; the premiere, incorporating new elements, took place at the Paris Opéra on February 24, 1979.

Lute. A generic name for a variety of string instruments familiar from innumerable Renaissance paintings. The body of the lute is shaped like half a pear;

its neck is turned back at the right angle. The fingerboard has embossed frets indicating the positions of the notes of the scale. The lute usually has five sets of double strings, plus a single string for the highest sound; they are plucked with the fingers. The tuning is in perfect fourths, with a third in the middle, the lowest string being G or A, and with a range of two octaves. The golden age of the lute was in the 16th and 17th centuries when it was the favorite instrument of the aristocracy. About the middle of the 18th century, it inexplicably lost its lure and joined the honorable company of other obsolete instruments.

Lute-like instruments existed in Mesopotamia in great antiquity, but they had only two or three strings, and there is no evidence that the familiar lute of the Renaissance actually descended by way of imitation or import of these precursors. Long-necked lutes existed in Persia and Arabia in the Middle Ages; their European variety was called *colascione* and usually had five strings. A small variety of the Arabian lute is called *'ud*. A lute-like instrument of Arabian provenance was the *tanbur*. The Russian *domra* was popular at the same time as the European lute. When it went out of fashion, it was superseded by the *balalaika*. The mandolin is of the lute family, and it has retained its popularity through the 20th century. Other types of lutes are the *mandola*, a large variety of the mandolin, and *bandora* (or *pandora*). Two very large lutes are the *theorbo* and *chiturrone*. None of these instruments, however, has the unique characteristic of a turned neck.

A whole musical literature was created for the lute at the time of its greatest popularity. Many collections of music written especially for the lute were published in the 16th and 17th centuries. It is from these books that music historians are able to trace the formal development of European dances, instrumental works, and vocal compositions. Most early lute music was written in tablature; the player was given a diagram of the strings and the position on which the fingers should be placed to secure the required notes or harmonies.

Lutenists enjoyed great renown in the Renaissance period, particularly in England. The English-born lutenist John Dowland, who was a contemporary of Shakespeare, commanded salaries equalling those of high officials. The Italian court lutenist Rizzio, who was brought to Scotland by Mary Stuart, assumed such power at the Scottish court that Mary's antagonists arranged for his assassination. Portraits of lutenists, both men and women, were favorites with the great painters of the Renaissance. Beginning with Chaucer, there are numerous references to lute players in English literature.

Luthéal. A mechanical attachment invented in 1919 by the Belgian piano manufacturer Georges Cloetens; it was to be placed on the metal framework inside the grand piano, imparting to it the sound of a clavecin. Ravel was quite fascinated by the potential of the luthéal and made use of it in the piano part of his violin piece, *Tzigane*. The luthéal failed to be attractive to the public or the music critics; accordingly, Ravel made another version of *Tzigane* for violin and piano, and still another version for violin with orchestral accompaniment. Ravel made further use of the luthéal in the original setting of *L'Enfant et les sortilèges*, but in the final version he decided to reproduce the effects of the luthéal by various orchestral timbres.

Lydian mode. Although the name is inherited from Greece, the Lydian mode is not identical with the ancient Greek mode of the same name. If projected onto the diatonic scale represented by the white keys on the piano, the Lydian mode would extend from F to F. Its arresting characteristic is the presence of the tritone between the tonic and the subdominant, the forbidding (and forbidden) *diabolus in musica*. Beethoven distinctly indicates the presence of the Lydian mode in the slow movement of his last String Quartet, op. 132. Chopin made the Lydian mode sound peculiarly expressive in some of his Slavic-like mazurkas.

Lyre. The most famous string instrument of ancient Greece. The strings ran along a sound box made of wood or tortoise shell and were played with a plectrum. It belongs to the same family as the Greek kithara but lacks the crossbars and other supports. The lyre, like the kithara, is the emblem of Apollo and is reproduced in numerous sculptures and drawings of him.

Lyrische Suite. A work for string quartet by Alban Berg, in six movements and set in the technique of 12-tone composition. Its lyric sentiment is emphatically expressed by a quotation from Wagner's Prelude to *Tristan und Isolde*. It was first performed in Vienna on January 8, 1927. A vocal finale was discovered later, and the work was first performed in this version in New York on November 1, 1979.

M

Ma Mère L'Oye (Mother Goose). Five children's pieces for piano four hands by Ravel, which he later orchestrated. The subjects are taken from the famous book of nursery rhymes by Charles Perrault. Ravel composed these pieces for two Parisian girls, one 10 years old and the other only 6, who gave the first performance of them at a regular concert in Paris on April 20, 1910.

Má vlast (My Country). A symphonic cycle by Bedřich Smetana, composed between 1874 and 1879. There are six sections: *Vyšehrad* (a historic town on the Danube); *Vltava* (the river on which Prague stands, known universally as the Moldau); *Šárka* (a legendary warrior woman); *Z českých luhův a hayüv* (*From Bohemia's Meadows and Groves*); *Tábor* (*The Camp*), which includes the melody of the Hussite war song; *Blanik* (a Bohemian hill on which the adherents of the martyred reformer Jan Huss congregated). Šárka is the leader of a fierce women's group in Bohemia that is engaged in a constant fight with the local knights. To overcome them, she lets herself be tied to a tree in the forest. One of the knights finds her and carries her off as a prize. As the knights celebrate her capture in their castle, they fall into a drunken stupor. Šárka then signals her female warriors to descend upon the castle and slaughter all the knights. This bloody event is set to music *con brio*, with a romantic duet for clarinet, representing Šárka, and cello, representing the knight who captured her. Whether by actual borrowing or through an extraordinary coincidence, the melody of the second movement, *Vltava* (*The Moldau*), was adopted in 1897 by the First International Zionist Conference in Basel; eventually it became the Israeli national anthem *Hatikva*, "hope." Investigators also found that this melody was remarkably similar to that of a Swedish song written in 1822, and it has also been traced to folksongs of Dutch and Polish origin.

Macbeth. The title of three discrete works based on Shakespeare's tragedy: (1) An opera by Verdi, first performed in Florence on March 14, 1847. The Italian libretto follows faithfully the main events of Shakespeare's play, but the opera is not one of Verdi's best. (2) An opera by Ernest Bloch, first performed in Paris on November 30, 1910. The score bristles with unorthodox harmonies and asymmetric rhythms and was judged severely by conservative Paris critics. (3) The first of seven remarkable tone poems by Richard Strauss, each based on an explicit story or a literary work, first performed in Weimar on October 13, 1890.

Macrotime. A term proposed by Karlheinz Stockhausen in 1955 to designate the duration of each rhythmic pulse, as quantitatively contrasted with micro-time, which is the number of vibrations of a given note.

Macumba. A ritual festival of Afro-Brazilians that is marked by a display of animal power and indeed related to primitive animalism. The festival includes elements of African and Indian folklore combined with Christian symbols, accompanied by music and dance, both believed to possess magical powers.

Madama Butterfly. An opera by Puccini, first produced in Milan on February 17, 1904. Lieutenant Pinkerton of the U.S. Navy is in Nagasaki and becomes enamored of a 15-year-old Japanese girl nicknamed Cio-Cio, Japanese for "butterfly." She is also formally referred to as Cio-Cio-San, the last word being the nobiliary particle corresponding to Madame. She and Pinkerton go through a Japanese marriage ceremony, which he knows is not legally binding. He then sails to the United States, leaving her behind. She has faith in his love for her and expresses her feelings in an aria based on a pentatonic theme that has become a favorite of the soprano repertory. When Pinkerton returns to Japan after three years, he brings with him his legal American wife. In the meantime, Cio-Cio-San has borne Pinkerton's son. She yields to Pinkerton's wife's entreaties to let her have the child. Cio-Cio-San then commits ritual hara-kiri while *The Star-Spangled Banner* is heard in the background. The score is remarkable in its bold innovations, making use of consecutive triads, unresolved discords, and percussive orchestral effects. There are also a fair number of pseudo-Japanese melodies.

Madrigal. In established historical usage, a liturgical or secular polyphonic composition of Italian extraction that flowered during the Renaissance but lapsed into obsolescence in the 19th century. The etymology of the word is uncertain. The most likely derivation is achieved by replacing *d* with *t* and *g* with *c*, thus relating the word to *mater*, "mother," in the sense of maternal love or belonging to Mother Church. The poetic form of the Italian madrigal arose in the 14th century and was marked by a fairly definite scheme in iambic pentameter. Such madrigals were usually pastoral in nature and continued to be popular with composers of the early Renaissance. A decided change in the madrigal style took place in the 16th century when the strict formality of the verses and tunes was abandoned in favor of a more relaxed, imaginative, and individual style, with polyphonic settings increased to four, five, and six parts. In the 17th century the role of the soloist became more and more pronounced; concomitantly, the polyphonic style gave way to homophony, forming a natural bridge to opera. Indeed, there developed a special genre of madrigal known as the madrigal opera, which was an immediate predecessor of the early *dramma per musica*, or opera proper. A madrigal opera is a group of madrigals united in content and forming a dramatic sequence. Another subspecies was the madrigal comedy, a type of commedia dell'arte that emerged early in the 16th century in Italy. It is formed by a chain of interconnected madrigals, suggestive of early oratorio. The most distinct specimen is *L'Amfiparnasso* by Orazio Vecchi, performed in 1594, which consists of a prologue and three acts of which 14 numbers are written in five-part madrigal style, without accompaniment.

Among important composers of Italian madrigals are Jacob Arcadelt, Cipriano de Rore, Andrea Gabrieli, Orlando di Lasso, Luca Marenzio, Don Carlo Gesualdo, and Claudio Monteverdi. Palestrina was the greatest writer of spiritual madrigals, as opposed to the secular type cultivated by most madrigalists. Elizabethan composers in England, among them William Byrd, eagerly followed the Italian model. A great impetus to the development of the English madrigal school was the publication in England in 1588 of a collection of Italian madrigals with English translations, *Musica Transalpina*.

Madrigali guerrieri e amorosi. A famous book of madrigals by Claudio Monteverdi, published in 1638. These "madrigals of war and love" for voices and instruments are written in the *stile concitato* ("excited style"), in this instance combining love with "warlike expression."

Maestro. An honorary appellation accorded, often without merit, to composers, conductors, teachers, and even to lower species of musical eminences. In Italian, the word conveys little more than a common term for a teacher, but when used by Englishmen, Americans, or Russians in addressing a musical celebrity, it sounds lofty and deferential.

Maggot. Far from being the repellent legless larva that infests putrefying bodies, in old English poetry *maggot* signified a pleasing whim. In music the word was attached to pieces of pleasurable content, often with a lady's name, as in *My Lady Winwood's Maggot*.

Magic. The magic rites of ancient times or of so-called primitive peoples in our time have always been accompanied by some musical performance, no matter how inchoate or artless. The myth of Orpheus, the godlike singer who could move people, particularly women, and even inanimate objects by his songs, is a classical invocation of artistic magic. Amphion was a magical player on the lyre; such was his skill that the stones used in the construction of the walls of Thebes were drawn into their proper places by his playing. The famous lines of William Congreve testify to the belief of this power: "Music has charms to soothe a savage breast, To soften rocks, or bend a knotted oak." Musical magic is inherent in religious incantations, which are products of man's primitive impulse to vociferate in joy or lament in sorrow. Certain rhythms assume a magical significance in the society in which they originate. The relentlessly repetitive drum beats of the jungle portend danger. In the 1920s the Cuban government forbade the manufacture and use of primitive Afro-Cuban drums (congas) because they affected the villagers so as to create serious disturbances and even revolts. To Jews in southern Russia, the very opening notes of the Russian czarist hymn suggested the beginning of a pogrom organized by groups of extreme monarchists, often led by the Russian orthodox priests and condoned by the police. The cantilation of the rabbis in a synagogue, the high-pitched songs of the Moslem criers from the minarets, the monotonous recitations of the Latin Catholic rosary, even the familiar strains of a lullaby, all partake of musical magic.

Epic literature of all nations and cultures is replete with instances of magical healing effected simply by intoning melorhythmic phrases that through constant use became associated with curative faculties. In the Finnish epic of *Kalevala*, the musical magician recites a spell related to the origin of a wound, whether inflicted by an animal or by a sword, and by revealing its nature exorcises the wound. The Siberian shamans accompany their healing rites by ululations and savage beating upon primitive tambourines or metal plates. The witch doctors of Haiti make noise first and begin their curative exercise only after the subject has become completely relaxed and submissive to incantation. The most ominous of all forms of magic, the sticking of pins into an effigy of a person to be ruined, is never performed in silence. Sinister cries accompany the imposition of taboo in primitive societies, and such cries inevitably assume the form of a musical incantation. Through constant repetition, the musical accompaniment of the ritual of taboo becomes a magical symbol of the act itself, so it is no longer necessary to utter any words or symbolic verbal sounds to impose a taboo on a house, a mountain, a river, or a person. The music alone suffices.

Priests, witch doctors, and military leaders alike apply magic by ruthless repetition of slogans, often in singsong fashion. This type of crude magic is also successfully plied by advertisers and politicians on the radio and television. An idiotically repetitive and musically repulsive jingle may drive the captive listener to distraction, but the commercial purpose is attained. Religious proselytism impressed magic on the "savages" during missionary work by endless repetition of Latin phrases that meant nothing to the possessors of the souls to be saved. The power of magical repetition is recognized in the endless incantations of *Ave Maria* in Catholic prayers or religious radio broadcasts. The musical exhibition in New York City in 1963 that featured the repetition 840 times of a vacuous piece by Erik Satie, *Vexations*, was a case of magic by cumulative stultification. Several composers in times past believed that their works were of magical origin and that they could transfer this magic to the audiences. Scriabin planned the composition of a *Mysterium* whose magical power would be such that its first performance would actually precipitate the end of the world, in which he himself and all participants in its performance would be consumed in an act of universal ecstasy. Whatever vestigial magic, musical and verbal, may still survive in its virgin state in such regions as the upper Amazon or in Polynesia, however, has now been polluted and denatured by a potent flow of musical "culture" by radio and other means of communication.

The Magic Flute. The last opera by Mozart, and the most complex, both musically and dramatically, produced in Vienna on September 30, 1791, less than ten weeks before Mozart's death. The German libretto is by Schikaneder, an impresario and actor; its labyrinthine entanglements are prodigious. The gorgeous music absorbs the listener entirely, letting the plot proceed on its irrational course. A youth falls in love with a portrait of the daughter of the Queen of the Night. He is given a magic flute to enable him to penetrate the fortress in which she is held captive somewhere in Egypt. His companion is a birdcatcher who has a set of magic bells capable of paralyzing any foe. After a series of perilous adventures, the youth and the queen's daughter are united and sing a hymn to the sun to symbolize the conquest of love and art over the powers of darkness. A partial clue to the story may lie in its heavy pseudooriental symbolism, such as was cultivated in the Masonic Order, of which both Mozart and his librettist were members. The hero is pursued by a serpent, which is killed by the female messengers of the protective Queen of the Night; the multiheaded serpent was a well-known masonic symbol. The lovers undergo an initiation similar to that of the Mason's Order and give a vow of silence, commonly administered in the French Order of Masons in the 18th century. Various theatrical scenes are modeled after the rituals of masonic lodges. The Egyptian pyramid, which is the locale of one of the scenes, is a famous masonic symbol (reproduced, incidentally, on the reverse side of The Great Seal of the United States). The similarity between the symbols used in the libretto and the masonic ritual gave rise to the fantastic tale that the Masons resolved to put Mozart to death for revealing Masonic secrets.

Magnificat. The most important hymn of the vespers service in the Roman Catholic liturgy, named for the opening word of the canticle of the Blessed Virgin Mary, "*Magnificat anima mea Dominum.*" The text is from Luke 1:46–55. Many pious composers wrote Magnificats as separate choral works.

In the Anglican church service, the Magnificat is a part of the evening prayer, using the English words, "My soul doth magnify the Lord."

The Maiden's Prayer (Prière d'une Vierge). Undoubtedly the most celebrated piano piece ever, written in 1851. Serious musicians deprecated it as a deplorable piece of sentimental salon music, but young ladies all over the world continued to play it in their stuffy drawing rooms. More than 100 separate editions of *The Maiden's Prayer* were published. The composer of this salon masterpiece was a 17-year-old Polish girl, Thekla Badarzewska. She died a few years after its publication and probably never knew what a poisoned gift she had bestowed upon the musical world. One heartless critic wrote in her obituary that her early death saved humanity from drowning in a flood of sentimental treacle.

Majority. A song by Charles Ives, composed in 1915. In the piano part it makes use of tone clusters to be played by pressing a strip of wood over the keys. The alternative title is *The Masses*.

Malagueña. An old Spanish dance tune in rapid triple time originating, as the name indicates, in Málaga. Its main harmonic characteristic is a repetitive cadential pattern from the tonic down to the dominant, harmonized by consecutive minor triads in root position.

Les Mamelles de Tirésias (The Mammary Glands of Tirésias). An opera buffa by Francis Poulenc, first produced in Paris on June 3, 1947. The libretto deals with transsexual transformation. Tirésias, weary of being a woman, ignites her bulging breasts, which rise and pop like balloons. Her husband, on the other hand, wants to be a woman. He succeeds brilliantly and gives birth to 40,000 children. In the end, they return to their original genders and appeal to the audience to breed energetically in order to repopulate the earth devastated by war. The score is glorified slapstick.

Mandolin. A string instrument of the lute family that originated in Italy in the 17th century. The name is the diminutive of *mandola*. The instrument is oval in shape and has four pairs of strings tuned like those of the violin (G, D, A, E). It is played with a plectrum called a mediator. Progressively larger sizes of the mandolin are the mandola, the mandoloncello, and the mandolone, the latter being the bass version. An ensemble consisting of mandolins combined with guitars is popularly known as a Neapolitan orchestra. Although the mandolin is generally regarded as a plebeian instrument, Mozart and Beethoven wrote for it. The mandolin is also included in Mahler's Symphony No. 7, in Schoenberg's *Serenade*, op. 24, and in Webern's *Fünf Stücke für Orchester*.

Manfred Symphony. A symphony by Tchaikovsky, first performed in Moscow on March 23, 1886. The work is inspired by Byron's famous poem depicting Manfred wandering in the Alps in search of oblivion. The score, in four symphonic movements, is often listed by literal-minded musicologists as Tchaikovsky's Symphony No. 7. Although brilliant and dramatic, *Manfred* is musically inferior to Tchaikovsky's full-fledged symphonies.

Mannheim school. The historical name attached to the performing activities of a group of musicians active at the court of the German city of Mannheim in the middle of the 18th century. The group developed a method of composition and performance that marked a radical departure from the monolithic style of the Baroque period. Their animator and mentor was the Bohemian master Johann Stamitz, who inaugurated in his symphonic works the principle of melodic guidance and symmetrical formal structure. In the works of the Mannheim school, harmony, too, underwent a decided change away from the rigid dependence on the figured bass. In performance, the Mannheim group introduced novel dynamic usages, the most important of which was the effect of continuous crescendo and corresponding diminuendo, in contrast with the antiphonal structure of mutually responsive sections of forte and piano in Baroque music. Among other innovations were arpeggiated chords, extensive tremolos, abrupt general pauses, pyrotechnical accents, simulated sighs, and various emotional devices almost romantic in nature. Regarding the orchestra, the Mannheim musicians cultivated greater independence of the wind instruments. Regarding form, there was a pronounced articulation of subsections in the minuet and the expansion of the sonata form to symphonic dimensions. The achievements of the Mannheim school soon became known in Paris and London and had considerable influence on the evolution of symphonic and chamber music. There was a great deal of opposition on the part of traditional and academic musicians who dubbed the innovations of the Mannheim school as mannerism. The circumstance that most of the Mannheim musicians came from Bohemia rather than from the main centers of German musical culture caused narrow nationalistic disdain. In a letter to Mozart, his father referred to the "overmannered Mannheim taste." There was no gainsaying the power of the Mannheim dynamic characteristics, however. A musician who heard the Mannheimers play reports that "their crescendo makes the listeners rise involuntarily from their seats, and gradually sink back out of breath with the corresponding diminuendo."

Manon. An opera by Jules Massenet, first produced in Paris on January 9, 1884. Manon, an emotionally perturbed 18th-century French girl, intends to become a nun but is diverted from her purpose by a dashing cavalier who carries her off to Paris. His father urges him to renounce the ways of the world and join the priesthood. Manon is arrested on suspicion of moral turpitude. Although her lover secures her freedom by bribing the authorities, she has no more strength to live and dies of inanition. In *Manon*, Massenet is at his sentimental best.

Manon Lescaut. An opera by Giacomo Puccini, first produced in Turin on February 1, 1893. A beautiful French girl intends to enter a convent, but a traveling companion induces her to join him in Paris. She becomes debauched by city life but agrees to take a ship to America with her lover. They make the voyage safely, but despite his solicitude, she dies in a "desert of Louisiana." The libretto differs from that of Massenet's opera *Manon*, but both are drawn from Prevost's novel, *Manon Lescaut*.

Manru. The only opera by Ignace Paderewski, first produced in Dresden on May 29, 1901. Manru is a dissolute gypsy; his wife, unable to bear his constant infidelities, kills herself. Manru is eventually destroyed by a man whose bride he has abducted. The opera is written in a conventional romantic manner. Despite Paderewski's fame as a virtuoso pianist, it was rarely produced even in his lifetime.

Maracas. A pair of gourds filled with dry seeds and shaken rhythmically to accompany popular Latin American dances. In the 20th century, maracas began to be used as percussion instruments in modern scores, quite independently from their ethnic content. Thus Prokofiev uses a pair in his patriotic oratorio, *Alexander Nevsky*; Varèse has a part for maracas in his "atomic" work, *Ionisation*.

March. A universal step corresponding to the natural alternation of the left and right foot in walking. (If there were a race of three-footed humans, they would march in waltz time.) Because uniform steps are essential in military practice, the march has become the chosen rhythm of armies all over the world. The word comes from the Latin *marcare*, "to mark." Although the time signature for a march is commonly 4/4, or alla breve, there are marches in 6/8 or 12/8, a type known as *Reitermarsch* ("rider march"), for binary time with rapid subdivisions in triplets that suggest a galloping horse. Schubert's song *Erlkönig* is a "rider march," descriptive of the desperate ride of a father with a dying son in his arms.

The most immediate function of the march is military; indeed, a military march, or, in French, *marche militaire*, is a distinctive musical form. A perfect example is found in Gounod's *Faust*. March time can be adapted to a variety of functions: a solemn religious march as exemplified by the "March of the Priests" in Verdi's *Aida*; a wedding march in Mendelssohn's music for *A Midsummer Night's Dream* and in Wagner's *Lohengrin*; a children's march as in Bizet's *Carmen*. Patriotic marches abound; of these the grandest is *La Marseillaise*. A category by itself is the funeral march, such as the slow movement in Beethoven's *Eroica* Symphony. The march from Chopin's Piano Sonata in B-flat minor is the one customarily performed at funerals; some frivolous American added the words "Pray for the Dead, and the Dead will pray for you.'' An example of a funeral march gone berserk is the set *3 Funeral Marches* by Lord Berners: *For a Statesman, For a Canary*, and *For a Rich Aunt*, the last naturally full of gaiety in anticipation of a lucrative inheritance.

Although most national hymns are in march time, there are numerous exceptions. *The Star-Spangled Banner* is in slow waltz time, as is the British national anthem, *God Save the King*. Elgar wrote five military marches under the general title *Pomp and Circumstance*, of which No. 1 is celebrated; its slow section, set to the words ''Land of Hope and Glory,'' is widely used as a commencement march in American schools. Sousa, the American ''march king,'' composed more than 100 military marches, of which *Stars and Stripes Forever* is one of the most rousing. Incidentally, the usual tempo of a marching tune in England and America is 80 steps per minute, which corresponds to the normal pulse beat.

Marche funèbre d'une marionette. A humorously intended orchestral piece by Charles Gounod, composed in 1873 as a funeral march for a puppet. The melody acquired popularity in the 1950s when the film director Alfred Hitchcock selected it as the ''signature'' tune for his television show.

Marche Slave. A piece for orchestra that Tchaikovsky wrote in 1876 to celebrate the liberation of Serbia from Ottoman rule. Its thematic materials combine Slavic and Russian elements, with the Russian czarist anthem emerging victorious. Although Tchaikovsky regarded it as a patriotic gesture of no musical significance, *Marche Slave* has become a regular repertory piece in Russia and elsewhere. It was first performed in Moscow on November 17, 1876.

Maria Stuarda. An opera by Donizetti, first performed in Naples on October 18, 1834, under the title *Buondelmonte*, with the historical characters of Mary Stuart and Queen Elizabeth changed to pacify the queen of Naples, who was horrified to learn that the opera represented the death of a revered Catholic queen of Scots. But outside the kingdom of Naples, the original libretto was restored, and the opera was produced at La Scala in Milan on December 30, 1835. The plot, largely borrowed from Schiller's famous romanticized drama, rewrites history. When Mary calls Elizabeth the bastard offspring of Henry VIII, Elizabeth sings ''Then you die'' and signs the death warrant. The music is most ingratiating.

Maria Theresia. Haydn's Symphony No. 48 (1769) in the sunny key of C major. It was so nicknamed because the Austrian empress Maria Theresia paid a visit at Esterházy's country estate where Haydn was employed and liked the symphony that Haydn played for her.

Mariachi. Mariachi bands are ever-present at festivities in Mexico City and other large towns in Mexico; they also supply entertainment in cafés and nightclubs. A typical mariachi group consists of violins, a large guitar, a trumpet, and Mexican percussion instruments. The origin of the word is obscure, but it is suggested that it represents a corruption of the French word *mariage*, and that it was first used during the brief rule of the Mexican Emperor Maximilian. Aaron Copland made use of typical mariachi tunes in his symphonic work *El Salón Mexico*, named after a once-popular nightclub in Mexico City.

Das Marienleben (The Life of Mary). A song cycle by Paul Hindemith to 15 poems by Rilke, depicting the life of the Virgin Mary. It was first performed at the Donaueschingen Festival on June 17, 1923. Hindemith revised the cycle in 1941 with the purpose of bringing out the voice part as the dominant factor in the contrapuntal structure.

Marimba. A Latin American percussion instrument akin to the xylophone. It has wooden bars that the player strikes with mallets. Beneath the bars, or keys, are resonators made of gourds. The marimba is of ancient origin, but in its modern form it was created in Guatemala early in the 20th century. From there it spread to the United States and later to Europe. Its range, at first limited, has eventually been expanded to six octaves.

The Marines' Hymn. This hymn is usually known by its opening line: "From the halls of Montezuma to the shores of Tripoli." The references are to the entry of American Marines in Mexico City in 1847 and the Marine landing in North Africa in the war against the Barbary pirates in 1805. The tune is from an operetta by Offenbach, *Geneviève de Brabant*, which was published in 1868, but it seems that Offenbach himself picked it up from some less dignified source. The uncopyrighted sheet music edition of the U.S. Marine Corps Publicity Bureau in 1918 attributed the text to an unidentified Marine officer during the Mexican war. How the words came to be latched on to an Offenbach air is a puzzle.

The Marriage of Figaro (Le nozze di Figaro). An opera by Mozart, first produced in Vienna on May 1, 1786. The Italian libretto is by Da Ponte, after Beaumarchais. In plot, this is a sequel to *The Barber of Seville*. Count Almaviva is married; Figaro, formerly a barber, is now the count's valet and wants to marry the countess's maid, but the count himself likes to flirt with her. The countess laments her husband's flighty ways, and Figaro stages complex stratagems to arouse the count's jealousy in order to bring him closer to his wife. The youthful page Cherubino is used by Figaro to play the suitor of the countess. As the count enters the house, the page puts on a maid's dress to hide his sex. (Since the part of Cherubino is entrusted to a soprano, the donning of a girl's dress actually restores the performer's original gender.) The complications increase exponentially, and the plot reaches the apex of its absurdity when an elderly female housekeeper whom Figaro has promised to marry is revealed as his own mother. But the more absurd the situations are, the more beautiful is the music.

La Marseillaise. The most beautiful of all national anthems, both in the patriotic text and the rousing melody. It was composed, or rather improvised on the spur of the moment, by Rouget de Lisle, a French Army officer in Strasbourg, on the night of April 24, 1792, and it was published almost immediately under the title *Chant de Guerre pour l'Armée du Rhin.* It was then widely sung as a patriotic song during the war with Austria. The title *La Marseillaise* was adopted later by a revolutionary volunteer group from Marseilles during the final phase of the French Revolution.

Mary Had a Little Lamb. The tune of this nursery rhyme is identical to the second section of the song *Good Night Ladies,* to the words "Merrily we roll along," composed by the American bandmaster E.P. Christy in 1847. The story of little Mary who took her lamb to school is supposed to be factual.

Le Maschere (The Masks). An opera by Pietro Mascagni, with the familiar characters of the commedia dell'arte engaged in traditional encounters. So great were the auguries of success for *Le Maschere* that the opera was produced on the same day, January 17, 1901, in six Italian cities: Milan (conducted by Toscanini), Venice, Turin, Verona, Genoa, and Rome (where Mascagni himself conducted). Only half-facetiously, Mascagni dedicated the opera "to my distinguished self." This simultaneous exhibition was a humiliating debacle, however. In Genoa, the audience hissed and booed so vehemently that the management had to lower the curtain without completing the performance.

Masque. A term for a spectacle or social assembly used in England during the 16th and 17th centuries. Such occasions featured a variety of artistic presentations, including poetry, drama, dance, and music. The subjects of such masques were usually taken from Greek mythology. Members of the aristocracy were themselves often engaged to perform the parts of shepherds and shepherdesses, benevolent gods and goddesses, and so on. Among poets whose masques were produced at the English court were Ben Jonson and Milton. A curious byproduct of the masque was the introduction of an "antimasque," which supplied entertainment between serious allegorical presentations. When opera was introduced in England, the masques became integrated with it and disappeared as an independent form.

Mass. The primary and the most solemn service of the Roman Catholic church. It includes recitation of the sacred texts, singing, and playing on the organ. The Mass is the most significant manifestation of religious music; its theory and practice through the centuries determined the development of polyphonic music in all parts of Europe before the Reformation. Virtually every composer in the musically productive Catholic countries—Italy, Germany, France, and Spain—wrote Masses. As a distinct musical form, the Mass reached its greatest flowering during the Renaissance period, when great masters of the Netherlands and Italy applied themselves to the composition of large religious works.

The word *Mass* comes from the Latin *missa*, the past participle in the Latin envoi at the conclusion of the Mass: *Ite, missa est*, which means "Go, it [the congregation] is dismissed." The most eloquent and devout Mass is the *Missa solemnis*, the High Mass, also known as *Missa cantata*, "sung Mass." A lesser mass is *Missa lecta*, the "read Mass," or Low Mass, which has no purely musical parts. The *ordinarium Missae*, the "Ordinary of the Mass," contains the chants that are included in every service and therefore in most Masses written by composers through the centuries that are performed not only in church but in concert. These divisions are Kyrie (Greek for "Lord"), an imploration of mercy: *Kyrie eleison, Christe eleison* ("Lord, have mercy, Christ, have mercy). Next is the Gloria: the priest intones *Gloria in excelsis Deo* and the chorus joins in with *Et in terra pax*. There follows the basic article of faith, the Credo, known as *symbolum apostolicum*. The fourth division is Sanctus, which in the High Mass is subdivided into two sections: Sanctus and Benedictus. The fifth division is the Agnus Dei ("The Lamb of God"), followed by the imploration *Miserere nobis* ("Have mercy on us"). The Kyrie is the only division of the Mass that is in Greek; the rest is in Latin.

Besides the Ordinary of the Mass, there is a group of divisions with texts to be sung on special days; the totality of these items is known as *proprium Missae*, the "Proper of the Mass." They consist of *psalmus ad introitum* (or simply "Introit"), which precedes the Kyrie; next are the Gradual and Tract, which are sung between the Gloria and Credo. The Credo is followed by the Offertory. The conclusion of the Proper of the Mass is *psalmus ad communionem*, after which the congregation is dismissed. Apart from these, there are also interpolations of lections ("readings") from the Bible. Although the Latin texts of the Mass are traditional, the melodies are not. There are hundreds of different settings of individual numbers of the Mass. An extremely important and musically fruitful extension of the Mass is the *Missa pro defunctis*, "Requiem Mass," so named because it opens with the Introit *Requiem aeternam dona eis Domine* ("Peace eternal give them, Lord").

Although the Mass is the most solemn religious service, it could not be separated entirely from the world outside the church. As a result, the songs of the common people began to intrude on the holy precincts of the Mass. This alien incursion, repellent as it must have seemed to the devout, produced some extremely original musical forms, among them the so-called *Missa parodia*, "parody Mass." This term does not, of course, imply the modern meaning of parody, or "imitative caricature," but preserves its original Greek meaning of *para-ode*, a "near song." The parody Mass reached its peak during the Renaissance, its principal feature being a free use of melodic material from Gregorian plainchant or secular madrigals and even folk songs; sometimes an entire motet or other choral composition was incorporated. Of such interpolations the most famous was the medieval popular song *L'Homme armé* (*The Armed Man*), which glorified the soldier. In this respect, a parody Mass is a compound or synthetic work. It is not to be derogated for that; great composers wrote Masses based on nonecclesiastical themes. The practice so shocked the orthodox that a council of the Roman church, held at Trent in the middle of the 16th century, issued a prohibition against using secular melodies as the cantus firmus in the Mass. A century and a half later Bach wrote his great B-minor Mass, and nearly another century later Beethoven composed his glorious *Missa Solemnis*. Schubert, Weber, Liszt, Franck, Gounod, and Bruckner wrote Masses marked by a grandeur of design that befits the subject.

Whereas the great Masses from Palestrina to Beethoven are polyphonic in structure, homophonic Masses were produced in the less devout 19th century. The Lutheran church retains most of the divisions of the Mass, as does the Anglican church. Such Masses are designed not for the ornate Gothic cathedrals but for the humble quarters of a parochial chapel. Sometimes separate items of the Mass, particularly the Gloria, attract a modern composer with the aim of stylization rather than reconstruction of the ancient model. Requiem Masses, which contain the dramatic section *Dies Irae*, somehow respond to the state of mind of the Romantic composer. Mozart, Berlioz, Verdi, and Brahms wrote Requiem Masses, and Britten contributed a moving *War Requiem Mass*. Leonard Bernstein composed a Mass, described as "a theater piece," to the texts of the Roman liturgy and popular American songs. Meanwhile, in the 20th century a serious attempt has been made to translate the Mass into the vernacular in each country with a Catholic community.

Mastersingers. The Guild of Mastersingers emerged in Germany after the end of the Crusades and the concurrent decline of the minnesingers. Socially they differed from the minnesingers, who were mainly aristocratic knights. The Mastersingers were men of the people who plied common trades, such as shoemaking and carpentry, and at the same time were devoted to music, organized communal singing, and cultivated folk arts. The founder of the Mastersingers is reputed to be one named Frauenlob (which means "praise of women"), who was also regarded as the last of the minnesingers. If such a connection link is accepted, then the birth of the Mastersingers can be dated in the early decades of the 14th century. The Mastersingers proved to be a very solid society that lasted well into the 19th century before finally dissolving under the pressure of modern professionalism. Wagner's opera *Die Meister-*

singer von Nürnberg reflects the atmosphere of the social and professional activities in the German townships of the 16th century. Most of the characters are historical, and Wagner makes use of actual melodies of the Guild. The German name for Mastersingers is *Meistersinger* (the German plural and singular forms of *singer* are identical).

La Matchiche. One of the most popular songs of modern times, written by a French vaudeville composer, Charles Borel-Clerc, in 1905 and published under various titles. *Matchiche* is a French form of the name of the genuine Brazilian dance *maxixe*. George Gershwin quoted it as a typical Parisian song in *An American in Paris*. A rhyme of sorts was made up to be sung to the tune in the United States: "My ma gave me a nickel, to buy a pickle; I didn't buy a pickle, I bought some chewing gum."

Mathis der Maler (Matthias the Painter). An opera by Paul Hindemith, to his own libretto inspired by the triptych of the painter Matthias Grünewald. The artistic career of Mathis is interrupted by a peasant uprising in 1542, and he espouses the rebel cause. Realizing that injustice is done in both camps, he withdraws from the materialistic world and dedicates himself to religious art. The score is permeated with the spirit of the German Renaissance in its choral-like structure; the savant polyphony is transparent; the idiom is modern but tonal. Despite the originality of the score and its ideological acceptability to the Nazis, Hitler's ministry put obstacles in the way of the production. Hindemith was a pure Aryan, but he was married to a woman who was half Jewish. The first production of *Mathis der Maler* took place in Zürich on May 28, 1938. Shortly afterward Hindemith emigrated to the United States. A symphonic version, drawn from the opera, was first performed in Berlin on March 12, 1934, Furtwängler conducting.

Le Matin (The Morning). Haydn's Symphony No. 6 (1761) in the key of D major. Some sense of the mists of early morning is conveyed by the adagio opening.

Mavra. An opera by Igor Stravinsky after a comic poem of Pushkin's, first produced in Paris on June 3, 1922. A girl in a suburban community near Moscow is engaged in a clandestine romance with a soldier. When her mother tells her to hire a cook, she brings in her lover disguised as a woman named Mavra. But he is careless and is caught unawares while shaving. He jumps out of the window and never returns. Stravinsky brilliantly stylizes the Russian folk inflections with angular rhythms and acrid harmonies.

Mazurka. A lively Polish dance in triple time that, as the name indicates, originated from a district in northern Poland, called Mazur in Polish. Its main characteristic is an off-beat accent and a syncopated first beat. The popularity of the mazurka is owed mainly to Chopin, who adorned its basic rhythmic design with ingenious chromatic pianistic embellishments. *Kujawiak* and *oberek* are distinctive varieties of the mazurka.

Médée. A "lyric tragedy" by Marc-Antoine Charpentier, one of the earliest French opera composers, first produced in Paris on December 4, 1693. The libretto is derived from the ancient Greek myth of Medea, the vengeful wife of Jason, whom she suspects of infidelity. She murders their own two sons in her wrath.

Médée is also an opera by Luigi Cherubini, first performed in Paris on March 13, 1797, modeled after the same myth. After lying fallow for a century and a half, the opera was revived with unexpected éclat in the middle of the 20th century.

Meditation. An elegy. The *Meditation* for solo violin in the opera *Thaïs* by Massenet is a favorite concert number. The coaxingly viscid *Ave Maria* by Gounod, superimposed on the Prelude in C Major of Bach's first book of *The Well-Tempered Clavier*, is subtitled *Meditation*.

The Medium. A music drama by Gian Carlo Menotti, to his own imaginative libretto in English, first produced in New York on May 8, 1946. The medium Madame Flora arranges for ghosts to speak to bereaved relatives through a hidden microphone. So realistic are the voices, produced by her daughter, that the medium begins to believe in their reality. In a panic, she shoots and kills her deaf-mute helper, whom she finds in the closet. The dramatic impact of the opera is considerable.

Meeresstille und glückliche Fahrt (Calm Sea and Happy Voyage). A concert overture by Felix Mendelssohn. Despite its reassuring title, the music is quite turbulent, but the voyage ends happily. The work was first performed in Berlin on April 28, 1828, and may be regarded as a companion piece to Mendelssohn's *Fingal's Cave*, which was written at about the same time.

Mefistofele. An opera by Arrigo Boito, first produced in Milan on March 5, 1868. Boito modeled his libretto after both parts of Goethe's great philosophical poem *Faust*. After the death of Marguerite, whom he had ruined, Faust is redeemed. The opera has excellent musical and literary qualities, but it never attained the success vouchsafed to Gounod's *Faust*.

Die Meistersinger von Nürnberg. An opera by Wagner, his first to include elements of comedy, produced in Munich on June 21, 1868, Hans von Bülow conducting. As in all Wagner's operas, the text is his own. The action takes place in Nuremberg in the 16th century. A singing contest is organized by the Guild of Mastersingers under the guidance of the cobbler Hans Sachs (a historical figure who played an important role in organizing singing societies in Germany in the 16th century). The first prize is the hand of Eva, daughter of the local goldsmith. Walter von Stolzing, in love with Eva, sings a supremely beautiful song, but the pedantic clerk Beckmesser faults him for violation of rules. (Wagner modeled Beckmesser after the Viennese music critic Eduard Hanslick, persistent opponent of Wagner; in the early sketches of *Die Meistersinger* Wagner used the name Hans Lick for Beckmesser.) After the prize is given to Walter, Hans Sachs explains the principles underlying the art of German song. The opera is interesting for its many realistic details. For instance, Eva, Beckmesser, and others call on the cobbler-mastersinger to have their shoes repaired. The contrapuntal texture of the music is glorious; unhampered by leitmotifs, the music flows with rhapsodic freedom.

Melodrama. During the past century, this term has acquired the meaning of a theatrical production calculated to excite the audience by piling up suspense upon suspense, with natural disasters adding to human conflict and individual misfortunes. The text of a typical melodrama corresponds in spirit to Gothic novels. Dramatic peripeteia, sudden reversals of fortune, mysterious portents and premonitions, often with supernatural overtones suitably illustrated by chromatic runs or tremolos on the diminished-seventh chord, are potent melodramatic devices. The genre was particularly popular in Russia, where it became known under the title *melodeclamation*.

Theatrical melodramas were highly successful in the 19th century and not only among socially disfranchised artistic groups. In stage presentations, the first half of the word *melodrama* was fortuitous, for there was no melos, no singing, no music in these productions. Melodrama in a purely etymological sense has had a long and respectable history. In 17th-century Italy, it was synonymous with opera. The first melodrama, so named specifically by its composer, was *Il Tito* by Marc Antonio Cesti, produced in 1666. In the early years of opera, the terms *melodramma* (two *m*'s in Italian), *tragedia lirica*, and *dramma lirico* were used interchangeably for a true opera. This practice continued through the 19th century in France, with operas often described as *drame lyrique* or *tragédie lyrique*. In the meantime, the term *melodrama* imperceptibly acquired the meaning of a theatrical performance in which lines were spoken with musical accompaniment. The first melodrama in this sense was probably *Ariadne auf Naxo* by Jiří Benda, produced in 1775, which greatly impressed Mozart when he heard it three years later. Zdenko Fibich wrote a trilogy of melodramas entitled *Hippodamia* that enjoyed numerous performances in Prague. Humperdinck enhanced the genre with his opera *Königskinder*, produced in 1897, by indicating the inflection of the spoken voice in written notes, marking the approximate level of pitch in each syllable. Schoenberg elevated melodrama to high art in his *Pierrot Lunaire*, which is specifically described as a melodrama in the score. In it Schoenberg introduced

Sprechstimme, inflected speech-voice, midway between speaking and singing. Parallel to these developments there emerged a more mundane and, by the same token, more popular type of melodrama incorporating the simultaneous use of recitation and music, as distinguished from *Singspiel* and *opéra comique*, in which the spoken dialogue and singing alternate. Schumann and Liszt wrote these kinds of melodramas. Prokofiev in *Peter the Wolf* and Walton in *Façade* made use of this technique.

Melody. A motion in successive tones having a self-governing sense of logical propulsion. The word *melody* is a compound of two Greek words, *melos* and *ode*, both pertaining to singing, *melos* referring to the totality of songs, and *ode* to a particular poem. In modern usage, melody is a tonal line vivified by rhythmic beat. To the Greeks, such a rhythmed melody was defined by another musical word, *harmonia*. In Western melos, a melody has harmonic implications, while the word *harmony* connotes a simultaneous sounding of several melodies or horizontal lines. Aesthetically, a beautiful melody must have a perfect balance between the high and low registers and a symmetric alternation of ascending and descending tonal groups. The main body of the melody is in the middle register, its center of gravity located between the extreme high and low registers. If melodies are analyzed with reference to these contrasts, it will be found that the number of high notes multiplied by the duration of each note equals the number of notes below the center of gravity, multiplied by the duration of each of these counterbalancing notes. The frequency of incidence increases toward the middle register, finally converging upon the melodic center of gravity. Rhythmic values have to be taken into consideration in such a statistical survey, so that in an ideal melody a long high note would be counterbalanced by a long low note, or by a succession of short low notes. Most melodies that achieve popularity move within the range of an octave between two dominants, in a major key, with the important points on the tonic, the mediant, and the upper dominant. These melodic notes are the third, the fourth, the fifth, and (for the upper tonic) the sixth partial tones in the harmonic series. It is therefore legitimate to conjecture that Western melodic lines are functions of the harmonic series, with preference given to the notes of the major triad. This is quite understandable; these notes are naturally produced by the bugle, horns without valves, and other wind instruments. The interpolated supertonic and subdominant complete a major pentachord, with the dominant duplicated below the tonic. The number of melodies so constructed is counted in thousands, if not millions, all of them in a major key, and many of them beginning with an ascending leap from the dominant to the tonic. Among famous examples are *La Marseillaise*, the last movement of Beethoven's Violin Concerto, Rossini's *William Tell Overture*, *Waltz of the Flowers* from Tchaikovsky's *Nutcracker Suite*, and *The Wedding March* from Wagner's *Lohengrin*. Melodies of this formation are not as numerous in minor keys as in major, but still they form a respectable inventory. Examples are the theme of the second movement of Tchaikovsky's Violin Concerto and that of *The Moldau* from Smetana's orchestral suite *Má vlast*. The latter theme, with some changes, has become the national anthem of Israel. There are also convincing tunes that are limited to harmonic notes only, the dominant, tonic, mediant, and dominant an octave above, resulting in a variety of bugle calls. George M. Cohan's World War I song *Over There* is based entirely on these open notes of the natural bugle. The first and the last movements of Mozart's *Eine kleine Nachtmusik* are derived from a subject contained between the two dominants of the key of G major. The finale of Haydn's *Military* Symphony in G major is also based on the seminal progression of the harmonic series from the third to the sixth partials. Numerous examples can be found by consulting the thematic catalogues of Classical sonatas and symphonies. Obviously, such an abundance of specific patterns cannot be the result of mutual influences among composers or any other factors. The derivation of all these melodies from the harmonic series is one of the most logically substantiated phenomena in melodic constructions, and therefore in all music. Harmonic implications of Classical melodies, and of a great majority of folk tunes of Western nations, are very much in evidence. The pendulum-like swing between the tonic and the dominant is the most frequent harmonic characteristic. An extraordinary and perhaps unique example is the melody based on ten repetitions of a single tone in the Allegretto of Beethoven's Symphony No. 7 within a symmetric period of four bars, with the harmonic formula of tonic, dominant, dominant, tonic. To choose a lesser example, *Chopsticks* begins with the upper voice repeated 12 times while the harmony swings from the dominant to the tonic.

Much theorizing has been done about the so-called force of gravity in melodic structures, which manifests itself in the musical necessity of reversing the melodic motion after the melody has reached its apogee or perigee, as the case may be. This does not mean, of course, that the melody must, like the King of France in the nursery rhyme, march up the hill with 40,000 men and then come back down again. The metaphor of gravity is applicable to the melodic rule that demands that after a wide leap the melody should come down at least one diatonic degree. It can be demonstrated by the feeling of absolute necessity that the leap up from the tonic to the submediant—from, say, A to F in the key of A minor—requires a détente by descending from F to E. Conversely, the drop from the dominant note E in the key of A minor down to the leading tone G-sharp requires an immediate ascent to the tonic A, and this quite independently from the consideration that the leading tone must ascend to the tonic anyway, at least in traditional melody and harmony. (This, of course, is not an absolute requirement; Grieg's melodies are notable for their peculiar fall from the leading tone to the dominant.)

Another resource of basic importance in traditional Western music is the sequence within the key, that is, a melodic pattern repeated on a different scale degree. Examples are legion. Beethoven's Symphony No. 5 opens with such a sequence, that of a falling third from the dominant to the mediant followed by a falling third from the subdominant to the supertonic. Typically, such sequences imply the familiar harmonic swing from the tonic to the dominant. A rather long sequence occurs toward the end of the Overture in Tchaikovsky's opera *Eugene Onegin*, having eight chain-links and descending fully two octaves.

Most melodies are contained within the octave from the dominant to the dominant, but continuous melodic lines extending over an octave are not rare. A remarkable example is the auxiliary theme in the last movement of Beethoven's Symphony No. 9, which begins on the tonic, rises to the sixth in the octave above, and ends on the tonic in that higher octave, with all melodic notes of equal rhythmic value. Although such an enlarged range is acceptable for instrumental passages, it is almost intractable for the human voice. The range of *The Star Spangled Banner* is an octave and a fifth, which makes it difficult to sing; futile attempts have been made to arrange it so that the second stanza could be transposed to a lower key. Wagner introduced the notion of *unendliche Melodie*, a romantically exaggerated description of a melody that naturally flows into the beginning of the next motif with an avoidance of perfect cadences. In English it is known as "endless melody," the term understood as being endless in the sense of a circle or any other closed curve.

Atonal melodies follow the structural plans of melodic lines that are entirely different from those of tonal melodies. Atonality excludes all triadic conformations and has no link with the harmonic series. The organized atonal systems, particularly the dodecaphonic techniques, follow their own rules of aesthetic structure, with the ideal of beauty derived from special considerations of intervallic motion. Even in dodecaphonic melodies, the center of gravity is present as the arithmetical mean of high and low notes.

The principles underlying the melodic structure of oriental songs differ radically from those of Western melos. There are no harmonic implications in oriental music; the scales themselves are formed from sets of intervals not necessarily contained within a Western scale. The study of non-Western melodies, therefore, must be relegated to a special discipline.

Melopœia. An ancient Greek term denoting all types of musical composition and performance. The word is a compound of *melos*, "song," and *poiein*, "to make." In Plato's *Symposion*, melopeia is described as the art of musical forms, whereas Aristotle defines it as the science of melody. The Aristotelian meaning was revived in the Renaissance in the theories of the Harmony of the Spheres. A rather tautological definition of the term is given by Mersenne: "Melopeia is nothing but the art of melody."

The Memphis Blues. A historically important song by W.C. Handy, which launched the blues as a musical genre. Handy originally wrote the tune as a campaign song for a candidate for mayor of Memphis, Tennessee. He published the song in 1912 as a piano solo; the lyrics were added in 1913. Handy, a black composer and trumpet player, lived long enough to enjoy its merited fame. In 1941, a movie musical, *The Birth of the Blues*, added to his glory, and after his death a postage stamp showing him playing the trumpet was issued by the U.S. Post Office.

Mephisto Waltz. There are four *Mephisto* Waltzes by Liszt of which the first, written in 1859, is the most famous. Its initial cumulative chord, formed by a series of perfect fifths separated by a minor sixth, was a great innovation at the time, and Liszt was berated by academic critics for taking harmonic liberties. Liszt's Mephisto is not Goethe's philosophic Beelzebub but a demonic spirit from *Faust* by the German poet Lenau. Liszt originally wrote his first *Mephisto* Waltz for orchestra as the second movement, entitled *Der Tanz in der Dorfschenke* (*The Dance in the Village Tavern*), to his score *Two Episodes from Lenau's Faust*. The second *Mephisto* Waltz was written in 1881, originally for orchestra and later transcribed for piano. The third Waltz, for piano, was written shortly before Liszt's death. The fourth, for piano, was published posthumously.

La Mer. A symphonic work in three movements by Claude Debussy, first performed in Paris on October 15, 1905. Although the piece is a song of the sea, Debussy was not too fond of sea travel, and even his infrequent trips to England were trying for him. The three sketches of this sea poem are impressions in instrumental colors of three aspects or events: *De l'aube à midi sur la mer* (*From Dawn to Noon on the Sea*), *Jeux de vagues* (*Play of Waves*), and *Dialogue du vent et de la mer* (*Dialogue of the Wind and the Sea*). The character of the music seems to justify the label of impressionism attached to *La Mer*, although Debussy himself deprecated this cliché borrowed from painting. From a purely analytical standpoint, the work is remarkable. The primary theme is pentatonic in structure; there are anamorphic variations that expand it into a whole-tone scale. Traditionally minded critics damned the work as formless (but isn't the sea itself without a stable form?). One American critic even drew up his own program for it, in which a sea traveler gets seasick and throws up in the last movement. When Erik Satie was asked which movement of *La Mer* he liked best, he said the first, *From Dawn to Noon*, and more specifically, "about quarter of eleven."

Mercury Symphony. Symphony No. 43 in E-flat major by Haydn (1772). The reason for this title is obscure, and who decided to name the symphony *Mercury* remains unknown. It is, however, clear that the eponymous Mercury referred to is the winged messenger of the gods, not the smallest planet of the solar system or the liquid metal.

The Merry Widow. An operetta by Franz Lehár, first produced in Vienna on December 28, 1905, under its German title, *Die lustige Witwe*. A rich Austrian widow is courted by a Slavic fortune seeker who finally corrals her in Paris. The recitative glorifying Maxim's restaurant in Paris was inserted by Lehár as a token of gratitude to the chef of that establishment, who gave him free meals during his impecunious Paris days.

Messe de Requiem. A sacred work by Gabriel Fauré, one of the most important Requiems of modern times, written in 1887. Its peculiarity is the omission of the Dies Irae; Fauré preferred to express faith, charity, and hope in his music rather than the vengeful drama of Doomsday.

Messiah. A great religious oratorio by Handel, which he wrote in a period of three and a half weeks, when he was living in Dublin, Ireland. (A word of caution: the title is simply *Messiah*, not *The Messiah*, as persistently misapplied in thousands of performances.) It was first performed in Dublin on April 13, 1742, with Handel himself conducting at the organ. A Dublin paper reported: "Words are wanting to express the exquisite Delight it afforded to the admiring crowded Audience. The Sublime, the Grand, and the Tender, adapted to the most elevated, majestick and moving words, conspired to transport and charm the ravished Heart and Ear." Although *Messiah* was a Lenten oratorio, it eventually became a standard choral work to be performed in the Christmas season as well. The score of *Messiah* lends itself to unlimited amplification; some London performances have numbered more than 3,000 singers and as many as 27 bassoons with other instruments in proportion. The English libretto is selected from the King James Bible. Although Handel never learned to speak English grammatically and his German accent was prodigious, he revealed an extraordinary sensitivity to the prosody of the English text. Handel's working score of *Messiah* was published in facsimile in 1974; it shows graphically the many changes Handel made in subsequent years, with some sections practically composed anew, others radically rearranged. Of the many famous numbers in the score, *Hallelujah Chorus* is the most familiar.

Metamorphosen. A mournful piece by Richard Strauss, scored for 23 string instruments. He wrote it at the end of the war that destroyed Germany in 1945 and concluded his manuscript with the words "In Memoriam." The work contains quotations from the funeral march from Beethoven's *Eroica* Symphony. It was performed for the first time in Zurich, Switzerland, on January 25, 1946.

Metronome. A mechanical device that beats time, indicating the tempo of a composition. It consists of a graduated pendulum that is adjusted by sliding a small weight up or down its length. The name is derived from the Greek words *metro* ("measurement") and *nomos* ("law"). The design most commonly used was invented by Johannes Nepomuk Maelzel about 1812. It is rumored, however, that Maelzel, who was something of a charlatan (he first acquired notoriety by exhibiting an "automatic" chess player, which concealed a dwarf chessmaster underneath the chessboard who moved the pieces by magnets), stole the idea of the metronome from an obscure Amsterdam mechanic named Winkel. However that may be, the initials MM (Maelzel Metronome) have for a century and a half adorned most student editions of Classical works. The marking "MM (quarter note) = 120" indicates that there are 120 quarter notes per minute. The proper beat can be obtained by setting the weight on the pendulum at 120. Each tick of the pendulum then counts for one quarter note.

Beethoven, who believed in the power of modern inventions (he patronized quacks in quest of a cure for his deafness), seized upon Maelzel's metronome as the perfect instrument to perpetuate the correct tempi of his works. However, his metronome marks were not practical. In one instance he converted an allegretto into prestissimo. Until lately, the metronome was a familiar pyramidal accoutrement perched on the piano in the drawing room of every teacher and student, but with the advance of technology it has been replaced by an unsightly cube that emits electronic beeps regulated by a dial. Some modern composers have discovered that the metronome clicks could be used as percussive beats. Ligeti, one of the most imaginative of the musical avant-garde, wrote a piece for 100 metronomes beating different tempi; visually, the spectacle is extraordinary.

Le Midi (Noon). Haydn's Symphony No. 7 (1761) and a sequel to his Symphony No. 6, also known as *Le Matin (The Morning)*. The music of *Le Midi* is in the bright key of C major to suggest the warm sun at midday.

Midsommarvaka (Midsummer Vigil). The first of three Swedish Rhapsodies for orchestra by Hugo Alfvén, his most celebrated piece. It was composed in 1904 and performed for the first time in Stockholm on May 10, 1904. It was produced as a ballet under the title *La Nuit de Saint-Jean* in Paris on October 25, 1920.

A Midsummer Night's Dream. Mendelssohn, who was the most prodigious of musical infant prodigies, wrote the overture for Shakespeare's *A Midsummer Night's Dream* at the age of 17. Later he composed additional music for the play, which included the *Wedding March*, to the tune of which thousands of happy, and millions of unhappy, couples have been wed. It was first performed in its entirety in Potsdam on October 14, 1843.

A Midsummer Night's Dream is also the name of an opera by Benjamin Britten, again based on Shakespeare, first performed in Aldeburgh, England, on June 11, 1960. The score is subdivided into set pieces; the idiom is deliberately eclectic, with elements of impressionism applied to the magical creatures and the realistic scene depicted in a folklike manner.

The Mikado. A comic opera by Gilbert and Sullivan, first produced in London on March 14, 1885, with the subtitle *The Town of Titipu*. Yum-yum is a delicious Japanese maiden whose guardian hopes to marry her. The heir to the Japanese throne, disguised as a minstrel, also loves her. Since in Japan flirting is punishable by death, periodical beheadings are frequently scheduled. However, the lord high executioner has an innate aversion to killing any living thing. When the Mikado's guilty son reveals his identity, the emperor is elated, cancels all executions, and lets his son marry Yum-yum. *The Mikado* was forbidden in Japan because it poked fun at the emperor.

Mikrokosmos. The title given by Béla Bartók for his six books of 153 progressive piano pieces for children. The remarkable innovation of this collection is its introduction of modal scales and asymmetric rhythmic patterns. Many pieces bear picturesque titles, such as *From the Diary of a Fly*; others indicate the technical substratum— for example, *Imitation Reflected* and *Accents*.

Military Symphony. Haydn's Symphony No. 100 in G major, the last of his 12 symphonies written for Salomon in London, where it was performed on March 31, 1794. The title is explained by the fact that the orchestration of the second movement includes not only the mandatory timpani but a triangle, cymbals, and the bass drum, practically an entire setup for Janizary music of the pseudo-Turkish type. This and the *Surprise* Symphony are the most popular of Haydn's symphonies.

Miniature score. Full scores of symphonic works, chamber music, and even complete operas began to be published in Germany in the 19th century. In pocket size, they were convenient to carry around for study purposes, or for reading while listening to the actual music played. The most active publisher of miniature scores was Eulenberg of Leipzig.

Minimalism. Music history has evolved from simple cellules for unaccompanied voice to grandiose edifices of sounds, including electronically produced tones. Then, like an enormous dinosaur whose very bulk made it impossible for him to find sufficient food to survive, the symphonic and operatic forms developed in the 19th century could no longer sustain their acoustical dimensions. As early as 1918, Stravinsky declared that music had reached its maximum dimensions and urged composers to write in limited forms. The direction from Lilliputian to Brobdingnagian works had to be reversed, creating a type of neo-Classical composition. But this was not enough; composers had to cope with the untempered growth of dissonant counterpoint and concomitant loss of the sense of harmony and tonality. Accordingly, composers of the last quarter of the 20th century restored triadic harmony. Modulations were reduced to phases; a single note would change in an arpeggio signalizing the formation of a new inversion, and remain there for a number of bars. Dissonances occurred now and then, but a consonant quietus would become the rule. A novel term emerged to describe the unexpected turn of events—*minimalism*, a musical synecdoche, *a pars pro toto*. It came to life in the form of a fossilized renewal mainly in America. Parallel to the purification of tonal masses, there was a gradual abandonment of rhythmic complexity. Repetitions of established patterns became the norm. Among pioneers of minimalism were La Monte Young, Terry Riley, Steve Reich, and Philip Glass. La Monte Young professed to revive the Pythagorean modes. Terry Riley in his piece entitled *In C* for any instruments actually held on to the key of C major until the last few bars, where he allows the passing entry of an F-sharp. Steve Reich reinforced his technique by a study of African drumming. Philip Glass enriched the uniformity of "phasing" by writing music for dadaistically imagined stage plays of inordinate length and heterogeneous content, such as *Einstein on the Beach*. More original is the minimalistic idiom of John Adams, whose music embraces in its points of inspiration such contrasting methods as in *Harmonium* for orchestra and the sensational opera *Nixon in China*.

Minnesingers. Medieval German minstrels who traveled through middle Europe singing lyric songs in royal German courts, ducal castles, and villages. Like their French counterparts, the trouvères and troubadours, they were mostly of noble birth and regarded their profession as an expression of knightly valor and idealistic dedication to the ladies of their hearts (*Minne* is "love" in Old German). With the end of the Crusades, and with a certain stabilization of the German states, the role of the minnesingers declined, and the cultivation of lyric or heroic songs gradually was transferred to the town guilds and local craftsmen.

Minstrels. Musicians employed by royalty and feudal lords in Europe during the Middle Ages. They served as entertainers, players upon the lute or the flute, jesters, and sometimes as participants in domestic and political intrigues. The term *minstrel* first appeared in the 14th century and was derived from the French *ménestrier*, literally, "a minister." With the decay of feudal society, the profession of minstrels assumed new forms. Thus, in America white minstrel groups were organized to perform in blackface in a repertoire of Negro spirituals with miscellaneous numbers known as "Ethiopian songs" in their repertory. Stephen Foster was the greatest composer of such songs, even though he never lived in the South and was not familiar with the conditions of Negro life or slavery.

Minuet. The most popular court dance in triple time danced by couples, distinguished by the stately grace of its choreography and the symmetry of its musical structure. The standard minuet consisted of three sections, of which the first and third were identical. The middle section, set in the dominant, subdominant, or in a relative key, was called *trio* because it was usually written for three instruments, whereas the minuet proper was usually arranged for a fuller ensemble. The French word for minuet is *menuet*, from the word *menu* ("little"). It is generally surmised that the minuet derived from a provincial French dance tune, but as a mature form it was introduced at the court of Louis XIV. Lully, who was court musician, wrote a number of minuets for royal balls. It is said that the king himself often ventured to dance to Lully's music, until his figure became too corpulent for choreographic exercise. The vogue of minuet dancing spread to all the courts of Europe; it was especially popular in Russia, Spain, and Italy, but less so in England and Germany. Eventually the minuet became an integral part of the Baroque instrumental suite and of Classical sonatas and symphonies. In the 19th century the minuet yielded its place in sonatas and symphonies to the more elaborate form of the scherzo, which, however, kept the time signature in 3/4 of the minuet as well as the characteristic interpolation of the trio.

Minute Waltz. A common name for Chopin's Waltz in D-flat major, op. 64, which is supposedly possible to negotiate in about one minute. Omitting the repeats, the time can be cut to 48 seconds. A modern electronic synthesizer can reduce the time to a few seconds

The Miraculous Mandarin. A pantomime by Béla Bartók. The subject is sordid; it relates the story of a mandarin's lust for a prostitute who is set on robbing him, but the mandarin is so sturdy that he survives all her accomplices' attempts to kill him. Because of both the subject and its dissonant music, the work had a difficult time obtaining performances. After its production in Cologne on November 27, 1926, it was taken out of the repertory by order of Mayor Konrad Adenauer, the future chancellor of West Germany.

Miroirs. A piano suite by Ravel, in five movements entitled *Noctuelles*, *Oiseaux tristes*, *Une Barque sur l'océan*, *Alborada del gracioso*, and *La Vallée des cloches*. They are the finest specimens of impressionistic piano writing. The mirrors of the title reflect nocturnal moths, wistful birds, a lonesome boat on the ocean, the morning serenade of a jester, and the valley of bells. The suite was first performed in Paris on January 6, 1906.

Miserere. The opening Latin word of the 50th Psalm, in the Roman Catholic numbering. The imploration, "Have mercy," is a part of the Holy Week Service known as Tenebrae, the darkness. There is a credible story that Mozart as a small boy attended the performance of a *Miserere* by the Italian composer Allegre in the Vatican, memorized the entire setting for nine voices, and wrote it down shortly afterward.

The Miserly Knight. An opera by Rachmaninoff, after a play of Pushkin, first performed in Moscow on January 24, 1906. The old miser has accumulated a treasure trove of gold, but he refuses to let anyone, even his own son, share in his fortune. In desperation the youth goes to the duke of the land for help. Thereupon his miserly father publicly accuses him of planning his murder, but as he utters the monstrous charge, he is seized with mortal pain and dies with the words, "Where are the keys to my treasure?" The score was composed when Rachmaninoff was only 22 years old; it has the charm of unpretentious romantic inspiration.

Miss Julie. An opera by Ned Rorem, after the drama by Strindberg, first produced in New York on November 4, 1965. The play is typical of Strindberg's preoccupations with social contradictions. Miss Julie is of noble birth; strangely, she falls under the spell of the family majordomo, who dominates her so fully that at his behest she robs her own father. Distressed and repentant, she commits suicide. The music is appropriately melodramatic, set in a moderately modernistic manner.

Missa Papae Marcelli. A historically important Mass bearing the name of Pope Marcellus II, composed by Palestrina in 1562. It is set in a homophonic style quite different from Palestrina's earlier polyphonic works. It is generally believed that Palestrina wrote this Mass at the behest of Marcellus in response to the papal criticism of the lack of clarity in the text of polyphonic religious works. This supposition is false, however, for Marcellus died in 1555, long before the Mass was written.

Missouri Waltz. A tune by Frederick Knight Logan (1871–1928), who was reluctant to admit its authorship because of its lamentable lack of musical quality. He published it as a piano solo in 1914, with his name on the cover as an "arranger." When the words were added in 1916, the sheet music sold a million copies and was adopted by the state of Missouri as its officiai song. Harry Truman loved to play the piece on the piano, and the *Missouri Waltz* became associated, for better or worse, with his image and his period.

Mr. Brouček's Excursions (also known as *The Adventures of Mr. Brouček*). A fantastic opera by Leoš Janáček in which a tipsy burgher imagines himself traveling to the moon (49 years before the actual landing on the moon in 1969) and back in time into the 15th century. The opera was produced in Prague on April 23, 1920.

Mitridate, Rè di Ponto. An opera by Mozart, first performed in Milan on December 26, 1770. Mozart was only 14 when he wrote this work. The libretto after Racine tells the dramatic story of Mithridates, king of Pontus, who loves a young Greek girl who is loved also by his two sons. All kinds of involvements ensue. Mithridates is fatally wounded in battle and urges his second son to marry the girl they all love.

Mixed media. An ultimate extension of opera was the unification of all arts; in this approximation it became a revival of the ancient ideal of Greek drama, supplemented by narration, homophonic singing, and dance. Wagner's *Gesamtkunstwerk* as outlined in his aesthetic writings was another attempt to bring about the conjunction of all arts. Scriabin dreamed of creating a *Mysterium* as a total art in which the entire audience would also participate. Leonard Bernstein programmed such a joint action in his secular and sacred Mass, in which the celebrants themselves became performers. In modern times, electronic sound, films, radio, and television have formed the totality of artistic means. The application of such diverse elements was eventually termed the *theater of mixed media*, which soon became popular among composers and performers. Stockhausen and Boulez formalized these techniques with the aid of the computer. The technique of collage, borrowed from surrealism, became the favorite medium of such composers. Improvisation played a major part in all such events. In some instances, the composer of a mixed-media work deliberately assigned instrumental parts to musicians who were totally unfamiliar with that particular instrument. A climactic event in mixed media was the production of the *Poème électronique* by Edgar Varèse in the pavilion of the Phillips Record Company at the Brussels World Fair in 1958. In the United States, much experimentation in mixed media was done in California by a group of composers who edited the ultramodern journal *Source*. In Italy, Luciano Berio and Sylvano Bussotti explored mixed-media composition. In Germany, Kagel experimented with photography of unfinished prints for use in mixed-media compositions. Perhaps the most ambitious project of mixed media was proposed by the American modernist Henry Brant, in which the concert hall, to be constructed of plywood, was to change its dimensions and geometric form according to the music performed in it.

Mixolydian mode. Although the word is Greek, the Mixolydian mode is not identical with the ancient Greek mode of the same name. If projected onto the diatonic scale represented by the white keys of the piano, the range of the Mixolydian mode would extend from G to G. To the modern ear it sounds like a major scale with a lowered seventh degree, devoid of a leading tone; it therefore lends itself naturally to attractive plagal cadences. Béla Bartók among others made effective use of the peculiarities of this mode.

Modality. A term used in modern music to describe a trend toward a revival of diatonic modes other than major and minor. A systematic avoidance of authentic cadences with a raised seventh degree in minor keys is the most important manifestation of modern modality; the favored cadence is the progression of the subdominant major triad to the tonic minor in the Dorian mode. Modulations into other keys are accomplished by direct landing on the intended tonic triad from any convenient point of the scale. Although seventh chords are freely used in modal works, the dominant-seventh chord, with its mandatory resolution into the tonic, is studiously avoided. Chromatic harmony is incompatible with the spirit of modality, but a chromatic melody may be harmonized in spacious triads, which keeps the feeling of modality. A corollary of modality is the use of harmonic progressions in triads rather than their inversions, often giving an impression of exotic origin. Debussy used triadic harmonies in modal writing to allude to Greek melos; Ravel exercised the charm of modality to conjure up the aura of times long past. The masters of the Russian national school, particularly Mussorgsky, resorted to modal progressions to evoke the spirit of Russian grandeur. Most curious is the application of broad modalities used by Stravinsky in *Le Sacre du printemps*, where, despite the prevalence of acrid dissonant harmonies, the inner triadic structures are always in evidence. Most modal compositions follow the basic rules of tonal connections in contrary motion, but some modern composers adopt the practice of moving triadic formations in parallel lines. Vaughan Williams, Prokofiev, Villa-Lobos, Casella, Aaron Copland, and others project the sense of modality by shifting triadic masses in parallel sequences. In most modal writings, pedal points supply a sonorous foundation, indicating the eventual tonic of the work.

Modulation. Transition from one key to another within a single composition. The idea of modulation dates back to the system of hexachords of Guido d'Arezzo, in which a modulation from one hexachord to another could be achieved by equating the syllabic degree in the initial hexachord to a syllabic degree of the terminal hexachord. For example, if La in the hexachord Ut, Re, Mi, Fa, Sol, La is renamed Mi, then a modulation is effected into the hexachord Fa, Sol, La, and so on, in which La is the third note. In polyphonic writing of the Middle Ages and the Renaissance, modulation was effected by a similar substitution of a degree of the scale. Such modulations produce a strange impression on the modern ear, leading some enthusiasts to proclaim the "modernity" of medieval composers. The cardinal principle operating in

such modulations has nothing to do with the precepts of tonal harmony that
were formulated centuries later; rather, such "sudden" medieval modulations
were justified by the acoustical primacy of the major chord, so that if in the
course of the composition the melody wandered into an alien field guarded
by a sharp or flat, the harmony adjusted itself to the new situation, forming
a major triad in the fundamental position. A remnant of this practice is found
in the familiar *tierce de Picardie*—that is, the "Picardy third"—the major
cadence of a piece in a minor key. As modality fell into desuetude and major
and minor keys became established as dual emblems of tonality, the procedures
in modulation were drawn according to the principle of kinship of keys having
the same number of sharps or flats in the key signature, or of neighboring
keys having one more or one less sharp or flat relative to the initial key. This
relationship was incorporated in a scientific looking "circle of fifths" in the
image of the face of a clock in which the sharps move clockwise and flats
move counterclockwise. Any composer desiring to modulate from one key to
another that was not "next door" in the circle of fifths had to make his way
through the intermediate stopovers, step by step. Departing from C major,
which is virginally clear of sharps and flats, with the destination of A major,
which has three sharps, one has to traverse successively the stops that have
one and two sharps in the key signature. This can be done by moving, for
variety's sake, first to a minor key having one sharp (that is, E minor) and
then to a major key having two sharps (that is, D major), and from there
moving to A major by a regular cadence. But what if a modulating traveler
had to go to a key four or five sharps away from the starting point? Surely
movement by steps across the clock of the circle of fifths would be tedious.
Providentially, each minor key has a major dominant, which enables the
modulating composer to jump four stops clockwise, in the direction of sharps.
For instance, the dominant of A minor is E major, a key that has four sharps
in its key signature. Emulating Guido d'Arezzo, we hit the dominant and then
declare it, by Guidonian *fiat* (which is a good Latin word that Guido might
have used, and which God used by saying *fiat lux*), the tonic of a new key,
E major. Starting from C major, then, we can detour to its relative minor
key, that of A minor, and from there make a direct transition to E major.
Suppose we want to go a little farther in the orbit, to B major, say, a key
with five sharps in its armature. We move to E minor, which is next door
to C major on the circle of fifths (as the relative minor of G major, having
one sharp), and from E minor we dash over to B major, which is the dominant of E minor. Now, starting again from the safety of the sharpless and
flatless key of C major, let us travel to a remote key in the flat direction,
say to D-flat major, which has five flats. To get there quickly, we declare
C major to be the major dominant of a minor key, to wit, F minor. Having
landed in F minor with supersonic speed, we proceed directly to D-flat major,

a key of which F minor is the mediant. We append a nice cadence, and the job is done.

The circle of fifths is not the only itinerary for modulation. There is a powerful resource in so-called chromatic modulation, in which neo-Guidonian substitution is effected by enharmonic change. Let us take the dominant-seventh chord in the key of E-flat, which is spelled B-flat, D, F, A-flat. Let us change A-flat enharmonically to G-sharp, a note identical with A-flat in sound but not in meaning, for G-sharp, being the top note of an augmented sixth, the bottom note of which is the former dominant B-flat, has an irresistible instinct to rise to A, while the bottom note B-flat has an equally irresistible instinct to sink to A. When both notes, following their instincts, land on an octave of A, we find ourselves in the locus of the cadential tonic 6/4 chord of D major (assuming that for euphony, we also raise F to F-sharp). The rest is just a matter of cadence. Robert Browning, who was a musically sensitive poet, set the process in verse. "The augmented-sixth resolved . . . leap of disimprisoned thrall/Into thy life and light, D major natural."

In chromatic harmony, chords are protean. Consider the diminished-seventh chord. Depending on one of its 24 musically possible spellings, it can instantly modulate to any of the 24 major or minor keys. No wonder it was called by Italian opera composers *accorde di stupefazione*, for, indeed, it stupefies the listener into catatonic suspense, particularly when played tremolo in the strings. Because the diminished-seventh chord consists of minor thirds that are free to move in parallel motion, dramatic chromatic rises and falls are quite convenient. Romantic operas, even by respectable composers, are full of such crawling chords, but even nonoperatic composers are not averse to taking advantage of this facility. In the coda of his B-flat minor Scherzo for piano, Chopin uses a series of ornamented diminished-seventh chords with nerve-tingling appoggiaturas in the middle voices that finally resolve into the long-anticipated key of D-flat major.

Moment-Groups. A term introduced by Stockhausen in the score of his work *Momente* (1962) to designate the premeditated or unpremeditated simultaneity of certain sounds produced by voices and instruments.

Mona. An opera by Horatio Parker, first staged at the Metropolitan Opera in New York on March 14, 1912, as the winner of a prize of $10,000 for an all-American opera. Despite the emphasis on Americanism (the librettist and the entire cast, with the exception of one minor part, were all Americans), the libretto itself was taken from an old British legend. Mona is the last defender of the Celtic Queen Boadicea who fought against Roman rule. The opera had only four performances; attempts at revivals foundered. Yet the music is not all bad. An interesting innovation is the assignment of certain keys to different characters; Mona is identified by the key of E-flat major.

Mona Lisa. An opera by Max von Schillings, first performed in Stuttgart on September 26, 1915. The whimsical libretto relates a married couple's visit to Florence. A local monk tells them the story of Mona Lisa, her husband Giocondo, and the love she nurtured for a Florentine youth, Giovanni. The smile on the lips of the woman tourist seems strangely familiar, and no wonder, for she is Mona Lisa rediviva, traveling with her husband, and the monastic teller of the story is Giovanni. The score is couched in an unrelieved Wagnerian idiom.

Der Mond (The Moon). An opera by Carl Orff, to his own text, after a fairy tale by Grimm, first produced in Munich on February 5, 1939. The story tells of four boys who steal the moon and use it as a bedside lamp. When they die, they arrange to take the moon with them to their graves. The sudden illumination arouses the dead. St. Peter comes down to restore order and puts the moon up in the sky where it belongs. As are most of Orff's operas, *Der Mond* is a theatrical spectacle, containing spoken dialogue, a pantomime, and several symphonic interludes in which a plethora of percussion instruments make interesting noises.

Il mondo della luna (The World of the Moon). An opera buffa by Haydn, first performed at the estate of Prince Esterházy where Haydn was music director, on August 3, 1777. An astronomer, fittingly named Dr. Ecclittico ("ecliptic," of course), drugs a rich Venetian and convinces him that he is on the moon and that the lunar authorities have ordered him to let his daughter marry her impecunious suitor. The music is spirited and ingratiating to the ears of inhabitants of any celestial body.

Money. Musicians do not manufacture material goods and therefore, like poets, must subsist parasitically. In times of catastrophic social disturbances, wars, famine, and plagues, music stops. In times of prosperity, musicians attach themselves to the dominant powers—the church, the royal court, educational institutions (which themselves must depend on the powers of the state), or wealthy merchants. In the church, and particularly in the most organized historical church of Rome, musicians performed the essential duties of writing for sacred services. When great royal courts emerged in the Middle Ages, kings, emperors, dukes, and other secular potentates employed musicians to lend decorum to their mundane preoccupations. With the emergence of industrial civilization, money kings took pleasure in sponsoring musical activities. Singers found easy employment in the church; instrumentalists were less in demand; composers had the least opportunity unless they acted also as performers, conductors of military bands, or instructors in universities. In current public demand for their services, a similar order exists; popular singers can make a fortune, but artists specializing in serious music rarely attract large audiences. A curious inverse ratio exists in relation to a singer's musical education or professional excellence and commercial success. Some of the most successful jazz and rock 'n' roll performers never learned to read music. Instrumentalists come second in popular acclaim; among them pianists enjoy the greatest opportunity for monetary success, followed by violinists and cellists. Symphonic conductors may be described as instrumentalists of the baton. Sometimes they have rivaled performing artists in public adulation, but because symphonic music is food for the sophisticates and the connoisseurs, and because conductors cannot pursue their profession with proficiency without an orchestra of great excellence, they may remain philosophers of music, even when they become idols of the audience. Infinitely more successful financially have been the leaders of dance bands, from the Waltz King Johann Strauss and the March King John Philip Sousa to the leaders of jazz bands and big swing bands.

In terms of both popular success and financial reward, composers are on the lowest rung of the ladder. Some composers of semi-Classical music and popular songs have achieved a certain prosperity, but composers of large symphonic works or chamber music have little hope of securing even a moderate income. The history of musical biography is a study in inauspicious beginnings and unhappy endings. Mozart wrote pathetic letters to a friendly banker asking for petty loans. (One of these letters sold some 200 years later to an autograph collector for a sum a thousand times as large as the loan requested by Mozart.) Beethoven flaunted his poverty with proud assertion of his status as a "brain owner." Tchaikovsky had a rich admirer in the person of Mme. von Meck, who gave him an annual grant. Wagner was put in a debtor's prison in Paris when he was already a well-known composer. Béla Bartók complained bitterly during his last years of life in America that he could not even find piano pupils to provide pocket money. A friendly Hungarian emigré arranged for Bartók to make a recording of his piano music, but sales were so poor that his friend doctored the royalty account to make it appear more respectable. (A picture postcard with Bartók's handwriting sold after his death for $165.) Schoenberg applied to the Guggenheim Foundation for a grant to enable him to complete his opera *Moses und Aron*, but was turned down. (A few pages of Schoenberg's orchestration of a Viennese operetta that he did as a young man were priced at several thousand dollars at an auction sale after Schoenberg's death.) Scriabin suffered desperate financial difficulties after the death of his Maecenas, the publisher Belaieff; sometimes, living in Switzerland, he even lacked enough money for a postage stamp. The situation of composers has improved considerably in the 20th century—in Europe, by the creation of government grants, prizes, and other awards to composers of serious music; and in America, by the formation of ASCAP and BMI, which protect composers' interests. Furthermore, "prestige" payments are often made by publishers to composers, the sale of whose works is not profitable commercially.

Mood Indigo. One of the earliest hits by Duke Ellington, popularized by his orchestra in 1930. It generated a whole series of imitations, depicting "color" moods from the deepest blue to the most cheerful red.

Moonlight Sonata. A popular but rather trivial title for Beethoven's *Sonata quasi una fantasia*, op. 27, No. 2, for piano (1801). An imaginative and sentimental German writer opined in print that the slowly rolling arpeggios of the opening movement reminded him of moonlight on the quiet surface of Lake Lucerne in Switzerland. The work is in C-sharp minor, in three movements. In the finale the wind whips up quite a little storm on the lake, and the moonlight is refracted violently.

Moresca. From the Spanish *morisca*, the Moorish dance. The moresca achieved popularity in Spain during the final phase of the struggle against Moorish power in southern Spain. It often contained a representation of a sword fight. The English Morris dance is apparently a late derivation of the moresca. Interludes of Moorish dances in exotic costumes were often included in French ballets of the period.

Morris dance. A characteristic English dance for men only. They wear exotic costumes and animal masks, apparently borrowing several features of the Spanish moresca, yet without losing its essentially English rhythmic verse. The Morris dance went into hibernation before its revival by British ethnomusicologists early in the 20th century.

Mosè in Egitto (Moses in Egypt). An opera by Rossini, first produced in Naples on March 5, 1818. The libretto follows the biblical narrative of the escape of the Hebrews across the miraculously distended Red Sea, and the destruction of the pursuing Egyptian army when the waters converge on them. Mussolini selected the opera to be performed at the gala reception for Hitler in Rome in 1935, oblivious to the fact that his antisemitic partner could have hardly enjoyed watching Jews escape.

Moses und Aron. An opera by Schoenberg, to his own text, left unfinished at the time of his death; its first act was produced posthumously in Zürich on June 6, 1957. The score is in the 12-tone idiom, with many episodes written in *Sprechstimme*. The religious conflict between spirituality and materialism, personified by Moses and his brother Aaron, underlies the text. Schoenberg gives indications in the score that an orgy staged around the idol of the Golden Calf should include the immolation of four naked virgins and other scenes of ancient depravity. A realistic production along these lines was attempted in London in 1965, but the alleged virgins wore loincloths. The omission of the second *A* in the German title was due to Schoenberg's triskaidecaphobia; if Aaron were spelled with two As, the sum of the letters in the complete title would have been 13.

Motet. This modest term embraces half a millennium of the most fruitful developments of polyphonic music, stretching from the Middle Ages to the Renaissance, and continuing through the period of the Baroque. The motet was cultivated in the church, both of the Roman Catholic and the Protestant rituals, as well as in multilingual secular practices. The term stems from *mot*, which in Old French signified a verse, strophe, or stanza. This is seemingly corroborated by the fact that the contrapuntal voice above the tenor, originally called *duplum*, acquired in the 13th century the name *motet* and carried a text. Franco of Cologne, writing in the 13th century, describes the motet as *discantus cum diversis litteris*, "a contrapuntal part with different texts." In the course of two centuries, the motet was supplemented by additional contrapuntal parts, some of them in the French vernacular. During the Renaissance, the confusion of bilingual texts and diverse rhythms led to the segregation of the Latin motet from the secular motet, which had absorbed numerous colloquial elements. Further developments, both unified and heterogeneous, are found in the great polyphonic works of the masters of the Flemish school—Ockeghem, Obrecht, and Josquin des Pres. Later, Palestrina in Italy, Victoria in Spain, Tallis in England, Hassler in Germany, and Goudimel in France contributed to the newly burnished art of the motet. In England the motet assumed homophonic forms, leading to the formation of a specific British type of anthem. In Germany, Schütz and, a century later, Bach, whose greatest work in the motet style was a score written for double chorus and eight solo voices, created the specific form of the German motet. The motet suffered an irreversible decline in the 19th century; the few composers who stubbornly cultivated it, particularly in Germany, did so more out of reverence for its Gothic past than out of inner imperative.

The Mother of Us All. An opera by Virgil Thomson, to a libretto by Gertrude Stein, first produced in New York on May 7, 1947. The mother of the title is Susan B. Anthony, the American suffragette who fought for women's right to vote. The cast of characters are two modestly abbreviated names, Virgil T. and Gertrude S. The music is disarmingly triadic but greatly sophisticated in its seeming simplicity.

Mother Machree. A semiclassical song by Ernst Ball written in 1910. It became one of the greatest Irish tearjerkers about mothers. *Machree* is an Irish word meaning "dear."

Mourning Symphony. Haydn's Symphony No. 44 in E minor (1771). The somewhat somber mood of the work must have suggested this nickname, which in German is *Trauersinfonie*.

Mozart i Salieri. A short opera by Rimsky-Korsakov, to a libretto after Pushkin's poem. It was first produced in Moscow on December 7, 1898. Pushkin's text gives literary sanction to a legend that spread shortly after Mozart's death, accusing the eminently respectable Italian composer Salieri (who was for a time a teacher of Beethoven) of poisoning Mozart. In Pushkin's poem and in the opera, Salieri declares that were Mozart allowed to live on, other composers, honest, industrious, but not blessed by genius, would be condemned to futility. Rimsky-Korsakov used authentic excerpts from Mozart's compositions as well as musical allusions to Salieri's opera *Tarare*, which Mozart prized highly.

Mozartiana. The fourth orchestral suite by Tchaikovsky, arranged from various instrumental and choral works of Mozart. It was first performed in Moscow on November 26, 1887.

La Muette de Portici (The Mute Girl of Portici). An opera by Daniel-François-Esprit Auber, first performed in Paris on February 29, 1828. The Neapolitan fisherman Masaniello leads a rebellion against Spanish rule; he is mysteriously murdered just as he achieves his goal of overthrowing the Spanish viceroy in Naples. In despair, his deaf-mute sister throws herself into the crater of Mt. Vesuvius during an eruption. The story has a historical foundation: An actual patriot named Masaniello led an uprising against Spain in 1647; he did get murdered, but Mt. Vesuvius erupted 16 years before it did in the finale of *La Muette de Portici*. When the opera was performed in Brussels in 1830, the people in the audience became so excited by this operatic cry for freedom that they spilled out into the streets demanding independence for Belgium; a year or so later they received it. *Post hoc ergo propter hoc?*

Murder of a Great Chief of State. A memorial work written by Darius Milhaud upon his learning of the assassination of President John F. Kennedy. He completed the work in a couple of days, and it was performed in Oakland, California, on December 3, 1963, less than two weeks after the tragic event.

Murky bass. A curious term of a puzzling origin applied to rudimentary accompaniment in broken octaves in the bass, which was much in use in Rococo music. Some philologists suggest that *murky* is an English word meaning exactly what it says: "unclear, obfuscating."

Musette. A French bagpipe popular in the 18th century. It was much more ornate in appearance than the Scottish bagpipe and was used in ballets given at the French court. Musette is also the name of a pastoral dance, characterized by a protracted drone. Musettes are found in many Baroque instrumental suites by French composers and also in the English Suite No. 3 of Bach. The middle section of the gavotte is often called musette, when it has a sustained drone on the tonic and dominant. An older name for the musette is *cornemuse*.

Music. A meaningful succession of perceptible sounds in temporal motion. These sounds may be single sonorous units (as in melody) or simultaneous combinations of several such units (as in harmony and counterpoint). The temporal motion may consist of sounds of equal duration (simple chant) or of unequal duration (rhythmed melody, or melorhythm). Melorhythms may be patterned symmetrically, in well-demarcated periods (corresponding to unchanged meter in versification), or in asymmetrical fragments. The perfection of a melorhythmic figure is determined by the balance between melody and rhythm. When melodic elements (tones) vary greatly in pitch, the rhythm may be allowed to remain quiescent; when the melody is confined to a few notes, and in extreme cases to a single note, then to be effective rhythm must show variety. This interdependence of melody and rhythm in a melorhythm may be expressed by the formula $R \times M = C$, where R stands for rhythm, M stands for melody, and C stands for an empirical constant. The validity of this formula may be verified by examining some folksongs or great melodies by famous composers.

Music is written by means of symbols or notes. A medieval monk, St. Isidore of Seville, stated in the 7th century that music is an art that can be preserved by oral tradition only because tones can never be notated. The history of musical notation has indeed been arduous, but for the past four centuries it has assumed a fairly uniform aspect. The height of a musical tone is measured by its relative position on a staff of five lines, with clefs indicating the selected pitch of a specific note, usually G, C, or F, placed on any of the five lines of the staff; the rest of the notes are calculated from the clef note, with each space and each line reckoning for one diatonic degree.

The word *music* is derived from the Greek words *musike techne*—that is, "the technique of the Muses." Euterpe, the muse of tragedy and flute playing, and Polyhymnia, the muse of songs, are regarded as the inspiring deities of music—Euterpe because in ancient Greece music was closely connected with tragedy, and theatrical spectacles were invariably accompanied by the playing on the flute; Polyhymnia because the beginning of music was marked by a multiplicity of songs. In the Middle Ages, theorists and theologians subdivided the art of music into several categories within an imaginary Harmony of the Spheres. These categories included *musica mundana* ("music of the universe"), *musica humana* ("harmony of body and soul"), and *musica instrumentalis* ("music as it is played"). *Musica vocalis* was added later, referring specifically to vocal music. A further development was *musica artificialis*, which was subdivided into the music of *chordae* ("strings"), *ventus* ("wind"), and *pulsus* ("percussion"). According to functional application, music was separated into two parts: *musica divina* ("church music") and *musica vulgaris* ("secular music," from *vulgus*, meaning "people," not "vulgar" in the pejorative sense).

The concept of music does not necessarily signify beauty or attractiveness; indeed, music of primitive peoples, which is beautiful to them, may appear chaotic and ugly to an outsider. Within the memory of many musicians, compositions by modern masters were condemned by critics as cacophonous. In his famous treatise on aesthetics *Vom Musikalisch-Schönen*, Hanslick defines music as "a tonally moving form." This definition begs the question, for the key word *tonally* embraces the "moving forms" of Liszt, Wagner, and other representatives of the "music of the future" which was anathema to Hanslick. Kant described music as "an artistic arrangement of sensations of hearing," which is logically acceptable, for it includes any subjectively artistic succession of musical elements. Hegel declared that the aim of music is "to render in sounds the innermost self which moves in itself according to the subjective feeling for one's ideal soul," a statement that is so involuted that it may describe any sound, or any combination of sounds, that expresses any kind of emotion. The most extreme manifestations of the modern avant-garde would find their place in the definition of music by the most rigid and most obfuscating of German philosophers, Schopenhauer, to whom the human will was the source of all action. He asserted that music is a "reflection of the will itself, revealing its very essence, whereas other arts treat but the shadows of the will." The Romantic poet Jean Paul describes music as "a reflected sound from a remote world." Inspired by the medieval concept of the harmony of the spheres, Schelling senses in music "the perceived rhythm and harmony of the observable universe itself." Musical theorists seeking to delimit music from other arts emphasize its unique capacity to convey emotions and meaning, to express spiritual and sensory phenomena in terms that use no language and no pictorial representation. Hegel himself admitted that music is "sufficient unto itself and therefore self-explanatory."

Great poets extolled music as a catalyst of passion and a motive force for bravery. Shakespeare expressed this quality in the ringing lines, "The man that hath no music in himself/ nor is not moved with concord of sweet sounds/ . . . let no such man be trusted." In his *Ode on a Grecian Urn*, Keats said that music should be perceived in silence: "Heard melodies are sweet, but those unheard are sweeter." Longfellow followed the philosophers in saying that "music is the universal language of mankind." Scientists seem to agree, to judge by the suggestion of an astronomer that a diagram of a Bach fugue should be included in a rocket sent outside the solar system on the chance that if intercepted it will be easier to decode by the hypothetical beings in distant galaxies than any other symbol.

In the Middle Ages music was part of mathematics, included in the Quadrivium of the universities. In poetic language, the word *numbers* means music. "Will no one tell me what she sings?" Wordsworth questioned, and surmised: "Perhaps the plaintive numbers flow/ For old, unhappy, far-off things." Leibniz said: "Music is a kind of counting performed by the mind without knowing that it is counting." This definition comes remarkably close to Bertrand Russell's description of mathematics as "the subject in which we never know what we are talking about, nor whether what we are saying is true.''

Music boxes. Mechanical musical instruments that were perfected shortly after the invention of clockwork, about the year 1200. The first mechanical music instrument was the barrel organ, manufactured for the archbishop of Salzburg in 1502. It had 350 pipes into which music was channeled from a barrel with flexible pins. This was followed by mechanical carillons, the best of which were made in Flanders and Holland in the 17th century. Chiming watches that played tunes appeared in France in the 18th century. The first true music box, in which steel tongues with a definite pitch were plucked by pins on a rotating cylinder, was made by Antoine Favre of Geneva in 1796. The music box industry reached its greatest development about 1870; it declined with the appearance of the phonograph, a rival too mighty for the tinkling pins and tongues. Apart from chiming watches, music boxes were manufactured in the form of snuff boxes and sewing boxes. Musical dolls are a form of music box that survives into the present time.

Music for Strings, Percussion, and Celesta. A highly original work for a small ensemble by Béla Bartók, in which percussion instruments play a major part. It was first performed in Basel on January 21, 1937.

Music journals. Before the advent of mass publication of general newspapers that included a special department devoted to the review of concerts, music criticism existed only in the form of theoretical discussions in learned pamphlets. Heated polemical exchanges accompanied the progress of *La Guerre des bouffons* during the famous Gluck-Piccini controversy in the 18th century. Germany was a pioneer in musical journalism; essays on technical subjects were published in connection with public performances. The first musical periodical containing critical evaluations of musical works was the *Allgemeine musikalische Zeitung*, founded in 1798 and published, with an occasional hiatus, until 1881. It was for this journal that Schumann wrote, at the age of 19, his unsigned article saluting Chopin as a genius. In 1834, Schumann founded his own publication, *Neue Zeitschrift für Musik*, dedicated to the propaganda of ''new'' music of a Romantic mold; after several interruptions it was reincarnated after World War I. The German music weekly *Signale für die musikalische Welt*, founded in 1841, lasted almost a century until World War II finally killed it off. The informative weekly *Allgemeine Musikzeitung* was also the victim of World War II after 70 years of a relatively prosperous existence. With the exception of Schumann's journal, these publications adopted a conservative, not to say reactionary, attitude toward the novel musical tendencies of each successive period. In France, *La Revue Musicale* continued its uncertain existence from 1827 to 1880, was revived under the same title in 1920, only to falter and eventually die of inanition. *Le Ménestrel* lasted more than 100 years after its founding in 1833, with the inevitable collapse during the Paris Commune and World War I; World War II put a finish to it. Its critical attitudes during the first century of its existence were definitely reactionary; it damned Wagner and Debussy with equal fervor. In England, the most durable monthly is *The Musical Times*, founded in 1844 and still going strong after nearly 150 years. In the United States, musical journals of opinion had a relatively brief life. In the 19th century, *Dwight's Journal of Music* enjoyed some respect; it was dull, and it damned Wagner.

In the meantime, artists of varying degrees of excellence, German, Italian, and Russian music teachers, and minor musicians of all calibers became commodities of the European musical market and commanded a great deal of advertising. In America these demands were met in a multiplicity of commercial music periodicals, of which *The Musical Courier* and *Musical America* were particularly prominent. They published weekly issues that featured dispatches by specially assigned European correspondents and reproduced excellent photographs of the current celebrities who bought advertising space. For a modest fee even for those times, these publications carried cover portraits of exotic-looking mustachioed tenors and ample-bosomed prima donnas, and occasionally even an American face. The ads informed on the activities of music teachers ("Mr. *X* has returned from Europe and will accept a limited number of exceptionally talented pupils"), voice teachers with Italian surnames ("Guarantee bel canto within six months by inhaling bottled compressed air from Naples"), "Miss *Y* triumphs in Muleshoe, Texas," and so on.

As the careers of these musical worthies became less and less profitable and interest in the artistic and amorous goings-on in the musical world waned, the journals languished and finally expired. *Musical America* survived as a shriveled appendix to *High Fidelity*. *The Etude* purveyed information to music lovers and amateurs; it published sentimental biographies of contemporary musicians, as well as simplified selections of some digestible compositions, but it, too, succumbed to the disenchantment of the times. In place of these publications there arose a crop of commercialized periodicals devoted to recordings, radio, and television, with only a sprinkling of informative material in their pages. Musicological journals carried on a precarious existence. In America, *The Musical Quarterly* has survived as a scholarly publication. In England, *Music and Letters* and *Music Review* purveyed selective information. There are music journals of some value in Italy. In Russia, the monthly *Sovietskaya Musica* furnished information on Soviet music. In Latin America, only the *Revista Musical Chilena* appeared with some regularity. The international avant-garde put out sporadic issues of great interest to their particular audiences. The most extreme of them was *Source*, published in the radical '70s in California (where else?), without visible financial support, printing the most fantastic samples of ultramodern productions lavishly illustrated in a variety of colors. It had a feverish existence for several years before collapsing.

Music therapy. A Sicilian youth suspected that his beloved was faithless. His suspicions were further inflamed by the sounds of flute music in the Phrygian mode. Seized by madness, he rushed into her house. Pythagoras, taking temporary leave of his mathematical calculations, took notice of the young man's condition and ordered the flute player to change from the Phrygian to the Dorian mode. This modification had an immediate soothing effect on the youth, who became philosophically calm. The ancient Greek Phrygian mode (which, it should be noted, corresponds to the Ionian mode in Gregorian chant, identical with C major) was regarded by the Greeks as most apt to cause hyperventilation in a human being. Alexander the Great was so sensitive to music that when a musician played a Phrygian air on the lyre he unsheathed his sword and slew one of his guests. The musician precluded further slaughter by switching to a less exciting mode. Aristotle tells of alleviating the pain of slaves by causing flute music to be played while they were being punished by flogging. Terpander pacified a menacing crowd of rebellious citizens by singing in benign modalities, accompanying himself on a seven-string lyre of his invention. So impressed were his listeners that they burst into tears and rushed to kiss the feet of their tyrant. Tyrtacus, the Athenian, was sent to Sparta on a mission to undermine the indomitable Spartan spirit by playing an elegy, *Eunomia* ("good law"), to them, but when he inadvertently changed to the martial Dorian mode, the Spartans rose in wrath and marched belligerently on Athens. Plato declared that civil obedience can be achieved by means of music. Indeed, public decrees were often recited in ancient Greece to melodious accompaniment on the lyre. Damon of Athens quieted drunken youths by playing spondaeic measures on the flute. Maecenas, the legendary patron of Roman poetry, cured his chronic insomnia by listening to distant sounds of music. The Phrygian mode was recommended by Theophrastus, favorite disciple of Aristotle, for cure of sciatica, with the vertical flute to be held close to the affected nerve ganglion. Many victims of melancholy regained their self-confidence when Phrygian tunes were played for them, Theophrastus reports. Flute playing in the Phrygian mode was also proposed by Caelius Aurelianus for temporary relief from lumbago and arthritis; at the sound of the flute, the ailing person would begin to tremble, thus stimulating the nerves affected and curing the disease.

Belief in the beneficial and curative properties of music persisted even when the modal dichotomy of the Phrygian and Dorian modes were replaced by "scientific" reasoning and experimentation. Peter Lichtenthal, in a remarkable volume, *The Musical Doctor*, published in 1811, suggests musical remedies for a variety of human ills; his list includes incidence of stupidity among school children, particularly girls, that yielded to music therapy. Quoting a contemporary French physician, he reports that a young girl, affected by irresistible nymphomania, became morally restrained when she was forced to listen to benign music three times a day.

"Music has charms to soothe a savage breast," William Congreve wrote, but the statement is not always true. If the chroniclers can be trusted, Eric the Good, king of Denmark, ordered all weapons removed from his reach before the court lutenist began to play for fear that he might be moved to violence by the sounds of music. So strong was this impulse, it is said, that the moment the lutenist began to play, the king rushed out, seized a sword and slew four men. On the other side of the ledger, King Philip II of Spain engaged the famous castrato Farinelli to sing for him nightly to allay his chronic melancholy. Farinelli sang the same four songs for the king every night for 25 years until the royal sufferer finally gave up the ghost.

One of the most bizarre chronicles of musical therapy concerns tarantism, an uncontrollable compulsion to dance, which erupted in Taranto, Italy, in the 15th century. This morbid choreographic condition was caused by the bite of the tarantula and according to contemporary reports could be cured by playing the Italian tarantella, a rapid dance in 6/8 time. The legend even found its way into some reputable music encyclopedias.

A plausible claim can be made, however, for the psychiatric benefit of music to help retarded and autistic children. Playing rhythmic dance music, particularly in binary meter (which corresponds to the natural alternation of steps, inspirations and expirations, and the diastolic and systolic heartbeats), may well have a soothing effect on disturbed individuals. The most beneficial tempo is 80 beats a minute, which corresponds to the normal pulse rate.

What kind of music should be played for medicinal purposes? As long ago as 1852, the German physiologist Lotze wrote in his book *Medizinische Psychologie*: "A careful study of melodies shows that we are completely ignorant of the circumstances under which the change from one type of nerve excitation to another corresponds to the physical substratum of the aesthetic sensations generated by the music." Some physicians assert that music can directly affect the seat of emotion in the cerebral cortex. Numerous experiments have been conducted on mental patients to find out what particular kind of music is best for them, but results are inconclusive. Musical statistics have been compiled by psychologists to prove that the piano music of Chopin and Rachmaninoff was good for unbalanced persons, while Stravinsky and Schoenberg upset their mental equilibrium. There is no denying that music can move masses of people to frenzy; the annals of political history are full of instances in which a revolutionary song inflamed the masses and led to victory. The Institute of Musical Therapy, organized in Poland in 1974, suggested the following musical program to be played before open-heart surgery for the beneficial effect on the patient as well as on the surgeon: Gavotte in A major by Gluck, *Clair de lune* by Debussy, *Siciliana* by Bach, and *Adagio* by Albinoni.

Musica ficta. The term, which literally means "fictitious music," originated in the 14th century to replace the misleading term *musica falsa*. Both terms described the practice of attaching accidentals, mainly sharps, to newly formed hexachords during the process of modulation. The expression *musica conjuncta* used by some writers is preferable because it alludes to the functional conjunction made between the hexachords by means of accidentals. Compilers of medieval Latin treatises fully realized how inadequate these terms were. In one of them, an anonymous author speaks of the new type of modulation as *non tamen falsa musica, sed inusitata* ("not so much false music, as unusual music"). But another anonymous author terms this "useless" music as *causa necessitatis et causa pulchritudinis cantus per se* ("for the reason of necessity and beauty, an independent melody"). Still another writer claims that *falsa musica non est inutilis immo necessaria* ("false music is not useless, but quite necessary"); this opinion is echoed by the positive pronouncement of Philippe de Vitry to the effect that *musica ficta sive falsa est musica vera et necessaria* ("*musica ficta* or *musica falsa* is true and necessary music").

The practical consequences of *musica ficta*, whatever the term itself might connote, were far-reaching. Medieval music theorists had followed the Guidonian Hand with slavish obsequiousness. Their cautious modulations had to be *in manu* ("in the hand"), but *musica ficta* led music to the regions *extra manum* ("outside the hand"), venturing into the territory that required remote sharps and flats—at first only F-sharp and B-flat, but later C-sharp and other accidentals. It should be remembered that B-flat, or *B rotundum* ("round B"), was very much "*in manu*," the flatting of B being necessary to avoid the "diabolic" tritone. This condition prevailed well into the 18th century. In the meantime, *musica ficta* generated subsidiary terms such as *vox ficta*, "fictional voice," a contrapuntal part containing extra sharps or flats, and *cantus fictus*, "fictional song," a theme written in an alien key. Not until the reluctant admission on the part of music theorists that all keys are intervallically alike and that notation was the *ancilla musicae*, the "maid-servant of music," were *musica ficta* and *musica falsa* absolved from the suspicion of falsity.

Musicology. The science of music. This term originated in France early in the 19th century (*musicologie*), was later adopted by German music theorists under the name *Musikwissenschaft*, and was domesticated in England and America as musicology. The province of musicology was at first limited to the gnostic division of musical knowledge, with an emphasis on abstruse historical and semantic subjects. Musicological dissertations were apt to be extremely circumscribed in their statements—for example, "certain conjectural elements in the Quattrocento French motet'' or ''the possible urban Iberian origin of the passacaglia.'' As the teaching of musicology expanded and embraced general historiography of music and even biography, PhD degrees were awarded by leading universities for dissertations with such titles as ''Plausible Deciphering of Beethoven's Notes to His Housekeeper Instructing Her to Buy Candles and Yellow Soap'' (the specification *gelbe* for the color of the soap was credited by the author to an eminent Beethovenologist) or ''New Data Establishing Schumann's Syphylitic Infection.'' Analysis of works, bibliographical studies of all kinds, and newfangled theories dealing with melody, harmony, or counterpoint, all gradually fell into the category of musicology until it became an all-embracing science of history, music theory, and musical biography. Although a study of national music was by definition a part of musicology, the increased investigation of non-European musical modalities led to the formation of a subsidiary branch of musicology, namely ethnomusicology.

Musique d'écurie. ''Music of the stable.'' A French designation for field music—that is, music played in unison by trumpets and signal horns.

Musique funèbre. A work for string orchestra by Witold Lutosławski, written in memory of Béla Bartók. It was first performed in Katowice, Poland, on March 26, 1958. Its introduction is based on a symmetric tune consisting of an ascending tritone and a descending semitone.

Die Mutter (The Mother). An opera by Alois Hába, to his own libretto, first performed in Munich on May 17, 1931. The story concerns the enmity between the children of the first and second marriages in a Czech family. The work is of historic significance because it includes quarter tones in the score to be played by specifically constructed instruments.

Muzak An American company that supplies ''canned music'' for public places such as restaurants, elevators, transportation terminals, waiting rooms, and occasionally restrooms. The kinds of music purveyed by Muzak usually consist of glutinous ballads and saccharine instrumental arrangements of popular songs. Driven to desperation, commuters brought a class action suit to show cause why this tonal pollution at Grand Central Terminal in New York City should not be declared a public nuisance. Surprisingly, they won.

Muzak was the brainchild of an Army general who was bemused by the commercial possibilities of ''wired radio'' as an entertainment medium. When the company was founded in 1934, it was in fact named ''Wired Radio, Inc.'' Later it was suggested to combine the popular brand name in photography, Kodak, with ''music,'' and the result was Muzak. Soon there were over 300 Muzak franchises around the world. Muzak executives like to describe themselves as ''Specialists in the Physiological and Psychological Applications of Music,'' and their product as ''a non-verbal symbolism for the common stuff of everyday living in the global village, promoting the sharing of meaning because it massifies symbolism in which not few but all can participate.''

Mysterious Mountain. An orchestral work by Alan Hovhaness, inspired by the mystic vision of a phantom peak somewhere in the Himalayas. The score is written in an impressionistic manner emphasizing colorful instrumental contrasts. It was first performed in Houston, Texas, on October 31, 1955, with Stokowski conducting.

Mysterium. An unfinished, in fact, uncommenced, crowning work of Scriabin that was to embody the synthesis of all arts and of all five human senses. He envisioned the *Mysterium* as a final sacrament, with himself as the high priest of the production. The work was to terminate in a universal ecstasy that would consume humanity in a mystical act marking the end of the manvantara, the theosophic era borrowed from Hindu cosmogony. The nearest approximation to *Mysterium* was Scriabin's *Poem of Ecstasy.* He planned an intermediate link between it and *Mysterium*, a composition for all media that he called a *Preliminary Act.* An unsuccessful attempt was made by a group of Russian musicians to orchestrate several of Scriabin's piano pieces of his last period and to arrange them in a suite approximating the idea of *Mysterium*.

Mystic Chord. The theosophic name that Scriabin attached to a chord consisting of six notes—C, F-sharp, B-flat, E, A, and D—which lies at the foundation of his last symphonic work, *Prométhée.* It is also known as the ''Prometheus chord.'' The chord was adumbrated in several of Scriabin's previous compositions, in which it usually resolved into the dominant-ninth chord by moving A to B-flat and F-sharp to G. Scriabin arrived at the formation of this chord intuitively, but later he rationalized its construction as consisting of higher overtones forming a six-tone scale from the eighth to the fourteenth overtones (C, D, E, F-sharp, A, B-flat). No one after Scriabin made use of the Mystic Chord, and it remains a solitary mausoleum.

Die Nachtschwalbe (The Night Swallow). A "dramatic nocturne" by Boris Blacher dealing with the life of a prostitute in a small German town who turns out to be an illegitimate daughter of the head of the vice squad. It was first performed in Leipzig on February 22, 1948, provoking quite a scandal because of its frankness in staging.

Natoma. An opera by Victor Herbert, first produced in Philadelphia on February 25, 1911, his only attempt to write in a grand operatic manner. The action takes place in California under Spanish rule. Natoma is an Indian girl in love with a U.S. Navy lieutenant, but she yields him to her rival, a white woman from Santa Barbara, and finds solace in the invocation to her ancestral Great Spirit.

Neapolitan cadence. A cadence in which the customary subdominant triad is replaced by the lowered supertonic in the first inversion, known as the Neapolitan sixth chord. The bass of the Neapolitan chord is the same as that of the subdominant chord; thus the substitution is logical. As in the regular cadence, the Neapolitan chord is followed by the dominant, often with an interpolation of the tonic 6/4 chord, ending on the tonic. The Neapolitan cadence, like the Neapolitan chord, received its name from its frequent use by composers of the Neapolitan school, particularly in the 18th century. A remarkable example of an instrumental composition that starts with the Neapolitan chord is the first Ballade in G minor by Chopin, which opens with a lengthy and elaborate cadenza based on the first inversion of the lowered supertonic of the key of G minor. Scriabin's Symphony No. 3, *Le Poème divin*, is nominally in C minor, but it begins with a Neapolitan cadence on D-flat.

Nearer My God to Thee. An American hymn composed by Lowell Mason about 1850. It became a standard song in Christian churches of the world.

Charles Ives quotes the tune in his Symphony No. 4 and other works to evoke the devotional atmosphere of old America.

Nelson Mass. A nickname for Haydn's Mass in D minor, written in 1798, in which a trumpet flourish in the Benedictus was supposed to suggest Nelson's victory at Aboukir. It is also called *Imperial Mass*.

Nero. An opera by Anton Rubinstein, first performed in Hamburg on November 1, 1879. In it Rubinstein tried to emulate the genre of French grand opera. In the last act Nero plays the anachronistic fiddle while Rome burns.

Neue Sachlichkeit. A movement launched in Germany after World War I to describe the "new objectivity" in drama, art, and music as a reaction against the hyper-Romantic tendencies of 19th-century culture. In music, it cultivated a functional *modus operandi*, pursuing well-defined objectives in clearly outlined forms. The economic necessity of cutting down the cost of production of musical presentations resulted in the creation of new, modern kinds of chamber opera, without a chorus, and with a partial return to Classical orchestral composition. In many respects, the movement coincided with the aims of *Gebrauchsmusik*.

Neues vom Tage (Daily News). An opera by Paul Hindemith, first produced in Berlin on June 8, 1929. The events of the libretto begin with a marital separation; another couple also becomes entangled in divorce proceedings. The libretto includes a bathtub aria that scandalized the critics. Another novelty was a chorus of stenographers at their percussive typewriters.

The New York Skyline. A graphic score that Heitor Villa-Lobos composed using his system of musical millimetrization, by which he transferred the outline of a painting or a photograph to music paper, allowing a semitone for every millimeter of the graph. The musical result was broadcast from Rio de Janeiro to New York for the opening of the Brazilian Pavilion at the New York World's Fair on April 7, 1940.

Night Flight (Volo di Notte). An opera by Luigi Dallapiccola, based on the autobiographical novel *Vol de Nuit* by Antoine de Saint-Exupéry, first produced in Florence on May 18, 1940. The story deals with a dramatic night flight over the Andes in a single-engine monoplane. Dallapiccola set it to music in a dynamic atonal idiom, verging on dodecaphony. The score includes spoken dialogue and a wordless passage of a disembodied voice warning the pilot of dangers facing him.

Night Flight is also the name of a tone poem by Gardner Read, inspired by the Saint-Exupéry book. It was first performed in Rochester, New York, on April 27, 1944.

A Night on Bald Mountain. An orchestral fantasy by Modest Mussorgsky. It pictures broom-riding witches who celebrate a Black Mass, but the church bells at midnight scare them away. Mussorgsky, who was diffident about his orchestration, left the score half finished. Rimsky-Korsakov completed it in his usual masterly fashion and conducted it for the first time, five years after Mussorgsky's death, in St. Petersburg on October 27, 1886.

Ninth chord. Although ninth chords are defined as chords consisting of a series of four superimposed thirds on any degree of the scale, their use is confined in practice to dominant-ninth chords. These chords were cultivated systematically by Wagner, Liszt, and Bruckner, always within a given tonality. The ninth chord requires five-part harmony for its totality; in four-part harmony, the fifth above the root is left out. The necessity of lowering the ninth to the dominant-seventh chord is felt very strongly in cadential formations—for instance, toward the end of the overture of Wagner's *Die Meistersinger*. The dramatic attraction of the ninth chord led Scriabin to the formation of his so-called Mystic Chord, which eliminates the fifth but includes an upper and lower appoggiatura to it. Debussy emancipated the tonal implications of the dominant-ninth chord by moving it in parallal formation, either chromatically or by minor thirds, without resolving. Numerous composers of the 20th century have used this device to create a feeling of vague harmonic uncertainty. The fascination of the ninth chord ceased abruptly with the decline of musical impressionism in the second quarter of the 20th century, and parallel ninth chords, once the darlings of modernism, were relegated to a type of "mood" music. Ninth chords built on degrees of the scale other than the dominant lack the proper euphony to provide much interest to composers of modern music, and examples of their use are few.

Nixon in China. A modern historical opera in two acts by John Adams, depicting, in fancifully realistic scenes, President Richard Nixon's trip to China in 1972, with Nixon as a baritone, Mao Zedong as a Wagnerian Heldentenor, and Nixon's wife, Pat, as a lively soprano. The world premiere was given in Houston, Texas, on October 22, 1987, and quite a few people made the trip from New York and other music centers to attend.

Les Noces (The Wedding). "Choreographic scenes with singing and music" by Igor Stravinsky, first produced by Diaghilev's Ballet Russe in Paris on June 13, 1923. It is scored for chorus, soloists, four pianos, and 17 percussion instruments. Because it is performed on the stage, it occupies an intermediate position between cantata and opera. The music is rooted in Russian folksong, but the harmonic and contrapuntal realization is propulsive and acrid, while always keeping within a diatonic framework. The libretto consists of four scenes that trace the rituals of a peasant betrothal and wedding.

Nocturne. A "night piece." The word suggests a nocturnal scene full of dreamy melodies set in euphonious harmonies. The nocturne emerged as a distinct genre of Romantic piano pieces early in the 19th century, primarily through the poetic creations of Chopin. The pioneer of piano nocturnes was the Irish composer John Field, but his pieces fall far below those of Chopin in quality. Even though nocturnes are creatures of the night, there is dramatic turbulence in the middle sections of some of Chopin's nocturnes. Schumann also wrote nocturnes, but, in conformity with the prevalent nationalistic sentiment of the time, he assigned to them a German name, *Nachtstück*. In Italian, the nocturne is *notturno*.

Nocturnes. An orchestral suite by Claude Debussy in three movements entitled *Nuages*, *Fêtes*, and *Sirènes*. It was first performed in its entirety in Paris on October 27, 1901. The first movement, "Clouds," is a musical monochrome; the clouds are bland, white and gray. The second movement, "Festivals," is full of rhythmic sounds and light. The third movement, which includes a female chorus, represents the laughing Sirens singing their seductive songs.

Noise. A collection of tonally unrelated simultaneous sounds of different frequencies and intensities, meaningless to musical or even unmusical ears. In radio transmission, noise is called static, and a similar electromagnetic disturbance in television is called "snow." White noise is an integral assembly of sounds of various frequencies.

Non nobis Domine. One of the most famous vocal canons of the second half of the 16th century, usually attributed to the great Elizabethan madrigalist William Byrd. Because the canon was not written out, it must be classified as a riddle canon; indeed, it can be sung in several different formations, all of them quite harmonious. It is set in three parts; the treble enters first, the middle voice then comes in a perfect fourth below, and the bass enters a fifth below the middle voice, that is, an octave below the upper tone. One of the voices may be inverted. In England, the canon is often sung as a grace before meals.

None. A part of the Roman Catholic Divine Office celebrated at the Ninth Hour, that is, at 3:00 P.M., the hour Jesus died on the cross, which was counted as the ninth hour from sunrise. The word comes from the Latin *ad nonam horam*, "at the ninth hour."

Norma. An opera by Vincenzo Bellini, first produced in Milan on December 26, 1831. Norma is the high priestess of the Druid temple in ancient Gaul during its occupation by the Romans. As behooves all operas, natural enemies fall in love. Here, not only Norma herself becomes involved with a Roman proconsul and bears him two children, but a virgin of the temple also loves him, in violation of her vow of chastity. The proconsul is caught desecrating the temple of the Druids, but Norma cannot put him to death as she ought to do in her capacity as high priestess. She confesses her own unchastity and ascends the punitive pyre with the proconsul for ritual incineration. *Norma* is Bellini's most melodious and most harmonious opera, a perennial favorite of the public of all races and geographical locations. The aria in which Norma appeals to the goddess of the Moon is a paragon of melodic beauty. Even Wagner professed his admiration for *Norma*.

The Nose. An opera by Dmitri Shostakovich, after the fantastic tale by Gogol, first produced in Leningrad on January 12, 1930. The story deals with the nose of a government functionary that mysteriously disappears from his face during shaving and goes off as an independent individual. All sorts of absurdities occur, interspersed with satirical darts at czarist bureaucracy. In the end, the nose resumes its rightful place, above the mouth and under the eyes, much to the owner's relief. The score is a brilliant exercise in grotesquerie. It includes an octet of janitors in dissonant counterpoint, a gigantic orchestral sneeze, and other effects. The production was greeted with great exhilaration by Soviet musicians but received a chilly reception by the Kremlin bureaucracy, in consequence of which Shostakovich was charged with imitating decadent Western models. Many years elapsed before *The Nose* was revived on the Soviet stage.

Notation. The craft of writing symbols to represent sounds. It took a millennium to develop a musical notation capable of even approximating the pitch and duration of each individual note. The Spanish theologian Isidore of Seville, who flourished in the seventh century, asserted that musical sounds could be transmitted from one generation to another only by oral tradition because they could not be properly notated. The old monk's pessimistic declaration seems to be prophetically fulfilled in many scores of the second half of the 20th century, which abandon all attempts at precise notation of pitch or duration, and resort instead to such approximations as *najwyszy dzwiek instrumentu* ("the highest possible sounds of the instrument"), a Polish direction given in the works of Krzysztof Penderecki, or instructions in a work by Karlheinz Stockhausen for the performer to strike any note on the piano and hold it indefinitely, or a similarly beguiling exhortation by John Cage: "This is a composition indeterminate of its performance, and the performance is of actions which are often indeterminate of themselves," or the declaration of the British ultramodernist Cornelius Cardew, the inventor of "scratch music" in which "the notation may be accomplished using any means, verbal, graphic, musical, or by collage."

Music of ancient Greece was notated by letters, some of them turned backward or upside down, apparently to indicate a certain type of interval. Toward the end of the first millennium of our era, an early system of notation appeared in the form of neumes, a Greek word for a nod, a sign, or a signal, indicating single notes or groups of notes (ligatures). Such neumes were placed directly in the text, above the lines, and indicated the rise or fall of the vocal inflection, graphically derived from the acute, grave, and circumflex accents. An acute accent, represented by an upward slant to the right, denoted the rise of a second, a third, or another small interval. With the establishment of square notation, the intervallic norms became more definite. Rhythmic values were determined according to an elaborate set of rules that varied from century to century and from country to country, so that the transcription of medieval chants became a matter of editorial discretion.

In time embryonic neumes developed into groups of notational cells that were embodied in graphic shapes and that assumed expressive Latin names, such as *punctum* ("point"), *virga* ("comma"), *pes* ("foot"), *clivis* ("declivity"), *scandicus* ("an ascent"), *climacus* ("climaxing"), *torculus* ("torque"), and *porrectus* ("erect"). These gave rise to symbols for ornaments in Baroque music. Thus *pes* became the lower appoggiatura and *clivis* an upper appoggiatura. *Scandicus* became an ascending double appoggiatura and *climacus* a descending double appoggiatura. *Torculus* was the ancestor of the inverted mordent and *porrectus* that of the mordent.

Mensural notation, or notation that can be measured, emerged in the middle of the 13th century, and its invention, or at least its codification, is usually ascribed to Franco of Cologne. In the early centuries of mensural notation, white notes of different shapes were used; black notes appeared in the course of time when a necessity for writing rapid passages arose. The standard notation of note lengths was the following: *maxima*, *longa*, *brevis* (or *breve*), *semibrevis* (or *semibreve*), *minima*, *semiminima*, *fusa*, and *semifusa*. Each of these equaled two or three notes of the next smaller durations; thus *maxima* had two *longas*, a *longa* had two *breves*, a *breve* had two *semibreves*, and so on. As if *maxima* were not long enough, a *larga* that had the value of two or three *maximas* was introduced. It is ironic that the *semibreve* (half-brief) note of the mensural notation became the longest note of modern notation, designated as a whole note, which occupies an entire bar in 4/4 time. It appears that in the Middle Ages time was running at a slower tempo. The shapes of these notes were either oblong or rhomboid, with or without stems attached. *Semiminima* was notated either as a black rhomboid with a stem stuck into it from above like a toothpick in an olive, or else as a white rhomboid with a flag. As musicians became more and more agitated in their rhythmical habits, additional flags were attached to the stems of small notes, and theorists ran out of qualifying prefixes, such as demi-, semi-, hemi-, and the like, with which to designate these very fast notes.

Arithmetically, in modern notation a whole note equals two half notes, a half note equals two quarter notes, and so on. In mensural notation, however, a note could equal either two or three of the next smaller notes. In modern notation a dotted half note equals three quarter notes, but in mensural notation the operation had to be indicated verbally or by a system of ligatures that are most misleading in view of the absence of barlines and other auxiliary symbols. The verbal clues were contained in the adjectives (in Latin, of course) *perfectum* or *imperfectum*. These words did not mean perfection or imperfection in the moral or physical sense but in the etymological Latin sense of completion and incompletion. *Perfectio* ("perfection") was the subdivision of a note into three smaller note values, subdivisions into two being imperfect. Furthermore, there were special terms for the mutual relationships between each pair of adjacent note values. The relationship between *brevis* and *semibrevis* was called *tempus*; the relationship between a *semibrevis* and *minima* was *prolatio* ("prolation"). If both *tempus* and *prolatio* were "perfect," the result was a bar of nine whole notes subdivided into three groups; if the *tempus* were perfect and the *prolatio* imperfect, this denoted three groups, each of which had two beats. If the *tempus* were imperfect but the *prolatio* perfect, then there were two divisions of three beats each. The "perfection" was symbolized by a perfect circle in the time signature; the "imperfection" was indicated by a semicircle that looks like a *C*. In modern notation we still use the sign of imperfection for the 4/4 time signature. (This symbol does not come from Common Time, an error frequently made in interpreting this binary time signature.) Some theologically minded music theorists of the Middle Ages suggested that triple time is perfect because it stands for the Trinity.

Painful complications ensue as we plunge more deeply into ligatures, groups of notes glued together or hanging to one another precariously by the corner of an oblong or to the side of a rhombus. Musicologists who are willing to devote their lives to the inscrutable mysteries of mensural notation come figuratively to blows in their internecine polemics. As a result, no two transcriptions of medieval manuscripts in mensural notation are in agreement.

In modern usage, fractional names designate musical notes: whole note, half note, quarter note, eighth note, sixteenth note, thirty-second note, sixty-fourth note, and so forth. Individual eighth notes have flags attached to them; groups of eighth notes are united by black beams. Sixteenth notes have two flags; their groups are united by double beams. Thirty-second notes have three flags and are united by triple beams, and so forth. Identical graphic symbols are used in all Western music, but the names may differ. Thus, in British usage half notes are called minimas, quarter notes are crotchets, eighth notes are quavers, sixteenth notes are semiquavers, thirty-second notes are demi-semiquavers, sixty-fourth notes are hemidemisemiquavers, and one-hundred-twenty-eighth notes are called semihemidemisemiquavers. A dot next to the note head adds 50 percent to the value of the note. Thus a half note has two quarter notes, and a dotted half note has three. The same augmentations by 50 percent are effected by dots placed after rests.

With the virtual disappearance of special signs indicating ornamentation (mordents, inverted mordents, etc.) in the 19th century, the present system of notation became an entirely workable method of writing notes that correspond precisely to the intended pitch and duration of each tone. The invention of the metronome made it possible to measure metrical units in fractions of a second. Interpretation remained a personal matter, but liberties could be taken only in dynamics, variations in tempo, and the like. True, the written notes did not always reflect the composer's ideal, and some great masters allowed themselves to write passages that could not be performed adequately or even approximately. Beethoven wrote sustained chords in some of his piano sonatas that could not be held by pedal without muddying up the harmony, or by the fingers which were occupied elsewhere. Schumann has a melody in his *Études symphoniques* for piano that is to be played legato in the bass but cannot be carried on without interruption.

The addition of the barline in the notational system is a great metric support, but the persistent habit of stressing the first beat has resulted in a brutalization of the basic rhythmic design. There are numerous examples in great masterpieces in which the composer seems to be following a different beat in his rhythmic design than appears in the metric arrangement. A musical person listening to the rapid finale of Schumann's Piano Concerto will hear an unmistakable rhythm of a slow Viennese waltz, but the conductor must square the apparent contretemps with the soloist. The trouble here is that Schumann notated this passage in rapid 3/4 with stresses on the first and third beats of the first bar and on the second beat of the second bar, the two bars forming a metric unit. A most extraordinary incongruence between the visual notation and auditory perception occurs in the first movement of Brahms's Symphony No. 1, where a rhythmic period of three eighth notes enters om the second beat of 6/8, with the accented notes overlapping the barlines. A modern composer would probably write a bar of 1/8 and then resume 6/8 time until the notated rhythm and meter coincide. Quite often the ear groups several bars into one unit in a fast tempo. When Beethoven indicates that the Scherzo of his Symphony No. 9 is to be perceived in *ritmo di tre battute* ("rhythm of three bars"), he reveals the inadequacy of notation and its incommensurability with auditory perception.

A system that pursued a totally different track from the generally accepted notation was tablature, which indicated graphically the position of each note on the lute, guitar, ukulele, and keyboard instruments. Tablatures were widely used by lute players beginning in the 15th century which then went out of use in the 18th century, together with the lute itself. After three centuries of almost total extinction, the tablature was revived in published editions for the guitar to enable popular performers who could not read music to pick out the necessary chords. The notation for the ukulele, a Hawaiian instrument of the guitar family that became popular in the United States in the first quarter of the 20th century, was always in the form of a tablature, resembling that of the lute but having no historic connection with it. A modern keyboard tablature, Klavarskribo, an Esperanto word for clavier writing that indicates the positions of notes on a diagram of the piano keyboard, was launched in Holland. The word *tablature* comes from the Latin *tabula*, ''board.'' The Italian term for tablature is *intabolatura*, ''intabulation.''

Ultramodern composers of the second half of the 20th century tried to remedy the ills of musical notation with the aid of science, at least as far as meter and rhythm were concerned. Instead of the uncertainties of tempo marks, time signatures, and rhythmical units in metrical frames, some ultramodern notation specifies the duration of each note in time units, usually in seconds or fractions of seconds. Visually, too, a whole note occupies all the room of a bar of 4/4 time, a half note takes up exactly one-half of such a bar, and passages in smaller notes are notated proportionately to the time they consume. In dynamics, the newest notation blithely specifies differences between pianissimo (pp) and pianississimo (ppp), fortissimo (ff) and fortississimo (fff), and so forth, up and down the dynamics range. The trouble is that human performers cannot execute such scientific niceties with any degree of precision or with the requisite aplomb. Electronic instruments come to the rescue.

Such is the perversity of human nature that just as musical notation seemed to achieve a scientific precision, composers of the avant-garde developed a yen for indeterminacy. Indeterminacy is a respectable scientific doctrine, and the theory of probabilities, which is closely related to it, has a mathematical aura that is quite idiosyncratic in its application. A human being is also a tangle of probabilities, however. It is logical, therefore, that ultramodern notation should have absorbed the human element. Xenakis, Stockhausen, Earle Brown, Bussotti, John Cage, and many others in Europe, America, Japan, and Greece have adopted a graphic notation that not only deals in probabilistic elements but that resorts to pictorial representations of human faces experiencing the prescribed emotions, from saintly tranquility to raging madness. When an occasional music staff is inserted in such scores, it may be covered with blobs of black ink or surrealistic geometrical curves. Verbalization of the basic elements of notation expands enormously here, and the performer is often urged to play or sing anything at all. Modern musicians are possessed by a desire to represent new music by visual images.

Notre Dame school. A school that flourished in Paris in the 12th and 13th centuries. Its greatest masters were Leoninus and Perotinus. Whether they were actually attached to the Cathedral of Notre Dame itself is a matter of conjecture, because the cornerstone of the famous church was not laid until the middle of the 12th century, and the construction was not completed for two more centuries.

Novachord. A newfangled electrical device designed to simulate the sound of any known or hypothetical musical instrument. It was invented by Laurens Hammond, who gave its first demonstration in the Commerce Department Auditorium, Washington, D.C., on February 2, 1939.

Novelette. A type of character piece for piano solo introduced by Schumann. It is characterized by a number of melodically unrelated themes that are united by a common rhythmic lift. Incidentally, the name does not mean "a little novel" as may be imagined. Schumann invented it to express his admiration for the English singer Clara Novello. This was not the first time that Schumann had engaged in such word play; he also wrote pieces that he described as *Wiecketten*, after the maiden name of his beloved wife, Clara Wieck. Novelette seems such a beguiling name that many composers have adopted Schumann's playful title, using the term precisely in the sense of "little novels." Did Balakirev, Liadov, and other composers of novelettes ever realize that they were unwittingly paying homage to Clara Novello?

Nummernoper. "Number opera." A fanciful term for an opera in which the principal ingredients—such as arias, vocal ensembles, and instrumental interludes—are clearly separated from each other, or are connected by recitative or spoken dialogue. Virtually all operas before Wagner were number operas, but an argument can be advanced that transitions between separate numbers create a continuity characteristic of music drama of the Wagnerian type. Wagner's theories virtually determined the operatic practice of the second half of the 19th century, but a return to the more formal type of number opera was marked in the 20th century. Modern composers, especially Stravinsky, successfully revived the genre and even took delight in emphasizing its archaic traits.

Nun's fiddle. A whimsical appellation common in Germany in the 14th century for the *tromba marina* because it was popular in convents.

Nuove musiche. Literally, "new musics." Originally the title of a selection of madrigals by the Florentine musician Giulio Caccini published in 1601, it became a slogan of the Camerata, a group of erudite poets, philosophers, and musicians who successfully reversed the musical trend of ever-increasing complexity of polyphonic music in favor of a simple homophonic style of solo arias and madrigals with simple harmonic accompaniments. So potent was the desire on the part of music lovers to return to the original sources of vocal music uncomplicated by artful devices that soon the entire period of the early

17th century was designated as the period of Nuove musiche. The monodic style of Nuove musiche gave birth to opera, oratorio, and cantata and inaugurated the era of the Baroque. The creators of Nuove musiche also established the historically important principle that the text should be the determining factor of musical expression rather than be subordinated to the prearranged melodic structure. The extreme development of Baroque polyphony reversed the stream toward greater complexity, but the predominance of the text over polyphony was once more proclaimed a century and a half later by Gluck and was popularized by Wagner and Debussy.

The Nutcracker. A famous ballet by Tchaikovsky, first performed in St. Petersburg on December 18, 1892. That Tchaikovsky could write this sunlit music in the same period as his mournful *Pathétique* Symphony proves, if proof is needed, that musical inspiration and accomplishment have nothing to do with the psychological states of a composer. The subject of the ballet is taken from the fairy tale *Casse-Noisette* by Alexandre Dumas, which in turn is borrowed from a tale by Hoffmann. A girl dreams of a fight between a nutcracker and mice. She helps the nutcracker, which then is transformed into a handsome prince who takes her into the magic land of sweets and candies. An instrumental suite drawn from the ballet score contains an overture, a march, and six dances: *Dance of the Sugar-Plum Fairy*, in which Tchaikovsky includes the celesta for the first time in any orchestral work, *Ukrainian Dance*; *Trepak*; *Arabian Dance* (coffee); *Chinese Dance* (tea); *Pastorale*; and *Waltz of the Flowers*.

O

O. The small letter *o*, placed over G, D, A, or E in a violin part or that of other string instruments, stands for zero and indicates that the notes so marked must be played on an open string (i.e., without depressing the strings with the fingers). The same symbol appears sometimes in the basso continuo part as a sign that only the bass note or its octave should be used in the accompaniment to a given passage without filling out the harmony. Violinists and other instrumentalists rarely use open strings in pure melodic passages, preferring stopped notes on strings a fifth below the available open string. In double stops, on the other hand, open strings are very handy, and they are virtually indispensable in triple and quadruple stops. Sometimes open strings are prescribed by the composer for reasons of euphony or symbolism. For instance, Saint-Saëns builds his *Danse Macabre* on the open strings, with the E string lowered a semitone to suggest the *diabolus in musica*. Alban Berg specifically indicates open strings in some passages of his Violin Concerto, the theme of which, although dodecaphonic, includes all four open strings of the violin. An anonymous string quartet erroneously attributed to Benjamin Franklin, the manuscript of which was discovered in Paris in 1945, is written entirely for open strings so that the rankest amateurs could play it, but the strings are tuned in an ingenious *scordatura*, so that unexpected and even dissonant harmonies can be formed.

Obbligato. A marking meaning "obligatory" in Italian terminology, originally applied to an instrumental part that was essential in the performance. Through some paradoxical inversion of meaning, the word *obbligato* began to be used, particularly in popular arrangements, to indicate that a part was optional. For instance, a song with cello obbligato would mean that such a cello part would be a desirable addition to the accompaniment but not obligatory.

Oberon. An opera by Carl Maria von Weber, first produced in London on April 12, 1826, with Weber himself conducting on his London tour. Oberon is King of the Elves; Titania is his Queen. Numerous oriental characters spring up here and there. Oberon's self-appointed task in life is to find a pair of lovers undeterred by any misadventure. He succeeds with the help of his magic horn. There is a grand reunion at the end, at the court of Charlemagne. The libretto (in English, because the opera was commissioned by the Covent Garden Theater in London) is magnificent in its absurdity. The glorious overture survives on the concert podium, but the opera is never (well, hardly ever) performed in its entirety.

Objets trouvés. A term introduced by avant-garde painters and sculptors and meaning exactly what it says, "found objects." Marcel Duchamp was probably the first to exhibit an *objet trouvé*, a urinal from a men's lavatory. Man Ray exhibited a sewing machine wrapped up in a piece of canvas, and Andy Warhol managed to create a sensation by selling a Brobdingnagian representation of a Campbell's soup can for a reputed sum of $70,000. A plate with remnants of an unfinished dinner was exhibited as an *objet trouvé*, as was "bagel jewelry," an actual bagel set in a jewelry box. Avant-garde composers made use of musical *objets trouvés* by the simple device of playing another composer's music. An example of an embroidered and encrusted *objet trouvé* is Luciano Berio's *Sinfonia*, incorporating whole chunks of music from Mahler, Ravel, and others.

Oboe. An important wind instrument in which the sound is produced with a double reed. It first appeared toward the middle of the 17th century in France. Its name is derived from the French word *hautbois*, which literally means "high wood." Its range is from B-flat below middle C up to about F over the treble clef staff. The oboe is rather limited in agility, in contrast to the lambent flute or the peripatetic clarinet. It compensates for these real or imaginary deficiencies, however, by the precision of its intonation and by the strength of its sound. Indeed, it can pierce through the entire orchestral fabric as easily as the trumpet. In orchestral writing, oboes are commonly used in pairs, like flutes, clarinets, and bassoons. As a solo instrument, the oboe is not as popular as the flute, clarinet, or even bassoon, but Handel wrote several concertos for it. It is difficult to imagine a solo recital even by a great oboe virtuoso, but such concerts have been given. As the mainstay of the orchestra, the oboe stands unchallenged. It is the oboe that gives the introductory A to tune up the orchestra.

Ocarina. A bulbous flute in the shape of a bird (*ocarina* is probably derived from the Italian word *oca*, a goose) with a mouthpiece and several perforations. Ocarinas are usually manufactured from baked clay; they are often used as whistles. Rimsky-Korsakov includes an ocarina tuned in an alternating scale of whole tones and semitones in the score of his opera-ballet, *Mlada*.

Ocean Symphony. The title given by Anton Rubinstein to his Symphony No. 2 in C major, written when he was only 24 years old. It was first performed in Leipzig on November 14, 1854, and became his most popular symphonic work. The *Ocean* Symphony was criticized as having "too much water and too little ocean," but it endured for half a century as long as its kind of expansive Germanic romanticism held sway. It became a ritual for the New York Philharmonic to open its seasons with the *Ocean* Symphony. Then suddenly something snapped. The work became unacceptable to music lovers, and it simply vanished from the repertory. *Sic transit Oceanus!*

Die Ochsenmenuett. A light opera by the Viennese composer Ignaz Xaver von Seyfried, first produced in Vienna on New Year's Eve, 1823. The silly libretto tells an unfunny and totally unsubstantiated anecdote about Haydn's composing a minuet for his favorite butcher, who sent him an ox as a token of his gratitude. The tune of the minuet was by Seyfried, but the rest of the opera was arranged from various authentic tunes by Haydn. Fortunately for the latter, he was long dead when *The Ox Minuet* was produced.

Octandre. A piece by Edgar Varèse for seven wind instruments and a double bass. *Octandre* means a flower having eight stamens. The piece was first performed in New York on January 13, 1924. Like all Varèse's works at first performances, it aroused shrieks of indignation and dismay from some music critics.

Octave. The only interval in the tempered system that is acoustically pure; it represents the ratio of vibrations of 2:1. The octave sound is the first partial note in the series of overtones and is therefore an integral part of any musical tone. The octave ingredient can be perceived quite clearly by a sensitive ear, even when a single tone is played, and it can be picked out with surprising clarity by silently holding down a piano key and then forcefully striking a key an octave below; the depressed key will respond with an octave sound loud and clear.

The octave is the only Latin-derived name for an interval in English musical terminology. In Latin, *octava* is the ordinal numeral, meaning the eighth, referring to the fact that the octave is the eighth degree of the diatonic scale. Different octaves bear special names, more or less acceptable in international nomenclature. The lowest octave, from the lowest C available on the piano keyboard, is called contraoctave; the next is the great octave, which is followed by the small octave. The octave that begins on middle C is the one-line octave and is usually designated by the letter *C* with a superscript, *C'*. It is followed by *C''*, *C'' ''*, and *C'' ''*. The earliest type of "polyphonic" singing was at the interval of an octave, with boys singing an octave higher than grown men. A curious explanation as to why the octave is the most perfect interval is given in an anonymous medieval music treatise: It is perfect because it was "on the eighth day that Abraham was circumcised.'' Actually, Abraham was quite old when he was circumsised, but his male descendants observed the ritual circumcision on the eighth day of their birth.

Ode. An orchestral work by Igor Stravinsky, in three parts—*Eulogy*, *Eclogue*, and *Epitaph*—written in memory of Natalie Koussevitzky, the famous conductor's wife. The *Eclogue* was originally intended as incidental music to the motion picture *Jane Eyre*, but the film was never produced, and Stravinsky made use of the hunting episode from it for the *Ode*. The work was first performed by the Boston Symphony Orchestra, with Serge Koussevitzky conducting, on October 8, 1943.

Ode to Napoleon. A score for speaking voices, piano, and strings by Schoenberg, written in 1942 in the middle of World War II. Schoenberg took for his texts Byron's poem in which Byron voices his wrath against Napoleon. In his score, Schoenberg makes use of a modified 12-tone technique, ending in a clear major chord. The work was first performed in New York on November 23, 1944.

Odhecaton. The title of the first printed collection of polyphonic music; it means "100 Songs" (*ode*, "song"; *hecaton*, "hundred"). The *Odhecaton* was printed by Petrucci in 1501; actually, there are only 96 songs in the collection, but its historical value would have been great no matter what the number of songs. Only nine of them have a text, but at the time the *Odhecaton* was published, instrumental tunes were commonly sung, and songs were often played on instruments.

Oedipe. An opera by Georges Enesco, first performed in Paris on March 10, 1936. The subject is drawn from the tragedies of Aeschylus and Sophocles, and the basic events of Greek mythology appear in the score. Oedipus inadvertently kills his father and mistakenly marries his mother, but he is vindicated at the tragic end as a victim of fate. The peculiarity of the score is that Enesco does not resort to stylization but internationalizes the theme, even to the point of making use of Rumanian melorhythms.

Oedipus Rex. An opera-oratorio by Igor Stravinsky, first performed in concert form in Paris on May 30, 1927, and on the stage in Vienna on February 23, 1928. To make the legend of Oedipus more timeless, Stravinsky arranged to have the libretto by Jean Cocteau translated into Latin. The music is majestically static, like a row of marble Doric columns. Significant musical phrases are relentlessly reiterated to drive their meaning into the mind of the listener. A narrator recites the events.

Of Thee I Sing. A musical comedy by George Gershwin, first performed in New York on December 26, 1931. The work is a savage thrust at an American presidential campaign conducted on the platform of love. The candidate,

Wintergreen, wins. Instead of marrying the winner of the contest for Miss White House, however, he elects a plainer girl who can really make corn muffins for White House functions. An impeachmemt process is avoided when the vice president, Throttlebottom, marries the beauty contest winner. The lyrics, by Gershwin's brother Ira, are incisive. The leading songs are "Of Thee I Sing" and "Love Is Sweeping the Country." Brooks Atkinson, drama critic of the *New York Times*, found the work "funnier than the government, and not nearly so dangerous." It was the first musical comedy to win a Pulitzer Prize.

Offertory. The fourth division of the Proper of the Mass in the Roman Catholic liturgy. The "offering" here is of bread and wine. The earliest musical procedure of the Offertory contained the reading of psalms, followed by a responsorial chant or some other antiphonal singing. In secular forms, many organ pieces bear the title *Offertory*, but most works of the type are religious motets in a polyphonic setting.

Oh, Bury Me Not on the Lone Prairie. One of those famous American songs whose origin is lost in the stagnant pools of ambiguous historicity. It was first published in 1907 and was included in the 1910 collection *Cowboy Songs* under the title "The Dying Cowboy." Next it appeared in an anthology of Southern ballads published in 1932, with the crucial first line, "Oh, bury me out on the lone prairie," reversing the original injunction not to.

Oh, Promise Me! This lyric promissory note was a last-minute insertion in the operetta *Robin Hood* by Reginald De Koven, produced in Chicago in 1890. The song became a nuptial hit, second in popularity only to Wagner's "Here Comes the Bride."

Oiseaux exotiques. A work for piano, wind instruments, and percussion by Olivier Messiaen in which are incorporated instrumental approximations of bird songs from exotic lands. It was first performed in Paris on March 10, 1956.

Ol' Man River. A song by Jerome Kern with words by Oscar Hammerstein II from their musical *Show Boat*, produced in 1927. Next to Stephen Foster's "Swanee River," it is the most glorious American river song, extolling the mighty Mississippi, which "just keeps rollin' along." Winston Churchill cited it as a song symbolizing the greatness of America.

Old Folks at Home. One of Stephen Foster's most famous songs; he wrote it in 1851 and subsequently sold it for a pittance to the famous minstrel group leader Christy, who then published it as his own. Only after Christy's copyright expired was the injustice righted and Foster's name given as composer in the new edition, but by that time he was dead. The song is commonly known under the title *Swanee River*. Actually, the name comes from the Suwanee River in Florida, whose name Foster, who never lived in the South, picked up from a map.

Oliphant. A Byzantine signal trumpet imported from the Orient and employed for ceremonial occasions. It was made from an elephant's tusk, hence its name. Philologically, the Old French spelling *olifant* is a verbal corruption of the word *elephant*. The instrument penetrated Europe from the East during the Middle Ages.

Olla podrida. "Rotten pot" in Spanish. The term is sometimes applied in the same meaning as the French *potpourri* (which also means "rotten pot") or *olio*—that is, a miscellany or medley of musical or comic dialogues and "exotic" dances at a burlesque show.

The Olympians. An opera by Arthur Bliss, first produced in London on September 29, 1949. The libretto, by J.B. Priestley, depicts the pathetic destiny of once-powerful Greek gods who are reduced to the status of itinerant actors and are allowed to return to Mt. Olympus only for a vacation once a year.

Ombra scene. A "shadow scene," or dramatic episode in opera, taking place in the nether regions, in a cemetery, or in a place where ghosts congregate. It is usually cast in the monodic manner of an accompanied recitative in triadic harmonies. For some reason, the key of E-flat major was *de rigueur* in such scenes. Ombra scenes abound in general pauses, tremolos, exclamations, and other emotional outbursts. The clarinet, French horn, and trombone are favorite instruments for shadow scenes in Baroque operas. Mozart introduces the ghostly statue of the Commendatore in *Don Giovanni* with an ominous trombone passage.

On Hearing the First Cuckoo in Spring. A symphonic poem by Frederick Delius, one of his most popular orchestral works. Its style is romantic, with impressionistic touches. It was first performed in Leipzig on October 2, 1913.

On Wenlock Edge. A suite for tenor, piano, and string quartet by Ralph Vaughan Williams, to a text selected from *A Shropshire Lad* by A.E. Housman. The music is full of spacious modalities and English refrains. It was first performed in London on November 15, 1909.

Ondes Martenot. An electronic keyboard instrument named after its French inventor Maurice Martenot; also known as Ondes Musicales. As in the Thereminovox and other early electronic instruments, the sound is produced heterodynamically, as a differential of two frequencies. It was first exhibited in Paris on April 20, 1928. Several composers have written works employing the Ondes Martenot, and André Jolivet even composed a full-fledged concerto for it.

Opera. In history, in literature, in art, in music, there comes a time when technical elaboration of available means reaches its limit, and a new turn in aesthetics becomes imperative. Such a point was reached in Italy, the historic progenitor of the art of music, toward the end of the 16th century, when a group of enlightened aristocratic men of science, poetry, and music assembled in Florence to discuss further advance in the arts. They assumed the modest name of Camerata, that is, a small chamber, and held regular gatherings in the villa of Count Giovanni Bardi. The participants besides Bardi himself included the poet Ottavio Rinuncini and the musicians Giulio Caccini, Jacopo Peri, and Vincenzo Galilei, father of the famous astronomer. Their project was to return music to the ideal of simplicity that was the essence of ancient Greek music. Accordingly, they published a collection, significantly entitled *Nuove musiche* ("new musics"), containing madrigals and airs by Caccini. The innovation of these pieces consisted in reducing music to a clearly outlined single voice with an accompaniment of static chords, expressly avoiding the polyphonic construction of the Renaissance masters. It was a state of musical entropy, in which the underlying matter remains stable in its solidity. Drawing a parallel from Greek philosophy, so beloved by the Florentine founders of the Camerata, the maxim of Heraclites, "all is flux," immanent in flexible counterpoint, is controverted by the opposing principle of Parmenides, "all is immovable," basic to uniformity of harmonic progressions. The idiom adopted by the "new" musicians was monody, as opposed to counterpoint. Their theatrical productions, marked by monodic harmony, were to be called *dramma per musica*, or "drama by means of music." In the course of time this new type of composition received the name *opera*, which in Italian means simply "work." The greatest contribution to the art of early opera was in the sublime productions of Monteverdi, who introduced such refinements as discords of the dominant seventh and boldly depicted natural events, such as a tempest, in his instrumental accompaniment.

Structurally and historically, opera is a continuation of a suite of madrigals connected by a definite story. An introductory ensemble for instruments established the mood of the work. There were obligatory arias, most of them built on a symmetric plan, with the cadence recapitulating the opening. There were brief duets and climactic choral ensembles. The dramatic development included, almost necessarily, an amorous encounter, an opposition of inimical forces, and a concluding resolution of conflicts. A proverbial "happy ending" was not a necessity in the *dramma per musica*, and the finale of a typical opera may have been tragic, with the main actors meeting death. The principal forms of opera were *opera seria*, with dramatic or tragic content, and *opera buffa*, devoted to entertainment. *Opera seria* included an abundant application of arias; *opera buffa* exercised the spirit of the dance.

From the very inception of opera there was the debate of which was more important: the story represented in the action or the music accompanying that action. The German musician Christoph Willibald von Gluck, who was active mainly in Vienna and Paris in the 18th century, militated against the undue prominence given to singers in operatic productions and maintained that the poetry of the text must be paramount; music was to be the servant of the drama unfolded on the stage. Gluck remained faithful to the origin of opera as a revival of Greek tragedy. The opponent of this view was the Italian Nicola Piccini who, like Gluck, was prominent in Paris. His style of composition was the very antithesis of Gluck's Grecian ideals, but he finally had to yield. Another operatic conflict arose in Paris in the middle of the 18th century, this time along national lines, as the Italian opera composers, who enjoyed the support of the French aristocracy, combatted the popular adherents of French nationalism. The famous philosopher Jean-Jacques Rousseau, himself a composer, went so far as to maintain that the French language, with its weak vowels and uncertain consonants, was unfit for singing. In an extraordinary reversal of his views, Rousseau himself wrote a popular opera with a French libretto.

Italy remained for nearly four centuries the grand mistress of opera. Composers around the world, even such an incomparable genius as Mozart, selected Italian texts for their operas. Italian singers captivated audiences of all nations; opera companies were administered by Italians. French opera was largely the creation of the Florentine music master Lully, who became also the chief composer of French ballet. Italians were greatly adept as librettists. Metastasio, a poet in his own right, supplied libretti to Gluck, Handel, Haydn, and Mozart. Da Ponte, who contributed the libretto to Mozart's *Don Giovanni*, led an adventurous life, was exiled from Europe for adultery, and went to America to teach Italian grammar at Columbia College in New York where he died at the age of nearly 90.

England tended to import Continental musicians to write theatrical music for the London Opera. Henry Purcell, the greatest English composer of the second half of the 17th century, bemoaned his compatriots' inability to write melodious music and proclaimed his determination to emulate the luscious melodies of sunny Italy in his own vocal works. In the 18th century, England was fortunate enough to engage Handel of Saxony as a royal musician to write operas for the London theaters. In opposition, another powerful British faction engaged Bononcini from Italy to provide operatic music. Their rivalry was immortalized in a celebrated stanza:

> *Some say, compar'd to Bononcini*
> *That Mynheer Handel's but a Ninny;*
> *Others aver, that he to Handel*
> *Is scarcely fit to hold a Candle:*
> *Strange all this Difference should be*
> *'Twixt Tweedledum and Tweedledee!*

Patronized by the King of England (who was himself a German, the founder of the Hanover dynasty), Handel wrote a number of operas to Italian libretti for the London stage, but they were unsuccessful. To the supreme good of all music, Handel turned to oratorio with English texts.

It has been said that England produced no opera composers of significance between Purcell and Britten. This ignores the novel type of ballad opera that flourished on the English stage early in the 18th century and its comic sequel, *The Beggar's Opera*, designed to entertain the masses rather than the aristocracy. The glorious musical comedies of the 19th century by Gilbert and Sullivan were direct descendants of ballad opera. Other composers of the 20th century, in addition to Britten, who wrote fine operas were Ralph Vaughan Williams, William Walton, and Michael Tippett.

Opera in the 19th century followed the spirit of the times in embracing Romantic and national ideals. Romantic nationalism was imbued with fantasy, which made it attractive to people of all categories. The first opera that successfully combined such diverse traits was *Der Freischütz* by Carl Maria von Weber. Its contents were colored by magic, its libretto was German, and its musical idiom was nationalistic. This Romantically nationalistic trend was crowned in Germany by the development of a totally different type of opera. The formal elements of arias, vocal ensembles, and independently conceived instrumental parts gave way to the revolutionary creations of Richard Wagner, who wrote his own German libretti on the subject of Germanic history and legend. Wagner's influence on the subsequent development of opera was universal; hardly any operatic composer in any country escaped the influence of his power and his imagination.

Italy continued to provide operas that were formal in structure and songful in treatment. Early in the 19th century this melodious and harmonious Italian operatic style became known as *bel canto* ("beautiful song"), with Donizetti, Bellini, and Rossini as its most proficient purveyors. Dramatic Italian opera was glorified by Giuseppe Verdi, born in the same year, 1813, as Wagner, and who lived a life so long that it projected into the 20th century. Verdi kept the basic elements of Classical opera intact: there was a stately orchestral overture that included melodic allusions to the most important motifs in the entire opera; there were inspired arias and beautifully fashioned vocal ensembles; there was also dramatic tension in the manner of contemporary Romantic literature. Verdi's theatrical art led to the development of the Italian *verismo*, the music drama of verity, whose most brilliant representatives were Puccini, Mascagni, and Leoncavallo. Paradoxically, the only practitioner of verismo on the modern American scene is an Italian, Gian Carlo Menotti, who has never become an American citizen although he has resided most of his life in the United States and has written his own libretti in English.

Opera in the 19th century greatly increased the number of acting parts and augmented their participation in ensembles, in duos, trios, quartets, quintets, sextets, septets, octets, and even nonets. The role of the orchestra was also expanded, with newly chromatic brass instruments enhancing the harmony. To govern this exudation of sound, a conductor was assigned to give necessary cues to singers and orchestral players. The opera plots, enriched by exotic flights of fancy, further complicated the scene. The result was a much inflated spectacle that became known as *grand opera*; its principal dispenser was the newly established opera theater in Paris. Its greatest contributor was Meyerbeer, a German-Jewish composer who established himself in Paris and produced one opera after another, each a veritable archipelago of insular episodes in which arias and choral ensembles were artfully landscaped. Other composers who devoted most of their time and energy to grand opera in France were Auber, Halévy, Gounod, Delibes, Saint-Saëns, and Massenet. Verdi, who never sought popular success abroad, agreed to write a grand opera, *Aida*, to celebrate the opening of the Suez Canal under French auspices. In all such grand operas it was required, for commercial purposes, to include a ballet. Even Wagner had to submit to the fashion by inserting a ballet scene in *Tannhäuser*, but his attempt to meet the Parisian requirements failed dismally when *Tannhäuser* was taken out of the repertory after a few performances. Grand opera presentations included by necessity large, and loud, choruses. Mark Twain, no admirer of European cultures, attended one such spectacle during his trip abroad and commented that the screaming on the stage was louder than during the big fire that burned down the orphanage in his home town.

Russian operatic nationalism arose powerfully with the production of Glinka's *A Life for the Czar* (the title had to be changed after the Russian Revolution to *Ivan Susanin*, after the hero of the opera). The so-called Russian national opera movement followed in the second half of the 19th century with a production of historical Russian operas by Rimsky-Korsakov, Borodin, and Mussorgsky. Tchaikovsky, who was their contemporary, did not join the national trend; instead he wrote operas to meet the Romantic spirit of the Russian people.

A curious type of political nationalism followed the Russian national school during the revolutionary period, a style described as *socialist realism*, which was declared by the Soviet government to be the only proper musical development. Accordingly, when Shostakovich produced his dramatic opera *Lady Macbeth of the District of Mtzensk*, in which he exposed the moral decay of old Russia, it was condemned by the Soviet critics and taken off the boards. It was not until years later that it was allowed to be performed again, but the offensive interlude representing, in a passage for sliding trombones, a sexual act was removed from the score. Prokofiev, too, was harshly criticized for his last opera, *Story of a Real Man*, even though it depicted a heroic deed of a Soviet pilot during World War II. This time, the official objection was the alleged excessive use of dissonances. It was eventually allowed to return to the stage, but by then Prokofiev had died.

Meanwhile, Wagner's influence remained incalculable among European composers, particularly in Germany. The greatest and most original opera composer in the Wagnerian mold was Richard Strauss, whose *Salomé* and *Elektra* reach the height of modern harmony and vocal complexity. National German opera, on the other hand, free of Wagnerian domination, is represented by Hindemith's *Mathis der Maler*.

In France, operatic development took a different course, that of impressionism, in which dramatic elements were understated rather than thrust forcefully upon the ear. The unquestionable masterpiece of this style was Debussy's *Pelléas et Mélisande*; in its score, the powerful dramatic events were conveyed in music by careful distillation of emotional expression.

Romantic nationalism was the natural style of operatic production among ethnic minorities within the sprawling Austro-Hungarian Empire. Smetana and Dvořák expressed their Czech sentiment mainly through their instrumental music, but they also wrote operas to libretti in the Czech language. A modern representative of Czech opera was Janáček, who excelled both in dramatic and fairy-tale spectacles. In Hungary, Kodály wrote a national comic opera *Háry János*; his close contemporary Béla Bartók limited his operatic activities to a short opera, *Bluebeard's Castle*.

Variegated as were opera productions at the threshold of the 20th century, a veritable upheaval took place when opera composers adopted the ultramodern technique of composition elaborated by Schoenberg and his disciples. Of these creations, *Wozzeck* by Alban Berg was clad in atonality (but not yet dodecaphony), dissonant counterpoint, and neo-Baroque terms. Schoenberg preferred limited operatic forms of expressionism, applying allusion without direct depiction and premonitions without realization, so that an atmosphere of penetrating mystery and mystical presentiment was established, exemplified by *Die glückliche Hand* and particularly his unfinished opera, *Moses und Aron*.

The United States has never been an operatic nation. Attempts to produce genuine native operas by 19th-century American composers resulted in poor imitations of contemporary Italian models. Although the Italian management of the Metropolitan Opera House in New York expressed its eagerness to present an American opera, it did not succeed in doing so until 1906, when it staged a short-lived opera by Frederick Converse. Its subsequent productions of American operas by Howard Hanson, Deems Taylor, Samuel Barber, and others inevitably failed. Opera was simply not in the American arteries and veins; American hearts did not respond to the old tinseled glory of European operatic grandeur. Instead, they created a new tradition of gorgeously crafted musical comedies that were half operas, half revues. Gershwin's *Porgy and*

Bess, announced as a "folk opera," became an American classic without adhering to the tradition of European opera. Finally, in the second half of the 20th century, American musicians inaugurated a modernistic operatic genre, a surrealistic collocation of contemporary events and dreamlike inconsistencies. The first work of this heterogeneous genre was the opera by Virgil Thomson, *Four Saints in Three Acts*, to a libretto by Gertrude Stein. Actually, there were in it many more saints than four and one act more than three, but this sort of oneiric inequity challenged and fascinated the listener. Systematic mixture of phantasmagorical reality in American opera was bewilderingly but somehow convincingly demonstrated in the hypnopompic opera *Einstein on the Beach* by Philip Glass. John Adams artfully combined a historic libretto with neo-Romantic minimalistic music in his would-be political opera *Nixon in China*. An utterly novel operatic event, cleverly named *Europera*, created by John Cage, consisted of a number of selections from European 19th-century operas chosen by means of chance operations. Its immediate impact on the audience was that of a *fata morgana*, a mirage of familiar motifs arranged in arbitrary sequences.

Opera buffa. Comic opera, generated as an opposite to *opera seria*. In a typical cast of an opera buffa, there are standard comic characters, some of which are borrowed from the commedia dell'arte. Opera buffa thrives on schemes and stratagems found in comedies of Shakespeare, Molière, and other classics of dramatic literature. Such plays are replete with mistaken identities, disguises, deceptions, and intrigues, but virtue triumphs in the end. The dupes forgive their tormentors, young couples are united, and the spirit of entertainment overcomes all the blatant absurdities in the action.

Opéra comique. This French term does not mean comic opera. When opéra comique became a regular art form in the 18th century, the word *comique* had dignified connotations, on a par with Dante's *La divina commedia*, which is anything but a comedy. The music of comic opera was of a light dramatic texture, often introducing concepts of morality and proper social behavior. In the 19th century in France, opéra comique denoted an opera with spoken dialogue. The Paris Opéra house (called the Opéra Comique) was originally the theater intended for the production of French dramatic works that contained musical numbers and spoken dialogues in about equal measure, but this opera house also mounted productions such as Bizet's *Carmen*, which could hardly be called comique.

Opera seria. Italian for "serious opera." It is virtually identical with the concept of grand opera; it denotes an eloquent music drama replete with emotional upheavals, tragic conflicts, scenes of triumph and disaster, with insanity, murders, and suicides filling the action. By tradition, an opera seria ought to have at least three acts but may well extend into five acts. It may also include ballet. The opposite of opera seria is opera buffa.

Operetta. Italian diminutive of *opera*; as such, it describes a short operatic production that includes spoken dialogue. The genre acquired popularity in the 19th century. Operetta composers, of whom the most famous were Johann Strauss in Vienna and Offenbach in Paris, subjected the gods and heroes of Greek mythology, so revered by opera composers, to merciful ridicule and used popular dances in place of the court ballets of old. Offenbach makes Orpheus dance the cancan, regarded in his time as shockingly vulgar. Gilbert and Sullivan, the twin geniuses of English operetta, directed their devastating wit against the upper classes of Great Britain in their *Pirates of Penzance.* In Vienna, the "Waltz King" Johann Strauss wrote light operettas without trying to demolish the society in which he lived, as in the perennial favorite *Die Fledermaus.* In the United States, operetta assumed the form of musical comedy, eventually known simply by its adjective, musical. *Show Boat* by Jerome Kern, *Of Thee I Sing* by George Gershwin, and *South Pacific* by Richard Rodgers presented an appealing mixture of romance and humor.

So-called serious composers avoided the contamination of popular musical theater. Neither Beethoven nor Wagner, neither Verdi nor Gounod ever wrote operettas. The Russians never practiced the art. Stravinsky wrote short operas, but the solemnity of their subjects and musical treatment prevented them from falling into the class of operetta.

Ophicleide. A large, deep-toned brass instrument. The name means literally "serpent with keys," derived from the Greek *ophis*, "serpent," and *kleidos*, genitive form of "key." George Bernard Shaw volunteered the information that his uncle played it and then "perished by his own hand." The ophicleide became extinct shortly after Shaw's uncle's suicide and was replaced by the tuba.

Opus number. The number assigned for chronological identification of a work, or group of works, by a particular composer. Unfortunately, composers and their publishers seldom were entirely accurate in coordinating the chronology with the opus numbers. For instance, Chopin's Piano Concerto in F minor, bearing the opus number 21, was actually composed a year earlier than his Piano Concerto in E minor, which bears the opus number 11. The use of opus numbers became an established practice in the 19th century, but it fell off among many modern composers. Mozart's works are identified not by opus numbers but by K. numbers, after Köchel, the first Mozart cataloguer. The word *opus* itself means "work" in Latin. Its common abbreviation is op.

Oratorio. The term oratorio is a metonymy. In Italian it defines a place to pray; its metonymy is a musical work of prayerful content. Oratorio originated about

1600 in Rome, anticipating by a year or so the development of opera in Florence. The spiritual father of oratorio was Philip Neri, who opened services combining sacred plays with choral episodes for the edification and enlightenment of youth, at a time when the Reformation in Europe was beginning to undermine the reigning Catholic church. For this he was beatified and later canonized, the only musician in all history to obtain sainthood. Whereas opera extolled the heroic deeds of mythological (mostly Greek) personages, oratorio glorified biblical events. The earliest composers of oratorio were Cavalieri and Carissmi, who used the Latin scriptures for their texts. The Germans were the first outside Italy to embrace the art of oratorio, using the vernacular. Thus Schütz produced a *Christmas Oratorio* in Dresden. Bach combined six cantatas into an oratorio to be performed on six successive days, from Christmas to Epiphany. After he settled in England, Handel produced a number of oratorios on biblical subjects to English words, culminating with *Messiah*, the best known oratorio in Christendom. Haydn's most elaborate oratorio was *Creation*. (A stagehand billed the London management "for help in Creation.") Ludwig Spohr wrote in English the oratorios *The Last Hours of the Saviour* and *The Fall of Babylon*. Mendelssohn contributed one of the greatest biblical oratorios in *Elijah*. Liszt glorified the Savior in his oratorio *Christus*. Saint Saëns composed a dramatic oratorio, *Le Déluge*, in an operatic style. Elgar contributed several oratorios in a characteristic grandiose manner. Modern composers modified the solemnity of classical oratorios by using advanced harmonic idioms; typical of these are Honegger's *King David* and Walton's *Belshazzar's Feast*. A type of composition defined as *secular oratorio* became popular in the 20th century; it made use of nonbiblical dramatic subjects, employing dissonant elements. Stravinsky's oratorio *The Flood* was written on a biblical subject but used dodecaphonic techniques.

Orchestra. Like so many basic terms in music (as, for example, *theater*, *symphony*, *chorus*, and *music* itself), the word *orchestra* is derived from ancient Greek usage; it designated the circular space in the theater, with seats of marble for important persons. By the process of metonymy, the musical group performing therein became itself known as an orchestra. As such, it comprised a variety of instruments. In the Classical period of the 18th century, the orchestra had a string section, a wind section, and a percussion section. The string section was subdivided into first and second violins, violas, cellos, and double basses; the wind section included the woodwinds of two flutes, two oboes, and two bassoons, and the brass, consisting of two French horns and two trumpets. To this was added the pair of kettledrums, tuned to the tonic and the dominant pitches of the principal key of the work. The clarinet was a later entrant; early symphonies of Mozart and Haydn lacked parts for clarinets. The trombone and bass tuba were included in the orchestra by the end of the 18th century to support the brass section, as was the double bassoon, which supplied a deep bass for the woodwinds. The English horn, tuned a fifth below the oboe, appeared as a symphonic instrument for the first time in a symphony of César Franck.

It was not until well into the 19th century that a symphony orchestra acquired a conductor, who stood between the first and second violin sections. There is a story, quite possibly true, that when the conductor of a Russian court orchestra under the Czars led an Imperial visitor through the orchestra, indicating the positions of the first and second violins, the visitor exclaimed: "Second violins in the Czar's orchestra! All must be first!" *Se non è vero, è ben trovato* ("If not true, it is well imagined").

With the advent of the novel form of symphonic poem in the middle of the 19th century, the orchestra was greatly expanded. A high flute known as the piccolo ("a little one") was added to augment the sonority; it was used for the first time in a symphony in the finale of Beethoven's Symphony No. 5. New instruments appeared, among them the so-called Wagner tuba, which was really a modified French horn. The saxophone (named after its inventor, Sax) entered the musical stage in the middle of the 19th century but was used in symphonic literature only as a curiosity; instead it had tremendous popularity in jazz. Then there were instruments that were employed once or twice in the entire orchestral literature—for instance, the heckelphone, a baritone oboe named after its inventor, Heckel. It had a part in the *Sinfonia domestica* of Richard Strauss. The piano entered the orchestra in the works of modern composers of the 20th century; other keyboard instruments included the celesta ("heavenly"), used already by Tchaikovsky, and the xylophone ("wood sound"). In addition, modernists included the time-honored guitar and mandolin. Drums of all kinds joined the percussion section of the orchestra, among them snare drums, bass drums, and such exotic instruments as congos, guïros, and claves. The placing of orchestral instruments underwent a sea change. In many orchestras, conductors placed both violin sections on their left and the cellos on their right. The violas were in the center, and the double basses were kept in the back of the orchestra. The woodwinds were usually placed in a front row facing the conductor, and the brass were disposed behind them. The drummers were given a spot wherever there was room for them.

L'Orfeo. A "fable in music" by Claudio Monteverdi, first performed privately in Mantua on February 22, 1607, and publicly two days later at the Court of Mantua. The libretto follows the familiar legend of Orpheus trying to recover his beloved Euridice from the Kingdom of the Dead. For aesthetic reasons, Monteverdi omitted the demise of Orpheus, who was dismembered by a mob of crazed corybantes. Instead, Orpheus is taken to Elysium by Apollo. The historical significance of *L'Orfeo* lies in its consistent monodic structure, in which the voice predominates, and in its orchestration, which includes clavicembalos, harps, trombones, cornetts, a clarino (a high trumpet), recorders, organs, and a large contingent of string instruments.

Orfeo ed Euridice. An opera by Christoph Willibald von Gluck, subtitled *azione teatrale per musica*, "theatrical action in music," first produced in Vienna on October 5, 1762, in Italian, with the part of Orfeo sung by the famous castrato Gaetano Guadagni. The work acquired its greatest historical significance after its performance with a French libretto in Paris on August 2, 1774. The opera demonstrates Gluck's doctrine of subordinating music to the text to achieve maximum dramatic verity. The story follows the Greek myth of the singer Orpheus trying to recover his beloved Euridice from the land of death, and losing her when he fails to obey the injunction not to look back at Hell's entrance.

Organ. The pipe organ is the largest of the keyboard instruments. Its very appearance is most imposing with its several rows of vertical pipes, usually arranged in a tasteful symmetrical position. It has two or more manuals, or keyboards, and a complex system of stops, or registers, that govern the tone color. It also has a pedal keyboard; a master organist must therefore be a virtuoso with his feet as well as with his hands. His musicianship must be of such a high caliber as to enable him to coordinate the multiple devices of his instrument in order to produce optimum results. The organ is thus a simulacrum of a full orchestra

A strict hierarchy is maintained in planning the manuals, but each manual, whatever its order of importance, can give an adequate rendition of the music. The most prominent manual bears the proud name of the great organ, which is supplied with the loudest stops. The second manual is the swell organ, which enables the organist to produce a tremendous crescendo. The third manual is called choir organ; it is used for the purpose of accompaniment. The solo organ is designed to bring out a special instrumental tone color. In large modern organs there is a fifth manual, the echo organ, which can produce the effect of a distant sound. The manuals are arranged in staircase-like steps, so that the great organ is the nearest to the player, and the echo organ is the highest. The order of the lower manuals may differ depending on the manufacturer. In any case, the organist's torso must be constantly exercised in reaching out for the various manuals. Considering that his feet must be very agile, the organist is obliged to perform physical work in excess of all other instrumentalists. Fortunately, there is a plethora of ingenious helping devices for the organist at the console. The pedal organ sounds an octave below the manuals. The stops of the pedal are so fixed that the sound may be lowered two and even three octaves. The stops are named according to the sizes of the sets of pipes that they activate. The normal pitch of the manual commands an 8-foot stop, called the open diapason stop, which opens a pipe approximately 8 feet long. Other pipes, 4 feet long and 2 feet long, sound respectively an octave or two octaves higher. In the low range, there is a 16-foot pipe and a 32-foot pipe, and even a 64-foot pipe, which will produce sounds two, three, and four octaves lower than the given note. Both the manuals and the pedals have special stops that can bring into play upper or lower octaves, or indeed all of them together, producing a gigantic unison that lends the particular magnificence to a cathedral organ. And that is not all. There are couplers by which two manuals can be connected, so that the organist can amplify the sound by playing on only one of these coupled manuals. And it is also possible to double the sound an octave above or below by these couplers. Furthermore, the organist can prepare the registration, that is, the system of stops, in advance so that he can start playing in octaves or double octaves, both in the manuals and in the pedals, and in desired tone colors. Special stops can be interconnected selectively or for the entire organ. Hence the expression "pulling out all the stops" to describe an organ in full glory, sound, and fury. (The metaphor obviously has sarcastic connotations when applied to a salesman or a politician.)

The names of the organ stops provide a whole inventory of acoustical terms. The king of the stops is the diapason stop, which implies a totality of tones (diapason means "through all" in Greek). Metaphorically, the word can be used in the same sense as gamut, meaning the entire compass of audible sounds from the lowest to the highest. Other stops are named after the instruments they attempt to imitate (flute, oboe, clarinet, bassoon, strings, and so on). Two registrations have poetic names—vox angelica and vox humana. Obviously, the first is supposed to convey the impressions of an angel singing solo and the second the voice of a human. Much sarcasm has been poured on the bland, effeminate tone of the angelic registration. And the human stop suggested to the celebrated 18th-century British historian, Dr. Burney, "the cracked voice of an old woman of ninety." Perhaps he had the bad luck to listen to a poor organist playing on a poor organ.

The spirit of competition in building larger and larger organs is particularly strong in the United States. The organ in the Chicago Stadium has six manuals and 828 stops. One of the most elaborate electronic organs ever built was constructed for Carnegie Hall in New York in 1974. It has 192 speakers in 29 cabinets and five manuals with a frequency range from 16 to 20,000 cycles. According to reports, the Convention Hall in Atlantic City boasts of a Brobdingnagian organ with seven manuals and 1,200 stops.

Organum. A term predominantly used for early polyphonic music that developed between A.D. 900 and 1200. Its earliest kind of composition consisted of a tenor part, with the addition of one, two, or at most three contrapuntal parts. The only intervals used were octaves and fifths, but perfect fourths resulted when the fifth note was inserted between two octave points. To the modern ear, such an organum sounds extremely arid and seems no more polyphonic than a mechanical duplication. This view is erroneous, for the actual practice of the masters of organum was much more free than the naked definitions implied. Indeed, contrary and oblique motions between the tenor and the contrapuntal voices were introduced as soon as the practice spread in general church usage. It became possible, for instance, to move from an octave to a fifth in contrary motion, and vice versa, and even use dissonant passing tones from one "legitimate" interval to another. Another century saw the development of melismatic organum in which contrapuntal parts were assigned florid passages, while the principal voice continued to hold the original tone. Hence its term *tenor*, that is, a "tenant," or "one who holds." With the advent of mensural counterpoint and notation, the art of organum became a complex discipline of polyphonic writing. The most notable achievements in this highly developed organum were reached by the two great masters of the Notre Dame school in Paris, Leoninus and Perotinus. The peak of the organum era of composition was achieved with the impressive *organa quadrupla*, in which the principal voice was accompanied by three intricate contrapuntal voices.

Orphée aux enfers (Orpheus in Hell). An opera by Jacques Offenbach, first produced in Paris on October 21, 1858. The gods of Olympus are here exposed as bumbling creatures intent on having their pleasure on Earth rather than in Heaven. Orpheus is in love with a shepherdess, and Jupiter is attracted by Eurydice, the wife of Orpheus. Abducted by Hades, Eurydice eventually becomes a Bacchante. The score includes a cancan, which shocked the sensibilities of some proper Parisians. Incidentally, Saint-Saëns makes a humorous use of the cancan from *Orphée aux enfers* in the section on the "Tortoise" in his *Carnival of the Animals*; the connection here is that Orpheus supposedly constructed his own lute from a tortoise shell.

Orphéon. A choral society in France in the 19th century with a membership recruited mainly among amateurs. It was named after the mythical singer Orpheus, whose art could enchant humans and animals alike and move inanimate objects. The Orphéon became an important branch of musical education in France; several periodicals were devoted to its activities, among them *La France Orphéonique* and *L'Echo des Orphéons*. In Barcelona, the Orfeo Catalán was organized with the purpose of performances of choral and other music. In Brazil, Villa-Lobos founded an "Orpheonic concentration," in which thousands of school children participated. The repertory of the original French Orphéon was enlarged by works specially written by Berlioz, Gounod, and others. In England, an Orpheonic Choral Festival was staged in 1860, with the participation of thousands. Toward the end of the 19th century, the extent of activities of the Orpheon abated, and in the 20th century the movement went into decline.

Ostinato. One of the few Italian terms in music that mean exactly what they say. The term means "obstinate" and came into musical usage about 1700 in the sense of *basso continuo obbligato*, "obligatory continous bass figure." The earliest dictionary definition, in Walther's *Musikalisches Lexikon*, was "that figure which once begun is continued, and never deviated from." A more modern and definitive description was given by Riemann: "Ostinato is the continued recurrence of a theme accompanied by constantly changing contrapuntal parts." Thus the practice of ostinato involves the dual elements of constancy: an "obstinate" constancy of the theme and the constant variations in contrapuntal voices. The ostinato is therefore both the binding and the diversifying substance of a musical composition.

Long before the term became part of musical terminology, the practice of repetition of the thematic phrase became common in motets and canons. Secular motives in medieval polyphonic compositions are particularly notable when regarded as early occurrences of ostinato figures. The street vendor's cry "fresh strawberries, wild blackberries" occurs in a French medieval motet. It must be observed, however, that such incidental uses of melodic and rhythmic repetition of a musical phrase are natural manifestations of folksongs and vocal compositions, and therefore they cannot be regarded as a conscious and technical application of the ostinato technique.

It is most tempting to seek the sources of ostinato in oriental music, particularly in the Indian ragas, or in modern jazz techniques, such as boogie-woogie, riff, and stomp, but such citations are misleading. Equally misleading is the notion of explaining composition in 12 tones as a manifestation of the ostinato technique. The true ostinato is the brainchild of the Baroque, and the forms in which ostinato is applied properly and consistently are the passacaglia, the chaconne, and their relatives. In these forms, the ostinato appears invariably in the bass and therefore becomes a true basso ostinato. The majestic creations of Bach in these forms are justly compared with the glorious achievements of Gothic architecture or epic poems in literature. With the waning of the Baroque in the middle of the 18th century, the use of the basso ostinato gradually declined. In Classical music, melody was the queen and the bass was the faithful servant. Obviously, such a base servant could not be obstinate. Indeed, Mozart and Haydn found the use of the governing basso ostinato artificial and "unnatural." Samples of *ritmo ostinato*, that is, "persistent rhythm" in the bass part, are found in Mozart's sacred music, but even in such works a certain variation of rhythmic figures is easily discernible.

Interest in the "artificial" devices of the ostinato technique revived toward the end of the 19th century. The finale of the Symphony No. 4 of Brahms has an ostinato. Max Reger, a Baroque revenant, wrote such passages like a Bach incarnate. The first opus number by Anton von Webern bears the title *Passacaglia*, implying an ostinato technique. In his opera *Lulu*, written in the 12-tone idiom, Alban Berg includes a similar ostinato movement. Implicit formations peculiar to the ostinato technique can be found in the piano works of Béla Bartók amd Hindemith. And, naturally, composers of neo-Classical music find the ostinato formula most congenial.

Otello. An opera by Giuseppe Verdi, first produced in Milan on February 5, 1887. The masterly libretto by Boito is faithful to Shakespeare's play from which it is derived, and the Italian text is exemplary. (The spelling "Otello," without an *h*, is proper in Italian.) Otello is a Moor who leads the Venetian army to victories over the Turks. Provoked by Iago, his malicious aide-de-camp, he suspects his wife Desdemona of infidelity and strangles her. When he finds out his monstrous error, he stabs himself to death. The opera, which Verdi completed at the age of 73, is remarkable for its departure from the style and idiom of his previous operas, toward the modern concept of music drama.

Over There. A celebrated patriotic song that George M. Cohan wrote in 1917 shortly after the United States entered the war against Germany. It sold more than 2 million copies of sheet music and a million phonograph records. Caruso sang it for the American troops. Cohan received the Congressional Medal of Honor for the song, which was featured in Cohan's 1942 movie biography, *Yankee Doodle Dandy.*

Overture. One of the most important genera of instrumental composition. Originally, the overture played only an ancillary role, as an opening to a play, opera, or ballet; in fact, the word *overture* comes from the French *ouverture,* an "opening." An overture to an opera served often as a thematic table of contents, with the tunes of the most important arias, choruses, and instrumental interludes passing in review and preparing the listener for the melodic joys that occur in the work. As a musical form, the overture made its first appearance in France in the 17th century, and the practice, particularly by Lully, gave rise to a special form of the so-called French overture, which consisted of two contrasting sections, the first being in a slow tempo marked by dotted rhythms and concluding on the dominant of the principal key, and the second part in a faster tempo, often culminating in a fugal development. This binary form later expanded into a ternary structure by the simple expedient of returning to the initial slow part, varied at will. The French overture was also much in use in instrumental suites. In the 18th century, the French overture went into decline and was replaced by the more vivacious Italian overture. The slow movement was placed in the middle between two fast sections; such a formation was obviously more exhilarating to the listener than the French genre in which the overture began and ended in slow motion. In early Italian operas, the overture was called *sinfonia*, that is, an instrumental section without singing, and, in more recent times, *preludio*. The "summary overture," which incorporates materials from the opera itself, is exemplified by Mozart's overtures to *Don Giovanni* and *The Magic Flute*, Beethoven's three *Leonore Overtures*, Weber's *Freischütz Overture*, all Meyerbeer's overtures, and virtually all overtures by Russian composers of the 19th century. Wagner's overtures to his early operas and *Die Meistersinger* belong to the category of summary overtures, but in his music dramas of the later period, and particularly in *Der Ring des Nibelungen*, he abandoned the idea of using material from the opera itself and returned to the prelude, usually of short duration, to introduce the opera. Richard Strauss followed the Wagnerian type of introduction in his own operas, and so did a great majority of modern opera composers, including Puccini and composers of the verismo school. Only the Russians of the Soviet period remained faithful to the Italian summary overture.

Overtures form an integral part of scores of incidental music for dramatic performances. In numerous cases, even operas by famous composers drop out of the repertory, while their overtures continue their independent lives on the concert stage. Performances of Beethoven's *Fidelio* are relatively rare, but his *Leonore Overtures* are played constantly. Rossini's opera *William Tell* has virtually disappeared from the repertory, but its overture is one of the most popular pieces of the concert repertory. A special genre of overture is the concert overture, not connected with and not intended for any opera. Among the most famous are the *Fingal's Cave Overture* by Mendelssohn, *Le Carnaval romain Overture* by Berlioz, the *Faust Overture* by Wagner, and two by Brahms, the *Academic Festival Overture* and the *Tragic Overture*. Beethoven's *Egmont Overture* is part of his incidental music to Goethe's *Egmont*; Mendelssohn's *Overture* to *A Midsummer Night's Dream* is an overture to Shakespeare's play. Among overtures in a lighter vein, the concert overture *Poet and Peasant* by Franz von Suppé achieved a tremendous popularity that has showed no signs of abating for well over a century.

Oxford Symphony. Symphony No. 92 by Haydn (1789), in G major. The title is misleading because Haydn did not compose it especially for the university town of Oxford, England, but had it performed there during his trip to England. He was rewarded for it by an honorary degree of Doctor of Music.

P

Pacific 231. A symphonic work movement by Arthur Honegger, first performed in Paris on May 8, 1924. The designation *231* indicates the number of wheels (2–3–1) on the American locomotive of the Pacific type. Honegger explained that he was as passionately infatuated with locomotives as other men are with horses or women. The score is a highly effective, although rudimentary, representation of accelerated motion, beginning with one note to a bar, and progressing through two, three, four, five, and six, picking up the tempo as a locomotive gains speed. There is a lyric middle section before *Pacific 231* puffs down to a stop.

A Pagan Poem. A work for piano and orchestra by the American composer Charles Martin Loeffler, inspired by an eclogue of Virgil, in which the central character is a sorceress. It was first performed in Boston on November 22, 1907, and its free mixture of archaic counterpoint and impressionistic colors pleased the public and the critics until this type of synthetic paganism went out of fashion.

Page turner. A necessary adjunct to the pianist in a chamber music ensemble and to a piano accompanist in song recitals. He (occasionally, she) sits on the player's left and turns the music score, holding the right tip of the page delicately between the fingers. Under no circumstances should the page turner put an arm across the pianist's field of vision. Any facial expression of aesthetic delight or, still worse, a grimace of disgust is impermissible. Any attempt at humming, rhythmic breathing, or similar musical or unmusical sounds are criminal offenses. An ideal page turner must be unobtrusive, respectful, and helpful. The American composer Pauline Oliveros raised the page turner to the status of a full-fledged participant in a piece titled *Trio for Violin, Piano, and Page Turner*.

Pagliacci. An opera by Ruggiero Leoncavallo, first performed in Milan on May 21, 1892, in which he made a deliberate effort to emulate the success of

Mascagni's *Cavalleria rusticana*, produced about two years before *Pagliacci*. He succeeded beyond all expectations; *Pagliacci* attained greater popularity than its model. Because the two operas are short, they are invariably paired like symmetric twins on operatic playbills and are commonly referred to as *Cav* and *Pag*. With these two works, Leoncavallo and Mascagni inaugurated a realistic movement in opera that came to be known as verismo. The correct title of Leoncavallo's opera is *Pagliacci*, not *I pagliacci*, as often listed. (The original manuscript score in the Library of Congress in Washington, D.C., has no definite plural article *I* on its title page.) There is, in fact, no reason why the Italian title should be retained at all, for it is translatable without any difficulty as simply *Clowns*. (Incidentally, the pronunciation is pah-lya-chee, not, as often monstrously perverted, pa-glee-ah-kee.) The story of *Pagliacci* is derived from an actual event when an actor killed his unfaithful wife after a theatrical performance in which they both took part. (Leoncavallo's father was the judge at the murder trial.) The opera is set as a play within a play; a group of traveling actors performs in a booth in the center of the stage. The cast of characters is that of the commedia dell'arte. Just before the curtain rises in the booth, the clown learns that his wife, who is Columbine in the play within the play, has a lover. He sings his famous aria (with which Caruso moved a generation of operagoers to tears), lamenting the necessity of putting on a clown's garb when his heart is breaking. As the play progresses, he begins to identify himself with the character of the drama. He demands to know the name of his wife's lover. Horrified at the reality of his actions, she refuses, and he stabs her to death. Her lover rushes in from the stage audience and is killed in turn. The clown then announces to the shocked spectators, "*La commedia è finita.*" (*Commedia* is the generic term for any play, including a tragedy.)

Palestrina. An opera by Hans Erich Pfitzner, to his own libretto, first performed in Munich on June 12, 1917. It is subtitled *Musikalische Legende* to account for its notion that Palestrina wrote his famous Mass for Pope Marcellus at the behest of the angels in order to convince the skeptical members of the Council of Trent that polyphony is, and ought to be, an integral part of church music. The score of *Palestrina* has its moments of academic grandeur.

Pampeana. The generic title that Alberto Ginastera attached to his works inspired by the music of the pampas. The first was for violin and piano (1947), the second for cello and piano (1950), and the third for orchestra, under the specific title *Pastoral* Symphony (1954).

Pandiatonicism. A "totally diatonic" technique of composition formulated circa 1937, freely dissonant in diatonic content, pyramidal in structure with large intervals in the low register, loyal to the primacy of the tonic, subdominant, and dominant in harmonization, and thus suitable for neo-Baroque works as written by Stravinsky, Casella, and others.

Panpipe. The most ancient of wind instruments, consisting of several reeds of different sizes bound together. It is the prototype of the mouth organ, with reeds arranged to produce a continuous diatonic scale. Panpipes exist in all primitive cultures. In South American countries they are known under various names: *antara* in Peru, *rondador* in Ecuador, *capador* in Colombia, and *sico* in Bolivia. In China, primitive panpipes are arranged in two mutually exclusive whole-tone scales, one of which is regarded as a masculine symbol and the other as feminine.

Pantoum. A Malaysian word describing a particular form of poetry popular in Indochina. In his search for exotic descriptions, Ravel attached it to the Scherzo in his Piano Trio, borrowing it from a poem by Victor Hugo.

Papillons. A piano suite of 12 pieces by Schumann, completed in 1831 and published as op. 2; they are descriptive of fleeting butterflies in feminine disguises. Schumann was inspired by the Romantic novel *Flegeljahre (Years of Indiscretion)* by Jean-Paul Richter. The lambent motive might well reflect Schumann's own indiscretion, for it is based on the notes A, E-flat, C, and B, spelling (in German nomenclature in which E-flat is Es, that is, S, and B is H) Asch, the town where he experienced his first infatuation. He used the same theme in his later piano work *Carnaval.*

Parable aria. A type of aria, much in vogue in the 18th century, in which the singer expresses emotions by way of a parable or metaphor. A famous example is the protestation of one of the ladies in Mozart's *Così fan tutte* that she will remain as firm as a rock in resisting temptation; the rock is the crux of the metaphor in the parable.

Paradiddle. A rhythmic drum roll consisting of four rapid, even notes struck with the right and left hands alternately. Paradiddle flamflam is a paradiddle followed by two notes of twice the value (e.g., four sixteenth notes followed by two eighth notes).

Paraphrases and transcriptions. When music became a democratic art in the 19th century, both the aristocracy and the middle class had pianos or harmoniums in their drawing rooms, and professional musicians found a new outlet for their wares. Music was brought to the people; opera and symphony had to be reduced to manageable proportions to be made accessible to the masses. Popular arias, marches, and ballet numbers from favorite operas were arranged by highly capable musicians for the common instrument of the century, the pianoforte. Amateur adults and young children were offered arrangements of Classical masterpieces that were not only musically adequate but also provided a social means of musical communication and entertainment. German publishers put out reams of musical literature for piano four hands or piano solo. Some great pianists, themselves composers of stature, were not averse to participating in this democratization of music. Liszt made piano transcriptions of opera and symphonic compositions, as well of songs of Schubert and Schumann; he also wrote fantasies on the motifs of current opera favorites. Liszt's teacher and Beethoven's pupil, Carl Czerny, took time off from writing his myriad piano exercises to publish arrangements of operatic airs. Such arrangements were eminently practical, acquainting music lovers with the operatic and symphonic music of the day.

Liszt introduced semantic distinctions among various categories of transcriptions. The most literal arrangement was, in his terminology, an *Übertragung* ("transference"); a more idiomatic transference was *Bearbeitung* ("reworking"). A free arrangement was a transcription; then followed a fantasia, sometimes further expanded as a "free fantasia" or "romantic fantasia." Liszt liked to call even more unrestricted free fantasias "reminiscences," or things remembered from listening to the music of this or that opera or symphony. As an auxiliary category, Liszt introduced the term *illustrations* for recurring thematic allusion. Finally, paraphrases united all characteristics of an arrangement, transcription, fantasy, or romantic fantasy, illustration, or reminiscence. To indicate the publishing category of a given transcription, Liszt sometimes used the word *Klavierpartitur* ("piano score").

Parergon zur Symphonia domestica. *Parergon* means leftovers. When Paul Wittgenstein, the one-armed pianist, asked Richard Strauss to write a special piece for piano left hand and orchestra for him, Strauss obliged by collecting disparate sections of his *Symphonia domestica*, and gave it to Wittgenstein, who played it for the first time in Dresden on October 16, 1925.

Paris Symphonies. The traditional generic category for Haydn's six symphonies, Nos. 82, 83, 84, 85, 86, and 87, written especially for performance in Paris in 1786.

Paride ed Elena. An opera by Gluck, first performed in Vienna on November 3, 1770. The libretto is based on the classical tale of Paris of Troy who kidnapped Helen, the beautiful wife of the king of Sparta. This is the third opera by Gluck, after *Orfeo ed Euridice* and *Alceste*, in which he formulated his basic principle that music should be the handmaiden of the text rather than its mistress.

Parody. A parasitic literary or musical genre that emerged in the 18th century and flourished in the 19th, particularly in opera. It usually followed on the heels of a successful, or merely notorious, theatrical production. Weber's opera *Der Freischütz* was lampooned in England as "a new muse-sick-all and seenick performance from the new German uproar, by the celebrated Bunnybear." Wagner's *Tannhäuser*, which suffered a notorious debacle at its first Paris production, engendered a number of French parodies, among them one entitled *Ya-Mein-Herr, Cacophonie de l'Avenir*. Occasionally, a parody anticipates the main event. One such parody, *Tristanderl und Süssholde*, was produced in Munich before *Tristan und Isolde* itself. This type of parody is quite distinct from the dignified parody Mass, in which the original Greek word still retained its philological connotation, *pare-ode*, or a "side-song."

Parsifal. A "sacred festival drama" by Richard Wagner. It was his last opera, produced in Bayreuth on July 26, 1882, less than a year before his death. The libretto, by Wagner himself, is drawn from the legend of the Holy Grail, the chalice from which Christ drank at the Last Supper. The religious symbolism of Parsifal is not easy to unravel. The King of the Grail allows himself to be seduced by the sorceress Kundry in the service of the magician Klingsor, who inflicts a grievous wound on the king. The wound can be healed only by the touch of the sacred spear, and only one pure of heart who has acquired wisdom through pity can take the spear away from Klingsor, who possesses it. Young Parsifal satisfies these requirements and is sent by the Knights of the Holy Grail to Klingsor's domain. Realizing the danger, Klingsor mobilizes a gardenful of flowermaidens to lure and confuse Parsifal, and as a further inducement to him, Kundry kisses him on the lips. This elicits from Parsifal the most baffling exclamation in all operatic literature, "The Wound!" Whatever hematological connection may exist between Kundry's lips and the king's wound, she instantly grasps its significance, and suddenly changes from a sorceress into a humble supplicant for salvation. Parsifal seizes the sacred spear that Klingsor hurls at him and makes the sign of the cross with it; the power of the Christian symbol utterly destroys Klingsor's kingdom. Parsifal makes his way to the Temple of the Holy Grail, where Kundry precedes him. The king bares his wound, and Parsifal heals it with a touch of the sacred spear. Parsifal then raises the Holy Grail into the air; at the sight of it the wretched Kundry collapses and dies. Parsifal is crowned king of the Grail. In *Parsifal*, Wagner keeps his system of leading motifs, but because of the religious content of the work, he also makes use of chorales and other sacred melodies. The harmonic and contrapuntal structure is purer and simpler than in Wagner's *Ring* tetralogy and his other music dramas.

Partbooks. Separate parts for singers or instrumentalists, in common use in the 16th century. Singers were seated around a table, each with an individual partbook, coordinating their singing by subtle signals, anticipation of breath, and so on, without using a general score. The practice of part singing from partbooks has been recently revived by various English singing groups.

Parthenia inviolata. A 17th-century collection of pieces for virginal bass viol, a companion volume to a printed collection of virginal music by William

Byrd, John Bull, and Orlando Gibbons. *Parthenia inviolata* does not mean an unviolated maiden but virginal pieces set for viol. The only complete copy of it is in the New York Public Library.

Particella. An abridged score; in Italian, the word means "a little part." Some composers prefer writing symphonic scores or even operas in arrangements for two or three staves, one for woodwinds, one for brass, one or two for strings, with the vocal part, if any, in small printing on top. A vocal score of a choral work such as an oratorio is usually published in the form of particella, with the orchestral part arranged for piano. Schubert and Wagner wrote some of their works first in particella form. Prokofiev systematically adopted this abridged form of orchestral writing and engaged a knowledgeable assistant to assemble the sections of such a particella into a full orchestra score according to his indications of instrumentation. A major part of the musical legacy of Charles Ives consists of piano arrangements with instrumental cues written in. Stravinsky composed *Le Sacre du printemps* first for piano four hands, which is essentially a particella. Many publishers now issue abridged scores for conductors, often with optional instrumental parts.

Le Pas d'acier. A ballet by Sergei Prokofiev, first performed by Diaghilev's Ballet Russe in Paris on June 7, 1927. The title means "the leap of steel" and features characters purported to represent the new industrial class of Soviet Russia. The score is appropriately discordant, and it created something of an inverse sensation among the anti-Soviet Russian émigrés in Paris who were shocked by this exhibition of "Bolshevik" music because Prokofiev himself was, technically speaking, an émigré in their midst. The Soviet critics, on the other hand, felt that Prokofiev used the very serious business of industrial construction in new Russia as an improper means to entertain the bourgeoisie with musical pap.

Passacaglia. A 17th-century dance form, probably derived from the Spanish *pasacalle*, from *pasar una calle*, "to pass through the street." The expression was applied in Spain to a procession of a chorus playing and singing in march time. In the 17th century, the passacaglia acquired the characteristics of a sui generis variation form. Its salient feature is an ostinato bass progression, with melodic and harmonic variations in the upper voices. In the Baroque period, the passacaglia became one of the most important instrumental forms for keyboard. Bach, Handel, Couperin, and Rameau all contributed to the perfection of the genre. In the 18th century it coalesced with the chaconne. The difference between the two forms is that the passacaglia is polyphonically constructed in a precise and rigorous style, whereas the chaconne is often chordal and homophonic.

Passion. As used in sacred music, this word has nothing to do with carnal desire. It retains its original Latin meaning of suffering, specifically the suffering of Jesus Christ on the cross. The great Bach passions are in the vernacular, and the characters, including Jesus and the apostles, speak and sing in German while the chorus supplies the narrative. There is a great deal of conventional melorhythmic symbolism: the passion, that is, the actual pain experienced by Jesus, is rendered in chromatics; the resurrection is set in clear major arpeggios; and the powers of the dark are expressed in the falling basses in broken diminished-seventh chords.

La Passione. Haydn's Symphony No. 49 in F minor, which he composed in 1768.

Pasticcio. An Italian term derived from *pasta*, "pastry" or "pie." The word is often used disdainfully to designate a motley medley of unrelated tunes by unrelated composers, arranged in a sequence with artificial connective tissue between numbers. Historically, pasticcio performed a useful function in acquainting music lovers with popular opera arias, dance movements, and concert pieces, presented as an appetizing plate of musical spaghetti. Unfortunately, the musical semantics of pasticcio departed from its original meaning as a tasteful concoction and began to be applied indiscriminately to sets of variations by several composers, musical nosegays offered to friends, and the like. The Viennese publisher Diabelli caused the publication of such a pasticcio by commissioning 51 composers to write variations on a waltz tune of his own. Beethoven obliged with 33 variations, which made Diabelli's name immortal. Several Russian composers (Borodin, Rimsky-Korsakov, Cui, and Liadov) got together to perpetrate variations on *Chopsticks*, and Liszt later added one of his own to their collection. Then there is the *Hexameron* for piano on the march theme from Bellini's opera *I Puritani*, written in 1837 by six composers, including Chopin and Liszt. The Italian avant-garde composer Luciano Berio concocted a bouillabaisse with chunks of Bach, Debussy, Ravel, and Mahler and called the result *Sinfonia*. Eventually, the word *pasticcio* lost whatever dignified connotation it had and became synonymous with an undifferentiated miscellany. In common usage, it is definitely derogatory. A story is told about a man attending the performance of a new opera who kept rising from his seat in the audience and bowing deeply in the direction of the stage. "Whom are you saluting?" a friend asked. "Mozart, Beethoven, Wagner, Verdi, and Puccini," he replied. That opera must have been a capital pasticcio.

A Pastoral Symphony. The third Symphony of Ralph Vaughan Williams, first performed in London on January 26, 1922. As was the case with Beethoven, who emphasized that the title of his *Pastoral* Symphony should be understood only as an expression and a sentiment rather than as a literal tone painting, so Vaughan Williams insisted that his *Pastoral* Symphony should be judged as pure music. The work, in four traditional movements, is typical of the contemplative nature of Vaughan Williams as a composer, for the music seems to bear an unspoken message. The finale contains a vocal part without words.

Pastoral Symphony. The proper title of this symphony by Beethoven is, in Italian, *Sinfonia Pastorale.* Its first performance took place in Vienna on December 22, 1808. It is Beethoven's Symphony No. 6, op. 68, and is set in the key of F major, which is often associated with pastoral moods. It is the only work of Beethoven having a program. There are five movements, and the descriptions by Beethoven himself are specific: (1) Revival of Pleasant Feelings upon Arriving in the Country; (2) Scene by the Brook; (3) Merry Gathering of Country Folk; (4) Thunderstorm; (5) Shepherd's Song of Joyful Gratitude after the Storm. Like many composers who first sketch out a descriptive program for their compositions and then retract the original tonal painting, Beethoven added a word of caution: "It is rather an expression of feeling than pictorial representation." However, the literalness of birdsongs in the score cannot be denied. There is the trill of the nightingale, the syncopated rhythm of the quail, and the familiar falling third of the cuckoo. And what could be more pictorial than the thunderstorms? Even the score looks like lightning bolts and heavy rainfall. And the serene conclusion gives the listener the feeling of the Austrian landscape after an invigorating rainfall.

Pathétique. A French adjective applied to musical compositions that are greatly emotional. It is not synonymous with the English meaning of "pathetic" in the sense of pitiful. Both words are derived from the Greek *pathos*, which means "suffering."

Pathétique Sonata. The name commonly applied to Beethoven's Piano Sonata in C minor, op. 13. The "pathetic"—that is, emotional—quality is dramatically expressed in its highly syncopated opening. The complete title is *Grande Sonate Pathétique*, written in French by Beethoven himself, as was the fashion of the day. (He composed it during the last year of the 1700s, the "French century.") The second movement in A-flat major is a set of variations on one of Beethoven's most engaging Rococo themes.

Pathétique Symphony. The common name of Tchaikovsky's Symphony No.6. The title was suggested to Tchaikovsky by his brother and biographer Modest after the work was already completed. It has four movements and is set in the somber key of B minor. Tchaikovsky conducted its first performance in St. Petersburg on October 28, 1893, nine days before he died of cholera. The music epitomizes Tchaikovsky's obsession with Fate. There are some extraordinary moments, such as a quotation from the Russian Mass for the Dead in the trombones. An exceptional feature is a "waltz in 5/4 time," as it came to be known, in the second movement. Tchaikovsky dedicated the *Pathétique* to his favorite nephew, Bob. He confessed that he loved it more than any of his works and that he actually wept while composing the music. He suffered when Bob failed to acknowledge the receipt of the score which Tchaikovsky sent to him. Although the work represented the utmost in human pessimism, it retains an unchallenged position in the Soviet Union where optimism is mandatory. Some extreme scholiasts of the official doctrine of socialist realism suggested an ingenious explanation of Tchaikovsky's general popularity: his music, with its constant minor modalities and melancholy melodic inflections, represents a solemn lamentation on the coffin of the ruling class of the Russian bourgeoisie, and, therefore, gives a proletarian audience a natural satisfaction to know that the enemy class had such a definite send-off. But this kind of dialectical nonsense was later abandoned in scholarly analysis of scientifically minded music critics.

Patter song. A rapid recitative in syllabic prosody, particularly effective in comic dialogues. The tessitura is in the middle register, and the singing approximates the parlando style. Mozart and Rossini excelled in the Italian patter song. The greatest master in English was Arthur Sullivan in setting Gilbert's witty lines in their comic operettas.

Paul Bunyan. A short, light opera by Benjamin Britten, to a libretto by W.H. Auden. It was first performed at Columbia University, New York, on May 5, 1941, when both Britten and Auden were in the United States. The story recounts the exploits of the legendary American frontiersman Paul Bunyan in a series of tuneful episodes. After being laid aside for 35 years, the opera was revived at the 29th Musical Festival at Aldeburgh, England, on June 4, 1976, as a bicentennial tribute to America.

Pause del silenzio. A symphonic suite by Gian Francesco Malipiero, expressing the sevenfold spirit of serenity, crudity, melancholy, gaiety, mystery, war, and savagery, leading to a pause of silence. The first part was first performed in Rome on January 27, 1918. Malipiero later wrote a sequel containing five "symphonic expressions"; it was performed for the first time by the Philadelphia Orchestra on April 1, 1927.

Pavane. A stately court dance in deliberate 4/4 time. The word was at one time supposed to have come from the Latin word *pavo,* or "peacock," because of the imagined similarity of the dance with the strutting step of the bird. But actually the pavane originated in the 16th century in Padua, Italy, and Pava is a dialect name for Padua. Because of its dignified choreography, the pavane became a favorite court dance in Europe and particularly in England during Elizabethan times. The tempo indication *Alla pavana* is also found. Many modern composers stylized the pavane in various novel ways. A common misspelling *pavanne* has taken root in some American samples of the pavane style.

Pavane pour une infante défunte. A piano piece by Ravel, written in 1899 and first performed in Paris on April 5, 1902. It is a fine stylization of a slow Spanish dirge, commemorating a deceased infanta, the royal princess.

Peacock Variations. The title sometimes used for the orchestral *Variations on a Hungarian Folksong* by Zoltán Kodály. It was first performed in Amsterdam on November 23, 1939. The work is based on an authentic Hungarian folk tune, *Fly, Peacock, Fly.*

Pedal point. A sustained note, usually in the bass (in French, *pédale inférieure*), and usually on the dominant or the tonic, or on both simultaneously. It is called *pedal point* as well as *organ point* because on the organ, an instrument on which the technique is particularly effective, it is played by the foot. A protracted organ point on the dominant usually heralds an authentic cadence on the tonic. So great is the bond, so strong the harmonic hold of the pedal point on the dominant, that it can support chords on all degrees of the diatonic scale, as well as modulations into the lowered supertonic or the lowered submediant in a major key. Among examples are the conclusion of the church scene in Gounod's *Faust*, the relevant passages in the overture to Wagner's *Die Meistersinger*, and the *Wedding Procession* in Rimsky-Korsakov's opera *Le Coq d'or*. Scriabin maintains a tonic pedal point in the finale of his *Le Poème de l'extase* for about five minutes. Cadenzas in piano concertos are based on a prolonged pedal point on the dominant in the bass. Cadences in fugal compositions are often reinforced by the pedal point in the bass, for instance, in the second fugue of the first book of Bach's *Well-tempered Clavier*. Pedal points in the bass can be sustained on the modern piano by the use of the middle, or sustaining, pedal. Pedal points in the middle voices (*pédale intérieure* in French) are relatively rare, but examples can be found in the high treble. Rimsky-Korsakov's *Scheherazade* concludes on such a high pedal point. Remarkably enough, some composers writing in an atonal idiom, or employing dodecaphonic techniques, occasionally use pedal points to establish the binding element missing in a system of composition that theoretically disenfranchises both the tonic and the dominant.

Peer Gynt. Incidental music that Edvard Grieg wrote for the introduction of Ibsen's famous drama of that name, which took place in Norway's capital Christiania on February 24, 1876. Two orchestral suites were drawn from it. The first is particularly celebrated; it contains the poetic pastorale *In the Morning*, followed by the mournful dirge *Ase's Death*, a mazurka-like *Anitra's Dance*, and the rather siniser rollicking piece *In the Hall of the Mountain*

King. The second suite, performed separately in Christiania on November 14, 1891, includes *Ingrid's Lament, Arab Dance, Stormy Evening on the Seashore,* and *Solveig's Song*.

Peer Gynt is also an opera by Werner Egk, first produced in Berlin on November 24, 1938. The libretto, drawn from Ibsen's great philosophical drama, tells of Peer Gynt's travels in search of adventure and pleasure. He visits Algiers, where Anitra dances for him; he courts the daughter of the King of the Trolls in his mountain palace. In the end, he returns to his ever-faithful Solveig, and dies in her arms. Egk's opera was unexpectedly praised by Hitler, who attended its first performance; this assured its success for a few brief years. However, Egk survived Hitler's deadly accolade; his *Peer Gynt* emerged into a Hitlerless world with its reputation for solidity and vitality intact.

Pelléas et Mélisande. A lyric drama by Claude Debussy, to a libretto drawn from Maeterlinck's tragedy of the same name. It was first performed in Paris on April 30, 1902, a date of historical significance, for Debussy's operatic masterpiece changed the face of the musical theater and inaugurated a new genre of music drama. Golaud finds Mélisande wandering in a forest. He marries her, but soon an affectionate though innocent alliance develops between Mélisande and Golaud's half-brother, Pelléas. When she lets her long hair fall from her window, Pelléas caresses it. Golaud's jealousy is aroused; he becomes violent. In a famous scene he drags Mélisande on the floor by her hair. In a triumph of understatement, she whispers, "I am not happy today." When Golaud finds her with Pelléas at the fountain in the park, he kills Pelléas. Mélisande is about to bear Golaud's child; dying in childbirth, she forgives her husband for his crime. So unusual is the music, so dramatic its departure from traditional French opera, that Paris music critics were bewildered. When Richard Strauss attended a performance of *Pelléas et Mélisande* in Paris, he turned to a friend during the first act and asked: "Is it going to go on and on like this?" To an uninitiated listener, Debussy's music appears static and monotonous. A Paris critic admitted by way of a compliment, "True, this music makes little noise, but it is a nasty little noise." Debussy's free use of unresolved dissonances, the frequent progressions of dominant-ninth chords, the unstable tonality, all contributed to critical incomprehension. It took many years for *Pelléas et Mélisande* to take its rightful place among operatic masterpieces.

Pelléas et Mélisande is also an orchestral suite by Gabriel Fauré, which he wrote as part of his sentimental incidental music for Maeterlinck's play. It was first performed in London on June 21, 1898. There are four movements; the most popular is the third, *Sicilienne*, which was arranged from Fauré's cello piece. Schoenberg, too, was fascinated by Maeterlinck's play and wrote a symphonic poem on the subject; he conducted its first performance in Vienna on January 26, 1905.

Pentatonic scale. As the etymology of the word indicates, this scale has only five tones to the octave. Pentatonic melodies were found in the ancient songs of geographically distant lands, in Scotland and Tibet, in China and pre-Columbian America, in Iceland and Australia. Is the pentatonic scale, then, some pangeographic, pananthropic root of natural inventions? No. The intervals between component degrees are different in Asian, African, and European scale formations. Western composers equate pentatonic scales to tonal progressions that can be played on the black keys of the piano keyboard. Such westernized scales can be classified as major and minor, major pentatonic being simulated by a scale starting on F-sharp of the "black key scale," and the minor pentatonic by one starting on D-sharp. Consecutive fifths and consecutive fourths are the formative intervals of pentatonic scales, and the harmonization usually tends to be based on pedal points on the presumed tonic and dominant. This music sounds alluringly exotic, but the resulting effect is hardly anything more genuine than an artificial *chinoiserie*. The best examples of modern pentatonic music are found in the works of Debussy and Ravel; Debussy uses the pentatonic scale in the middle section of his piano piece *Voiles*, and Ravel, in the third piece of his suite *Ma Mère L'Oye*, entitled *The Empress of the Pagodas*. The Chinese themselves would never recognize such Gallic pagodas as their own. Among modern operas containing materials from the pentatonic structures of the Orient are Puccini's *Madama Butterfly*, which employs Japanese melodic patterns, and *Turandot*, which presents examples of pseudo-Chinese melodies. Actually, the most common Japanese mode, although pentatonic, contains a semitone and so cannot be reduced to a "black key" scale. On the other side of the world, Irish and Scottish melodies are derived from pentatonic scales that are structurally quite different from oriental exemplars. Unfortunately, some of the best known Irish melodies have apparently been inaccurately transcribed. There seems to be considerable evidence that the initial leading tone in *Londonderry Air* should be a minor third, not a minor second, below the tonic.

Percussion. Not all instruments now classified in the percussion group really percuss, that is, strike (from the Latin verb *percutere*, which forms *percussus* as its past participle). Classified as instruments of percussion are also some of concussion, that is, shaken instruments such as the increasingly popular Latin American shaker maracas; instruments of friction, such as the güiro; and castanets, which are clapped together. Because most percussion instruments perform largely a rhythmic function, the definition of "rhythm" instruments, which has been gaining acceptance in jazz, should be considered an alternative for "percussion" instruments. There is a tendency to include keyboard instruments among percussion instruments, but this would be historically and functionally misleading. Although the piano and its predecessor, the harpsichord, are indeed percussed, their function is not rhythmical. On the other hand, the celesta (which looks like an upright piano), the marimba, and the xylophone all have keyboards and are customarily included in the percussion section. The German terms *Schlaginstrumente*, "strike instruments," and *Schlagzeug*, "strike things," also fail to include concussion and friction.

In the orchestral scores of the Baroque and Classical periods, percussion was relegated to a subordinate position and often notated on an extra line. The kettledrums, usually in pairs tuned to the tonic and the dominant, reinforced the bass and were often placed below the bass line in the score. Those instruments without a definite pitch—the bass drum, cymbals, triangles, and so on—were imports described as Janizary music, because they were included in the military bands of Turkey, led by the court musicians of the Sultan. Among percussion instruments of a definite pitch, the most important are the glockenspiel, the xylophone, and the celesta, all of them pitched in the treble. The glockenspiel has a penetrating bell-like sound and is often used whenever an exotic color is invoked. The glockenspiel is the magic bell in the score of Mozart's opera *The Magic Flute*. Tchaikovsky makes effective use of it in the *Chinese Dance* of his *Nutcracker Suite*. Glockenspiel is German for "bell-play," and the German term is retained in English. The xylophone, which means literally "wood sound," is a newcomer in Western orchestral literature, although it was known under the name of *Holzharmonika* ("wood harmonica") in the 16th century. It is frequently used in modern scores because of its clear and articulate timbre. The celesta is a relatively recent invention. The first composer to use it was Tchaikovsky in the *Dance of the Sugar-Plum Fairy* in his *Nutcracker Suite*. Another type of celesta manufactured in the 20th century is the dulcitone; its "dolce" tone is obtained through the substitution of steel bars by clear and overtone-free tuning forks. The marimba, a Latin-American keyboard instrument with resonators attached underneath, and the vibraphone, which is electrically amplified, are the latest entries in popular and serious modern music. Darius Milhaud wrote a concerto for the marimba, and several composers have included the vibraphone in their works.

Russian opera composers often use church bells in their scores: Tchaikovsky in his *1812 Overture*, Rimsky-Korsakov in *The Legend of the Invisible City of Kitezh*, Mussorgsky in the conclusion of *A Night on Bald Mountain* (they were actually added by Rimsky-Korsakov in his revision of the work). Khatchaturian added a lot of bells in his Symphony No. 2 to glorify the Russian resistance to the Nazi invasion in World War II; in fact, this symphony has been called "Symphony with a Bell." Bell-like sounds are produced by other instruments made of metal: the cymbals that are struck together, the large gongs and tamtams, the triangle, and a variety of jingles such as sleigh bells. The tambourine has a drum head with little cymbals attached.

Drums, big and small, have furnished realistic effects in a number of scores in which military references are made, or to portray an execution, as in *Till Eulenspiegel* by Richard Strauss or the *Robespierre Overture* by Litolff. In his Symphony No. 5, Carl Nielsen has an interlude for a side drum in which the player is instructed to keep drumming, as if determined to interrupt the progress of the music itself. The bass drum looks and sounds impressive enough to suggest ominous events. Chinese blocks have a percussive sound almost as clear and penetrating as that of the xylophone, except that their pitch is indefinite. Among other percussion instruments, claves are an integral part of Latin-American popular bands; the instrument has also been adopted in many modern scores. Its sound is produced by striking together two pieces of resonant hardwood.

A tremendous expansion of the role of the percussion section in modern orchestral scores has put drummers in a privileged position in the orchestra. Some percussion parts demand real virtuosity, for instance, Stravinsky's *L'Histoire du soldat*, in which a single performer must handle several instruments in a truly acrobatic fashion. Carl Orff elevated the rhythm instruments to a commanding position in elementary schools. Percussion ensembles specializing in music expressly written for percussion have proliferated in Europe and America; a notable piece in this category is *Music for 18 Musicians* by Steve Reich. And there is at least one masterpiece of percussion literature, *Ionisation* by Edgar Varèse, scored for 42 percussion instruments and two sirens.

The Perfect Fool. A comic opera by Gustav Holst, to his own libretto, first produced in London on May 14, 1923. In it, Holst ridicules by means of stylistic allusions both German and Italian conventional opera.

Perfect pitch. An innate capacity to name a note by its absolute frequency of vibrations, as contrasted with relative pitch which is the ability to name an interval between two notes. The gift of absolute pitch is invariably discovered in early childhood, being manifested by the child's ability to identify instantly and without fail a note played on a piano or another instrument. This gift is the most obvious symptom of inherent musicality; a child thus endowed cannot avoid becoming a musician. But perfect pitch is not a passport to either virtuosity or ability to compose. A number of great musicians did not possess it, among them Berlioz, Wagner, Tchaikovsky, Ravel, and Stravinsky. Some musicians, particularly singers, can simulate the sense of absolute pitch by assaying the stress on the vocal cords that is required to reproduce the note in question. Despite repeated claims by educators, perfect pitch cannot be attained by ear training. The acuteness of perfect pitch varies greatly when recognition of chords is tested. Some modern musicians are capable of naming correctly a highly complex conglomerate of sounds without a moment's hesitation. Especially difficult to discern are chords containing two perfect fifths separated by a major seventh (e.g., D, A, A-flat, and E-flat, in this order of ascendance). Because the frequency of vibrations assigned to the standard A has tended to rise during the past 100 years, particularly in America, European musicians of the older generation are apt to hear contemporary orchestras as if the music were transposed a semitone higher, in which case perfect pitch becomes an acoustical nuisance. Physiologically, perfect pitch is analogous to precise recognition of colors in the visual spectrum; in both cases the criterion is the unfailing ability to name the frequency of vibrations in the corresponding spectrum. It is interesting that an overwhelming majority of blind musicians have perfect pitch. Some evidence suggests that even now perfect pitch exists among tribes living in isolated communities. One such community has been discovered in the Hawaiian Islands, where the natives could not recognize their own songs when sung on a different pitch level. It may be maintained that Greek ethos and the spiritual characteristics of various Greek modes depended not on the difference of the component intervals between successive degrees of the scale but on the actual pitch of such scales.

La Périchole. An operetta by Jacques Offenbach, first performed in Paris on October 6, 1868. La Périchole is the nickname of a Peruvian street singer in the 18th century when Peru was under Spanish rule. She loves her singing partner, but the Spanish viceroy hires her as a member of his court staff. She undergoes all kinds of temptations but in the end returns to her lover. This is one of the most famous operas of Offenbach; several tunes from it are exceedingly popular.

Peter and the Wolf. A symphonic fairy tale by Sergei Prokofiev for narrator and orchestra, written for the Moscow Children's Theater in a couple of weeks to his own text. Peter is a Soviet boy who takes care of his pet animals, including a bird, a duck, and a cat. When a wolf invades his domestic zoo, Peter organizes a hunt, rounds up the predator, and takes him to the zoo. The score pursues a didactic purpose, each animal being represented by a different instrument and theme. It was first performed on May 2, 1936, and became enormously popular all over the world.

Peter Grimes. An opera by Benjamin Britten, his most popular, first produced in London on June 7, 1945. The libretto is taken from a 19th-century poem. The music is alternately lyric and tragic; the symphonic interludes, descriptive of the sea, and particularly one imitating the cries of the gulls, are very fine. Peter Grimes is a fisherman whose apprentice is lost at sea. Everyone suspects Grimes of murder, and he is enjoined at the inquest not to hire other apprentices. He disobeys the order and hires a new helper, who falls off a cliff to his death. A sympathetic sea captain advises Grimes to leave the village; he sails off on his boat and perishes at sea.

Petrouchka. Stravinsky wrote this most strikingly Russian work while away from Russia, completing it in Switzerland when he was only 28 years old. The famous bitonal combination in the score, which became known as the "Petrouchka chord," is a superposition of C-major and F-sharp major triads, white keys against black keys on the piano keyboard, falling easily under the fingers of both hands. Stravinsky played sketches of *Petrouchka* for the famous Russian impresario Diaghilev, who thought the music would make an excellent ballet. The scenario represents the Russian spring carnival, featuring a puppet show. "Petrouchka" is an affectionate nickname for "Peter." He falls in love with a beautiful ballerina but is thwarted by a rich Moor who throws poor Petrouchka out. There is a pathetic interlude, with Petrouchka's motif derived from the broken bitonal chord. For his basic materials, Stravinsky made ample use of popular street songs of old Russia, but he also borrowed some Austrian waltzes and even French chansonettes. There is an imitation of the barrel organ with its seductive disharmonies. *Petrouchka* was performed in the Diaghilev series of Russian ballets in Paris on June 13, 1911, and was an immediate success. Debussy was greatly impressed by it, and in a private letter he described Stravinsky as a young savage who swept away all the musical rules and conquered the listeners. Strangely enough, *Petrouchka* was criticized by some Russian critics who said that Stravinsky betrayed his national heritage by a vulgar and distorted treatment of native songs to please the decadent Parisian tastes. Some American critics found the score unfit for a concert performance because it smacked of circus and vaudeville. But all such fault-finding was soon forgotten. After 75 years, the score of *Petrouchka* still stands as a remarkable specimen of true musical modernism.

Der Philosoph. Symphony No. 22 in E-flat major (1764) by Haydn. As in all of Haydn's symphonies, the title was invented by some unknown person for some unfathomable reason.

Phonograph. The idea of preserving the sound of speech or music occupied the minds of poets and scientists for centuries. In the domain of fable, sound was captured in lead pipes. When the nature of sound was proved to be airwaves that could be recorded by attaching a stylus to a tuning fork and traced as a series of sinusoidal zigzags on a rotating blackened cylinder, the problem seemed to be near solution. All that had to be done was to play back the grooves on the cylinder with a sharp point, and the original sound produced by the tuning fork would be returned. In 1877, Thomas Alva Edison attached a sensitive membrane to a stylus that impressed grooves on a wax cylinder.

By retracing the grooves with the same stylus, the membrane was set in reciprocal motion, and Edison heard the sound of his own voice reciting "Mary Had a Little Lamb." He named this new invention *phonograph* ("sound writing" in Greek). Many epoch-making inventions appear simultaneously, and indeed Edison had a close rival in the Paris inventor Charles Cros, who developed a talking machine that he named *parlephone* ("speaking sound"). Edison exhibited his phonograph at fairs and scientific meetings, but for many years it was regarded merely as an amusing toy. The rendition of the voice was squeaky and scratchy, but progress was rapid. A horn attached to the recording membrane above the cylinder amplified the sound so that it could be heard at a distance. Edison visited Russia in 1890 and showed his instrument to eminent musicians, who were tremendously impressed. Rimsky-Korsakov signed an endorsement: "I heard the phonograph and I marveled at this invention of genius. Being a musician I can foresee the possibility of wide application of this device in the domain of musical art. A precise reproduction of talented interpretations of musical compositions, of outstanding singing voices, recording of folk songs, and improvisations by the means of the phonograph can be of incalculable importance to music. The phonograph also possesses the amazing capacity of accelerating and slowing down the tempo and to transpose. Glory be to great Edison!" Rimsky-Korsakov's vision proved to be correct; in 1894, the Russian collector of folksongs Eugenie Lineva undertook a series of trips in the Volga region with a specially constructed phonograph to record native music and published her authentic findings.

A decisive step in transforming an entertaining toy into an important musical instrument was the invention by Emile Berliner of a phonograph disc in 1888. Despite the flat disc's obvious advantages, Edison continued to manufacture cylinders, introducing some improvements but not yielding the field to the disc before 1929. In the meantime, the phonograph became a major industry, particularly in America. In 1900 the Victor Talking Machine Company adopted as its advertising symbol a picture of a dog listening to "His Master's Voice" on a disc phonograph. So famous became the dog and the slogan that the phonograph itself assumed the name of this company, Victrola. In England, the common term was Gramophone.

The great drawback of the early phonograph was its limited length and the bulk of its discs. Each side of the disc could play only four minutes and thirty seconds, and when records were made of symphonies and operas, individual movements had to be split into several sections. Just as the invention of the phonograph itself was a natural development of known scientific facts, so the method of increasing the duration of the music on a single disc was substantially enlarged by a seemingly obvious improvement. By increasing the number of grooves on the disc and simultaneously slowing down the number of revolutions per minute from 78 to 33⅓ or 45, it became possible to produce the so-called long-playing record, with each disc accommodating nearly half an hour of music. Furthermore, manufacturers began making records out of a plastic material that was lighter than the shellac of the old 78s and was unbreakable. An opera recorded on a 78 required many discs that weighed several pounds, whereas on the new LPs, the same opera could be recorded on two or three discs.

At the same time, progress was made in simulating natural hearing by placing microphones at strategic positions when making a recording. Soon the first step toward a "surrounding" sound was made with the introduction of binaural recording; by 1958 the technique was expanded to stereophonic recording, commercially known as stereo, from the Greek word *stereos*, "solid." Recording through four channels, which gave a vivid impression of being surrounded by sound, was introduced in 1970 under the name *quadraphonic*. Finally, in the 1980s the unsurpassable and theoretically ultimate improvement was made with the invention of the compact disc, or CD. The stylus was dispensed with, and by some magic the sound was transferred onto the disc by laser. Old recordings were not scrapped, however. Using ingenious methods of salvaging and amplifying early recordings, the voices of Caruso, Adelina Patti, and others were resurrected. At the same time, successful recordings were made of the playing of famous composers, among them Debussy, Paderewski, and Scriabin, from well-preserved paper rolls of the pianola. By the last quarter of the 20th century, the phonograph industry has become a multibillion-dollar business. Its prosperity is nourished by untold millions of albums recorded by the great stars of rock'n' roll, country music, and a wide variety of so-called pop artists. The slang expression "in the groove" testifies to the popularity of the recording industry. Some small recording companies specialize in novelties, reviving forgotten masterpieces of the past or giving a chance to modern composers to record their works. As a result of these activities, large record libraries have catalogues covering the entire course of music history and providing invaluable educational material for students and music lovers.

Phrygian mode. Although the name is inherited from Greece, the Phrygian mode is not identical with the ancient Greek mode of the same name, which corresponds to the Ionian ecclesiastical mode. If projected onto the diatonic scale on the white keys of the piano, the Phrygian octave would extend from E to E. The plagal mode corresponding to the Phrygian mode is Hypophrygian, with the ambitus extending from the dominant B of the Phrygian mode to the next dominant, and thus becoming identical in construction, although not in function, with the Locrian mode.

Piano. The most popular musical instrument in the home and on the concert stage. The piano was invented in the first decade of the 18th century by

Bartolommeo Cristofori, who called it a *Gravicembalo col piano e forte* ("a clavichord with soft and loud"). This rather clumsy description was soon abbreviated to pianoforte or (particularly in Russia) fortepiano. Subsequently, it became known under its present name, a rather inadequate and illogical name for an instrument that was invented to achieve both soft and loud sonorities. The most important innovation of the piano, as distinguished from its keyboard predecessors, the harpsichord and clavichord, is in its mechanism of sound production. On the clavichord, the tone was produced by metal tangents striking the string, and on the harpsichord the strings were plucked. In the piano the sound is produced by hammers striking the strings from below. Although the mechanism activating the hammers seems simple, the technical construction of the pianoforte required a great deal of ingenuity and inventive skill. The hammers had to fall back to their original position after striking the strings without accidentally rebounding, and then a soft damper that is lifted when the key is struck must quickly fall back on the string to keep it from continuing to reverberate. If rapid repetition of the same note is needed, a special device makes the hammer drop to an intermediate height between the original position and the strings, so that it can strike the string again in an instant. Dampers are absent in the extreme upper register of the piano because the thin strings do not sustain enough resonance to require damping. A pianist may find it rewarding and intriguing to play rapid and loud passages in the uppermost octave on the keyboard and listen to the curious effect of an acoustic cloud or "white noise" that lingers for a fraction of a second.

To produce a sound an octave deeper, a string must be doubled in length. If all piano strings were of the same thickness, then the string for the lowest C in the bass, seven octaves below the highest C on the keyboard, would have to be 128 times as long as the string for the high C, an obvious structural impossibility. An examination of the soundboard under the lid of a grand piano shows that the bass strings are much thicker than the treble strings, and it is through a combination of increased thickness and increased length that the bass strings can be accommodated within the wing-like shape of the piano. Curiously enough, Beethoven adopted the German name *Hammerklavier* for the sonatas of his last period; the word simply means a hammer keyboard (hammer in German is *Hammer*). The piano strings in the bass range are single for each tone; in the middle range, they are paired to give more resonance; and in the extreme treble there are three strings to each tone to enhance the resonance still more. Modern pianos have three pedals; the farthest right (the loud pedal) releases all the dampers and causes the piano to give out a resonant harmony that includes the sounds of all the keys played while the pedal is held down. It is therefore properly applied only in passages of a predominantly chordal consistency. Unfortunately, many amateur pianists become addicted to the loud pedal even when the harmony is not uniform, thus producing a chaos of unrelated sounds but at the same time covering up possible wrong notes that become drowned in the tonal mass. The left pedal (the soft pedal) shifts the entire keyboard slightly to the right, with the result that the hammers strike the bass strings obliquely, thus diminishing their volume; the hammers strike only two out of three strings for each tone in the middle and upper registers. That is why the application of the soft pedal is often marked in Classical scores as *una corda* (one string), or *due corde* (two strings), depending on the shift. When the left pedal is to be released, the action is indicated by the words *tre corde*. A third pedal was added later between the soft and loud pedals for the special purpose of holding up the damper over an individual string, thus enabling the pianist to sustain some notes selectively.

The range of the early pianoforte was about the same as that of the contemporary harpsichord, about four and a half octaves, the upper limit being F above the staff of the treble clef. Because of the lack of higher notes, 18th-century composers for piano often had to transpose the recapitulation section in sonata form an octave lower in the middle of a sequence, as in Mozart's famous C major Sonata, K. 545. Similar sudden transpositions occur in Beethoven's early sonatas. The range of the piano keyboard was extended rapidly in the 19th century and soon stabilized in its present standard keyboard of seven octaves and a minor third, from deep A to high C. The Austrian firm of Bösendorfer manufactured early in the 20th century a piano with an added sixth below the low A, but it remains a curiosity and seldom is used in concert.

Editors of Classical piano music have been preoccupied with the problem of adapting works written for a limited range so as to make use of the normal keyboard of modern pianos. Such a revision raises the speculative question whether Mozart would have taken advantage of the newly available higher notes—as, for instance, in the recapitulation of his C major Sonata—to avoid the awkward shift of register. Beethoven actually had a chance to revise his earlier sonatas for publication when the range of the keyboard was extended within his lifetime, but he failed to do so, possibly because he felt disinclined to spend time on such a revision. It certainly would have been worthwhile to change the written lowest A to G-sharp in the octave cascade of G-sharp in Ravel's *Jeux d'eau* whenever this piece is performed on a Bösendorfer piano that has the crucial extra notes in the bass.

Picardy third. The philosopher Jean-Jacques Rousseau, also a professional composer and music scholar, described as *tierce de Picardi* the common practice of ending a work written in a minor key with a major tonic chord containing the major third at its base. The reason was that the usage was particularly strong in the French region of Picardie, where there were numerous cathedrals and organs. There is no mystery, however, for the acoustic reasons in concluding a work on a chord with a major third, an interval that is part of the overtone series, whereas the tonic minor third is not. Examples can be found literally by the millions, in the cadences of chorales, in the coda of each of Bach's fugues in minor keys, and so on. The principle of the Picardy third is also extended into whole sonatas and symphonies in minor keys, in which a work in a minor key ends in a major key. The most resplendent illustration of this is Beethoven's Symphony No. 5 in C minor, which ends in resounding C major.

The Picture That Is Turned Toward the Wall. A hand-wringing and heart-rending song by Charles Graham, executed by him in 1921. It became a hit with the Salvation Army, the Women's Christian Temperance Union, and other organizations that allow no leeway for sin. The picture that was turned toward the wall was that of a farmer's daughter who went off with a (horrors!) man. Chromolithographs in gaudy colors, showing the farmer in the process of turning his daughter's picture toward the wall, enjoyed great popularity in the 19th century.

Pictures at an Exhibition. When his friend Victor Hartmann, a rather mediocre Russian painter, died, Mussorgsky was disconsolate. After going to a posthumous exhibition of Hartmann's pictures, he wrote in 1874 a suite of short piano pieces, each descriptive of one of the paintings. That Hartmann's name is remembered at all is owed to Mussorgsky's genius of musical pictorialism. Among the more striking musical portraits are *An Old Castle, Ballet of Un hatched Chickens in Their Eggshells, The Hut of Baba Yaga*, and the triumphant *Great Gate of Kiev*. Music lovers know *Pictures at an Exhibition* mainly by the brilliant orchestration made by Ravel in 1922.

Pierrot Lunaire. A song cycle for speaking voice, piano, flute (and piccolo), clarinet (and bass clarinet), violin (and viola), and cello by Arnold Schoenberg, first performed in Berlin on October 16, 1912. As in his *Gurre-Lieder*, which uses poems by a non-German translated into German, so the text of *Pierrot Lunaire* (which means "Moonstruck Pierrot") is taken from 21 poems by a Belgian poet, Albert Giraud, rendered into German. The music is a tour de force of fascinating contrapuntal artifices, with instrumental timbres and the speaking voice forming an absorbing network of aural impressions.

The Pines of Rome. A symphonic poem by Ottorino Respighi, first performed in Rome on December 14, 1924. The music describes, by deft allusion, four pine groves in and around Rome. The score introduces an innovation, a recording of a nightingale.

Il Pirata. An opera by Vincenzo Bellini, commissioned by the Teatro alla Scala and first performed there in Milan on October 27, 1827. The pirate is a disillusioned swain whose beloved marries a duke. When his pirate ship is wrecked on his native shore, he tracks down his successful rival, slays him, but is caught and condemned to hang. The twice-bereaved bride lapses into that dependable operatic refuge, lyrical madness. The pirate chorus is rhythmically stimulating.

The Pirates of Penzance. An operetta by Gilbert and Sullivan, subtitled *The Slaves of Duty*, first produced in New York on December 31, 1879. The hero is apprenticed to be a pirate on his 21st birthday. Because he was born in a leap year, however, he would not reach majority until the year 1940, a very remote future date indeed at the time of the operetta's production. After many verbal confusions, the pirates abandon their dismal calling and proclaim their undivided loyalty to Queen Victoria.

Pitch. Acoustically, pitch is determined by the frequency of vibrations of a given tone. The smaller the sound-producing instrument, the higher the pitch; a whistle is small and its pitch is high; the bass tuba is large and its pitch is low. On string instruments and on the piano, the shorter and thinner the string, the higher the pitch. A relatively few musicians possess perfect pitch, a faculty that enables them to name without fail any note within the audible range. Perfect (or absolute) pitch is innate; persons who were not born with it cannot be trained to acquire it, any more than a color-blind person can be trained to tell red from green. Relative pitch, however, enables a person to name the interval between two pitches; this ability can be acquired.

Those who are particularly obtuse in recognizing even relative pitch may be taught to identify intervals through their similarity to the pattern of a well-known song. A minor second is the initial interval of *Dark Eyes*; a major second is the one in *Yes, Sir, That's My Baby*; a minor third is the opening interval of Brahms's *Lullaby*; a major third constitutes the surprise in the *Surprise* Symphony of Haydn. A perfect fourth is the most frequent initial interval of national anthems and folk songs, and examples are many: *La Marseillaise* has the most easily recognizable ascending fourth. The augmented fourth is the "forbidden" interval in traditional music, although it is the love interval in the song *Maria* from Bernstein's *West Side Story*. The perfect fifth is the opening interval of *Twinkle, Twinkle Little Star*; a minor sixth is the opening interval of the Yiddish song *Bei mir bist du schön*; a major sixth opens *My Bonnie Lies Over the Ocean*. The interval of a minor seventh, which implies an immediate modulation into the dominant key, is the opening interval of the words "There's a place for us" from the song *Somewhere*, also from *West Side Story*. As to the major seventh, it is an unthinkable interval to begin a tune with, except in atonal music. The octave is encountered frequently as an initial interval; *Clair de lune* by Debussy is an example, as is the song *Somewhere over the Rainbow*.

All the preceding examples account for ascending intervals. It would be of interest to compile a similar list of initial intervals of popular melodies in the downward direction. Here are a few random samples: the theme of Beethoven's Symphony No. 5 is a falling major third; the initial interval of "Land of Hope and Glory" is a descending minor second, moving from the tonic to the leading tone; a descending minor third introduces *The Sidewalks of New York*; the opening of *The Star-Spangled Banner* descends to a perfect fifth through a minor third.

Plagal cadence. A cadence in which the tonic is preceded by the subdominant rather than by the dominant. The word *plagal* comes from the Greek for "oblique." After 1500 the authentic cadence almost completely displaced the plagal cadence, which retained its hold only on the conclusion of hymns with the words "Amen."

Plagal modes. In Gregorian chant, plagal modes were formed by shifting the range a fourth below that of the corresponding authentic mode to a fifth above. This derivation is denoted by adding the prefix *Hypo* (below) to the authentic mode. The plagal mode retains the same "tonic" note (called *finalis*) as its authentic partner. On the white keys of the piano keyboard, the Dorian mode extends from D to D; the Hypodorian mode would extend from A a fourth below D to A a fifth above D but with a final landing back on D. This gravitation distinguishes it from the authentic mode extending from A to A, the Aeolian mode, which resolves on its own *finalis* of A.

Plagiarism. This embarrassing word is derived from the Latin noun *plagiarius*, "kidnapper." It was used for the first time in the sense of an illicit appropriation of another writer's work by the Roman poet Martial and eventually became a universal term in all languages. The essential element of plagiarism is deliberate intent. Remembered folk sayings, reminiscences of proverbial expressions, or verses from classical works of literature do not constitute plagiarism. As for musical plagiarism, it must be realized that the most naturally attractive melodies in Classical music are derived from the diatonic scale and that rhythmic arrangements of such melodies are limited to certain symmetric formulas within a binary or a ternary meter. This makes accidental coincidences almost inevitable. Still, eager plagiarism hunters devote considerable time and effort to prove that there is nothing new under the musical sun, and they exult in pointing out that the great opening theme of Beethoven's *Eroica* is identical to that of an early Mozart overture, thus brilliantly demonstrating that the three notes of the major triad can be arranged in a variety of ways in 3/4 time. The theme of the finale of Mozart's *Jupiter* Symphony in C major is identical in its structure and rhythm to the main theme of the finale of Haydn's Symphony No. 13 in D major, written many years before

Mozart's time. In the middle of the 18th century, the German writer and composer Friedrich Wilhelm Zacharias proposed to compile a source dictionary of such unintentional as well as intentional borrowings. In 1731 an otherwise respectable Italian composer Giovanni Bononcini, who was a serious rival of Handel for royal and aristocratic favors in London, made the grievous error of submitting to the Academy of Ancient Music in London a madrigal by the contemporary Italian composer Lotti as his own. When this reckless act of patent plagiarism was discovered, Bononcini was disgraced and had to leave England. Handel himself, however, was not averse to borrowings of whole arias from other composers for use in his operas. Fortunately for him, this practice remained unknown in his time, and he was buried in Westminster Abbey with great solemnity. (Poor Bononcini became involved in a venture of making gold from base metals in association with a criminal charlatan and eventually sought refuge in Vienna where he died in obscurity.) In fact, an early edition of the *Encyclopedia Britannica* referred to Handel as "a common thief and shameless borrower." Musical petty larceny was treated with benign tolerance in the 18th and 19th centuries, forgivable since the financial profit was meager. The situation changed in the 20th century when popular music became big business. The copyright laws protected the composer only partially; if the plagiarist disguised his handiwork sufficiently, the intent to defraud could not be proven in a court of law. Indeed, fraudulent claims of plagiarism against successful publishers and composers of popular tunes launched by the writers of songs bearing only a superficial similarity to the money-making productions became so common in the United States that publishers often bought off such claimants to avoid costly defense procedures. In a handwritten decision, Learned Hand, United States Judge in New York City, ruling in a case involving the composer of the popular song "I Didn't Raise My Boy to Be a Soldier," put a plague on both parties by declaring, "The defendant is a casual composer of melodies, though he has small knowledge of musical notation and small skill in playing. I am aware that in such simple and trivial themes as these it is dangerous to go too far upon suggestions of similarity. For instance, the whole of the leading theme of the song is repeated literally from a chorus of *Pinafore*, though there is not the slightest reason to suppose that the plaintif ever heard of the opera. It is said that such similarities are of constant occurrence in music and that little inference is permissible." The situation is different when a quotation of a famous song is deliberately made for purposes of characterization or as a historical reference, as for instance, the *Marseillaise* in Tchaikovsky's *1812 Overture* and Giordano's opera *Andrea Chénier*, or *The Star-Spangled Banner* in Puccini's *Madama Butterfly*. When Stravinsky used the tune of *Happy Birthday to You* in a symphonic dedication to Monteux on his 80th birthday, however, he ran afoul of the copyright and had some trouble having it performed. A most interesting coincidence is found between an early song by Liszt and the principal phrase in the introduction to Wagner's opera *Tristan und Isolde*; the notes are exactly the same without transposition. Wagner was very close to Liszt, so there may have been a subconscious reminiscence of chromatic procedures that was not realized by either of them.

The Planets. An orchestral suite by Gustav Holst, first performed in its entirety in London on November 15, 1920. There are seven movements, corresponding to the seven planets known before the discovery of Pluto. The designations of these movements are mythological: *Mars, the Bringer of War*; *Venus, the Bringer of Peace*; *Mercury, the Winged Messenger*; *Jupiter, the Bringer of Jollity*; *Saturn, the Bringer of Old Age*; *Uranus, the Magician*; and *Neptune, the Mystic*. The work is by far the most celebrated of Holst's productions; the Jovian joviality of the Jupiter movement is particularly striking.

Plants and music. In a wacky book, *The Secret Life of Plants*, a claim is made in all seriousness that plants are "tuned to the Music of the Spheres" and react sensitively to music. An Indian authority has testified that by playing ragas to an appreciative audience of asters, petunias, onions, sesame, radishes, sweet potatoes, and tapioca he proved "beyond any shadow of a doubt that harmonic soundwaves affect the growth, flowering, fruiting, and seed-yields of plants."

An American horticulturist piped some music into greenhouses, claiming it caused his plants to germinate more quickly and bloom more abundantly and more colorfully. A Canadian botanist played a recording of Bach's violin sonatas in his garden, with the result that despite the poor quality of soil, wheat grew better than in the richest earth, demonstrating conclusively that "Bach's musical genius was as good or better than material nutrients." Inspired by these experiments, a botanist in Illinois played a recording of Gershwin's *Rhapsody in Blue* for some plants; they "sprouted earlier than those given the silent treatment, and their stems were thicker, tougher, and greener."

The acme of scientific experimentation with the harmonic life of plants was achieved by a mezzo-soprano who was a regular soloist at Denver's Beach Supper Club. She played the taped musical notes C and D on the piano every second, alternating with periods of silence; as a result, her African violets, drooping at first, began to flower joyously. No lover of rock 'n' roll, she successfully proved that squashes hated rock music so much that they actually grew away from the transistor radio broadcasting it and even, in their desperation, tried to climb the slippery walls of the greenhouse. On the other hand, the cucurbits curled around the radio speaker broadcasting Beethoven and Brahms. When she exposed corn and zinnias to rock music, they grew in abnormal shapes and finally withered and died. Plants subjected to the sounds of "intellectual, mathematically sophisticated music" reacted with such enthusiasm that they bent toward the source of the music at angles of more than 60 degrees, some of them entwining the loudspeaker. Well, Victor Hugo heard a tree sing when bathed in light, *"L'Arbre,' tout pénetré de lumière, chantait,"* but then, he was a poet.

Player piano. A mechanical device that combines the principles of air stream propulsion and percussive hammer action for automatic reproduction of a performance on the piano. A roll of very strong paper, perforated in such a way that the holes made on it correspond in pitch and duration to the notes originally played on the piano, is rotated on a cylinder. The pitches are represented by the horizontal parameter, and the duration, including rests, by the vertical. Because the cylinder rotates, a rapid scale registers visually as a terraced pattern. To reproduce the original performance, a stream of air is passed through the perforations to activate the corresponding hammers, which then strike the piano strings and simultaneously depress the keys of the piano keyboard. The visual impression of such automatic piano playing is that of a magical performance by the invisible fingers of a phantom pianist.

The player piano, under various trademarks such as the Pianola and the Welte-Mignon, became highly popular after its introduction late in the 19th century, and its popularity did not diminish until the advent of the modern phonograph. Several composers, among them Stravinsky and Hindemith, recorded specially written works for the player piano. The defect of the pianola and similar reproductive mechanical instruments, however, was a lack of dynamic nuance. In 1957 piano rolls made by Welte-Mignon early in the century were discovered. In their manufacture, columns of incompressible mercury were used to register precise pressure on the piano keys, making it possible to have faithful renditions of performances played by famous pianists of the time. These performances were then re-recorded on the phonograph, restoring with a remarkable fidelity the manner of playing by Paderewski and other famous musicians.

The player piano has the unique capacity of enabling a composer to make perforations directly on the roll guided by desired measurements, and modern composers have availed themselves of this facility. The most remarkable results were achieved in this technique by the American composer Conlon Nancarrow, who has constructed a number of études and other pieces by direct perforation on the roll, resulting in melodic, harmonic, and rhythmic patterns of extreme complexity and utmost precision that could not be played by any human pianist or even any number of pianists.

The Plough That Broke the Plains. An orchestral suite by Virgil Thomson, arranged from his background music for a documentary film produced in 1936. It depicts the joys and miseries of American farming.

Pochette. French for "little pocket." It is the name given to miniature violins carried by ballet instructors in their pockets for use at rehearsals.

Le Poème de l'extase (The Poem of Ecstasy). The fourth Symphony by the Russian mystic composer Alexander Scriabin. It had its first performance, however, not in Russia but in New York by the Russian Symphony Society conducted by Modest Altschuler on December 10, 1908. The work justified its title. Scriabin provided a multitude of sectional subtitles in French detailing the intermediate states leading to ecstasy, which is represented by 53 consecutive bars of exultant C major in its final musical orgasm.

Le Poème divin (The Divine Poem). An orchestral work by Scriabin, first performed in Paris on May 29, 1905. It is Scriabin's first work of mystic inspiration; the titles of its four movements are indicative of this mystical program: *Grandiose*, *Luttes*, *Voluptés*, and *Jeu divin*. The work is in C minor, with an ending in resonant C major, *"avec une joie éclatante"* ("with a resounding joy").

Poème électronique. A work by Edgar Varèse for sounds entirely electronically produced. It was commissioned for the Philips Pavilion at the Brussels World Fair in 1958, with the sound projected stereophonically from 400 loudspeakers distributed throughout the building.

Poème satanique. A piano piece by Scriabin, composed in 1903. Curiously enough, this "satanic" piece is set in the celestial key of C major; Scriabin was decidedly on the side of the angels.

Point. A musicomathematical term used to enhance the impression of profundity by avant-garde composers in the last third of the decaying 20th century. When attentively examined in context, it means a convergence of autonomous sounds resulting either at optimum white noise comprising all pitches, or the geometrical zero in absolute silence; such points can be arrived at by various acoustical encounters.

Polemics. Music theorists are not fighters, and their polemical exchanges are rarely spiced with invectives commonly encountered in political campaigns. Still there are a few famous battles in music history. One Giovanni Spataro inveighed mightily against the renowned lexicographer Gafurio, calling him "Maestro of errors." The entire title is worth reproducing: *Lucid and most probative demonstration of Maestro Zoanne Spatario* [the name varies] *a Bologna musician against certain frivolous and vain accusations of Franchino Gafurio (Master of errors) brought to light, Bologna, 1521.* Few scholars could wade through this vast tirade, but the little book remains a characteristic document. Four hundred years after its issuance, it was translated and published in German.

Of more interest are attacks leveled at Monteverdi by an obscure contemporary, Giovanni Maria Artusi, under the self-asserting title, *L'Artusi, ovvero delle imperfettioni della moderna musica*, published in Venice in 1600. Not content to attack Monteverdi, Artusi also shot a fusillade against his own teacher, Zarlino, and against Vincenzo Galilei (father of the famous astronomer). Galilei, too, attacked Zarlino for his theory that major and minor triads are mutual mirror reflections of their component major and minor thirds. Monteverdi dismissed Artusi's attacks in a brief paper entitled *Ottuso accademico* (*Obtuse academician*), but apparently he was sufficiently nettled to take a glancing blow at his detractors in the preface to one of his own books of madrigals. The famous *Guerre des bouffons* that rent asunder the French musical community in the middle of the 18th century lacked personal attacks and concentrated on the dispute between the adherents of the Italian *buffi* ("comedians") and the proponents of French national opera. Louis XV and his powerful mistress Madame de Pompadour sided with the French national school, while Rousseau and the encyclopedists, supported by the queen, favored the melodious and harmonious ways of Italian operas. Rousseau fulminated against writers of opera in French, a language that he regarded as inferior for singing, but he failed to attack the personalities. As a result, the whole *Guerre des bouffons* remained a war of abstractions.

Political tonalities.   Major keys are optimistic. Minor keys are pessimistic. This dichotomy dates to the Renaissance, and it was restated with all the power of government by the first Commissar of Education of the Soviet Union, Anatoly Lunacharsky, who declared in his introductory speech at a Moscow concert on December 10, 1919:

> Major keys possess the characteristics of lifting a sound a semitone. By their exultant sense of joy such sounds elevate the mood; they cheer you up. By contrast, minor keys droop; they lead to a compromise, to a surrender of social positions. Allow me, as an old Bolshevik, to formulate this observation: Major tonalities are Bolshevik music, whereas minor keys are deeply rooted in Menshevik mentality.

Still, Bolsheviks love the music of Tchaikovsky even though 85 percent of his works are set in minor keys. The resolution of this anomaly has been proposed by the learned theorists of the Society of Proletarian Musicians: Workers and peasants enjoy the music of Tchaikovsky because it eloquently celebrates the funeral of the enemy class, the bourgeoisie. Q.E.D.

Polka.   Despite its name suggesting a Polish origin (*polka* means "a little Polish girl"), the polka is a Bohemian dance in rapid tempo in 2/4 time. It originated in Prague about 1847 and almost immediately spread all over Europe. In this process it lost its specific Bohemian characteristics and became a popular salon dance. Johann Strauss wrote a famous *Pizzicato Polka* and many other composers followed suit. Stravinsky wrote a *Circus Polka* for a dance of elephants in an American circus.

Polonaise. The most distinctive dance of Poland, invariably set in a dignified triple time. *Polonaise* is the feminine adjective in French of *La danse polonaise*. Examples of polonaises are found in instrumental works of Bach, Beethoven, and Schubert, but it was Chopin who elevated the polonaise to the heights of artistry in his piano music.

Polska. Paradoxically, this dance form, whose name is the feminine adjective of Poland in the Polish language, corresponding to the French *polonaise*, is not Polish but Swedish. The polska must have originated shortly before the Thirty Years' War in the 17th century in which Sweden was actively involved. In its domesticated Swedish rhythms, the polska is akin to the mazurka.

Polymetry. Consistent use of different meters in different voices. Polymetric schemes are implicit in numerous Classical and Romantic works called *imbroglios*. Explicit polymetry occurs in modern works in which different parts bear different time signatures. A polymetric design is central to the second movement of Ives's symphonic set *Three Places in New England*, representing the meeting of two marching bands playing out of sync. Originally, Ives incorporated the two different meters of the two bands in a uniform time signature, but a published edition provides an optional notation in which a whole bar of one marching band in 4/4 time equals 3/4 of the other band, so that three bars of the slower band has the same duration as four bars of the faster band. Among examples of implicit polymetry not marked as such by time signatures is the coda of Schumann's Piano Concerto, where the systematic syncopation in the piano part in 3/4 time results in a polymetric combination of 3/2 in the piano part versus two bars of 3/4 in the orchestra. In Gershwin's *I Got Rhythm*, the implicit polymetry consists of one bar in 2/16 time, four bars of 3/16 time, and one bar of 2/16 time, adding up to 16/16, that is, 4/4, which is the notated time signature. Sometimes the term *polymetry* is applied inaccurately to a succession of different time signatures. The proper term for such usages is *changing meters*.

Polyphony. A musical term so pregnant with historical and structural significance that it is dissolved in its own universality. The term stems from the Greek words *poly*, "many," and *phone*, "sound"; in ancient Greek, the word bore a derogatory meaning of multivoiced chatter. In a medieval treatise, polyphony is described as *modus canendi a pluribus diversam observantibus melodiam*, "a method of singing a 'diverse melody' from many components." In the musical lexicon published by J.G. Walther in 1732, *polyphony* is defined simply as "a many-voiced composition." In the 19th century, polyphony was identified with counterpoint in which each voice has a destiny of its own, as contrasted with homophony, in which the melody is a dominating part with the rest of the musical fabric subordinated to it harmonically. The dichotomy of polyphony and harmony has been described in geometric terms as horizontal and vertical coordinates of musical composition. The term *linear counterpoint* gained some acceptance in the 20th century to emphasize the prevalent horizontality of polyphonic ingredients. In a polyphonic composition, the individual parts are interdependent and mutually accommodating in forming a euphonious ensemble. Contrapuntal imitation is a polyphonic system par excellence, the fugue being the summit of polyphonic technique.

Polyphony culminated with the great works of Bach and went on a decline almost immediately after his death; indeed, the rush toward homophony was led by one of Bach's own sons. (In place of diversity in unity, which was the essence of polyphonic composition, the masters of Classical music of the second half of the 18th century and the succeeding four generations of Romantic composers made melody paramount and harmony its ancillary coordinate.) An artistic development of the polyphonic technique was hampered by rigid rules of contrapuntal practice; thus, second inversions of triads were forbidden because of the presence of the objectionable perfect fourth between the bass and upper voices; melodic progressions of the augmented fourth, or tritones, were deprecated. In Bach's time, music students were physically punished by a painful strike of the instructor's cane on the knuckles of the hand for using the tritone. Theorists went to inordinate lengths to account for apparent violations of the rules of strict polyphony by postulating the existence of a putative missing voice. Thus one eminent scholar, confronted with the use of the supertonic-seventh chord in a Classical work (which was not kosher, according to the orthodox members of the faith), explained it as a dominant-eleventh chord with a missing bass and third.

In the 20th century, Max Reger revived the art of polyphony with extraordinary success; his teacher, Hugo Riemann, told him in all seriousness that he could become a second Bach if he so desired. Reger failed to become a second Bach, but he did produce a large amount of respectable polyphony. The technique of composition with 12 tones related only to one another, as promulgated by Schoenberg, is an avatar of strict polyphony. In this system, polyphonic voices are all derived from a single basic theme; both the horizontal and vertical lines—melody and harmony—are coalesced in the governing series of 12 tones. Strict polyphony, in its purely structural aspects, which includes canonic imitation, fugue, and the devices of inversion (retrograde, augmentation, and diminution), is a doctrine scientifically conceived and precisely executed. The complexity of a double fugue with a second subject as the melodic inversion of the principal theme, or *dux*, is exemplified in the A-minor fugue of the first book of Bach's *Well-Tempered Clavier*. Polyphony may be an obsolescent art, but it remains a Gothic wonder of human genius.

Polyrhythmy. A term properly used to denote the concurrence of several different rhythms. All polyphonic music entails the use of different rhythms at the same time, but to qualify for the description *polyrhythmic*, such rhythms must be maintained for a considerable number of bars in each individual part. One of the most remarkable examples of polyrhythmy is found in Chopin's *Fantaisie-Impromptu* for piano, where groups of four sixteenth notes in the right hand are accompanied by triplets in the left hand.

Polytonality. The use of several tonalities simultaneously. This technique is commonly associated with modern music, but anticipations of polytonal practice can be found in polyphonic music of the Renaissance, when tonality was liquescent and elements of divergent keys clashed against one another. Such fortuitous tonal encounters, however, resulted from totally different antecedents than did intentional polytonality. The earliest example of intentional polytonality is actually found in Mozart. He amused himself by composing a piece entitled *Ein musikalischer Spass* (*A Musical Joke*) wherein strings and horns played in different keys, and the final cadence was polytonal. The subtitle of the piece, *Die Dorfmusikanten* (*Village Musicians*), reveals Mozart's purpose of making fun of untutored village players.

Approximations of polytonality, or rather bitonality, can be found in the synchronization of the lowered supertonic-sixth chord with the dominant triad in a Neapolitan cadence. In this coupling, two triadic harmonies, having their tonics at the distance of a tritone, collide with a curiously euphonious effect. Stravinsky formalized this polytonal usage in *Petrouchka*, in which the triads of C major and F-sharp major coagulate in close proximity. More explicitly, Darius Milhaud used the same combination in the score of his ballet *Le Bœuf sur le toit*. Strictly speaking, however, this bitonal usage does not constitute integral polytonality, which demands the use of the simultaneous combination of four different triads, aggregating to all available notes of the tempered scale. It is entirely possible, of course, to arrange an integral panchromatic chord containing all 12 notes of the tempered scale in groups that would spell out all 24 major and minor triads and assign such triads to different instrumental groups so as to make them stand out individually, but the separation of the triadic groupings may be acoustically difficult.

Pomp and Circumstance. A generic title for orchestral marches by Edward Elgar. The title comes from Shakespeare's *Othello*. The most famous of these marches is Elgar's first; its middle section has been set to the words "Land of Hope and Glory," and it is used by almost every American school as a processional at graduation ceremonies. The first two marches were introduced in Liverpool, England, on October 19, 1901.

Pop! Goes the Weasel. A famous Anglo-American nursery rhyme in gig time. The word *weasel* here had nothing to do with the rodent but was the name of a household utensil, like a flatiron. *Pop* was the colloquial word for the pawnshop, so that the lines "that's the way the money went, pop! goes the weasel" described the predicament of a poor Englishman who had to hock his flatiron. In the American version, the weasel is definitely an animal.

Pop music. A somewhat disdainful term for popular music in which emphasis is placed on its peculiarly common aspects. Because it is a degraded form of semiclassical music, and semiclassical music in turn is a downgraded form of Classical music, pop music may be described as Classical music on the third remove. Of the principal attributes of Classical music, pop music retains a rhythmic symmetry and a rudimentary harmonic basis reduced to essential triadic progressions, sometimes curiously modal in their plagal proclivities. In a sense, pop music may be regarded as folk music, which is also the product of unlettered masses isolated from the mainstream. But whereas folk musicians sing, dance, and play on native instruments without a thought of merchandising their inventions, pop musicians serve the commercial world. Just as pop art imitates the most vulgar methods of advertising and portrays in its poster-like productions canned goods, encapsulated nudes, or industrial junk, so pop music follows the familiar themes of modern life in its most sordid and even lethal aspects—drugs, booze, stimulants. Folk music unites an inarticulate past of people into an ethnic unit; pop music fractures the people's art into an inchoate mass. Historically regarded, the success of pop music among young people in most industrial countries of the world, principally the United States, England, and West Germany, has its precedent in the religious fanaticism of the whirling dervishes of Islam and the flagellants of the Middle Ages.

Porgy and Bess. A famous opera by George Gershwin, to a libretto by his brother Ira, based on a contemporary American play by DuBose and Dorothy Heyward. It was first performed in Boston on September 30, 1935. The startling innovation of the opera was its selection of a subject from Negro life; the cast of characters consisted entirely of black Americans. Porgy is a cripple; Bess is his girl. He kills her former convict lover, is arrested, but is released for lack of evidence. In the meantime, Bess is spirited away to New York by a worldly gent with an engaging nickname, Sportin' Life. At the end of the opera, Porgy is still looking for Bess. Several songs from the opera have become classics of American music, including "I Got Plenty o' Nuthin'," "Bess, You Is My Woman Now," and "It Ain't Necessarily So," which irreverently casts doubt on the most cherished stories of the Bible. The musical idiom of *Porgy and Bess* is an artistic recreation of Negro spirituals, jazz, and blues.

Posthumous works. The expression is barbaric, for how can a work occur after the death of its author? Dictionaries give an alternative definition as "published after death." But what about a work that has been played numerous times during the composer's lifetime but was published only after his death? This distinction is so important that it has led to numerous debates about the nature of the federal copyright law and to at least one serious lawsuit, brought in 1973 by Peter Bartók, son of Béla Bartók, against the composer's publishers Boosey & Hawkes, concerning the renewal of the copyright of Bartók's *Concerto for Orchestra*. The copyright of a work must be renewed after 28 years. Both Peter Bartók and the publishers applied for the renewal of the copyright. The U.S. Copyright Office declined to decide who had the right to have the copyright renewed. Because the *Concerto for Orchestra* was published after the composer's death in 1945, the publishers claimed the right to renew the copyright, but Peter Bartók asserted his right as the lawful heir to his father's estate and declared that the work in question was performed several times during his father's life and therefore could not be regarded as posthumous. The judge ruled in favor of the publishers, basing his findings on the specific meaning that the word *posthumous* conveys in regard to works published after an author's death. The judge cited the usage of the word that has been accepted since the middle of the 19th century, with a specific reference to a work by Chopin that was published as a posthumous opus in 1855, six years after his death, although it had been written in 1828 and first performed in 1830. He ruled, therefore, that because the definition of the word in the field of music had applied for more than a century to any composition published after the death of its composer, Boosey & Hawkes had the right to renew the copyright.

Le Postillon de Longjumeau (The Postilion of Longjumeau). An opera by Adolphe Adam, first performed in Paris on October 13, 1836. The coachman of a *carosse de diligence* develops a fine tenor voice in the course of announcing schedules and destinations. He rides to Paris and fame. There he courts by proxy a rich Paris lady. In one of those coincidences that can happen only in opera, the object of his attention turns out to be his lawful wedded wife, whom he deserted in Longjumeau. There are no recriminations between the two because both made good in a new life, and their marriage is happily reaffirmed. The opera enjoys a regular run in French opera houses.

Potpourri. A collection of musical numbers having a motley variety of unrelated refrains and fragments. In an enlarged sense, potpourri has been used by music publishers, particularly in Germany, for any collection of favorite arias or instrumental pieces, and the word itself (which means "rotten pot" in French) did not acquire its somewhat derogatory meaning until much later. Modern composers of the neo-Classical persuasion revived the genre of potpourri in a nostalgically attractive manner, as a series of disconnected musical sketches.

Prague Symphony. The name commonly applied to Mozart's Symphony No. 38 in D major, first performed in Prague in 1787, bringing Mozart expressions of admiration in the public and in the press, the like of which he had rarely tasted in Vienna. Mozart was very fond of Prague.

Prayers of Kierkegaard. A work for soprano solo, chorus, and orchestra by Samuel Barber, inspired by the writings of the Danish mystic philosopher Kierkegaard. The music is appropriately ascetic, but its contrapuntal fabric is acrid. The work was first performed in Boston on December 3, 1954.

Prelude. An introductory piece to a large work; also an independent composition. The word comes from the Latin *praeludium*, "pre-play." The French term is the same as in English, except for an accent, *prélude.* In Italian, it is *preludio,* in German, *Vorspiel.* The earliest instrumental preludes correspond to the etymological signification of the term; they consist usually of introductory chords and arpeggios and a brief melody with a homophonic accompaniment. During the Baroque period, preludes served as introductions to an instrumental suite, usually for piano or organ. The most remarkable introductory preludes are those paired with fugues in Bach's *Well-Tempered Clavier,* each in the key of the fugue that follows. In the 19th century, however, the prelude was emancipated and became an independent form. Chopin's Preludes for piano are not preambles to anything but self-sufficient compositions. Debussy, Rachmaninoff, and Scriabin followed Chopin in fashioning their piano preludes. The opening "Promenade" in Mussorgsky's piano suite *Pictures at an Exhibition* is of the nature of a prelude; similar Promenades are interposed between numbers in the rest of this suite, where they assume the role of interludes. The antonym of *prelude* is *postlude.* In Hindemith's piano suite *Ludus Tonalis,* the postlude is the optical inversion of the prelude, obtained by playing the pages of the prelude upside down and adjusting the accidentals.

Prélude à l'Après-midi d'un faune. Beyond question the most poetic creation of Debussy's impressionistic genius, scored for a small orchestra in which the woodwinds, horns, harps, and a pair of antique cymbals form an exquisite image. Inspired by a poem by the French symbolist Stéphane Mallarmé, it depicts a sensuous faun's silent contemplation of nymphs and other creatures of the woods on a sunny afternoon. It was first performed in Paris on December 23, 1894. For a subsequent performance, the program carried a note explaining that the complete text of the poem could not be printed as it would be too gross for young girls attending the concerts. An American music publishing house issued an arrangement of the work with a picture of a fawn on the cover; the publisher did not know the difference between the Greek godlet faun and a young deer.

Les Préludes. A symphonic poem by Liszt, first performed in Weimar on February 23, 1854, with Liszt himself conducting. The title is taken from a poem by Lamartine, in which the poet asks the rhetorical question: What is life but a series of preludes? The music is successively dramatic, lyrical, and solemn.

Prepared piano. A term introduced by the American composer John Cage in the early 1940s; a more fitting description would be *altered piano*, or still more precisely, *piano with an altered timbre*. The alteration consists of placing miscellaneous objects upon, around, or under the strings of a piano, an operation that affects the sound of the piano in various ways, producing buzzing effects, muting, and resonance. Among the objects Cage introduced to serve the alteration are paper clips, safety pins, clothespins, screws of different sizes, cardboard, rubber wedges, pencil erasers, wires, metal strips, and the like. Cage's *Sonatas and Interludes* (1946–1948), a major work for prepared piano, was performed in January 1949 in Carnegie Hall; the work earned him awards from both the Guggenheim Foundation and the National Institute of Arts and Letters, for "having thus extended the boundaries of musical art."

Prima donna. Literally, "first lady," a term applied to the leading soprano in opera. *Prima donna assoluta* is an absolute prima donna, superior to the *seconda donna* or *prima donna altra*. The cult of the prima donna reached its height in the 19th century. A typical prima donna was an ample-bosomed Italian or German soprano possessing great lung power. The chronicles of opera are replete with tales about temperamental prima donnas engaging in fistfights and invective with other prima donnas over the size of lettering of their names on theatrical posters, the space allocated in their private rooms at the opera house, the extent of publicity, the efficiency of the hired claque, and so on.

Primitive music. A term generally applied to songs created spontaneously by untutored musicians of exotic provenance, with the implication of artlessness in a positive sense and lack of artfulness in a negative sense. The term also suggests a certain condescension on the part of educated musicians; conversely, musicians surfeited by an abundance of art music seek fresh inspiration in primitive folksongs and dances as a source of new techniques. Thus Picasso was inspired by the artless productions of primitive cultures in creating his own superprimitive art; similarly, Stravinsky sought new resources in the asymmetrical melodies and rhythms of ancient Russian songs. A lack of musical education thus becomes an advantage in the eyes and ears of a modern artist who has reached an impasse at the end of uncontrolled amplification of available resources. What Charles Ives had to say about primitive village musicians who are artistically "right" even when they play wrong notes strikes at the core of this contradiction. It is a remarkable paradox of musical culture that the most popular melodies of the world are of anonymous authorship, the creations of the collective genius of a race.

Prince Igor. An opera by Alexander Borodin, produced posthumously in St. Petersburg on November 4, 1890. Borodin, who was a professor of chemistry, neglected his musical compositions and failed to complete the score of *Prince Igor*; this task devolved on Rimsky-Korsakov and Glazunov. The libretto is based on a Russian 12th-century chronicle recounting the story of the heroic Russian warrior, Prince Igor. He is about to lead his army against the Mongol invaders, the Polovtzi, when an unpredicted eclipse of the sun throws his superstitious soldiers into disarray. (*Prince Igor* is the only opera with a solar eclipse.) The celestial phenomenon is of sinister import; Igor suffers defeat and is captured. The Polovtzian khan treats him royally in captivity, however, and is willing to let him go free provided he promises not to go to war against him again; the khan also offers him his choice of the beautiful slave girls who stage the famous Polovtzian dances. Igor rejects all these allurements; he eventually escapes and rejoins his faithful loving wife. The music represents the most gorgeous panoply of Russian orientalism.

Printing and publishing of music. Almost immediately after the appearance of Gutenberg's Bible set from movable type, experimenters began to set musical notes in type. The first book with printed musical examples was *Psalterium*, set in type in 1457 in Gutenberg's workshop. An important development in music printing was the use of woodblocks in which complete musical examples, notes, and lines were carved out and inked. This method was particularly handy for books on music theory in which the text alternated with musical examples. These early specimens were usually printed in very large notes and widely separated lines. A significant advance toward modern printing was made by the Venetian printer Petrucci, who began printing music books in the first year of the 16th century; he may well be considered the Gutenberg of music printing. He also printed the first tablatures for the lute.

Early printed music involved a double process. The lines of the staff were printed first, usually in red, and then black notes were superimposed. Toward the end of the 16th century metal plates began to be used, with both the lines and notes engraved by hand. In the 18th century, music engraving reached the point of a graphic art, particularly when punches and hammers were applied. Professional craftsmen sometimes accepted work in music engraving; Paul Revere, the American patriot who was a silversmith by trade, became the first in the United States to engrave music. The 18th-century French violinist and composer Jean Marie Leclair entrusted the engraving of his music to his wife, who was a trained toolmaker. (Leclair was stabbed to death in his home; evidence strongly pointed to his wife as the killer, for the wounds were inflicted by metal punches such as were used in music engraving.) Decisive progress in music printing was made by using lithography, that is, printing from a stone surface with a viscous ink, a process developed by the German printer Senefelder in 1796. Carl Maria von Weber apprenticed himself to Senefelder and introduced some improvements of his own in lithography. Type printing, in which musical symbols had to be placed on the staff separately by hand, was perfected in the second half of the 18th century. This method was used concurrently with copperplating and lithography for special purposes, such as the reproduction of musical examples in theory books. The greatest era of music printing from copper plates was reached in the middle of the 19th century. Beautiful editions of instrumental music, orchestral scores, and complete operas were published by the German publishers Schott, Peters, and particularly Breitkopf & Härtel. Excellent editions of works by Russian composers, financed by the wealthy Russian merchant Belaieff, were printed on the German presses in Leipzig.

The 18th century was dominated in England by the publishing house of Walsh, which began issuing fine editions of Handel's operas and also reprinted many works by continental composers. Several important publishing enterprises emerged in Great Britain in the 19th century and have prospered unflaggingly into the last part of the 20th; they are Chappell, founded in 1810, and Boosey, founded in 1816. Boosey's competitor was Queen Victoria's trumpet player, Hawkes, who formed an independent printing shop specializing, like Boosey, in orchestral and chamber music. In 1930, the inheritors of Boosey and of Hawkes joined in a highly successful publishing house, Boosey & Hawkes. Another important British publishing house was Novello, established in 1829 and concentrating on choral music. Others are the firms of Curwen, Augener, and Chester, which became active in the middle of the 19th century.

The United States, even after its independence, continued to import its music from the former mother country. Among the earliest American publishers, or rather importers, of music was Benjamin Carr, who emigrated to America after the Revolution and set up the first American music store, Carr's Musical Depository, in Philadelphia. The first important American-born publisher of music was Oliver Ditson, who established a business as a music seller in Boston in 1835 and continued in business for over a century. The American dependence on Great Britain for music publishing continued until the middle of the 19th century, when it was taken over by German immigrants. The year 1861 marked the foundation of the most important music publishing firm in the United States, established by Gustav Schirmer. Another German-born music publisher, Carl Fischer, settled in New York and founded an important publishing organization in 1872. Among American-born music publishers, Theodore Presser opened his own business in 1883. An important source of income for American music publishers was the representation of European publishers who held the rights on lucrative operas, popular orchestral pieces, and pedagogical literature.

Italy occupies an important position in music publishing, thanks to their almost exclusive rights on famous Italian operas. The firm of Ricordi, formed in 1808, holds the richest grants of Italian operatic literature. The entire stock of plates and publications was wantonly destroyed in 1943 in a barbarous air attack on Milan, the site of the Ricordi publishing house, but like a musical phoenix it emerged from the ashes and resumed its important position in the world of music. In Austria, Hungary, and the Scandinavian countries, local publishers maintain a close cooperation with the large German and English publishing houses. Among French publishers the firm of Durand, founded in 1870, became the most important as well as prosperous. The Editions Salabert, organized in 1896, proliferated into the lucrative field of popular arrangements of theater music. Before the Revolution Russia had several important publishers that supplied the Russians with European music literature and also published works by Russian composers. Among them, Jurgenson, Tchaikovsky's publisher, played a significant role in championing Russian music; Belaieff generously sponsored the publication of music by composers of the Russian national school. Koussevitzky, with his very rich wife, founded his own firm with the specific purpose of publishing works by modern Russian composers, among them Scriabin, Stravinsky, and Prokofiev. After the Revolution, the Soviet government nationalized all Russian publishing houses and established the Central State Publishing House. Because the Soviet government was the sole publisher, problems of expenses were solved within the general budget of the State. It therefore became possible for Russia to publish music extensively, almost extravagantly. For instance, all 27 symphonies of Miaskovsky have been published from engraved plates, including the orchestral parts. Collected works of Russian Classical composers are systematically issued. Even composers less known in Russia and quite unknown abroad get their works published as a matter of routine. Similar policies in publishing music exist in other socialist states of Poland, Yugoslavia, Czechoslovakia, Rumania, and Bulgaria.

Program music. An inadequate description of music that by its melodic and rhythmic contours suggests a landscape, an action, a sentiment, or a historic scene. Perhaps *descriptive music* would be a more accurate term, but the expressions program music and programmatic music are solidly established in English-speaking countries. The term has also entered the German music lexicons as *Programmusik*, and in French, *musique à programme*. In the 19th century, the preferable term for program music was *tone painting*. A pioneer in program music was Liszt. His ideas were developed by many German composers of the second half of the 19th century, culminating in the tone poems of Richard Strauss. Abstract mathematical terms became the ultimate development of program music in the works of Edgar Varèse. The Romantic notion that music can express something realistic was attacked on philosophical and aesthetic grounds in the famous tract *Vom Musikalisch-Schönen* by the greatest musical reactionary who ever lived, Eduard Hanslick. He wielded his caustic pen as an influential critic in Vienna. With casuistic cunning, Hanslick quoted an array of German writers to support his claims for truthfulness in music. Mattheson, a contemporary of Bach and Handel, who certainly were not composers of program music, is quoted as saying, "In writing a melody, the main purpose should be to express a certain emotion." Another famous 18th-century theorist, Friedrich Wilhelm Malpurg, wrote: "It is the composer's task to copy nature, to express the vital stirrings of the soul and the innermost feelings of the heart." The music historian Johann Nikolaus Forkel equated music to rhetoric. Hanslick then quotes several weighty German dictionaries that define music as "the art of expressing sensations and states of mind by means of pleasing sounds," and "Music is the art of producing sounds capable of expressing, exciting, and sustaining feelings and passions." A professor of aesthetics is quoted with obvious distaste by Hanslick as stating that "each feeling and each state of mind has its own inherent sound and rhythm." No wonder that Hanslick as a critic became an inveterate opponent of Liszt and Wagner and an exuberant admirer of Brahms, a composer who never demeaned himself by painting a landscape in music. But what about Beethoven's *Pastoral* Symphony? Would Hanslick condemn it also? No, for Hanslick had a perfect rebuttal of this in Beethoven's own words written on the score: "*Mehr Ausdruck der Empfindung als Malerey*" ("More of an expression of feeling rather than painting").

Imitation of sounds in nature, particularly the singing of birds, are obvious sources of literal program music and are imitated in a number of compositions centuries before the movement of Romantic program music became pronounced. Among famous examples are *La Poule* by Rameau, imitating the cackling of hens; Couperin's *Les abeilles*, with its murmurations of innumerable bees; *The Cuckoo* by Daquin; and the three birds in Beethoven's *Pastoral* Symphony. In literary musical narratives, the earliest example is a set of biblical stories written for harpsichord by Kuhnau, *The Seasons* by Vivaldi, and Karl Ditters von Dittersdorf's 12 symphonies illustrating Ovid's *Metamorphoses*. Probably the most explicit piece of symphonic program music is the *Symphonie fantastique* of Berlioz, written by him to express his love for the Shakespearean actress Harriet Smithson. Among Liszt's symphonic poems, the ones that have direct literary connections are *Les Préludes* and *The Faust Symphony*. Litolff composed an overture *Robespierre*, in which the falling of the severed head of Robespierre into the basket is rendered as a thud on the bass drum. A sneeze is illustrated in both the opera *The Nose* by Shostakovich and in *Háry János* by Kodály. Sounds of industry were reproduced with varying degrees of verisimilitude in numerous works of modern music. In his *Pacific 231*, Honegger created a stimulating impression of an American locomotive gathering speed by the simple device of increasing the number of accented beats in each succesive bar. The whirring of an early airplane propeller is realistically imitated in a piece entitled *The Aeroplane* by the American composer Emerson Whithorne. The Italian Futurists attempted to emulate the noises of 20th century city life by the use of megaphones. The stroke of midnight is sounded by the chimes in the score of Mussorgsky's *A Night on Bald Mountain*. The clatter of steel-making is realistically illustrated by the shaking of a sheet of metal in the ballet *Iron Foundry* by the Soviet composer Alexander Mosolov.

The infatuation with the idea that music must mean something recognizable to the listener led to the regrettable practice of affixing imaginative but more often trite nicknames to musical compositions whose composers never intended to write programmatic music. It is ironic that most of the familiar titles attached to Mendelssohn's *Songs Without Words* are the products of the publisher's eagerness to attract romantically inclined players. The title *Spring Song* does not appear in Mendelssohn's manuscript. Haydn's symphonies and string quartets received popular nicknames that represent the general eagerness to seek familiar images in the sounds of music. Even so, it is as difficult to trace the rationale of some of these titles as it is to conjure up the animal figures in the constellations of the zodiac seen by ancient stargazers. Among Haydn's symphonies we have *The Philosopher*, *The Schoolmaster*, and *The Absent-Minded Man*. Only the *Surprise* Symphony, which in German has a more concrete description, *Paukenschlag* ("Drumstroke"), has a musical meaning behind the title, because in the second movement there is a sudden loud chord at the end of the theme, inserted there supposedly by Haydn to wake the somnolent ladies in the audience. Among some puzzling titles of Haydn's string quartets are the *Razor* Quartets. The *Emperor* Quartet, however, has a perfect explanation: It contains the tune that became the national anthem of Austria. There is no explanation why Mozart's great C major Symphony should be called *Jupiter*. Nor is there any reason to call Beethoven's E-flat Piano Concerto the *Emperor* Concerto. Both nicknames were apparently invented in England.

Even when the composer himself expressly denies any programmatic significance, descriptive nicknames stay put. The so-called *Raindrop* Prelude of Chopin is supposed to have been inspired by raindrops falling on the roof of his house on the island of Mallorca, but he expressly denied this tale. More to the point is the title *Revolutionary* Étude, which is marked by rebellious upward passages in the left hand; it was composed by Chopin at the time Warsaw was captured by the Russians, leading to the partition of his beloved fatherland. The nickname for Chopin's *Minute* Waltz seems obvious, but no human pianist can play it in 60 seconds flat, with all the repeats.

A literal example of program music is *Symphonia domestica* by Richard Strauss, in which the composer portrayed in music the daily bath of his infant son; the exact time, seven o'clock, is represented by the chimes' striking seven. Tchaikovsky's *Pathétique* Symphony is a piece of program music after the fact; the descriptive title was attached to it after the score was completed. It is interesting that it contains a passage in the trombones from the Russian Mass for the Dead, as if Tchaikovsky had a premonition of his death that occurred several days after the first performance of the work. There is no objective way to determine whether a composition "means" something from just listening to it. Tchaikovsky expatiated at great length in his letter to his patroness Mme. von Meck that his Symphony No. 4, dedicated to her, represented the inexorability of Fate. Mahler gave programmatic titles to several of his symphonies, *Titan* for No. 1, *Summer Morning's Dream* for No. 3, *The Giant* for No. 5, but he subsequently withdrew all these titles and insisted that he had never authorized anyone to use them for identification. Schoenberg, to whom music was a pure art, yielded to the request of his publisher to attach titles to his *Five Orchestral Pieces*. And years later, he was even willing to change the title of the third piece, originally called *The Changing Chord*, to *Summer Morning by the Lake!* In his *Kinderszenen* for piano, Schumann depicted a child's moods, of which *Träumerei* is the most moving. In his *Pictures at an Exhibition*, Mussorgsky presented a series of action scenes.

Any composition, no matter how abstract or classically sober, can be interpreted as an image. Modern ballet composers often use movements from symphonic works for choreographical spectacles of a romantic nature with suitable titles attached to them. Some pieces of program music would lose their attraction if they were deprived of their titles. The witty interlude "Pianists" in *The Carnival of Animals* of Saint-Saëns would be pointless were it not for the inclusion of pianists among the animals of the title. In some pieces of program music, the title becomes more important than the music itself. This is particularly true about the humorous creations of Erik Satie, whose music would hardly be the same without those fantastically oxymoronic titles, such as *Heures séculaires et instantanés* ("Century long instantaneous hours"). Sometimes composers yield to the temptation of attaching programmatic titles to their works only to delete them later. Stravinsky's *Scherzo fantastique* was inspired by Maeterlinck's *Life of the Bees*; he even added specific subtitles, such as *Queen Bee's Nuptial Flight*, to parts of his score, but he later denied this derivation.

The principle of absolute beauty in music so eloquently proclaimed by

Hanslick is opposite to the doctrine of socialist realism, as propounded by the theoreticians of the Soviet Union, who insist that all music must have a specific meaning. The musical philosophy of the People's Republic of China goes even further in espousing the primacy of programmatic music. In January 1974, the official organ of the Communist party of the Chinese Republic published a leading article entitled "Works of Music Without Titles Do Not Reflect the Class Spirit" and specifically condemned the Piano Sonata No. 17 by "the German capitalist musician, Beethoven" and the Symphony in B minor by the "Romantic Austrian capitalist musician, Schubert."

Charles Ives was certainly a composer of program music, using the United States as his inspiration. In his symphonic *Fourth of July*, he assembled a heterogeneous orchestra with a wildly dissonant climax representing the explosion of multicolored fireworks. In his memo on the work, he wrote: "It is pure program music—it is also pure abstract music," and he added a quotation from Mark Twain's *Huckleberry Finn*: "You pays yer money, and you takes yer choice." George Antheil insisted that his *Ballet mécanique*, scored for several player pianos, two airplane propellers, doorbells, and a plethora of drums, was not program music of a mechanical world but "the most abstract of the abstract."

Prologue. An introductory part of an opera. Wagner described his music drama *Das Rheingold* as the *Vorabend* ("Prologue") to the main trilogy of *Der Ring des Nibelungen*. A typical short prologue is that sung before Leoncavallo's *Pagliacci*; here it is used in a Shakespearean sense, signifying a person who addresses the audience to explain the meaning of the play. The prologue is different from an overture in that it is short and contains no allusions, verbal or musical, to the action. An overture, in most cases, is a musical table of contents of the opera to follow.

Prométhée (Prometheus). The crowning work of Alexander Scriabin, subtitled *Le Poème du feu* (*The Poem of Fire*), with a reference to Prometheus who stole fire from heaven. The score calls for an important piano part, organ, choruses, full orchestra, and a special instrument that Scriabin called in French *clavier à lumières* ("keyboard of light") and in Italian *luce* ("light"). This instrument was supposed to produce changing colors that would inundate the concert hall. The score is musically built on the so-called Mystic Chord, consisting of six notes, C, F-sharp, B-flat, E, A, and D, which Scriabin regarded as a concord of a higher order. *Prométhée* was first performed by Koussevitzky in Moscow on March 15, 1911, with Scriabin playing the piano part; no attempt was made to introduce the color organ.

Prompter. A rather important person in opera, seated in a small pit in the proscenium with the score in front of him (or her), who gives cues to singers. Such a prompter is introduced in the whimsical opera *Capriccio* by Richard

Strauss. In the last act of *Tristan und Isolde*, a prompter is sometimes ensconced under the dying Tristan's couch. In France, Germany, and Russia, the prompter is called *souffleur*, that is, "one who breathes"; in Italy, he is known as *Maestro suggeritore*, "a master suggester." Incautious prompters have been known to hum the tune. One such suggester, named Adriano Petronio, cued the singers at a performance at the Metropolitan Opera House in New York in the sextet from *Lucia di Lammermoor* so loudly that the ensemble was facetiously referred to by the habitués as the "septet from *Lucia*."

The Proms. An affectionate abbreviation for the Promenade Concerts of London, which began in 1837 in imitation of Paris's popular concerts launched by Philippe Musard in 1833. The programs consisted usually of ballroom dances, overtures, and occasionally short pieces of choral music. In London, the Promenade Concerts were given in the summer in Drury Lane Theater, which was turned into an "agreeable promenade in hot weather." The name of the concerts was firmly established by 1840. The eccentric French musician Julien was the first conductor of these concerts; he was followed by the German August Manns in 1859. In 1875 the Italian Luigi Arditi conducted Promenade Concerts at Covent Garden. In 1893, Henry Wood took over the series, and his name became forever associated with the most brilliant period of the Promenade Concerts, which by then had come to be known as The Proms. On the night of May 10, 1941, the concert hall was hit by Nazi aerial bombardment, but The Proms did not expire. The concerts moved to the Royal Albert Hall. In 1944, The Proms were officially named The Henry Wood Promenade Concerts, as homage to the conductor, who died on August 19, 1944. Among his successors were Sir Adrian Boult, Sir Malcom Sargent, Sir John Barbirolli, and Sir Colin Davis. A great deal of avant-garde music was featured in The Proms programs, such as *The Whale* by John Tavener (August 1, 1969) and Tim Souster's *Triple Music II* and *The Soft Machine*, a rock piece offering including such tunes as *Esther's Nose Job* and *Out-Bloody-Rageous* (August 13, 1970).

Le Prophète. An opera by Giacomo Meyerbeer, first produced in Paris on April 16, 1849. The prophet, based on a historical figure, is John of the town of Leyden, leader of the Anabaptist sect in the 16th century. In order to assert his self-proclaimed divine status, he denies his identity and repudiates his mother. When his beloved Bertha realizes what he has become, she stabs herself to death. The army of the Holy Roman Empire advances on the "prophet's" lodgings. His palace is set afire, and he perishes alongside his forgiving mother. The coronation march accompanying the prophet's entry into the cathedral is famous.

Der Prozess (The Trial). An opera by Gottfried von Einem to a libretto drawn from the morbid novel by Kafka, first performed in Salzburg on August 17,

1953. The opera comments on the fate of the victim of a monstrous bureaucracy who is tried on unnamed charges. A recurrent rhythmic pulse serves as a sinister leitmotif.

Psalm. One of the most important categories of prayerful biblical poems to be sung with instrumental accompaniment. The word comes from the Greek word meaning "to pluck." Innumerable works, from the simplest plainchant, have been set to texts from the Book of Psalms. Biblical tradition holds that King David wrote the Psalms and sang them; he is therefore known as the Psalmist.

Pseudonyms. Pseudonyms in literature are common; women novelists often assumed masculine names to facilitate publication of their works. In music, pseudonyms are rare, except where a dignified composer writes undignified music. In the beginning of his career, MacDowell published a number of short pieces under various pseudonyms. The real name of the British composer of light music Albert William Ketelbey was William Aston. Professional composers of popular songs often wrote under pseudonyms. Vladimir Dukelsky, a serious symphonic composer, adopted the *nom de plume* of Vernon Duke in writing popular songs. Particularly widespread is pseudonymity among singers, both in opera and on the popular stage. Because Italians are proverbially associated with excellence in opera, many non-Italians, eager to make an opera career, have assumed Italian names. Thus the American soprano Lillian Norton became Nordica. At the turn of the century, the belief was that a musician with an Anglo-Saxon name could not write successful songs and that a surname ending in "ski" (to imitate a Polish suffix) or "ska" for women was essential. Thus, the British pianist Ethel Liggins became Ethel Leginska, but it did not help her American career much. A flight from obvious Jewish names was pronounced among musical performers until recently. In the beginning of his spectacular career, Leonard Bernstein was strongly advised to change his name, but he indignantly refused and did rather well under his real name.

Psychology. Like all artists, professional musicians have an exaggerated *amour propre*. Composers, representing as they do the intelligentsia of the musical profession, are the least prone to self-aggrandizement, but even they are apt to be intransigent about the uniqueness of their talent. Schoenberg regarded composition derived from folk materials as devoid of aesthetic value and defended his abstract musical philosophy of music, with considerable vehemence. On a less dignified plane are the vanities of performing musicians in their desire to climb the ladder of fame and fortune. Anecdotes abound. The pianist Vladimir de Pachman would applaud himself at a public concert. To enhance his social status, the pianist Sigismond Thalberg supported the rumor that he was the illegitimate son of a minor German duke. The American musician and composer Silas Gamaliel Pratt said to Wagner, to whom he was introduced, "You are the Silas Gamaliel Pratt of Germany." The musical psychology of singers, at least in times past, was motivated by the lowest of animal instincts. Operatic prima donnas would tear each other's hair out for the honor of being classified as prima donna assoluta, thus qualifying for larger posters or a more sumptuous carriage.

In popular credence, musicians were often regarded as not responsible for their actions. Even the fundamentalist sect of Jehovah's Witnesses, so rigid in its absolute obedience to the laws of the Lord that it takes no exception to the cruel ruling in Deuteronomy 22:20–21 ("if virginity be not found for the damsel, then they shall bring out the damsel to the door of her father's house, and the men of her city shall stone her with stones that she die"), finds extenuating circumstances for King David's sin of adultery and murder that "as an outstanding musician he most likely was an emotional man."

Pulcinella. A ballet by Igor Stravinsky, consisting of a number of Italian dances based on various works by Pergolesi and others. (The authenticity of these sources has, however, been cogently questioned.) The ballet score, composed for Diaghilev, was first performed by the Russian Ballet in Paris on May 15, 1920. Stravinsky arranged a concert suite from the score, and this was first performed by the Boston Symphony Orchestra on December 22, 1922. He also transcribed some of the movements of the suite for cello and piano, and for violin and piano, under the title *Suite italienne.* Despite the feminine ending, Pulcinella is a male character that appeared in the Italian commedia dell'arte in the 17th century, depicted as a deceitful scoundrel.

I Puritani di Scozia (The Puritans of Scotland). An opera by Vincenzo Bellini, first performed in Paris on January 24, 1835, a few months before Bellini's untimely death. The libretto is derived, after several translations and re-translations from French and Italian, from Walter Scott's novel *Old Mortality.* The Puritans are the Roundheads, fanatical followers of Oliver Cromwell. The action takes place in 1649 after the execution of the Stuart King Charles I of England. A noble Cavalier, faithful to the king's cause, is engaged to the daughter of a Puritan, but he fails to appear at the altar, being otherwise engaged in getting the widowed queen out of Cromwell's murderous clutches. His bride is bewildered by his unexplained defection and goes insane. Her mad scene rivals in effectiveness that of Donizetti's *Lucia di Lammermoor,* which is also derived from the writings of Walter Scott. Having saved the queen, the faithful bridegroom returns to his beloved, causing her to regain her mental faculties. But, oh horror! Cromwell's soldiers surprise them and carry the hapless youth to the execution block; once more his bride-to-be lapses into madness. But lo! A trumpet fanfare announces a new victory for Cromwell and his magnanimous decision to grant amnesty to his foes. Once more the situation is saved. As if on cue, the bride regains her senses, and a happy chorus congratulates them. The popularity of *I Puritani* in the 19th century was enormous. The famous male duet of two Roundheads was performed at the premiere by two of the loudest singers in Europe; as Rossini quipped, they must have been heard as far as Mt. Vesuvius. The same duet was the subject of the *Grandes variations de bravoure sur la marche des Puritans* for piano by Liszt.

Q

Quadrille. A French ballroom dance, whose name is derived from the Latin word for a "square," through the Spanish *quadrilla*, "four dancing pairs." Its main figures are *Le Pantalon*, *L'Été*, *La Poule*, and *La Pastourelle*, with a finale. The quadrille attained its greatest popularity in the early 19th century, in Europe (including Russia) and America.

Quarter tones. The attraction of quarter tones for modern composers is explained by the desire to develop a finer and more subtle means of musical expression. Quarter tones, or their approximate intervals, existed in the enharmonic scale of ancient Greek music. A pioneer of the modern revival of quarter tones was Julian Carrillo of Mexico, who published a treatise on *Sonido 13* in 1895, the number 13 referring to the tonal resources beyond the chromatic scale. Alois Hába of Czechoslovakia codified the usages of quarter tones in his *Neue Harmonielehre*, published in 1928. The first quarter-tone piano (with two keyboards tuned a quarter tone apart) was built in 1924. Rimsky-Korsakov's grandson Georg founded a quarter-tone society in Leningrad in the 1920s. The Russian composer Ivan Wyschnegradsky, who made his home in Paris, wrote quarter-tone music for two pianos tuned a quarter tone apart. Charles Ives wrote a chorale for strings in quarter tones as early as 1914. Several systems of notation for quarter tones have been proposed, the most logical of which is the one by Hába using slashed signs for flats and sharps. Ernest Bloch used quarter tones in his Piano Quintet, notated simply as flatted or sharped notes.

Quartet for the End of Time (Quatuor pour la fin du temps). A work for violin, clarinet, cello, and piano by Olivier Messiaen, in eight movements, a devotional meditation on the end of time. He wrote it while a prisoner of war in Germany and had it performed in the prisoners' camp Stalag 8A, Görlitz, Silesia, on January 15, 1941.

Quattro pezzi sacri (Four Sacred Pieces). Choral pieces that Verdi wrote in 1896 in his very old age when he turned toward religious music after the composition of his last opera, *Falstaff*. They are *Ave Maria*, *Laudi alla Vergine Maria*, *Stabat Mater*, and *Te Deum*. A curious scale occurs in *Ave Maria*; Verdi found it in a musical journal where it was called *scala enigmatica*. Just what was especially enigmatic in this scale is difficult to fathom. It is simply an altered major scale with the lower supertonic and raised subdominant, dominant, and submediant, but it does create the feeling of a whole tone scale in the middle section.

The Queen. Symphony No. 85 in B-flat major (1785) by Haydn, the fourth in a series of six symphonies that Haydn wrote for performance in Paris. The title, usually listed in French, *La Reine*, is explained by the fact that Marie Antoinette heard it seven years before she died on the guillotine.

Queen of Spades. An opera in three acts by Tchaikovsky, after Pushkin's tale, first produced in St. Petersburg on December 19, 1890. A Russian army officer tries to elicit the secret of three winning cards from an old woman who has received them from the magician Cagliostro. His strange demand frightens the old woman, and she dies, but her ghost appears to him in a lifelike hallucination and gives him the three winning cards: 3, 7, ace. He gambles on these cards and wins on the first two. But instead of picking up the winning ace, he draws the queen of spades for the last winner-take-all stake and loses everything. The card face of the queen grimaces at him, and he recognizes the old woman in it. He goes out and kills himself. The score is highly dramatic and is in constant repertory in Russia, although it is not frequently staged elsewhere.

Quintenquartett. The String Quartet op. 76, No. 2 (1797), by Haydn, in the key of D minor. Its nickname refers to the interplay of fifths in the first movement. The quartet is also known as the *Bell* or the *Donkey*. Furthermore, the minuet in it became known as the *Witch Minuet* because of its supposedly bewitching quality.

Quintuplets. A group of five notes of equal duration played against a normal grouping of four or three notes. An interesting example of a whole section of quintuplets in eighth notes against a waltz rhythm of 3/4 is found in the *Dance of the Mermaids* in Rimsky-Korsakov's opera *Sadko*.

Quodlibet. Latin for "as you like it." As cultivated by medieval students in Central Europe, it was a free medley of popular melodies, religious hymns, and cosmopolitan madrigals. No wonder the French name for the quodlibet was *fricassée*, "stewed meat." The secret attraction of such stews was the joy of recognizing familiar tunes in an otherwise solemn context. Great Bach himself succumbed to the lure of the quodlibet by combining two popular melodies in the last movement of his *Goldberg Variations*. In modern times, a quodlibet formed by the superposition of the Russian song *Dark Eyes* and Chopin's F minor Étude was popular among Russian conservatory students. Another popular modern quodlibet is a combination of the tunes *La Matchiche* and *Petite Tonkinoise*.

Quotations. Musicians are seldom artists in words, and good literary quotations on music were mostly supplied by poets. Here are some samples: "Music is love in search of a word" (Sidney Lanier). *"O laborum dulce lenimen medicumque"* ("O sweet emollient and medicine"; Horace). "Sweet melody repaireth sad hearts" (Robert Burton). *"Incitamentum amoris musica"* ("Music is an incitement to love"; a Latin proverb). "Music is a calculation performed by the mind without knowing that it is counting numbers" (G.W. Leibnitz). "If one hears bad music it is one's duty to drown it in conversation" (Oscar Wilde). "Heard melodies are sweet, but those unheard are sweeter" (John Keats). *"De la musique avant toute chose"* ("Music before anything else"; Paul Verlaine). "Music has charms to soothe the savage breast" (William Congreve). The following are all from Shakespeare: "How sour sweet music is when time is broke and no proportion kept!" "If music be the food of love, play on." "I never heard so musical a discord, such sweet thunder." "That man that hath no music in himself nor is not moved with the concord of sweet sound is fit for treasons, stratagems, and spoils. Let no such man be trusted. Mark the music." "The Music of the Spheres! Rarest sounds! Most heavenly music!" Then there are others. "All nature is but art unknown to thee, all discord, harmony not understood" (Alexander Pope). "The skin of all of us is responsive to gypsy songs and military marches" (Jean Cocteau). "Listen to music religiously as if it were the last strain you might hear" (Thoreau). "A true music lover is one who on hearing a blonde soprano singing in the bathtub puts his ear to the keyhole" (Anonymous). "Hell is full of musical amateurs. Music is the brandy of the damned" (George Bernard Shaw). *"Les sanglots longs de violons"* ("The long sobs of violins"; Baudelaire). "Hallelujah! Praise God in His Sanctuary; Praise Him with the blast of the horn; Praise Him with the psaltery and the harp; Praise Him with the timbrel and dance; Praise Him with stringed instruments and the pipe; Praise Him with the loud-sounding cymbals; Praise Him with the clanging cymbals! Hallelujah!" (Psalm 150). "So smooth, so sweet, so silvery is thy voice, melting melodious words to lutes of amber" (Robert Herrick). "There's music in the sighing of the reed/ there's music in the gushing of the rill/ there's music in all things, if men had ears" (Byron). "There are the three great chords of might/ and he whose ear is tuned aright/ will hear no discord in the three/ but the most perfect harmony" (Longfellow). "And music: what? That burst of pillared cloud by day/ and pillared fire by night, was product, must we say/ of modulating just, by enharmonic change/ the augmented-sixth resolved—from out the straighter range/ of D-sharp minor—leap of disimprisoned thrall/ into thy life and light, D major natural.'' (Robert Browning). The American composer Charles Ives noted his opinions in memos and diaries: ''Beauty in music is too often confused with something that lets the ears lie back in an easy chair.'' ''Why do I like these things . . . Are my ears on wrong?'' ''My God! What has sound got to do with music!'' ''Is it the composer's fault that man has only ten fingers?'' ''It may be possible that a day in a Kansas wheat field will do more good for an American composer than three years in Rome.'' ''In some century to come school children will whistle popular tunes in quarter tones.''

R

Radio opera. When radio was in its infancy, the musical community became worked up by the idea of channeling opera into homes. The utopian dream seemed to be the *renouveau* of the prospect described in the novel *Looking Backward: 2000–1887* by the American writer Edward Bellamy, who in 1887 was so impressed by the miracle of the telephone that he boldly prophesied that in A.D. 2000 people would be able to listen to music on the telephone, with special programs transmitted from a central station each day from 5:00 to 7:00 P.M. Radio opera did not need telephone wires, but essentially the idea was the same as Bellamy's. Listeners still had to use earphones when excerpts from *Pagliacci* were broadcast from the Metropolitan Opera in New York in 1910. The first complete broadcast of an opera was that of *Hänsel und Gretel*, transmitted from Covent Garden in London on January 6, 1923. On September 7, 1924, *Aida* was broadcast from the Metropolitan Opera. On March 16, 1930, Beethoven's *Fidelio* was broadcast from Dresden by transatlantic radio. Apparently the first opera ever written specifically for broadcasting was Charles Wakefield Cadman's *The Willow Tree*, transmitted from New York on October 3, 1933.

The greatest flowering of radio opera came by way of the phonograph. With the development of long-playing records, it was possible by the 1950s to put entire operas, even obscure ones, on the air because of the fortunate arrangement whereby no royalties had to be paid for broadcasting phonograph records. It might seem that television would bring about a real revolution in expanding the walls of an opera house to embrace the entire world. This was not to be, however, because of the cost of television productions. The most successful opera written especially for television was *Amahl and the Night Visitors* by Gian Carlo Menotti, commissioned by NBC in 1951 for a Christmas show and repeated annually (with but one omission) at Christmas time.

Raga. A unique system of scales used in music of India that represents not only a succession of certain intervals (not necessarily corresponding to the tempered scale) but that also carries a meaningful relationship to spiritual values. For listeners attuned to the infinite gradations of the semantics of the ragas, the correspondences exist not only with human moods, such as joy or sorrow, loneliness and waiting, love and revulsion, but also with a definite time of the day or season of the year. The playing of the ragas by native musicians assumed, therefore, a mystical and magical quality of meditation and communication. The subtlety of moods and modes of the raga may well elude an outsider, and therefore a long session of Indian music played on native string instruments (vina, sitar, tambura, etc.), bamboo flutes, and horns, accompanied by a variety of percussion instruments, may appear monotonous because of its lack of harmonic combinations, but such impressions are fallacious. Whereas the scales of the ragas are pentatonic in their primary structure, supplementary tones may be added, increasing the scale to seven degrees. The scale is enriched through the subtle "bending" of each tone, depending upon the skill and mood of the performer and raga. The hierarchy of the primary and secondary tones of the ragas is strictly observed, and transition from one raga to another, akin to Western modulations, cannot be made within the same performance. The primary notes of the scale are usually emphasized by a rhythmic stress.

The notation of the ragas is difficult for Western musicians because of the improvisatory nature of native performances. The rhythmic structure of the ragas is additive and cumulative. It is additive in the sense that divisions containing different numbers of beats in each are added to form a rhythmic unit of considerable complexity, often making an arithmetic progression (e.g., 2, 3, 4, 5, or 3–5–7); it is cumulative because such rhythmic units are repeated to form larger segments. To an uninitiated listener, it appears magical that a group of native performers, playing without scores and without a visible signal by a principal player, can strike several drums or sound several instruments together after a long count of beats. This ability is explained by the fact that professional native musicians can conceive such units, usually consisting of prime numbers, as 19 or 37 beats. To this capacity must be added the constant rhythmic variations that are skillfully but instinctively fitted into the main metrical divisions.

The Indian raga *tanam* involves breaking up words into syllables and rearranging them in different orders. The word *tanam* is derived from the Sanskrit *anantam*, "endless." This syllabification creates derivative rhythmic patterns because the vowels in Sanskrit are quantitative, long and short. The melodic lines in *tanam* consist of the repetition of short rhythmical phrases. When the lines are played on the vina, the rhythm produces a constant alternation of plucked and pulled strings with periodic silences that are an integral part of the melody.

Ragtime. An indigenous form of American music that emerged as a unique manner of piano playing in American saloons, barrooms, bordellos, and burlesque houses. In vulgar speech, such pianists were referred to as "perfessors" (professors). It was natural that the custodians of music as the art of the beautiful were outraged by the vogue of ragtime. *The Musical Courier* erupted in righteous indignation in an editorial entitled "Degenerate Music," published in its issue of September 13, 1899: "A wave of vulgar, filthy, and suggestive music has inundated the land. Nothing but Ragtime prevails. . . . Our children, our young men and women are continually exposed to the contiguity, to the monotonous attrition of this vulgarizing music. It is artistically and morally depressing, and should be suppressed by the press and pulpit," The pulpit obliged with fire and brimstone. "The cannibalistic rhythmic orgies are wooing our youth along the primrose path to Hell!" But there were also voices raised in defense of ragtime. *The Musical Record* of Boston pointed out sarcastically that "if ragtime were called *tempo di raga* or *rague temps*, it might win honors," and prophesied that the day would come when ragtime would be recognized as a genuine American art. Indeed, European composers, free from American prejudices against its own art, turned an attentive ear to ragtime. Debussy used the ragtime rhythm for *Golliwogg's Cakewalk* in his piano suite *Children's Corner*. A decade later Stravinsky wrote an instrumental piece entitled *Ragtime*. The great American composer Charles Ives wrote music inspired by ragtime. Scott Joplin, the black genius of American popular music who began his career as a bordello pianist, left a signal mark on ragtime, with such well-known compositions as *Maple Leaf Rag* and *The Entertainer*.

The Rake's Progress. An opera by Igor Stravinsky, first performed in Venice on September 11, 1951. The English libretto was written by W.H. Auden and Chester Kallman; the title is from a series of satirical lithographs by the 18th-century artist Hogarth. The story is a parable; the rake of the title is led into a series of adventures. He marries a bearded lady of the circus and invests a fortune in a device that grinds stones into flour and makes bread. He gambles for his soul with the devil, and although the devil loses the game, the rake loses his mind. The moral pronounced in the epilogue is very much in the manner of 18th-century fabulists: "For idle hearts and hands and minds, the devil finds work to do." The music is set in a neo-Baroque manner, with an ostentatious cultivation of formal arias, recitatives, choral intermezzi, and other settecento accoutrements. The rhythmic scheme is alive with angularities and asymmetries in the characteristic Stravinsky vein. The counterpoint is acrid and dissonant, the texture pandiatonic, the orchestration economic, with the cembalo serving as the connective tissue of the musical organism.

Rákóczy March. One of the most celebrated tunes in music history. Francis Rákóczy was the leader of the 1703 Hungarian rebellion against the Austrians, but the tune bearing his name did not appear until a century later. János Bihari, a Hungarian gypsy violinist attached to a Hungarian regiment during the Napoleonic wars, is credited as actual composer. The march was first printed in 1820 in a collection of popular Army marches and quickly became a favorite. Liszt played it as a piano solo during his tour of Hungary in 1838, and later incorporated it into his *Hungarian Rhapsody* No. 15. Berlioz arranged the *Rákóczy March* for orchestra in 1846 under the title *Marche Hongroise* and also included it as a separate number in his oratorio *The Damnation of Faust*.

The Rape of Lucretia. A chamber opera by Benjamin Britten, first performed at the Glyndebourne Festival in England on July 12, 1946. The libretto, based on a legend from Roman antiquity, glorifies the virtue of Lucretia, who refuses to submit to the imperious Roman commander. To prove his superiority, he rapes her. She summons her husband and recounts her tragedy and shame before sinking a dagger into her breast. The musical idiom of the score is philosophically restrained quite in opposition to the traditional operatic manner.

Rasoumowsky Quartets. The usual listing of Beethoven's three string quartets, op. 59. Count Rasoumowsky was the Russian ambassador to Vienna and liked to play the violin. The attribution demonstrates how immortality could be bought for little money by commissioning a great composer to dedicate a piece to an important official or a wealthy man. In the first two quartets of this group, Beethoven used a Russian popular song that he picked up from a German collection. For this reason, the *Rasoumowsky* Quartets are also known as the *Russian* Quartets.

Realism. A musical genre adopted by several composers of the 19th century determined to bring music closer to humanity. Realism differs from the simple imitation of sounds in character pieces such as *The Music Box*, *The Nightingale*, *The Brook*, *The Cuckoo*, and the like. Rather, it attempts to reflect in musical terms the reality of existence. The most logical application of realism is in vocal music, particularly in opera. The emergence of *dramma per musica*, which was the beginning of opera, was prompted by the desire to express the inflections of common speech in music. Among early opera composers, Caccini stated his aims as creating a melody "by means of which it would be possible to speak in musical tones." His contemporary Jacopo Peri spoke of applying in opera "the accents that we unintentionally employ at moments of profound emotion." Wagner sought to intensify the power of ordinary speech, but his use of leading motifs precluded true realism. It was left to the Russian composers of the national school, particularly Dargomyzhsky and Mussorgsky, to declare their determination to articulate in popular Russian accents the arias and particularly the recitatives in their operas. In this they opposed the Italian and German ideals of music for music's sake. The Italian operatic realism was applied in the school of verismo. A specific type of realism motivated by a political purpose arose in the Soviet Union under the somewhat specious genre of socialist realism. A modern excrescence of musical realism is vocal surrealism, in which accents of common speech are intentionally displaced. Sometimes such distortion serves the purpose of rendering the illiterate speech of the people. Stravinsky subjected the natural inflections of Russian speech in the vocal parts of his *Les Noces* to surrealistic distortions. In the score of his opera *The Rake's Progress*, he departs completely from the natural prose of the English libretto, shifting the accents toward the weak syllables to produce the effect of forceful angularity.

Realization. An edited arrangement of an old work; an adaptation for a specific purpose. This term came into use in the 20th century, favored particularly by English composers and arrangers. An arrangement required complete fidelity to at least the melody, rhythm, and harmony of the original, whereas a realization has a greater degree of freedom in transcribing the original harmony.

Rebec. A precursor of the violin that originated in Islamic nations in Asia. It found its way to Spain and France where it remained popular until the violin displaced it. It had only three strings and was rectangular or trapezoidal. This instrument was also known by the Arabic name, *rabab*.

Recital. A word invented by the manager of Liszt's concert appearances in London to convey a suggestion of a narrative and so to please romantically inclined music lovers. The term is applied only to a solo performance, particularly by a pianist, a singer with accompanist, a violinist with accompanist, and so on, but not to a trio or quartet.

Recitative. A musical narrative, as contrasted with arias and other formal parts in an opera or oratorio, which carries the action from one aria to another. In early opera, *recitativo secco* was the common practice, with singers reciting a musical phrase following the accents and inflections of the spoken language accompanied by a bare minimum of chords played on the harpsichord (hence *secco*, "dry"). In the 19th century, the demarcation between the accompanied recitative and the aria tended to be less distinct, until in Wagner's music dramas they coalesced into one continuous song, the "endless melody."

Recorder. A vertical flute popular during the early Baroque period, and later superseded by the transverse flute. Recorders of all compasses from bass to treble were used as solo instruments in chamber ensembles under such names as sopranino recorder, descant, treble recorder, and *flauto d'Eco*, which is included in Bach's fourth *Brandenburg* Concerto. After being dormant for more than a century, the recorder had a spectacular revival, fostered by instrument dealers, in the 20th century.

The Red Poppy. A ballet by Reinhold Glière, first performed in Moscow on June 14, 1927. The title symbolizes the blossoming of revolutionary sentiment in China. The score includes a *Sailor's Dance* based on a popular Soviet song; there are also snatches of the *Internationale*. In the apotheosis, the visiting Soviet sailors and Chinese revolutionaries swear eternal friendship.

Reed. A hollow tube closed at one end; the essential part of reed instruments. Reeds made of a light, flexible material such as cane are capable of a wide range of pitches when attached to a long pipe with a series of holes that are covered to obtain different notes. Such wind instruments are commonly divided into two categories: single reeds such as the clarinet and saxophone, and double reeds such as the oboe and bassoon. In a double reed instrument, the two reeds vibrate against each other. (In a brass instrument, the lips perform the function of the second reed.) Reeds made of a hard metal that produce only one pitch are used in the harmonium, accordion, and organ reed stops.

Reformation Symphony. Mendelssohn's Symphony No. 5 in D minor, first performed in Berlin on November 15, 1832. It is called *Reformation* because the final fourth movement is based on the Lutheran chorale, *Ein' feste Burg*.

Refrain. In poetry and music, a repeated section that follows the principal part of the poem or song; it is also called *chorus* because the main stanza or verse is performed solo and the following chorus is by an ensemble. The word *refrain* is derived form the Latin *refractum*, "fragmented," in the sense of a periodic recurrence. In Italian, it is *ritornello*, a little thing that returns; in Spanish, *estribillo*; in old English, *burthen*; in Russian, *pripev*, literally, "by-song." A refrain often repeats the last line of the verse with the same text and melody, particularly if it summarizes the moral of the song. A religious refrain may be a single word *Amen* intoned by the congregation in response to the minister or cantor. In Spain, a common refrain is *olé*, expressing enthusiasm by a crowd.

Reggae. A unique kind of popular music native to the island of Jamaica, emerging in shantytowns there around 1965. It combines elements of black "soul" singing with superimposed sentiment of social rebellion and is rooted in African rhythms. Reggae is the native way of pronouncing "regular."

Rehearsal. Literally, re-hearing; a practice session for a chamber music ensemble, a song recital, a symphonic work, an opera, jazz band, and so on. A prerequisite for a fruitful rehearsal is a willingness to achieve a mutual accommodation among the participants so as to achieve proper balance in harmony, fluctuations of tempo, and dynamic equilibration. Basic elements can be agreed upon in advance, but subtler nuances have to be felt intuitively. An anecdote is related about a rehearsal of a cello sonata, when the cellist asked the pianist to play softer. "I can't hear myself," he complained. "You're lucky," the pianist retorted, "unfortunately, I can." The collision of vanities at rehearsals is a constant hazard. When the violinist Henryk Wieniawski toured the United States with Anton Rubinstein in the 1870s, the two were not even on speaking terms. According to reports, however, their mutual animosity did not affect the excellence of their performances. An abominable practice of "deputy players" exists in France at rehearsals so that often the personnel of the orchestra that plays the actual concert is different from that at the rehearsal. When an orchestra player told Toscanini at a Paris rehearsal that he would send a deputy to play the concert, Toscanini said, "Then I will send a deputy to conduct the concert," and walked off the podium. Rehearsal is not a happy term. It is better in French: *répétition*; in Italian, *prova*; or in German, *Probe*, a "try-out."

Relâche. An "instantaneous ballet" by Erik Satie, first produced in Paris on November 29, 1924. The word *relâche* ("release") is used to announce the cancellation of a performance. At the performance the curtain bore in huge letters the inscription *"Erik Satie est le plus grand musicien du monde"* ("Erik Satie is the greatest musician in the world"), adding that those who disagree with this estimate are urged to leave the hall.

Religiosity. Religious symbolism left many traces in musical notation. Perfect time consisting of three beats is defined in the medieval treatises as being an attribute of the Christian Trinity. Even in secular works, composers showed piety. Haydn signed most of his symphonies with *"Deo soli gloria"* or *"Finis laus Deo."* Bruckner dedicated his Symphony No. 9 *"An meinen lieben Gott."* When the English composer Arnold Bax was asked to contribute a program note for one of his symphonies, he declined, explaining that the music was dictated to him by God. Performing musicians, not many of whom are naturally religious, have been known to rely on divine help for the quality of their performances, but some are apt to denounce God when they fail. When it rained on the day of the American debut of the Russian bass Sibiriakov, he shook his fists at the skies and cried out: "If God has such weather for Sibiriakov's concert, then God is a bastard!" The adulation of symphonic conductors leads some of them to accept the projected God-like image. "I know who you are," gushed a Boston dowager entering the reception room of Serge Koussevitzky. "You are God!" "I know my responsibilities," Koussevitzky replied imperturbably. When the mercurial Artur Rodzinski took over the New York Philharmonic, he decided to dismiss 14 players. But, he assured the manager, he would first seek divine counsel. The next morning he declared: "God spoke to me, and He said, 'Fire the bastards!' "

Renard. A chamber opera by Igor Stravinsky, first produced in Paris on May 18, 1922. Subtitled "A fable about a fox, a rooster, a cat, and a ram, a merry spectacle with singing and music after popular Russian fairy tales," it tells of a fox outfoxed by less sophisticated animals. The score demonstrates Stravinsky's dexterity in a modernistic distillation of folksong materials.

Repetend. A word derived from a Latin gerund, meaning "to be repeated," that can be usefully applied to a musical phrase constantly repeated for many bars, such as the protracted ending of the initial theme in the first movement of Beethoven's *Pastoral* Symphony, in which the violin figure is repeated ten times. Concluding chords in a Classical coda are typical conventional repetends. Modern composers tend to do away with repetends; Prokofiev ends the march in his opera *Love of Three Oranges* with a single C-major chord, where his Classical and Romantic predecessors might have had 16 or 32 chords.

Répétiteur. A French title for an opera coach, the humblest functionary in the realm of grand opera whose tedious duty is to make singers keep time. These musical menials acquire valuable practice and sometimes rise to conductorship. The remarkable Greek conductor Dimitri Mitropoulos served as répétiteur at the Berlin Opera early in his career.

Reservata. This term, which is an abbreviation of *Musica reservata*, is a philosopher's stone of musical historiography, for its meaning is arcane, its origin recondite, its connotations cryptic, and its function enigmatic. *Musica reservata* first appeared in print in *Compendium Musices* by Adrian Coclico in 1552. On etymological grounds, one is tempted to translate the word *reservata* as "reserved," in the sense of being exclusive, connoting a style of composition appreciated only by expert musicians. An alternative explanation of the term is that the element of "reservation" indicated a restricted use of ornamentation.

Retrograde. A pedantic melodic device often encountered in polyphonic works, much beloved by composers of puzzle canons, and usually prefaced by them with fanciful phrases such as *Vade retro me, Satanas* ("Get Thee behind me, Satan," Mark 8:33), *Ubi alpha ibi omega* ("Where alpha is, omega is too"), *Canite more Hebraeorum* ("Sing in the Hebrew manner," from right to left), and (the most famous designation) *cancrizans* (walking like a crab). In the minuet of his Symphony No. 47, Haydn explicitly marked *al rovescio*, meaning it could be played backward without any change of the original music. Bach's *Musical Offering* has a two-part canon in which the original subject is sounded simultaneously with its retrograde form. Beethoven has a crab motion in the final fugue of his *Hammerklavier* Sonata. A remarkable example of a very melodious and harmonious piece representing a combination of the original and its retrograde form is exemplified by an anonymous canon, erroneously attributed to Mozart, which can be played by two violinists reading a page across the table from one another, so that one of the players performs the tune beginning with the last note and ending with the first note of his vis-à-vis partner. The wonder of it is that the result is in perfect harmony, and that a sharp applies to two different notes in the opposite parts without creating an unresolved dissonance.

After a century of neglect, the technique of retrograde motion staged a revival in the music of the 20th-century Vienna school. Schoenberg has a retrograde canon in No. 18 of *Pierrot Lunaire*, as does Alban Berg in the middle section of his opera *Lulu*. Retrograde motion is of fundamental importance in 12-tone music, in which two of the four principal melodic forms of the tone row include retrograde and inverted retrograde. There are numerous synonyms for retrograde motion: *Krebsgang*, *al rovescio*, *alla riversa*, and *recte et retro* (straight and backward).

Revolutionary Étude. The popular name of Chopin's Étude, op. 10, No. 12, in C minor for piano, supposedly composed when Chopin heard the sad news of the occupation of Warsaw by the Russians. The stormy surging scales in the left hand lend credibility to this story.

Revue. A generic term for a theatrical spectacle in which singing, speaking, dancing, and entertainment of all types are combined into a package that has no pretense of inner cohesion or unified plot. Each sketch in a revue is self-sufficient; the genres vary from sentimental ballads and duets to satire on topical subjects, from classical dances to popular marches. Revues originated in France in 1830 under the reign of the "bourgeois" king, Louis Philippe. A *Revue de fin d'année* was actually a review of events of the year past. In the second half of the 19th century, such revues were called *variétés*. The most brilliant and the most daring revue of the first quarter of the 20th century was the theater named Folies Bergère (that is, follies of the district of Bergère). In the 19th century, the boldest exhibition of the female body was involved in the cancan, which titillated tourists and provided puritans with subjects for sermons on the decay of public morality. After a century of oppressive censorship by the Society for the Prevention of Vice in New York, uninhibited gaiety exploded in the American musicals, as musical comedies came to be known.

Rhapsody. A Romantic form of composition that became popular toward the end of the 18th century. The word is derived from the Greek verb *rapto* ("to sew together") and the noun *ode* ("chant"). In Homeric times, itinerant singers, called rhapsodes (literally, "weavers of songs"), recited their odes at festivals and political events. The rhapsodic forms were revived during the end of the 18th century, when Christian F.D. Schubart published a collection of songs entitled *Musicalische Rhapsodien*. In the 19th century, the meaning of rhapsody was expanded to include instrumental compositions without singing. Liszt wrote a series of piano works under the title *Hungarian Rhapsodies*.

Brahms composed several rhapsodies for piano. Among other composers who wrote rhapsodies were Dvořák, Glazunov, Ravel, and Enesco.

Rhapsody in Blue. A famous work for piano and orchestra by George Gershwin, first performed by him in New York on February 12, 1924. This was the first piece of symphonic dimensions that used the idiom of the blues; a saying went that Gershwin "made an honest woman out of jazz." The piece is both lyrical and dramatic; its expansive melody and pleasingly modernistic harmonies made *Rhapsody in Blue* a landmark in American music.

Rhapsody in Rivets. The subtitle of the Rhapsody No. 2 for piano and orchestra by George Gershwin, which he wrote for Koussevitzky and the Boston Symphony. Gershwin was the piano soloist in the Boston premiere on January 29, 1932. Rivets in the title (which Gershwin later discarded) refers to the rhythmic sound of the riveting being done by construction workers throughout the streets of New York City.

Das Rheingold. The opening music drama, designated as *Vorabend* ("fore-evening"), of Wagner's great tetralogy, *Der Ring des Nibelungen*, to his own loftily poetical text strewn with evocative Germanic neologisms. The maidens of the river Rhine guard the gold, which is not just a precious yellow metallic element with the atomic number 79, but a magical substance. Whoever forges a ring out of the Rhine gold will be master of the world. The Nordic gods who mill around their castle in Valhalla are no less quarrelsome than the gods of Mt. Olympus and are beset as much as the Greek gods by trouble with disobedient underlings. The dwarf Alberich of the Nibelung family renounces his love in order to obtain the gold; from it he forges the baneful ring of the Nibelung. Wotan, the Nordic Jupiter, succeeds in stealing the ring from the incautious Alberich, who then pronounces a curse upon it. Wotan has to contend with the giants Fasolt and Fafner, who demand payment for their work in building Valhalla. Although Wotan offers them the body and soul of the goddess of youth Freia in partial payment, they demand the gold as well. Having obtained it, the giants quarrel and the more vicious one, Fafner, slays the other. Realizing that Valhalla must be protected against foes, Wotan procreates nine Valkyries, stallion-riding warrior maidens generously endowed with brass-plated bosoms. Their main task is to take the bodies of slain heroes to Valhalla where they can be restored to life and protect the stronghold. Wotan also begets human children, Siegmund and Sieglinde, who in turn beget Siegfried. Wotan's hope is that Siegfried, the ideal of a Nordic hero, will track down the giant Fafner, recapture the ring, and return it to the Rhine maidens. A whole encyclopedia of leitmotives is unfolded in *Das Rheingold* and stored away for future use in the remaining parts of the tetralogy. Not only the gods, giants, and dwarfs are characterized by these leading motifs.

Objects or ideas involved in the action, the ring itself, the curse imposed upon it, the magic helmet that can transform a person into various human or animal shapes—each of these is also represented by an individual leitmotif.

Rhenish Symphony. The subtitle given by Robert Schumann to his Symphony No. 3 in E-flat major. Exceptionally, it is in five movements, but the penultimate movement, descriptive of the Cologne Cathedral, may be regarded as an intermezzo. The title is justified because in this work Schumann intended to reflect life in the Rhine countryside. It was first performed, appropriately, in the Rhenish town of Düsseldorf on February 6, 1851.

Rhythm. The animating element of all music, and the essential formative factor in melody. A melody divested of rhythm loses its recognizable meaning, whereas rhythm without melodic content may exist independently. Rhythm must be distinguished from meter, which is an expedient grouping of rhythmical units. St. Augustine made a distinction between meter and rhythm in his treatise *De musica*, and it still holds true: "Every meter is rhythm, but not every rhythm is also meter." The simplest rhythm beyond the monotonous repetition of the same note value is an alternation of a long and short note, corresponding to the trochee in poetry. The metrical arrangement of such a rhythmic figure may be 3/16, 3/8, or any multiples of these fractions. The ear cannot distinguish one bar of 6/8 from two bars of 3/8, except by applying the extraneous considerations of known forms or depending on the tempo. The famous *Barcarolle* from Offenbach's *The Tales of Hoffmann* can be perceived aurally as a waltz unless one knows that a barcarolle must be in 6/8 time. One of the most remarkable instances of a complete divorce between meter and rhythm occurs in the finale of Schumann's Piano Concerto, in which the ear registers a leisurely waltz time while the conductor fights against the aural rhythm by giving the downbeat on a rest every other bar. One of the most common cross rhythms is the superposition of triple and duple rhythms in Spanish popular dances such as the accentuation of 3/4 over a meter marked 6/8. The compound meters of 5, 7, and 11 beats in a measure usually represent two rhythmic groups. The "waltz" in Tchaikovsky's Symphony No. 6 is in 5/4 time, with the rhythmic figures easily separated into two sections of 2 and 3 beats each. In Rimsky-Korsakov's *Dance of the Mermaids* from the opera *Sadko*, the quintuple rhythms are primal, not divisible into groups. In Russian and Bulgarian music, the metrical units of 8 beats are sometimes split into rhythmic groups of 3 plus 3 plus 2.

In the 20th century, there has been a marked tendency among modern composers to write music without barlines, thus abolishing metrical groupings altogether. More durable was the attempt to equate rhythm with meter at all times, changing the time signature when the rhythmic figure was altered. *La Danse sacrale* in Stravinsky's *Le Sacre du printemps* is an example of such subordination of meter to rhythm. An intriguing case of incommensurability between meter and rhythm is found in Gershwin's song *I Got Rhythm*, in which the square measure of 4/4 is in effect subdivided into one bar of 1/8, four bars of 3/16, and one bar of 1/8. Boris Blacher introduced the method of "variable meters" with time signatures in which the numerator increases by one in each successive bar until a bar of five beats is reached, whereupon the metrical numerator decreases by one beat in each measure. Elliott Carter used what he called "metrical modulation," wherein a subordinate rhythm in a given metrical set becomes the primary meter, and the former primary meter is reduced to a subordinate position. Rhythmical figures without a common denominator relative to the principal metrical set are found in numerous modern works in which groups of notes, usually in prime numbers such as 5, 7, 11, 13, 17, or 19, are bracketed against an approximate number of beats within the principal meter. In the compositions of the avant-garde, both meter and rhythm are often replaced by durations given in seconds or fractions of a second. In his book *New Musical Resources*, Henry Cowell proposed new shapes of musical note values making possible subdivisions into any kind of rhythmic groupings.

The most common rhythms found in folksongs of all Western lands, and inherited in Classical, Romantic, and some modern works, generally follow the prosody of verse. It is remarkable how potent such simple rhythms are in common melodic progressions. A major or minor scale played in trochaic meter will yield an attractive tune. As an example, one may try an arrangement in the rhythm of the trochee of the minor hexachord with a pause in every cadential fourth measure, whereupon the same rhythm continues in retrograde motion. Here is an example of a tune in which capital letters represent longer notes and small letters shorter notes: A b C d E f E; D c B a B; C d E f E d C; B a B c A (the last A is cadential). The interdependence of melody and rhythm is expressed in the term widely used in Spanish writing on music, *meloritmo*, or "melorhythm." It deserves incorporation into other languages.

Rhythm and blues. A type of popular music generated in the Harlem district of New York, performed by small groups, usually with singing. Its metrical division follows the model of the blues and is closely allied to boogie-woogie. Because of its syncopated rhythm, rhythm and blues was also known as the Harlem Jump. Later it was amalgamated with rock 'n' roll as a subspecies.

Ricercar. One of the most important musical forms of the Renaissance era. It is also one of the most vaguely defined forms, encompassing elements of canon, fugue, fantasy, and early sonata. *Ricercar* (or *ricercare* or *ricercata*) is the Italian verb meaning "to seek, to search, to research." Early in the 16th century, ricercar retained its literal meaning of "trying out," as in tuning the lute and playing improvisatory arpeggios and melodic fiorituras as a sort of preamble in the tonality of the intended principal section of a work. An Italian 16th-century theorist describes the ricercar as a sequence of *"suoni licenziosi"* (not in the sense of licentious sounds but of sounds arranged with a certain degree of license) to be played *senza arte* ("without artifice, artlessly"). Vincenzo Galilei, the father of the great astronomer, who was an important music theorist of the 16th century, wrote about a musician who played "a fine ricercar with his fingers" and then began to sing. Originally, the ricercar was a prelude to a song, to a keyboard composition, or to a dance tune played on a lute, but within a century it assumed an independent significance comparable to a fugue and a sonata, having a contrapuntal style far removed from its pristine "artlessness." When Bach presented his *Musical Offering* to Frederick the Great of Prussia, he chose the ricercar as the center of his work and devised an acrostic in Latin, *Regis Iussu Cantio Et Reliqua Canonica Arte Resoluta* ("By the King's Command the theme and additions resolved in canonic style"). The ricercar lapsed into innocuous desuetude in the 19th century but was revived in the 20th century by several composers, among them Stravinsky, Martinů, and Malipiero, when the slogan "Back to Bach" became fashionable.

Rienzi. An early opera by Wagner, produced in Dresden on October 20, 1842, when he was 29 years old. The full title is *Cola Rienzi, der letzte der Tribunen* (*Cola Rienzi, the Last of the Tribunes*). The libretto is by Wagner himself, derived from the historical novel by Bulwer Lytton. Rienzi was called the last of the tribunes because he tried to restore Roman self-government. The action evolves in the framework of the internecine struggle between leading Roman families in the 14th century. Rienzi and his sister perish with a handful of his adherents in the flames at the capitol in Rome. The Overture, with its stirring trumpet calls, is popular as a concert number, but the opera is rarely performed in its entirety.

Rigaudon. A dance originating in the 17th century in southern France. Set in alla breve time, it usually opens on an upbeat and has a middle trio section. The rigaudon was often part of the instrumental suites of the 17th and 18th centuries. Ravel included a rigaudon in his piano suite *Le Tombeau de Couperin*.

Rigoletto. An opera by Verdi, to a libretto based on Victor Hugo's play *Le Roi s'amuse*, first performed in Venice on March 11, 1851. Rigoletto, a deformed court jester, mocks an aggrieved father whose daughter was seduced by a libidinous duke and is cursed by the victim of his insensitive raillery. The curse is prophetic, for his own daughter is debauched in turn by the despicable rake. Incensed, Rigoletto hires an assassin to kill the duke and deliver his body in a sack at the door of a tavern. But when he arrives there at midnight, he hears the ineffable duke singing his immortal and immoral antifeminist aria, *La Donna è mobile*. Horrified, he opens the sack and finds his dying daughter, who had been stabbed by mistake when she went on a midnight tryst with the duke. "Maledizione!" he cries out, recalling the curse. The opera is a perennial favorite. The duke's aria is sung by myriad tenors; there is also a magnificent vocal quartet. Liszt wrote a paraphrase for piano on the themes from *Rigoletto*.

Der Ring des Nibelungen (The Ring of the Nibelung). Wagner's great tetralogy, described by him as "a stage festival play for three days and a preliminary evening." The entire cycle was produced for the first time in Bayreuth on four evenings: August 13, 14, 16, and 17, 1876. The individual titles of the four operas are *Das Rheingold*, *Die Walküre*, *Siegfried*, and *Götterdämmerung*. The cycle is musically united by a whole encyclopedia of leading motifs identifying not only the personages involved but also objects and ideas. Wagnerian statisticians have counted as many as 90 leading motifs in the cycle, and special manuals have been published to guide the listener through the melodic jungle.

Rispetti e Strambotti. A string quartet by Gian Francesco Malipiero, commissioned by the Elizabeth Sprague Coolidge Foundation and first performed in Pittsfield, Massachusetts, on September 25, 1920. *Rispetti* ("respects") are poetic forms of old Italian madrigals; *strambotti* are peasant love songs. The contrast between the aristocratic and the rustic forms constitutes the musical content of Malipiero's work.

Ritardando. A gradual slowing down; it is to be distinguished from *ritenuto*, which means holding back, establishing a slower tempo at once. A propensity for unauthorized and musically unjustified ritardando is an abiding sin of many performers who cover up technical deficiency and inability to play difficult passages in proper tempo. One American singer, when told by the exasperated accompanist that ritardandi could not be tolerated in Figaro's rapid aria from Rossini's *Barber of Seville*, retorted, "I didn't make any ritardando; I just slowed down a little."

Robert le diable. An opera by Giacomo Meyerbeer, with the libretto by the French writer Eugène Scribe, first produced in Paris on November 21, 1831. Robert, a medieval duke in Palermo, is half human, half devil. When he falls in love with a Sicilian girl, his father, the devil-in-chief, keeps him from winning a crucial tournament, the prize of which is her hand. But Robert is aided by his virtuous half-sister (who has no satanic blood in her veins) and wins his bride after all. The opera was tremendously successful in the 19th century and enjoys sporadic performances even in the 20th century.

Rock 'n' roll. The most powerful type of American popular music; it erupted in the middle of this century and has continued to grow irrepressibly. The origin of the term dates back to the motion picture *Transatlantic Merry-Go-Round*, produced in 1934, which featured a song, "Rock and Roll," with music by Richard A. Whiting and lyrics by Sidney Clare. There is no inkling in the rhythmic and harmonic characteristics of this song of the type of rock 'n' roll that developed some two decades later. Stylistically, rock 'n' roll, or simply rock, is an outgrowth of swing music and rhythm and blues.

Rock owes its popularity to small radio stations that pioneered in broadcasting rock records promoted commercially by a special class of music announcers known as disc jockeys, or DJs (that is, riders on record discs). One of the earliest specimens of mature rock was the song "Crazy, Man, Crazy," recorded in 1953 by Bill Haley and the Comets. A Cleveland DJ named Alan Freed is generally credited with popularizing these songs under the generic term rock 'n' roll. In 1956 the landscape of rock 'n' roll was brightened by the rise of Elvis Presley. Dressed in outlandish attire and sporting three-inch-long sideburns, he sang accompanying himself on an electric guitar, gyrating suggestively around his lower axis—a body language that earned him the moniker Elvis the Pelvis. Rock 'n' roll suffered a temporary eclipse when it was discovered that DJs accepted bribes from recording companies for pushing their rock records, a practice that became known as "payola." An even greater scandal erupted in the 1970s when executives of a major recording corporation admitted that they pampered their best-selling rock artists into signing exclusive contracts through wine, women, and, most reprehensible of all, drugs.

No scandal could stop the inexorable march of rock 'n' roll, however. In 1960 Chubby Checker and his innovative dance, the Twist, added a new beat to rock 'n' roll, operating in the newfangled discotheques, successors to nightclubs, which used long-playing records amplified to the threshold of pain. Then came the Beatles of Liverpool, England, taking their appellation from "beat." Whereas the American product was raucous, vulgar, and visceral, the Beatles emphasized sophistication while propagating universal sentiments of human friendship, love, and fascination with mind-boggling drugs. The initials of one of their songs, *Lucy in the Sky with Diamonds*, spell LSD, which is a powerful hallucinogen. In August 1969, rock 'n' roll culminated in the gigantic festival near Woodstock, New York, when tens of thousands of young people converged on a farmer's field, disdaining the hardships of travel, feeding, and sleeping in order to be among their rock idols.

Guardians of public morals, and even medical doctors, became concerned with the spiritual and physiological effects of rock on young people. Examinations of the auditory capacities of habitual rock players and their customers revealed a loss of hearing in the upper ranges. In 1975 the pastor of a Baptist church in Florida cited statistical records to the effect that 984 out of 1,000 teenage girls who became pregnant out of wedlock committed fornication while rock music was being played. Even plants seem to react adversely to the sound of rock. In a book entitled *Noise: The New Menace*, the author claims that all plants exposed to rock leaned away from the sound, as if trying to escape the noise, and would not bloom.

Rococo. The name of an architectural style of the 18th century characterized by shell-like ornaments; the word comes from the French word *roc*, "shell." As in architecture, so in music, the Rococo style emerged in the second half of the 18th century as a reaction against the elaborate style of Baroque music.

The Roman Carnival Overture. The most successful overture that Hector Berlioz wrote. It was actually an arrangement of materials from his unsuccessful opera *Benvenuto Cellini*. Cellini was a notorious profligate, so it is not surprising that the overture is full of sensual joy. Berlioz conducted its first performance in Paris on February 3, 1844, under its French title *Le Carnaval romain*.

Romance. A term of wide and vague application. Most specifically, it describes the type of Spanish poetic narrative in the manner of the ballad. In France and Russia the term *romance* often refers to any short art song composed of several stanzas. In German, it is spelled *Romanza*, and designates a brief instrumental work of a romantic nature.

Romantische Sinfonie. The name given by Anton Bruckner to his Symphony No. 4, in the key of E-flat major. As in most Bruckner symphonies, there are four movements. The themes are spacious, and the development is rich and resonant. Bruckner made three major revisions of the work; it was first performed in its final form in Vienna on January 22, 1888.

Romeo and Juliet. An overture-fantasy by Tchaikovsky, first performed in Moscow on March 16, 1870. This was Tchaikovsky's first important orchestral work. It opens with a chorale, which is followed by a series of spasmodic syncopated passages illustrative of the strife between the two warring houses in Shakespeare's drama. The highest point of the overture is the flowing lyric theme of love that has charmed audiences all over the world for more than a century.

Romeo and Juliet is also a ballet by Sergei Prokofiev, first produced not in Russia but in Brno, Czechoslovakia, on December 30, 1938. The work did not reach the Soviet stage until January 11, 1940, when it was produced in Leningrad. It is one of the most engaging ballets by Prokofiev; he drew two orchestral suites from it.

Romeo et Juliette, a symphonic work by Hector Berlioz, was first performed in Paris on November 23, 1839. In this piece, scored for voices, chorus, and orchestra, Berlioz creates a type of Romantic oratorio with musical episodes taken from Shakespeare, of which the scherzo *Queen Mab* is a prodigious display of orchestral coruscation.

Rondo. An instrumental form often used as the finale of Classical symphonies, concertos, and sonatas. Historically, terminologically, and perhaps structurally, the rondo is derived from the French *rondeau* and connotes the form of a round. In the instrumental rondo, the main subject, often called *refrain*, recurs regularly in the basic key and intervening episodes appear in related keys. Sometimes these episodes are expanded to create secondary thematic sources. Variations are widely applied, and there is usually a coda to conclude the work.

Rosalia. A term of opprobrium used with reference to the modulating sequence to a key a major second higher. The term comes from a once popular Italian song, *Rosalia, mia cara.* The Germans called this type of modulating sequence *Cousin Michel*, after an old German song of that name, or contemptuously, *Schusterfleck* (a "shoemaker's patch"). But Beethoven, Schubert, Liszt, and Bruckner used the rosalia type of sequence most admirably for dramatic effect.

Der Rosenkavalier. An opera by Richard Strauss, to a libretto by his most imaginative collaborator, Hugo von Hofmannsthal, first produced in Dresden on January 26, 1911. The intricacy of the plot, with its manifold entanglements, amatory crosscurrents, cross-dressing, and contrived mistaken identities, is in the most extravagant manner of 18th-century farce. The action takes place in Vienna in Mozart's time. The personages embroiled in the comedy are the Feldmarschallin (the wife of the fieldmarshal), a young count whom she takes as a sporadic lover, an aging baron, and a nubile lady whom the baron proposes to marry. According to the quaint custom of the time, the prospective bridegroom must send to his betrothed a young messenger carrying a rose; the Feldmarschallin selects her own young lover for this role. Naturally, the Rose Cavalier and the young lady fall in love. The scene becomes further confused when the Feldmarschallin orders the young cavalier to put on a servant girl's dress to conceal his presence in her bedroom. Dressed as a girl, he attracts the attention of the foraging baron, and to save the situation, agrees to a tryst with him. As if this were not enough, the part of the Rosenkavalier is entrusted to a mezzo-soprano, so that when he (in actual appearance and physiological gender, she) changes his/her dress, the actress singing the role actually engages in double transvestitude. The finale unravels the knotted strands of the plot. The music is almost Mozartean in its melodious involvement; the Viennese waltzes enliven the score. After the morbid and somber scores of his earlier operas *Salomé* and *Elektra*, Strauss proved that he could combine bel canto with musical invention.

Le Rossignol (The Nightingale). An opera by Igor Stravinsky, first produced in Paris on May 26, 1914. The Chinese emperor is dying, and his life is supported by the singing of a nightingale. When the Japanese ambassador thoughtlessly presents the emperor with a mechanical nightingale, the real bird flies away, and the emperor's health declines dangerously. As a discordant funeral march is played, the real nightingale is brought in, and the emperor regains his strength. The moral seems to be that human ills ought to be left to natural cure. The score is extremely dissonant, with harmonies built on the tritone and the major seventh.

Rotulus. A roll of parchment sheets sewn together, which was the usual form of books in ancient times up to the 4th century and remained in use for another millennium for musical manuscripts. Several medieval motets owe their preservation to the sturdiness of such rotuli.

Round. A perpetual canon, usually in three parts. The entrances of the voices are rhythmically equidistant; the melody, invariably in a major key, is built on the tonic triad so that the counterpoint is in thirds and a complete triadic harmony is achieved when all the voices come in. *Frère Jacques* is a famous example.

Rovescio. Italian for "reverse"; in music it signifies a melodic inversion. A famous example is Contrapuntus VI in Bach's *Die Kunst der Fuge*. The 18th variation in Rachmaninoff's *Rhapsody on a Theme of Paganini* is a precise melodic inversion of the theme; because the theme is encompassed by a minor triad, its inversion becomes a melody in major. Some Baroque composers used the word *rovescio* (and its cognates *riverso* and *rivolto*) in the sense of retrograde motion. The postlude of Hindemith's *Ludus Tonalis* represents (allowance made for shifting accidentals) both an inversion and a retrograde movement. A curiosity is a piano toccata by Ronald Binge entitled *Vice Versa*, which can be read *al rovescio*, in both senses of the word. It can also be played upside down without any change in the music.

La Roxelane. Haydn's Symphony No. 63 in C major (1779). The feminine title may be explained by the fact that the Allegretto from this symphony is a variant of the French song *Roxelane*. However, the approximation is stretched.

Rubato. More properly termed *tempo rubato*, it literally means "stolen time," and is applied to a free treatment of the melody, allowing for ritardando, which must, however, be compensated by a subsequent accelerando so that the measure remains constant and the accompaniment is not disrupted. The practice is the musical equivalent of the saying, "to rob Peter to pay Paul."

Rudepoema. A piano work by the Brazilian composer Heitor Villa-Lobos which he wrote for the pianist Artur Rubinstein. The title means "rude poem" in the sense of unrestrained savagery. Indeed, it is technically so difficult that for many years only the greatest virtuosos could tackle it. Villa-Lobos subsequently arranged it for orchestra and conducted its first performance in Rio de Janeiro on July 15, 1942.

Rugby. *Mouvement symphonique No. 2* by Arthur Honegger, which describes a rugby game in kinetic rhythms. It was first performed in Paris on October 19, 1928, and was subsequently played, appropriately so, during the intermission at an international rugby match between France and England, in Paris on December 31, 1928.

Rumanian Rhapsodies. Two orchestral works by the greatest composer of Rumania, Georges Enesco. The first is especially popular. They were first performed in Bucharest on March 8, 1903, conducted by Enesco himself, who was only 21 years old at the time.

Rusalka. An opera by Dvořák. "Rusalka" is the Slavic name for a water nymph who drowned herself after her beloved prince, whom she tempted to join her in the water. The opera was first performed in Prague on March 31, 1901, and proved to be quite popular.

Ruslan and Ludmila. An opera by Mikhail Glinka, first produced in St. Petersburg on December 9, 1842. The libretto follows Pushkin's fairy tale of that name. Ludmila, daughter of the Grand Duke of Kiev, is betrothed to the valiant Russian knight Ruslan, but during the wedding feast she mysteriously vanishes as the scene darkens and lightning and thunder rend the skies. The Grand Duke promises her hand to anyone who will find her. Two suitors besides Ruslan take part in the hunt, but Ruslan is helped by a benign magician. He discovers that Ludmila was abducted by the sinister magus Chernomor (the name means "Black Mortifier"), whose might resides in his long beard. This gives an obvious clue to the resolution of the problem. Ruslan is confronted with horrendous obstacles, most spectacularly a huge severed head guarding Chernomor (the part of the head is sung by a vocal quartet), but he regains his beloved. The score contains interesting harmonic innovations such as whole-tone scales, and it is profoundly imbued with Russian folksong inflections.

Russian music. Russian national music reflects the characteristics of the nature of Russia itself. The central plateau of Russia is a flat prairie separated by the Ural mountains from Siberia and by the Caucasian chain from Asia Minor. The melodies of the Russian people are appropriately spacious, formed by brief diatonic sections and marked by asymmetrical structures. The diatonic themes of Russian songs are usually confined within a tetrachord or a pentachord, in a major or a minor mode. Russian songs of great antiquity are apt to be in a slow measured time, but peasant songs employ lively dancing rhythms. Melodic and rhythmic figures in Russian songs often form sequential groups in related scales, so that a melody in a major tetrachord is imitated by a similar progression in the corresponding minor mode, a minor third below. When a theme is cast in an asymmetrical rhythm of five, seven, or eleven units, the tempo is apt to be slow and leisurely. Another distinct characteristic of natural Russian melos is a cadence of a falling fourth, from the subdominant to the tonic. It seems legitimate to draw a parallel between such open intervals and the vast distances between populated localities in Russia. We find this construction in such popular tunes as *The Volga Boatmen's Song*, in Borodin's symphonies, and in Stravinsky's *Le Sacre du printemps*. In scale patterns, Russian melodies are apt to make use of the lowered submediant to form the harmonic major scale. The radio signature of the official evening broadcasts in Soviet Russia uses a popular Soviet song, *Moscow Nights*, set in a minor key with a characteristic falling fourth in the final cadence.

Beethoven made use of two Russian folksongs in his string quartets dedicated to the Russian ambassador in Vienna, Rasoumowsky, using material from a collection published in St. Petersburg in 1790. Balakirev and Rimsky-Korsakov published extensive collections of Russian folk songs. Glinka is usually regarded as the "father of Russian music," for he was the first to create two important operas based on Russian subjects, *A Life for the Czar* (1836) and *Ruslan and Ludmila* (1842). A proud proclamation of national musical independence came on the occasion of a symphonic concert of Russian music given in St. Petersburg in 1867 when the Russian writer Stasov greeted the musicians represented on the program as a "mighty little company" strong enough to challenge comparison with the European masters. The composers were Balakirev, Borodin, Cui, Mussorgsky, and Rinsky-Korsakov. To these illustrious names was added that of Glazunov as a true inheritor of the spirit of Russian nationalism. Tchaikovsky, who lived in Moscow, was not connected with the nationalist group of the St. Petersburg "Mighty Five" and represented the universal style of romantic composition.

The most innovative composer of modern times was Igor Stravinsky, who left Russia in 1914 and wrote his essential nationalistic works, based on Russian sources, as an émigré living in Switzerland and France; among them were *The Firebird*, *Petrouchka*, and *Le Sacre du printemps*. A most peculiar development took place in the Soviet Union, a style described by its theorists as "socialist realism," which demanded the observation of basic musical materials treated according to the notions of revolutionary changes in society, resolutely opposing so-called "formalism," and excluding the use of free dissonant writing. Accordingly, one of the most significant composers of the Soviet period, Dmitri Shostakovich, was subjected to violent denunciation by Soviet officals for his alleged adherence to Western trends. Similarly attacked were Prokofiev, Miaskovsky, and Khatchaturian. Fortunately for Russian music, the reactionary tide that swept Russia during its darkest times was turned, and Russian composers regained their freedom to write music according to their natural inspiration.

S

Le Sacre du printemps (The Rite of Spring). The most celebrated score of the 20th century, written for Diaghilev's Ballet Russe by Igor Stravinsky. Its production in Paris on May 29, 1913, created a public scandal that reverberated mightily through music history. The ballet is subtitled "Scenes of Pagan Russia" and portrays in jagged, ponderous sequences the ancient rites as perceived by a highly sophisticated and imaginative modern musical mind. The basic melodic material is reduced to the diatonic tetrachord, but the harmonic dressing is harshly polytonal and the orchestration is arranged in huge blocks and globes of sound; the angular rhythms are set in constantly changing meters. The difficulties created for conductors and instrumentalists are enormous, and decades elapsed before *Le Sacre* could be handled by ordinary performers. The impact of the score was incalculable; hardly a single composer anywhere in the world escaped its powerful influence.

Sadko. An opera by Rimsky-Korsakov, first produced in Moscow on January 7, 1898. The libretto is based on an ancient Russian epic. Sadko is a popular minstrel in Novgorod, the first capital of Russia. He has mercantile dreams of selling wares abroad, a dream that is fantastically realized when a flock of swans on Lake Ilmen, who are the feathered daughters of the King of the Ocean, take him to their abode on the bottom of the lake. He catches magic goldfish that turn out to be made of real gold. He returns to Novgorod a rich man. *Sadko* is a paradigm of the Russian fairy tale opera. *The Song of India*, sung by a Hindu merchant visiting Novgorod, is a perennial favorite on the concert platform. The score of *Sadko* abounds in bold innovations. A chorus in 11/4 meter was regarded so difficult to perform that Russian opera choristers devised a line of 11 syllables as a mnemonic aid: "Rim-sky-Kor-sa-kov-is-al-to-ge-ther-mad!"

En Saga. A tone poem by Jean Sibelius, first performed in Helsingfors on February 16, 1893, conducted by Sibelius himself. With this work Sibelius established his individual musical style; it is based on a motif in a minor mode that reflects the millennial Scandinavian spirit—introspective, strong, and persevering. The work is indeed a saga of Finland.

St. François d'Assise. An opera by Olivier Messiaen, his first, to his own libretto based on the mystical life of St. Francis, whose devotion was not limited to humans but also embraced birds and God's other creatures. Messiaen himself was a devoted birdman who collected songs of the flying species and used them with melodic twits, twirls, and trills of his own. The opera was produced at the Paris Opéra on November 28, 1983.

St. Louis Blues. A celebrated song that W.C. Handy wrote in 1914; it stabilized the form of blues, anticipated in his previous success, *The Memphis Blues*. The sheet music sales and recordings of *St. Louis Blues* leaped into millions.

The Saint of Bleecker Street. A music drama by Gian Carlo Menotti, to his own libretto, first produced in New York on December 27, 1954. The action takes place in an Italian section of Greenwich Village in New York. An Italian girl believes she has the sacred stigmata, but her agnostic brother derides her. He himself is ridiculed by his girlfriend for his devotion to his sister, and in an argument he accidentally kills the girlfriend. He flees, returning to Bleecker Street as his sister enters the convent. But now she becomes overwrought emotionally and dies as she pledges her vow.

Salomé. An opera by Richard Strauss, to a libretto from the original French play by Oscar Wilde. It was first performed in Dresden on December 9, 1905. The story, obliquely connected with the biblical narrative, is centered on Salomé, stepdaughter of Herod, tetrarch of Judea. John the Baptist, imprisoned by Herod, is brought out to the palace at Salomé's request. She is fascinated by him, even though he curses her, and she brazenly cries, "I want to kiss your mouth!" Herod, who lusts after Salomé, asks her to dance for him. She agrees on condition that he will fulfill her unspoken wish and performs the sensuous Dance of the Seven Veils. The reward she demands is the severed head of John the Baptist. Herod tries to dissuade her from her monstrous intention but yields in the end. When the head is brought out on a platter, Salomé mocks it. "You wouldn't let me kiss your mouth!" she cries, and kisses it passionately on the lips. Provoked beyond endurance by this act of depravity, Herod commands the guards to kill her. The score is a masterpiece of stark realism, set to music of overwhelming power, ranging from exotic melodiousness to crashing dissonance. The opera aroused vehement opposition when it was staged at the Metropolitan Opera in New York on January 22, 1907; the moralistic uproar in the public and press was such that the management was compelled to cancel further performances. It took two decades for the American public to mature sufficiently to absorb the opera.

The story of Salomé is told quite differently in *La Tragédie de Salomé*, an orchestral suite by Florent Schmitt, first performed in Paris on November 9, 1907. Here Salomé throws the head of John the Baptist into the sea, and the waters flow red like blood. A bolt of lightning strikes the palace and destroys it. The music dramatically illustrates these events in dark, dissonant harmonies.

El Salón Mexico. An orchestral piece by Aaron Copland, inspired by Mexican tunes. The title refers to a dancehall in Mexico City in which Copland heard a native group play Mexican popular music. The first performance of the work was given in Mexico City on August 27, 1937, with Carlos Chávez conducting; it became one of Copland's most popular works.

Salon music. The type of music that flourished in Paris and Vienna in the 18th century, a salon being the drawingroom in aristocratic mansions, and salon music therefore satisfying the need for light entertainment. Liszt complained of the *"atmosphère lourde et méphitique des salons"* ("heavy and ill-smelling salon atmosphere"). During his Paris sojourn, the German poet Heine voiced his despair at the universal proliferation of light piano music "that one hears in every house, day and night," adding that "at the very moment of the writing of this report a couple of young ladies in the neighboring house are playing a morceau for two left hands." The word *salon* gradually became synonymous with Biedermeier culture. Chopin was not averse to writing piano music designed for salon performances, and Schumann described him as the *"vornehmste Salonkomponist"* ("most elegant salon composer"), and his famous Waltz in A-flat major as a *"Salonstück der nobelsten Art, aristokratisch durch und durch"* ("salon piece of the most noble art, aristocratic through and through"). Lesser composers frankly entitled their works *Études de Salon*, *Petites Fleurs de Salon*, and the like. Perhaps the most "mephitic" (to use Liszt's word) was *Prière d'une Vierge* (*The Maiden's Prayer*) by a young Polish girl named Thekla Badarzewska, which spread through Europe and America with an irresistible force of distilled sentimentality. Although salon music largely disappeared with the cataclysmic outbreak of World War I, social salons continued to be maintained by wealthy hostesses in Paris and other music capitals. Countess de Polignac, the daughter of the American sewing machine manufacturer Singer, who married a French aristocrat, commissioned works by Stravinsky, Manuel de Falla, and others for performance at her musical matinées.

Salon orchestras were organized for performances of light music in cafés, cabarets, and the houses of the rich. The minimal ensemble was the piano trio. The so-called Vienna type of salon orchestra consisted of a "seated" violinist, a "standing" violinist, as well as cello, flute, and percussion. The

Berlin salon ensemble added the clarinet, cornet, trombone, viola, and double bass; the Paris salon orchestra usually employed piano, violin, cello, flute, cornet, and drums. Special editions were published for these orchestras to enable them to play light overtures or dance suites in "theater arrangements," in which there were cues in the piano parts to replace the missing instruments. Although salon music was deprecated for its low taste, the salon orchestra performed a positive educational role, providing Classical and semi-Classical music in workable arrangements.

Salsa. A Latin American dance that originated in the Caribbean islands, most notably in Cuba, with traceable African roots. The word *salsa* means "sauce" in Spanish; the dance may have received its name because of its hot, peppery, acrid, and pervasive rhythm over a hypnotically repetitive melodic line. Its meter is invariably 4/4, with quarter notes alternating with eighth notes in syncopated beats.

Sambuca lincea. A curious enharmonic harpsichord, so named by its inventor Fabio Colonna, who was also known under the name of Linceo; *sambucus* is Latin for "elder tree," from which the instrument was built. Constructed about 1600, it was tuned according to a complicated scheme combining pure acoustic Pythagorean intervals with various tempered adjustments. To accommodate this diversity, the octave of the sambuca lincea was divided into 17 notes; in all, there were 50 strings.

Samson et Dalila. An opera by Camille Saint-Saëns, first performed in Weimar to a German libretto on December 2, 1877. It tells the familiar story of Delilah, the priestess of the Philistine temple, who entices the Hebrew warrior Samson, and during his sleep cuts his hair, which is the source of his physical power. He is then blinded, chained, and taken to the Philistine temple in Gaza. There, summoning his remaining strength, he breaks the pillars supporting the roof, bringing the temple down on himself and on the miscreant worshippers. Because of restrictions on theatrical representation of biblical characters, the opera was not performed on the stage in France until 1892, and not in England until 1909.

Sanglot. French for a sob, a "tearful sigh"; an emotional appoggiatura, common in female arias with interjections such as "Oh!" "Ah!" or "Hélas!" An effective sanglot can be achieved by a closing of the vocal box. Such a *coup de glotte* was a great specialty of Caruso, in his rendition of such arias as Canio's *Vesti la giubba* from *Pagliacci*.

Sapho. Charles Gounod's first opera, produced in Paris on April 16, 1851. The libretto describes in melodramatic terms the life of the Greek poetess who flourished on the island of Lesbos. Jules Massenet also wrote an opera of this title, but its libretto was based on a story by Alphonse Daudet. It was first produced in Paris on November 27, 1897.

Saraband. A dance step in triple time, popular in the 17th and 18th centuries, which became an integral part of the Baroque instrumental suite. The origin of the word is conjectural; it has been variously traced to Arabia through Moorish Spain, to Mexico and to Panama. Ironically, one of the earliest mentions of the word occurs in the ruling of the Spanish Inquisition in Mexico in 1583, which forbade performing the saraband on penalty of a fine and imprisonment, apparently due to its supposed immoral and suggestive nature. Half a century after its proscription in Spain, the saraband quietly slithered into France and even into Elizabethan England. It received its highest sanction by being given a place of honor in the instrumental suites of Bach and Handel.

Satzlehre. A theory of polyphonic composition, a compound German word consisting of *Satz* in the sense of contrapuntal rules, and *Lehre* or "study"; a more complete term is *Tonsatzlehre,* "study of tonal settings." It is distinguished from other theories of composition in that it is not preoccupied with the acoustical, harmonic, or intervallic elements of chords and contrapuntal combinations but is concerned mainly with the larger considerations of structure and style.

La Scala. The most famous Italian opera house, founded in 1778 in Milan. Its full name is Teatro alla Scala. Although it is popularly imagined that the theater owes its name to the spectacular steps leading to its portals (*scala* is ladder in Italian), the theater was actually named after Regina della Scala, the wife of the Duke Visconti of Milan. It opened on August 3, 1778. A whole galaxy of Italian composers—Rossini, Donizetti, Bellini, Verdi, and Puccini—had their operas premiered at La Scala, and great conductors, including Toscanini, presided over these performances. In August 1943 La Scala was almost entirely destroyed by the insensate Allied air attack on Milan. It was rebuilt in 1946 with the financial assistance of musicians and music lovers from all over the civilized world and was reopened on May 11, 1946, with Toscanini conducting. The restoration was remarkably faithful. The Teatro alla Scalla has six tiers, four of which are taken over by 146 boxes lined with elegant multicolored fabrics, with the lighting provided by a sumptuous chandelier. In 1955 the Teatro alla Scala gave birth, in a splendid parturition, to an offspring called La Piccola Scala, suitable for performances of chamber opera and modern ballet.

Scat. A type of jazz singing in which meaningless syllables or vowels are inserted into the vocal line. It must be rhythmical, and the need to maintain a certain beat or syncopated phrase prevails over the requirement of verbal sense. The scat technique became amalgamated with bebop, itself a word that consists of two meaningless scat-like syllables.

Schandeflöte (Shame flute). A heavy vertical flute made of iron that was hung on a tight ring around the neck of a town fifer in medieval Germany who was condemned to public disgrace for the crime of playing too many wrong notes in the performance of his duties. A sign was placed on his jacket spelling out the extent of his inharmonious conduct.

Scheherazade. A symphonic suite by Rimsky-Korsakov, based on *The Thousand and One Nights*, first performed in St. Petersburg on November 3, 1888. The connecting link within the suite is a brief violin solo representing the narrative of the sultan's most resourceful wife, who saves herself from his customary execution of each of his wives after the wedding night by telling him exciting serial tales requiring continuation. The score is a paradigm of orchestral brilliance. Its synthetic orientalism even influenced composers in Arab countries.

Schelomo. A "Hebrew rhapsody" by Ernest Bloch for cello and orchestra, first performed in New York on May 3, 1917. *Schelomo* is the original Hebrew word for Solomon; the solo cello portrays the eloquent voice of the wise king of the Hebrews.

Schenker system. A theory of musical analysis proposed by the Austrian musicologist Heinrich Schenker that reduces the melody and harmony to the *Urlinie*, the fundamental line, governing the melodic design, and the bass line *Grundbrechung*, "ground breaking." The process of analysis is in several stages. The actual composition is defined as foreground; its partial reduction is middleground; its final schematization, the background, constitutes the *Ursatz*, that is, the ultimate irreducible structure, representing the summation of the *Urlinie* and the *Grundbrechung*. These successive stages are obtained by a series of *Züge*, or "motions." Because the overtone series is the basic source of the *Ursatz*, the Schenker system postulates the absolute preponderance of the tonic major triad, with the subdominant and dominant triads as its derivatives and with minor triads accounted for by Procrustean adjustments. In his original historical exposition, Schenker covers the period from Bach to Brahms (Wagner is omitted). Analysis of chromatic harmony is made by further adjustments. Following this modus operandi, it is possible to analyze even modern works, but the artificiality of the Schenker system becomes increasingly evident with every successive step.

Scherzo. A "jest" in Italian, but the term was applied with widely varied significance. In the 16th century, *scherzo* meant a vocal composition in a light manner, but such titles as *Scherzi sacri* ("sacred scherzos") are also found in music literature. In the second half of the 18th century, the term was standardized to mean instrumental composition in 3/4 or 3/8 time in a rapid tempo. Structurally, the scherzo was a modification of the Classical minuet; in the 19th century, it often replaced the minuet in sonatas, chamber music, and symphonies. Like the minuet, the scherzo contains a contrasting middle part, the trio (so named because originally it was written for three instruments only). In most Classical symphonies, the scherzo was placed in the position formerly occupied by the minuet, that is, as the third movement, but Beethoven shifted it to the second movement in his Symphony No. 9. In the course of time, the scherzo became an independent instrumental work. Chopin elevated it to a music form of prime importance. His piano Scherzos are extensive, virtuosic compositions, although they keep their ternary form. Paul Dukas called his orchestral poem *L'Apprenti Sorcier* a scherzo. Stravinsky wrote an orchestral work entitled *Scherzo fantastique*, inspired by Maeterlinck's essay on the life of bees.

Scherzo à la russe. A sophisticated potpourri of Russian folklike motives by Igor Stravinsky scored for a jazz big band was written for a radio broadcast in 1944. He conducted the orchestral arrangement of it in San Francisco on March 22, 1946.

Schlitztrommel. German for "slit-gong," or "slit-drum"; in French, *tambour de bois*. A large drum in use for centuries among the tribes of central Africa and Australia, it is similar to the teponaxtle of South America. It is made of a large log with a slit along its trunk; two different tones are produced by striking to the right or to the left of the slit. In the jungle, it serves as a method of communication; simple messages of danger, joy, death, or war are transmitted through rhythmic beats. Some modern composers, among them Carl Orff and Stockhausen, have used the *Schlitztrommel*.

Schluss. German for "conclusion," when music embraces the totality of the final section of a composition. The last movement of a large work is sometimes referred to in German as *Schluss-Satz*, "conclusion part." The *Schluss* in a simple chant may be limited to two notes, the *penultima vox* ("next-to-last voice") and *ultima vox* ("last voice"), to use the terminology of the medieval Latin treatises. The ideal *Schluss* in Classical music occurs in Mozart's Symphony No. 39 in E-flat major, which concludes with a simple restatement of the principal theme, suggesting a signature in Gothic characters. The most prolix *Schluss* is that of the Symphony No. 2 of Sibelius, consisting of a seemingly interminable succession of ascending scales, which, upon reaching the sixth degree of the key, retreat to the leading tone in the lower octave, only to resume their Sisyphus-like ascension. The most abrupt *Schluss* occurs with the C-major chord at the end of Prokofiev's march from the *Love of Three Oranges*. The most numbing C-major *Schluss* is found in the finale of the Piano Concerto No. 1 by Shostakovich. By definition, the *Schluss* must be a unison or a concord, but Chopin and Schumann sometimes ended an individual number in a suite of pieces on an unresolved dominant-seventh chord. The final chord in Mahler's grand symphony *Das Lied von der Erde* is a discord. In atonal writing, a dissonant ending is required, unless it happens to be a single tone lost in midair, pianissimo. Toward the middle of the 20th century, several composers, among them Stockhausen, Earle Brown, and John Cage, developed a concept of works without an ascertainable *Schluss*, wherein any moment of a composition may be either a beginning or an end.

Schola cantorum. A "school of singers." The term goes back to the seventh century, when such a school was established in Rome for teaching proper Gregorian chant. Pope Pius X decreed in 1903 that similar singing schools should be established in all Catholic churches. The name was also used by academic organizations not connected with the church, notably the Schola Cantorum in Paris, founded in 1894.

School Days. A song by Gus Edwards, introduced by him as a vaudeville act in 1907. It proliferated spontaneously and became a standard in American grade schools, encouraging school children to study reading, 'riting, and 'rithmetic, with a caveat that otherwise they might be exposed to the hickory stick.

The Schoolmaster (Der Schulmeister). Haydn's Symphony No. 55 in E-flat major (1774). There is some didactic presentation of the musical material in its second movement, hence the title. It is not known who attached the pedagogical name to the work.

Schwanda the Bagpiper. An opera by Jaromir Weinberger, first performed in Prague on April 27, 1927, under the Czech title *Švanda dudák*. Schwanda's expertise on the bagpipe is such that he wins the affection of the frosty queen, nicknamed Ice Heart. When she discovers that he has a wife, she sentences him to death. He flees her wrath, but because of a thoughtless blasphemy he commits, he is sent to Hell. A friendly magician wins his soul in a rather dishonest card game with the devil, and Schwanda is freed. He returns to his patient and loyal wife. The Polka and Fugue from *Schwanda* are perennially popular at light symphonic concerts. Weinberger's subsequent works, written after he emigrated to the United States, were dishearteningly unsuccessful. Despondent, he took poison and died in his Florida home.

Der Schwanendreher (The Organ-Grinder). A concerto for viola and small orchestra by Paul Hindemith; he himself played the solo viola part at its premiere in Amsterdam on November 14, 1935. The organ-grinder of the title is a minstrel who plays folk tunes from the Middle Ages and Renaissance that he has heard during his travels. The title literally means "the swan turner," referring to the swan revolving on top of the organ-grinder's instrument.

Schwanengesang. A collection of songs by Franz Schubert, written in 1828 and published posthumously in Vienna. The title was selected by the publisher to indicate that these Lieder were Schubert's swan songs. To be sure, swans cannot sing; they croak or grunt, but the phrase is beyond ornithological rectification.

Die schweigsame Frau (The Silent Woman). An opera by Richard Strauss, first produced in Dresden on June 24, 1935. The plot follows the outline of *Epicœne* by Ben Jonson. A cantankerous old man, appropriately named Morosus, is looking for a wife who will keep silent. His nephew turns up with a theatrical group that includes his own wife, whom he introduces to his uncle as "the silent woman." A fraudulent marriage contract is drawn between her and the old man, but as soon as she moves into his house she begins to behave like a garrulous shrew. The old man is distraught by this transformation and is only too glad to restore her to her lawful husband, his nephew, and even give him money. The score represents the humorous strain in the music of Strauss, in the manner of *Der Rosenkavalier*.

Scordatura. An Italian term stemming from *discordatura*, "mistuning." The practice arose in the 16th century to facilitate the playing of the lute in different keys. Scordatura received its highest development in early Baroque music, with composers ingeniously changing the tuning of string instruments to enable them to play easily in keys of several sharps or flats. A pioneer of scordatura was Heinrich von Biber, whose "mystery sonatas" are systematically arranged in scordatura so that the violins, violas, and cellos become in effect transposing instruments, each string having its own transposition. Under such conditions, not only the notes but the intervals between the strings become altered. Vivaldi applied scordatura in several concertos. The visual appearance of the music, notated in traditional clefs, suggests a modernistic cacophony. An anonymous string quartet incorrectly attributed to Benjamin Franklin uses different scordaturas for different instruments in different movements. Thus, a quartet of absolute amateurs, playing on opens strings only, could produce a fairly intricate contrapuntal work. With the progress of instrumental techniques, scordatura lost its raison d'être, but modern composers occasionally use it to secure a fundamental harmony in a minor key by tuning down a semitone the two lower strings of a violin, viola, or cello. In the coda of Tchaikovsky's *Pathétique* Symphony, the melodic line descends to F-sharp, but the violins playing the passage have to stop at their lowest note, G, and the final F-sharp has to be taken over by other instruments. To avoid this frustrating sense of incompleteness, Leopold Stokowski when performing the work instructed the violinists to tune down the open G string to F-sharp, a procedure that can be classified as scordatura.

Score. The vertical notation of a piece of music for several instruments or voices in which the individual parts are placed one below another so that the music can be read in its totality. An orchestral score lists all instruments, with the woodwinds on top, brass instruments in the middle, and the strings in the lower section. Percussion is placed between the brass and the strings. In concertos, the solo parts are placed immediately above the string section, as are the vocal parts and choruses in operas, oratorios, and other vocal scores. The first page of a complete orchestral or operatic score must list all instruments as a sort of inventory, with instruments in the high range placed above those of the lower range; the bottom line of a score is occupied by the double bass part. To save space, the staves of instruments that have rests on a particular page in the score are omitted, and only the active parts are printed. First and second flutes and other paired instruments usually share the same staff in the orchestral score, although it is often necessary to split individual string sections into several staves when they play *divisi*, that is, divided. The task of an orchestral or operatic conductor, in surveying these musical masses under his command, is complicated by the fact that clarinets, the English horn, French horns, and trumpets are transposing instruments. Some 20th-century composers, notably Prokofiev, have written the parts of transposing instruments in the key of C, so that the conductor does not have to be confounded by the polytonal look of the score, gazing at a clarinet part with one sharp in the key signature while the strings have one flat. In chamber music with piano, the piano part is invariably placed below the other instruments, which in turn are disposed according to their relative pitch. Thus, in a string quartet the first violin is on top, then the second violin, the viola, and at the bottom, the cello.

Scotch Symphony. The name usually assigned to Mendelssohn's Symphony No. 3, op. 56, in A minor, first performed in Leipzig on March 3, 1842. The most Scottish of the four movements is the second, Vivace, which seems to have Scottish modalities. Mendelssohn dedicated the work to Queen Victoria.

Scratch Orchestra. An organization founded in 1969 by the British avant-garde composer Cornelius Cardew. He defined it as "a large number of enthusiasts pooling their resources (not primarily musical) and assembling for action." He further declared that "the word music and its derivatives are not understood to refer exclusively to sound. Each member of the orchestra is provided with a notebook (or a scratchbook) in which he notates a number of accompaniments performable continuously for indefinite periods."

Scythian Suite. The first important orchestral score by Sergei Prokofiev, first performed, with Prokofiev conducting, in Petrograd on January 29, 1916. The subtitle of the suite is *Ala and Lolli,* the names of Scythian gods. The finale describes the sunrise in sonorous displays of B-flat major. Prokofiev was very conscious of the importance of the sun and even circulated a questionnaire among his friends inquiring simply: "What is your opinion of the sun?" The solicited opinions turned out to be 100 percent positive.

Sea Symphony. The subtitle of the Symphony No. 1 of Ralph Vaughan Williams, for vocal soloists, chorus, and orchestra to texts from Walt Whitman. It is in four movements: *A Song for All Seas, All Ships*; *On the Beach at Night Alone*; *The Waves*; and *The Explorers*. Vaughan Williams conducted its first performance at the Leeds Festival on October 12, 1910.

The Seasons. Haydn's famous oratorio, written on the threshold of the 19th century. It is usually listed under its English title because the work was based on an English poem by J. Thomson. The text was translated into German and published as *Die Jahreszeiten*. It was first performed at the Schwarzenburg Palace, Vienna, on April 24, 1801. "The Seasons" is also the title of a group of string concertos by Vivaldi.

The Second Hurricane. A children's opera by Aaron Copland, first performed in New York on April 21, 1937. The work was written for performance by nonprofessional young musicians. The libretto bears the imprint of a newspaper story. A group of children organize aid to victims of a flood in the Ohio Valley after a hurricane. They charter a plane and fly there with food and medicine, but the hurricane strikes for the second time in the same location, and the rescuers themselves have to be rescued. The music is rhythmic, lyrical, energetic.

Self-quotations. Composers are apt to amuse themselves by quoting appropriate passages from their own works. In the score of *Don Giovanni*, Mozart takes pleasure in quoting the admonition to Cherubino from *The Marriage of Figaro*, "Non più andrai." Wagner quotes *Tristan und Isolde* in the score of *Die Meistersinger*. Richard Strauss rather brazenly quotes themes from his previous tone poems in the score of *Das Heldenleben*, in which he himself is the titular hero unafraid of the petty assaults of critics.

Selma sedlák (The Sly Peasant). An opera by Antonin Dvořák, first performed in Prague on January 27, 1878. The beautiful Betrushka, daughter of a rich peasant, loves a hired hand, but her father wants her to marry a prosperous villager. Enter new characters: the duke and duchess. The duke is struck by the beauty of Betrushka; her lover then conceives the idea of securing ducal help for his own marriage. Betrushka persuades the duchess to put on her dress. When the duke makes amorous advances to the disguised duchess, she slaps his face. Thereupon all false identities are straightened out, everybody forgives everybody, and the two young people are united in happy matrimony. What with subplots involving the duke's servants, there are obvious similarities in the story to *The Marriage of Figaro*, but Dvořák's music can hardly be compared with Mozart's.

Semiramide. An opera by Gioachino Rossini, first produced in Venice on February 3, 1823. Semiramide, the queen of Babylon, conspires with her lover to kill the king. This done, she takes another lover, a young barbarian, but to her horror she discovers that he is her own son by a previous union. When her first lover attacks her son, she intercepts his dagger and dies; thereupon, her son slays her first lover and by hereditary rights becomes king. The opera is seldom performed, but the overture is a concert favorite. A number of other composers wrote operas on the subject, among them Porpora, Gluck, Salieri, Cimarosa, Meyerbeer, and, in the 20th century, Respighi. None of these is ever performed.

Semper Fidelis. A march written by John Philip Sousa in 1886 while he was leader of the Marine Band. He dedicated it to the U.S. Marine Corps.

Semper Paratus. A song by Capt. Francis Saltus von Boskerck of the U.S. Coast Guard. He published it in 1928, and it has since become the official march of the Coast Guard.

Sensemayá. An "indigenous incantation to kill a snake" for voice and orchestra by Silvestre Revueltas, with words by the Afro-Cuban poet Guillen. It represents a voodoo ritual. It was first performed in a revised version for large orchestra without voice in Mexico City on December 15, 1938.

Sequence. An extremely fruitful technical device that achieved its greatest flowering in Baroque music. In a sequence, a thematic phrase is imitated in the same voice a degree higher or lower without altering its rhythmic pattern. In its simplest form, a sequence has two segments that effectively connote the tonic and dominant harmonies. Examples of such sequences are found by the thousands in Classical works. The theme of Mozart's Piano Sonata in A major, K. 331, is typical; the opening notes of Beethoven's Symphony No. 5 and the subsequent phrase also constitute such a tonic-dominant sequence. Sequences are called *tonal* if they move along a given key; they are *real* if they are true as to the precise interval and thus represent a modulation. The longest tonal sequence occurs toward the end of Tchaikovsky's overture to *Eugene Onegin*; it has eight segments and descends fully two octaves by consecutive degrees. Real sequences are effective when they modulate through major and minor keys in the direction of flats in the cycle of fifths, making use of dominant-seventh chords. For instance, the first inversion of the dominant-seventh chord of F major would be followed after its resolution into the tonic triad by the first inversion of the dominant-seventh chord of D minor, resolving into D minor, followed by the first inversion of the dominant seventh of B-flat major, and so on. Also effective are modulating sequences generated by the descending chromatic bass—for example, the third inversion of the dominant-seventh chord in G resolving into the first inversion of G major followed by the third inversion of the dominant-seventh chord in F resolving into the first inversion of the F-major triad, and so forth. It is particularly effective when the leading tone is in the melody.

A curious revulsion against the employment of sequences arose in the 20th century. Some modern composers completely renounce all sequential formulas as automatic devices impeding the flow of free invention. However, composers of the neo-Baroque persuasion have ostentatiously revived the use of sequences, particularly tonal sequences, often with the purpose of emphatic stylization.

In Gregorian chant, the term *sequentia* was applied to a long melismatic chant, originally without words but later supplied with syllabic texts. Sometimes the verse had only a single word, "alleluia," repeated many times. These early ecclesiastical sequences eventually gave rise to important medieval forms such as the *estampie*. They have no historical or musical connection with the tonal sequences of Classical music.

Serenade. A term derived from the Italian word *sera*, "evening," and its derivative, *serenata*, "evening song," but the more remote verbal origin is *serena*, "serene," as applied to a cloudless sky and inferentially to a state of peaceful contentment. In the 16th century, serenade acquired the meaning of an evening song, performed by a lover before a fair lady's window; it was habitually accompanied on the lute or guitar and delivered at day's end. A serenade is a favorite device in opera. An interesting example of a mock serenade is an aria by Mephistophélès in Gounod's *Faust*. About the second half of the 18th century, the literal meaning of serenade expanded to denote any piece of entertainment music, becoming practically synonymous with *divertimento*. An instrumental serenade is usually scored for a small ensemble and designed for an open-air performance or a festival occasion. Mozart wrote his *Haffner Serenade* for a wedding in the family of Sigmund Haffner, burgomeister of Salzburg. In the 19th century, the title *serenade* was often attached to any instrumental work scored for a small instrumental group.

Serenade for String Orchestra. A work of symphonic proportions by Tchaikovsky, first performed in Moscow on January 28, 1882. Tchaikovsky said that in it he paid his debt to Mozart, and he deliberately imitated Mozart's manner. The music has more of the spirit of the Baroque, however, and its finale makes use of the Russian song *Under the Green Apple Tree*. When Tchaikovsky thought he imitated somebody, he invariably composed original music.

Serpent. A wind instrument actually constructed in the shape of a snake. It was first manufactured in France about 1600 and consisted of several pieces of wood bound together by a leather covering. Despite its ungainly appearance and the considerable difficulty in handling it, the serpent served an important function in providing the deep bass in military bands in support of the bassoon. The serpent was also known as a Russian bassoon because it was regularly used in Russian military bands. It was still in use in the first half of the 19th century, but Berlioz damned it as a monstrosity. This damnation was the serpent's last hiss.

Serse (Xerxes). An opera by Handel, first produced in London on April 15, 1738. Two brothers in ancient Persia are in love with the same girl, but Xerxes loses out despite his royal stature. The opera rates very low among Handel's creations, but it contains the celebrated aria *Ombra mai fu* known to the musical multitudes simply as *Handel's Largo*. Its text, "The Shade Never Was," was apparently meant to be satirical because here Xerxes, standing in the desert under a single tree, comments upon its cooling shade.

Servilia. An opera by Rimsky-Korsakov, first produced in St. Petersburg on October 14, 1902. It takes place in Rome in A.D. 67. A young tribune, Valery, loves Servilia, daughter of a Roman senator who is accused of treason by the Emperor Nero and exiled. Servilia is crushed by the internecine domestic fights and expires in the arms of her lover. This is one of the two operas by Rimsky-Korsakov not based on a national Russian story (the other was *Mozart and Salieri*).

Shawm. An early form of oboe, very popular in the Renaissance, which went out of use in the 17th century. It was shaped like a bassoon and was made of a long piece of wood with a curved metal bell. At the height of its popularity, the shawm came in all sizes, providing a range from bass to high soprano. The word comes from the French *chalémie*, via the German *Schalmei*. The bass shawm was called *bombarde* in France and *Pommern* in Germany; in Italy it was known as the *piffaro*, "a whistling pipe." When George Bernard Shaw, in his days as a music critic, received a letter addressed to G. B. Shawm, he thought it was a spelling error until someone told him that it was an obsolete wind instrument producing a forced nasal sound.

Short octave. A deficient lowest octave in early keyboard instruments; it omitted the chromatic tones and used black keys to sound the notes usually assigned to the white keys, with only B-flat kept in its proper position. The short octave had only five white keys and three black keys. The white keys were tuned for E, F, G, A, B, and the black keys for the sounds of C, D, and B-flat. An alternative tuning was C, F, G, A, B, for white keys, and D, E, B-flat for the black. The rationale for the omission of chromatic tones except for B-flat was that chromatics were used very seldom in the deep bass register in keyboard compositions of the Baroque period. There were also advantages. Thanks to the short octave, organists or harpsichordists could play chords in widely spread positions because the stretch of the short octave was only five white keys. In his E-minor Toccata for harpsichord, Bach has a difficult interval of the tenth in the bass, but in the short octave it would require the stretch of only one octave. The retention of the B-flat in the short octave is explained by the great frequency of that note as a keynote.

The Sicilian Vespers (I Vespri Siciliani). An opera by Verdi, first produced in Paris on June 13, 1855, at the Grande Exposition under the French title *Les Vêpres siciliennes*. The subject was not relished by the French audience, for it dealt with the expulsion of the French from Sicily in the 13th century. The Vespers of the title are the church bells rung by a patriotic Sicilian noblewoman as a signal for the expected uprising. The opera ends in a massacre of the French. Not a major Verdi opera, it is surprisingly tenacious in the world's opera houses.

Le Siège de Corinthe. An opera by Gioachino Rossini, first performed in Paris on October 9, 1826. The story deals with a daughter of the governor of Corinth who refuses to submit to the commander of the Turkish army besieging Corinth as the price of its relief. She dies with her father in the city ruins. Since the first production of the opera happened to take place during the Greek uprising against the Turks, to which the French were highly sympathetic, it won a particularly warm reception. Actually, the score was a revision of an opera on a similar subject first produced in Naples on December 3, 1820, under the title *Maometto II (Mahomet II)*.

Siegfried. A music drama, the third of Wagner's cycle *Der Ring des Nibelungen*, first produced in Bayreuth on August 16, 1876, as part of the inaugural Bayreuth Festival. Siegfried is the incestuous child of Siegmund and Sieglinde, children of Wotan. He is guarded by the Nibelung dwarf Mime. Wotan predicts that a hero will emerge who will make the mighty sword with which to kill the murderous giant Fafner, magically transformed into a dragon. Siegfried fulfills Wotan's prophecy, forges the sword, and slays Fafner. Inadvertently, he touches the hot gore of the slain dragon; putting his finger to his lips, he suddenly becomes aware that he can understand the language of the birds. Siegfried also reads the mind of Mime and realizes that Mime plots his death. He kills the malevolent dwarf and goes forth to his next adventure, to rescue Brünnhilde, the disobedient Valkyrie who was punished by Wotan and placed on a rock surrounded by a ring of fire. He reaches her as she lies in deep sleep and puts the fateful ring of the Nibelung, now in his possession, on her finger. He awakens her with a kiss. The score contains some of the most gorgeous episodes in Wagner's tetralogy; the scene with the birds is poetic.

Siegfried Idyll. A piece for a small orchestral group that Wagner performed in his home on Lake Lucerne as a surprise for the birthday of his wife, Cosima, on Christmas Day 1870, celebrating the birth of their son Siegfried. In the manuscript the work is titled simply *Symphonie*. In its score, Wagner made use of several leading motifs from his opera *Siegfried*. Siegfried Wagner was to become an opera composer, known as "the little son of a great father."

Sight reading. Before the system of notation was firmly established, sight reading included perforce a great deal of improvisation within the given meter and key. Choirboys were trained to sing mensural music by sight. Contemporary chronicles report the case of a 14-year-old chorister known as *frater Georgius* from Pisa who could sing at sight from the most intricate parts of polyphonic music. The real challenge to professional musicians came in the 19th century when to read at sight a difficult piece of piano music required a superior ability to coordinate melody, harmony, and rhythm.

Piano accompanists to singers and instrumentalists are routinely supposed to be able to play their parts and follow the soloist without a rehearsal, so that playing *a prima vista* or, to use the French term, *à livre ouvert* ("at the open book"), became a necessity in a practical concert career when little time was available for rehearsal. A particularly difficult task is to reduce a full orchestral score at sight on the piano. It involves instantaneous transposition of transposing instruments, coordinating string and wind groups at a glance, and reducing all this to a pianistically feasible arrangement, without losing the tempo and component contrapuntal rhythms. It can be managed with a traditional score, in which harmonies can be assumed to be compatible in various instrumental groups, but in a modern score, where atonality is a tonal hurdle and polytonality a common hazard, such an instantaneous piano reduction is tremendously difficult.

Sinfonia Antarctica. The Symphony No. 7 of Ralph Vaughan Williams, scored for soprano, female chorus, and orchestra, first performed in Manchester, England, on January 14, 1953. In this work Vaughan Williams used the background music he wrote for a motion picture on Sir Robert Scott's expedition to the Antarctic, where Scott perished in 1912. The music abounds in special effects while preserving its balance between drama and the contemplation of eternity. The words are taken from Shelley, Coleridge, and John Donne, ending with quotations from the notebook of Scott.

Singakademie. A historically important musical institution organized in Berlin in 1791 to present concerts of vocal music. In 1829, Mendelssohn conducted in the Berlin Singakademie a performance of Bach's *Passion According to St. Matthew* that greatly contributed to the renewed appreciation of Bach's music.

Singing. The repetitive emission of sound energy in a sequence of melodious tones. It is the most natural vocal action of humans, birds, and some marine animals such as whales. When the witty Austrian tenor Leo Slezak was asked how early he began studying voice, he replied, "I vocalized the chromatic scale when I was six months of age." The human organ that produces the melodious sounds within a definite range is the voice box in the larynx. The impulse to sing (or to speak) is generated in the muscles of the diaphragm, which pushes air upward into the lungs, and from there into the larynx and the vocal cords, which are set in periodical vibrations. The ability to produce sounds of tonal purity and definite pitch constitutes the art of singing. A singer has no instrument outside his or her own body to practice on, so voice training requires nothing more than the control of the vocal cords and the propulsion of air from the lungs. The range of the singing voice is usually not more than 30 tones, but these tones can be modulated in an extraordinary versatility of inflexions and dynamic nuances. A professional singer is able to project the voice with great subtlety in degrees of power ranging from the faintest pianissimo to a thundering fortissimo. For some mysterious reason, Italians, and particularly Neapolitans, are peculiarly gifted at singing. The annals of opera are replete with Italian names. Opera companies all over the world, from Italy to Russia, England, the United States, and South America, were until recently Italian musical colonies. There are exceptional cases of men and women extending their voices by training. The American composer Henry Cowell was able to sing practically the entire audible range, from the lowest notes of the bass to the highest treble. Hans Werner Henze wrote a work for voice and orchestra that demands a similarly fantastic vocal range, and there are singers who train themselves to satisfy this requirement. In works by avant-garde composers, singers are given parts requiring the production of all kinds of physiological sounds, such as howling, shrieking, hissing, grunting, moaning, buzzing, gurgling, chuckling, and coughing. There are even individuals who can sing upon both inhaling and exhaling ("circular breathing"), so that they can sustain a note indefinitely. Finally, there are freaks who can sing through the nose. The avant-garde composers take advantage of all such methods of voice production. A special technique in singing is *Sprechstimme*, literally, "speech-voice," which preserves the inflection upward or downward but does not require tonal singing.

Singspiel. A theatrical piece with interpolated musical numbers, particularly popular in the 18th century. The difference between the Singspiel and a full-fledged opera lies in the use of spoken dialogue, but this distinction became less pronounced when purely operatic works admitted dialogue as part of the action. Many features of the Singspiel were adopted in German Romantic opera.

Sir John in Love. An opera by Ralph Vaughan Williams, first produced in London on March 21, 1929. The story deals mainly with Falstaff; the text is selected from Shakespeare's comedy *The Merry Wives of Windsor*. A famous arrangement of the English folksong *Greensleeves* is in this opera.

Sisyfos. An orchestral work by Karl-Birger Blomdahl, symbolizing the hopeless struggle of Sisyphus who is condemned to push a large stone uphill only to have it roll down again from the summit. The music is appropriately pessimistic. It was first performed in Stockholm on October 20, 1954.

Six Épigraphes antiques. A group of pieces written for piano four hands by Claude Debussy and first performed by him and the composer Jean-Jules Roger-Ducasse in Paris on March 15, 1917. The *Épigraphes* were later orchestrated by Ernest Ansermet. Debussy always felt an affinity with ancient Greek prosody, and these pieces are instances of his Grecian moods.

Skyscrapers. A ballet by John Alden Carpenter, first performed in New York on February 19, 1926. This was the first theatrical work inspired exclusively by the American urban landscape. Elements of jazz are much in evidence.

Slap-bass. The manner of playing on the double bass by slapping the strings with the palm of the right hand for rhythmic effect.

Slavonic Dances. Two sets of orchestral dances that Dvořák wrote in 1878 and 1886. These dances are not mere transcriptions or inventions based on authentic Slavonic tunes but original creations of Dvořák in the manner of Slavic folksongs; the melodies employ Ukrainian, Serbian, Polish, and, of course, Czech rhythms. Dvořák also arranged them for two pianos.

The Sleeping Beauty. A ballet by Tchaikovsky, first performed in St. Petersburg on January 15, 1890. The scenario is taken from a classical tale. An evil fairy, scorned at the royal court, dooms a young princess to die when she comes of age. A good fairy transforms the seeming death into a deep sleep, from which the princess awakens when a prince charming, providentially named Desire, kisses her. The score is one of Tchaikovsky's most poetic creations. Particularly popular is the Waltz. A suite of five numbers has been drawn from the score.

The Snow Maiden. An opera by Rimsky-Korsakov, first produced in St. Petersburg on Febrary 10, 1882. The Snow Maiden is the delicate offspring of incompatible parents, Frost and Spring. At the peril of her life, she must not let warmth, physical or emotional, enter her heart. A young villager is captivated by her icy beauty and follows her wherever she goes. Her mother warns her to keep away from the destructive rays of the sun as summer approaches. The girl ignores her mother's warnings and melts away like spring snow. The opera is one of the most poetic productions of the Russian operatic stage, but it is rarely staged outside Russia.

Soggetto. Italian for "subject," used particularly in the Italian titles of contrapuntal and fugal works. A curious form of such a subject is *soggetto cavato* ("excavated subject"), in which the subject is derived from the letters, syllables, or vowels in a name. BACH is a typical modern example of an excavated subject because the letters correspond in German nomenclature to the notes B-flat, A, C, and B-natural. When only vowels are "excavated" from a name, they are assimilated with the vowels of the hexachord of Guido d'Arezzo, ut, re, mi, fa, sol, and la. Josquin wrote a Mass for Hercules, Duke of Ferrara, based on a subject "excavated" from the Latin dedication: "Hercules Dux Ferrarie." The vowels here are e, u, e, u, e, a, i, e, which correspond to the solmization syllables re, ut, re, ut, re, fa, mi, re, that is, D, C, D, C, D, F, E, D. "Excavated" subjects have been used by several modern composers applying equalizations to the complete alphabet. Mario Castelnuovo Tedesco devised birthday cards in which the name of the recipient was "excavated" by arranging several successive alphabets in English corresponding to the chromatic scale. This method generates melodic patterns at angular intervals.

Le Soir. Haydn's Symphony No. 8 in G major (1761) and a sequel to *Le Midi*, his Symphony No. 7. Sometimes it is called *La Tempesta*. The music is not too tempestuous, however, and the evening mood of the title is unperturbed.

Solmization. A system applied to the teaching of singing that is derived from the method of Guido d'Arezzo, in which the initial notes of every successive line in the *Hymn to St. John* happen to form a diatonic hexachord, the corresponding syllables being ut, re, mi, fa, sol, and la. The word *solmization* denotes the practice of singing sol-mi. Sol is the fifth note of the hexachord beginning with ut, but mi in the Guidonian system is the third note of another hexachord, based on F, and thus corresponds to la in the original hexachord. In singing practice, solmization is also known as sol-fa, from which the word *solfeggio* is derived. It gave origin to the rather deplorable way to facilitate singing at sight by intoning the syllables do, re, mi, fa, sol, la, ti (the latter being a substitute for si). In the system of tonic sol-fa, these syllables can be sung for all seven degrees of the major scale in any key. Hence, the system is known as that of the "movable do." The advantage that is gained in teaching singing classes and school choruses is offset by the aberration from the absolute pitch of the written note. To indicate chromatics, the vocables are changed to the vowel *e* for sharps and the vowel *a* for flats. Further modifications have been introduced by instructors to make their charts self-consistent, but the method is unfortunately flawed at its original invention.

El Sombrero de tres picos (The Three-Cornered Hat). A ballet by Manuel de Falla, first performed in London by Diaghilev's Ballet Russe on July 22, 1919.

The picaresque story centers on the governor of a Spanish province who tries to seduce the comely wife of a local miller and carelessly leaves the emblem of his authority, a Napoleonic three-cornered hat, on the premises. All kinds of nonsensical peripeteia ensue. The music sparkles with Spanish rhythms.

Somebody Loves Me. An engaging song written by George Gershwin for the 1924 season of the Broadway revue "George White Scandals," named for its producer. The same three magic words were used as an incipit in a song by Hattie Starr, the first female composer on Tin Pan Alley in 1892, but she was no Gershwin.

Son et lumière. A spectacle that involves sound and light, originating in France about 1950 and therefore usually known under the French name. The text of a typical *son-et-lumière* spectacle relates to the history of the monument around which it is enacted. Whenever possible the producers try to record realistic sounds such as cannon fire, the shouts of a crowd, and so on. A special score, often of electronic sounds, enhances the spectacle. Because of the authenticity of the carefully researched narrative, the spectacles also have educational value. Since 1960, such productions have been staged at the Tower of London, with its grim background of imprisonment and execution, and at the jubilee celebrations in Persepolis in Iran, the Acropolis in Athens, Napoleon's tomb in Paris, and Independence Hall in Philadelphia.

Sonata. Like most forms in music history, the sonata takes its name from the Italian language, in which it means something to be sounded, as *cantata* means something that is sung. A sonata is a wordless musical composition to be performed on a single instrument, usually the piano, in which case it is specifically designated as piano sonata. When written for two instruments, say violin and piano or cello and piano, it is called a violin sonata or a cello sonata. Any other instrument can be coupled with piano; thus there is the clarinet sonata, flute sonata, viola sonata. Paul Hindemith composed sonatas for every orchestral instrument with piano, including a tuba sonata.

The history of the sonata begins in the Baroque era, where it appears as a trio sonata, scored for two instruments, usually violins, and cello accompanied by a keyboard that filled in the harmony. It became even more specialized with the terms *sonata da chiesa*, a piece to be performed in church, and *sonata da camera*, to be played in a hall or chamber. Eventually the term *sonata* was limited to works written exclusively for keyboard. Bach's teacher Kuhnau is generally credited with having written the first programmatic sonata, with a descriptive title, *Biblical Sonata*. What became known as the Classical sonata was set in three movements. The first, usually in energetic fast tempo, was the formative element in which there was an exposition presenting two contrasting themes in two contrasting keys (tonic and dominant), a development of thematic material, and a recapitulation wherein the two principal themes appear in the same key (tonic). The second movement was a meditative song-like piece, and the third movement might be a lively scherzo or a boisterous rondo, with a recurring rapid principal subject alternating with other refrains.

While Mozart and Haydn perfected the art of the Classical sonata, Beethoven expanded it. His 32 piano sonatas are a panoply of fantasies, melancholy soliloquies, and stormy displays of passion. Many of them bear fanciful titles, not always approved by the composer. The sonata remained a favorite vehicle for composers for the piano. Schubert wrote 21 piano sonatas; Mendelssohn, Chopin, and Brahms each wrote three; Schumann contributed six. Liszt composed a long, protracted, single-movement sonata. MacDowell gave picturesque titles to his four piano sonatas: *Tragica*, *Eroica*, *Norse* (on Nordic themes), and *Keltic* (on Irish themes). Scriabin's ten sonatas are sonatas by name only; in their form they are free fantasias. Charles Ives wrote a mammoth *Concord* Sonata, in which the four movements were named after writers from Concord, Massachusetts.

Song. Singing, the most natural faculty of the human condition, must have emerged at the dawn of civilization, even before articulate speech. A song may be limited to a single ejaculation of pitched sound, a manifestation of sexual attraction, or a savage war cry; it may be a succession of sounds, in monotone or in varying pitch levels. Rhythm is an integral part of a song even at the most primitive stage; this intrinsic union is expressed in the Spanish language by the term *meloritmo*, in which melos, "melody," carries a definite rhythmic line. The simplest melorhythm is illustrated by the series of sounds produced by an American Indian slapping himself on the mouth in rhythmic succession. Composers of the avant-garde who have discovered the fascination of the primitive in music as well as in painting and poetry are apt to cultivate elementary melorhythms as a relief from the complexity of the modern arts. It is tempting to summarize the history of human song as a progression from the primeval monotone to the explosive monumental discord of modern times and back again to the primordial molecule of song.

In a modern lexicographical sense, a song is a relatively short composition, either spontaneously generated by an anonymous mass of people or consciously devised by a musically trained person. It is a paradox of music history that the popularity of an individual song is inversely proportionate to the eminence of its composer. The excellence of a primitive song resides in its very brevity and its limited tonal compass. The greatest artistic substance was achieved by the German Lied ("song"); its ABA structure is commonly called *song form*. This formula prescribes that the first part of a song be repeated identically, with but a slight alteration at the ending, after a contrasting middle part.

A Song of Summer. An orchestral piece by Frederick Delius, first performed in London on September 17, 1932. One of his final works, it was dictated note by note by Delius to a musical amanuensis, Eric Fenby, after he was struck with blindness and paralysis.

Songs Without Words. A group of piano pieces by Felix Mendelssohn. Most of the individual titles—such as *Spring Song*, with its centrifugal rapid passages, and *The Bee's Wedding*, with its buzzing chromatics—are the inventions of publishers. Only three titles were given by Mendelssohn himself: *Gondola Song*, *Duetto*, and *Folksong*. The German title of the whole collection is *Lieder ohne Worte*.

Songspiel. A hybrid English-German designation of a modern satirical opera, cabaret, or vaudeville show that emerged in Germany after World War I. The English word *song* had in German a narrowed meaning of "cabaret song." Kurt Weill's opera *Mahagonny* bears the designation *Songspiel*.

La Sonnambula. An opera by Vincenzo Bellini, first produced in Milan on March 6, 1831. The libretto is by the French writer providentially surnamed Scribe, who had a knack for turning out implausible operatic libretti. The somnambulist of the title is an orphan girl betrothed to a villager in Switzerland early in the 19th century. The marriage is nearly wrecked when she wanders in her sleep into the bedroom of a visiting nobleman who courts the proprietress of the local tavern. Nobody believes that she wandered into the visitor's room in her sleep, but as they argue pro and con, she appears on the ledge of the house singing a sad aria. Her bridegroom is reassured of her fidelity. The score is full of beautiful melodies and fully justifies Bellini's name (*bellino* means "pretty" in Italian).

Sonnenquartette. A nickname for Haydn's Six String Quartets, op. 20, which he wrote in 1772. The sunny title has nothing to do with the music of these quartets but is explained by the engraving of a rising sun on the cover of an early edition of the quartets.

Sonology. A term introduced in some American music schools in the last third of the 20th century to describe the study of sound as a structural unit in composition and the laws governing both the acoustical nature of sound and its artistic application to music in the theater and concert hall.

Soprano. An Italian term for the highest female voice, derived from the medieval Latin *superanus*, "standing over." The normal range of the soprano voice is two octaves, from middle C upward. Some vocal parts call for a "voice soprano," meaning a natural voice of a preadolescent boy. Soprano also indicates the highest type of musical instrument, such as soprano saxophone, soprano recorder, and the like.

Soubrette. An ingenue soprano role, a typically seemingly naive but clever and designing servant girl in French and Italian operas and operettas. Such are Susanna in *The Marriage of Figaro* and Papagena in *The Magic Flute*. A coloratura soubrette is exemplified in Rossini's *The Barber of Seville* and by Zerbinetta in *Ariadne auf Naxos* of Richard Strauss. Curiously, the term *soubrette* (which means "little kitten"), though French, is used mainly in Germany. In old French, *soubret* meant "cunning," or "shrewd." In Italian, the term is usually *servetta*.

Sound. A generic name for all humanly audible sensations produced by sound waves ranging from about 16 to 25,000 cycles per second. Low tones generate long sound waves; high tones generate short sound waves. Dogs can hear ultrasonic frequencies of vibrations that are far higher than is the human range, and bats hear frequencies still higher. A pure tone unencumbered by overtones, such as is produced by the tuning fork, generates a sinusoidal sound wave that can be schematically represented as a semicircle above a horizontal line followed by a similar semicircle below that line. Two such semicircles form a cycle of the sound wave. The total number of cycles for any given period of time, usually a second, is called the *frequency of vibrations* of the sound waves. The pitch of a sound is measured by the frequency of vibrations per second. Low sounds, or low pitches, have a low frequency; high pitches have high frequencies. When a frequency is tripled, we hear an octave and a fifth above. When a frequency is quadrupled, we hear a pitch two octaves above the original sound. This order of frequencies is called a *series of overtones*, or a *harmonic series*, and the entire system of traditional harmony is based on it. The ratios of vibrations can be arithmetically derived from it: the octave ratio is 2:1; a fifth, 3:2; a fourth, 4:3, and a major third, 5:4.

The relative strength of the overtones produced by the sound of a musical instrument determines its timbre, or tone color. Middle C on the piano, on the violin, or on the flute has the same frequency of vibrations per second, but their difference in timbre is immediately recognizable. Sound waves created by each instrument are compounded by the sound waves of the overtones involved, and the resulting curve is no longer sinusoidal but complex, having several peaks. When many instruments play together, sounding different pitches, the resulting total sound wave requires a complex geometric study to reconstruct its components. A person with a musical ear, particularly a person who has the sense of perfect pitch, can make this analysis instantly and name all the pitches and all the tone colors constituting the resulting sound.

The loudness of a tone depends on the amplitude, or the swing, produced by the vibrations of a sounding body. The amplitude can be observed visually by plucking a string and watching it vibrate. Noise is a sound without a definite pitch. When the entire spectrum of tones and noises is produced together, the effect is called white noise, analagous to the mixture of all the colors of the rainbow making up the color white.

Spinet. A keyboard instrument of the harpsichord family, closely related to the virginal. Its shape is more like that of the modern grand piano than the virginal, which is rectangular. The spinet was popular during the 18th century and then abruptly disappeared from the musical scene. The modern instrument now called *spinet* has little in common with the venerable Baroque instrument; it is simply a small upright piano.

Spring Sonata. A fairly common nickname for Beethoven's Sonata for violin and piano, op. 24 (1800–1801), particularly in Germany (*Frühlingssonate*). The key of the *Spring* Sonata, F major, is often associated with a revival of nature and love.

Spring Symphony. The name that Schumann attached to his Symphony No. 1 in B-flat major, op. 38. He wrote it during the winter months, but it was the happiest time of his life; he had just married his beloved Clara. The Symphony is in the traditional four movements and was first performed in Leipzig on March 31, 1841.

    Spring Symphony is also a work for voices and orchestra by Benjamin Britten. Unpretentiously arranged to words from English poems glorifying springtime, the work ends with an allusion to the coming of summer with the medieval English round, *Sumer is icumen in.* It was first performed during the Holland Music Festival in Amsterdam on July 9, 1949.

Staccato. Italian for "detached." A type of articulation opposed to *legato*, and consisting of a series of detached notes, usually in rapid tempo. In *forte* it becomes *martellato*, and in *pianissimo* and fast tempo it is sometimes described as *virtuoso staccato*. Staccato is equally effective on the piano and on string instruments, where the bow does not rebound from the strings as it does in *sautillé*.

Stadler Quintet. The name assigned to the Clarinet Quintet, K. 581 (1789), of Mozart, who wrote it for the virtuoso clarinet player Anton Stadler.

Standing ovation. Unanimous and tumultuous applause at the end of a particularly exciting musical performance, when the audience is so transported by admiration for the artist, conductor, singer, pianist, violinist, or other musician that through some body chemistry the listeners are impelled to rise from their seats and clap their hands mightily and sometimes even rhythmically, joyously abandoning themselves to unrestrained vociferation and, in extreme cases, animalistic ululation. The spontaneity of such manifestations, however, is often suspect (as are similar outbursts of collective enthusiasm for politicians).

The Star-Spangled Banner. The national anthem of the United States. The tune is that of *The Anacreontic Song*, which was first published in London about 1780; it is ascribed to John Stafford Smith, a member of the Anacreontic Society in London, formed as a whimsical glorification of the Greek poet Anacreon, famous for his odes to love and wine. The words are by Francis Scott Key, who was inspired by the sight of the American flag still waving at Fort McHenry near Baltimore during the British bombardment of it on the night of September 13, 1814. The poem was printed in a broadside under the title "Defence of Fort McHenry," to the tune *Anacreon in Heaven*. Although *The Star-Spangled Banner* was a de facto national anthem in the 19th century and was used as such by the United States Army and Navy, it did not become the official American anthem until March 3, 1931, when President Herbert Hoover signed a bill to that effect. Because of the awkward range of the tune, extending to an octave and a fifth, several attempts—all abortive—have been made to transpose the second part of the song to a lower key. The anthem has been used to symbolize the United States in numerous compositions, including Puccini's opera *Madama Butterfly*. Some American states have statutes against the mutilation or disfigurement of the melody or harmony of the anthem; such a law was invoked by the Boston police to preclude a performance of Stravinsky's arrangement of the anthem at a Boston Symphony Orchestra concert in 1942.

Steel band. A kind of ensemble that was developed spontaneously in Trinidad, with the instrumentation provided by steel barrels discarded by local oil companies. The players, called Panmen, select drum tops that are dented in such a way that each dent produces a different tone. By further manipulating these drum tops, a whole diatonic scale can be produced. The natives who have absorbed the sounds of American and British popular music have learned to form whole orchestras of steel drum tops, performing in four-part harmony. The highest pitch is called *ping-pong*, and the bass is called *boom*. The steel band is usually supplemented by several pairs of maracas and guïros. The songs are of the calypso type, with the text commenting on topical events.

Stentorphone. An extremely loud open diapason pipe in a large organ, named after the legendary Greek hero Stentor in the Trojan War who could outshout fifty enemies.

Stiffelio. An opera by Verdi, first produced in Trieste on November 16, 1850. It failed miserably, and no wonder. The libretto was static. Stiffelio, an evangelical minister, faces a problem: His wife allowed herself to be seduced by a local reprobate. As a Christian, should he forgive her? As a man, should he throw her out? The Italian censors stepped in and their intervention gave the opera its coup de grâce. Still, there was music to salvage, and Verdi tried to graft it to another opera called *Aroldo*, but it failed, too.

The Stone Guest (Kamennyi gost). An opera by Alexander Dargomyzhsky, after Pushkin's poem of the same name. The score, left unfinished at Dargomyzhsky's death, was completed by Rimsky-Korsakov and Cui. The first performance took place in St. Petersburg on February 28, 1872. The Stone Guest of the title is the statue of the Commendatore slain by Don Juan. Not only does Don Juan try to seduce his widow, but he also invites the statue to supper. The marble handshake of the Stone Guest crushes Don Juan, and he falls dead. The opera is of importance because of Dargomyzhsky's fruitful attempt to treat the inflections of Russian speech realistically rather than in a conventional operatic style.

Stradivario. A choreographic fantasy by Gian Francesco Malipiero, set for dancing instruments that defend themselves from a thief trying to steal a Stradivarius violin. It was first performed in Florence on June 20, 1949.

Street cries. Street vendors used to peddle their wares in melodious jingles before the age of commercialized trade; each product had its own recognizable tune. Such street cries were common in France as early as the 13th century, and they were often incorporated into contemporary motets. Street cries were also used by English composers of the early Renaissance; notable are those for fresh oysters and hot mutton pies. Newsboys often sold their papers in 19th-century London with a pleasant modal lift. Charpentier's opera *Louise* includes a quodlibet of peddlers of carrots and other vegetables. Even Bach included the popular tune *Cabbage and Turnips* at the end of his great *Goldberg Variations*. In the present century, Luciano Berio's *Cries of London* is unusual. It is scored for eight voices, to authentic vending tunes. The tune urging customers to buy garlic is especially amusing. In Cuba, Brazil, and Argentina, knife sharpeners and shoeshine boys open up a whole symphony of vendors' tunes at early tropical sunrise. Street organs with reed pipes used to be a ubiquitous sight and sound in Italy, with a monkey passing a hat for donations. A story is told that Verdi, annoyed by street organs playing the tune *La donna è mobile* from *Rigoletto* before his window, paid off the street musicians to stop playing or change their song.

Stretto. Italian for "straitened" or "narrowed." A stretto usually occurs at the climax of a composition, when thematic and rhythmic elements have reached the point of saturation. A classical example is the prestissimo finale of the second act in Mozart's *The Marriage of Figaro*. A stretto at the end of an impassioned aria or a dramatic duet is virtually synonymous with a cabaletta. Particularly effective is a stretto in a fugue, in which the "straitening" process is achieved by piling up the subject, the answer, and their fractional particles in close succession, producing the effect of accelerated canonic imitation. The point is that whereas in the exposition a stretto can be achieved by a purely dynamic process, in a fugue such a stretto is a profound polyphonic exercise that has to be foreordained by the configuration of the theme and the answer at the inception of the fugue.

Stride piano. A jazz piano style that retained elements of ragtime. The melody, encrusted in muscular harmonies, is accompanied by the skeleton bass that "strides" between single notes on the strong beat of the measure and chords on the weak beat in a regular oom-pah rhythm.

String instruments. Pedantic fidelity requires that the harp and piano be described as string instruments, for their sound is produced by plucking or striking the strings, but a wise tradition reserves the term *string instruments* for members of the violin family, in which the strings are brought into vibration primarily by bowing. String instruments manipulated by plucking, such as the lute, guitar, balalaika, mandolin, banjo, and some oriental instruments, are usually included in a category of their own. Another important distinction between these two categories of instruments is that on traditional string instruments, which include the violin, viola, cello, and double bass, the player must find the notes with four fingers of the left hand by groping, whereas the guitar, lute, and the like have frets, or marking points, indicating the position of the twelve notes of the chromatic scale. It is noticeable visually that the distances between frets diminish for each successive chromatic interval. The violin string measuring $13\frac{1}{2}$ inches sounds an octave higher when it is stopped in the middle point—that is, at the distance of $6\frac{3}{4}$ inches from the peg and the bridge. But the next octave takes only a quarter of the string to span, and the next octave only $\frac{1}{8}$ of the string. Thus even a mediocre violinist must develop an extraordinary capacity for judging small distances by touch. String instruments can be organized in any combination; even a duet for violin and double bass has been written. The most common combinations, in addition to an unaccompanied string instrument, are string quartet, string quintet, string sextet (often including the double bass), and a string orchestra.

String quartet. Historically, the most significant type of chamber music. A string quartet consists of two violins, viola, and cello. Such an ensemble provides a rich four-part harmony and an articulate interplay of contrapuntal forms, especially canon and fugue. Opportunities for expressive and effective solo parts are many, with the solo instrument accompanied by the other three instruments; episodic duos and trios furnish another resource. Goethe compared the playing of a string quartet with "a conversation of four educated people." The first violin is a natural leader. The second violin is the leader's faithful partner; the somewhat derogatory expression, "to play second fiddle," suggests its subordinate function. The viola fills the harmony and emerges as an important member of the quartet, usually in canonic passages. The cello holds the important duty of the bass voice, determining the harmony; its sonorous arpeggios lend an almost orchestral quality to the ensemble. The employment of special effects such as pizzicato and the availability of double stops contribute further to the harmonic richness of string quartets.

Claims for the priority of composing string quartets have been made for several composers of the 17th century, but the first composer of stature to establish the string quartet as a distinctive musical form was Haydn, who wrote 83 string quartets. (This is not, however, the maximum; Boccherini wrote 102.) Mozart's string quartets brought the art of the string quartet to its highest flowering in the 18th century; his *Dissonanzenquartett* aroused a heat of controversy because of its innovative use of seemingly dissonant harmonic combinations. Beethoven's last quartets caused contemporary critics to state that they were the products of the composer's loss of hearing.

The taste for and attraction of string quartets have sharply declined in the modern era. Debussy, Ravel, and Stravinsky wrote only a single string quartet each. Schoenberg and Bartók revived the form with considerable departures from tradition; Schoenberg even used a vocal solo in one of his. Russian composers continued to cultivate string quartets assiduously. Shostakovich wrote 15 of them. The traditional structure of a string quartet is that of sonata form, consisting of four movements and usually including a minuet or a scherzo.

String quintet. A chamber music ensemble of five string instruments, usually two violins, two violas, and cello. The most prolific composer of string quintets was Boccherini, who wrote twelve; Mozart wrote six; Beethoven wrote three (of which two are really arrangements of other works); Mendelssohn wrote two, as did Brahms. Schubert's great C major Quintet is scored for two violins, viola, and two cellos.

String trio. An ensemble of three string instruments, usually violin, viola, and cello; historically, it is an offshoot of the trio sonata. Haydn wrote as many as 20 trios for two violins and cello; Mozart and Beethoven also contributed to the form. Schoenberg's String Trio is set in the 12-tone idiom.

Stück. A common German name meaning a "piece"; *Klavierstück* is a piece for piano. A Yiddish variant is *shtick*, a slang expression for a cheap vaudeville routine.

Study in Sonority. A work for ten violins or multiples of ten by Wallingford Riegger, in which the G strings of the violins are tuned down to E. The piece is set in dissonant counterpoint with megachords containing from eight to twelve different notes. It was performed for the first time in Philadelphia by Leopold Stokowski on October 30, 1923, using forty violins.

Sturm und Drang. A literary movement in Germany during the last quarter of the 18th century; the name is from the title of a popular play by one Klinger. It became eponymous with a growing sentiment among the youth of the time for "storm and stress" in leading a rebellion against conservatism in social politics and art. In music it presaged the Romantic style of composition, which strove to express inner sentiments. Schumann's struggle against musical Philistinism and the programmatic concepts of many of his works are direct descendants of *Sturm und Drang*.

Suite. A musical form designating a succession of mòvements unified only by a homonymous key. The most important of this category is the Baroque suite, composed of several dance forms. It generally consisted of allemande, courante, sarabande, and gigue. Several optional movements, mostly derived from popular dances, could be interpolated between the sarabande and gigue, notably a minuet and gavotte. Bach diversified the form of instrumental suites by assigning to them the adjectives "English" and "French," referring to their presumed national provenance. Bach also wrote keyboard suites in the form of partitas.

The character of the suite was changed radically in the 19th century. Whereas Bach, Handel, and other Baroque composers followed the contrapuntal style of composition, composers of the later centuries regarded the suite mainly as an assemblage of variegated movements, often arranged from operas, ballets, and theater music. Sometimes such suites became the only viable remnants of a score of incidental music—for instance, in the suite *L'Arlésienne* of Bizet, or *Peer Gynt* of Grieg. Tchaikovsky's *Nutcracker Suite* is one of the most popular examples of the genre. Neo-Classical composers of the second quarter of the 20th century, notably Stravinsky and Hindemith, have made a serious effort to revive the Baroque suite, with a titillating titivation of the ancient forms by means of dissonant treatment.

Suite bergamasque. A group of four piano pieces written by Claude Debussy between 1889 and 1905, in the form of a classical suite. Its third movement is the famous *Clair de lune*. Debussy took the title *Suite bergamasque* from the alliterative lines in Verlaine's poem *Clair de lune*: "masques et bergamasques." The term *bergamasque* is derived from the dance from Bergamo, Italy.

Sumer is icumen in (Summer is coming in). The initial words of the earliest known canon, written for four voices, with the harmony formed by a double organ point, or pedal (which is designated as *pes*, "foot," in the original manuscript). The canon is of English origin, and the original parchment manuscript is in the British Museum. The title above the music is *Rota*, "round." A controversy exists as to the date of its composition; the estimate varies between 1250 and 1320. Dr. Willard Libby, inventor of the carbon

14 method of dating, was approached to help establish the date with scientific accuracy; he expressed his willingness to undertake the task if about an ounce of the original manuscript could be spared to be burned in order to analyze its ashes chemically. No attempt has been made to approach the Curator of Rare Manuscripts at the British Museum with this proposition. The text of the canon is as follows: "Sumer is icumen in/ Lhude sing cuccu!/ Groweth sed, and bloweth med,/ And springth the wude nu/ Sing cuccu!"

Summer Morning's Dream (Ein Sommermorgentraum). The subtitle of Mahler's Symphony No. 3 as given in the original manuscript. The work is set in the key of D minor (but the manuscript also marks it as being in its relative key of F major). It is in six sections, each with a romantically descriptive communication: "The summer marches in," "What the flowers tell me," "What the animals tell me," "What Men tell me," "What Angels tell me," accompanied by voices, and "What love tells me." Mahler conducted the first complete performance in Krefeld, Germany, on June 9, 1902; there were partial performances of separate movements in 1896.

Summer Night on the River. A symphonic sketch by Frederick Delius, set in a characteristically Romantic manner. It was first performed as a companion piece to another tone poem of his, *On Hearing the First Cuckoo in Spring*, in Leipzig on October 2, 1913.

Sun-Treader. A symphonic work by Carl Ruggles inspired by a line from a poem by Robert Browning, "Sun-treader, light and life be thine forever." The work is set in a powerful dissonant idiom, in which contrapuntal layers are constantly lifted and lowered in a titanic harmonic struggle. It was first performed in Paris on February 25, 1932.

Suor Angelica. An opera by Giacomo Puccini, first produced by the Metropolitan Opera in New York on December 14, 1918, as the second part of his operatic triptych *Il Trittico*; the first part was *Il Tabarro* and the third *Gianni Schicchi*. Sister Angelica, who abandoned her own child, enters the convent to redeem her sin. When she learns that the child is dead, she takes poison. Because of the sincerity of her repentance, the Madonna appears to her holding Angelica's transfigured child in her arms; Angelica receives her absolution. Puccini's own sister was a nun. When he finished the vocal score, he played it for her at the convent.

Surprise Symphony. Symphony No. 94 in G major by Haydn. This is the third of the twelve so-called *London* Symphonies Haydn wrote for the concerts conducted by the German violinist Salomon in London. The surprise is furnished by the sudden loud chord at the end of a quiet opening theme of the slow second movement. The anecdote is often told that Haydn put the loud chord in to wake up the somnolent English ladies who went to concerts for a nice refreshing nap, but when it was first performed in London, March 23, 1792, the papers failed to note such an effect. One critic said that the loud chord suggested to him the discharge of a musket on a pastoral scene when a shepherdess lulled herself to sleep contemplating nature and a distant waterfall. No shepherdesses attended the London premiere of the *Surprise* Symphony. As if to disabuse people of such stories, German catalogues list the *Surprise* Symphony simply as *Paukenschlag*, "Drumstroke" Symphony.

Surrealism. Surrealism in art is the superposition of extraneous elements on reality. If tonality is accepted as musical reality, then polytonality could be described as musical surrealism, with the surrealistic effect supplied by the addition of unrelated tonalities. The term *surrealism* was introduced into modern literature and art by the Polish-born French poet Guillaume Apollinaire, who subtitled his play *Les Mamelles de Tirésias*, "Drame surréaliste." In this play the surrealistic elements consist in the translocation of secondary sexual characteristics, wherein the husband sprouts a pair of mammaries while his wife sheds hers. Francis Poulenc wrote an opera on the subject employing polytonality. Erik Satie was the chief apostle of musical surrealism, which found its manifestation primarily in his oxymoronic titles such as *Heures séculaires et instantanées* ("Century-old or instantaneous hours") or *Crépuscule matinal de midi* ("Morning Twilight at Noon"). Numeric surrealism is employed by Virgil Thomson in his opera *Four Saints in Three Acts*, which really has about two dozen saints and is set in four, not three, acts. Operatic surrealism is exemplified by *The Nose* by Shostakovich, after Gogol's tale, in which the nose escapes from the face of a government functionary and assumes an independent existence, including even sneezes. In the "jazz" opera, *Jonny spielt auf* ("Jonny Strikes Up") by Ernst Křenek, a jazz player surrealistically surmounts the terrestrial globe. In Hindemith's *Hin und Zurück* ("Forth and Back"), the action is a palindrome, whereby the opera ends at its starting point. Stravinsky's ballet *Petrouchka*, in which puppets are more real than their manipulators, is surrealistic; in this work Stravinsky exploits the tonal polarity of C major and F-sharp major as an example of harmonic surrealism. The same type of bitonality is used by Darius Milhaud in his ballet *Le Bœuf sur le toit* ("Bull on the Roof"), which depicts incongruous events in an American saloon. In the ballet *The Miraculous Mandarin* by Béla Bartók, the fantastic surrealism of the action (in which the Mandarin is impervious to mortal wounds as long as lust attaches him to a prostitute) is illustrated by a discordant musical score. The French philosopher Henri Bergson describes music itself as a surrealist phenomenon, for it imposes a tonal language upon the world in which the primary means of communication is through verbal expression.

A *Survivor from Warsaw*. A cantata by Arnold Schoenberg for speaker, male chorus, and orchestra, first peformed in Albuquerque, New Mexico, on November 4, 1948. The words are by Schoenberg himself, in English; the text narrates the story of a Jew who survived the Nazi horrors in Warsaw. The Nazi commands are uttered in German, and the work concludes with the singing of a Hebrew prayer. The score's acrid 12-tone setting adds to the tension.

Suzuki method. A pragmatic teaching method developed by the Japanese violinist Shinichi Suzuki, the leader of the Talent Education Movement. Based on repetition of a simple tune, it seems to be successful with very young children, especially those between the ages of four and eight, who are taught to play the violin by imitating the teacher's physical movements and the teacher's placement of the fingers on the strings.

Swan Lake. A ballet by Tchaikovsky, first performed in Moscow on March 4, 1877. The scenario is the quintessence of Romanticism. A young girl loved by a prince is changed by witchcraft into a swan. She can be saved only if he identifies her in the swan lake, but he fails, selecting the wrong swan. His beloved perishes, and he jumps from a cliff into the water to his death. The score contains some of Tchaikovsky's best Romantic music; an instrumental suite has been drawn from the ballet.

Swan song. The legend that swans sing beautifully at the approach of death is of ancient origin. Plato states that dying swans sing so sweetly because they know that they are about to return to the divine presence of Apollo to whom they are sacred. Another Greek writer reports that flocks of swans regularly descend on Apollo's temple during festive days and join the choir. Lucian, skeptical as ever, made a journey to the swan breeding grounds in Italy and inquired among the local peasants whether they ever heard a swan sing. He was told that swans only croak, cackle, and grunt in a most disagreeable manner. So-called mute swans maintained on the royal preservation in England are not voiceless; they growl, hiss, and even trill. Despite these unpleasant characteristics, the swan with its graceful long neck (eighteen vertebrae, as compared with the giraffe's seven) remains a symbol of beauty and poetry. Rossini was called the Swan of Pesaro, his birthplace. Although he had a self-deprecating sense of humor, it never occurred to him how ambiguous this compliment was from the ornithological standpoint. In his *Carnival of the Animals*, Saint-Saëns assigns his beautiful cello solo to the swan; it inspired Anna Pavlova's famous dance creation, *The Dying Swan*. Sibelius wrote a symphonic poem entitled *The Swan of Tuonela*, with a mellifluously nasal English horn solo representing the song of the dying swan. (Tuonela in Finnish folklore is the land of death.) A group of Schubert's posthumous songs was given the title *Schwanengesang* (*Swan Song*) by the publishers. Yet no composer has dared to reproduce the true sound of the swan's song; not even the bassoon in its lowest register is ugly enough to render justice to a dying swan's croaking. In Hans Christian Andersen's tale *The Ugly Duckling*, a swan egg is deposited in a nest of ducks; after it is hatched, the white swan is an ugly duckling compared with its adopted siblings. Prokofiev wrote a poetic ballad for voice and piano based on this tale.

Sweet Adeline. This song, once a staple of barbershop quartets, was written by the American musician Henry W. Armstrong and published in 1903; it was named in honor of the famous Italian prima donna Adelina Patti, who was having one of her recurrent farewell concert tours in America at the time. When sung in characteristic close harmony with chromatic intercalations, *Sweet Adeline* eventually acquired a peculiar odor of an amiable state of male inebriation.

Swing. Swing music is a natural product of the jazz era, which created a demand for larger bands and a great volume of sound. The advent of swing music coincided with the development of the radio industry when, in the 1930s, millions could hear concerts broadcast into homes. As the name seems to indicate, swing symbolized an uninhibited celebration of the youthful spirit of the age. Big bands of the swing era were usually catapulted into syncopated action by a clarinetist, a trumpet soloist. or a saxophone player. The instrumentation of a big swing band derived from its jazz predecessor, with clarinet, saxophone, trumpet, trombone, percussion, and piano as its mainstays. If a jazz band with its small contingent of instruments roused the keepers of morals to protest, that was nothing compared with the furor of indignation against the swing music of a big band and its alleged immoral influence on the youth of the 1930s and 1940s. Once more the clergy held the forefront of the assault against the evils of the new music. "Swing Bands Put 23,400 in Frenzy," "Jitterbugs Cavort as 25 Orchestras Blare," "Pastor Scores Swing as Debasing Youth—Declares It Shows an Obvious Degeneracy in Our Culture" ran the headlines of *The New York Times*. Loud swing music late at night so upset the sensitive burghers in the once peaceful boroughs of Greater New York City that they went to court to muzzle the swingers. They lost. *The New York Times* reported the result in its issue of June 30, 1938: "2 A.M. Swing Music Upheld by Court. Residents Lose Pleas to Curb 15-Piece Band. Can't Sleep, They Assert. But Magistrate Rules That Lively Strains Do Not Disturb the Peace." Revenants from another century added literary denunciations of swing as "music which squawked and shrieked and roared and bellowed in syncopated savagery." But visitors from Europe were more kind. "I love swings," Stravinsky was quoted as having said in his Russianized English. "It is to the Harlem I go. It is so sympathetic to watch the Negro boys and girls dancing and to watch them eating the long, what is it you call them, hot dogs. It is so sympathetic. I love all kinds of swings." In 1945, Stravinsky demonstrated his faith in swing by composing his *Ebony Concerto* for clarinet and band. Eventually swing music was not loud enough, and in the course of time yielded to the louder sound of rock 'n' roll.

Sympathetic strings. Strings of resonance that are not played on but that vibrate "sympathetically" to reinforce the regular melodic strings. They were much in use in old string instruments, such as the viola d'amore. Some piano manufacturers add sympathetic strings above the strings in the treble to add resonance to the tinny sound of the upper range of the piano; such extra strings are called *aliquot strings*.

Symphonia. A medieval term that means "consonance," in contrast with *diaphonia*, "dissonance." In Baroque music, the term was used indiscriminately for all genres of ensemble, but eventually a symphony became a specific form of orchestral composition. Richard Strauss used the old meaning of the term in his *Symphonia domestica*, a work that is not a real symphony.

Symphonia domestica. An autobiographical symphonic work by Richard Strauss, conducted by him for the first time in New York on March 21, 1904. The work describes a day in the family of Richard Strauss. When the clock strikes 7 o'clock, the new baby is given a bath. Admiring relatives exclaim "Just like Papa!" or "Just like Mama!", depending on whether they are paternal or maternal relatives. A domestic argument is introduced by a double fugue.

Symphonic Dances. An orchestral work by Paul Hindemith, in four movements, first performed in London on December 5, 1937. The score was originally designed for presentation as a ballet based on the life of St. Francis, but later Hindemith decided to write a different score for that purpose, entitled *St. Francis*, with the subtitle *Nobilissima Visione*.

Symphonic Metamorphosis on a Theme by Carl Maria von Weber. An orchestral suite by Paul Hindemith that makes an anamorphic use of various themes of Weber's four-hand piano music and theater scores. The work was first performed in New York on January 20, 1944.

Symphonic poem. A fanciful term for an orchestral composition that is inspired by a literary work, a mythological legend, a historical event, or a patriotic invocation. Such compositions were often described as "program music" that tells a story. Liszt is credited by most music historians as the progenitor of the symphonic poem. Examples are his *Faust* Symphony, containing movements named after personages in Goethe's epic; *Hamlet*, after Shakespeare; *Tasso*, named after the Italian poet of the Renaissance but inspired by poems on Tasso of Byron and Goethe; and *Mazeppa*, depicting the extraordinary career of the 17th-century Ukrainian leader who changed allegiance from Russians, Poles, and Swedes to Ottoman Turks in order to achieve independence for the Ukraine. Tchaikovsky's symphonic poems were related to Shakespeare (*Romeo and Juliet*) and Dante (*Francesca da Rimini*). Russian composers were fond of the narrative rendered in music. Balakirev entitled his largest symphonic work simply *Russia*. Rimsky-Korsakov's symphonic poem *Sadko* is drawn on an ancient Russian tale that he also used in an opera. Mussorgsky composed a symphonic poem, *A Night on Bald Mountain*. Borodin wrote a descriptive symphonic piece, *In the Steppes of Central Asia*. Liadov produced three miniature symphonic poems on Russian folk tales: *Baba Yaga*, *Enchanted Lake*, and *Kikimora*. Glazunov contributed to the genre in his symphonic poem *Stenka Razin*, based on the life of the 17th-century Russian peasant rebel. Quite apart from the Russian national school stands Scriabin, whose symphonic poems *Le Poème de l'extase*, *Le Poème divin*, and *Prométhée* draw their inspiration from mystic sources. The national Czech composer Smetana wrote six symphonic poems in the form of an orchestral suite under the title *Má vlast* ("My Country"). Dvořák composed five symphonic poems, all based on Czech legends. The greatest contribution to the form of symphonic poem was made in modern times by Richard Strauss, but he preferred to describe them as *tone poems*. They include *Don Juan*, *Tod und Verklärung* (*Death and Transfiguration*), *Till Eulenspiegel*, *Also sprach Zarathustra* (*Thus spoke Zarathustra*), and *Ein Heldenleben* (*A Hero's Life*).

Symphonie fantastique. Of all musical compositions of the age of Romanticism, the *Fantastic* Symphony by Berlioz is the most literal and also the most literary. Consider its inception: Berlioz attended in Paris a performance of *Hamlet* given by the Shakespearean Company of London, with Harriet Smithson as Ophelia. Instantly infatuated with her, he walked the streets of Paris in a state of fantastic obsession. He decided to express his passion in the language he knew best—music. In the work, Miss Smithson is identified by a recurrent theme which Berlioz calls *idée fixe*. There are five movements: *Dreams and Passions*, *A Ball*, *Scene in the Fields*, *March to the Gallows*, and *Walpurgisnight's Dream*. The Symphony was first performed in Paris on December 5, 1830, but Miss Smithson did not attend. Eventually they met and married. He spoke no English. She spoke no French. They were unhappy. Miss Smithson died, a victim of premature senility. It turned out that Berlioz wrote the *March to the Gallows* of the score long before he beheld the Shakespearean Miss Smithson, and he incorporated it into a composed overture. The *idée fixe* was an earlier idea of the *Symphonie fantastique* ex post facto. Incongruously, the printed score is dedicated not to his beloved, but to the Emperor of All the Russias, Nicolas I. Why? Berlioz, romantic soul that he was, also had proper regard for earthly necessities. During his concert tour to Russia in 1847, he was advised to seek the imperial favor in the hope of obtaining a pecuniary reward. So he put the name of the Emperor on the opening page of his symphony. There is no record of his receiving any emolument; the Czar was notoriously insensitive to art.

Symphony. The most significant and most complex form of musical composition, which in its Classical form represents the supreme achievement of Western music. The term has undergone protean changes during its history. It comes from the Greek word *symphonia*, "sounding together." During the Middle Ages, *symphonia* was translated into Latin as *consonantia* or *concordantia*, "consonances" or "concords." The consonant intervals of the octave, fifth, and fourth were called *simplices symphoniae*. The word for a composer was *symphonista*. In the 17th century, the term *symphonia* was divested of its general meaning as a musical composition, being used exclusively for an instrumental ensemble without voices. It was also applied to instrumental overtures or interludes in early operas.

In the first half of the 18th century, the instrumental sinfonia was formally stabilized as a composition in three symmetric movements: Allegro, Andante, and Allegro. The opening Allegro was of the greatest evolutionary importance, for it followed the germinal form of the sonata, with clearly demarcated sections that became defined by theorists as exposition, development, and recapitulation. Haydn is commonly regarded as the "father of the symphony," but in fact several composers before his time wrote orchestral works that already comprised the formal elements of symphonic style. Particularly important among these predecessors were the musicians of the Mannheim school who emphasized contrasts of style, tempo, dynamics, and instrumental combinations. The era of the Classical symphony began in the second half of the 18th century. Its most illustrious representatives were Mozart and Haydn; a legion of opaque luminaries labored in obscurity in Central Europe and in Italy throughout the Classical period. Most Classical symphonies included a supernumerary dance movement, usually a minuet. Despite the vaunted versatility of the symphonic form, its structure was essentially uniform.

A revolutionary change in the history of the symphonic form occurred in the 19th century. The form of a symphony became individualized. Symphonies were no longer manufactured in large quantities, according to a prescribed formula. They acquired individual physiognomies; the *Eroica* Symphony of Beethoven is a famous example. In his Symphony No. 9, Beethoven added a chorus, an extraordinary innovation at the time. Schubert failed to complete one of his most famous symphonies, which became forever known as the *Unfinished* Symphony. Bruckner discarded his first symphony, which he chose to describe as *Zero* Symphony. Four symphonies by Dvořák remained unpublished in his lifetime, creating havoc in their numbering in later years. As a result, his most famous symphony, *From the New World*, which was originally catalogued as No. 5, has been renumbered as No. 9. Several early symphonies by Mendelssohn have been added to his catalogue by later editors. Symphonies of the Romantic period were often autobiographical. Berlioz wrote a grand orchestral work that he entitled *Symphonie fantastique*, as a musical confession of his love for the Shakespearean actress Harriet Smithson. Liszt selected two literary epics, Dante's *La divina commedia* and Goethe's *Faust*, on which to base his symphonies.

Several composers who proclaimed themselves fervent nationalists wrote symphonies in a traditional Romantic style. Among the greatest was Sibelius, who assigned national Finnish subjects to his symphonic poems but whose seven symphonies bear no programmatic subtitles. The nine symphonies of Mahler are Romantic revelations of the most intense character. Saint-Saëns was a grandiloquent symphonist. Bizet's youthful Symphony in C major, which he discarded, was rediscovered more than half a century after his death and became a favorite. Debussy and Ravel never wrote symphonies, and it is only in the 20th century that modern French composers, particularly Milhaud and Honegger, have contributed to the genre. The Russians remain faithful to the traditional form of the symphony. Tchaikovsky wrote six symphonies. Glazunov wrote eight, Scriabin and Rachmaninoff composed three each. Shostakovich produced fifteen, several of which include vocal soloists and chorus. The champion symphonist in Russia was Miaskovsky, who wrote twenty-seven symphonies. Virtually every Russian composer of the Soviet period has written symphonies in idioms varying from neo-Classical to moderately modernistic. Strangely enough, Germany and Austria, the countries that created and maintained the art of symphonic composition, showed a decline of symphonic production in the 20th century. Perhaps the fact that Wagner, the master of musical minds in post-Classical Germany, devoted his energies totally to the musical theater (his youthful symphony was not published until many years after his death), drew the German composers of the post-Wagnerian generation away from symphonic composition. Richard Strauss wrote two symphonies, *Symphonia domestica* and the *Alpine* Symphony, but they are panoramic and symphonic in name only. Hindemith was not a Wagnerian but, rather, a modern follower of Reger, but neither he nor Reger wrote symphonies in the traditional formal manner.

The three great composers of the modern Vienna school, Schoenberg, Berg, and Webern, did not compose works of truly symphonic dimensions. Stravinsky, who began his career as a follower of Rimsky-Korsakov's pictorial symphonism, wrote several symphonies, but they were closer to the pre-Classical type of sinfonia than to the traditional Classical or Romantic symphony. After Haydn's symphonic journeys to London, England became a willing receptacle of German music. In the 20th century, Elgar wrote two grand symphonies, and Vaughan Williams wrote nine, some of them highly modern in idiom. Arnold Bax composed seven symphonies. Of the younger generation, William Walton wrote two. Benjamin Britten, generally regarded as the most remarkable English composer of the 20th century, never felt the symphonic urge; his works in symphonic form approach the manner of orchestral suites. The Danish composer Carl Nielsen wrote six symphonies, with explicit programmatic content expressed in such subtitles as *Expansive* Symphony and *Inextinguishable*. The most prolific Italian composer of symphonies was Malipiero, who wrote at least ten, several of which he equipped with suggestive subtitles.

In the United States, among composers who pursued the symphonic career steadfastly through the years are Roy Harris, who wrote fourteen, and Walter Piston, William Schuman, David Diamond, Peter Mennin, and Vincent Persichetti, who wrote eight symphonies each. Howard Hanson, who proclaimed his faith in Romantic music, wrote six symphonies. Of Aaron Copland's symphonic works, the most significant is his Symphony No. 3, which includes his famous *Fanfare for the Common Man*, quoted in extenso. A unique American symphony is the Symphony No. 4 of Charles Ives, which consists of four movements written at different times and in widely divergent idioms. His Symphony No. 1 is entirely academic; his Symphony No. 2 is a powerful Romantic work; his Symphony No. 3 is in a far more advanced, modernistic idiom, but it is still within traditional confines.

The main structure of a symphony during the two centuries of its formulation has not radically changed. The lively scherzo replaced the mannered minuet. The four traditional movements were often compressed into one. The general tendency early in the 20th century was to reduce the orchestra to the bare bones of the Baroque sinfonia. In his *Symphony of Psalms*, Stravinsky eliminates the violins altogether in order to conjure up the desired aura of austerity. The piano—not a symphonic instrument per se, and never used in the symphonies of Schumann, Mendelssohn, Tchaikovsky, Brahms, or any other composer of the Romantic century regardless of their individual styles— became an unexpected guest in the symphonies of the 20th century, with an obvious intent to provide sharp articulation and precise rhythm. Shostakovich wrote an important piano part in his Symphony No. 1.

Symphony for Organ and Orchestra. The first symphonic work by Aaron Copland, first performed in New York on January 11, 1925, with Copland's teacher Nadia Boulanger playing the organ. Walter Damrosch conducted and gratuitously declared to the audience after the performance that a youth who could write such music at the age of 24 would be capable of murder a few years later. Copland failed to fulfill this prophecy.

Symphony of a Thousand. A nickname of unknown origin for the Symphony No. 8 of Mahler, in the key of E-flat major. The title was justified by the fact that the work requires a huge ensemble with vocal soloists, two mixed choruses, and a boys' chorus, as well as a battery of percussion instruments. It was first performed in Munich on September 12, 1910. Mahler never sanctioned the nickname, but he wrote extravagantly about the significance of the work: "In this Symphony the whole universe begins to sound in musical tones; it is no longer human voices, but planets and suns that are in motion here." The *Symphony of a Thousand* is in effect an oratorio. It consists of two lengthy choral sections, the first based on the medieval Pentecostal hymn, *Veni, Creator Spiritus*, and the second a rendition of a philosophical part of Goethe's *Faust*.

Symphony of Psalms (Symphonie des Psaumes). A work by Igor Stravinsky for chorus and orchestra, which he dedicated "to the glory of God on the occasion of the 50th anniversary of the Boston Symphony Orchestra." Because of a postponement of the Boston performance, the actual world premiere of the *Symphony of Psalms* was given not in Boston but in Brussels on December 13, 1930. The Boston Symphony performance followed one week later. The text is in Latin, as it was in Stravinsky's previous vocal work, *Oedipus Rex*. By using an ancient language, Stravinsky intended to emphasize the timeless character of the music.

Symphony with a Bell. A subtitle used by Soviet commentators for the Symphony No. 2 of Aram Khatchaturian, first performed in Moscow on December 30, 1943. The music depicts the horrors of the Nazi assault on Russia and the heroism of the Soviet people, symbolized by the recurring bell motif.

Symploche. A rhetorical musical device in which the beginning of a musical phrase serves also as its ending. A highly artistic example is the initial phrase of the ending to Mozart's Symphony No. 39 in E-flat major.

Syncopation. One of the most powerful sources of rhythmic diversification. The word comes from Greek grammatical usage and was applied to the omission of a letter or a syllable, a process resulting in a *syncope*, "a clashing together of two separate elements." (Syncope is also the skip of a heartbeat, due to cerebral ischemia.) In mensural notation, syncopation was used to make changes in the main stress. The consequence of such rhythmic displacement was the generation of a discordant tonal combination that had to be resolved into a consonance. In contrapuntal theory, syncopation is classified as the fourth species of counterpoint. Syncopated notes were initially marked as auxiliary ornaments and were often written in small notes placed before the principal note. Suspension and appoggiaturas furnish the characteristic elements of dissonant syncopation. In the works of the Romantic era, syncopation served to enhance the emotional stress.

Syncopation is the spice of music in dance forms. Viennese waltzes create an effect of syncopation by stressing the third beat of the measure; the mazurka tends to accent the second beat; the march emphasizes the main beat but supplies syncopation in smaller rhythmic divisions within square time. Ragtime and jazz elevated syncopation into a principal device of composition. But oddly, the latest manifestation of American popular music, rock 'n' roll, largely abandoned syncopation in favor of a stultifying uniform rhythm with the accent on the strong beat of the measure. On the other hand, reggae, a style of popular music originating in Jamaica that infiltrated the American pop scene in the second half of the 20th century, derives much of its interest from syncopated rhythms.

Syrian chant. A Christian hymnody that was in use in the early Christian communities in Syria. Whatever oriental influences can be traced in both Byzantine and Gregorian chant must have come through Syria.

T

Il Tabarro (The Cloak). An opera by Giacomo Puccini, produced as the first part of *Il Trittico (The Triptych)* by the Metropolitan Opera in New York on December 14, 1918. The story deals with a love triangle among the bargemen on the Seine River. The barge owner suspects his helper of conducting an affair with his wife. He kills him, covers the body with his wife's cloak, and then kills her, too.

Tafelklavier. The German name for square piano, constructed similarly to the clavichord and specifically adapted for hammer action as distinct from the harpsichord in which the strings are plucked. The French square piano, called *piano carré*, was first manufactured in 1742. It became very popular in England and in the United States before yielding to the upright piano.

Tafelmusik. Literally, "table music" in German; it was known mostly by its French name, *musique de table. Tafelmusik* designated the type of entertainment provided for banquets and similar festive occasions. Respectable composers contributed to the genre; a typical example is Telemann's instrumental suite *Musique de table*. There is a witty spoof on *Tafelmusik* in the finale of the second half of Mozart's opera *Don Giovanni*, where a band plays selections from various operas including Mozart's own. The French composer Delalande published in 1703 a collection of *"symphonies qui se jouent ordinairement au souper du Roy."* This sort of music "ordinarily played at the King's supper" was disdained in the 19th century, but the hedonistic composers of the 20th century revived it gleefully.

Tagelied. Literally, a "day song"; a poem of farewell made popular by the minnesingers. *Tagelieder* are usually songs of partings between lovers, sung at sunrise. Wagner has such a one in the second act of *Tristan und Isolde*, in the form of a warning against imminent danger. In France and other Latin countries, the *Tagelied* is known as *alba* or *aubade*, a "morning" or "dawn" song.

Take Me Out to the Ball Game. A song by Albert von Tilzer, introduced by him in vaudeville in 1908. It became the unofficial anthem of American baseball. The composer himself did not attend a ball game until some 20 years after he wrote the song.

A Tale About a Real Man. An opera by Sergei Prokofiev, first produced in an unofficial preview in Leningrad on December 3, 1948. The libretto was based on an actual episode in World War II in which a Soviet flyer lost both feet in combat but was patriotically determined to continue in active duty even though he had to wear prostheses; he succeeded brilliantly in aerial combat. Prokofiev hoped to vindicate himself with this opera against Soviet bureaucrats who accused him of pursuing decadent Western ways—a false hope, for the opera was savagely attacked by official Soviet critics as failing to achieve the correct line of socialist realism. The opera was revived in Moscow on October 8, 1960. The hero glorified in the opera attended the performance in person, but Prokofiev himself was dead.

The Tales of Hoffmann. An opera by Jacques Offenbach, based on stories of the German fabulist E.T.A. Hoffmann. In it, Hoffmann himself is represented as telling in three acts the stories of his three great loves: one with a lithe mechanical puppet, one with a blithe Venetian courtesan, and one with a tubercular German maiden. Offenbach died before completing the score, which was partly orchestrated by Guiraud for its posthumous première in Paris on February 10, 1881. The second act contains the famous *Barcarolle*.

Tambour militaire. A small drum used in military bands. It has no definite pitch but produces a dry, well-articulated sound in the tenor register. As a rhythmic instrument, it is used in symphony, opera, and even chamber music. Carl Nielsen gives the tambour militaire an important part in his Symphony No. 5, instructing the player to beat the drum following its own rhythm "as if trying to interfere with the rest of the orchestra." A solo on the military drum introduces the execution by hanging of Till Eulenspiegel in the score of that title by Richard Strauss. Varèse gives the military drum the leading "tenor" part in his *Ionisation*.

Tambourine. A popular instrument of Spanish origin, consisting of a single drumhead bordered by a ring with a number of metallic jingles. The tambourine can be played in a variety of ways, by shaking, thumping, plunking, clicking, striking against the knee or against the opposing hand. The sound produced is dry and short, with no resonance or reverberation. The tambourine is regularly used to accompany Spanish dances. Bizet makes use of it in *Carmen*, Rimsky-Korsakov in his orchestral score *Capriccio Espagnol*, Debussy in *Ibéria*, and Ravel in *Rapsodie espagnole*. A tambourine of biblical times, *timbrel*, was furnished with several pairs of bronze jingles, which the biblical damsels shook to attract male attention. One extant specimen, unearthed in Babylon and dating back to about 2700 B.C., has ten pairs of bronze jingles and is beautifully ornamented with precious stones. According to the Bible, Miriam, sister of Moses, used a timbrel during the Exodus from Egypt.

Tambourin is the French spelling of tambourine; etymologically, it is the diminutive of *tambour*. The tambourin consists of a cylindrical drum covered with skin on both ends; it is possibly of Arab origin. Tambourin is also the name of an old dance in Southern France that was accompanied by a pipe and a tambourin. Rameau wrote a piece for clavecin entitled *Tambourin*, with rhythmic imitations of the characteristic beat of the instrument.

Tanam. A technique of playing Indian ragas by breaking up words into syllables and rearranging them in different orders. *Tanam* is derived from the Sanskrit *anantam*, "endless." This syllabification creates derivative rhythmic patterns because the vowels in Sanskrit are quantitative, long and short. The melodic lines in tanam consist of the repetition of short rhythmical phrases; when played on the vina, the rhythm produces a constant alternation of plucked and pulled strings; periodic silences constitute an integral part of the melody.

Tancredi. "*Melodramma eroico*" (Heroic melodrama) by Gioachino Rossini, with the libretto derived from Tasso's poem *Gerusalemme liberata* ("Jerusalem liberated"), combined with Voltaire's *Tancrède*, wherein the hero is victorious in war against the infidels and claims the faithful lady of his heart in marriage. It was Rossini's first marked success as an opera composer; its first performance took place in Venice on February 6, 1813.

Tango. A celebrated dance of Argentina, danced by a couple. Attempts have been made by some respectable lexicographers (including some editions of Webster's dictionary) to derive the word from the Latin *tangere*, "to touch"; however, all evidence points toward a native onomatopoeic derivation, possibly imitative of the drumbeat. Musically, the tango has the characteristics of the habanera; both are in 2/4 time with a dotted rhythmical figure in the accompaniment. The first section is set in a minor key and the second in major. The tango quickly became popular in Europe in the years immediately preceding World War I. Its frank sexuality shocked the guardians of morality, and protests were voiced by the clergy and government authorities, so that the Argentine ambassador to France found it necessary to state that the tango was the product of bordellos and was never tolerated in decent Argentine society.

Tannhäuser. An opera by Richard Wagner, to his own libretto, first produced in Dresden on October 19, 1845. Wagner described the score by the word *Handlung*, "an action." The complete title is *Tannhäuser und der Sängerkrieg auf dem Wartburg* (*Tannhäuser and the Singing Contest on the Wartburg*).

Tannhäuser was a historical figure, a German minnesinger who led a wandering life in the 13th century and participated in a crusade. In Wagner's opera, Tannhäuser succumbs to the pleasures of the flesh in the Venusberg, a mountain in central Germany in whose caves, according to medieval legends, the goddess Venus herself held court. He yearns to return to his own world, however, and to his beloved Elisabeth. He joins a group of pilgrims in the valley of the Wartburg; among them is his friend Wolfram (who was also a historical figure). A singing contest is held in the Wartburg castle. Tannhäuser shocks the assembly by singing a song in praise of Venus. He is expelled from the Wartburg and joins the pilgrims on their way to Rome where he hopes to obtain absolution from the Pope. Wolfram sings a song appealing to the evening star (that is, Venus) for protection of Elisabeth. Having failed to obtain forgiveness in Rome, Tannhäuser returns home and encounters a funeral procession; it is that of Elisabeth. He collapses before her coffin and dies. He achieves redemption when the papal staff, brought back from Rome by the pilgrims, sprouts leaves. The opera marks a turning point in music history as an artistic affirmation of the Romantic ideal.

Tantric chants. Ritual singing of Hindu sects, designed to attain purification of soul and body and combined with body exercises such as yoga. The text of the chants is fashioned from the mystic syllables of the sacred mantras, and the symbols are inspired by the diagrams of the ritual mandalas. Some Tibetan chants last more than seven hours.

Tanzhalle. A dance hall; a place of entertainment that flourished in Berlin and elsewhere in Germany in the first third of the 20th century in which sexual contact was facilitated between customers.

Tap dance. A type of American dance in which distinct rhythmic patterns are provided by the tapping of the performer's feet on the floor. Typical tap shoes have metal plates on the soles. Tap dancing in wooden shoes was called buck-and-wing dancing; in soft-shoe dancing the performer shuffled on the floor. In 1952 the American composer Morton Gould wrote a *Concerto for Tap Dancer and Orchestra* in four classical movements.

Tapeur. A rather unkind description of a pianist accompanying dance rehearsals, from the French verb *taper*, ''to pound.''

Tapiola. A symphonic poem by Jean Sibelius, a commissioned work first performed in New York on December 26, 1926. Tapiola is the god of Finnish forests, and the music is appropriately somber and majestic.

Tarantella. A rapid Italian dance in 6/8 time, popular in the 19th century. It is named after the Italian city of Taranto. According to legend, the playing of the tarantella cured tarantism, an uncontrollable impulse to dance that is supposedly caused by the bite of the tarantula. However, medical investigations of persons bitten by the tarantula have revealed no such choreographic symptoms.

Tarare. An opera by Antonio Salieri, first produced in Paris on June 8, 1787. The libretto, written specially for Salieri by Beaumarchais, deals with a soldier of fortune named Tarare, who is in mortal combat with the king of the fabled town of Ormuz (or Hormuz) on the Persian Gulf. Tarare wins the battle and becomes king. The opera was immensely successful in its first production in Paris and later in an Italian version under the title *Azur, Re d'Ormus* in Vienna. *Tarare* was one of the earliest operas to introduce an element of oriental mysticism. Mozart liked *Tarare* very much; his own opera *The Magic Flute*, embodying similar images, was produced four years later.

Taras Bulba. A rhapsody for orchestra by Leoš Janáček, after Gogol's novel, first performed in Brno on October 9, 1921. The piece depicts the struggle of the Cossacks against Polish domination in the 15th century, and it involves Bulba's younger son, who betrays his land for the sake of a Polish girl. Bulba takes him prisoner among Polish soldiers and shoots him to death.

Tartini tones. The differential tones produced by playing double stops in perfect nontempered tuning. They were first described by the Italian composer and theorist Giuseppe Tartini in 1714 as *terzo suono*, "third tones," and idiomatically known also as "wolf tones."

Te Deum. One of the most celebrated songs of praise in the Roman Catholic liturgy, regarded as one of the last extant examples of the *psalmus idioticus* (*idioticus* here, of course, does not mean idiotic but rather "vernacular" or "idiomatic"). It is also known as an Ambrosian hymn, although it has never been proved that St. Ambrose was the author. It is furthermore one of the most favorite texts for musical settings. A Te Deum is essentially a hymn of thanksgiving, salutation, or commemoration. Handel wrote a Te Deum for the Peace of Utrecht, and Berlioz contributed one for the Paris Exposition. Other famous works to use this text are by Bruckner, Dvořák, and Verdi. In the 20th century, Benjamin Britten, Kodály, and Vaughan Williams each wrote a Te Deum.

Te Deum Symphony. The usual designation of Anton Bruckner's Symphony No. 9, which he never completed. Before his death he suggested that his choral work *Te Deum* might be used in place of the unfinished finale; the symphony was first performed in this version in Vienna on February 11, 1903.

Teaching. George Bernard Shaw put an unfair kibosh on teachers when he delivered his dictum: "Those who can, do; those who cannot, teach." True, many retired virtuosos turn to teaching when they can no longer perform.

True, also, to some of them the teaching profession is merely a vehicle to exercise their misanthropical disappointment at failing to become great artists. Ancient Greek legend has it that Hercules slew his music teacher Linus with his own lyre when he reprimanded Hercules for playing a wrong note. Still, music teaching is an honorable profession. From time immemorial, music traditions have been carried from one generation to another by devoted elders. Instruction in singing and playing was essential in ancient cultures, primarily in religious rituals. Music was also an integral part of Greek tragedy that included poetry and dancing. The musical tradition was preserved in the early centuries of Christianity by monks who taught the traditional rules of plainchant to apprentices and novitiates. In the 11th century, Guido d'Arezzo promulgated the first systematic method of music theory by arranging a system of hexachords represented by the positions on the palm of the left hand.

Secular teaching of music was part of the Quadrivium in medieval universities, in which music theory was included among the four mathematical arts, the other three being arithmetic, geometry, and astronomy. Music as taught in the Middle Ages was mostly concerned with mathematical relationships between the length of a string or air column and the pitch, as well as the numerical proportion of pitches producing a certain interval. Theology played a great role in medieval music science. Triple time was called *tempus perfectum*, a term explained by the theological doctrine of the perfect Trinity.

At the time of the Renaissance, the teaching profession was mainly in the hands of church organists. Music aspirants flocked from all over Europe to study with Girolamo Frescobaldi at the Vatican, where he was organist early in the 17th century. Bach and Handel undertook an arduous journey to Lübeck to hear the great Buxtehude play the organ, hoping to succeed him at his post after his death. Because the stipulation for succession was marriage to one of the incumbent's daughters and all of Buxtehude's five daughters were extremely unattractive, both Bach and Handel demurred. Music history gained much from this misadventure. Handel, having gone to London, did not teach music professionally, but Bach became the music master of the St. Thomas School in Leipzig, where he had many students, including his own sons. Royal houses habitually engaged a music master to teach the princesses the art of playing the lute, harp, and singing. Mary Stuart engaged an Italian lutenist, David Rizzio, who was suspected of being her lover; he was eventually murdered by the Scottish court clique. A singing master was often a comic character in opera; an example is Don Basilio in Rossini's *Barber of Seville*.

Institutional music teaching originated in Italy in the 16th century. Such music schools were known as conservatories, in the literal sense of the word, for they were founded to provide "conservation" for orphaned or ailing girls. In fact, these conservatories were called *ospedali*, that is, "hospitals." A French musician, visiting one of these "hospitals" in Venice early in the 18th century, reported his enchantment with the singing girls: "They sing like angels. There can be nothing more ravishing than to watch a young girl in a white frock with a spray of pomegranate flowers over her ear perform for her audience." Soon conservatories and other music schools spread all over the world. Italian musicians established a virtual monopoly on the teaching of singing, whereas the Germans specialized in teaching composition and theory. In the 20th century, the Russians invaded musically underdeveloped countries mainly as piano teachers. Other Slavic countries, particularly Bohemia and Poland, sent the surplus of their music educators abroad. A geographical map of this historic migration of music teachers from Central and Eastern Europe is edifying, for it seems to prove that the musical Garden of Eden was located in a relatively small area of Central Europe. Travel to Germany in quest of musical education became universal in the 19th century; a great number of British, American, and Russian composers participated in this pilgrimage, and simultaneously German musicians traveled to Great Britain, Russia, and the United States in search of employment and fortune. Not until the middle of the 19th century did French music teachers acquire a similarly lucrative reputation. In the 20th century, one French teacher in particular, Nadia Boulanger, established a regular "boulangerie" of students from all over the world. Her American composer-students included Aaron Copland, Virgil Thomson, Randall Thompson, and Roy Harris. British and American music teachers finally asserted themselves in the 20th century.

The genealogy of private music teaching gives us a vivid panorama of music history: Haydn taught Beethoven, Beethoven taught Czerny, Czerny taught Liszt, Liszt taught Siloti, Siloti taught Rachmaninoff. In his last years in Weimar, Liszt used to receive young pianists, mostly female, who played for him. Too often, Liszt dozed off while listening to a student play, but as soon as she stopped, he would wake up and murmur, "Schön" ("nice").

Great national schools of composition often arose as a result of mutual teaching, in or out of a conservatory. Rimsky-Korsakov received his early instruction from Balakirev. Subsequently, Rimsky-Korsakov himself became the teacher of two generations of Russian composers, including Stravinsky. Among celebrated composers who were active as teachers of composition and directors of national conservatories were Vincent d'Indy and Gabriel Fauré in France, Max Reger in Germany, and Dvořák in Bohemia. In the violin field, no one was greater than Leopold Auer, from whose fiddle nursery in St. Petersburg came Jascha Heifetz, Mischa Elman, and hundreds of other violinists.

Among the great piano teachers was Theodor Leschetizky, who taught Paderewski; several of Leschetizky's consecutive wives, the most replendent among them being Anna Essipoff, became distinguished teachers themselves.

Tobias Matthay taught three pianistic generations in London; the Matthay System, as his teaching method was known, became a passport to educational competence in England and America. Isidor Philipp established himself in Paris and taught many pianists who made fine careers. David Popper taught quite a few good cellists and wrote pleasing pieces for the cello. As for singing, Manuel García was the first true professional teacher; his daughter, the fabulous Malibran, was one of his pupils. He was also the inventor of the laryngoscope, used to probe the voice box in the larynx. To enumerate former opera stars who became great teachers is tantamount to compiling an inventory of singers. The greatest opera singers, Chaliapin and Caruso, never descended from their pedestals to teach, however.

The Telephone. An opera by Gian Carlo Menotti, to his own libretto, first produced in New York on February 18, 1947. Menotti engagingly describes the opera as *L'Amour à trois*, the third member in the collective amour being the telephone itself; it is constantly in use because its female owner is a compulsive talker. After many attempts to attract attention, her desperate suitor calls her on the phone from the corner drugstore to propose marriage. The story is trifling, but *The Telephone* has become a popular success.

Temperament. A calculated alteration of the acoustical values of musical intervals to make possible the division of the perfect octave into 12 equal semitones. Theorists and performing musicians struggled for centuries to find a practical way of reconciling the perfect octave with the natural perfect fifths between the second and third partial of the harmonic series, the perfect fourth, and the major third. It is arithmetically impossible to equate any multiple of 3:2, which represents the ratio of frequencies of vibrations for the pure untempered fifth, with any multiple of 2:1, which is the ratio of frequencies of vibrations for a perfect octave. It is but a visual deception that the cycle of 12 fifths on a piano keyboard equals the cycle of seven octaves, with their common terminal on the highest C of the keyboard. Actually, the final acoustic perfect fifth would reach the hypothetical tone B-sharp, a few vibrations above the C of the last octave. Consequently, to avoid the chaos of unequal division, it is necessary to contract a pure fifth to the ratio of an imperfect tempered fifth, which would be less than its theoretical 3:2. The same adjustment is necessary for every interval. By sacrificing the acoustical purity of the fifth, the fourth, and other intervals of the generative harmonic series, it became possible to play a tune beginning on any key at all and modulate freely from one key to another. Bach sanctioned this acoustical sacrifice in his two volumes of *The Well-Tempered Clavier*, each containing 24 preludes and fugues in every key in chromatic order. This also settled the problem of enharmonic sounds, such as B-sharp and C, or F-sharp and G-flat, which in pure intonation would have been mutually different. In fact, Bach wrote one of his fugues in two enharmonic versions, E-flat minor and D-sharp minor, as if to emphasize the equality of enharmonic tones and its corollary, the equal division of the perfect octave into 12 semitones.

Der Templer und die Jüdin (The Templar and the Jewess). An opera by Heinrich Marschner, produced in Leipzig on December 22, 1829. The libretto is based on Walter Scott's novel *Ivanhoe*, concentrating on Ivanhoe's abortive love for a Jewess. The opera was very popular in its time; Schumann used an aria from it, *Du stolzes England, freue dich!* ("Thou proud England, rejoice!") in the 12th variation of his *Études symphoniques*, the reason being that he dedicated the work to his English friend the composer William Sterndale Bennett, wishing in this manner to gratify Bennett's patriotic feelings.

Tempo. An Italian word meaning "time" or "movement" in a suite or symphony. Its universal meaning in all languages, however, is the speed of musical performance. The marks indicating tempo are also universally Italian: largo, adagio, andante, allegretto, allegro, presto, and prestissimo. These definitions are often qualified by words of caution such as *ma non troppo* or *poco*. The first attempt to put some precise meaning into these vague Italian modifiers was made by the learned German flutist, composer, and theorist, Johann Quantz, who wisely selected the natural human heartbeat of 80 beats per minute as the norm. Taking 4/4 as the basic time signature, he assigned the exact duration of the pulsebeat to a half note in allegro, to a quarter note in allegretto, and to an eighth note in adagio. The invention of the metronome, a scientific measurement of the tempo, seemed to have standardized this precise terminology. Performers often disregarded the metronome markings by composers. Thus the timing of Toscanini's performance of the Funeral March in the *Eroica* made in 1935 scored only 52 eighth notes a minute, 35 percent slower than Beethoven apparently intended. Some modern composers, particularly Stravinsky, abandoned the traditional Italian tempo marks altogether and replaced them by the metronome number. Because Stravinsky insisted on precision in the performance of his works and abhorred Romantic aberrations, his metronome marks were absolute.

The rediscovery of recordings of great artists of the past disclosed a shocking departure from tempo markings as suggested by the composer. The sentimental leanings among German musicians and theorists of the second half of the 18th century, epitomized in the word *Empfindung*, "affection," and their desire to achieve a perfect human expression in performance led to constant shifts of tempo and dynamics—an astonishing practice contradicting the modern idea of the precise and ordered execution of Classical works. Even Mozart's father commented favorably on the device of "stolen time," an anticipation of the Romantic *rubato* so despised by modern interpreters. The tendency in the 20th century regarding tempo is generally in favor of precision, away from unauthorized ritardandos (so commonly resorted to in difficult technical passages), and *Luftpausen* ("air pauses"). Toward the middle of the 20th century, however, a curious counterreaction set in. Music critics and the general public began to complain about the metronomic monotony of modern performers. An unscientific nostalgia spread through the music world. Once again, as in the preceding century, "personality" was hailed as preferable to the fidelity to the printed music. Even composers themselves welcomed flexible tempi affected by celebrated interpreters as "vitalizing" the music.

The Tender Land. An opera by Aaron Copland, first performed in New York on April 1, 1954. The tender land of the title is the American Midwest. A young harvest worker has a summer romance with a farm girl, but he is indecisive about marriage. Eventually he leaves the farm. Her love is more profound, and she sets forth in search of him. The score represents Copland's modern lyricism at its best.

Tenor. The highest and most expressive male voice. The word tenor comes from the Latin *tenere*, "to hold." This derivation is explained by the fact that the cantus firmus in early vocal polyphony was given to the tenor voice, whose function was to hold the melody while other voices moved contrapuntally in relation to it. In operatic history, tenors enjoyed the greatest social and financial success as well as female adulation. But tenors were also traditionally regarded as being mentally deficient; an Italian joke lists the degrees of comparison, "stupido, stupidissimo, tenore." Tenors seem to be the natural product of the soil of the Italian peninsula, with Naples having the greatest density of tenors, among them Enrico Caruso. But Caruso was anything but "stupido." He had wide literary interests; he was also talented in pencil drawings. Another non-stupid tenor was Leo Slezak, who had a Viennese kind of wit, often at the expense of his fellow singers.

The ordinary range of the tenor voice is two octaves, from C below middle C to C above it. The tenor part is usually notated in the treble clef, but it sounds an octave lower. In some opera scores, the tenor part is indicated by a combined tenor and treble clef. The mark of distinction for great tenors is their ability to hold high C for a long time, often ignoring the musical and harmonic necessity to let go. Old film prints of tenor arias in opera show tenors running up to the footlights of the stage during a highly dramatic duet to project a high C into the audience and then retreating to join an awaiting soprano.

Tenth Symphony. An unfinished work of Gustav Mahler. Two movements only are extant, *Adagio* and *Purgatorio*; they were first performed posthumously in Vienna on October 12, 1924. In them, Mahler's idiom reaches the ultimate of complexity for his time, making use of extremely dissonant combinations of tones. The handwritten inscriptions in the manuscript point toward serious mental turbulence: "Madness possesses me! Devil, come and seize me, the cursed one!" The British musician Deryck Cooke completed the Symphony, making use of some of Mahler's sketches and fragments. His version received the approbation of Alma Mahler, the composer's widow. Cooke's full performing version was given its premiere in London on August 13, 1964.

Terraced dynamics. The Baroque style of dynamic changes by a direct transition from one degree of loudness to another. The term was introduced by Busoni in German as *Terrasendynamik*. Terraced dynamics were in common usage in the Baroque era, perhaps owing to the inability of the cembalo to graduate the sound with a distinct change from *piano* to *forte* or vice versa. In the Elizabethan period, explicit indications such as lowd (loud), lowder (louder), softer, and the like were in use. Beethoven favored terraced dynamics in the form of *subito piano* after *forte*. During his neo-Classical period, Stravinsky began to cultivate terraced dynamics almost exclusively, to symbolize his use of Baroque manners.

Tessitura. Italian for "texture," used to indicate the proportionate use of high or low register in a given vocal range. If high notes are preponderant, the tessitura is said to be high, as in most coloratura soprano parts; if low notes are frequent, the tessitura is said to be low.

The Testament of Freedom. A work for chorus and orchestra by Randall Thompson, with a text from the writings of Thomas Jefferson. It was first performed at the University of Virginia, of which Jefferson was the founder, on April 13, 1943, and has had numerous subsequent performances.

Tetrachord. A group of four diatonic degrees derived from ancient Greek scales in which it was used invariably in a descending progression. However, the medieval tetrachord was counted upward, and this natural ascent was retained in subsequent centuries. As a result, the names of the Church modes that developed from conjunct or disjunct tetrachords forming an entire diatonic scale were different from the Greek modes. The musical quality of the tetrachord was determined by the placement of the semitone in the diatonic progression. Thus, the Phrygian tetrachord was formed by the placement of the semitone between the first and the second degrees; in the Aeolian and Dorian tetrachords, the semitone was between the second and third degrees; in the Ionian and Mixolydian modes, the semitone occupied the place between the third and fourth degrees. The Lyrian tetrachord is formed by successive whole tones.

Text-sound composition. A medium that germinated in the Dada movement in the first quarter of the 20th century and was revived, making use of magnetic tape and other electronic devices, in the second half of the 20th century. Text-sound works emphasize the sonorous element independent from the meaning, if any, of the words recited; such compositions hark back to prehuman cries through ritualistic incantation and Pentecostal glossolalia or else may project into the future with the aid of computers, synthesizers, and stereophonic sound engineering. The medium developed among modern poets, sound engineers, and composers in Sweden and was picked up by American composers. Among the latter, Charles Amirkhanian achieved a degree of true virtuosity.

Thaïs. An opera by Jules Massenet, first performed in Paris on March 16, 1894. The libretto is drawn from the ironic novel by Anatole France. A monk in Egypt is horrified by the depravity of the courtesan Thaïs and dreams of converting her. He succeeds rather well. He conducts her through the desert, where they reach the convent and she takes her vow as the bride of Christ. The monk then undergoes a reversal, now craving not the spirit but the flesh of Thaïs. To exorcise the obsession, he flagellates himself violently but in vain. Meanwhile, Thaïs attains spiritual perfection and dies a true Christian. The instrumental solo *Meditation* from the score is a perennial favorite.

Thematic catalogue. An inventory of musical works by an individual composer arranged according to the genre (operas, symphonies, chamber music, solo works) or by opus number, and supplemented by musical incipits, that is, opening themes of the works catalogued. Such catalogues may be compiled by composers themselves or by their publishers. Haydn entrusted his copyist with compiling a thematic catalogue of his works, "which I can recall at present, from the age of 18 until my 73rd year of life." The Haydn catalogue contains errors of both omission and commission; at least two symphonies are listed as having identical initial phrases. Mozart also began cataloguing his compositions, but a complete thematic catalogue of his works was first put together by a botanist named Köchel, who had a passion for inventories. Thematic catalogues now exist for a majority of important composers and a minority of unimportant ones. Some extensive catalogues include information about the provenance of the manuscripts, details concerning various editions, and other similar data. In catalogues of German composers published after World War II, the notation *verschollen* ("disappeared," "vanished without a trace") makes its ominous appearance, alluding to the unconscionable looting of such manuscripts by the occupying armies.

Theme and Variations: The Four Temperaments. A work for string instruments with piano by Paul Hindemith, in which he set out to describe in musical terms the four temperaments of medieval medicine: *Melancholic*, *Sanguine*, *Phlegmatic*, and *Choleric*. The work was first performed in Boston on September 3, 1940.

There's a Long, Long Trail. A Western ballad by Zo (Alonzo) Elliott, who wrote it in 1913 while a student at Yale University. Shortly afterward he went to England, where he had the piece published. Eventually it became a standard song of World War I. President Woodrow Wilson himself once sang it at a White House dinner.

Thésée. An opera by Jean-Baptiste Lully, first performed in Paris on January 12, 1675. Theseus was the legendary hero who vanquished in Crete the bull Minotaur, whose annual diet was seven youths and seven maidens. Although a hero in Crete, Theseus proved to be a reprobate when he abandoned Ariadne; she had helped him find the way out of the labyrinth where the Minotaur dwelled by giving Theseus a thread ("Ariadne's thread") to guide him. Numerous epics and dozens of operas have been written with Theseus as the central character.

Three Blind Mice. This perennial popular children's song is probably the earliest printed nonreligious tune in music history. It was published in 1609 as a round for three voices, and this is still the setting which is sung in English-speaking countries.

Three New England Sketches. An orchestral work by Walter Piston in which he portrays his impressions of the seaside, the summer evening, and the mountains, the parts of a landscape he as a New Englander knew so well. The suite was first performed in Worcester, Massachusetts, on October 23, 1959.

Three-Page Sonata. A piano piece by Charles Ives, written in 1905, and so entitled for the obvious reason that it had only three pages. Ives marked at the point of recapitulation: "Back to First Theme—all nice Sonatas must have First Theme."

Three Places in New England. One of the most important works in American music, composed by Charles Ives between 1903 and 1914. The three places are the St. Gaudens monument in Boston Common, Putnam's Camp in Redding, Connecticut, and the Housatonic at Stockbridge. The music evokes memories of the Civil War; characteristically, Ives quotes fragments of popular American hymns and ballads in the music. The score represents a fantastic web of polytonal and polyrhythmic combinations. In 1930, Ives reduced the original score to the contingent of a chamber orchestra at the request of Nicolas Slonimsky, who gave its first performance in New York on January 10, 1931, with his Chamber Orchestra of Boston. This reduction became the standard of all subsequent performances of the work until the rediscovery of the original score for large orchestra, which was published posthumously about 1980.

Threni. A work for solo voices, chorus, and orchestra by Igor Stravinsky, to the Latin text of the Lamentations of Jeremiah. As in *Canticum sacrum* and (partly) in *Agon*, Stravinsky employs in this score some serial devices. *Threni* ("tears") was first performed in Venice on September 23, 1958.

Through the Looking Glass. An orchestral suite by Deems Taylor inspired by the wonderful tale of Lewis Carroll. It is in four movements: *The Garden of Live Flowers*, *Jabberwocky*, *Looking Glass Insects*, and *The White Knight*. The music is romantic and effective. It was first performed in New York on March 10, 1923, and was quite popular for a while, until musical tastes changed, plunging it into oblivion.

Another 20th-century composer, David del Tredici, equally enamored of Carroll's whimsical tale, produced an entire series of "Alice" works for amplified vocalist and orchestra. Some of these pieces also called for a rock group (electric guitars and saxophones) and folk group (banjo, mandolin, accordion, and so on). Del Tredici's "Alice" works include *An Alice Symphony* (1969), *Adventures Underground* (1971), *Vintage Alice: Fantascene on a Mad Tea Party* (1972), *Final Alice* (1976), *Child Alice* (1980), and *All in the Golden Afternoon* (1983).

Thrush. Slang expression for a female singer, especially one of popular songs. The real thrush is a coloratura triller among songbirds. Spike Hughes declared in a letter to *The Times* of London in the 1930s that "all thrushes sing the tune of the first subject of Mozart's Symphony No. 40 in G minor (K. 550), and phrase it a sight better than most conductors. The tempo is always dead right and there is no suggestion of an unauthorized accent on the ninth note of the phrase."

Till Eulenspiegels lustige Streiche (Till Eulenspiegel's Merry Pranks). A symphonic work by Richard Strauss; the title bears an amplifying elucidation, *nach alter Schelmenweise*, "after an old roguish manner." The piece was first performed in Cologne on November 5, 1895. Till Eulenspiegel is a hero of many medieval folk tales and is blamed for a variety of practical jokes. In the score, he pays the supreme penalty on the gallows, and his angular mischievous motif is cut off at the drumstroke marking his hanging. This is followed by an epilogue repeating his original lyrical tune. The surname *Eulenspiegel* means "owl mirror."

Time field. A topographical term used in structural modern music in which the temporal relationship is established spontaneously between the sounds (as independent acoustical phenomena) and the performer (whose reactions to these sounds determine the player's next action).

Timpani. The accepted Italian term for kettledrums; the common misspelling *tympani* is unjustified. The Italian word is the plural of *timpano* and is ultimately derived from the Greek word for a membrane. The French word is *timbales*, and in German it is *Pauken*. The timpani are the only percussive instruments in the orchestra with a definite pitch. In Classical symphonies and overtures, the timpani are usually written in pairs, tuned to the tonic and the dominant. Structurally, the timpani consist of hemispherically or parabolically shaped drums that look like large kettles covered with a treated animal hide. The screws around the rim increase or relax the tension of the membrane so that the pitch can be regulated accordingly. Modern kettledrums are equipped with pedals that can change the pitch with greater precision; later developments have led to the manufacture of a genuinely chromatic instrument. In the 19th century, the number of timpani in the orchestra increased; Wagner's *Ring* tetralogy requires four; Berlioz, in his passion for grandiosity, scored the movement *Tuba mirum* in his *Grande Messe des Morts* for sixteen. Uncommon tuning is found in Beethoven's symphonies; particularly remarkable is the tuning in an octave F to F in the Scherzo of his Symphony No. 9, where it is applied antiphonally. A foreboding ostinato on the solo kettledrum occurs in the transition from the Scherzo to the finale in Beethoven's Symphony No. 5. The indication *timpani coperti* is synonymous with *timpani sordi* and means "covered" or "muted" timpani; the desired effect is achieved by covering the head of the instrument with a piece of fabric.

Modern composers are apt to write timpani parts that require acrobatic virtuosity in manipulating several instruments, playing on the rim, making a glissando with the chromatic pedals, retuning while performing a rapid trill, and the like. Solo timpani occur in many modern works, and there are even timpani concertos. Alexander Tcherepnin composed a sonatina for timpani and piano. The opening phrase of John Vincent's *Symphonic Poem after Descartes* opens with a timpani solo in the rhythm of the Cartesian maxim, *Cogito ergo sum*. The American composer and percussion virtuoso William Kraft composed a Timpani Concerto that was premiered in Indianapolis on March 9, 1984.

Tin Pan Alley. A now obsolescent description originated around 1910 of the section of New York City on Broadway between 28th and 42nd streets where most popular songs were launched. It came to be associated with anything connected with popular songs.

Titan Symphony. The name originally attached to Mahler's Symphony No. 1 in D major, but Mahler disavowed this title. The work is a symphonic poem in two parts, the first part being described by Mahler as *From the Days of Youth*, and the second as *Commedia umana* ("human drama," as opposed to Dante's *divina commedia*). The main subject corresponds to the melody of the second song of Mahler's cycle *Lieder eines fahrenden Gesellen* (*Songs of a Traveling Companion*). The Symphony was first performed in Budapest on November 20, 1889.

Titles. In Classical music, titles of compositions usually describe the form and content of the work. Such forms as symphony, sonata, prelude, cantata, and opera may have been changeable through the centuries of their evolution. Thus *sinfonia* meant any instrumental composition or an orchestral interlude in an opera; it was only in the 18th century that it acquired the meaning of a symphony in the modern sense of the word. The advent of Romantic music made the problem of suitable titles acute. Time and again, composers would assign a programmatic title to a symphony or other work, only to repudiate it at a later time for fear that the music would be interpreted as ancillary to the story. What can be more explicit in its programmatic outline than Beethoven's *Pastoral* Symphony, with its realistic storm and three bird calls? Yet on second thought Beethoven carefully marked the score "More of an expression of feeling rather than painting." Mahler's romantic imagination prompted him to give all kinds of specific titles not only to his symphonies in their entirety but also to individual movements; later, however, he denied any such programmatic implications. So violent was he in his renunciation that when he was questioned about the meaning of one of his symphonies at a banquet, he raised his glass as if for a toast and exclaimed, "Let the programs perish!"

Such repudiations are particularly baffling when a literary work lies at the foundation of a typically Romantic composition. Berlioz boldly transplanted his early overture *Les Francs-juges* into the *Symphonie fantastique* where it became a *March to the Gallows*. To unify it with the rest of the *Symphonie*, he inserted a couple of bars of the *idée fixe*, the common theme of the work. He did even better: to save the labor of copying the old overture he pasted on the *idée fixe* of the old manuscript, replacing a bar of rests. Thus the "Frank Judges" became the "March to the Gallows." Mendelssohn's *Fingal's Cave*, inspired by his visit to northern Scotland in 1829, was originally entitled *The Solitary Island*. A fascinating instance of a composer's decision to affix new programmatic titles is illustrated by Schoenberg's *Five Orchestral Pieces*. In the original, they bore abstract titles without any programmatic content. Forty years later, yielding to the importunities of his publisher to "humanize" the titles, Schoenberg agreed to change the title of the third piece, *The Changing Chord*, to *Summer Morning by the Lake*. The titles that Scriabin selected for many of his works are theosophic, and he was often willing to listen to suggestions from his close intellectual associates. It was his brother-in-law, Boris de Schloezer, who suggested to him that the opening motif of his Symphony No. 3, *Le Poème divin*, is a proclamation of self-assertion: "I am!" This notation appears in the final manuscript and in the published score. And it was Modest Tchaikovsky, the brother of the composer, who suggested the name *Pathétique* for the Symphony No. 6.

Toccata. A term denoting a keyboard piece that takes advantage of the articulated clarity possible with keyboard instruments and that is written to display the virtuosity of its performers. The word comes from the Italian verb *toccare*, "to strike" or "to touch." In the 16th century, the term was understood as a prelude or an improvisation before the central section of a composition, particularly in organ playing. In the 17th century, the toccata assumed a more precise definition as a keyboard composition in a rapid tempo, in steady rhythm. In the 19th century, composers applied the term to a type of work that would otherwise be called *étude*. Debussy and Prokofiev wrote piano toccatas marked by brilliant technical display. Among modern composers who contributed to the genre were Busoni, Reger, and Stravinsky.

Tom Jones. An opera by François Philidor, first performed in Paris on February 27, 1765. The libretto is taken from the famous novel by Fielding, *Tom Jones, The History of a Foundling.* Tom is a scalawag who takes his pleasures where he finds them, but he loves Sophia Western in earnest. Her father, however, plans a rich marriage for her. It turns out in the end that Tom is really a nephew of the country squire and therefore is of enough nobility to marry Sophia. Byron called the character of Tom Jones "an accomplished black-guard," but in the opera Tom is a romantic lover.

Tombeau. French for "gravestone"; a genre of instrumental composition dedicated to the memory of a dignitary or a friend. In 1920, a number of French composers contributed memorial pieces to a collection entitled *Tombeau de Debussy.* The form of a memorial tombeau is also reflected in the titles *Threni* (Latin), *Tears* (English), *Plainte* (French), and *Lamento* (Italian). The same function of reverential remembrance is expressed by the title *Homage*, as in *Hommage à Rameau* by Debussy and *Homage to Ives* by Aaron Copland. Ravel's *Le Tombeau de Couperin*, a piano suite, is a fine example of a 20th-century tombeau; it was conceived as a tribute to François Couperin, the great master of the French Baroque. It contains six movements in 17th-century forms, with superinduced pandiatonic ornaments. Ravel orchestrated four of the movements, which were performed for the first time in Paris on February 28, 1920.

Tonality. A concept that embraces all pertinent elements of tonal structure, including both melodic and harmonic juxtapositions that determine the collective tonal relations—that is, a basic loyalty to a tonal center. The term is relatively new, having originated in France about 1820. It was universally adopted with requisite flexional changes in German, English, Italian, Spanish, and Russian nomenclature. Tonality does not determine a definite key; a composition may modulate widely from the outset and travel far from the original key, and yet it adheres to the sense of tonality as long as it follows the tonal structure. The antonym of tonality is *atonality*, a type of composition in which tonality is rejected. The guardian of tonality is the key signature, and no matter how many times this key signature is changed during a given composition, the sense of tonality remains as long as each individual section establishes a definite key.

Tonarium. A catalogue of medieval chants. A complete tonarium was usually organized according to the principal eight tones of Gregorian chant, including antiphons, communions, introits, and responsories.

Tone cluster. This picturesque term was invented by Henry Cowell at the age of 18. A tone cluster consists of a row of adjacent tones—diatonic, pentatonic, or chromatic. Cowell applied them systematically in many of his compositions, such as *Amiable Conversations* for piano, in which diatonic clusters are used in the right hand on white keys and pentatonic clusters are employed in the left hand on the black keys. Small tone clusters can be performed on the piano keyboard with fists or the palm of the hand; extensive tone clusters of two octaves or more require the use of the entire forearm, from the fist to the elbow. The idea is not entirely new; composers of "battle pieces" applied tone clusters using the palm of the hand, mostly in the bass, to imitate a cannon shot. A curious piano piece *Alpine Storm* by the German-American composer George Kunkel specifies the use of the palm of the left hand to produce the effect of thunder. Independently of Cowell, Charles Ives employed tone clusters to illustrate the "celestial railroad" in the Hawthorne movement of his *Concord* Sonata, produced by gently pressing a wooden plank down on the keys in the treble to create sympathetic vibrations.

Tone color. A widely used term for timbre. As tonometric experiments demonstrate, the peculiar tone color of a musical instrument or of the human voice depends on the relative strength of harmonics produced by the fundamental tone. A note produced on one instrument differs as much from the same one produced on another instrument as the tone color of one voice differs from that of another. The tone color of the flute is perceived as the purest of all instruments because it is rich in upper octave harmonics. The clarinet, on the other hand, generates a harmonic series characterized by the fifth over an octave. The oboe owes its penetrating sound to having harmonics of practically the same mutual strength. The harmonics of string instruments are also abundant in all registers. Schoenberg has introduced the idea of a scale of tone colors, so that a succession of identical pitches on various instruments would form what he called the *Klangfarbe* scale.

Tonight We Love. This song, filched from Tchaikovsky's Piano Concerto No. 1 by an unscrupulous Broadway hack, became popular in 1941. Around 1950, someone in Hollywood with a wry sense of humor published a song entitled "Everybody's Making Money but Tchaikovsky."

Tonus. In the Middle Ages, *tonus* designated a mode. In the 16th century, a system of 12 modes was established, comprising six authentic and six plagal modes. The complete theory of the tonus was expounded upon by Glareanus in his treatise *Dodecachordon* (meaning "12 modes"), published in 1547. Zarlino changed the order of the modes in his *Istitutioni harmoniche*, published in 1558, placing the Ionian mode at the head of the list. With this he instituted the C major scale as the fundamental tonal progression.

Top. A child's toy in the shape of an inverse cone. When wound up, it produces a humming sound of a fairly definite pitch. It is used in some avant-garde works, including *A Celtic Requiem* by John Tavener, which calls for "a top in E-flat."

Torch song. An American slang term for a ballad of despair and lovelorn lamentation, usually sung by a "thrush" or "canary" (female singer) with sobbing cadenzas. The term came from the expression "to carry a torch," to care for someone deeply, especially without reciprocation. Torch songs were the creations of the jazz and swing era of the 1930s and 1940s. They were revived in 1970 with a more explicit sexual content, often reaching hysterical extremes at constantly recurring climaxes. The term wilted, melted, and went into innocuous desuetude when sex became open.

Toreador Song. The famous march song from Bizet's *Carmen*. There is no such word as *toreador* in Spanish; a bullfighter is *torero*, and the correct term for the man who kills the bull in the ring is *matador*.

Torquato Tasso. An opera by Gaetano Donizetti, first produced in Rome on September 9, 1833. The central character is Tasso, the famous poet of the Italian Renaissance. The Duchess Eleonora falls in love with him when he reads poetry to her, but her brother, the reigning Duke of Ferrara, wants her to marry the Duke of Mantua, and gets rid of Tasso by putting him in a madhouse.

Tosca. An opera by Giacomo Puccini, first produced in Rome on January 14, 1900. The libretto is derived from a drama by Sardou, which in French is *La Tosca*. The action takes place during the turbulent summer of 1800 in Rome. Napoleon's army advances into Italy and is greeted by Italian patriots as liberators from the oppressive Austrian rule. Tosca is a famous opera singer; her lover, the painter Cavaradossi, shelters a political refugee and becomes the target of persecution by the sinister chief of the Roman police, Scarpia. Captivated by Tosca's beauty, Scarpia seeks to bargain her favors against Cavaradossi's release from prison. In desperation, she agrees to submit to him, whereupon Scarpia issues an order for a pretended execution of Cavaradossi, using blank cartridges. "As in the case of Palmieri," he adds ominously. Confident of her lover's escape, Tosca takes advantage of Scarpia's amorous relaxation and stabs him to death. But Scarpia had outwitted Tosca:

"In the case of Palmieri" was a code message to the soldiers to make the pretended execution real. Cavaradossi falls at the stake; after the soldiers are gone, Tosca rushes to him, but he does not rise. Distraught, she hurls herself to her death from the prison's parapet. The score introduces many bold harmonic innovations—consecutive triads, unresolved dissonances, and whole-tone scales. At the same time, the exquisite art of Italian bel canto is beautifully exercised. Tosca's lament at the cruelty of fate and Cavaradossi's moving cavatina are among the finest arias in the operatic repertory.

Tostquartette. The collective name for Haydn's 12 quartets, opp. 54, 55, and 64 (1788–1790), dedicated to the amateur violinist and industrialist Johann Tost of Vienna. The fifth quartet is nicknamed *Razor* Quartet. It seems that Haydn, annoyed at the bluntness of his straight razor, swore to trade his next string quartet for a sharp razor. Johann Tost, eager to oblige, produces a good razor and gets the dedication.

Die tote Stadt (The Dead City). An opera by Erich Wolfgang Korngold, produced in Hamburg and Cologne on the same day, December 4, 1920. The libretto is Germanically morbid, but the score is one of the most effective operas of the post-Wagner era. A widower faithful to the memory of his wife is struck by a resemblance to her in a young dancer whom he learns to love. In her desire to please him, she thoughtlessly makes a wig of his late wife's hair. Provoked by this act of sacrilege, he strangles the girl. But welcome relief is granted to him (and to the spectators): The whole sequence of events was but a dream.

Die toten Augen (The Dead Eyes). The most successful opera by Eugène d'Albert, first performed in Dresden on March 5, 1916. The libretto deals with a blind woman miraculously cured by Christ. The miracle has its disadvantage, however; as she regains her sight, she realizes how ugly her husband is. Disappointed, she yields her favors to a Roman centurion. Her husband kills himself, and she, too, commits suicide.

Totentanz. "Dance of death." A morbid genre cultivated during the Middle Ages in poetry, painting, and music. It evoked the image of Death dancing with its prospective victim. Even in the songs of youth, expectation of death was often the principal motive, as in *Gaudeamus igitur*, which warned youth to enjoy life before *nos habebit humus* ("the earth will have us"). Liszt wrote a piece for piano and orchestra entitled *Totentanz*, also known under the French name, *Danse macabre*. He was inspired by the frescos in the cemetery of the town of Pisa that represented Death mowing down indiscriminately the rich and the poor, the old and the young. Throughout the composition, the ominous strains of *Dies Irae* are heard. It was first performed in The Hague on April 15, 1865.

Toy Symphony. Symphonies ostensibly written for children to perform were popular in the 18th century. The most famous of them, the *Toy* Symphony, was originally attributed to Haydn, but it was found to be a movement in an instrumental suite by Mozart's father, Leopold. The toys in the orchestra are a rattle, a triangle, and several squeakers to imitate the cuckoo, the quail, and the nightingale.

Tragic Overture. The proper title of one of the two symphonic overtures of Brahms, the other being the *Academic Festival Overture*. The *Tragic Overture* is in D minor, a tonality often having solemn and tragic connotations in Romantic music. It was first performed in Vienna on December 26, 1880. A number of commentators exerted their verbal ingenuity to depict the music in terms of inexorable fate, sin and redemption, passion and purification, and the like. The tragic element can easily be heard in the ominous sounding beats of the timpani and in the mighty blasts of the trombones. But there is a spirit of pastoral serenity in the second theme and its development.

Tragic Symphony. A descriptive appellation sometimes attached to Mahler's Symphony No. 6 in A minor. The tragic element is supplied in the orchestration by a large variety of percussion instruments, among them a hammer, which seems to symbolize Doomsday. The work is in four parts and was first performed in Essen, Germany, on May 27, 1906.
　　Tragic Symphony is also a common nickname for Schubert's Symphony No. 4 in C minor, which he composed at the age of 19.

Tranfjädrarna (The Crane Feathers). An opera by Sven-Erik Bäck, from a Japanese Noh drama dealing with a bride who is really a bird. It was performed for the first time on the Stockholm radio on February 28, 1957.

Transatlantic. An opera by George Antheil, to his own libretto, first performed in Frankfurt on May 25, 1930. In it an American presidential candidate is searching for a suitable bride in various locales around New York. The tunes are jazzy, evoking the innocence of the eponymous transatlantic nation in search of elusive maturity.

The Transposed Heads. An opera by Peggy Glanville-Hicks, to her own libretto drawn from Thomas Mann's novel, first performed in Louisville, Kentucky, on March 27, 1954. A Hindu woman, unsure of her choice between her genius of a husband and her handsome simpleton lover, proposes that they decapitate themselves and transpose their heads. Bewildered by the resulting severed heads and decapitated torsos, she commits suicide. The score is rhythmically nervous and understandably dissonant.

Transposition. Performance of a composition in a higher or lower key in order to adjust to the range of a given voice or a more convenient and more effective tonality in an instrumental work. Most common transpositions are made in song anthologies, usually from the original setting for a high voice to a lower range.

Trauersinfonie. Haydn's Symphony No. 44 in E minor (1772), so nicknamed because of its mournful character. *Trauer* in German means "mourning."

Träumerei. A quintessential Romantic piano piece by Robert Schumann from his suite of 14 character pieces entitled *Kinderszenen*, which he wrote in 1838. *Träumerei* is a German collective noun connoting light dreaming. The piece is in the romantic key of F major, with sweet modulations into relative major and minor keys. It was selected as a memorial to be played by Soviet military bands in place of the funeral march at the ceremonies for Soviet soldiers killed in World War II.

Travesti. Opera roles in which women sing the parts of young men. Examples are Cherubino in Mozart's *The Marriage of Figaro*, Octavian in *Der Rosenkavalier*, and Siebel in Gounod's *Faust*. The British sometimes call this operatic practice "breeches-part," translated from the German word *Hosenrolle* ("pants role"). Travesti is the past participle of the French verb *travestir*, "to disguise."

La Traviata. An opera by Verdi, first produced in Venice on March 6, 1853. The libretto is drawn from the French play *La Dame aux camélias* by Alexandre Dumas *fils*. The Italian title is untranslatable; it is the feminine past participle of the transitive verb *traviare*, "to lead away from the right path," which is derived from *trans*, "across," and *via*, "path" or "way." The English translation proposed in some reference works, *The Wayward One*, obviates the morally important point that La Traviata of the tale was not wayward by nature. To render justice to the title, it would have to be translated "A person of the female gender who has been diverted from the way of the righteous." Young Violetta is La Traviata, an already well-established courtesan. She meets a dashing gentleman, Alfredo, who proclaims his ardent love for her. They rent a villa together near Paris. Alfredo's father is dismayed by his son's misalliance and begs Violetta to let him go. She complies and announces to Alfredo the end of their affair; he takes temporary leave of her but on returning finds her dying of consumption. After some vocalizing, she dies in his arms. *La Traviata* is one of the most tuneful of Verdi's operas. There is a famous scene of drinking a toast, known as *brindisi*. There are poignant arias. The subject of the opera seems to have shocked the sensibilities of some mid-19th-century opera-goers. The London papers expressed outrage that "the ladies of the aristocracy" should be allowed to attend a production "to see an innocent young lady impersonate the heroine of an infamous French novel who varies her prostitution by a frantic passion." *La Traviata* has survived, however, and retains its popularity.

Trecento. The Italian designation for the 14th century, its art, literature, and music. By extension, this designation embraces the period from about 1325 into the first decades of the 15th century. In music, it is a period characterized by the effloresence of polyphonic secular music with texts in the vernacular. The most important forms of the Trecento are madrigal and caccia.

Treemonisha. An opera by Scott Joplin that describes the life of an abandoned black baby girl found under a tree by a compassionate woman named Monisha and therefore christened Monisha of the Tree, or Treemonisha. It was composed in 1911, two years before Joplin's death, and received its first stage performance in Houston on May 23, 1975, orchestrated by Gunther Schuller, who also conducted the performance.

Trees. A semiclassical song by Oscar Rasbach to the words of Joyce Kilmer. The seminal message of the song is that only God can make a tree. The musical prosody of the setting is peculiarly awkward, and the tessitura is poorly managed. Why this song became popular on the concert circuit is difficult to fathom.

Tremolo. A popular embellishment consisting of a repeated alternation of two notes in rapid tempo, regarded as a powerful device to produce dramatic tension. In his preface to the operatic madrigal *Il combattimento di Tancredi e Clorinda*, Monteverdi describes the tremolo as the most expressive dynamic device of the *stile concitato*, illustrating as it does Tancredo's unwitting fatal wounding of his beloved Clorinda. The use of the tremolo for dramatic effect reached its greatest popularity in the 19th century, particularly in opera. It later degenerated into melodrama and soon vanished from the realm of serious composition altogether, except for comical effects.

Triad. As the name indicates, a chord consisting of three notes. Modern music theory recognizes four types of triads: a major triad, consisting of a major third superimposed by a minor third; a minor triad, consisting of a minor third topped by a major third; a diminished triad, consisting of two minor thirds, one on top of the other; and an augmented triad, formed by two conjunct major thirds. The major and minor triads are fundamental to the determination of a key; the diminished triad is regarded as a discord because it contains a diminished fifth; the augmented triad is also a discord because it contains an augmented fifth even though the augmented fifth is enharmonically equivalent to a minor sixth. In a daring display of modernity, the Russian composer Vladimir Rebikov ended the score of his opera *The Christmas Tree*, written in 1903, on an augmented triad and was criticized for his audacity. In the 20th century, some music critics tried to deprive the triads of their specific connotations as consisting of two thirds, and they extended the notion of a triad to any chord containing three notes, even chromatically congested three notes. Analogously, a group of two notes was described as a dyad.

The Trial of Lucullus. An opera by Roger Sessions, first performed in Berkeley, California, on April 18, 1947. The Roman general Lucullus is dead, but before entering the Elysian Fields he must defend himself against the accusation of being a mass murderer. The jury is not impressed by his recital of military victories and unanimously condemns him. The libretto by Bertolt Brecht was originally intended for a radio play as an allegorical indictment of Hitler. Paul Dessau also wrote an opera with this title.

Tricesimorprimal temperament. An outlandish division of the octave into 31 equal intervals, proposed by the 17th-century Dutch astronomer Christiaan Huygens. This sesquipedalian term comes from the Latin adjective for the numeral 31.

Tricotet. A type of melody that was improvised, sung, danced, and played on instruments by minstrels in the Middle Ages. It was completely devoid of specific form. French Baroque composers gave the name tricotet to fanciful sections of instrumental suites.

Trill. A melodic embellishment in which a given note occurring on the strong beat alternates rapidly with a diatonic degree above it. The practice of trilling was cultivated in France in the 17th century and was sometimes picturesquely described as *tremblement*, "shake." In German it is *Triller*, in Italy, *trillo*. The word *trilleta* is the Italian diminutive for the trill, and *trillo caprino* is an irregular trill, or, literally, a "goat's trill," from *capro*, "goat." A graphic symbol for a trill is a wavy line, extending according to the length desired. In modern instrumental writing, the trill invariably begins on the principal note, but in the Baroque period the trill usually began on the note above the principal note.

Trio. A generic term for a composition employing three instruments or three vocal parts. The piano trio is scored for violin, cello, and piano. A trio set for violin, viola, and cello is usually called a string trio. Haydn wrote a number of trios for two violins and cello; Beethoven also contributed to this type of trio. Among piano trios, the greatest exemplars are those of Beethoven, Schumann, Mendelssohn, Brahms, and Tchaikovsky. Trios for piano, clarinet, and cello were written by Mozart and Khatchaturian. The term *trio* for the central section of a minuet or scherzo is a relic of the Baroque era, when it was actually written for three instruments, such as two oboes and bassoon.

Trio sonata. The most important genus of instrumental Baroque music. Despite its name, the trio sonata is scored for four instruments, two in the high range and two in the low range. The upper parts are usually played by two violins and the lower parts by cello and cembalo, the latter taking care of the basso continuo by supplying the harmonic skeleton of the work. In pre-Classical music, the upper parts were often taken over by viols and cornetti and the lower parts by a viola da gamba and cembalo. There are specimens of trio sonatas written for a considerably larger ensemble, but even in such cases the texture is in three principal parts; to emphasize this peculiarity, the composer often added the words *a tre*. Two principal genera of trio sonatas are *sonata da chiesa* ("church sonata") and *sonata da camera* ("chamber sonata"). Handel wrote 28 trio sonatas, including six scored for two oboes and bass; Vivaldi wrote 12; Bach's most famous trio sonata is his *Musical Offering*, which he wrote for Frederick the Great. Toward the middle of the 18th century, trio sonatas evolved into piano trios, with the piano part appearing as cembalo redivivus, not only filling in the harmony but having an independent role melodically and contrapuntally.

Il trionfo dell'onore (Triumph of Honor). An opera by Alessandro Scarlatti, first performed in Naples on November 26, 1718. The hero (or rather, the villain) of the opera courts two ladies at once. When the honest suitor of one of them nicks him in a duel, the villain decides to marry the unattached lady. The opera is historically important as one of the earliest examples of the Neapolitan opera buffa.

Trionfo di Afrodite (The Triumph of Aphrodite). A scenic cantata by Carl Orff, to his own libretto derived from Greek and Latin poems, first performed in Milan on Febrary 13, 1953. In lieu of a dramatic plot, the work portrays the initiation into marriage according to the sacred rites of Aphrodite. The idiom is monodic, austere, and stylistically formalized so as to suggest an archaic ambience.

Triple dot. Three dots placed to the right of a note augment its duration by one-half plus one-fourth plus one-eighth its value, each subsequent dot adding half the value of the preceding dot. Triple dots are rare. An example is found in Rimsky-Korsakov's opera *Tsar Saltan*.

Triskaidekaphobia. Fear of the number 13 (*tris*, 3; *kai*, and; *deka*, 10; *phobia*, fear). Among musicians, Rossini and Schoenberg possessed it in an extreme measure. In addition to triskaidekaphobia, Rossini was afraid of Fridays; he died on November 13, 1868, which was a Friday. Schoenberg was mystical about the sinister meaning of 13 in his own life; he was born on the 13th of the month and regarded it as an ill omen. Even in numbering bars in his compositions, he systematically omitted number 13. When he began to compose his opera *Moses und Aaron*, he realized that the number of letters in the title was 13. To exorcise triskaidekaphobia, he removed the second *a* to make *Aron*. He was seriously upset when he was tactlessly reminded by a jocular friend on his 76th birthday that 7 plus 6 equals 13. He died on July 13, 1951, 13 minutes before midnight, at the age of 76.

Tristan chord. A somewhat arbitrary designation of the Wagnerian chord consisting of F, B, D-sharp, and G-sharp, which occurs in the second measure of the Prelude to the opera *Tristan und Isolde*. The upper voice ascends chromatically, the alto and bass descend chromatically, and the tenor drops a minor third down to form the dominant-seventh chord of the key of A, thus establishing the Tristanesque connection with the opening note, which is A. The chord and the succeeding cadence are fundamental to melodic and harmonic transformations of the principal leading motives of the entire score. So unusual was it for the music of the middle of the 19th century that Wagnerophiles built a whole mystique about it in the theory of chromatic harmony. The notorious Wagnerophobe, the critic Hanslick, said that the chromatics of the Prelude to *Tristan und Isolde* reminded him of an old Italian painting representing a martyr whose intestines are being slowly unwound on a reel.

Tristan und Isolde. An opera by Wagner, to his own libretto, first performed in Munich on June 10, 1885. The story is derived from an ancient Cornish legend. King Mark of Cornwall sends his nephew Tristan to fetch his chosen bride Isolde, a princess of Ireland. During the sea voyage, Isolde falls so deeply in love with Tristan that only death can save her from disgrace. She asks her lady attendant to give her poison, but the woman prepares a love potion instead. After drinking it, both Tristan and Isolde become consumed with passion. Isolde marries King Mark but continues to keep secret trysts with Tristan; their love duet is surpassingly moving in its chromatic sensuousness. Tristan, wounded by the king's henchman, is taken to his castle in Brittany. Isolde comes to visit him; a shepherd plays a tune on his wooden trumpet which is a signal that Isolde's ship is approaching. Tristan, still bleeding from his wound, rushes to meet her and expires lovingly. The concluding scene is Isolde's own *Liebestod*, or "love death," expressing a mystical belief that the deepest light of love can be fulfilled only in the deepest night of death. The score is the apotheosis of Wagner's system of leitmotifs. Wagner's annotators have painstakingly catalogued in the score the themes of love, death, day and night, love potion, fidelity, suspicion, exultation, impatience, and malediction. *Tristan und Isolde* is couched in a highly chromaticized idiom. For modernists, the Prelude to *Tristan und Isolde* is a prophetic vision of atonality; Alban Berg inserted its opening measures into his atonal *Lyric Suite*. Debussy, whose attitude toward Wagner was ambivalent, made fun of the Prelude in his whimsical *Golliwogg's Cakewalk*. Wagner chose to give the name Isolde to the illegitimate daughter born to him by Cosima von Bülow on April 10, 1865; during this time, Cosima's husband, Hans von Bülow, was conducting strenuous rehearsals of *Tristan und Isolde*.

Tritone. The interval of the augmented fourth, containing three whole tones, as in F to B. It was a forbidden progression in the building of hexachords.

One of Bach's chorales begins with three whole tones in succession, aggregating to a tritone, to the words, *"O schwerer Gang"* ("Oh, difficult step"). In medieval Latin treatises on music, the tritone was called *diabolus in musica*. *Vexations* by Erik Satie (circa 1895) for piano, to be played, according to Satie's own prescription, 840 times in succession, is based entirely of tritones in the right hand in parallel motion (except one diminished fourth, which may be and probably is a misprint), the harmony being incomplete diminished-seventh chords (with a couple of incomplete dominant-seventh chords tossed in).

Il Trittico (The Triptych). A group of three short operas by Puccini: *Il Tabarro*, *Suor Angelica*, and *Gianni Schicchi*. The entire triptych was performed for the first time at the Metropolitan Opera in New York on December 14, 1918.

Trois morceaux en forme de poire. A characteristic title of three piano pieces by Erik Satie, which he wrote in 1903 as a rebuttal to reproaches that his music was formless. Obviously, pieces "in the shape of a pear" cannot be said to be shapeless. A color picture of a pear appeared on the title page of the published edition.

Trois petites liturgies de la Présence Divine. A work by Olivier Messiaen, scored for celesta, vibraphone, maracas, gong, tam-tam, piano, Ondes Martenot, and string orchestra. The text is drawn from religious writings of St. Paul, St. Thomas, the Apocalypse, and the Song of Songs, as well as from scientific writings on medicine, botany, geology, and astronomy. It was first performed in Paris on April 21, 1945.

Trois Préludes flasques. One of Erik Satie's piano suites in which the title is more important than the music. The adjective *flasques* ("flabby") refers to the deliberate shapelessness of the piece.

Trombone. The bass instrument of the trumpet family. The name is the Italian augmentative of *tromba*; the suffix *one* (pronounced oh-nay) indicates bigness. (For instance, *capo* is "chief"; *capone*, "big chief.") The trombone is the only instrument that changes its shape physically during performance; the player draws the sliding tube in or out, the lower notes being produced by extending the tube and the higher notes by drawing the tube in. For this reason the trombone is called sliding trombone. No orchestral instrument can sound *Dies Irae* more ominously than the trombone. The trombone announces in doom-laden tones the entrance of the statue of the Commendatore in Mozart's *Don Giovanni*, summoning the profligate protagonist to a ghostly supper. Beethoven reserves the appearance of the trombone for the glorious finale of his Symphony No. 5. The range of the tenor trombone, which is the one most often used in the orchestra, is from E below the bass clef to C an octave above middle C. The bass trombone is tuned a fourth lower. There is also a double-bass trombone that is an octave below the tenor trombone. It is rarely used, and to play it one must possess very strong lungs. Sometimes a pedal pump is attached to help the player to blow. Richard Strauss makes use of it in *Elektra*, as does Varèse in *Arcana*.

Tropes. Progressions of notes in Gregorian chant that have characteristic melismas. The term is often used in medieval treatises interchangeably with church modes. Originally the term applied to rhetorical figures of speech defined by Quintilian as *verbi vel sermonis a propria significatione in aliam mutatio* ("a change from the proper meaning of a word into another"). The musical texture of the medieval tropes annexed in the course of time all kinds of intrusive modalities, including secular tunes. The proliferation of unorthodox tropes and the supposed melismatic pollution of Gregorian chant caused the Council of Trent, held in the middle of the 16th century, to proscribe all such usages, allowing only those melodic figures that had become firmly ingrained into traditional ecclesiastical chants.

Les Troqueurs (The Tricksters). A comic opera in one act by Antoine Dauvergne, first performed in Paris on July 30, 1753. Two young men try to outwit their girl companions who in turn outwit them by arousing unjustified jealousy. The piece is a trifle, but it made history as the opening of the famous literary and aesthetic squabble known as the *Guerre des bouffons* ("War of Comedians"). *Les Troqueurs* was the response of the nationalistic group of French men of the theater, supported by the king himself and his mistress the Marquise de Pompadour to the proponents of Italian opera. *Les Troqueurs* was supposed to prove that the French could also write entertaining music *dans le goût Italien* ("in the Italian taste"), as opposed to the rather tedious lyric operas of Lully and Rameau, full of Greek mythology and opaque allegory. The success of the opera gave impetus to the composition of light, short theatrical pieces with music. However, the director of the French Opera Theater, fearful that a purely French product would not attract the public accustomed to the Italian type of entertainment, did not reveal the name of the composer until *Les Troqueurs* had become a definite success.

Troubadour. The generic name for poets and singers who roamed the country in Provençe in the 12th and 13th centuries; in their local tongue they were known as *trobador*, or *tropator*, that is, "the composers of tropes." The art of the troubadours gradually penetrated into Northern France, where they became known as trouvères; in Germany they were called minnesingers. The troubadours originated many types of popular French songs, such as *alba* (later *aubade*) and *pastorela* or *pastourelle*. A considerable number of songs composed by the troubadours have been preserved.

Trout Quintet. The Piano Quintet in A major (1819) by Franz Schubert, the penultimate fourth movement of which is a set of variations on Schubert's song, *Die Forelle* (*The Trout*).

Trouvère. The historic name describing medieval French poets and singers who flourished in the domain of the *langue d'oeil*, so named to describe Frenchmen who used the word *oeil* for the affirmative particle, *oui*, as distinct from the Provençal *langue d'oc* for the troubadours, to whom the affirmative was *oc*. The songs of the trouvères created a profusion of literary and musical forms, known under the collective title of *Chansons de geste* ("Songs of deeds"); they also cultivated the forms of rondeau, ballade, virelais, motets, and the instrumental estampies. Amazingly enough, thousands of trouvère songs have been preserved in medieval chansonniers. The word is probably derived from the French verb *trouver*, "to find."

Il Trovatore (The Troubadour). An opera by Verdi, first produced in Rome on January 19, 1853. It merits the inverted prize for the most impenetrable libretto in the history of opera, but the score contains some of Verdi's finest inventions, among them the celebrated *Anvil Chorus*. The Troubadour leads the rebellion against the King of Aragon whose army is commanded by the Troubadour's own brother, Conte di Luna. The brothers are not aware that they are kith and kin; to complicate matters further, they love the same girl. Enter a mysterious gypsy woman named Azucena, who tells the Troubadour the dreadful story that her own mother was unjustly accused of slaying the baby brother of Conte di Luna and was put to death for her alleged crime. Actually the baby was saved, and the Troubadour was that baby. Azucena is arrested as a spy and condemned to die the same fiery death as her mother. The Troubadour, who believes Azucena to be his mother, tries to save her life but is captured by Conte di Luna. The Troubadour's bride, Leonora, begs Conte di Luna to release him, and the unspeakable count agrees provided she give herself to him. She submits but takes a slow-working poison to escape her unwelcome lover. She goes to the tower where the Troubadour is kept and brings him the message of his freedom. The poison begins to work, and she dies in his arms. At that moment Conte di Luna arrives and orders the Troubadour executed after all. As the Troubadour dies, Azucena reveals to the Conte di Luna that he was his brother.

Les Troyens (The Trojans). An opera by Hector Berlioz. The complete score was so long that Berlioz decided to split it into two parts; only the second part, *Les Troyens à Carthage*, was performed during his lifetime, in Paris on November 4, 1863. The entire work, including the first part entitled *La Prise de Troie*, was produced posthumously in Karlsruhe, Germany, on December 6, 1890. The libretto, based on Virgil's epic on the Trojan war, ends with the suicide of Dido, the Queen of Carthage, after her abandonment by Aeneas.

?!

Trumpet. The most ancient instrument of the human race. The Latin name for it was *tuba*; in medieval hymns it was the trumpet of Judgment Day. When the Doomsday trumpet is represented in actual compositions, however, its part is usually given to the trombone. It is a dogma in books on orchestration that a single trumpet equals in its sonority the entire orchestra. The most obvious dramatic use of the trumpet is that of a military summons. In Beethoven's opera *Fidelio*, the trumpet announces the arrival of the new governor who is to establish justice. In *Carmen*, it summons Don José to the barracks. The trumpet can also be meditative and even philosophical, particularly when muted, as in *The Unanswered Question* by Charles Ives.

For centuries, the trumpet was limited to natural harmonic tones and had to be tuned to the key of a work in which it was used. To effect a modulation to a lower key, the trumpet player had to insert an extra tubing into his instrument; to modulate to a higher key, the tubing had to be shortened. It was not until the 19th century that efficient trumpet keys were invented that made it possible to play an entire chromatic scale. But before then, the trumpet parts in the works of Mozart, Haydn, and even Beethoven used mainly the tonic and the dominant of the principal key. Wagner wrote a part for a wooden trumpet in the third act of *Tristan und Isolde*, but it is usually played by the English horn.

The trumpet was standardized in the second half of the 19th century, as a transposing instrument in B-flat that sounds a major second below the written note. The alto trumpet in F is used in many scores by French composers, among them *España* by Chabrier. In Germany, Russia, England, and the Netherlands, the B-flat trumpet is used almost exclusively; it is marked *in B*, B being the German designation for B-flat. French and American composers increasingly have used a trumpet in C, which does not transpose. The trumpet plays an important role in jazz; most jazzmen call it, with poetic nonchalance, a "horn," bringing about confusion in colloquies with so-called serious musicians, to whom a horn is a French horn. The range of the trumpet is from its written note F-sharp below the treble staff to the written C above the staff. The lowest note in the B-flat trumpet is therefore E in actual pitch. Some virtuoso trumpeters can overblow the range for several notes above the high C. Louis Armstrong, the legendary jazz trumpeter who was called Satchmo (as an abbreviation of "satchel mouth"), once hit high C 280 times in succession. It was the trumpet that brought down the walls of Jericho: "And it came to pass, when the people heard the sound of the trumpet, and the people shouted with a great shout, that the wall fell down flat" (Joshua 6:20).

Trumpet Voluntary. A celebrated tune mistakenly attributed to Purcell. Actually, it was written by Jeremiah Clarke, an obscure contemporary of Purcell whose only notorious act was when he shot himself for the love of a lady. The original title of Clarke's piece was *Prince of Denmark's March*; he wrote it with many a trumpet flourish to glorify the arrival in England of Prince George of Denmark, consort of Queen Anne.

Tuba. The brass instrument in the bass range of the orchestra, where it supplies a harmonic foundation for the trombones above it. It is manufactured in three sizes: tenor, bass, and double bass. The latter is an octave below the tenor tuba. There are also the so-called Wagner tubas, which are smaller than the common variety and more mellifluous. They were specially designed for Wagner's music dramas as performed at the Bayreuth Festivals and are therefore known as Bayreuth tubas.

Tuning. By universal convention, orchestral tuning begins with the oboe giving an A of the middle octave, which, in most orchestras, is pitched at 440 vibrations per second. The rest of the orchestra instruments then adjust themselves to this pitch. In the process, some sort of inchoate arpeggiating is spontaneously performed by the various instruments. A story is told about an oriental potentate who went to a concert in Paris and was asked which piece he liked best. "The beginning," he replied. "Just before the man with the stick came in." The modern Russian composer Shchedrin wrote a movement in his Symphony No. 2, subtitled *Prelude VII*, which imitates the tuning of an orchestra. In piano tuning, it is necessary to reconcile the difference between the perfect fifth and fourth of the tempered pitch with the acoustical pitch derived from the series of overtones. On the piano, fifths and fourths have to be altered to make the cycle of 12 fifths equal to seven octaves. The piano tuner arrives at this equation by making sure that tempered fifths produce about 47 beats a minute, made audible by the slight increase and decrease of the loudness of the principal tone.

Tuning fork. A metal fork giving the pitch of A above middle C, which, according to prevailing international agreement, has 435 to 440 cycles per second, depending on the standard pitch in a given country. Tuning forks can be manufactured in different sizes if the thickness and length are varied proportionately.

Turandot. An opera by Giacomo Puccini, left unfinished at his death and first performed in this incomplete version at the Metropolitan Opera in New York on November 16, 1926. Later on, Franco Alfano added an ending using Puccini's thematic material, and it is in this form that *Turandot* is usually performed. The score is remarkable in many respects; in it, Puccini attempted bold experimentation, approaching polytonality and atonality. Because Turandot is a Chinese princess, Puccini made use of pentatonic scales supposedly oriental in their intervallic content. The libretto stems from *The Arabian Nights*. Princess Turandot announces that she will marry only a man wise enough to solve three riddles proposed by her; the price of failure is death. Her palace begins to look like a mortuary as one after another contender fails the quiz. But she meets her match in a prince of Tataria, a Mongol tribe at war with China. He solves all her riddles, ludicrous as they are, but she begs him to release her from an obligation to marry. He agrees if she guesses his own name. The only person who knows his name is a Tatar slave girl; she is tortured on Turandot's order and stabs herself to death to avoid the disclosure. Eventually Turandot guesses that his name is Love. This realization makes it possible for her to marry him.

Turangalîla. A grandiose symphony by Olivier Messiaen, in ten sections inspired by Indian ragas as a paean to love (*Turangalîla* means "love song" in the Hindi language), conceived in a rhythmic idiom of tremendous complexity and scored for orchestra, Ondes Martenot, and solo piano. It was first performed by the Boston Symphony Orchestra, conducted by Leonard Bernstein, on December 2, 1949.

Turkey in the Straw. An American square dance whose tune is identical with that of the song *Zip Coon*, published in New York in 1934. It was probably a variant of Irish hornpipes, which were popular early in the 19th century.

The Turn of the Screw. An opera by Benjamin Britten, after the psychological novel by Henry James, first produced in Venice on September 14, 1954. A governess is placed in charge of a young boy and girl in a dismal house in the English countryside. Two former servants, now dead, seemed to exercise a mysterious hold on the children's minds, and the governess herself entertains a neurotic belief in a strange posthumous influence. In questioning the boy, she brings him to a catatonic stage; his weak heart gives way and he dies. The opera, like the novel, leaves the mystery of reality and superstition unsolved. The score is expressionistic; there is a modified application of dodecaphonic techniques. The thematic "screw" is turned in 15 interludes connnecting the opera's eight scenes.

Twelve-tone music. This term is the translation of the German compound noun *Zwölftonmusik*, a method of composition in which all themes are composed of 12 different tones of the chromatic scale, promulgated by Schoenberg in 1923. Schoenberg's own definition, which he regarded as the only correct one, is "the method of composition with 12 tones related only to one another." About 1940, the Greek-derived term *dodecaphony* ("twelve-toneness") came into use as the synonym of the method. Several composers before Schoenberg wrote themes containing all twelve different tones, but they never organized such subjects in contrapuntal and harmonic structures. The Austrian theorist Joseph Matthias Hauer in particular asserted priority of dodecaphonic composition; he even made a rubber stamp that he used on his stationery affirming himself as the "spiritual protagonist and, despite many bad imitators, still the only capable composer of twelve-tone music." Schoenberg dismissed Hauer's claim in a characteristic statement: "If I were to escape the danger of being called an imitator, I had to disclose my secret. I called a meeting of friends and students, to which I also called Hauer, and gave a lecture on my new method. Everybody recognized that it was quite different from that of others."

Twinkle, Twinkle, Little Star. A melody that first appeared in the middle of the 18th century; the tune is probably derived from a French folksong. The French text, *Ah, vous dirai-je, maman,* is the earliest of many settings in many languages. Mozart wrote a set of piano variations on this theme during his sojourns in Paris. The words of *Twinkle, Twinkle, Little Star* are by a Londoner, Jane Taylor, and were published in 1806 in a collection, *Rhymes for the Nursery.*

Tzigane. A gypsy rhapsody for violin and orchestra by Maurice Ravel, which he wrote for a Hungarian violinist named Jelly d'Arányi. The music is attenuated rather than forcibly imposed. Originally, Ravel wrote it for violin and *luthéal,* a piano with a mechanical attachment placed over the strings to make it sound almost like an organ. It was performed for the first time in London on April 26, 1924, with Ravel at the *luthéal.*

U

Uirapurú. A symphonic poem by Heitor Villa-Lobos, first performed in Buenos Aires on May 25, 1935. Uirapurú is a legendary jungle bird, which is a handsome youth underneath his feathers. He is fascinated by a jungle maiden, but a jealous Indian kills him. In death he becomes a bird again. The score presents a colorful musicorama of tropical birds of the Brazilian jungle.

Una corda. "One string," an indication directing the pianist to use the soft pedal, which moves the entire keyboard, and with it the hammers, slightly to the right so that the hammers strike only one string instead of two or three. When the composer wishes to restore full sonority, the indication is *tre corde* ("three strings"). Beethoven was the first to use these terms systemically in his piano works.

Una cosa rara. An opera by Vicente Martín y Soler, first performed in Vienna on November 17, 1786. The work reflects the fascination with exotic subjects; its libretto is drawn from the history of the Ottoman Empire. The opera was probably the first to include a Viennese waltz; another distinction is the use of the mandolin as an accompanying instrument in a serenade. Mozart quoted an aria from *Una cosa rara* in *Don Giovanni*.

The Unanswered Question. An instrumental work composed in 1908 by Charles Ives, sometimes subtitled *A Cosmic Landscape*. The trumpet propounds the "unanswered question" in an atonal setting, echoed by woodwinds and strings. The components in the score are written at different tempi in different meters. The work was not performed until some half century after its inception, but then it became famous.

Undertow: Choreographic Episodes for Orchestra. A ballet suite by William Schuman, representing the case history of a psychopathic individual. It was first performed in New York on April 10, 1945.

Undine. An opera by Albert Lortzing, first performed in Magdeburg on April 21, 1845. A water nymph marries a mortal, by which act she is assured of gaining an immortal soul. When her husband betrays her with a human female, she avenges herself by enticing him to join her in her native watery realm, where he drowns. Another opera with the same title and a similar story was written by the German fabulist E.T.A. Hoffmann, who was an amateur composer; it was first produced in Berlin on August 3, 1816.

Unfinished Symphony. A profoundly romantic semisymphony by Franz Schubert, his No. 8. It is in the melancholy key of B minor. By the irony of fate it became Schubert's most famous orchestral work. Schubert wrote it at the age of 25 as a token of acknowledgment of his election as an honorary member to the musical societies in Linz and Graz in 1822, but why did it remain incomplete? The manuscript contained two movements and a few bars of the third movement, a scherzo. According to a version promulgated in a wretched movie, Schubert wrote the Symphony for one of his high-born female students as an expression of his love for her. She thanked him but explained that the disparity of their stations prevented any thought of marriage. "Then let my symphony, like my love for you, remain unconsummated," poor Schubert is supposed to have said. On Schubert's centennial in 1928, an international competition was held for the completion of the *Unfinished*. The prize was given to a Swedish composer who declared afterward that his score was a deliberate imitation of the style of the judges of the competition. An interesting coincidence: A younger contemporary of Schubert, Norbert Burgmüller, also left an unfinished symphony at his death at the age of 25; this symphony was, like Schubert's, in the key of B minor.

The Unicorn, The Gorgon, and the Manticore. A "madrigal fable" by Gian Carlo Menotti, first performed in Washington, D.C., on October 21, 1956. The story, by Menotti himself, tells of a poet who takes out on three successive Sundays a pet unicorn, a gorgon (Medusa was one), and a manticore (one-third man, one-third lion, and one-third scorpion).

Unison. Literally, "sounded as one." The interval zero. To play in unison is to play the same note in the same octave position.

Universe Symphony. An unfinished project of Charles Ives for which he made sketches between 1911 and 1916. It was intended, in his words, to be a "contemplation in tones of the mysterious creation of the earth and firmament, the evolution of all life in nature, in humanity, to the Divine."

Unterhaltungsmusik. Literally, "conversation music." A category embracing all types of musical compositions designed to please and entertain rather than impress and enlighten.

Urtext. A magic word conjuring up an idea of absolute authenticity in literary or musical works. Most of these editions are the product of the codifying and cataloguing that is peculiarly Germanic. The prefix *Ur* signifies the primeval or primordial state; *Ursprache* is the hypothetical first language underlying all other languages. In music the Urtext represents the original manuscript as set down on paper by the composer.

The passion for the Urtext is a peculiar obsession of 20th-century music scholars. Their predecessors treated the classics in a rather cavalier fashion, freely altering the notes and harmonies. Bach has been the favorite object of their unwelcome solicitude. There is the notorious case of an editor's adding a bar to furnish a transitional chromatic harmony in Bach's C major Prelude from the first book of *The Well-Tempered Clavier*. Editions of Beethoven's piano sonatas by Hans von Bülow and others treat the Urtext with little respect. On the other side of the spectrum, however, worshipful editors do not dare to correct even the most obvious of errors. Yet one can never be sure, in editing modern works, whether seeming errors were not intentional. A copyist who tried to "correct" some "wrong" notes in a manuscript of Charles Ives, was told in no uncertain terms by Ives, who wrote in the margin of his manuscript. "Do not correct; the wrong notes are right." On the other hand, when a respectful copyist questioned a misplaced accidental in the proofs of one of Rimsky-Korsakov's scores, the great master of Russian music retorted in the margin: "Of course it is an error. I am not someone like Debussy or Richard Strauss to write wrong notes deliberately."

Ut. The opening syllable of the first line of the hymn used by Guido d'Arezzo, corresponding to the tonic of the mode. Because *ut* lacked a vowel at the end and was therefore difficult to sing, it was changed to *do*, except in French nomenclature, where *ut* remains in proper usage; *Ut majeur* is C major. *Ut* is the only syllable in Guido's hymn that constitutes an entire word; the rest of the notes are the initial syllables of nouns or verbs. *Ut* is the Latin concessive particle; the first line reads *Ut queant laxis* ("That they might be relaxed . . .").

Utrecht Te Deum. Handel's hymn praising God and Queen Anne of England on the occasion of peace concluded in Utrecht, Holland, marking the end of the war of the Spanish succession in 1713. It was first performed, along with another of his sacred works, *Jubilate*, on July 17, 1713.

V

V Studni (In the Well). An opera by Wilhelm Blodek, first performed in Prague on November 17, 1867. A young girl is in a quandary as to whether to wed a rich widower or an impecunious but handsome youth. A wise village woman advises her to look in the well to see whose face is reflected in the water. Both contenders find out about it, and each climbs a tree next to the well to make sure that his face appears. The old widower falls into the well, but the youth keeps his balance and gains the girl's hand. The opera enjoyed considerable success in its day; in Germany it was known under the title *Im Brunnen*.

Vaganti. Medieval university students who roamed freely from school to school; hence the name, a cognate of "vagabond." Even though the vaganti lived outside the framework of established society, they were divided into superior and inferior strata, the highest of them belonging to the category of clericus, an educated class, and the lowest to the nondescript group of goliards. The distinctive characteristic of the vaganti was their dedication to poetry and music. Not being constrained by the strictures of the church, they indulged their fancy in songs glorifying the delight of the senses, drink, and secular games. The famous student song, still heard in European universities, *Gaudeamus igitur*, expresses this joy of living, with the verse, typical of the spirit of the vaganti, *meum est propositum in taberna mori* ("it is fated that I should die in a tavern"). A remarkable collection of songs by the vaganti, known as *Carmina Burana*, was discovered in 1803 in a Benedictine monastery in Bavaria; several songs in this collection were popularized in a choral arrangement made by Carl Orff in 1937.

Le Vaisseau fantôme (The Phantom Ship). An opera by Pierre-Louis Dietsch, first performed in Paris on November 9, 1842. It is of historic interest because Wagner wrote his own opera on the same story, which was performed under the title *Der fliegende Holländer (The Flying Dutchman)*.

La Valse. A choreographic poem for orchestra by Ravel, who wrote it as a dream recollection of a Viennese waltz heard at the Austrian Imperial Court in 1855. The waltz rhythm is perceived through an acoustical fog, but gradually the oneiric shape becomes more and more dominant until it overwhelms the senses with a powerful explosion of sonority. *La Valse* was first performed in Paris on December 12, 1920.

Valse triste. Next to *Finlandia*, the most popular work of Jean Sibelius; it is lyric and full of natural grace. *Valse triste* was originally scored for strings only as part of the incidental music to the play *Kuolema* (*Death*) by Sibelius's brother-in-law, Arvid Järnefelt, which was produced in Helsingfors on December 2, 1903. Sibelius conducted the first performance of the chamber orchestra version of this work in Helsingfors on April 25, 1904.

Valve. A significant device for brass instruments that came into use about 1815. Before then, trumpets and horns could play only natural tones and were limited to a definite key. In the orchestral scores of Classical works, the parts of trumpets and horns, commonly set in a variety of pitches, compelled the player to use several different instruments or insert extra tubing manually in order to change the tuning. The valve instruments obviated this laborious procedure by increasing or decreasing the total length of the tube with the aid of valves or pistons. Modern horns and trumpets have three valves to lower or raise the pitch. As a result, a full chromatic scale can be played. Because the tubes cannot be made proportionate in the precise mathematical relation required, some chromatic tones have to be rectified by combining several valves; numerous methods of manufacturing are provided for this purpose. An alternate to piston valves is supplied by rotary valves.

Vamp. A preludizing jazz accompaniment, usually consisting of a succession of chords against an ostinato figure in the bass to set the rhythmic pace for a song.

Vampuka, the African Bride. A satirical opera by an obscure Russian composer, Erenberg, first produced in a Russian cabaret, The Crooked Mirror, in St. Petersburg on January 30, 1909. It derides the conventions of grand opera on exotic subjects, with numerous direct quotations from *Aida* and *L'Africaine*. The satire had an extraordinary success in the sophisticated circles of old Russia, and its popularity was such that the name Vampuka entered the language, signifying operatic nonsense.

Vanessa. An opera by Samuel Barber to a libretto by Gian Carlo Menotti, first produced at the Metropolitan Opera in New York on January 15, 1958. During a stormy night Vanessa awaits the return of her lover Anatol, as she has done for 20 years. A young man appears seeking shelter; it is the son of her lover, now dead, and his name is also Anatol. Over the chasm of a generation, Vanessa falls in love with him and actually marries him. In the meantime this present-day Anatol has spent a perilous night with Vanessa's niece, who subsequently suffers a miscarriage. As her aunt departs for Paris with Anatol, the niece settles down for long years of waiting for her brief lover's return. The music is passionately romantic but is set in a sophisticated modern framework.

Variable meters. A scientific-sounding definition of the metrical system introduced by Boris Blacher in his piano work *Ornamente*, composed in 1950. The device is deceptively simple: the first bar has two beats, the second bar has three, and so on, following the ascending arithmetical progression, then reversing the process in a descending progression. Other German composers adopted Blacher's variable meters, among them Karl Amadeus Hartmann in his Concerto for Piano, Wind Instruments, and Percussion, and Hans Werner Henze in his String Quartet.

Variations. Variety is the spice of life, and variations are the sweet adornments of melody. The simplest formula is the Air with Variations in which the theme is embroidered by added notes. Such notes are placed a diatonic degree above or below the tune; in a more advanced development, the basic melodic elements are subjected to harmonic variations, which in turn become the points of departure for further ornaments. In the Middle Ages, ornamentation in church modes was a form of elementary variations, and the symbols often bore picturesque descriptions, such as *clivis* (cliff), *scandicus* (ascent), and *climacus* (descent). In Baroque music these terms became grace notes. As time went on, variations grew more and more complicated. Thus a variation on a tune in a major key could be a similar tune but in minor. At the request of Diabelli, a publisher, Beethoven wrote a collection of variations for piano that are almost unrelated to the given theme. In most variations, the theme is supposed to be stated, full and unadorned, in the beginning. The French composer Vincent d'Indy, however, reversed the order in his *Istar Variations*: the Babylonian goddess of that name goes through seven gates, at each of which she deposits some of her garments, until she emerges naked in the last movement, which is the original theme. Elgar challenged the critics to identify the hidden subject of his *Enigma Variations*. There probably is none; Elgar simply described the characters of his friends in these variations. But the enigma remains.

Variations for Orchestra. An important work by Schoenberg, the first consciously composed in the 12-tone method. It was first performed in Berlin on December 2, 1928. In this work Schoenberg uses the sequence of tones B-A-C-H (B-flat, A, C, B-natural), which is woven into the basic 12-tone subject.

Variations on a Nursery Song. A piece for piano and orchestra by the Hungarian composer Ernö Dohnányi, who performed as soloist in its first performance in Berlin on February 17, 1914. The nursery song of the title is the

French air *Ah, vous dirai-je, maman*, which is celebrated as the alphabet song in several languages. The score is dedicated to "the enjoyment of lovers of humor and to the annoyance of others."

Variations on a Rococo Theme. A work for cello and orchestra by Tchaikovsky, first performed in Moscow on November 30, 1877, by his colleague at the Moscow Conservatory, the cellist Fitzenhagen. Tchaikovsky imagined the Rococo style as the expression of "light carefree joy," characteristic of the late 18th century, "quite different," as he wrote in one of his published articles, "from the disheveled romanticism of later times. . . . I found for a Rococo theme a nice little tune in the manner of the gavotte." Altogether there are seven variations.

Variations on a Theme by Frank Bridge. An orchestral work written by Benjamin Britten in homage to his teacher, the English composer Frank Bridge. It was first performed at the Salzburg Festival on August 27, 1937. The theme is taken from Bridge's *Three Idylls*; there are ten variations in all.

Varsovienne. A mazurka, named after the city of Warsaw; it originated in France coincidental with a great upsurge of sympathy for the unsuccessful Polish rebellion against Russia in 1848. The tune became popular again among intellectuals during the abortive Russian revolution of 1905.

Vaudeville. In present usage, vaudeville conveys the idea of a light variety entertainment, but the word is actually of a dignified and ancient origin, derived from *Chanson du vau de Vire*, that is, "Song of the valley of Vire," which is part of the department of Calvados, France, renowned for its farcical folksongs. In the Renaissance period, vaudeville often figured in morality plays in the form of lyrical madrigals. In the 18th century, vaudeville became synonymous with any kind of entertainment. Mozart used a vaudeville skit explicitly named as such in the conclusion of his opera *The Abduction from the Seraglio*. In the 19th century, comedies with musical episodes were called *vaudevilles*. Finally, in the entertainment industry of the 20th century, particularly in America, vaudeville was degraded to its lowest position in art as a variety show.

Les Vendredis. The French title of two sets of pieces for string quartet, 16 in all, by Russian composers, including Borodin, Rimsky-Korsakov, Glazunov, and Liadov, so named to observe the hebdomadal meetings on Fridays (*Vendredis*) held at the house of the publisher Belaiev in St. Petersburg in the early 1900s.

Venetian school. A generally accepted and convenient designation of the style of composition that developed in Venice in the 16th century, with the participation of several important organists from the North, especially from the

Low Countries. San Marco Cathedral, with its magnificent architectural plan of symmetric enclaves that make it possible to produce antiphonal choral works of a truly stereophonic quality, was the center of the Venetian school. The first acknowledged master presiding over the principal organ at San Marco was Adrian Willaert, appointed maestro di capella in 1527; he was not an Italian but a Belgian from the town of Bruges. He instructed the great Italian madrigalist Andrea Gabrieli in the art of chromatic modulation. Gabrieli in turn taught his nephew Giovanni Gabrieli to adapt choral techniques to the treatment of the orchestra, particularly in the contrasting alternation of massive sonorities, thus popularizing the effect known as the echo, in which a given melody is repeated softly. A long series of great organists at San Marco Cathedral included Claudio Merulo and the theorist Zarlino. It has been claimed also that the great Flemish organist Sweelinck made a trip to Venice and became one of the builders of the Venetian school, but this has been refuted by documentary evidence; Sweelinck in fact never went to Venice. Undoubtedly, the Venetian school of composition, orchestration, and choral treatment exercised a profound influence on composers in Germany, among them Hieronymous Praetorius, Michael Praetorius, and Hans Leo Hassler.

Verfasser. A German word for author, or editor. As a postscript to the last unfinished fugue of Bach in his *Art of the Fugue*, his son Philip Emanuel wrote: "At this point *der Verfasser* died."

Verismo. The realistic type of drama, literature, and music in Italy that evolved in the last decades of the 19th century as a reaction to conventional Romantic art. The aesthetic principle of verismo is to represent elements of verity (from *vero*, the Italian adjective for "true"). The first truly veristic opera was Mascagni's *Cavalleria rusticana* (*Rustic Chivalry*), which won an Italian publisher's first prize and was produced with great éclat in 1890. Inspired by the success of the opera, Mascagni's contemporary Leoncavallo produced in 1892 his own veristic opera, *Pagliacci*, which also became extremely successful.

Verklärte Nacht (Transfigured Night). A work by Arnold Schoenberg, set for string sextet, which he wrote in 1899 when he was 25 years old, long before he initiated his method of composing with 12 tones related only to one another. It was first performed in Vienna on March 18, 1902. The title is taken from a poem by a contemporary writer describing the acceptance by a woman's lover of paternity of a child conceived by another man. The score is almost Wagnerian in its expansive harmonies.

Vers la flamme (Toward the Flame). Scriabin's piano "poem," op. 72, composed in 1914. It expresses his esoteric ideas of a perpetual ascent toward the regenerating flame of the final ecstasy postulated in the theosophic doctrine.

The music is delicate and subtly nuanced. There is no key signature, suggesting an atonal setting.

Die Verschworenen (The Conspirators). An opera by Franz Schubert, produced posthumously in Vienna on March 1, 1861. The subject follows the plot of *Lysistrata* by Aristophanes, wherein the wives of the Crusaders announce a marital strike until their husbands formally repudiate war.

Vespers. The seventh canonical hour of the Divine Office of the Roman Catholic liturgy, to be performed, as the name indicates, at dusk, about 6 o'clock in the afternoon. The Latin name is *vesperae*. Vespers is the most important service in the Office insofar as its applicability to musical composition goes, for it includes a variety of chants, hymns, and a Magnificat. Secular forms are commonly admitted in the Vespers, and this dispensation encouraged composers to set Vespers and Magnificats as independent works in a polyphonic style. Monteverdi wrote several Vespers, and Mozart composed two Vespers for a large ensemble.

La Vestale. An opera by Gaspare Spontini, first produced in Paris on December 15, 1807. A Roman captain, Licinio, is busy conquering Gaul. In distress, his betrothed applies for a position as a vestal virgin; upon examination she is found to be a *virgo intacta* and is allowed to join the vestals. Licinio refuses to guard her virginity and upon return to Rome invades the vestal premises, extinguishing the holy flame in the process. The vestal is sentenced to death for her failure to protect the flame, but she is saved when a bolt of lightning strikes the scene and relights the sacred fire. This celestial intervention is interpreted as of divine origin, and the lovers are reunited in matrimony.

Vexations. A piano piece by Erik Satie, in which he stipulates that it should be repeated 840 times. On September 9, 1963, in New York, a group of dedicated avant-garde musicians carried out Satie's instructions literally, using pianistic relays. The total duration of this marathon performance was 18 hours and 40 minutes.

Vibraharp. A percussion instrument introduced in America early in the 20th century; in its popular form, it has metal bars connected with an electrical current causing a vibrato. Alban Berg used it in the score of his unfinished opera *Lulu*.

Vibraslap. A shaker manufactured around 1970 to replace the Latin American instrument *quijada del burro* ("jawbone of an ass"). In the genuine jawbone, the teeth rattled percussively when struck with the palm of the hand or produced a dental glissando when brushed with a stick. The vibraslap is a wooden shell with small metal pieces inside.

Vibrato. A coloristic effect achieved in singing by letting the stream of air out of the lungs about eight times per second through the rigid vocal cords; ideally, the pitch should remain the same to avoid an irrelevant trill. Vibrato is used in playing wind and especially string instruments, with a slight oscillation of the pitch through a barely perceptible motion of the left hand and finger pressure on a sustained tone.

La Vie parisienne. An opéra-bouffe by Jacques Offenbach, first produced in Paris on October 31, 1866. Two swains await the arrival by train of their mutual object of adoration, but she spurns them both. Frustrated, one of them tries to seduce a Swedish baroness while the other assumes the role of admiral of the Swiss navy. Secret trysts are held; a traveling Brazilian sings an infectious matchiche. These are easily penetrable disguises, but at the end each swain finds a complementary damsel. *La Vie parisienne*, an affectionate spoof on life during the Second Empire under Napoleon III, enjoyed considerable success in Paris.

Villanella. A type of secular song that originated in Naples in the 16th century. Its musical format was marked by a deliberately rustic style and was cultivated by educated composers who wished to combat the absolute domination of the madrigal type of vocal music. Such villanellas often were of topical content and regional in application. The French spelling is *villanelle* or *villanesca*.

Vingt-quatre violons du Roi. A string ensemble, known as the *grande bande*, that was attached to the courts of Louis XIII, Louis XIV, and Louis XV. It comprised 24 violins and other string instruments. The *petite bande* had only 16 players. The ensemble was made famous by Lully, who conducted it for many years.

Viola. A string instrument tuned C, G, D, and A, a fifth lower than the violin. Physically, it is only one-seventh larger than the violin, and its tone lacks the brilliance of the violin without having the deep philosophical quality of the 'cello. It is no wonder, therefore, that the viola rarely plays a leading part in chamber music or in the orchestra. An exception is *Harold in Italy* by Berlioz, which has an important viola part.

Viola d'amore is an archaic instrument about the size of the violin but lacking its perfect proportions. The number of strings varies from five to seven; in addition, there are sympathetic metal strings under them, imparting a silvery resonance to its sound. The English diarist Evelyn commented on "its sweetness and novelty." The mysterious name of the viola d'amore may have the prosaic explanation that its scroll above the pegbox was often made in the shape of Cupid's face. The viola d'amore was very popular in Baroque music, and Bach used it in several of his works. In modern times, the viola d'amore was mostly used for its evocative value, as in the *Sinfonia domestica* of Richard Strauss.

Viola bastarda is an old string instrument with six strings, tuned alternatively in fifths and fourths. Its strange designation as a bastard viola is explained by the fact that it looked like an illegitimate offspring of the viola da gamba and the viola d'amore. In English, it is called *lyra viol*.

Viola da braccio, or "arm viola," is an obsolete string instrument that eventually developed into the modern violin. The *viola da spalla*, or "shoulder viola," is similar to the viola da braccio. The *viola piccola* is a "little viola," an obsolete string instrument of the viola family.

Violin. The best known, the most expressive, and the most artistic instrument of the string family. Poets and storytellers have extolled the violin as the most human instrument, capable of an extraordinary variety of expression—merry and sad, boisterous and tranquil, frivolous and meditative. The physical aspect of the violin is easy to describe. Its oval body is modified by two elliptic depressions across its waist. There are two symmetrical sound holes in the shape of large cursive *f*'s. The violin has four strings, tuned G, D, A, and E, in fifths, that are held at one end by a string holder and supported by a bridge above it. The strings are maintained in their tension by four pegs in a peg box. A fingerboard is under the strings. The body of the violin has the function of a resonator box. The resonance is at its strongest at the vibrating center of the violin. The strings are activated into sound by a bow strung with horsehair. There are no frets or other marks on the fingerboard to guide the violinist, as the guitar player is guided. The violinist must therefore develop a secure sense of the placement of the finger on the fingerboard to play in tune.

The first plausible ancestor of the violin was the Arab instrument known under the name *rabab*, which penetrated into Western Europe and became known there under the name *rebec*. In England, the rebec was called *fiddle*, without the derogatory sense that this name later acquired. The shapes of these instruments varied until the present form was fashioned by the great violin makers of Cremona in the late 17th century. The most celebrated of the Cremona masters was Antonio Stradivari (or Stradivarius). The label "Antonius Stradivarius Cremonensis fecit anno . . ." glued to the inner surface of the back of the violin and visible through the *f* holes is (if genuine) a guarantee of the excellence of the instrument. There are some 540 Stradivarius violins in existence, although the authenticity of some is in doubt. Their monetary value depends on pedigree; some "Strads," as they are affectionately known, that belonged to famous violinists fetch as much as half a million dollars each. The secret of the art of Stradivarius and his workshop has been unsuccessfully probed by generations of violin manufacturers, who have sought the solution in the peculiar quality of the wood from the forests of the Cremona region or in the quality of the varnish. Stradivarius and his apprentices were not educated men; the drawings of violins and other string instruments that Stradivarius left do not shed light on his mysterious skill. Attempts have been made, using the most modern tools of analytical science, to create perfect copies of the Strads, but in vain. Some indefinable elements (perhaps the proportionate distribution of overtones, or the quality of resonance, or the position of the vibrating center) elude the research.

The word *violin* is derived from the Italian *violino*, the diminutive of *viola*. *Violino* was also used for viola in old scores. Thus *violino ordinario* designated the modern viola; the *violino piccolo* was synonymous with the violin as we know it, although it now connotes a small version of the instrument, used for teaching children. The violin became a favorite instrument in the hands of early virtuosos of the 18th century. Its technique expanded through many ingenious devices such as harmonics, double stops, and pizzicato. Violin virtuosity attained its apogee with Paganini, whose wizardry on the instrument was documented in detail by contemporary reports.

Violin Concerto in E Minor. One of the most popular repertory pieces of every violinist in every part of the world, composed by Felix Mendelssohn. It is in three movements, with the middle movement, Andante, forming a perfect contrast with the outer Allegro movements. Mendelssohn wrote this Concerto for the violinist Ferdinand David, who played it for the first time in Leipzig on May 13, 1845. Because Mendelssohn and David were Jewish, some irreverent person set the opening theme to the words: "Oh, Moishe, Oh, Moishe, the business is no good." The Nazis prohibited performances of the Concerto, so it was not heard in Germany from 1933 to 1945.

Le violon d'Ingres. The famous French painter Ingres was a good amateur violinist and liked to play the violin for relaxation. The expression *le violon d'Ingres* acquired the sense of an avocation, a hobby.

Violoncello. The most songful instrument in the lower range of the string family. Like the violin and viola, it has four strings; the tuning is C, G, D, and A, an octave below the viola. Relatively few violoncellists have achieved worldly success comparable to that of Paganini and other wizards of the violin, but the names Casals, Piatigorsky, Rostropovich, and Yo-Yo Ma testify to the power of the 'cello. The word *violoncello* is the diminutive of *violone* and literally means "little big viola." A *violoncello piccolo* is a little violoncello, a name attached to the five-string 'cello used in some works by Baroque composers. The abbreviation *cello* is commonly used in England and America; in this form the diminutive suffix alone is retained.

Viols. The generic type of string instruments that attained universal popularity in the 17th century. Three sizes of viols were in use, classified by their French names: *dessus de viole* ("top of the viola," i.e., treble viol), *taille de viole* (tenor viol), and *basse de viole* (bass viol). The bass viol was called *viola da* *gamba* in Italian, "the viol of the leg," and was the precursor of the modern 'cello. An ensemble of viols was called in England a "chest of viols," or "consort of viols." The viols were tuned like the lute, in fourths above and below the central interval, which was a third. The bass viol was tuned D, G, C, E, A, and D; the tenor viol was tuned A, D, G, B, E, and A; the treble viol was tuned an octave above the bass viol. To these was added the *pardessus de viole*, tuned a fourth above the treble viol.

Virginal. A keyboard instrument of the harpsichord family, extremely popular beginning with the reign of the Virgin Queen Elizabeth I of England. A natural surmise that virginals received their name from the unmarried queen is refuted by pre-Elizabethan German publications in which the term *virginal* was already being used. The earliest collection of music for the virginal, published in Britain in 1611, bore the revealing title *Parthenia, or The Maydenhead of the first musicke that was ever printed for the Virginalls*. It included dances, mostly pavanes and galliards, by British composers of the time. A sequel was published under the title *Parthenia Inviolata*, which of course did not mean inviolate virgin but designated virginal music set for viola "invioled," arranged for viol.

Virtuosity. From the Latin *virtus*, not in the sense of morality but in the sense of ability or value. For the last two centuries, virtuosity has become exclusively the virtue of artists, and specifically musicians; no one speaks of a virtuoso carpenter, a virtuoso cobbler, or a virtuoso obstetrician. A musical virtuoso must possess above all else a superlative technique. The first virtuosos in this sense were church organists. Of these, Frescobaldi acquired legendary fame. His biographers claim that 30,000 people flocked to hear him at St. Peter's in Rome. In later centuries, the term *virtuoso* was applied mostly to instrumentalists, particularly pianists and violinists. Virtuosity reached its peak in the 19th century. Paganini was the first violin virtuoso in the modern sense; his own compositions of transcendental difficulty testified to his expertise, which was also described many times by professional musicians who heard his concerts. Liszt candidly declared that his aim in performance was to emulate Paganini's violin on the piano. Liszt's great rival in piano virtuosity was Anton Rubinstein, whose thundering octaves were, to believe reliable critics, overwhelming in their impact on listeners. In terms of world acclaim, Paderewski was a true heir to Liszt and Rubinstein, but surviving recordings have raised doubts as to his place in the pantheon.

Vogelquartett. The *Bird* Quartet by Haydn, op. 33, No. 3 (1781), in the key of C major, so nicknamed because some of the trills and mordents in its melodies sound like an aviary in turmoil. It is also identified with one of a group known as *Gli Scherzi*, or "The Jokes."

Voice production. This curious term, widely used by singing teachers, is postulated upon the physiological misapprehension that the human voice can be "directed" or "projected" from the head, from the chest, or from the epiglottis by conscious effort. The only source of the human voice is the larynx, and the only resonator is the pharynx, but many professional singers are convinced that the lower notes travel from the vocal cords to the thoracic cavity and that the head voice is monitored from the top of the head. With the invasion of the United States by Italian singing teachers late in the 19th century, and by Russian singers after World War I, the mythology of voice production assumed the status of a science. A Russian singer who organized an American opera company urged his students to "exercise the muscles of the brain" and was quite unimpressed when told that the brain had no muscular network. There is no harm in using the terms *chest voice* and *head voice* if both the teacher and the student understand that they are using metaphors. It must be remembered, however, that great natural singers such as Caruso and Chaliapin developed their glorious voices never knowing whether they sang from the chest, from the head, or from the epiglottis.

Volga Boatmen's Song. The most famous Russian folksong, whose ancient origin is indicated by its melodic structure with its typical falling cadential fourth. Its Russian title is *Burlaki*, which means "Boat Haulers," that is, men who pulled boats upstream on the Volga River while singing a heaving strain. The Volga boatman is also the subject of a celebrated painting of Repin.

Voluntary. A partly improvised organ piece used in the Anglican church service. As the word indicates, the piece is "volunteered" in a variety of styles. Traditionally, it was written in a polyphonic idiom having elements of imitation. English composers of the 17th and 18th centuries wrote many such voluntaries. The British organists applied the term *voluntary* to any kind of improvisation, particularly one using the loud cornet stop.

Von Heute auf Morgen. An opera by Arnold Schoenberg, first produced in Frankfurt on February 1, 1930. The score makes use of the full-fledged method of composition with 12 tones. The title, which translates to *From Day to Day*, describes the daily effort of a housewife to retain the affections of her indifferent husband.

Voodoo. A ritual on the island of Haiti that comprises a whole complex of songs, dances, and the orgiastic beating of drums. A voodoo ritual is based on the magical mythology of the black population and is derived from the religious practices of their African ancestors.

Vorspiel. The German word for a prelude, prologue, or overture. Wagner treated the *Vorspiel* as an introduction in a very broad sense and designated the entire opera *Das Rheingold* as *Vorspiel* or prologue of his tetralogy *Der Ring des Nibelungen*.

The Voyage of Edgar Allan Poe. An opera by Dominick Argento, his third stage work, written in an expansively romantic and ingratiating songful manner. The libretto describes Poe's dream in which he recapitulates the nostalgic and painful memories of his life, focusing mainly on his child bride, who died before him. It was first produced in Minneapolis on April 24, 1976.

The Voyevode. A symphonic ballad by Tchaikovsky, first performed in Moscow on November 18, 1891. This work has no connection with Tchaikovsky's opera of the same name but is inspired by Pushkin's translation of a poem by Mickiewicz. It has some merit, although Tchaikovsky himself referred to the score as "a piece of rubbish."

W

Die Wacht am Rhein. A rousing patriotic German hymn, written by Carl Wilhelm in 1840, which exhorted the Germans to keep "watch on the Rhine." It became famous during the Franco-Prussian War of 1870–1871, when the Germans not only maintained their watch on the Rhine but actually crossed the river in Alsace and appropriated the city of Strasbourg, which became Strassburg in German, until its recovery by France after World War I.

Wait (Wayte). A town watchman in the Middle Ages whose duty was to keep order in the streets at night and announce the time. The waits figure in the Bible, in the repeated query, "Watchman, what of the night?" Waits often serenaded incoming travelers in their stagecoaches; they were also employed to provide music for ceremonial occasions.

Waldstein Sonata. The common title of Beethoven's Piano Sonata No. 21, op. 53, in C major, written in 1803–1804. It is dedicated to Count Waldstein, a friend and patron of Beethoven, hence the title. The opening movement is remarkable for its dramatic intensity.

Die Walküre. The second music drama of Wagner's cycle *Der Ring des Nibelungen*, produced at the opening of the Bayreuth Festival on August 14, 1876. *Die Walküre* begins with the meeting of Siegmund and Sieglinde, the mortal children of Wotan. When Sieglinde shows Siegmund the magic sword, Nothung, which Wotan drove deep into a tree and which can be pulled out only by a hero, Siegmund performs the task. Sieglinde becomes enraptured; she abandons her brutal husband, Hunding, and flees with her brotherly lover. But Wotan comes to the aid of Hunding and orders his nine warlike daughters, the Valkyries, not to lend support to the lovers. Siegmund is killed by Hunding when Wotan shatters the magic sword in Siegmund's hands. Wotan's favorite Valkyrie, Brünnhilde, disobeys Wotan's orders. As punishment, Wotan places her on a high rock and surrounds it by a ring of fire; only a hero can break through the fire and rescue her. This hero is Siegmund and Sieglinde's son

507

Siegfried. She had died in childbirth, and Siegfried is tended by the Nibelung dwarf, Mime, in his cave. Mime hopes that the young hero will be the one to kill Mime's great enemy, the giant dragon Fafner. The most famous symphonic episode from the opera is *The Ride of the Valkyries*, in which the sturdy Teutonic amazons disport themselves on top of cloud-covered rocks; Wagner's thematic use of the arpeggiated augmented triads here is notable. *The Magic Fire*, illustrating Brünnhilde's imprisonment by a fiery ring, is another popular tableau in the opera. In it, the most important leading motifs of the opera, including Wotan's imperious command, Brünnhilde's lament, the slumber motif, and the sparkling magic fire itself, are all combined in a gorgeous Wagnerian panoply.

Walpurgis Night. May 1st is the feast day of St. Walpurgis, an 8th-century English abbess. Walpurgis Night is the Witches' Sabbath held on the peak of Mt. Brocken in the Harz Mountains. Faust attended it in Goethe's poem; Berlioz has a scene of the Witches' Sabbath in his *Symphonie fantastique*. Gounod includes a scene during Walpurgis Night in his opera *Faust*. *Dies Irae* is commonly used as a motto in virtually all musical representations of the Walpurgis Night.

Waltz. The most famous ballroom dance in 3/4 time, generated in Austria toward the end of the 18th century. Choreographically, it consists of a pair of dancers moving around an imaginary axis, resulting in a movement forward. In the 18th century, the waltz was regarded as a vulgar dance fit only for peasant entertainment. In 1760 waltzing was specifically forbidden in Bavaria by a government order. The waltz began to receive social acceptance in the wake of the French Revolution when it became fashionable even in upper social circles on the continent. England withstood its impact well into the 19th century. A story is told about an English dowager who watched a young couple waltzing and asked incredulously, ''Are they married?'' The first representation of a waltz-like dance on the stage occurred during a performance of the opera *Una cosa rara* by Martín y Soler in Vienna in 1786. The waltz attained its social popularity during the Congress of Vienna in 1815; at that time it was known under the name of ''Vienna Waltz.'' In France it assumed different forms, in 3/8 or 3/4 time, as an andante, allegretto, allegro, or presto.

As a musical form, the standard waltz consisted of two repeated periods of eight bars each. The earliest printing of a waltz in this form was the publication of 12 concert waltzes by the pianist Steibelt in 1800; these were followed by a collection of waltzes by Hummel for piano published in 1808. Such concert waltzes were extended by the insertion of several trios, multiple reprises, and a coda, lasting nearly half an hour in all. During the 19th century, the concert waltz became a favorite among composers for piano. It found its greatest artistic efflorescence in the waltzes of Chopin.

The waltz grew into an industry in Vienna. Joseph Lanner and Johann

Strauss, Sr., composed hundreds of waltz tunes to be played in Viennese restaurants and entertainment places. Johann Strauss, Jr., raised the waltz to its summit as an artistic creation that at the time served the needs of popular entertainment. He was justly dubbed "the Waltz King." When Brahms was asked to autograph a waltz tune for a lady, he jotted the initial bars of *The Blue Danube Waltz* of Strauss, with a characteristic remark, "Unfortunately, not by me." Apart from *The Blue Danube Waltz*, properly entitled *On the Beautiful Blue Danube*, Strauss, Jr., wrote several other perennial favorites such as *Tales of the Vienna Woods*, *Voices of Spring*, *Vienna Blood*, and *Wine, Women, and Song*. All these waltzes were really chains of waltz movements. The waltz gradually became acceptable as a symphonic movement. Berlioz has a waltz in his *Symphonie fantastique*. Tchaikovsky includes a waltz in his Symphony No. 5, as does Mahler in his Symphony No. 9. Ravel glorified the waltz in his orchestral piece *La Valse*. Thus, in less than a century, the waltz, which began as a somewhat vulgar dance tune, took its place next to the minuet as a legitimate concert form.

Waltzing Matilda. An old Scottish song, first published in 1818. The words are of Australian origin, fitted to an old tune and published in Sydney in 1903. Matilda is not a girl's name but Australian slang for knapsack, and waltzing means bouncing, not dancing the waltz. In fact, the tune is in 4/4 time, not waltz time. The song, tremendously popular among Australian troops during the two world wars, almost assumed the status of a second national anthem.

War and Peace. An opera by Sergei Prokofiev, first produced in Leningrad on June 12, 1946. Prokofiev did not specify the number of acts and emphasized that the production should be announced as being in 13 scenes. He originally planned to have the opera presented in two parts on two consecutive evenings, but eventually he compressed it to fit a single evening. The cast of characters numbers 72 singing and acting *dramatis personae*. The work attempts to embrace the epic breadth of Tolstoy's great novel from which the libretto was extracted by Prokofiev and his second wife, Myra Mendelson. The opera opens with a "choral epigraph," summarizing the significance of Napoleon's invasion of Russia in 1812. Interlaced with military events are the destinies of the Rostov family and the dramatic story of Pierre Bezuhov. The concluding words of the victorious Field Marshal Kutuzov, "Russia is saved," unquestionably were intended by Prokofiev to echo the recent Russian experience in fighting off another invasion, that of Hitler. The musical idiom is profoundly Russian in spirit, but there are no literal quotations from folksongs. The melodic, rhythmic, and harmonic realization is recognizably that of Prokofiev's own.

War Requiem. The work Benjamin Britten wrote to commemorate the restoration of the Cathedral of Coventry, mostly destroyed by bombing in World

War II. Its first performance took place in the cathedral on May 30, 1962. The text includes six movements from the traditional Latin Requiem Mass and nine antiwar poems by Wilfred Owen.

Warsaw Concerto. A semiclassical piece for piano and orchestra by the English composer Richard Addinsell. It was written as part of the music for the film *Dangerous Moonlight*, produced in 1942 as a dramatic depiction of the Nazi destruction of the Polish capital. Unaccountably, the *Warsaw Concerto* became enormously popular.

Water Music. The music that Handel wrote for his royal patron King George I of England, to be played on an open barge during the king's sailing party on the Thames River on July 17, 1717. Three orchestral suites were subsequently drawn from *Water Music*, consisting of hornpipes, minuets, and other dances. Publishers seized on its success and printed numerous arrangements of it under the title *The Celebrated Water Musick*.

We Shall Overcome. A hymn of considerable antiquity that has become in its modern form the marching song of the American civil rights movement. Its melodic and harmonic outline is traced to the 18th-century anthem *O Sanctissima*.

Weber's Last Thought. A waltz for piano, a copy of which was found among Carl Maria von Weber's manuscripts when he suddenly died in London in 1826. Assuming that it was a work by Weber (why else would he have kept the manuscript among his personal effects?), it was published under the sentimental title *Weber's Last Waltz* or *Weber's Last Thought*. The piece became popular; the German composer Johann Pixis wrote a piano fantasy on it. He sent a copy to another minor German composer named Carl Reissiger, who, to his astonishment, recognized in it one of his own *Danses brilliantes*, which he had presented to Weber just before Weber died. *Weber's Last Thought* proved to be Reissiger's middle-age waltz.

Die Weihe der Töne (Consecration of Sounds). The Symphony No. 4 of Ludwig Spohr, subtitled "a characteristic tone painting in the form of a symphony," and written in 1832. There are four programmatic movements: (1) *Largo*, representing stark silence of nature before the creation of sound, followed by *Allegro*, portraying the actual sounds of nature; (2) *Andantino*; (3) *March*; *War Music*; *Battle*; *Return of the Victors*; and (4) *Funeral*; *Consolation in Tears*.

The Well-Tempered Clavier. The accepted English translation of the German title, *Das Wohltemperierte Clavier*, of Bach's great collection of 48 paired preludes and fugues (often referred to as simply "The 48"), in two volumes, each containing 24 preludes and 24 fugues in all major and minor keys arranged in chromatic order, alternating in major and minor keys. Consequently, all odd-numbered preludes and fugues are in major keys, and all even-numbered ones are in minor keys. The first prelude and fugue in each of the two books is in C major; the last prelude and fugue in each is in B minor. It is easy to determine the key from the number, and the number from the key. If the number is odd, subtract 1 and divide the result by 2, which will give the count of semitones up from C and will determine the tonic of the key. Thus Prelude or Fugue No. 15 will be in a major key since 15 is an odd number, and specifically in the key of G major (15 − 1 = 14; 14 ÷ 2 = 7; 7 semitones from C is G). For even numbers, subtract 2 and then divide the result by 2. Thus, Fugue No. 16 will be in the key of G minor (16 − 2 = 14; 14 ÷ 2 = 7). To find the number from a given key, the procedure must be reversed. Count the number of semitones from C to the tonic of the prelude or fugue in question, and then multiply it by 2. If the key is major, add 1; if the key is minor, add 2. The G major Prelude and Fugue must therefore be No. 15 (the interval from C to G is 7 semitones; 7 × 2 = 14; since the tonality is major, add 1; 14 + 1 = 15). The Prelude and Fugue in C minor must be No. 2; the interval from C to C is 0; 0 × 2 = 0; since this is in a minor key, add 2 to the result: 0 + 2 = 2. The complete German title of "The 48" can be rendered into English as follows: "The Well-Tempered Clavier, or Preludes and Fugues through all tones and semitones, relating to the major third, that is, Ut Re Mi, as well as those relating to the minor third, that is Re Mi Fa. Compiled and prepared for the benefit and practice of young musicians desirous of learning, as well as for the entertainment of those already versed in this particular study, by Johann Sebastian Bach, Anno 1722." (What a didactic apologia for an epoch-making work!)

The term *well-tempered* refers to the use of equal temperament, in which the octave is divided into 12 equal semitones, and the tuning is such that the transposition is possible without altering the ratio of frequencies for different intervals. Bach's achievement was the apotheosis of even-tempered tuning. It must be noted, however, that Bach had a precursor in the person of J.K.F. Fischer, who published a quarter of century earlier a collection of 20 preludes and fugues in 19 different keys, characteristically entitled *Ariadne musica* (with the allusion to Ariadne, whose guiding thread helped Theseus to find his way out of the Cretan labyrinth). Bach must have known Fischer's work; in fact, some of Bach's fugal subjects are similar to Fischer's.

A legion of well-meaning editors labored mightily over the publication of Bach's *Well-Tempered Clavier* in order to arrive at the proper understanding of various tonal and rhythmic ambiguities in the text. One editor had the temerity to insert a supernumerary bar in the C-major prelude of the first book, ostensibly to smooth down the uncomfortable transition between two unrelated diminished-seventh chords; his daring emendation is even adopted in school editions. The English Bachologian Ebenezer Prout amused himself by setting the subjects of each one of Bach's 48 fugues to humorous verses, some of them not without wit. For Fugue No. 7 of the second book, he had this: "When I get aboard an ocean steamer/ I begin to feel sick." The words "feel sick" come up on a trill. The Fugue No. 22 of the first book, which is rather intricate, inspired him to write, "Oh, dear! What shall I do? It's utterly impossible for me to play this horrid Fugue! I give it up!" And the chromatic countersubject of the same Fugue is quite emotional: "It ain't no use! It ain't a bit of good! Not a bit, not a bit!"

Werther. An opera by Jules Massenet, first performed in Vienna on February 16, 1892. The libretto is extracted from Goethe's celebrated short novel, *The Sorrows of Young Werther*. Werther is a young man nurturing an overpowering passion for a girl who reciprocates his affection on a philosophical level but marries a more pragmatic person. Werther then borrows a pistol from her husband and shoots himself. She rushes to his side, and he has the ultimate gratification of dying in her arms. A wave of suicides followed the publication of Goethe's novel among young males wallowing in the misery of unrequited love. In his opera, Massenet extracted the last fluid ounce of tearful emotion afforded by the libretto.

West Side Story. A musical play by Leonard Bernstein with lyrics by Stephen Sondheim. It was first performed in Washington, D.C., on August 19, 1957. The work demonstrates Bernstein's ability to fashion authentically American theater music. The dramatic theme of the play deals with the massive migration of Puerto Ricans to New York City. Two rival youth gangs, the Jets, composed of white boys, and the Puerto Ricans, nicknamed the Sharks, fight each other like latterday Montagues and Capulets. Tony of the Jets is a counterpart of Shakespeare's Romeo, and Maria, sister of the leader of the Sharks, is Juliet. Tony and Maria arrange for a clandestine meeting; their song *Tonight* is one of the most appealing love ballads in American musical theater. Also remarkable are Tony's invocation, *Maria*, and her vivacious confession, *I Feel Pretty*. The tension erupts in a savage "rumble" ballet. In a climactic fight, Tony's friend Riff is knifed to death. In revenge, Tony kills Maria's brother Bernardo; Tony himself dies at the hands of a Shark. The film version of *West Side Story*, released in 1961, received ten awards for excellence.

Westminster Chimes. This familiar tune was composed about 1794 by William Crotch; at least he is credited with its composition. In 1860, "Big Ben," the bell in the clock tower of the Houses of Parliament, was equipped with a mechanism for sounding the Westminster Chimes. The opening four notes are identical with a phrase that occurs in Handel's *Messiah*, to the words, "I know that my Redeemer liveth." This must be a coincidence; these four notes, consisting of the mediant, tonic, supertonic, and lower dominant, occur in thousands of melodies. Vaughan Williams interpolated the Big Ben tune in his *London* Symphony.

When Johnny Comes Marching Home. A Civil War song published in 1863; it became a nostalgic ballad of Union soldiers returning home from the battlefields. The words and music were credited at the time of publication to Louis Lambert, which was the pseudonym of Patrick Gilmore, the celebrated bandmaster. Because bandmasters of the 19th century had the habit of freely appropriating folksongs, or even songs by known contemporary composers (as Christy did in publishing "Ethiopian" songs by Stephen Foster under his own name), it may well be that *When Johnny Comes Marching Home* is an arrangement of a preexisting popular song; the modal character of the tune suggests Irish or Scottish provenance.

Whole-tone scale. A tonal progression in whole steps, thus using only six different notes and avoiding tonal triads and major or minor scales. Whole-tone progressions became popular in the late 19th century to convey a sense of mystery or mortal danger, as they could be easily harmonized with the ambiguous augmented triad. Rossini used the whole-tone scale in one of his posthumously published piano pieces. Glinka applied modulations along the steps of whole tones to describe the horrors of the magician's abode in his opera *Ruslan and Ludmila*. Puccini runs down the whole-tone scale in the bass to announce the arrival of the brutal police chief in *Tosca*. In his piano piece *Voiles (Sails)*, Debussy casts the first and third sections in whole tones, while setting the middle section in the pentatonic scale. Film composers have been apt to entrust to the trombones the whole-tone scale to describe Nazis or other brutal types, but such obvious devices to instill shudders have gradually disappeared from artistic usage.

Will You Love Me in December As You Do in May? A song by Ernest Ball, written in 1905 with words by James Walker, who was later elected mayor of New York City. Walker used the song in his political campaign. It was eventually played at his funeral.

William Tell. An opera by Gioachino Rossini, first performed in Paris on August 3, 1829, under the French title *Guillaume Tell*. Its overture is a popular concert piece. The subject is taken from a turbulent chapter in the history of Switzerland. William Tell is a Swiss patriot famed for his skill in archery. The brutal governor of the province tests his markmanship by ordering him to split with an arrow an apple placed on the head of his small son. William Tell passes the test, then turns the weapon on the tyrant and kills him with a single shot.

Woodwinds. The group of instruments in the orchestra originally made of wood and played by blowing (flute, piccolo, oboe, English horn, clarinet, bass clarinet, bassoon, double bassoon). In modern times, flutes and piccolos are made of metal, but they are nevertheless included in the woodwind category. A woodwind quintet is a technically inaccurate name for an ensemble consisting of four woodwind instruments and a French horn, which is a member of the brass family.

Wozzeck. An opera in three acts, subdivided into 15 scenes, with libretto and music by Alban Berg, first produced in Berlin on December 14, 1925, courageously conducted by Erich Kleiber (courageously because rehearsals of the enormously complicated atonal score required months of time and portended much trouble on the part of the orchestra, singers, and audience). Alban Berg fashioned the libretto from an obscure unfinished play by an obscure young German dramatist, Georg Büchner, who died of typhus in 1837 at the age of 23. The subject was taken from real life, the tragic story of an ordinary army barber named Woyzeck (*Wozzeck* was a misspelling, a result of Büchner's illegible handwriting). Woyzeck was content living with his unwedded girlfriend Marie, who bore him a child. But she becomes a temporary mistress of the dashing drum major of the army, and in a fit of jealousy Wozzeck kills her. The actual soldier Woyzeck was sentenced to death for his crime. In Büchner's drama he drowns himself in a lake.

The musical structure of Berg's opera is most unusual. Although it is fiercely atonal, each of its sections is modeled after a specific musical form: a classical suite, a rhapsody, a military march, a passacaglia, a rondo, a sonata allegro, a fantasy, a fugue, a scherzo, a set of variations, an invention, an interlude, and a perpetuum mobile. The reviews of the first performance were savage. Opined one Berlin critic: "As I left the theater last night I had a sensation not of coming out of a public institution but out of an insane asylum. On the stage, in the orchestra, in the hall, plain madmen. Among them the shock troups of atonalists, the dervishes of Arnold Schoenberg. In Berg's music there is not a trace of melody. There are only scraps, shreds, spasms, and burps." Curiously enough, another composer, Manfred Gurlitt, chose the same subject independently from Berg for his own opera *Wozzeck*, which was produced in Bremen on April 22, 1926, only four months after Berg's great work, but it could not withstand the comparison and soon faded from the musical scene.

The Wreckers. A grand opera by Dame Ethel Mary Smyth, who was renowned also as a militant suffragette (she spent two months in a British jail for it). The opera was originally set to a French libretto as *Les Naufrageurs*, but it was first produced in a German version as *Strandrecht* in Leipzig on November 11, 1906. The story deals with the inhumanity of villagers on the Cornish coast of Britain (the wreckers of the title) who asserted their right to rob and murder the shipwrecked sailors (the *Strandrecht* of the German title). The score is full of Wagnerian strife and fire, laden with a multiplicity of leading motifs.

Wunderkind. When an eager and hopeful mother (or, less frequently, father) notices that her darling child bangs on the keyboard of a piano, she perceives the breath of musical genius. Most child prodigies are pianists or violinists. There are but few wunderkinder of the 'cello and hardly any of a wind instrument. Wunderkinder are often kept chronologically young by their parents' cutting down their ages as they outgrow short pants. Mozart's father advertised his genius son as being 8 years old during several successive years. Child conductors are rare, but at least one of them made a meteoric career early in the century. It was Willy Ferrero, an American-born Italian boy who toured Europe as a symphonic conductor at the age of 8, arousing wonderment among audiences in France, Italy, and Russia. He ended his career as a provincial opera conductor. Another wunderkind conductor was Lorin Maazel, who led symphony concerts at the age of 9, eliciting invidious comparisons with a trained seal; he has since become one of the world's leading conductors. Child composers are even more of a rarity than performing wunderkinder. Mozart was the greatest among them. Mendelssohn achieved a fantastic mastery of musical composition at a very early age. Schubert wrote inspired songs at the age of 17. But neither Beethoven nor Brahms was a precocious composer; nor was Wagner, Tchaikovsky, or Stravinsky. Erich Wolfgang Korngold evinced comparisons with Mozart when he wrote a piano trio at the age of 12. He was introduced to Mahler, who exclaimed, "A genius! A genius!" Korngold wrote operas at the age of 18, but his star dimmed with age. Escaping European turmoil, he emigrated to Hollywood and became known as a film composer. Ineffable sadness surrounds the parade of red-cheeked little boys in velvet pants and little girls in white dresses whose pictures used to adorn the advertising pages of European and American music magazines of the *fin de siècle*. Whatever happened to them? Not even the most dogged efforts of musicographical hounds were able to trace them to their final retreats in some unknown home for the aged.

X

Xochipilli Macuilxochitl. "Imagined Aztec music" for wind instruments and Mexican percussion by Carlos Chávez. He conducted the first performance in New York on May 16, 1940. The Aztec words of the title are the attributes of an Aztec god.

Xylophone. A keyboard percussion instrument with resonant hardwood keys arranged like piano keys and played with sticks or mallets; the name of the instrument was derived from the Greek word for wood (*xylo*). Predecessors of the modern xylophone, found in many parts of the world, consist of a few wooden bars of different lengths that produce different tones. They were usually laid out on straw, and therefore became known among explorers as *Strohfiedel* ("straw fiddle"). Reversing the trend, European and American xylophones were imported into Latin America and Africa and became domesticated there as a kind of piano with wooden keys. Saint-Saëns used the xylophone to great effect in his *Danse macabre* to suggest the rattling bones of the disembodied ghosts. Many composers of the 20th century have included the xylophone in their symphonic scores.

Xylorimba. A hybrid keyboard instrument, with combined features of the Polynesian xylophone and African marimba, in which the resonance gourds are eliminated. Xylorimbas are used in works by some modern composers.

Y

Yankee Doodle. A mystery song of American music. A reference to the title is found in a libretto to an American ballad opera produced in 1767; the tune was first printed in 1794. During the American Revolution, the song was already popular. For a long time, the British believed that the tune was sung to mock the ragged American revolutionists, but Americans themselves played it as an expression of a certain swaggering confidence in their cause.

Yes, We Have No Bananas. An American nonsense song, concocted in 1923 by Frank Silver and Irving Cohn, who claimed that their inspiration came from a Greek fruit peddler who nodded his head to signify that yes, he did not have any bananas. But Greeks nod their heads to signify the negative and shake their heads for the affirmative, so the Greek merchant had perfect ethnic logic on his side. Humorless musicologists point out that the first four notes are identical with the opening of the Hallelujah Chorus from Handel's *Messiah*. So what else is new?

Yodeling. A time-honored type of singing in rural mountainous Switzerland. The earliest yodel call is found in a collection entitled *Bicinia Gallica, Latina, Germanica*, published in 1545, where it is described as "The Call of a Cowherd from Appenzell."

The Young Person's Guide to the Orchestra. Variations and fugue by Benjamin Britten. The subject is taken from a piece of incidental music of Henry Purcell. Britten cleverly brought out various instruments as soloists one after another, so the eponymous young person can really learn how orchestral instruments sound. The piece was written in 1945 as part of an educational film entitled *Instruments of the Orchestra*. It was first performed in Liverpool on October 15, 1946.

Youth Symphony. The nickname of Prokofiev's Symphony No. 7 (his last), which he wrote to glorify the spirit of Soviet youth. Ostentatiously melodious

517

and harmonious, it provided a balm on Prokofiev's soul after the denunciation
of his music that was hurled at him by the Soviet music functionaries in 1948.
The first performance of the *Youth* Symphony took place in Moscow on
October 11, 1952. A few months later, Prokofiev was dead.

Yurupari. A very long wooden trumpet used by the Brazilian Amazon Indians,
who consider it to be taboo to women and strangers. Oscar Wilde mentions
these primitive instruments in his novel *The Picture of Dorian Gray*, speaking
of exotic and dangerous hobbies of his hero in whose collection there are
"mysterious yuruparís of the Rio Negro Indians, that women are not allowed
to look at."

Z

Z mrtvého domu (From the House of the Dead). An opera by Leoš Janáček, first performed posthumously in Brno on April 12, 1930. Its libretto is drawn from the somber novel of Dostoyevsky, centered on the destiny of the Czarist exile who bears traits of Dostoyevsky himself. When he is freed, his fellow prisoners symbolically release an eagle from its cage.

Zarzuela. Spanish light opera with spoken dialogue. The name is derived from the Royal Palace La Zarzuela, near Madrid. Performances of zarzuelas at the Spanish court were interspersed with ballets and popular dances. With the massive intrusion of Italian opera into Spain in the 18th century, the zarzuela lost its characteristic ethnic flavor, but it was revived by national Spanish composers of the second half of the 19th century, among them Ruperto Chapí, Joaquín Valverde, Amadeo Vives, and Federico Chueca. The modern type of zarzuela, known as *genero chico*, embodied elements of the Viennese operetta and later annexed American jazz rhythms. Zarzuelas taking up an entire evening were called *zarzuela grande*; a *zarzuelita* is a small zarzuela.

Die Zaubergeige (The Magic Violin). An opera by Werner Egk, first performed in Frankfurt on May 19, 1935. The libretto deals with a peasant who receives a magic violin from an earth spirit; it has the power to fulfill any wish except love. When the peasant meets a girl of his heart, he surrenders the violin in exchange for love.

Zauberoper. A German term for a "magic opera," that is, an opera in which supernatural forces intervene in human affairs. A typical example is Weber's *Der Freischütz*.

Zémire et Azor. A pastorale by André Grétry, first performed in Fontainebleau on November 9, 1771. Azor is a royal prince transformed into a monstrous creature as punishment for his brutal self-conceit and overweening arrogance. Only love can restore his human shape; he receives it from Zémire. Ludwig

Spohr wrote an opera on the same subject that was performed in Frankfurt on April 4, 1819.

Zeppelins erste grosse Fahrt. A dramatic symphony by August Bungert depicting the initial flight of the German dirigible *Graf Zeppelin*. It was first performed in Coblenz on December 1, 1909.

Zero Symphony. This is the way Bruckner described his early Symphony in D minor, written in 1864, which he eventually discarded. It was not performed until May 17, 1924. Its music is in a pleasing Romantic vein, but the score lacks philosophical introspection characteristic of Bruckner's numbered symphonies.

Ziegfeld Follies. A famous series of spicy revues decorated with a panoply of beautiful girls inaugurated in New York City on July 8, 1907, by Florenz Ziegfeld. The follies became the cynosure of the American musical theater until Ziegfeld's death in 1932. Songs and sketches were by various hands with topical subjects. Musically, the most successful "follies" were the ones by Irving Berlin, who contributed many of his most enduring tunes, including *A Pretty Girl Is Like a Melody*, to the 1919 edition. Berlin wrote the entire score and lyrics for the 1927 revue, which contained his songs *You Gotta Have It* and *Learn to Sing a Love Song*.

Der Zigeunerbaron (The Gypsy Baron). An operetta by Johann Strauss, Jr., first produced in Vienna on October 24, 1885. A baron is abducted from his palatial estate as an infant. Returning as an adult, he finds the place occupied by a crowd of gypsies, among them a charming girl with whom he immediately falls in love. Fortunately for the sense of social privilege, she, too, turns out to be of noble blood. The overture, full of Viennese gaiety, is a perennial favorite.

Zingaro. A male gypsy; *zingara* is a female gypsy. The word is used mostly in such derivations as *zingaresca*, "gypsy tunes"; *alla zingarese*, "in the gypsy manner"; and so on. Liszt, who identified Hungarian folksongs with those of wandering gypsy bands, used the notation *alla zingarese* in a number of his pieces.

Zither. A folk instrument popular in Bavaria and Austria that is capable of producing considerable harmonic sonority. It is built of a wooden soundbox that may have as many as 40 strings, of which several are melody strings used similarly to those of a violin, with stops helped by a fretted fingerboard and using the fingers of the left hand to determine the note. The strings are plucked with a plectrum, while the accompaniment is produced by the fingers of the right hand. In Finland a popular form of zither is called *kantele*.

Zukunftmusik. A term coined by Wagner to describe what he regarded as the "music of the future." (*Zukunft* in German means "future.") Wagner's opponents turned this lofty phrase into a derisive description of his music.

Zwischenfälle bei einer Notlandung (Incidents at an Emergency Landing). An operatic "reportage" for instruments and electronic devices by Boris Blacher, first performed in Hamburg on February 4, 1966.